"*The true voyage of discovery lies not in finding new landscapes, but in having new eyes.*"

—MARCEL PROUST (1871–1922, French Novelist)

Wild at Heart has a sewn, lay-flat binding and
only gets better with use.

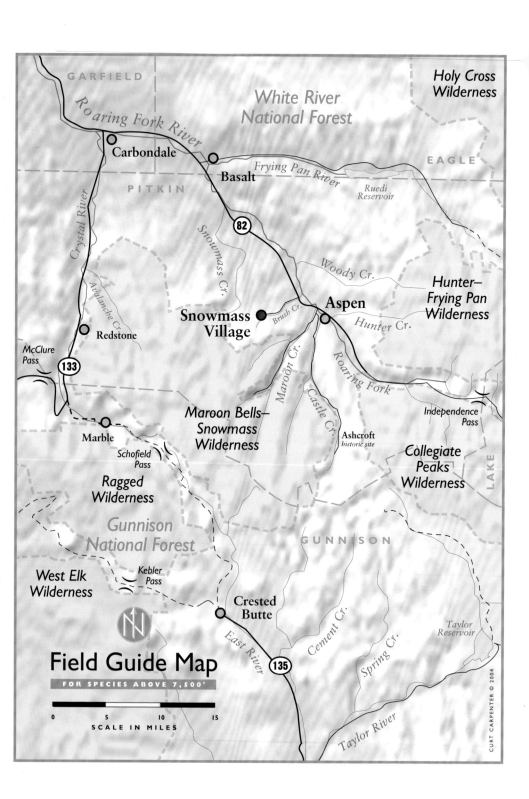

Field Guide Map

FOR SPECIES ABOVE 7,500'

0   5   10   15
SCALE IN MILES

GARFIELD

White River
National Forest

Holy Cross
Wilderness

EAGLE

Roaring Fork River

Carbondale

Basalt

Frying Pan River

Ruedi
Reservoir

PITKIN

82

Crystal River

Snowmass Cr.

Woody Cr.

Hunter–
Frying Pan
Wilderness

Avalanche Cr.

Snowmass
Village

Brush Cr.

Aspen

Hunter Cr.

Redstone

McClure
Pass

133

Maroon Cr.

Roaring Fork

Castle Cr.

Independence
Pass

Maroon Bells–
Snowmass
Wilderness

Ashcroft
historic site

LAKE

Marble

Collegiate
Peaks
Wilderness

Schofield
Pass

Ragged
Wilderness

Gunnison
National Forest

GUNNISON

West Elk
Wilderness

Kebler
Pass

Crested
Butte

Cement Cr.

Taylor
Reservoir

East River

135

Spring Cr.

Taylor River

CURT CARPENTER © 2004

SNOWMASS VILLAGE

Wild at Heart

A FIELD GUIDE TO PLANTS, BIRDS & MAMMALS

**Snowmass · Aspen
& the Colorado Rocky Mountains**

Janis Lindsey Huggins
Author and photographer
www.highcountrywild.com

Mammal track illustrations by Delia Malone
Plant illustrations by Darcy O'Donnell & Janis Huggins

Additional photos by other photographers as credited
History, Trails and Geology chapters authored as credited

DISTRIBUTED BY

WHO PRESS

PUBLISHED BY THE TOWN
OF SNOWMASS VILLAGE

Additional support from Susan and Mark Beckerman in memory of Rachel Ballenzweig,
who loved the mountains and all the living things found there.

With a heart full of gratitude to Jim and Moja Lindsey, the two most wonderful parents a person could have, and in loving memory of my grandmother, Birdie Lee Lindsey, who was my inspiration to live surrounded by plants and the natural world.

Distributed by
Who Press
PO Box 548
Moab, UT 84532
www.whopress.com
whopress@yahoo.com

Printed in China through Global Interprint

Includes bibliographical references and index
ISBN 978-1-882426-31-7

New Library of Congress Control Number: 2008905043

Cover and Book Design: Christina Watkins
Project Manager: Janis Lindsey Huggins
Project Director: Dawn Barton Keating, West Elks Consulting
Slide Scanning: John Belobraidic, Missoula, Montana
Layout Design and Production: Eric Auer and Janis Lindsey Huggins
Print-ready Production: Marjorie DeLuca, Aspen Graphic Services
Editors: Dave Reed, Jody Cardamone and Hensley Peterson
Illustrations: Delia Malone (mammal tracks), Darcy O'Donnell (plants), Janis Lindsey Huggins (plants)
Technical Editors: Delia G. Malone, wildlife biologist
  Jody Cardamone, Aspen Center for Environmental Studies, head naturalist
  Arvind Panjabi, Rocky Mountain Bird Observatory, ornithologist
  Kevin Taylor, Teton Science School, botanist
  Dr. Ronald Hartman, University of Wyoming, Department of Botany, Rocky Mountain Herbarium, curator
  Lisa Tasker, E. M. Ecological, LLC, Natural Resource and Restoration Consulting, principal ecologist-botanist
  Dr. Bruce Bryant, Scientist Emeritus, U.S.G.S., geologist

CAUTION: This field guide is not intended in any form to be a "how to" manual for consuming wild plants. We do not advise experimentation by readers, and we caution that many plants in the mountains, including some used in traditional medicine, are poisonous and harmful.

Funding for this book was provided by the Town of Snowmass Village, Snowmass Land Company, the Aspen Skiing Company and Susan and Mark Beckerman.

CONTENTS

ACKNOWLEDGMENTS

Completing an in-depth project really does take "a village"—a host of both old and new friends and family who have offered their expertise, encouragement, support, experience and invaluable time to help see me to the finish.

Metamorphosis from my dream to reality began in 1994 when the Town of Snowmass Village (TOSV) approved two new residential subdivisions: Two Creeks and The Pines.

As a condition of that approval, the TOSV required the developer, Snowmass Land Company (SLC), to provide funding for a book to educate the homeowners on the wealth of wildlife and native plants within the subdivisions. Seeing an opportunity to reach a much wider audience, town wildlife specialist Dawn Barton Keating and SLC President Jim Wells decided instead to produce a field guide that would apply to both residents and visitors of the Brush Creek watershed and similar habitats in the entire upper Roaring Fork Valley. Combining existing funding for the original concept from SLC and additional funding approved by the Town Council, the TOSV contracted with me in June 2000 to research, write and produce a more expanded field guide for this area. What I thought would be a quick, one-year project evolved into a 4-year labor of love to adequately address the large number of species present here.

My heartfelt thanks and sincere appreciation to everyone who helped build this book:

Dawn Barton Keating, project director for *Wild at Heart* and former wildlife specialist for the Town of Snowmass Village. Dawn wrote Trails and History and was invaluable in her efficient handling of financial details.

Delia Malone, wildlife biologist, helped me write and proof the Bird and Mammal text, was my wildflower lookout during the two summers of photographing plants, and drew the mammal tracks with an artful, yet experienced, eye.

Darcy O'Donnell, currently a junior in the Visual Arts and Design Academy at Santa Barbara High School completed over thirty plant drawings—her first published illustrations. Darcy's cartoons have appeared in the *Santa Barbara Independent*, and her paintings are exhibited at SB City College and the SB Arts Fund Gallery.

David Hiser, photographer extraordinaire, taught me how to photograph plants. Little did I know that his advice would include getting out in the wee hours of the morning to capture plants in the right light and without wind!

Digital Arts Aspen ??

Kathy Darrow, botanist and author (*Wild about Wildflowers*) from Crested Butte, gave me the courage to take on this project and inspired me with her enthusiastic love for wild places. The *Key to Plant Families* is her production.

Garry Zabel, professor of geology at Colorado Mountain College, and **Sylvia White,** geologist, spent many months writing and perfecting the Geology chapter. Flight time for aerial photos was courtesy of **Greg Rippy.**

Kevin Taylor, botanist and guide for Rocky Mountain Biological Lab (RMBL) and Teton Science School proofed the Plants text with a critical eye to detail. The many wonderful walks he guided kept me inspired.

Arvind Panjabi, ornithologist with the Rocky Mountain Bird Observatory, Fort Collins, Colorado, proofread the Birds text and answered lots of questions.

Dr. Ronald Hartman, Rocky Mountain Herbarium, Department of Botany, University of Wyoming, proofed technical details regarding nomenclature and characteristics, verified the identity of photographs and responded quickly to umpteen e-mails.

Dr. Bruce Bryant, Scientist Emeritus, U.S.G.S., graciously edited Geology.

Christina Watkins, *Wild at Heart*'s designer from Prescott, Arizona, offered an expert's guiding hand through the morass of details that come with producing a book.

John Belobraidic, Missoula, Montana, spent countless hours converting slides to refined digital images, and cheerfully shared his expertise throughout the entire project.

Dave Reed, editor, made the text more consistent throughout and produced a better book.

Jody Cardamone and **Hensley Peterson** made this book shine! They spent many months working on the final edit. Jody, head naturalist at Aspen Center for Environmental Studies, polished, wordsmithed and provided technical editing, while Hensley made sure grammar, punctuation and style were accurate. Words cannot describe their incredible effort on this project!

Eric Auer, production, took the maze of text, photographs and drawings and put it into book form (with Janis as his sidekick).

Marjorie DeLuca, Aspen Graphic Services, handled final production, refining the layout files to make them printer-ready—with a very masterful eye for detail.

Martha Moore Benson, A.H.G., proofed text on medicinal values of plants and all the Latin names of plants and birds. Her continuous encouragement was invaluable.

Anita Manchester proofread, ran errands, and even kept me fed—besides spending days coordinating over 410 photo scans with the proper plant—a tedious task!

Peggy Lyon, head field botanist for the Colorado Natural Heritage Program, and **Lisa Tasker**, owner of E.M. Ecological, LLC, helped immensely with identifying plant specimens, proofing text and answering endless questions.

Heather Hopton, the late board member of the local Audubon Society, loved herons and monitored the nesting populations in this valley for many years. I am so grateful for the many hours she spent helping me write the heron section, and miss her greatly.

Jonathan Lowsky, Pitkin County wildlife biologist, proofed the early Mammals text.

Dr. Dave Clark, Dr. Michelle Balcomb and **Dr. John Emerick** are all early pillars of my foundation in botany, biology and ecology and helped me develop a love for plants, birds and mammals during endless hours outdoors.

Dr. Marc Bekoff, Professor of Ecology and Evolutionary Biology at the University of Colorado at Boulder, offered his experienced guidance regarding coyote behavior.

Bill Boineau was my savior through the maze of computer problems.

Renee Fleischer continually encouraged me to see the light at the end of the tunnel.

Walnut House Films did an excellent job of developing hundreds of rolls of film from my Nikon F-100. Thanks to Trent Burkholder for his patience and expertise.

Many very talented photographers provided great additional photos for the book.

A very special thanks to my loving and extremely patient partner of twenty-six years, my husband, **George Huggins**, owner/broker, Huggins & Company Real Estate, who helped proofread, cross referenced page numbers, edited photos, organized and sent packages, cooked and cleaned dishes—more than he would have liked—and gave me wonderful, stress-reducing backrubs. Never-forgotten, my Mom and Dad—**Jim and Moja Lindsey**, my brothers and sisters—**Moja Lynn**, **Leigh Anne**, **Dan** and **Jim**, my step-daughter **Lauren**, and last—but never least—my faithful canine companion, **Molly Brown**, who all supported me 24/7 through the joys, trials and tribulations of writing this book.

I will be grateful to everyone until Mt. Daly erodes to a final grain of sand!

Regardless of the incredible efforts of the above people, I take full responsibility for possible errors in the text or species identification. Any comments, or questions about the text or mystery plants you find, are very welcome. Contact me at janis.huggins@comcast.net or P. O. Box 6188, Snowmass Village, CO 81615.

INTRODUCTION

In the end we conserve only what we love. We will love only what we understand. We will understand only what we are taught.

—BABA DIOUM, International Union for
Conservation of Nature, Senegalese poet

Welcome to the upper Roaring Fork Valley, situated in one of the most beautiful settings in the Rocky Mountains! Many residents and visitors alight in this mountain mecca hoping to find solitude, renewal and adventure. Surrounded by the White River National Forest, within which are found three designated wilderness areas—Maroon Bells–Snowmass, Hunter–Frying Pan and Collegiate Peaks—the valley is literally located in the heart of the wild.

This book fulfills a dream I have had since coming to the valley in the late 1960's—to give people identification and natural history information on as many of the local plant, mammal and bird species as possible. After years of study, obtaining a degree in natural sciences and botany, and working as a naturalist guide in both summer and winter, my dream evolved into an intense desire to share what I have learned over the years with others who love the outdoors. Thanks to the Town of Snowmass Village who provided the primary funding and support, this field guide came into being. It includes a discussion, with photos, of 423 plants, 112 birds and 49 mammals, as well as chapters on local ecology, geology, history and trails. By focusing on the upper Roaring Fork Valley, this book is able to cover a large number of the species found here, eliminating the need for a virtual library in your pack. The goal is to provide a bridge between the technical key and a coffee table picture book.

While trails, history and geology focus on Snowmass Village and the Brush Creek Valley, the plants, mammals and birds are indigenous to similar montane, subalpine and alpine habitats throughout the Colorado Rocky Mountains.

The value we place on any given plant or animal is really a reflection of what we know about it and its place in our surroundings. The earth's human population is increasing exponentially, imposing an ever-greater burden on wild ecosystems. We are being called to insure the survival of wild species and the habitats on which they depend. My hope is that readers will use this book to expand their understanding of the rich natural diversity around us, by delving further into the

t. Daly looms
ove Snowmass
illage at sunrise.
David Hiser

intricate world of each species and exploring their integral place within mountain ecosystems.

With this in mind, allow yourself some time away from the everyday rush. Let the wonderful mountain air lure you outside to explore and experience the sensuousness of nature—its visual beauty, sounds, textures and even tastes—to hear the earth speak, revealing nature's inner wisdom.

Janis working on Rim Trail plant survey

Immense pleasure is often found in the details. Listen for the sweet song of a yellow warbler among the willows, or the call of a male flicker reverberating through the forest. Search for snowberries bejeweled with early morning dew, or wander in search of whimsical yellow monkey flowers while listening to the delightful trickle of a moss-bound stream. Take a moment to inhale the soft anise fragrance of sweet cicely leaves, the crisp smell of wild mint, or the pungent aroma of crushed fir needles. Meditate to the lonely howl of a coyote on a starlit night—or simply sit a while as the mountain breeze strokes your cheek. Discover for yourself the meaning of "wild at heart."

USING THIS FIELD GUIDE

A Swedish botanist of the 18th century, Carl von Linnaeus, created what is now the universal system for the division of the plant and animal kingdoms into distinct groups. In the Linnaean system, each kingdom is divided into a progression of subdivisions based on similarities within each group, in the following descending order: division (in plants) or phylum (in animals), class, order, family, genus and species.

For simplicity, this guide deals only with the last three, each chapter being organized by family, with genus and species listed for each individual. This is similar to understanding what lineage you are from, identifying with your last name (genus) and then having that special first name (species) that separates you from others (but lacks identity without your last name). Each species is listed alphabetically by one of its common names with the scientific name(s) below. In Plants, non-flowering plants are first, followed by flowering plants. To help you identify a plant, there is a Color Guide to Flowering Plants covered in this book on page 57, followed by a Plant Family Key. Birds and mammals are listed in taxonomic order as you would find them in most field guides.

There are pros and cons to capitalizing common names of species. In the interest of smoother reading and continuity—and with apologies to the American Ornithological Union—this guide gives all common names in lower case. Measurements are given in the traditional English system, with metric conversions in parentheses.

My Help Is in the Mountain

My help is in the mountain
where I take myself to heal
the earthly wounds
that people give to me.

I find a rock with sun on it,
And a stream where the water runs gentle,
And the trees which one by one
Give me company.
So must I stay for a long time,
Until I have grown from the rock,
And the stream is running through me,
And I cannot tell myself from one tall tree.
Then I know that nothing touches me,
Nor makes me run away.
My help is in the mountain
That I take away with me.

—NANCY WOOD, from the book *Hollering Sun*

derson Ranch
le Hildur and Bill
derson were in
idence, ca. 1946.
rtesy Aspen
storical Society

HISTORY

*Everybody needs beauty as well as bread, places to play
in and pray in, where nature may heal and give
strength to body and soul alike.*

—JOHN MUIR

History of the Brush Creek Valley

Snowmass Village is a very young community located in the Brush Creek Valley. It went through a dramatic evolution from Native American hunting grounds to modern year-round recreational resort within a short eighty-year period.

Before the arrival of European settlers, the Ute people had migrated annually from their winter camp at lower elevations to spend the summer hunting, fishing, and gathering wild foods along Brush Creek and the many other streams that make up the Roaring Fork drainage. Known as the Yuuttaa or "People of the Shining Mountains," the Ute tribe consisted of seven bands whose estimated population of 4,000 people inhabited roughly 150,000 square miles of western Colorado, Utah and northern New Mexico. Isolated and protected by their mountainous environment, the Utes were able to avoid contact with the European Settlers much longer than most North American tribes.

The first white settlers arrived in the area in the late 1870's and early 1880's, lured by the discovery of silver and gold. With them came conflict with the native people. By 1880, the Tabequache band and their famous Chief Ouray had been banished to a reservation in northeast Utah.

Mount Daly was named by the 1874 Hayden Survey party in honor of then-president of the National Geographic Society, Augustus Daly.

However, Western Colorado was soon settled by miners and homesteaders. Unlike Aspen, the area around what is now Snowmass Village boasted no silver, however the open meadows along Brush Creek attracted cattle and sheep ranchers. Eventually, nineteen ranches were to occupy the Brush Creek Valley. Some of these ranches are recalled today in the names of streets, subdivisions and

3

trails. Sinclair Road, the Melton Ranch Trail and Subdivision, and the Anderson Ranch Arts Center are all named after families that first settled the valley.

With the repeal of the Sherman Silver Purchase Act in 1893, Aspen's prosperous silver mines closed down. Aspen too became a ranching community, and the Roaring Fork Valley settled into a way of life for the next several decades, often referred to as the "Quiet Years."

After World War II, spurred by the return of soldiers from the Army's Tenth Mountain Division and the efforts of industrialist-visionary Walter Paepcke, Aspen began a renaissance as ski resort and cultural center. In 1958, inspired by the success of the Aspen, Aspen Highlands and Buttermilk ski areas, entrepreneur and Olympic skier Bill Janss began buying up ranches in the Brush Creek Valley with the dream of building a new resort. By 1961, he had acquired six ranches at the base of Baldy and Burnt Mountains, which included the 380-acre Anderson Ranch. His ambition was to build a ski area in partnership with friend and Aspen Skiing Corporation President D.R.C. Brown on Forest Service land, to be served by a European-style ski community developed on 3,300 acres of private land.

Designed by local architect Fritz Benedict, Snowmass-at-Aspen (sometimes referred to as West Village) opened in 1967 with five chairlifts, fifty miles of ski trails, seven hotels and six restaurants. Radiating outward from the Snowmass Village Mall, it was one of ten villages originally planned by Janss for the Brush Creek Valley. Five times the size of Aspen,

HILDUR HOAGLAND ANDERSON, 1907–2002

One woman especially embodied the spirit of Snowmass Village during her lifetime, which spanned much of the community's history from the early ranching years to the recent past. Born in Aspen in 1907, Hildur Hoagland moved with her family three years later to a ranch in the Brush Creek Valley, where the Hoaglands raised cattle, sheep, wheat and hay. She lived on the ranch for more than 40 years, attending the community's one-room schoolhouse, now called the Little Red Schoolhouse. She married Bill Anderson, raised four children in the original ranch house, which is now the Anderson Ranch Arts Center's office building, and taught in schools throughout the area. To be closer to her teaching job in Aspen, the family moved back there in 1953 where they also ran Anderson Stables. As a teacher, mentor, rancher, musician (she is remembered for her accordion playing) and parent, Hildur Anderson received many awards during her remarkable life. She was inducted into the Aspen Hall of Fame in 1994. When she died in 2002 at the age of 94, her contributions to the Roaring Fork Valley were recognized in the Congressional Record. The Little Red Schoolhouse's Hildur Anderson's Toddler Center is named in her honor.

THE NAMING OF LOCAL LANDMARKS

SNOWMASS—The developers, rather than use the name of the area above Divide Road called "Snowmesa" for their ski area, chose to borrow the name of the drainage and community over the ridge known as Snowmass. They thought it sounded better and seemed more appropriate.

BURNT MOUNTAIN AND BIG BURN—Named for the large area at the top of the mountain that burned before 1879, the fire attributed either to Indians trying to drive out the settlers or to settlers trying to clear land.

KRABLOONIK—Means "bushy eyebrows" in the Eskimo language, named after a lead sled dog belonging to Dan MacEachen, owner of the restaurant and kennel.

ELK CAMP—Site of a traditional elk hunting camp.

SNEAKY'S SKI RUN—Named after the area's first mountain manager, Jim "Sneaky" Snobble.

WHISPERING JESSE SKI RUN—Named after the lift construction crew boss, Jesse Caparrella.

NAKED LADY SKI RUN—Named after the lift construction crew tacked a Playboy centerfold to a nearby tree.

Buttermilk and Highlands combined, the ski area boasted the highest lift-served skiing terrain in the country.

Bill Janss left behind a legacy and a vision for Snowmass Village as a planned, environmentally friendly mountain community that still influences land-use decisions today. Although much of his plan never came to fruition, he envisioned a network of small villages separated by open space and connected by a transit system, with architectural guidelines encouraging the use of native stone and timber as building materials. To make the development "harmonious with nature," the Janss Corporation spent $250,000 during initial development for underground utilities to preserve scenic vistas.

With the Janss Corporation and the Aspen Skiing Corporation promoting the area's outstanding natural beauty, scenery and year-round recreation, a real estate boom ensued. In 1968, Brush Creek Road was paved, and a post office was opened, giving Snowmass Village its own zip code and distinguishing it from Snowmass, referred to now as Old Snowmass, further downvalley. Snowmass Village was incorporated as a town in 1977. The original acreage purchased by the Janss Corporation was split up and changed hands many times. Notable among the owners were Jim Chaffin and Jim Light's Snowmass Corporation, which developed the Snowmass golf course; the Federal Deposit Insurance Corporation (FDIC), which took title to the land in 1986 after the default of the previous owners; and the Snowmass Land Company (SLC), which

5

developed the Divide, Horse Ranch and East Village, now known as Two Creeks and The Pines subdivisions. SLC sold the remainder of their land to Aspen Skiing Corporation, some of which has been developed into the new Base Village.

At the time of this writing, Snowmass Village has an estimated 3,600 dwelling units, a year-round population of nearly 2,000 and the ski area has a capacity of 12,000 people per day. Again, it stands on the verge of potentially major changes, with the planned Base Village development and associated on-mountain improvements.

Fast-paced development and accompanying prosperity have not come without environmental consequences. Brush Creek was channelized and denuded in many places, resulting in extreme silting of the river, killing the native trout. The Burnt Mountain elk herd's migration corridor was pinched to 10% of its former size and weeds invaded meadows and mountainsides, outcompeting some of the native vegetation. With greater awareness a new, more environmentally aware chapter of Snowmass Village's history has begun, as the community endeavors to reconcile development with environmental protection. The Town has instituted wildlife protection standards in its land use code, enforced by a part-time staff wildlife biologist. Significant funds have also been allocated to improve fish habitat along Brush Creek. As part of the effort, the Town Council has funded this book to enourage better understanding and protection of the local environment. In contrast with the early years of the resort, large development projects today must undergo rigorous review and community debate.

In 1997, the Aspen Skiing Company established an Environmental Affairs Department, which hosts environmental education programs on the ski area and provides grants to local groups seeking to protect or restore the local environment. Since its inception, they have won numerous environmental awards. The hope is that through these efforts and the national environmental planning requirements for public lands, the rich and remarkable mountain ecosystems found on Baldy and Burnt Mountains can be preserved.

A Road, a Creek and a Community in Maturation is a document that still guides much of the community's planning efforts. It outlines three of the underlying values shared by local residents: public support for a resort and hospitality-based economy; public expression of the pioneering spirit; and stewardship of the environment. Emboldened by these values, the challenge will be for now and future residents of Snowmass Village to truly become a new People of the Shining Mountains, deserving of the title.

INTERESTING HISTORICAL FACTS

- In 1963-65, in order to promote the soon-to-be ski resort, the developers of Snowmass-at-Aspen offered powder tours for $10 a day, including lunch.

- Ridge Run was Snowmass's first residential development, completed in 1967. Robert McNamara, then Secretary of Defense, built one of the first houses there, reflecting the prominent people drawn to Snowmass in the early days.

- In 1967, there were only two phones in the Brush Creek Valley, one at the log cabin where Hildur Anderson grew up and the other at the construction trailer on Fanny Hill.

- In 1966, a lot in the Melton Ranch subdivision cost $6,500.

- A room at the Silvertree Inn in 1967 was $25 a night.

- The Maroon Bells–Snowmass Wilderness Area, which borders the ski area, was designated as part of the national wilderness system in 1964. As far back as 1934, it was part of the Maroon-Snowmass Primitive Area and the Snowmass State Game Refuge, acknowledging the area's scenic and wildlife values.

Original Little Red Schoolhouse on Owl Creek Road, looking toward what is now the Rim Trail

COURTESY ASPEN HISTORICAL SOCIETY

TRAILS

Climb the mountains and get their good tidings. Nature's peace will flow into you as sunshine flows into trees. The winds will blow their own freshness into you, and the storms their energy, while cares will drop off like autumn leaves.

—JOHN MUIR

ore than a dozen trails are accessible from Snowmass Village. Ranging in length from one to nine miles (1.6-14.5 km.), they offer a wealth of diversity in terrain and scenery. It is here that one may encounter many of the birds, mammals and plants that surround Snowmass Village. Nine of the most popular trails are described below, intending to give some idea where to look for those species covered in this field guide. Although large mammals such as bear, mountain lion and bobcat do live in these mountains, sightings are not common as they are very secretive in their lifestyle. Learning their tracks and other sign is the best way to "see" them. Also, remember that sightings of plants and birds mentioned is dependent on the time of the year. For more detailed route descriptions, please refer to a local hiking guide in combination with a copy of the trail map published by Snowmass Village, which is available in town offices and local shops. Take water and snacks and be prepared for inclement weather.

A note about trail closures: Snowmass values its wild elk and deer populations, requiring certain trail closures during migration, calving and winter feeding activities. This is especially critical in the spring when recreational pursuits could disturb both migration and calving, so please heed the closures and use other trails during those times.

TRAILS ACCESSED OFF DIVIDE ROAD	TRAILS ACCESSED OFF BRUSH CREEK ROAD
Ditch Trail	**Rim Trail**
East Snowmass Creek Trail	**Tom Blake Trail**
Maroon-Snowmass Trail	**Anaerobic Nightmare Trail**
Nature Trail	**Government Trail East**
	Government Trail West

Ditch Trail

Habitat types: Aspen and mixed-conifer forests, riparian areas. **General location:** Near Krabloonik restaurant and dog kennels. **Elevation:** Start: 8,950 ft. (2728 m) at Divide Parking Lot. Finish: 8,800 ft. (2682 m) at East Snowmass Creek. **Access points:** Top of Divide Road. Parking is available in Lot E. Signed trailhead at the western edge of the parking lot. **Length:** 1.7 miles (2.7 km) one way. **Trail closures:** None. **Route description:** Follows an old irrigation ditch most of the way, traversing a number of ski runs near Chair Lift #5. The nearly level grade makes it an easy walk for the whole family. It also provides convenient access to the East Snowmass Creek Trail (see below). **Ownership:** U.S. Forest Service. The first mile crosses land leased by the Aspen Skiing Company for the Snowmass Ski Area.

What to look for: Fireweed, Calypso orchid, spotted coralroot, western bracken fern, Greene mountain ash, red elderberry, rattlesnake-plantain orchid, mitrewort, twisted stalk and wild hollyhock. Engelmann spruce and lodgepole pine. Sharp-shinned hawk, warbling vireo and red-breasted nuthatch. Ants "milking" aphids on fireweed, "bear trees" (see page 409), mule deer and porcupine. Panoramic vistas and wooden benches for rest and reflection.

Notes of interest: East Snowmass Creek and natural springs in the vicinity provide water for Snowmass Village. Head gates at the end of the trail direct stream flow to the town.

East Snowmass Creek Trail (No. 1977)

Habitat types: Spruce-fir to alpine tundra, riparian areas. **General location:** Maroon Bells–Snowmass Wilderness Area. **Elevation:** Start 8,360 ft. (2548 m) at main trailhead, or 8,800 ft. (2682 m) at end of Ditch Trail. Finish: 12,000 ft. (3658 m) at Willow Lake trail junction. **Access points:** Accessible by two access points. The easier option is to park in the Ditch Trail parking lot and walk almost to the end of the Ditch Trail from the top of Divide Road; cross over East Snowmass Creek on a wooden bridge to a trail that switchbacks up a hill to join the main East Snowmass Creek Trail. The other access point is the main trailhead, reached by driving from the top of Divide Road west down a dirt road (rocky, but negotiable by most 2-wheel-drive vehicles) past the Krabloonik kennels and restaurant, for 1.5 miles (2.4 km) to an intersection with Snowmass Creek Road in the valley floor; continue straight ahead at this intersection for 300 ft. (90 m) to the trailhead, on the left near a wooden bridge. Using this access point, you will have a steeper climb to reach the same point where this trail intersects the easier Ditch Trail. **Length:** 8.5 miles (13.7 km) one way. **Trail closures:** None. **Route description:** Follows East Snowmass Creek, climbing steeply in some places to East Snowmass Pass at 12,680 ft. (3865 m), and

East Snowmass Creek meadows in July

then descends via switchbacks to a junction for Trail No. 1978 for Willow Lake and Willow Pass. This is one of the longest and most difficult trails in the Snowmass Village area, providing access to the krummholtz and tundra zones. It passes through lush mountain meadows, cool spruce-fir forests and a series of steep avalanche chutes, indicated by scattered broken trees swept down by massive snowslides from the peaks above. **Ownership:** U.S. Forest Service.

What to look for: Wet areas are abundant with false hellebore, mountain bluebell, larkspur, rosy paintbrush and monkshood. Twinflower, glacier lily, spotted saxifrage, brook saxifrage and snowbed draba. Clark's nutcracker, hermit thrush, American pipit and brown-capped rosy finch. Bighorn sheep, mountain goat, bobcat, yellow-bellied marmot and pika. Also, keep an eye out for dark scars on aspen trees made by the claws of climbing bears or larger patches from browsing elk.

Notes of interest: This remote drainage is important as wildlife habitat. Elk use it as part of their summer range, bighorn sheep winter here and mountain goats are present year-round on cliffs high above the valley floor.

Maroon-Snowmass Trail (No. 1975)

Habitat types: Aspen and mixed-conifer, spruce-fir, alpine tundra. **General location:** Maroon Bells-Snowmass Wilderness Area. **Elevation:** Start: 8,400 ft. (2560 m) at trailhead. Finish: 10,980 ft. (3347 m) at Snowmass Lake. **Access points:** From the top of Divide Road, proceed west for 1.5 miles (2.4 km) down a dirt road past Krabloonik kennels and restaurant to an intersection in the valley floor. The road is rocky, but negotiable by most 2-wheel-drive vehicles. Continue straight at this intersection for a few hundred more yards passing the trailhead for East Snowmass Creek on the left and arriving at a large dirt parking lot. The trail

Snowmass Mountain

begins on the east side of the parking lot. **Length:** 8.3 miles (13.4 km) one way. **Trail closures:** None. **Route description:** Follows Snowmass Creek, climbing gradually and culminating in spectacular views of Snowmass Lake. This popular route is often taken as a full-day hike or the first leg of an overnight backpack. The many delightful areas along the entire length of cascading Snowmass Creek invite shorter hikes as well. Of particular interest are the beaver ponds approximately one mile up the trail. **Ownership:** U.S. Forest Service, within the Maroon Bells-Snowmass Wilderness Area.

What to look for: Tasselflower, blue and western red columbine, pipsissewa, wood nymph, stinging nettle, shooting star, monkeyflower, and Whipple's penstemon. Beaver, bighorn sheep, mountain goat, yellow-bellied marmot and pika. Belted kingfisher, ruby-crowned kinglet, American dipper, fox sparrow, Wilson's warbler and white-tailed ptarmigan. Enormous boulders left by melting glaciers, called glacial erratics.

Notes of interest: This route is a core trail in the Maroon Bells-Snowmass Wilderness Area, linking up to other Maroon Bells trails and providing access to many alpine areas including Trail Rider Pass, Snowmass Mountain, West Snowmass Creek and Pierre Lakes.

Nature Trail

Habitat types: Aspen and mixed-conifer forests. **General location:** Trail parallels Divide Road. **Elevation:** Start: 8,900 ft. (2713 m) near Krabloonik parking lot. Finish: 8,700 ft. (2652 m) at Parking Lot 7. **Access points:** The easiest route is to hike downhill from the top of Divide Road back to the Snowmass Village Mall. Park at the Krabloonik restaurant and kennels and walk south across Divide Road to the trailhead marked with a sign for the Sleigh Ride Trail; keep walking along Divide Road for another 600 ft. past the Sleigh Ride trailhead to the Nature Trail trailhead. Access is also possible from the Snowmass Mall by starting from the north end of Parking Lot 7 at a marked trailhead sign. **Length:** 1 mile (1.6 km). **Trail closures:** None. **Route description:** A short hike along a section of Brush Creek that has never been developed. Popular with school groups, bird-watchers and guided hikes because of easy access, gentle terrain and lush vegetation. Travels through aspen groves, conifer stands and flower-filled meadows, providing some of the best examples of local mountain plants. **Ownership:** The trail passes primarily through town-owned land except for a section in the middle of the trail that is owned by the Ziegler family. To date, the Zieglers have graciously allowed access through their property on the trail.

What to look for: Twisted-stalk, green bog orchid, false hellebore, monkshood, green gentian, horsetail, large-leaved avens, giant angelica, white checkermallow and aspen sunflower. Currant and gooseberry. Engelmann spruce with its butterscotch-smelling bark. Lazuli bunting, olive-sided flycatcher, yellow warbler, Swainson's thrush and golden-crowned kinglet. Mule deer, raccoon, red fox, pine squirrel middens and "bear trees" (see p. 409).

Notes of interest: Provides a good example of what Brush Creek looked like before development. Compare the diverse variety of plant and animal species on this stretch of the creek with the lower stretches that have been channelized and developed.

Rim Trail

Habitat types: Oak-mountain and sagebrush shrublands, aspen and mixed-conifer forests. **General location:** Traverses the upper northern rim of Snowmass Village. **Elevation:** Start: 8,600 ft. (2621 m) at the left of the Mountain View Apartments. Finish: 7,850 ft. (2393 m) along Horse Ranch Drive. **Access points:** Access the west end at Mountain View Apartments on Brush Creek Road or the east end off Brush Creek Road at the Rodeo parking lot. Access is also possible at the halfway point from the top of Sinclair Road. All three access points are marked with trailhead signs. Parking is available at the top of Sinclair Road and at the Rodeo parking lot. From the Rodeo lot, follow the paved bike path north along Horse Ranch Drive for .8 mile (1.3 km) to the trailhead. **Length:** 7 miles (11.3 km) one way. **Trail clo-**

Spectacular view from the Rim Trail

sures: The eastern section from Sinclair Road to Horse Ranch is closed October 30–June 20 for big game winter range and migration. **Route description:** After climbing 1.3 miles (2.1 km) from the Mountain View trailhead to a ridge, the trail undulates across sage meadows and through aspen forests, providing expansive views of Snowmass Ski Area, Wildcat Ranch and adjacent wilderness. Short steep sections may be quite slippery when the Mancos Shale soil is wet. Horseback riders use the eastern section above Horse Ranch, and mountain bikers may be encountered throughout. **Ownership:** The eastern section above the Horse Ranch subdivision bisects 650 acres of town-owned open space.

Trail sign explains spring trail closures.

What to look for: Pasqueflower, lanceleaf spring beauty, prairie smoke, sulfur-flower, sugarbowl, northern rock jasmine, mariposa lily, mountain candytuft, ball-head waterleaf, penstemon, double bladderpod, arrowleaf balsamroot, and blue-eyed Mary. Mountain mahogany, bitterbrush and gooseberry. Western tanager, golden eagle, black-headed grosbeak, mountain bluebird, green-tailed towhee, Lewis's woodpecker and red-tailed hawk. Elk, deer, porcupine, coyote and red fox.

Notes of interest: This area provides important winter range for 200-600 mule deer and elk, hence the closure of the eastern portion of the trail to human use eight months a year.

Tom Blake Trail

Habitat types: Aspen and mixed-conifer forests, riparian areas. **General location:** The trail traverses west to east from near the top of Faraway Road to Sinclair Divide on Owl Creek Road. **Elevation:** Start: 8,900 ft. (2713 m) at East Ridge Lane. Finish: 8,350 ft. (2545 m) Owl Creek Road. Access points: The trail can be accessed at several different points, but they are hard to find or do not have parking. The best approach is to be dropped off at the East Ridge Road trailhead, 1.5 miles (2.4 km) up Faraway Road and walk eastwards, downhill on the prettiest section; or be dropped off at the Sinclair Divide trailhead and walk west, or uphill. It is also possible to start at the Mall and access the trail via the Ridge Run Trail which cuts across Assay Hill. Another route is to walk up Stark's Trail near the Two Creeks parking lot until it joins the Tom Blake Trail. **Length:** 3.7 miles (6 km) one way. **Trail closures:** April 25–June 20 for elk migration and calving.

Route description: Beginning at East Ridge Lane, the trail traverses along the lower ski slopes above the Two Creeks and Pines subdivisions through dense stands of aspen, spruce and fir. **Ownership:** Crosses through a number of residential areas. A conservation easement protects the open space values of the eastern section. A small upper section above Two Creeks subdivision crosses U.S. Forest Service land.

What to look for: Richardson's geranium, bittercress, western coneflower, curly-headed goldenweed, hemlock parsley, cowbane, and whole hillsides of cow parsnip. Douglas-fir and gooseberry. Cooper's and sharp-shinned hawks, house wren, great horned owl and evening grosbeak. Mule deer, elk and long-tailed weasel. Aspens scarred by climbing bears and hungry elk.

Notes of interest: Dedicated to the late Tom Blake, who served as a visionary Snowmass Village Town Council member and Pitkin County Commissioner. Tom's trail provides access to four popular mountain bike trails: Stark's, Sequel, Government Trail East and Anaerobic Nightmare.

Anaerobic Nightmare

Habitat types: Aspen, spruce-fir forests. **General location:** Above Two Creeks and the Pines subdivision. **Elevation:** Start: 8,600 ft. (2621 m). Finish: 9,200 ft. (2804 m). **Access points:** Accessed via either the Tom Blake Trail or Government Trail East and serves as a connector trail between the two. **Length:** 1 mile (1.6 km). **Trail closures:** April 25–June 20 for elk migration and calving. **Route description:** Intersects with Tom Blake trail about 1 mile (1.6 km) from the eastern Tom Blake trailhead off Owl Creek Road. The junction is signed. Climbs steeply, though not as steeply as its name implies, through thick stands of aspen, spruce and fir trees until joining with Government Trail East at a marked intersection. **Ownership:** U.S. Forest Service.

Lauren Huggins takes a breather on Anaerobic Nightmare.

What to look for: False Solomon's seal, heartleaf arnica, coneflower, giant lousewort and baneberry. Brown creepers, red-breasted nuthatch, evening grosbeak and great horned owl. Black bear sign such as rocks turned over to look for ants. Elk, mule deer and pine squirrel.

Notes of interest: Mixed stands of aspen and grasses in this area provide good calving habitat for elk, which is why the trail is closed during spring.

Government Trail East (No. 1980)

George Huggins and Molly Brown hike the Government Trail.

Habitat types: Aspen, mixed-conifer and spruce-fir forests, riparian areas. **General location:** Snowmass Ski Area to the outskirts of Aspen. **Elevation:** Start: 9,400 ft. (2865 m at Elk Camp Work Road. Finish: 8,000 ft. (2438 m) at Iselin Park. Access points: Drive up Wood Road for 1 mile (1.6 km). Continue straight onto Pine Lane for 0.2 mile (0.3 km) until pavement ends. Proceed east onto the dirt Elk Camp Work Road across ski runs and under chair lifts. Park at a marked trailhead after 1 mile (1.6 km). Trail begins to the left (east). Can also be accessed midway by hiking up the Tom Blake and Anaerobic Nightmare trails. **Length:** 5.6 miles (9 km) one way. **Trail closures:** May 15–June 20 for elk migration and calving. **Route description:** From the Snowmass Ski Area, the trail traverses lower Burnt Mountain and Buttermilk Ski Area, undulating past small streams, meadows, aspen groves and lodgepole pine forests before crossing Maroon Creek and coming out at Iselin Park. A popular trail for hikers thanks to its diverse scenery; also sought out by experienced mountain bikers, who relish the rocky, technical sections. **Ownership:** Almost entirely on U.S. Forest Service land. The ski area sections are leased from the Forest Service by the Aspen Skiing Company.

What to look for: Mountain maple, mountain bluebell, fireweed, thimbleberry and sweet cicely. Douglas-fir, subalpine fir and Engelmann spruce. Blue grouse, yellow-rumped warbler, Cooper's hawk and western wood-pewee. Racoon, marten, deer, porcupine, pine squirrel and long-tailed weasel.

Notes of interest: Bisects prime elk calving habitat and the migration route for the Burnt Mountain elk herd.

Government Trail West

Habitat types: Spruce-fir and aspen forests, riparian areas, ski run meadows. **General location:** Snowmass Ski Area. **Elevation:** Start: 9,400 ft. (2865 m) at Elk Camp Work Road. Finish: 8,900 ft. (2713 m) at junction with Ditch Trail. **Access points:** Accessed off the Elk Camp Work Road. Drive up Wood Road for 1 mile (1.6 km). Continue straight onto Pine Lane for .2 mile (.3 km) until pavement ends. Proceed east onto the dirt Elk Camp Work Road across ski runs and under chair lifts. Park at a marked trailhead after 1 mile (1.6 km). Government Trail West begins across the road from the Government Trail East trailhead in a grove of aspen trees. The western end can be accessed off the Ditch Trail, with the route back to Elk Camp Work Road mostly uphill. **Length:** 3.5 miles (5.6 km) one way. **Trail closures:** None. **Route description:** From Elk Camp Work Road, the trail heads west across a series of ski runs until it merges with the Ditch Trail. **Ownership:** Entirely on U.S. Forest Service land, leased by the Aspen Skiing Company for the Snowmass Ski Area.

COURTESY TOWN OF SNOWMASS VILLAGE

Popular single track with mountain bikers

What to look for: Scouler's willow (with red-naped sapsucker nectar holes—see p. 312), pink pyrola, one-sided wintergreen, mountainlover, Drummond's willow, russett buffaloberry and Wolf's currant. Red-naped sapsucker, northern flicker, mountain and black-capped chickadees and three-toed woodpecker. Giant pine squirrel middens, mosses, pixiecup lichen, "bear trees" (p. 409) and outstanding views.

Notes of interest: Popular with mountain bikers. A good place to compare undisturbed areas with ski runs, where grading and timber removal have changed the vegetation and kept trees and shrubs from maturing. Ski runs mimic avalanche chutes somewhat, as they are open meadows kept in early succession by annual clearing for winter recreation. There are some positive benefits to this. Deer, for example, can rest and hide in the forest by day and graze on the open ski runs during the evening. Ski runs also allow for a variety of sun-loving and shade tolerant plants to grow in close proximity.

BACKCOUNTRY ETHICS

A thing is right when it tends to preserve the integrity, stability, and beauty of the biotic community. It is wrong when it tends otherwise.

—ALDO LEOPOLD

In response to a growing body of research on wildlife-human conflicts, and changes to vegetation and water sources from backcountry users, seven guiding principles have been developed by public land agencies and national outdoor schools. These Leave No Trace principles (LNT) or Backcountry Ethics were developed to ensure that we and future generations have the opportunity to enjoy quality outdoor experiences by embracing individual codes of conduct that minimize our effect on the wild.

The LNT Seven Principles:
- **Plan ahead and prepare**
- **Travel and camp on durable surfaces**
- **Dispose of waste properly**
- **Leave what you find**
- **Minimize campfire impacts**
- **Respect wildlife**
- **Be considerate of other visitors**

We urge you to share the backcountry with others, human and otherwise, by practicing these principles during your outdoor adventures.

Dos and Don'ts on the Trail:
Do yield to uphill traffic on the trail
Do help prevent erosion—stay on the trail and avoid shortcuts
Don't feed the wildlife
Don't pick the wildflowers

Elk Seasonal Ranges

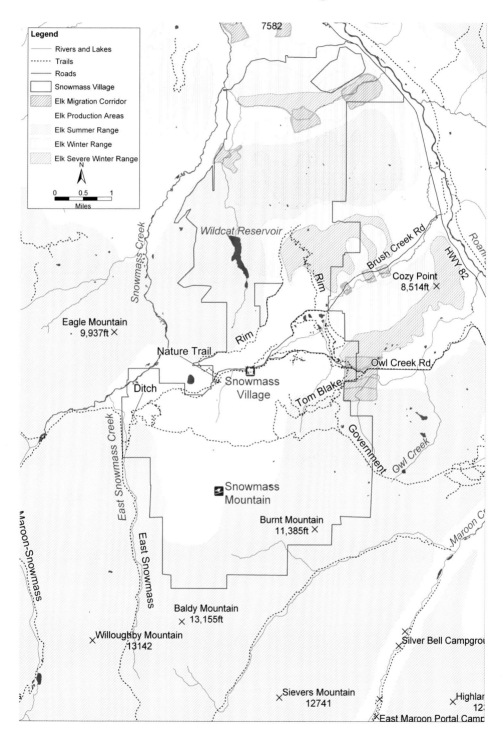

Legend
--- Rivers and Lakes
······ Trails
── Roads
▢ Snowmass Village
▨ Elk Migration Corridor
Elk Production Areas
Elk Summer Range
Elk Winter Range
▨ Elk Severe Winter Range

N

0   0.5   1
Miles

7582

Wildcat Reservoir

Snowmass Creek

Rim

Brush Creek Rd

HWY 82

Roar...

Cozy Point
8,514ft ✕

Eagle Mountain
9,937ft ✕

Rim

Nature Trail

Owl Creek Rd

Ditch

Snowmass
Village

Tom Blake

Owl Creek

East Snowmass Creek

Government

Maroon-Snowmass

East Snowmass

Snowmass
Mountain

Burnt Mountain
11,385ft ✕

Maroon C

Baldy Mountain
✕ 13,155ft

Willoughby Mountain
✕ 13142

Silver Bell Campgrou

Sievers Mountain
✕ 12741

Highlan
✕ 12

✕ East Maroon Portal Camp

rrison Formation,
Camp
nis Huggins

GEOLOGY

*The hills are shadows, and they flow from form to form and
nothing stands; they melt like mists, the solid lands, like clouds
they form themselves and go.*

—ALFRED, LORD TENNYSON, *In Memoriam*

Snowmass Trailside Geology

Snowmass Village is located in the southern Rockies, on the northeast edge of the Elk Mountains at an elevation of 8,000 ft. (2438 m). The geologic history of these mountains is truly fascinating and includes examples where ancient seas, rivers, beaches and mountains have come and gone several times. To the east of Snowmass Village is the Sawatch Range, which marks the Continental Divide and is known for containing Colorado's highest peaks.

About 50–70 million years ago, a period of mountain uplift called the Laramide Orogeny began shaping the Rocky Mountains. The forces responsible for the Laramide Orogeny are found in tectonic plates—large sections of the earth's crust that are in constant motion. These plates sometimes slowly crash into one another, such as those that are building the Himalayas right now, or sometimes slide over one another creating a buildup of energy which when unleashed affects landscapes on the overriding plate. A sliding scenario was the force behind the Laramide Orogeny, as the North American plate slid rapidly, geologically speaking, over the Pacific plate, causing the interior of the North American plate to buckle and form the Rocky Mountains. The last 3 million years of erosion, primarily due to glacial periods, have added the final touches to the mountains seen today.

The highest areas around Snowmass Village began forming about 34 million years ago, when magma welled up into existing sedimentary rock layers, which then cooled approximately 10,000 ft. (3048 m) beneath the surface creating "domes" of a granite-like rock called granodiorite. The spectacular peaks on the western horizon, Mount Daly, Capitol Peak and Mount Sopris, are remnants of these magma domes that have been exposed through erosion. Daly's signature diagonal stripe is a younger intrusion of a slightly

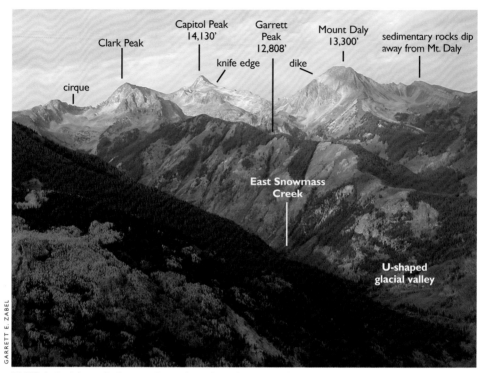

PLATE 1. Aerial view looking southwest from above Snowmass Village. Note the light-colored sedimentary rock layers of the Eagle Valley Evaporite (see Geologic Section, p. 29), and the red layers of the Maroon Formation dipping north away from the original "dome" of Mount Daly. Also note the U-shaped glacial valley of East Snowmass Creek. Other glacial features include the horn of Capitol Peak, its arête (knife edge) and cirques.

different composition that cut through the older granodiorite. A layer like this that cuts across existing rock is called a dike.

For an incredible 360-degree view of the above peaks, hike up the Rim Trail switchbacks starting at the Mountain View Condominiums at the intersection of Brush Creek Road and the Divide Road (see map on p. 28). Far to the northeast the gently sloping peak of Basalt Mountain is a remnant volcano that was active around 10 million years ago. Like Hawaii's volcanoes, this one produced sheet-like lava flows, the remnants of which form a layer of gray-black basalt 1,000 ft. (305 m) thick at the top of the mountain. Southeast of Basalt Mountain, north of Highway 82 and across from Aspen Village, is a slope covered with dark gray, angular rubble. These talus fields are remnants of a cinder cone—a very small volcano that formed a hill—now called Triangle Peak. This was the most recent volcanic activity in the upper Roaring Fork Valley, occurring about 1.4 million years ago.

Unlike the granodiorite peaks to the west and the volcanic features to the north, much of the geology surrounding Snowmass Village is composed of shale, sandstone and mudstones, all formed as layers of sedimentary rock millions of years ago (see p. 29).

Notice that all of the surrounding rocks on the Rim Trail look the

Basalt Mountain
10,866'

Rim Trail

Wildcat Reservoir

Triangle Peak

GARRETT E. ZABEL

PLATE 2. The view from near the top of the Elk Camp ski lift. Snowmass Village and the Rim Trail can be seen at the left of the photo.[1]

same. Layers of similar rock type and age are given formation names, and the name for these gray rocks is Mancos Shale. This formation was created from muddy sediments deposited by the Cretaceous Seaway, a shallow sea that covered most of the interior of North America about 75–100 million years ago. Locally, Mancos Shale contains small marine fossils, including cone-shaped baculites. Pieces of this shale may be black where plants decayed long ago, leaving a thin layer of carbonaceous material.

Looking south, find the ski runs of Big Burn on the slopes of Baldy Mountain, and those of Elk Camp on Burnt Mountain, which is east of Baldy. Garrett Peak, just west of Big Burn and across East Snowmass Creek Valley, is easily visible when walking or skiing Sneaky's ski run. All of these mountains are composed of sedimentary rock layers. Now, turn to the west to see Eagle Mountain, the nearest and smallest peak. Approximately halfway down the mountain, a small rocky outcrop of Entrada Sandstone is all that is visible in this area of the same host rock found in Arches National

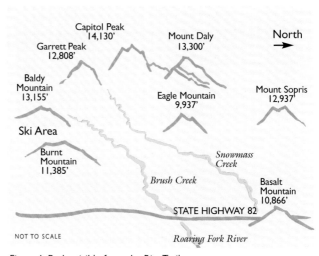

Capitol Peak
14,130'

Mount Daly
13,300'

North →

Garrett Peak
12,808'

Baldy
Mountain
13,155'

Eagle Mountain
9,937'

Mount Sopris
12,937'

Ski Area

Burnt
Mountain
11,385'

Snowmass
Creek

Brush Creek

Basalt
Mountain
10,866'

STATE HIGHWAY 82

NOT TO SCALE

Roaring Fork River

Figure 1. Peaks visible from the Rim Trail

23

Park in Moab, Utah.

At the top of the ridge, about 1.5 miles northwest of the junction of Highway 82 and Brush Creek Road, is a small outcrop of tan sandstone of the lower Mesaverde Formation. Only a remnant of this 66–70 million-year-old formation is seen here, though elsewhere in the southwest it can be hundreds of feet thick and may contain coal deposits. The top of this formation, where intact, was the last rock formed before the extinction of the dinosaurs.

The Rim Trail also crosses several small faults, where sections of rock were shifted up or down during the process of mountain building. Highway 82, near the Snowmass Village turnoff, parallels a major fault that puts the 300 million year old Maroon Formation and the overlying 240 million year old State Bridge Formation to the east up against 75 million year old Mancos Shale. Heading toward Highway 82 on Brush Creek Road, surrounded by gray Mancos Shale, look east across the Roaring Fork Valley to see those red cliffs and hillsides of the Maroon and State Bridge Formations. To the west of Snowmass Creek, Eagle Mountain is cut by a north-south–trending fault that pushed rocks up to the east and dropped them down on the west.

Views of Mancos Shale hillsides from Brush Creek Road.

When hiking, biking, skiing or boarding down the Big Burn, you are on Dakota Sandstone, formed 100 million years ago from the beach sands of the advancing Cretaceous Seaway. Did dinosaurs walk this beach? Although none have been found here, dinosaur footprints have been found in Dakota Sandstone on the Front Range near Denver.

The pink, red, tan, white and green layers of the Morrison Formation seen above and behind the Big Burn, and from Elk Camp (see chapter heading photo), are renowned for containing many of the large dinosaur fossils found in other areas of the United States. These rocks are Jurassic in age (150 million years old) and formed on a floodplain before the Cretaceous Sea advanced over North America. The many colored layers

PLATE 3. Looking south from the Patrick Virtue bench on the Ditch Trail at glacial and landslide deposits on top of the Sam's Knob sill. Note the vertical fractures within the sill, called columnar jointing. The baked Mancos Shale underlies the sill.

are the result of volcanic ash carried by wind and water from volcanoes to the west and deposited as sediments. Red and pink rocks formed in oxygen rich areas where the layers were exposed to air, while green and gray layers formed in an oxygen poor environment where they were covered by ash.

For another spectacular view, summer or winter, ride the Sam's Knob lift to the top. Why is Sam's Knob a knob? It formed when magma squeezed between, or intruded into, existing rock layers and cooled to form a ridge of granodiorite, or a sill. A sill is an intrusion that is parallel to existing rock layers and does not cut across layers, as does a dike. This ridge remains because it is more resistant to erosion than surrounding rock layers. The Sam's Knob sill is about the same age as the dike that forms the stripe on Mt. Daly. The exposed solidified magma of the Sam's Knob intrusion can be seen from two locations—where the Lunchline Trail curves just above the Ullrhof Restaurant, and on the Ditch Trail about 1.5 miles (2.4 km) from the village where the Patrick Virtue bench overlooks Snowmass Creek Valley and Mount Daly. From the bench, notice where heat from the intruding magma baked the Mancos Shale below it, hardening and darkening it. Also, look for the vertical columnar shapes of the intrusion's light gray-tan granodiorite on the cliff face. During cooling, this type of rock creates fracture blocks, causing the rock to erode and break along those joints (Plate 3).

The varicolored jumble of rocks above and along the trail were deposited by landslides unleashed when the water from melting glaciers saturated the above mountainsides. Glaciers hundreds of feet thick

Closeup of Dakota Sandstone (see Plate 3), viewed from the upper part of the Powderhorn ski run.

periodically filled the valleys in the Snowmass Village area from about 2 million to 10,000 years ago. Moving like enormous ice bulldozers, they widened and deepened the drainages over thousands of years, scouring out sheer, rocky bowls called cirques at valley heads and leaving behind piles of broken, transported rock called moraines. Some of the most challenging terrain at the Snowmass Ski Area is appropriately named the Cirque. When multiple glaciers originate near a high point, their cirques form a jagged pinnacle known as a horn. When cirques and glacial valleys develop adjacent to each other, a knife-edged ridge called an arête is created. Capitol Peak, "Colorado's Matterhorn," is a textbook example of these glacial features (Plate 1).

Farther along the Ditch Trail, large boulders called erratics are scattered throughout the aspen forest. Seemingly out of place, these huge rocks were moved from their original locations higher up the valley by the massive force of glaciers and then dropped as the glaciers melted.

To see the oldest rocks near Snowmass Village, cross the log bridge over East Snowmass Creek at the end of the Ditch Trail and continue to the Maroon Bells-Snowmass Wilderness boundary sign. Look east (left as you move up the hill) and notice the red rocks at the base of the cliffs. This is the Maroon Formation, named for the deep-red rock also exposed in the Maroon Creek area, below the famous Maroon Bells. Most of Garrett Peak is also made up of the Maroon Formation.

These massive red rocks formed from sediments deposited as the Ancestral Rocky Mountains began eroding about 310 million years ago into the area between them, known as the Central Colorado Trough (figure 2). Massive streams and debris flows of rocks, mud and sand eventually filled the trough to a maximum thickness of over 3 miles (4.8 km). Distinct layers are easily seen where the Maroon Formation is exposed. Petrified mud cracks, ripple marks, cross beds of sand, reptile tracks, and even raindrop imprints can be found revealing the history of the rocks. Hematite, an iron mineral, gives the formation its rust-red color.

Geologic history repeats itself, and these rocks were broken and moved when they became part of the glacial and landslide deposits along the Ditch Trail. Once again, the old rocks are being recycled as future rock-forming debris and sediment.

Recognizing some of the changes that occurred in the past as seas

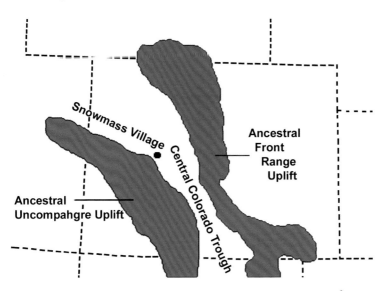

Figure 2. Ancestral Rocky Mountains of Colorado. Modified from Hoy and Ridgway.[2]

deepened and then retreated (depositing sand [now sandstone] in shallow water, and mud [now shale] as waters deepened) makes one realize there is more mystery in these mountains than is seen on the surface. With a little imagination, the granitic rocks become molten as they were long ago, bubbling and oozing far below ground. Hiking through this geology rich area, feel the uplift and weathering down of great, ancestral mountains and listen for the many ancient stories being told.

Note: For a broader understanding of geological events of the Rocky Mountains and upper Roaring Fork Valley, refer to references listed under References in the Appendix.

Geological Formations of Snowmass Village

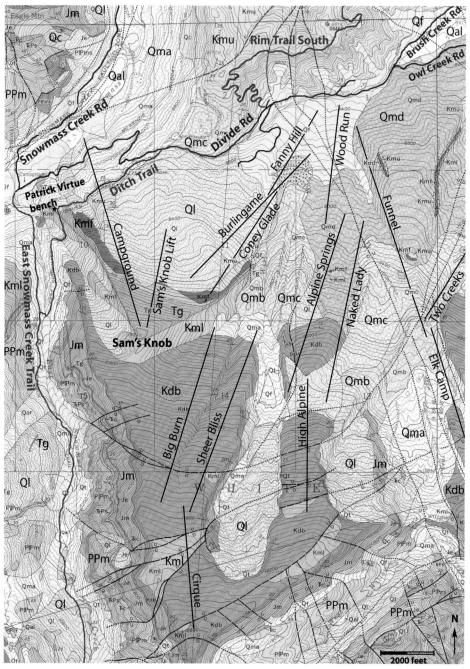

Modified from "Geologic Map of the Highland Peak Quadrangle," Bryant, 1972 by Garrett Zabel

SEE GEOLOGIC SECTION FOR KEY

Geologic Section of Exposed Rocks in the Snowmass Village Vicinity and Map Key

Eras	Geologic Period	Age of area feature	Formation name & map symbols (see p. 28)	Special area features
Cenozoic	**Quaternary** (present to 1.8 million years)	Up to present—1.8 million years	**Gravels Qal, Qc, Qf Glacial deposits** as moraines **Qma,b,c** or **d** (a is youngest) Landslide deposits **Ql**	Glacial features such as moraines, landslide deposits, cirques, aretes, horns and erratics. Other features include alluvial fans and colluvium (rock fall).
	Tertiary (1.8–65 million years)	32–34 million years	**Granodiorite** **Tg**	Forms Capitol Peak, Mt. Daly, Mt. Sopris and Sam's Knob sill.
Mesozoic Era/Cenozoic Era Boundary known as **K-T Boundary**		65 million years Boundary not seen here.		Evidence is not found locally, but this is known as the time of the dinosaur extinction caused by either asteroid impact or volcanism, or both.
Mesozoic **Age of Reptiles**	**Cretaceous** (65–144 million years) This period marks the beginning of flowering plants. Dinosaurs reign.	70 million years	**Mesaverde Formation**	Massive amounts of decomposed plants in ancient delta deposits create coal now mined nearby.
		75 million years	**Mancos Shale** **Kmu, Kmf, Kml**	Most of the rock at Snowmass Village is this. It can contain carbonaceous material and fossils.
		100 million years	**Dakota Sandstone** **Kdb**	Light color, very hard rock that forms the Big Burn area.
	Jurassic (144–208 million years) Dinosaurs!	150 million years	**Morrison Formation** **Jm**	Red, green and gray striped rocks famous for containing dinosaur fossils; visible from top of Elk Camp.
		160 million years	**Entrada Sandstone** **Je**	Yellow-tan rocks that form small cliffs locally; in Utah these rocks form the red arches in Arches National Park.
	Triassic (208–248 million years) Frogs and turtles followed by mammals birds & dinosaurs	208 million years 240 million years	**Chinle Formation State Bridge Formation** **Tc, TPs**	Mostly red to red-orange rocks on the east wall of East Snowmass Creek canyon.
Paleozoic Era/Mesozoic Era Boundary		248 million years		This period marks the time of mass extinction when 96% of marine invertebrate species disappeared and is the closest time to total extinction of life on earth.
Paleozoic **Age of Fishes**	**Pennsylvanian-Permian** (248–323 million years) Time of the supercontinent, Pangaea. Insects evolve to giant size; 14 inch spiders!	300 million years	**Maroon Formation** **PPm**	Tropical storms break down the Ancestral Rockies, forming mud and rock debris, which formed deposits of bedded, dark red rock.
		Rocks not exposed near Snowmass Village		Sand and mud from the Ancestral Rockies deposited near to and in a sea between the mountain ranges. Periodic evaporation of the sea formed gypsum, anhydrite and salt.
		310 million years	**Gothic and Eagle Valley Evaporite**	
		320 million years	**Belden Formation**	Mud and sand from the initial uplift of the Ancestral Rockies deposited in a sea along with limestones.
	Mississippian (323–354 million years) First reptiles	340 million years	**Leadville Limestone**	Leadville Limestone and the Belden Formation hosted rich silver deposits discovered at Aspen in 1879.
	Cambrian through Devonian age rocks are beneath the surface here but are exposed in the Glenwood Canyon (354–545 million years)			Sandstone, dolomite and limestone deposited in shallow sea covering large region.
Precambrian/ Proterozoic	**Precambrian** (545 million to 4.6 billion years)	1.4–1.7 billion years	**Precambrian Granodiorite and Gneiss**	Rocks that formed about six miles deep in the earth are exposed locally in the Aspen area.

ECOLOGY

*Those who contemplate the beauty of the earth find reserves of
strength that will endure as long as life lasts.*

—RACHEL CARSON

Mountain Life Zones
and Ecosystems

Snowmass Village is located on Brush Creek, a tributary of
the Roaring Fork River, which flows into the Colorado
River. All of these watersheds are located in the
Southern Rockies Ecoregion, which includes much of
Colorado as well as parts of southern Wyoming and
northern New Mexico.[1] An ecoregion is a large geographical
area containing a diversity of ecosystems within a landscape of similar topography, geology, soils, plant communities and weather. An
ecosystem develops from the interaction between living organisms
and their physical environment, resulting in a recognizable community of plants and animals. Where the physical factors of soil, water
and climate vary within an ecoregion, so do the ecosystems. The
concept of ecosystems can be applied to a particular plant community, to defined microhabitats within each plant community or to a
larger group of plant communities that function together. For
example, an ecosystem may be an oak-mountain shrubland, an aspen
or spruce-fir forest, a microhabitat within one of the larger ecosystems, such as a small meadow, pond or a damp cliff face, or it could
refer to the entire Southern Rockies Ecoregion.

Ecologists traditionally group Colorado ecosystems into "life
zones"—foothills, montane, subalpine and alpine—defined by certain
plant communities and their associated ecosystems. Elevation, latitude and topography affect the temperature, winds and growing season, which in turn affect the type of plant community or communities that make up the ecosystems within each life zone. Changes
with elevation occur because for every 1,000 feet (305 m) of elevation gain, the temperature decreases by 3 degrees F (16 degrees C),
which is the equivalent of traveling 600 miles (966 km) north. This
field guide covers life zones in this area from approximately 7,500

feet (2286 m) to 14,000 feet (4267 m), leaving out those at lower elevations.

The ecosystems within these life zones are complex and dynamic, representing thousands of years of adaptations by living things to the natural processes occurring within them. Whenever competition, available moisture, plant or animal diversity or exposure within an ecosystem changes suddenly (as with the introduction of non-native species), the structure, function and composition of natural communities can easily be degraded.

Following are descriptions of the local ecosystems by life zone. Elevations listed are approximate due to the many variables that can affect the upper and lower limits of different plant communities, and thus, the life zones.

A list of common plants and wildlife associated with each ecosystem is found at the end of its description. These are not meant to be complete, but rather to give a picture of the type of plants found there. Many species listed are found in several ecosystems, but are more typical of some.

RIPARIAN AND WETLAND

Riparian and wetland ecosystems occur throughout the montane, subalpine and alpine life zones. Their common feature is the occurrence of plants that require saturated soils during at least part of the growing season. "Riparian" refers to the relatively lush vegetation areas adjacent to streams, rivers, ponds and other open water. It is a transitional zone between true aquatic and drier upland or terrestrial environments. Riparian areas are a type of wetland because they depend on the presence of water, but the soils do not retain as much water as true wetlands, which include marshes, bogs, fens, seeps or springs.[2] Scientists classify different types of true wetlands by where they occur, the type of soils present and their source of water, such as runoff, precipitation or ground water.

Riparian habitat

Since the elevation, latitude or climate of riparian and wetland ecosystems is not as important to their existence as is the presence of periodically saturated soils, many of the same plant and wildlife species found in them are common to similar areas throughout North America.[3]

Beaver ponds create wetlands.

Together, riparian and wetland ecosystems occupy less than 3% of Colorado's land area, yet are home to approximately 40% of the plant species, as well as 75% of the birds and 80% of the mammals that live in or migrate through the state. Wildlife depends on these areas for habitat, food, nesting sites, corridors for movement and cover from predators for all or part of the year.[4]

Besides the key role these systems play in the daily lives of plants and wildlife, they are fundamentally important to the health of the greater ecosystem, which includes humans. The lush vegetation is the base of a much larger food chain linking aquatic insects, fish, birds, mammals and decomposers.

Riparian and wetland soils and plants are critical in moderating natural flood processes, absorbing water from runoff and recharging ground water, which in turn percolates back into rivers and streams maintaining flows during the dry season. Riparian and wetland soils and associated plants also filter out water impurities and contaminants, such as pesticides and heavy metals before they can enter streams. Pools and beaver ponds allow sediment to settle, which would otherwise move downstream smothering aquatic plants and insect larvae that wildlife depends upon for food. Over-bank flooding in riparian areas can deposit sediments that replenish nutrients and build soil in upland habitats.

Shade from riparian and wetland vegetation maintains cooler water temperatures, which supports a higher concentration of dissolved oxygen. If the vegetation dies or is removed, many of the organisms that inhabit these areas become stressed because of the increase in temperature and decrease in oxygen, and may not survive. Stream species, such as trout, caddisfly, stonefly and mayfly for example, do best when the water temperature is less than 55 degrees F (13 degrees C).

About 40–60% of Colorado's original riparian and wetland areas have already been altered.[5]

Both riparian and wetland systems are very sensitive to disturbance. Residential and commercial development, building and maintenance of trails and roads, over grazing, peat mining, dams and water diversions can all result in degradation of these ecosystems.

Some riparian areas and wetlands can be characterized by the trees and shrubs that grow there, but others may occur as meadows and marshes without any woody vegetation. Lower elevation riparian is dominated by blue spruce and cottonwood with strapleaf, sandbar, Bebb's and whiplash willows present, whereas there is a shift to aspen and Engelmann spruce with Drummond's, mountain and Booth's willows as the elevation increases. Planeleaf, short-fruit and Wolf's willows form thickets at even higher elevations in alpine wetlands. Below is a brief list of typical plants and animals found in riparian and wetland ecosystems of this area.

Plants

Trees and Shrubs
aspen (*Populus tremuloides*)
blue spruce (*Picea pungens*)
chokecherry (*Prunus virginiana*)
Engelmann spruce (*Picea engelmannii*)
gooseberry and currant (*Ribes spp.*)
hawthorn (*Crataegus erythropoda*)
mountain alder (*Alnus tenuifolia*)
mountain ash (*Sorbus scopulina*)
mountain maple (*Acer glabrum*)
narrowleaf cottonwood (*Populus angustifolia*)
red-osier dogwood (*Cornus sericea*)
river birch (*Betula occidentalis*)
shrubby cinquefoil (*Potentilla fruiticosa*)
twinberry honeysuckle (*Lonicera involucrata*)
wild rose (*Rosa woodsii*)
willows (*Salix spp.*)

Herbaceous Plants
American speedwell (*Veronica americana*)
arrowleaf senecio (*Senecio triangularis*)
bittercress (*Cardamine cordifolia*)
brook saxifrage (*Saxifraga odontoloma*)
cattails (*Typha latifolia*)
checkermallow (*Sidalcea candida*)
cowbane (*Oxypolis fendleri*)
false hellebore (*Veratrum californicum*)
field mint (*Mentha arvensis*)
grass-of-Parnassus (*Parnassia fimbriata*)
giant angelica (*Angelica ampla*)
horsetail (*Equisetum arvensis*)
large-leaved avens (*Geum macrophyllum*)
marsh marigold (*Caltha leptosepala*)
monkeyflower (*Mimulus guttatus*)
monkshood (*Aconitum columbianum*)

mountain bluebells (*Mertensia ciliata*)
northern green bog orchid (*Limnorchis hyperborea*)
Parry's primrose (*Primula parryi*)
rose gentian (*Gentianella amarella*)
star gentian (*Swertia perennis*)
St. John's wort (*Hypericum formosum*)
watercress (*Nasturtium officinale*)
water hemlock (*Cicuta maculata*)
wild iris (*Iris missouriensis*)
willowherb (*Epilobium hornemannii*)

Grasses and Grass-like Plants
baltic rush (*Juncus arcticus* var. *balticus*)
beaked sedge (*Carex utriculata*)
Colorado rush (*Juncus confusus*)
Hall's rush (*Juncus hallii*)
Nebraska sedge (*Carex nebrascensis*)
small-winged sedge (*Carex microptera*)
swordleaf rush (*Juncus ensifolius*)
tufted hairgrass (*Deschampsia cespitosa*)
water sedge (*Carex aquatilis*)
woodrush (*Luzula parviflora*)
woolly sedge (*Carex lanuginosa*)

Beaver lodge

Birds

great blue heron (*Ardea herodias*)
Canada goose (*Branta canadensis*)
mallard (*Anas platyrhynchos*)
wild turkey (*Meleagris gallopavo*)
spotted sandpiper (*Actitis macularia*)
Wilson's snipe (*Gallinago gallinago*)
great horned owl (*Bubo virginianus*)
violet-green swallow (*Tachycineta thalassina*)
Lewis's woodpecker (*Melanerpes lewis*)
olive-sided flycatcher (*Contopus cooperi*)
western wood-pewee (*Contopus sordidulus*)
Cordilleran flycatcher (*Empidonax occidentalis*)
willow flycatcher (*Empidonax traillii*)
warbling vireo (*Vireo gilvus*)
American dipper (*Cinclus mexicanus*)
Swainson's thrush (*Catharus ustulatus*)
yellow warbler (*Dendroica petechia*)
MacGillivray's warbler (*Oporornis tolmiei*)
Wilson's warbler (*Wilsonia pusilla*)
western tanager (*Piranga ludovicana*)
white-crowned sparrow (*Zonotrichia leucophrys*)
fox sparrow (*Passerella iliaca*)
song sparrow (*Melospiza melodia*)
Lincoln's sparrow (*Melospiza lincolnii*)
Cassin's finch (*Carpodacus cassinii*)

Mammals

water shrew (*Sorex palustris*)
montane shrew (*Sorex monticolus*)
masked shrew (*Sorex cinereus*)
American beaver (*Castor canadensis*)
deer mouse (*Peromyscus maniculatus*)
meadow vole (*Microtus pennsylvanicus*)
montane vole (*Microtus montanus*)
muskrat (*Ondatra zibethicus*)
western jumping mouse (*Zapus princeps*)
long-tailed weasel (*Mustela frenata*)
raccoon (*Procyon lotor*)
mink (*Mustela vison*)
northern river otter (*Lutra canadensis*)
coyote (*Canis latrans*)
black bear (*Ursus americanus*)
raccoon (*Procyon lotor*)
long-tailed weasel (*Mustela frenata*)
striped skunk (*Mephitis mephitis*)
elk (*Cervus elaphus nelsoni*)
mule deer (*Odocoileus hemionus*)

Young mink

MONTANE FORESTS AND SHRUBLANDS

7,000–9,500 ft. (2134–2896 m)

Diverse ecosystems distinguish the montane life zone. Slopes that face south or west are usually dominated by oak-mountain and sagebrush shrublands, while the moist and cool north- and east-facing slopes are covered by aspen and mixed-conifer forests, with intervening riparian and wetland ecosystems making up the patterns. Following are descriptions of the ecosystems associated with the montane life zone in this area.

Oak-Mountain Shrublands 5,500–8,500 ft. (1675–2591 m)

MONTANE FORESTS AND SHRUBLANDS

Mule's ears and lupine brighten oak-mountain shrublands.

Oak-mountain shrub communities occupy mostly south- or west-facing slopes, where solar radiation is strong, temperatures are relatively high and soils are dry and rocky. In the Brush Creek watershed, these shrub communities thrive on dense clay soils derived from Mancos Shale. In other areas of the Roaring Fork watershed, this same community is found on other soils, but they all share sunny, relatively dry locations. Distinct dark green clumps of Gambel oak are interspersed with serviceberry, chokecherry, mountain mahogany, antelope bitterbrush and sagebrush.

Oak-mountain shrublands can be a transitional ecosystem between pinyon-juniper woodlands or the large sagebrush shrublands of lower elevations and aspen or mixed-conifer forests at higher elevations. It is possible to find a few scattered Rocky Mountain junipers in this habitat. Pinyon pine is rare, although an occasional pinyon may be found up to 9,000 feet (2745 m) in the Roaring Fork drainage. Small pockets of aspen or Douglas-fir ecosystems may occur within these shrublands on shaded, more north-facing slopes where temperatures are cooler and moisture more prevalent.

Thick vegetative cover, along with an abundance of berries, seeds and other forage, makes this very important wildlife habitat. Bears gorge on the chokecherries, serviceberries and acorns in the fall, storing fat in preparation for hibernation. Elk and deer prefer oak-mountain shrublands as winter habitat and many birds find secure nesting, resting and feeding sites here. Watch for the colorful spotted towhee singing from the top of a shrub as his distinctive red eye glistens in the sunlight. Predators such as coyotes, foxes, bobcats and birds of prey feast on the plentiful rodent population. Red-tail hawks regularly soar overhead as they scout this area.

Because native wildlife species depend so heavily on this habitat, the disruption of oak-mountain shrublands for development of other uses can have a great impact on them. Residents and builders can help by preserving native shrubs where possible, and using native vegetation in landscape plantings.

Plants

Shrubs

antelope bitterbrush (*Purshia tridentata*)
broom snakeweed (*Gutierrezia sarothrae*)
chokecherry (*Prunus virginiana*)
Gambel oak (*Quercus gambelii*)
mountain mahogany (*Cercocarpus montanus*)
mountain sagebrush (*Artemisia tridentata* var. *vayseyana*)
mountain snowberry (*Symphoricarpos rotundifolia*)
Oregon grape (*Mahonia repens*)
rabbitbrush (*Chrysothamnus* spp.)
rock goldenrod (*Petradoria pumila*)
Utah serviceberry (*Amelanchier utahensis*)
wax currant (*Ribes cereum*)

Herbaceous Plants

arrowleaf balsamroot (*Balsamorhiza sagittata*)
common lupine (*Lupinus argenteus*)
Rollins' bladderpod (*Physaria rollinsii*)
dwarf bluebells (*Mertensia fusiformis*)
fringed sagewort (*Artemisia frigida*)
golden smoke (*Corydalis aurea*)
longleaf phlox (*Phlox longiflolia*)
mat penstemon (*Penstemon caespitosus*)
mule's ears (*Wyethia amplexicaulis*)
multi-flowered phlox (*Phlox multiflora*)
narrowleaf paintbrush (*Castilleja linariifolia*)
Nelson's larkspur (*Delphinium nuttalianum*)
northern rock jasmine (*Androsace septentrionalis*)
pasqueflower (*Anemone patens*)
pink plumes (*Geum triflorum*)
pussytoes (*Antennaria* spp.)
scarlet gilia (*Ipomopsis aggregata*)
sugarbowl (*Clematis hirsutissima*)
sulfurflower (*Eriogonum umbellatum*)

Grasses and Grass-like Plants

bottlebrush squirreltail (*Elymus elymoides*)
elk sedge (*Carex geyeri*)
fringed brome (*Bromus ciliatus*)
Indian ricegrass (*Stipa hymenoides*)
junegrass (*Koeleria macrantha*)
mutton grass (*Poa fendleriana*)
Thurber's fescue (*Festuca thurberi*)

Birds

golden eagle (*Aquila chrysaetos*)
red-tailed hawk (*Buteo jamaicensis*)
blue grouse (*Dendragapus obscurus*)
band-tailed pigeon (*Columba fasciata*)
common nighthawk (*Chordeiles minor*)
Lewis's woodpecker (*Melanerpes lewis*)
broad-tailed hummingbird (*Selasphorus platycercus*)
dusky flycatcher (*Empidonax wrightii*)
plumbeous vireo (*Vireo plumbeus*)
Steller's jay (*Cyanocitta stelleri*)
western scrub jay (*Aphelocoma californica*)
common raven (*Corvus corax*)
blue-gray gnatcatcher (*Polioptila caerulea*)
mountain bluebird (*Sialia currucoides*)
Townsend's solitaire (*Myadestes townsendi*)
orange-crowned warbler (*Vermivora celata*)
Virginia's warbler (*Vermivora virginiae*)
MacGillivray's warbler (*Oporornis tolmiei*)
black-headed grosbeak (*Pheucticus melanocephalus*)
lazuli bunting (*Passerina amoena*)
green-tailed towhee (*Pipilo chlorurus*)
spotted towhee (*Pipilo maculatus*)

Mammals

dwarf shrew (*Sorex nanus*)
Nuttall's cottontail (*Sylvilagus nuttalii*)
least chipmunk (*Tamias minimus*)
golden-mantled ground-squirrel (*Spermophilus lateralis*)
bushy-tailed woodrat (*Neotoma cinerea*)
rock squirrel (*Spermophilus variegatus*)
deer mouse (*Peromyscus maniculatus*)
marmot (*Marmota flaviventris*)
montane vole (*Microtus montanus*)
western jumping mouse (*Azpus princeps*)
coyote (*Canis latrans*)
red fox (*Vulpes vulpes*)
black bear (*Ursus americanus*)
mountain lion (*Felis concolor*)
bobcat (*Lynx rufus*)
striped skunk (*Mephitis mephitis*)
elk (*Cervus elaphus*)
mule deer (*Odocoileus hemionus*)

Sagebrush Shrublands Up to 8,500 ft. (2591 m)

MONTANE FORESTS AND SHRUBLANDS

KATHERINE DARROW

Sagebrush shrublands are found in the montane zone, usually intermittent with oak-mountain shrublands. They are also found at higher elevations where mountain big sagebrush can adapt to colder landscapes with well-drained soil.[6] Although preferring full sun, they can tolerate shade and higher levels of organic matter than other big sagebrush varieties occuring at lower elevations.

Historically, sagebrush shrubland dominated the drier land in the valley bottoms, which is also the most desirable for agriculture and residential development, making it one of the most threatened ecosystems in rapidly developing mountain areas. Although there are some large stands along Snowmass Creek Road, most sagebrush in Brush Creek and the upper Roaring Fork valleys has been cleared or seriously fragmented. The smaller isolated patches that remain are largely incapable of supporting the birds that rely on extensive sagebrush habitat for their survival, such as Brewer's sparrow, sage sparrow and sage grouse. Where sagebrush has not been removed, overgrazing by cattle and sheep in many places suppressed native perennials and encouraged invasion by non-native species such as cheatgrass. Once compromised, sagebrush shrublands rarely recover without active human management because non-native grasses allow fire to spread more easily, seeds that would replenish an area are destroyed and mycorrhizal fungi necessary for seed establishment are lost.

In summary, plants and animals that depend on this habitat for winter range, nesting or foraging are compromised when the ecological integrity of the shrublands is degraded by the invasion of non-native species, conversion to other uses, and alteration of natural fire patterns.

Arrowleaf balsamroot

Plants

Trees and Shrubs

mountain big sagebrush (*Artemisia tridentata* var. *vaseyana*)

antelope bitterbrush (*Purshia tridentata*)

mountain snowberry (*Symphoricarpos rotundifolius*)

rabbitbrush (*Ericameria nauseosa*)

Rocky Mountain juniper (*Juniperus scopulorum*)

Utah serviceberry (*Amelanchier utahensis*)

Herbaceous Plants

arrowleaf balsamroot (*Balsamorhiza sagittata*)

broom snakeweed (*Gutierrezia sarothrae*)

common lupine (*Lupinus argenteus*)

larkspur (*Delphinium nuttallianum*)

mariposa lily (*Calochortus gunnisonii*)

mule's ears (*Wyethia amplexicaulis*)

multi-flowered phlox (*Phlox multiflora*)

narrowleaf paintbrush (*Castilleja linariifolia*)

pussy toes (*Antennaria rosea*)

salsify (*Tragopogon dubius*)

scarlet gilia (*Ipomopsis aggregata*)

tall pentsemon (*Penstemon strictus*)

sulfurflower (*Eriogonum umbellatum*)

Grasses and Grass-like Plants

bottlebrush squirreltail (*Elymus elymoides*)

Indian ricegrass (*Stipa hymenoides*)

junegrass (*Koeleria macrantha*)

muttongrass (*Poa fendleriana*)

needle-and-thread grass (*Stipa comata*)

sandberg bluegrass (*Poa secunda*)

Mammals

dwarf shrew (*Sorex nanus*)

desert cottontail (*Sylvilagus audubonii*)

least chipmunk (*Tamias minimus*)

Wyoming ground squirrel (*Spermophilus elegans*)

golden-mantled ground squirrel (*Spermophilus lateralis*)

rock squirrel (*Spermophilus variegates*)

deer mouse (*Peromyscus maniculatus*)

montane vole (*Microtus montanus*)

badger (*Taxidea taxus*)

coyote (*Canis latrans*)

red fox (*Vulpes vulpes*)

mountain lion (*Felis concolor*)

bobcat (*Lynx rufus*)

elk (*Cervus elaphus nelsonii*)

mule deer (*Odocoileus hemionus*)

Birds

red-tailed hawk (*Buteo jamaicensis*)

golden eagle (*Aquila chrysaetos*)

American kestrel (*Falco sparverius*)

common raven (*Corvus corax*)

black-billed magpie (*Pica pica*)

blue-gray gnatcatcher (*Polioptila caerulea*)

green-tailed towhee (*Pipilo chlorurus*)

sage sparrow (*Amphispiza belli*)

vesper sparrow (*Pooecetes gramineus*)

lark sparrow (*Chondestes grammacus*)

Brewer's sparrow (*Spizella breweri*)

Red fox

Aspen Forests 7,500–9,500 ft. (2286–2896 m)

MONTANE FORESTS AND SHRUBLANDS

JUDY HILL

Aspen forests define seasons here in the mountains. Spring arrives with dangling aspen catkins followed by new, lime-green foliage, which expands into summer becoming the whispering of quaking leaves.

Autumn is resplendent with color as whole stands change to gold, orange, crimson and bronze. Too soon, winter surrounds the graceful trunks with swirling snowflakes. Original "survivors," aspens are found as small twisted trunks at timberline, stalwart on arid slopes of the West's desert basins and thriving on our moist Colorado slopes, reigning over more of North America than any other tree.

Bark beetle galleries are created when beetle larvae hatch from eggs laid under aspen bark, as they burrow out, eating the nutritious tissue just beneath the aspen bark.

Aspen forests are next in importance to riparian and wetland ecosystems in the arid West for the essential role they play in the lives of an estimated 500 species, from bears to fungi, because of the wide array of micro-habitats they contain.[7]

Dark expressive "eyes," the elongated black knots on an aspen's trunk are the result of continual self-pruning of lower limbs receiving inadequate light. This self-pruning opens up the understory, allowing for growth of the many different layers of vegetation common to an aspen forest.

They also prevent erosion by controlling runoff, as they filter water through their soils ensuring that clean water spills into the valley's streams.

Beneath the green canopy, dappled sunshine, rich alkaline soil and a leaf litter sufficient to hold moisture support a diverse understory which provides an array of wildlife with plentiful food, as well as cover and habitat for nesting and denning. "Honeydew," a honey-like substance secreted by aphids feeding in the canopy, often covers the vegetation below with a shiny varnish.

Aspen trees reproduce by sending out suckers, which produce trees that are a genetic clone of the mother tree. Even though each tree in such a clone develops its own root system, and the original roots probably wither away, the clone is still considered a single organism since the stems are all genetically identical. While most aspens are short-lived at 50 to 70 years, an entire clone could be thousands of years old—some speculate even a million.[8] Although the dominant color of fall aspens is a brilliant yellow-gold, leaves of some clones may turn contrasting shades of orange or red. A clone may also collectively leaf out earlier or later than others.

Aspen trees are quite vulnerable to fungus, insects and disease. This results in dead and dying trees scattered throughout the forest. However, these trees are critical to cavity-nesting birds such as woodpeckers and flickers who excavate their nests in the soft wood of these trunks. If abandoned, secondary cavity nesters, which include chickadees, western bluebirds, house wrens, red and white-breasted nuthatches and swallows, will come in and raise families in these aboreal apartment houses.

Aspen forests are typically considered successional. This means they are eventually replaced by a more stable plant community such as subalpine fir, Douglas-fir or Engelmann spruce, which grow up in the shade aspens provide. These climax communites often replace aspen or lodgepole pine forests, usually the first to colonize areas after natural or manmade disturbance. However, if an aspen grove is isolated from such seed sources or the conditions for successional changes to occur, it may maintain itself continually. Aspens probably have not generally reproduced by seed germination since the last ice age, about 10,000 years ago, but they can do so in the right circumstances—as they did after the 1988 Yellowstone National Park fire.

"Pando," an aspen clone in Utah's Wasatch Mountains, consists of over 47,000 male stems spread over 106 acres (43 ha), and is estimated to weigh 6,500 tons (5896 metric tons)—making it one of the world's largest organisms.[9]

Black bears may climb aspens in search of food or to mark their territory. Their front claws make slashing marks as they drag themselves up; just beneath those, you can see where the rear claws punched into the trunk for support (see "Bear Trees" on p. 409).

When winter browse is scarce, elk will feed on the living bark of aspens, stripping it from the bottom up as they don't have upper incisors. They don't "girdle" trees as porcupines do, but may remove enough bark to kill trees during severe winters. Longer and wider scrapes are caused by buck deer or bull elk rubbing the tree to remove itchy antler velvet.

Plants

Trees and Shrubs

chokecherry (*Prunus virginiana*) .
common juniper (*Juniperus communis*)
mountain ash (*Sorbus scopulina*)
mountain gooseberry (*Ribes inerme*)
mountain snowberry (*Symphoricarpos rotundifolius*)
red elderberry (*Sambucus racemosa*)
serviceberry (*Amelanchier alnifolia*)
thimbleberry (*Rubus parviflorus*)
wild rose (*Rosa woodsii*)

Herbaceous Plants

aspen thistle (*Cirsium clavatum* var. *osterhoutii*)
baneberry (*Actaea rubra*)
beauty cinquefoil (*Potentilla gracilis* var. *pulcherrima*)
blue columbine (*Aquilegia coerulea*)
common lupine (*Lupinus argenteus*)
Engelmann aster (*Aster engelmannii*)
false Solomon's seal (*Maianthemum racemosum*)
Fendler's meadowrue (*Thalictrum fendleri*)
giant lousewort (*Pedicularis procera*)
mountain parsely (*Pseudocymopterus montanus*)
northern bedstraw (*Galium boreale*)
Porter's loveage (*Ligusticum porteri*)
purple clematis (*Clematis occidentalis*)
Richardson's geranium (*Geranium richardsonii*)
scarlet paintbrush (*Castilleja miniata*)
star Solomonplume (*Maianthemum stellatum*)
western sweetroot (*Osmorhiza occidentalis*)
western coneflower (*Rudbeckia occidentalis*)
western valerian (*Valeriana occidentalis*)

Grasses and Grass-like Plants

blue wild rye (*Elymus glaucus*)
elk sedge (*Carex geyeri*)
mountain brome (*Bromus carinatus*)
orchard grass (*Dactylis glomerata*)
slender wheatgrass (*Agropyron trachycaulum*)
timothy (*Phleum pratense*)

Birds

sharp-shinned hawk (*Accipiter striatus*)
Cooper's hawk (*Accipiter cooperii*)
red-tailed hawk (*Buteo jamaicensis*)
blue grouse (*Dendragapus obscurus*)
northern pygmy owl (*Glaucidium gnoma*)
northern saw-whet owl (*Aegolius acadicus*)
great-horned owl (*Bubo virginianus*)

broad-tailed hummingbird (*Selasphorus platycercus*)
Williamson's sapsucker (*Sphyrapicus thyroideus*)
red-naped sapsucker (*Sphyrapicus varius*)
hairy woodpecker (*Picoides villosus*)
downy woodpecker (*Picoides pubescens*)
northern flicker (*Colaptes auratus*)
western wood peewee (*Contopus sordidulus*)
olive-sided flycatcher (*Contopus cooperi*)
warbling vireo (*Vireo gilvus*)
Steller's jay (*Cyanocitta stelleri*)
tree swallow (*Tachycineta bicolor*)
violet-green swallow (*Tachycineta thalassina*)
black-capped chickadee (*Poecile atricapillus*)
mountain chickadee (*Poecile gambeli*)
white-breasted nuthatch (*Sitta carolinensis*)
house wren (*Troglotydes aedon*)
mountain bluebird (*Sialia currucoides*)
Swainson's thrush (*Catharus ustulatus*)
yellow-rumped warbler (*Dendroica coronata*)
pine grosbeak (*Pinicola enucleator*)
Cassin's finch (*Carpodacus cassinii*)
evening grosbeak (*Coccothraustes vesperitinus*)

Mammals

masked shrew (*Sorex cinereus*)
montane shrew (*Sorex monticolus*)
Nuttall's cottontail (*Sylvilagus nuttalii*)
snowshoe hare (*Lepus americanus*)
least chipmunk (*Tamias minimus*)
marmot (*Marmota flaviventris*)
deer mouse (*Peromyscus maniculatus*)
montane vole (*Microtus montanus*)
meadow vole (*Microtus pennsylvanicus*)
long-tailed vole (*Microtus longicaudus*)
western jumping mouse (*Zapus princeps*)
porcupine (*Erethizon dorsatum*)
coyote (*Canis latrans*)
red fox (*Vulpes vulpes*)
black bear (*Ursus americanus*)
raccoon (*Procyon lotor*)
short-tailed weasel (*Mustela ermina*)
long-tailed weasel (*Mustela frenata*)
striped skunk (*Mephitis mephitis*)
bobcat (*Lynx rufus*)
elk (*Cervus elaphus nelsonii*)
mule deer (*Odocoileus hemionus*)

Mixed-Conifer Forests   7,500–10,000 ft. (2286–3048 m)

MONTANE FORESTS AND SHRUBLANDS

Mixed-conifer ecosystems refer to montane coniferous forests that are transitional between lower-elevation pinyon-juniper woodlands and cooler, higher-elevation forests of mostly continuous spruce-fir. Although often a hodgepodge of Douglas-fir, lodgepole pine, subalpine fir, and Engelmann spruce, the mix is usually dominated by one of the first two species. Occasionally, ponderosa pine and limber pine are added to the mix. In this area, those dominated by Douglas-fir occur on north-facing slopes as well as in shaded ravines. Those forests dominated by lodgepole pines often grow at the same elevations in drier, well-drained soil as pioneering trees after some type of disturbance, such as fire, blowdown, insect infestation or avalanche. Lodgepole pines may form large uniform stands so thick with skinny, straight trees that little sunlight reaches the ground. Over time, natural processes such as fires or insect infestation naturally thin out these stands and will produce more open, park-like landscapes with larger trees.

Aspen, a pioneering tree like lodgepole, can be found in these mixed-conifer forests, occurring as small stands or random trees in sunny areas where the soils are holding more moisture. No bird, plant or mammal species is specific only to this mixed-conifer forest type; however, the following species are commonly encountered.

Plants

Shrubs
bilberry (*Vaccinium myrtillus*)
buffaloberry (*Shepherdia canadensis*)
common juniper (*Juniperus communis*)
snowbrush (*Ceanothus velutinus*)
mountain lover (*Paxistima myrsinites*)
Scouler's willow (*Salix scouleriana*)
Wolf's currant (*Ribes wolfii*)

Herbaceous Plants
calypso orchid (*Calypso bulbosa*)
heart-leaf arnica (*Arnica cordifolia*)
one-sided wintergreen (*Pyrola secunda*)
pipsissewa (*Chimaphila umbellata*)
striped coralroot orchid (*Corallorhiza striata*)

Birds
gray jay (*Perisoreus canadensis*)
Steller's jay (*Cyanocitta stelleri*)
mountain chickadee (*Poecile gambeli*)
white-breasted nuthatch (*Sitta carolinensis*)
red-breasted nuthatch (*Sitta canadensis*)
ruby-crowned kinglet (*Regulus calendula*)
brown creeper (*Certhia americana*)
hermit thrush (*Catharus guttatus*)
yellow-rumped warbler (*Dendroica coronata*)
red crossbill (*Loxia curvirostra*)
pine siskin (*Carduelis pinus*)
western tanager (*Piranga ludoviciana*)

Mammals
snowshoe hare (*Lepus americanus*)
uinta chipmunk (*Tamias umbrinus*)
pine squirrel (*Tamiasciurus hudsonicus*)
porcupine (*Erethizon dorsatum*)
marten (*Martes americana*)

THE SUBALPINE ZONE: SPRUCE-FIR FORESTS

9,500–11,500 ft. (2896–3505 m)

Ascending in elevation, a nearly continuous band of deep verdant green, interspersed with thriving wildflower meadows and steep mountain streams, eventually replaces the diverse plant communities that characterize the montane elevations. The dominant ecosystem in the subalpine zone,

Engelmann spruce and subalpine fir form dense forests covering Elk Camp slopes beneath cliffs of the Dakota Formation.

these cool, moist spruce-fir forests are marked by an almost cathedral-like quiet, broken only occasionally by a scolding pine squirrel, the brusque call of a bold Steller's jay or the liquid song of a hermit thrush. The dense shade and the acidic soil derived from decomposing conifer needles will not support the diversity found under open canopies with alkaline soils.

Aspen and lodgepole pines, typical pioneering trees of the montane zone, will intermix with spruce-fir wherever natural disturbances such as blowdowns, deaths from insect infestations, fire or avalanches create openings that allow more sunlight-dependent species to grow.

Spruce-fir forests collect and retain more snowfall than any other zone, capturing snow blown off exposed alpine areas. When spring arrives, steady snowmelt fills the creeks and streams of the Roaring Fork watershed that eventually flow into the Colorado River, providing water for areas west of the Continental Divide. Unfortunately, much of this water is now being diverted east to the burgeoning Front Range, leaving fish high and dry.

GEORGE P. HUGGINS

Subalpine stream meanders through wildflower meadows.

Fragmentation by logging, road-building, trails, house construction and ski areas, all whittle away at the heart of the forest habitat. Many sensitive species such as marten and Canada lynx require larger territories and need unbroken forests to survive. These human activities also create barriers to animal movement, cause erosion and water pollution, provide corridors for invasion of weedy species, and allow easier human access that can disturb wildlife. Damage from disruption is slow to heal because of the short growing season and cold winters.[10]

Plants

Shrubs

bilberry (*Vaccinium myrtillus*)
bog birch (*Betula glandulosa*)
buffaloberry (*Shepherdia canadensis*)
Colorado currant (*Ribes coloradense*)
common juniper (*Juniperus communis*)
mountain lover (*Paxistima myrsinites*)
red elderberry (*Sambucus racemosa*)
red raspberry (*Rubus idaeus*)
shrubby cinquefoil (*Potentilla fruiticosa*)
wild rose (*Rosa woodsii*)
Wolf's currant (*Ribes wolfii*)

Herbaceous Plants

alpine cinquefoil (*Potentilla subjuga*)
broad-leaf arnica (*Arnica latifolia*)
heart-leaf arnica (*Arnica cordifolia*)
one-sided wintergreen (*Pyrola secunda*)
parrot's beak (*Pedicularis racemosa*)
pink pyrola (*Pyrola asarifolia*)
red columbine (*Aquilegia elegantula*)
Jacob's ladder (*Polemonium pulcherrimum*)
striped coralroot (*Corallorhiza striata*)
thimbleberry (*Rubus parviflorus*)
twinflower (*Linnaea borealis*)
wood nymph (*Moneses uniflora*)
woolly golden aster (*Heterotheca villosa*)
Wooton's groundsel (*Senecio wootonii*)

Forbs of subalpine meadows

American bistort (*Polygonum bistortoides*)
common lupine (*Lupinus argenteus*)
daffodil senecio (*Senecio amplectens*)
death camas (*Zygadenus elegans*)
graceful buttercup (*Ranunculus inamoenus*)
green gentian (*Frasera speciosa*)
harebell (*Campanula rotundifolia*)
Aspen sunflower (*Helianthella quinquenervis*)
northern paintbrush (*Castilleja sulphurea*)
Parry's gentian (*Gentiana parryi*)
rosy paintbrush (*Castilleja rhexifolia*)
scarlet paintbrush (*Castilleja miniata*)
subalpine larkspur (*Delphinium barbeyi*)
mountain bluebells (*Mertensia ciliata*)
yarrow (*Achillea millefolium* var. *lanulosa*)

Grasses and Grass-like Plants

alpine bluegrass (*Poa alpina*)
arctic bluegrass (*Poa arctica*)
elk sedge (*Carex geyeri*)
fringed brome (*Bromus ciliatus*)
mountain brome (*Bromus carinatus*)
reedgrass (*Calamagrostis canadensis*)
slender wheat grass (*Elymus trachycaulus*)
smooth wild rye (*Elymus glaucus*)
Thurber's fescue (*Festuca thurberi*)
tufted hairgrass (*Deschampsia cespitosa*)
woodrush (*Luzula parviflora*)

Birds

northern goshawk (*Accipter gentiles*)
blue grouse (*Dendragapus obscurus*)
boreal owl (*Aegolius funereus*)
broad-tailed hummingbird (*Selasphorus platycercus*)
olive-sided flycatcher (*Contopus cooperi*)
gray jay (*Perisoreus canadensis*)
Steller's jay (*Cyanocitta stelleri*)
common raven (*Corvus corax*)
Clark's nutcracker (*Nucifraga columbiana*)
mountain chickadee (*Poecile gambeli*)
brown creeper (*Certhia americana*)
red-breasted nuthatch (*Sitta canadensis*)
white-breasted nuthatch (*Sitta carolinensis*)
ruby-crowned kinglet (*Regulus calendula*)
golden-crowned kinglet (*Regulus satrapa*)
Townsend's solitaire (*Myadestes townsendi*)
hermit thrush (*Catharus guttatus*)
dark-eyed junco (*Junco hyemalis*)
pine grosbeak (*Pinicola enucleator*)
red crossbill (*Loxia curvirostra*)
pine siskin (*Carduelis pinus*)

*. . . nature shows us only
surfaces, but she is a million
fathoms deep.*

—RALPH WALDO EMERSON

Mammals

masked shrew (*Sorex cinereus*)
montane shrew (*Sorex monticolus*)
Nuttal's cottontail (*Sylvilagus nuttalii*)
snowshoe hare (*Lepus americanus*)
least chipmunk (*Tamias minimus*)
marmot (*Marmota flaviventris*)
pine squirrel (*Tamiasciurus hudsonicus*)
northern pocket gopher (*Thomomys talpoides*)
deer mouse (*Peromyscus maniculatus*)
bushy-tailed woodrat (*Neotoma cinerea*)
long-tailed vole (*Microtus longicaudus*)
montane vole (*Microtus montanus*)
pine marten (*Martes americana*)

long-tailed weasel (*Mustela frenata*)
ermine (*Mustela erminea*)
porcupine (*Erethizon dorsatum*)
coyote (*Canis latrans*)
red fox (*Vulpes vulpes*)
black bear (*Ursus americanus*)
bobcat (*Lynx rufus*)
Canada lynx (*Lynx canadensis*)
elk (*Cervus elaphus nelsonii*)
mule deer (*Odocoileus hemionus*)
bighorn sheep (*Ovis canadensis*)

THE LAND OF ELFIN TIMBER

Krummholz, derived from the German for "crooked wood" or "elfin timber," refers to the upper limits of the subalpine zone, where strong winds, blowing snow and ice crystals, frigid temperatures and intense solar radiation reduce stands of spruce and fir to prostrate, stunted mats. A short growing season of 40–90 days at this elevation largely prohibits seed production. Regeneration typically occurs when wind-carried seeds from trees at lower elevations find protected nooks in which to germinate. Clumps of krummholz spread by "layering" when heavy snow pushes the branches to the ground, allowing them to take root. These tree islands create their own microhabitats as they grow away from the prevailing wind, providing protected niches for wildflowers that are too tall to survive on the adjacent tundra. A mix of species from the subalpine and alpine are found here. Krummholz trees may look like a miniature collection of flag-topped shrubs, but many of them are as old as the towering spruces and firs only 1,000 vertical feet below.

THE ALPINE ZONE

11,400 ft. (3470 m) and above

DAVID HISER

When the growing season becomes so short that trees cannot gather enough energy to put on woody growth, the limit of tree growth, or treeline, occurs, marking the lower limit of alpine life zones—sometimes referred to as tundra. Appearing barren and desolate at first, a closer look reveals the varied pattern of microclimates, each supporting a unique ecosystem. This engaging world of Lilliputian plants hugs the ground, having adapted to survive a severe climate where temperatures often drop far below freezing, and ice crystals become piercing daggers driven by winds that may reach 100 mph (161 km/hr). Mats of tiny alpine and snow willows grow only a few inches high, while many plants grow protected in sheltered cracks and crevices of rocky outcrops. Many alpine plants have evolved waxy, furry or red pigmented armor to protect their tender foliage from the intense solar radiation found there. In fall, as photosynthesis slows and green chlorophyll pigments break down, the red anthocyanins become more obvious in plants such as alpine avens and king's crown, cloaking alpine meadows with crimson.

The perennial is queen of the alpine. Perennial plants are already established and ready to flower during very brief frost-free growing seasons, typically only sixty days or less. Scientists speculate that the female stigma of some plant species has evolved to be receptive for a longer period of time in the alpine, because there are fewer insects available for pollination.

Mammalian predators such as mountain lion and coyote come to hunt in the rolling landscape during the summer, but leave for lower elevations as winter approaches, following elk and mule deer to lower elevations. Birds,

King's crown, rosy paintbrush, alpine avens and American bistort grace alpine meadows.

such as the golden eagle and prairie falcon, also hunt here during the summer and fall, but migrate to lower elevations when the snow hides their prey.

Plant communities in the alpine zone are primarily determined by snow deposition patterns, though pocket gopher activity can dramatically alter the community mix. Following are

47

brief descriptions of the microecosystems that together shape the alpine.

Fellfields

Moss campion

Fellfields are rocky, exposed areas typically blown free of snow, where hardy cushion and mat-forming plants cling tightly to available soil with roots that grow thick and deep. Common plants include moss campion (*Silene acaulis*), alpine sandwort (*Minuartia obtusiloba*), alpine forget-me-not (*Eritrichum nanum* var. *elongatum*), alpine pussytoes (*Antennaria media*), yellow stonecrop (*Sedum lanceolatum*), alpine clover (*Trifolium dasyphyllum*), big-rooted spring beauty (*Claytonia megarhiza*), pygmy bitterroot (*Lewisia pygmaea*), mountain dryad (*Dryas octopetala*), northern rock jasmine (*Androsace septentrionalis*) and drabas (*Draba* spp.). Over time, leaf and soil debris accumulate among fellfield cushions, providing a more hospitable climate for less hardy plants and eventually transforming fellfields into meadows.

Snowbank Communities

Glacier lily

Large snowbank communities exist where snow deposition patterns create snowbanks that linger long into spring, and even right into summer, severely limiting the growing season. Once the snow melts, only a few hardy forbs, lichens, mosses, sedges and rushes can withstand these conditions. Sibbaldia (*Sibbaldia procumbens*), glacier lily (*Erythronium grandiflorum*), snowlover (*Chionophilia jamesii*) and snow buttercup (*Ranunculus adoneus*) are a few flowering plants that thrive here.

Wet Meadows

Wet meadows and small pools form in low areas downslope from snowbank communities, where the slowly melting snow provides a perfect microclimate for water-loving plants. Marsh marigold (*Caltha leptosepala*) and elephantella (*Pedicularis groenlandica*) flourish here. Also look for queen's crown (*Sedum rodanthum*), Rocky Mountain fringed gentian (*Gentianopsis detonsa*), alpine willow (*Salix arctica* var. *petraea)*, snow willow (*Salix reticulata*), alpine lousewort (*Pedicularis*

Fringed gentian

sudetica subsp. *scopulorum*), Parry's primrose (*Primula parryi*), glacier lily (*Erythronium grandiflorum*), globeflower (*Trollius albiflorus*), alpine avens (*Geum rossii*), snow buttercup (*Ranunculus adoneus*), bog saxifrage (*Saxifraga oregana*), sibbaldia (*Sibbaldia procumbens*) and James' snowlover (*Chionophila jamesii*). Water from wet meadows and snowbank communities moves down through the soils to become the headwaters of streams.

Tundra Turfs and Meadows

Turfs are drier areas made up of dense turfs of grasses such as tufted hairgrass (*Deschampsia cespitosa*) and sedges, primarily tiny kobresia (*Kobresia myosuroides*), that are blown free of snow throughout most of the winter. In contrast, tundra meadows have deep, rich soils that hold more moisture and support an abundant diversity of wildflowers. These include alpine sunflower (*Tetraneuris grandiflora*), a furry golden "giant" of the meadows, and slender American bistort (*Polygonum bistortoides*), a favorite food of white-tailed ptarmigan. Also look for snow willow (*Salix reticulata*), alp lily (*Lloydia serotina*), alpine avens (*Geum rossii*), sky pilot (*Polemonium viscosum*), alpine bistort (*Polygonum viviparium*), arctic gentian (*Gentiana algida*), king's crown (*Sedum integrifolium*), subalpine fleabane (*Erigeron peregrinus*), Parry's lousewort (*Pedicularis parryi*), rosy paintbrush (*Castilleja rhexifolia*) and western

King's crown

yellow paintbrush (*Castilleja occidentalis*). Both areas are important sources of forage for grazing elk.

Willow Carrs

Willow carrs are shrub communities occurring throughout both the subalpine and alpine where deep snow provides enough moisture to support thickets of low willows, typically Wolf's (*Salix wolfii*), planeleaf (*S. planifolia*) and short-fruit (*S. brachycarpa*). Look for rosy paintbrush (*Castilleja rhexifolia*), monkshood (*Aconitum columbianum*), buttercups (*Ranunculus* spp.), star gentian (*Swertia perennis*), bog saxifrage (*Saxifraga oregana*) and mountain bluebells (*Mertensia ciliata*) in their midst. Willow carrs provide important protective cover and food for white-tailed ptarmigan and mule deer and nesting habitat for white-crowned sparrows and willow flycatchers.

Star gentian

Alpine sorrel

Talus Fields, Cliffs and Rock Crevices

Talus fields are slopes where coarse, blocky rock rubble has tumbled from the fractured walls of cliffs, broken loose by the freezing and thawing of water. Some of these rocky slopes are rock glaciers, slowly creeping downslope as they are pulled by gravity and the freeze/thaw action of ice deep in the rocks. Goldbloom saxifrage (*Saxifraga chrysantha*) and big-rooted spring beauty (*Claytonia megarhiza*) are two charming plant species found here. Other plants include yellow stonecrop (*Sedum lanceolatum*), alpine sorrel (*Oxyria digyna*), blue columbine (*Aquilegia coerulea*), common alumroot (*Heuchera parvifolia*), mountain thistle (*Cirsium scopulorum*), spotted saxifrage (*Saxifraga bronchialis*) and whiplash saxifrage (*Saxifraga flagellaris* var. *crandallii*). These plants are also commonly found on cliffs and in rock crevices.

The shrill piping of pikas, small rabbit-like mammals, frequently breaks the silence, warning others of their species to find cover among the rocks. Look for rosy finches, which are found only in this part of Colorado.

Alpine avens

Gopher Gardens

Gopher gardens are the most diverse of alpine plant ecosystems. These areas have literally been rototilled by the burrowing of northern pocket gophers. Rodents with powerful digging claws, they spend their lives underground tunneling, feeding on roots and plants which they pull down through the soil and cleaning their passageways by carrying soil to the surface in special external cheek pouches. Plants common to these disturbed soils are alpine bluebells (*Mertensia alpina*), alpine avens (*Geum rossii*), sky pilot (*Polemonium viscosum*) and alpine sunflower (*Tetraneuris grandiflora*). Areas that are dug repeatedly may be dominated by tufted hairgrass (*Deschampsia cespitosa*), arctic sagewort (*Artemisia norvegica*) or Parry's clover (*Trifolium parryi*). See also page 394 for northern pocket gopher.

Birds
white-tailed ptarmigan (*Lagopus leucurus*)
horned lark (*Eremophila alpestris*)
American pipit (*Anthus rebescens*)
brown-capped rosy finch (*Leucosticte australis*)
white-crowned sparrow (*Zonotrichia leucophrys*)

Mammals
montane shrew (*Sorex monticolus*)
pika (*Ochotona princeps*)
marmot (*Marmota flaviventris*)
northern pocket gopher (*Thomomys talpoides*)
deer mouse (*Peromyscus maniculatus*)
meadow vole (*Microtus pennsylvanicus*)
elk (*Cervus elaphus nelsonii*)
mule deer (*Odocoileus hemionus*)
mountain goat (*Oreamnos americanus*)
big-horn sheep (*Ovis canadensis*)

Overview of Plant Communities

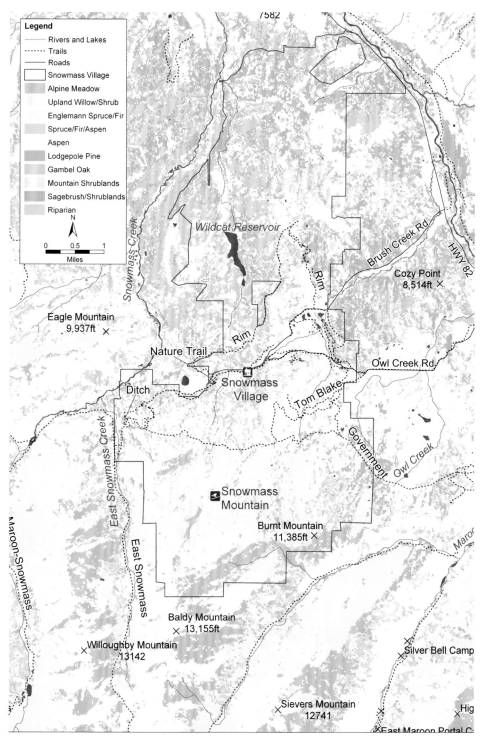

PLANTS

*How deeply with beauty is beauty overlaid . . . the ground
covered with crystals, the crystals with mosses and lichens and
low-spreading grasses and flowers, these with large plants
leaf over leaf with ever-changing color and form, the palms
of the firs outspread over these, the azure dome over all like a
bell flower, and star above star . . .*

—JOHN MUIR

An immersion into the plant kingdom reveals a world of
wonder brimming with intricate design, vivid color,
fantastic form and heady fragrance—from the tiniest
moss to the tallest tree beneath the "azure dome" of
the mountain sky.

Snowmass Village and the upper Roaring Fork Valley are the
perfect places to learn about mountain plants in their natural setting. With such a variety of plant communities to choose from,
the possibility for becoming acquainted with new plants is almost
endless!

Prepare to indulge your senses. Take along a magnifying
hand lens to examine the tiniest parts of a flower, perhaps sparkling
golden pollen spilling from the ruby anthers of brook saxifrage.
Inhale the heady sweetness of stemless evening-primrose or the
spicy scent of crushed sagebrush leaves. Relish the texture of fuzzy
mullein foliage or prickly borage fruit against your skin.

Visit plants at various times of the day or the season to know
their forever changing appearances. Spring is a good time to watch
different leaf shapes emerge from soil moist with snowmelt as they
pierce the decomposing latticework of last season's leaves. When
summer arrives, savor the kaleidoscope of color as meadows burst
into bloom. Visit again when the flowers have withered and
matured into elaborate forms of fruit and seed, rustling and swaying
in brisk autumn winds. Come at sunrise to see flowers glistening
with dew and drenched in color, then return on sunny afternoons
as insect pollination intensifies with busy bees stuffing their leg
pockets full of pollen, and as insects of every kind visit flower after
flower to gather nectar.

Following plants through the seasons develops a background
for identification when they have no flowers. Each page of the following chapter is a magical excursion into the complex world of
mountain plants to help you identify and understand them.

alypso Orchids
nis Huggins

When identifying plants, it is always best to get down on the plant's level. Do not pick flowers or break branches. Taking flowers only as photos or exquisite images in the mind's eye will ensure that plants continue to delight others year after year. Many beautiful native plants are now available commercially at nurseries in the valley for those who would like to grow them.

GEORGE HUGGINS

Janis shares plant stories with fellow hikers.

USING THIS CHAPTER

This chapter is organized by plant family, meaning a plant can be recognized by the particular characteristics shared within that family. By learning these traits, an educated guess can be made as to where to begin when searching for a new plant in the field guide. If unfamiliar with family characteristics, and the plant has flowers, then start with the **Color Guide to Flowering Plants** on page 57. There is also a **Key to Plant Families** on page 67. For evergreen trees and shrubs, as well as ferns and horsetails, please refer to the photos within the short **Non-flowering Plant section** on page 71. Consider the following when using this chapter:

• Plant families are divided into **non-flowering** and **flowering plant groups**. Within each of those groups, the families are listed alphabetically by common name, as is each individual plant within the appropriate family. Trees and shrubs are all listed within their family.

• Learning plants by families is more interesting than just learning plants by flower color or shape. For example, the shrubs chokecherry and wild rose are related to the herbaceous alpine avens, so it makes sense that they share historical uses.

- To include more species in the book, an alternate format without natural history paragraghs is used when multiple species, usually the same genus, have similar attributes (alternate format groups listed alphabetically within the family—e.g., Penstemon Group). Willows, grasses, rushes and sedges are in same format. Only a brief description and photo are included.

- **Sources for common names:** *Flora of North America*, the author, or Jody Cardamone, head naturalist for Aspen Center for Environmental Studies.

- Sources for **scientific names** (in italics): *A Checklist of the Vascular Plants of Colorado*, from the Rocky Mountain Herbarium, Department of Botany at the University of Wyoming, by Dr. Ronald L. Hartman and B. E. Nelson (http://www.rmh.uwyo.edu). The goal is to provide traditional scientific names that will be recognized by most visitors from the United States and around the world. [Bracketed] synonyms refer to alternate nomenclature from the *Catalog of the Colorado Flora: A Biodiversity Baseline*, by William A. Weber and Ronald C. Wittmann of the University of Colorado Museum. Dr. Weber's field guide *Colorado Flora—Western Slope* is currently the most complete technical key available for Colorado plants.

- **Non-native plants** are marked with an asterisk (*). Plants also on the **Pitkin County Noxious Weed List** (see p. 269) are marked with this symbol: Ⓦ

- **Natural history uses are in green:** When plants have aromatherapy, ceremonial, edible, garden, medicinal, revegetation or wildlife uses.

- **Plant descriptions** in two parts, the first part being a paragraph of essential identification information as follows:

COMMON NAMES OR LATIN?

Learning common names is a good introduction to plants, but studying their personality and history is a giant step in gaining deeper insight into the plant's value to humans, wildlife and surrounding ecosystems. Learning the Latin scientific name is also important, as they are typically more consistent worldwide than common names, and are necessary for anyone involved in scientific research, restoration work, native plant gardening or use of plants as medicine or food. Common names may be the ones used most often, but they are not as dependable, varying by locality. A single plant may have ten common names or sometimes the same common name is used for several different plants.

For example, many people refer to the local corn lily (*Veratrum tenuipetalum*) as "skunk cabbage," because its early growth resembles the broad basal leaves of the "real" skunk cabbages (the Western *Lysichiton americanum*, or *Symplocarpus foetidus* in the Northeast), which are in the Arum family (Araceae). Corn lily is also called false hellebore and Veratrum. This isn't just confusing—it can be very dangerous. The "real" skunk cabbages are edible after preparing them correctly, whereas Veratrum is strictly poisonous.

Life zone/ecosystem refers to the habitat where a plant can be found, as described in the Ecology chapter.

Flowering dates are a rough estimate for this area only and may be affected by a number of factors in any mountain environment. Similar habitats found at different elevations are subject to a wide range of physical influences such as variations in annual and seasonal moisture, temperature and sun exposure due to elevation or directional aspect. Thus, plants that tolerate a wide range of elevation will flower at different times of the season in varying locations. The ovary of a flower matures into a characteristic fruit, which carries the seeds. **Fruit** types follow the flowering dates.

Characteristics is intended to complement the photo and lead to accurate identification of the plant while comparing it with similar plants. In addition, **a ruler** is printed in the back of the book on p. 470 to help with measurements. Unless mentioned otherwise, **all plants are native perennials, shrubs or trees.** A **magnifying hand lens,** available at nature centers and some office supply stores, is very helpful for observing tiny flower parts, although you can reverse binoculars and look through the opposite way.

- The second, more **descriptive paragraph** covers folklore, historical and current uses, recent research, plant reproduction and other interesting information.

- Any information on medicinal or other uses of plants is provided only to briefly acquaint readers with the fascinating natural history of each species. Anyone wanting to explore these subjects further should consult additional resources which go into greater depth, or contact the appropriate professional.

Some plants that are described may not have a known history or practical use, but they can still be appreciated for their intrinsic beauty and for their place in our intricate natural ecosystems—whether for their air-cleaning role, the oxygen they provide, as food or shelter for living species, as erosion control or for the nutrients they provide when they decompose into the soil.

> ### DO NOT EAT, PICK OR DIG PLANTS!
>
> In light of potentially harmful or poisonous properties of many plants, this book does not recommend that readers consume plants in any form. Any decision to do so is at your own risk and discretion. The medicinal herb market is placing tremendous pressure on many wild species. Interested readers are urged to purchase only cultivated herbs from reliable sources, rather than those that are gathered from the wild, or "wildcrafted."
> **Visit United Plant Savers** at unitedplantsavers.org

> Two excellent websites for Colorado wildflowers are www.swcoloradowildflowers.com and Colorado Native Plant Society's webpage, www.conps.org.

Color Guide to Flowering Plants

Family name is listed with page number for each plant.

Honeysuckle—129   Pink—178   Sandalwood—199   Parsley—162   Lily—133

Dogwood—109   Lily—135   Mustard—148   Parsley—162   Lily—134

Buckwheat—94   Gentian—116   Saxifrage—199   Saxifrage—200   Parnassus—123

Buckwheat—95   Pea—171   Saxifrage—200   Sunflower—232   Lily—136

Burreed—97   Sunflower—250   Violet—258   Valerian—255   Buttercup—102

Buckthorn—93   Pink—179   Rose—190   Sunflower—224   Rose—191

Snapdragon—206	Lily—132	Sunflower—236	Morning-Glory—146	Rose—194
Phlox—176	Rose—192	Snapdragon—209	Dogwood—109	Sunflower—239
Lily—135	Gooseberry—121	Sunflower—236	Primrose—184	Saxifrage—201
Buttercup—103	Madder—138	Mustard—151	Parsley—164	Sunflower—241
Gentian—115	Heath—126	Sunflower—237	Sunflower—243	Saxifrage—202
Mustard—151	Parsley—165	Honeysuckle—129	Waterleaf—260	Lily—136

Ev-Primrose—112 Parsley—168 Pink—182 Pink—179 Pea—170

Sunflower—249 Valerian—256 Rose—198 Mallow—139 Purslane—186

Rose—196 Sunflower—253 Gooseberry—122 Purslane—186 Mint—144

Pink—181 Sunflower—227 Heath—128 Heath—127 Orchid—158

Parsley—167 Orchid—159 Buttercup—106 Geranium—119 Gooseberry—120

Orchid—160 Mallow—139 Heath—125 Mallow—140 Pea—173

Geranium—119	Snapdragon—208	Pink—180	Rose—193	Snapdragon—212
Pea—171	Ev-Primrose—110	Stafftree—217	Purslane—187	Primrose—185
Mustard—149	Mint—145	Honeysuckle—129	Stonecrop—218	Milkweed—143
Mint—144	Borage—90	Phlox—175	Pea—173	Dogbane—109
Pink—180	Snapdragon—207	Primrose—184	Gooseberry—121	Heath—127
Heath—125	Phlox—176	Sunflower—252	Sunflower—238	Honeysuckle—130

Gooseberry—121

Mint—145

Heath—125

Pea—169

Phlox—176

Lily—137

Gentian—116

Honeysuckle—130

Waterleaf—259

Snapdragon—214

Rose—197

Snapdragon—208

Rose—190

Buttercup—99

Buttercup—104

Ev-Primrose—111

Sunflower—251

Barberry—86

Sunflower—251

Buttercup—104

Buttercup—106

Sunflower—226

Rose—195

Bellflower—87

Snapdragon—214

Mustard—150

Verbena—257

Gooseberry—122

Sunflower—224

Gentian—116

Bellflower—87 Phlox—177 Borage—90 Borage—91 Stonecrop—218

Buttercup-106 Gentian—117 Snapdragon—204 Pea-172 Orchid—159

Waterleaf—260 Buttercup—105 Snapdragon—204 Phlox—175 Snapdragon—212

Gentian—117 Buttercup—100 Buttercup—100 Borage—92 Buttercup—101

Snapdragon—215 Sunflower—227 Snapdragon—205 Flax—113 Phlox—177

Mint—144 Snapdragon—215 Sunflower—228 Iris—131 Parsley—167

Honeysuckle—129   Rose—191   Gooseberry—121   Lily—136   Sunflower—222

Gooseberry—191   Gooseberry—191   Rose—198   Lily—134   Sunflower—223

Buttercup—99   Rose—197   Rose—190   Rose—188   Rose—188

Heath—124   Lily—136   Mallow—140   Sunflower—244   Sunflower—244

Oleaster—156   Rose—196   Sunflower—235   Sunflower—220   Rose—189

Lily—134   Lily—136   Cactus—107   Mustard—147   Sunflower—245

Snapdragon—208 Mustard—150 Sunflower—230 Ev-Primrose—112 Sunflower—222

Sunflower—230 Sunflower—245 Sunflower–233 Snapdragon—210 Sunflower—252

Sunflower—231 Parsley—164 Buttercup—102 Parsley—165 Sunflower—238

Sunflower—245 Snapdragon—209 Sunflower—234 Snapdragon—210 Sunflower—228

Mustard—150 Pea—172 Violet—258 Snapdragon—212 Mustard—152

Sunflower—235 Fumitory—114 Rose—192 Barberry—86 Sunflower—242

Mustard—153	Buckwheat—96	Saxifrage—202	Sunflower—240	Willow—263
Rose—196	Sunflower—248	Sunflower—254	Sunflower—240	Willow—265
Sunflower—233	Sunflower—349	Sunflower—255	Sunflower—242	Cattail—108
Mustard—153	Sunflower—244	Stonecrop—219	Mustard—152	Mustard—148
Spurge—269	Honeysuckle—130	Pea—174	Buckwheat—94	Sunflower—229
St. John's wort—216	Borage—92	Snapdragon—205	Willow—265	Willow—264

Buckwheat—97   Willow—266   Birch—89   Buttercup—102   Grass—272

Buttercup—101   Sunflower—229   Plantain—183   Saxifrage—201   Rush—275

Mare's Tail—142   Maple—141   Parsley—163   Mustard—148   Rush—275

Sunflower—250   Oak—155   Rose—193   Currant—121   Sedge—274

Goosefoot—122   Parsley—168   Birch—88   Buttercup—105   Grass—272

Nettle—154   Willow—268   Phlox—177   Sunflower—232   Buttercup—104

KEY TO PLANT FAMILIES

Choose the description in each pair of the key that best fits the plant you are trying to identify. Follow the numbers through the key to arrive at the plant family (in bold) to which the plant belongs.

1A. Plant with true flowers–(4)
1B. Plant with cones or spores–(2)

2A. Trees with needles or scales–(3)
2B. Ferns or other spore producing plant–**FERNS and ALLIES**

3A. Trees with needles over ½" (13 mm) long–**PINE**
3B. Trees or shrubs with scales or very short (< ½" or 13 mm) needle-like leaves–**JUNIPER**

4A. Parasitic plants lacking chlorophyll (not green)–**ORCHID**
4B. Not parasitic (green)–(5)

5A. Plants aquatic, wholly or partially submerged–(6)
5B. Plants not aquatic, though may grow near or in water, not submerged–(7)

6A. Plants with long, grass-like leaves floating on water surface. Flowers in bur-like clusters–**BURREED**
6B. Plants stiff and upright with leaves in whorls–**MARE'S TAIL**

7A. Shrubs or trees–(**KEY A**)
7B. Herbaceous–(**KEY B**)

KEY A

1A. Plants with thorns or spines on twigs or stems–(2)
1B. Not thorny or spiney–(4)

2A. Leaves not lobed or pinnate and having 3 prominent veins from the base–
BUCKTHORN
2B. Leaves not as above–(3)

3A. Flowers small, tubular, producing a pea-sized black or red berry–
CURRANT
3B. Flowers large, showy, with 5 pink petals; producing a leathery red fruit–
ROSE

4A. Flowers in catkins, i.e. long tassels of minute flowers–(5)
4B. Flowers not in catkins–(7)

5A. Leaves lobed, fruit an acorn–**OAK**
5B. Leaves not lobed, fruit otherwise–(6)

6A. Low-growing shrubs of wet areas; leaves roundish, slightly serrate–**BIRCH**
6B. Trees or shrubs; leaves may be long and narrow or broad with a pointed tip–
WILLOW

7A.   Low-growing shrub, usually not more than 2 feet (61 cm) high—(8)
7B.   Upright shrub, usually more than 2 feet (61 cm) high—(9)

8A.   Flowers 4-petaled, salmon-pink, tiny (<¼" or 6 mm)—**STAFF TREE**
8B.   Flowers bell-shaped—**HEATH**

9A.   Leaves alternate, covered with whitish scales—**OLEASTER**
9B.   Leaves opposite—(10)

10A. Leaves lobed; flowers not showy; fruit a "winged" samara—**MAPLE**
10B. Leaves simple—(11)

11A. Flowers showy, tubular, in pairs—**HONEYSUCKLE**
11B. Flowers small, white, in clusters; shrubs with bright red stems—**DOGWOOD**

KEY B

1A.   Flowers in heads, appearing to be one flower, but composed of many small disk and/or ray flowers—**SUNFLOWER**
1B.   Flowers not in heads—(2)

2A.   Stems and/or leaves succulent—(3)
2B.   Stems and leaves not succulent—(5)

3A.   Plant armed with spines—**CACTUS**
3B.   Plant without spines—(4)

4A.   Leaves opposite or basal—**PURSLANE**
4B.   Leaves alternate—**STONECROP**

5A.   Flowers irregular; not radially symmetrical—(6)
5B.   Flowers regular; radially symmetrical—(16)

6A.   Leaves compound or deeply lobed—(7)
6B.   Leaves simple, entire, or toothed—(7)

7A.   Spur present on back of flower—(8)
7B.   Spur absent—(9)

8A.   Yellow or pink flowers; stamens 6—**FUMITORY**
8B.   Blue or purple flowers; stamens many—**BUTTERCUP** (Larkspur)

9A.   Flowers pea-like; fruit a pod—**PEA**
9B.   Flowers not pea-like; fruit not a pod—(10)

10A. Flowers tubular, or with a long "snout"—**SNAPDRAGON**
10B. Flowers not tubular or with a snout—(11)

11A. Flowers similar to garden violets or pansies—**VIOLET**
11B. Flowers not like violets—(12)

12A. Stems square; leaves opposite; flowers pink, lavender, or blue—(13)
12B. Stems not square; leaves basal or alternate—(14)

13A. Plant with minty odor; flowers strongly "2-lipped"—**MINT**
13B. Plant lacking minty aroma; flowers not strongly "2-lipped"—**VERBENA**

14A. Flowers small, in ball-like clusters—**VALERIAN**
14B. Flowers not in ball-like clusters—(15)

15A. Flowers dark blue/purple, with hood-like upper petal—**BUTTERCUP** (Monkshood)
15B. Flowers variously colored, usually with sac-like lower petal—**ORCHID**
15C. Flowers tiny, papery, arranged in long spikes; leaves basal—**PLANTAIN**

16A. Leaves with parallel veins, often flat, grass-like; flower parts in 3's or 6's—(17)
16B. Leaves with netted or branching veins, leaves various; flower parts in 4's or 5's— (19)

17A. Tall (>4 feet or 122 cm) plants of wet areas; flowers clustered in long brown spikes—**CATTAIL**
17B. Plants shorter, though may be in wet areas; flowers not as above—(18)

18A. Ovary inferior; flower parts attached to the top of the ovary—**IRIS**
18B. Ovary superior; flower parts attached below the ovary—**LILY**

19A. Petals united, flowers conspicuous—(20)
19B. Petals separate, or flowers small and inconspicuous—(30)

20A. Plants with milky sap—(21)
20B. Plants without milky sap—(22)

21A. Flowers bell-shaped; not fragrant—**DOGBANE**
21B. Flowers complex, not bell-shaped; often fragrant—**MILKWEED**

22A. Leaves basal—**PRIMROSE**
22B. Leaves on stem—(23)

23A. Leaves opposite or whorled—(24)
23B. Leaves alternate—(25)

24A. Flowers tiny, white or greenish; leaves whorled—**MADDER**
24B. Flowers larger, variously colored, often blue or purple; leaves whorled or opposite (some members of this family appear to have separate petals, but on close inspection, they are united at the base)—**GENTIAN**

25A. Plant a vine—**MORNING GLORY**
25B. Plant not a vine—(26)

26A. Leaves simple—(27)
26B. Leaves lobed or divided—(28)

27A. Slender plants with bell-shaped flowers and pointed petals; fruit a single capsule—**BELLFLOWER**
27B. Plants more robust than above, often with stiff hairs on stems and leaves; flowers with rounded petals; fruit of four nutlets—**BORAGE**

28A. Stamens many (>10), united in a tube around the style—**MALLOW**
28B. Stamens 5—(29)

29A. Corolla a long narrow tube flaring to 5 petals—**PHLOX**
29B. Corolla a short broad tube; flowers often arranged in spiral cymes— **WATERLEAF**

30A. Flowers small and inconspicuous—(31)
30B. Flowers showy, though individual flowers sometimes small and arranged to present as one large "flower"—(32)

31A. Leaves opposite; plants with stinging hairs; flowers long, greenish clusters dangling from leaf axils—**NETTLE**
31B. Leaves alternate; flowers in clusters or upright spikes in leaf axils—**GOOSEFOOT**
31C. Leaves basal—**SAXIFRAGE**

32A. Individual flowers small (<¼" or 6mm), clustered or arranged to present as a larger inflorescence—(33)
32B. Individual flowers larger, not clustered to present as a larger inflorescence—(34)

33A. Leaves simple—**BUCKWHEAT**
33B. Leaves compound—**PARSLEY**

34A. Petals in 4's—(35)
34B. Petals in 5's—(36)

35A. Inferior ovary—**EVENING PRIMROSE**
35B. Superior ovary—**MUSTARD**

36A. Leaves stiff, leathery, holly-like with sharp pointed lobes—**BARBERRY**
36B. Leaves not as above—(37)

37A. Stamens numerous (>10)—(38)
37B. Stamens as many or twice as many as petals—(39)

38A. Floral parts attached to a cup-like hypanthium—**ROSE**
38B. Floral parts not attached to a hypanthium—**BUTTERCUP**

39A. Flowers light blue; plant slender, of open meadows—**FLAX**
39B. Flowers not blue—(40)

40A. Leaves compound or deeply lobed—**GERANIUM**
40B. Leaves simple—(41)

41A. Leaves chiefly basal, plus a single leaf on the stem; flowers white—**PARNASSIA**
41B. Leaves not as above; flowers variously colored—(42)

42A. Leaves alternate—**SANDALWOOD**
42B. Leaves opposite—(43)

43A. White or pink flowers; plants generally of dry areas—**PINK**
43B. Yellow flowers; plants found in wet, marshy areas—**ST. JOHN'S WORT**

NOTE: If you haven't placed your plant in a family with this key, there is a possibility that the family is not covered in this book. For more a more thorough and precise key, consult Weber's *Colorado Flora: Western Slope* (2001). For another useful, simple key, consult the *Rocky Mountain Flower Finder* (1990) by Janet L. Wingate or the *Alpine Flower Finder* by Janet L. Wingate and Loraine Yeatts (1995).

Non-Flowering Plants

FERNS AND FERN ALLIES

Ferns, horsetails and clubmosses belong to an ancient group of plants, reproducing by spores rather than by seeds as flowering plants do. Some are members of the earliest lineage of vascular plants. A few of the more visible species in this group are included here, although a coverage of other non-seed-producing plants, such as mosses, clubmosses and liverworts, is beyond the scope of this guide.

FERN FAMILY

Most ferns thrive in a moist, humid environment, the dry mountainous West being an unlikely place for them to grow in great numbers. However, there are several local species to be found nestled under cliffs, rock ledges or along crevices associated with springs and streams, as well as bracken fern, a species of dry open areas in aspen forests.

Ferns are remnants of tree-sized plants that dominated the earth's flora more than 300 million years ago during the Carboniferous Period, or the Age of Ferns. They still reproduce through an ancient process called "alternation of generations," meaning they alternate between sexual and asexual generations in order to complete their life cycle. Unlike flowering plants, which have "female" pollen-receiving pistils and "male" pollen-containing anthers, ferns reproduce by means of spores produced in tiny cases called sporangia. Sporangia are grouped together in clusters called sori, which are usually located on the underside of the leaf. Fern spores fall to the ground and grow into small heart-shaped plants, called prothallia, or the gametophyte generation. These in turn produce inconspicuous male and female structures, where sperm from the male structure fertilizes an egg from the female via a droplet of water. The fertilized egg then grows into the familiar, more visible fern plant, or the sporophyte generation.

Although ferns have been considered a single family, the Polypodiaceae, the trend is to divide them into multiple families. There are about 12,000 species of ferns worldwide. Families associated with local fern species are listed in each description.

Moonwort, Grape Fern

Botrychium lunaria

(Adder's Tongue family—Ophioglossaceae)

Life zone/ecosystem: Montane to subalpine. Mountain meadows and forest edges. **Characteristics:** Rare. Mostly under 6 in. (15 cm), slightly succulent. Two types of branches; sterile frond divided into 4–6 pairs of crescent- or moon-shaped (thus, lunaria) leaflets, closely spaced or overlapping; smooth edges of each leaflet (pinnule) at 90°–180° angle. Tip of fertile frond bears spores in sporangia, or grape-like clusters.

Diminutive emerald jewels, these tiny ferns are very unusual and difficult to spot. Seeming to have materialized from a land of herbal lore and make-believe, moonworts were once thought to remove the shoes of horses that trod on them, so watch your step! Moonworts were also considered magical, gathered in moonlight by witches and necromancers to create powerful potions and protective amulets.[1] Several species of moonworts exist in this area, but differences are so subtle they often baffle even the experts. Although not all moonworts have crescent-shaped leaflets, all have one frond divided into two branches, one fertile and the other non-fertile, green for photosynthesis.

Lanceleaf grape fern (*Botrychium lanceolatum*) is a fairly common subalpine botrychium.

Rock Brake Fern

Cryptogramma acrostichoides
[*C. crispa*] (Rock Brake family—Cryptogrammaceae)

Life zone/ecosystem: Montane to alpine. Rocky places. **Characteristics:** Fairly common. Fronds either fertile or sterile, but not both. Edges of leaf's pinnate divisions (pinnae) on fertile frond are rolled over the sori, creating podlike structures. Sterile fronds have no spore structures.

This fern's unusual bright-green fronds make it easy to identify. It grows in tufts from fissures in boulders of rock falls or scree fields, actually appearing to "break" the rock. Quite hardy for a fern, it can withstand extended periods of drought.

Western Bracken Fern

Pteridium aquilinum
var. *latiusculum*
[*Pteridium aquilinum*
susp. *lanuginosum*]
(Bracken family–
Dennstaedtiaceae)

Life zone/ecosystem:
Montane. Dry open aspen
forests. **Characteristics:**
Uncommon. Large leathery
leaves, sometimes surpassing
3 ft. (1 m) in length; arise
singly from underground
stems. Edges of pinnae are rolled over
sori for protection.

Bracken ferns grow in most regions of the world, from the tropics to the northern and southern temperate zones. Those who consider fern fiddleheads a wild gourmet treat need to beware of bracken fiddleheads as they contain carcinogens that have been linked to stomach cancer.[2] Farmers are well aware that this fern, which probably evolved to repel chewing insects, can be fatal to livestock. Sheep seem to be the most resistant to these toxins. Scientists still do not understand the purpose of the distinct nectar glands on the young leaves of bracken, because ferns, unlike flowering plants, have no need to lure pollinators. A Swiss botanist has proposed that the glands are for excreting excess sugar when vigorous growth of the young leaves begins to slow down.

ONE COMMON, ONE RARE

MOUNTAIN BLADDER FERN (*Cystopteris montana*) is listed in *Colorado's Guide to Rare Plants.* The broadly triangular fronds, 2–5.5 in. (6–14 cm) long, are divided into three main branches. Found in moist, rich soil of subalpine spruce-fir forests.

DARCY O'DONNELL

FRAGILE BLADDER FERN (*Cystopteris fragilis*) is the most common fern from montane to alpine. The delicate fronds, 8 in. (20 cm) or less, are pinnate with sharp-toothed pinnae that are typically perpendicular to the frond's rachis. *Cystopteris* is a genus of the Ladyfern family (Athyriaceae).

HORSETAIL FAMILY

Equisetaceae

G iant horsetails, called Calamites, grew up to fifty feet tall during the Carboniferous Age of the Paleozoic Era, more than 300 million years ago. Although miniscule by comparison, today's horsetails (or "scouring-rushes") are their descendants. They still have basically the same structure, with leaves reduced to small scales attached to sheaths surrounding a grooved stem.

Recent gene research has determined that horsetails and ferns are the closest relatives of seed plants.[3] Horsetail reproduction is primarily vegetative through the sprouting of extensive rhizome systems, but also sexually through an alternation of generations similar to ferns. Fertile stems have terminal cones filled with spores, which are equipped with elaters—long appendages that expand and contract with changes in humidity to dig spores into the soil surface. When the spores germinate, they produce a tiny plant called a prothallus, only a few cells thick. Each prothallus then produces either eggs or sperm. Eggs are fertilized when sperm from the male swim to the egg-bearing female prothallus, perhaps during rain or runoff. The resulting embryo grows into a horsetail plant.

Field Horsetail

Equisetum arvense

MEDICINAL · WILDLIFE

Life zone/ecosystem: Montane to subalpine. Wet to partially dry meadows, marshy areas, streamsides.
Characteristics: Common. height 2–24 in. (5–60 cm). Simple brown fertile stem (see inset) is unbranched, topped with cone-like reproductive structure containing spores; dies after spores released. Only bushy green sterile stems remain, resembling a horse's tail. Sterile stems are jointed and hollow, bearing up to 20 whorls of slender branches, with inconspicuous, scale-like leaves connected at the base to form a band at each stem node, or joint. Horizontal rhizome systems may extend up to 7 ft. (2 m) beneath soil's surface.

Miniature forests of bushy horsetail stems look soft and green, but the illusion quickly vanishes when you rub the silica-laden branches between your fingers. The high content of this scratchy mineral made this plant useful to pioneers for scouring cooking pots and utensils and to Native Americans for polishing pipes, bows and arrows. Europeans also used horsetail in place of fine steel wool for the fine sanding and polishing of new furniture. Today, herbal pharmacologists tout horsetail as one of nature's richest sources of silicon in a form easily assimilated by the body. In *The Green Pharmacy*, author Dr. James Duke suggests trying horsetail for treating bursitis and tendonitis, citing studies that show silicon plays an important role in health and resilience of cartilage and connective tissues such as tendons. It has also been used to heal fractures and torn ligaments. Chemical constituents in this herb may affect blood pressure. Although horsetail is low in nutritive value and rarely consumed by deer and elk, bears sometimes include it in their diet.

The following three species are less common in our area, and differ from field horsetail in that they lack the fern-like sterile stems, having only green, fertile, unbranched stems with a spore-containing cap. Their leaves are also reduced to tiny scales fused to sheaths at joints on the vertically ridged stem. Functional and medicinal uses are the same for all species.

Northern Scouring-rush, Slender Scouring-rush

Equisetum variegatum [*Hippochaete variegata*]

Sand bars along streams. Uncommon. Spore cones are sharp-pointed as in tall scouring-rush, but the whole plant is shorter and narrower, and the stems are only 0.12 in. (3 mm) wide.

Smooth Scouring-rush

Equisetum laevigatum [*Hippochaete laevigata*]

Moist soil. Uncommon. Annual, up to 3.3 ft. (1 m). Sheaths with only small band on top. Spore cones with rounded tip. Stems die back each winter.

Tall Scouring-rush

Equisetum hyemale [*Hippochaete hyemalis*]

Moist soil. Common. Grows 12–39 in. (30–100 cm). Stems, which persist several years, bear sharp-pointed spore cones and have sheaths usually with a dark band at both base and top. Often found growing in large patches. May hybridize with smooth scouring-rush.

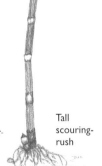

Tall scouring-rush

GYMNOSPERMS

Gymnosperm is Greek for "naked seed," which is a reference to the fact that plants in this group do not produce seeds in the enclosed ovary of a flower. Plants that bear their seeds in cones, or conifers, account for the lion's share of gymnosperms and are quite common in this region. Most conifers are evergreen, with green needle-like or scale-like leaves. Yews, cycads, and ginkgo, not present here, are included in this family.

CYPRESS FAMILY   *Cupressaceae*

Trees and shrubs of this family are intensely aromatic. Their mature leaves are usually scale-like and either opposite or whorled (may be awl-shaped when young), in contrast with the needle-like leaves of the pine family. Some species bear both male pollen cones and female seed-bearing cones on the same plant, whereas others have both all-male and all-female plants. The female cones are usually woody, but may be fleshy or berry-like. For example, juniper berries, are actually cones with fleshy scales that are very tightly compressed. Junipers are the only members of this family residing in our area. "Cedar" is loosely applied to members of this family, but true cedars are in the pine family and native only to Mediterranean and Himalayan regions.

Common Juniper

Juniperus communis var. *depressa* [includes *J. communis* vars. *montana* and *saxatilis*]
EDIBLE · GARDEN · MEDICINAL · WILDLIFE

Life zone/ecosystem: Montane to subalpine. Dry forests and forest openings and Oak-mountain shrubland.
Female seed cone: Small green berries in leaf axils, maturing to frosty blue berries 2nd or 3rd year. **Male pollen cone:** Petite pollen cones at tips of branches resemble fragile pine cones. **Characteristics:** Common. Sprawling evergreen shrub up to 3 ft. (1 m) tall. Varieties of this species may grow to small trees. Needle-like leaves are awl-shaped, sharp-pointed, and usually in whorls of 3; bluish-green, bearing a white stripe on top and lighter green undersides. Male pollen cones and female cones usually on separate shrubs. Limbs often smeared with black residue, a type of fungus that results from being covered by snow for long periods.

Not only are junipers one of the most widespread woody plants on earth, but a host of their food and medicinal uses have prevailed for centuries. Native Americans have relied on different parts and preparations of juniper as remedies for colds, coughs, rheumatism, sore throat, tuberculosis, urinary infections and indigestion. They also consider junipers spiritual plants, burning branches during ceremonies to cleanse the place and to purify the spirit, while crushed leaves are popular as incense in many cultures. Scientific studies show that juniper gives off a disinfecting gas when burned, explaining why both Europeans and the Chinese historically burned juniper to fumigate homes and hospitals during epidemics. Modern herbalists use preparations of various parts of common juniper to treat urinary tract and bladder infections, mixed with soothing herbs to protect against potentially damaging effects of juniper oils on the kidneys. Berries can be toxic in large quantities! Although wild-food gourmets use mature berries in marinades for wild game, the berries are best known for their use in making gin, named for the berry's Dutch name, *ginever*. Juniper berries are important food for wildlife, such as blue grouse, Townsend's solitaires, coyotes and cottontails.

Rocky Mountain Juniper, Rocky Mountain Red Cedar

Juniperus scopulorum [*Sabina scopulorum*]

EDIBLE · MEDICINAL · WILDLIFE

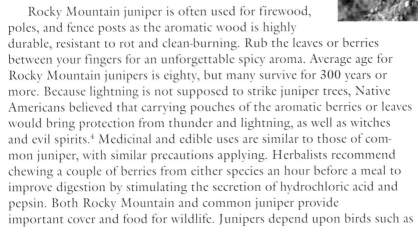

Life zone/ecosystem: Montane. Oak-mountain shrubland. Usually drier, south-facing slopes with sagebrush and scrub oak; also along streams and creeks. **Male pollen cone:** Same as common juniper. **Female seed cone:** Usually less than 0.28 in. (7 mm) in diameter, 2-seeded, and smaller than **Utah juniper** (*J. osteosperma*). Smaller and paler blue than common juniper. **Characteristics:** Fairly common. Small tree, 3–33 ft. (1–10 m). Scale-like leaves barely overlap and closely hug branches; young leaves possibly needle-like. Slender, tapering, and droopy branchlets differ from more stout branchlets of similar Utah juniper, found at lower elevations. Trunk gray to reddish-brown with shredding bark; gnarled and twisted with age.

Rocky Mountain juniper is often used for firewood, poles, and fence posts as the aromatic wood is highly durable, resistant to rot and clean-burning. Rub the leaves or berries between your fingers for an unforgettable spicy aroma. Average age for Rocky Mountain junipers is eighty, but many survive for 300 years or more. Because lightning is not supposed to strike juniper trees, Native Americans believed that carrying pouches of the aromatic berries or leaves would bring protection from thunder and lightning, as well as witches and evil spirits.[4] Medicinal and edible uses are similar to those of common juniper, with similar precautions applying. Herbalists recommend chewing a couple of berries from either species an hour before a meal to improve digestion by stimulating the secretion of hydrochloric acid and pepsin. Both Rocky Mountain and common juniper provide important cover and food for wildlife. Junipers depend upon birds such as robins, Townsend's solitaires, and bluebirds—which feed on the berries—to disperse their seeds. Seeds pass unharmed through the bird's digestive system, emerging to germinate in a new location. Elk, mule deer and bighorn sheep will eat the berries when other forage is scarce.

HOW OLD ARE THEY?

Maximum known ages for many tree species are listed by Rocky Mountain Tree-ring Research, Inc. in Fort Collins, Colorado. Visit their website at http://www.rmtrr.org/oldlist.htm. The following are maximum known ages for several species:

Species	Age	Location
Douglas-fir	1,275	Northern New Mexico
Douglas-fir	1,350	Vancouver Island, Canada
Engelmann spruce	911	Central Colorado
Rocky Mountain juniper	1,889	Northern New Mexico
Gambel oak	401	North Central Arizona

PINE FAMILY
Pinaceae

Members of this ancient family are commonly referred to as conifers, which are cone-bearing trees and shrubs with needle-like leaves and usually fragrant resinous sap. Their tiny male cones produce pollen, which is carried on the wind to fertilize ovules produced on the scales of larger, woody female cones. Female seed cones first appeared in the Permian era, 250 million years ago with the first conifers, probably originating from the reduction of large fertile branches—the cone axis having been modified from the main branch, the seed-producing scales from cone-bearing branches and bracts from leaves. Winged seeds are typically released when the cone scales separate and open at maturity, the wings providing easy lift for wind distribution away from the mother tree. Conifers also reproduce by skirting, where they send out new roots and shoots from limbs that come in contact with the ground.

Bristlecone pine is one of the world's oldest living plants and is considered rare in our area, but there is a small population near Marble, Colorado. Bristlecone fossils have been found in the Creede Oligocene formation in Colorado, dating from 27–35 million years ago.[5]

When endeavoring to identify conifers, be sure to consider needle shape, bark, female cone size and shape, and tree shape. Individual traits are sometimes variable and can be confusing.

JUDY HILL

Blue spruce along the Roaring Fork River. Branches on older tree to right have become more ragged and outstretched. Heavily-furrowed bark of mature spruce in upper right photo.

Cones of blue spruce (upper), and Engelmann spruce (lower).

Blue Spruce
Picea pungens
EDIBLE · GARDEN · WILDLIFE

Life zone/ecosystem: Montane and subalpine. Prefers lower, wetter sites than Engelmann. Usually riparian, occasionally on moist, north-facing slopes. **Female seed cone:** Papery cone 2.5–4 in. (6–10 cm), containing paired winged seeds. **Male pollen cone:** In small clusters on underside of twig ends. **Characteristics:** Common. Slow-growing conifer reaching 70–100 ft. (21–30 m). Stiff blue-green needles are very sharp, diamond-shaped in cross section; glaucous with white stripe. Compared to Engelmann spruce, young twigs under magnification are hairless; cones much larger; grayish-brown bark may appear scale-like when young, but lacks reddish color of mature Engelmann; mature bark usually furrowed; shape of old-growth trees more "ragged" from a distance, whereas Engelmann more triangular or somewhat parabolic with age; new growth of both species may be bluish.

Regal and beautiful, the blue spruce is the state tree of Colorado and Utah, the ragged outstretched branches of very old trees often calling to mind the expressive arms of a graceful dancer. Famous for its color, blue spruce has been very popular in the landscape industry since the 1860's. *Pungens* means "sharp," referring to the almost spine-tipped needles. Hybrids with Engelmann spruce are possible and do occur in the Roaring Fork Valley.[6]

Douglas-fir
Pseudotsuga menziesii var. *glauca*
EDIBLE · GARDEN · MEDICINAL · WILDLIFE

Life zone/ecosystem: Montane to lower subalpine. Moist slopes, often among aspen and spruce-fir. **Female seed cone:** Cone with 3-pointed "mouse-tail" bracts, resembling legs and tail of mice diving for cover; borne from the base of, and underside of, each scale; scattered over the tree; mature from pale green to cinnamon brown; seed winged at tip. **Male pollen cone:** Small and reddish-brown. **Characteristics:** Pyramid-shaped tree with loosely drooping branchlets, usually 80–180 ft. (25–55 m) tall in the Rocky Mountains. May form almost pure stands. Flat needles, bluish green to bright green on top with one groove; pale with 2 white stripes, which contain stomata, or pores, on lower surface; arranged spirally, each on small stalk attached to the droopy stem. Buds at ends of branches glossy, mahogany-colored and pointed. Bark of young trees smooth with resin-filled blisters; mature bark deeply grooved and thick.

Grove of Douglas-fir. The contrast with aspen gold shows the loose conical shape typical of this species.

Cinnamon-brown cones with whimsical "mouse-tail" bracts make this one of the most recognizable conifers. Pseudotsuga means "false hemlock," but Douglas-fir is neither a hemlock or a true fir. Douglas-fir cones are pendant and fall to the ground intact, whereas true firs have erect cones with scales that drop off at maturity. Douglas-fir is one of the most important commercial timber trees, popular for

UNUSUAL DEFORMITIES ON CONIFERS

"Witches' broom" is a large congested mass of stunted branches often found on spruce and fir. It is caused by broom rusts (Uredinale fungi), of which there are several species. Fir broom rust (*Melampsorella caryophyllacearum*) completes a portion of its life cycle on herbaceous chickweeds, while spruce broom rust (*Chrysomyxa arctostaphyli*) uses kinnikinnik as a secondary host. These rusts propagate through windborne or waterborne spores, which must infect both hosts before completing their life cycle. One tree cannot be infected by another tree directly. Thread-like bodies called mycelia originate from the spores, invading and causing a cancer-like reaction that deforms the tree's tissue, but is not fatal to the tree. Witches' brooms can be confused with dwarf mistletoe (see p. 83) or physiological deformations; however, yellowing needles, orange pustules on the undersides of leaves and the trait of shedding all needles each fall are indicative of broom rust. These nest-like deformities provide resting and nesting places for small mammals.

particle board, paper, plywood, and structural timber. Native Americans used the wood for spears, tools, hooks, barbs and poles. The pitch was applied to seal the joints of implements, caulk water vessels, and fasten moccasins—some even chewed it as gum. They also used it in medicinal salves to heal cuts and skin irritations, and made it into a tea for colds. Rarely, trees develop frost-like globules of sweet granular white resin on the branches and cones. Ethnographers mention that some tribes ate this "Douglas-fir sugar" as a confection or used it as a sweetener. Douglas-firs also provide important food and cover for wildlife. Numerous songbird species, such as Clark's nutcracker, chickadees, red-breasted nuthatch, red-winged crossbill, dark-eyed junco and pine siskin, extract the seeds from cones or forage for fallen seeds. The needles are an important winter food for blue grouse, and mule deer browse on trees during winter into early spring. Pine squirrels cache large quantities of cones for later use and chipmunks, mice, voles and shrews eat seeds from the forest floor. Try crushing a few needles for a heady balsamic fragrance.

MYSTERIOUS "PINEAPPLES" AT BRANCHES' TIPS?

Cooley's galls form at the tips of blue and Engelmann spruce twigs after the female Cooley spruce gall adelgids, aphid-like insects, mature in spring and lay their eggs on branch tips. When the larvae hatch, they crawl to the base of needles to feed on new growth, causing the branch tip to swell and form a protective gall around them. During mid-summer, a hole forms at the base of each needle, allowing the new winged females to exit and start the cycle again. The galls look pineapple-like when green, becoming dried and brown like cones after the larvae's departure.

Engelmann Spruce
Picea engelmannii
EDIBLE • GARDEN • MEDICINAL • WILDLIFE

Engelmann spruce cones are typically clustered at the top of the tree.

Young spruce cone

Life zone/ecosystem: Subalpine. Prefers higher, drier slopes than blue spruce. **Female seed cone:** Cinnamon-brown papery cones average 1–2 in. (2.5–5 cm) long, smaller than blue spruce; mostly in upper 1/3 of tree; winged seeds. **Male pollen cone:** Yellow to purplish-brown, scattered all over tree.

Characteristics: Common. Long-lived conifer, averaging 250–450 years and reaching 45–130 ft. (14–40 m); greatest known height 179 ft. (54.5 m). More triangular-shaped than blue spruce when mature, yet not as spire-like as subalpine fir. Tall, old trees often cylindric in the body, narrowing at top and bottom. Needles stiff, moderately sharp, diamond-shaped in cross section, attached singly to stem; thick woody base remains when needle removed. New twigs minutely hairy under magnification. Bark scaly and rich reddish-brown to grey; bark scales flake off easily. Aromatic pitch smells like butterscotch. Needles and buds contain natural antifreeze, allowing some spruces to withstand intense winter temperatures as low as −112 degrees F (−80 degrees C).

The ancient European cathedral was actually built in such a way as to reproduce the quiet, peaceful feeling of a spruce-fir forest—quiet that is enhanced by a thick layer of decaying needles and fallen trunks. The soil is very acidic and supports many unusual plants, such as parasitic pinedrops and striped coralroot. The crowded canopy blocks out most sunlight. Although the conditions preclude a wide diversity of life,

SPRUCE OR FIR?

For positive identification, learn this ditty about their needles: "Friendly, flat, flexible fir versus sharp, stiff, spiky spruce." Rolling the needles between your fingers will tell you whether needles are square like a spruce, or flat like a fir.

Mature Engelmann spruce with Mt. Sopris in the background

spruce-fir forests do provide valuable winter habitat for wildlife. Tiny winged spruce seeds are an important food source for birds and small rodents; deer and bighorn sheep enjoy the twigs; and porcupines eat the cambium. During the fall, pine squirrels stockpile hundreds of spruce cones in their food middens, which are spongy piles of cone scales at the base of trees that can grow to huge proportions after generations of use. Spruce wood is lightweight, fine-textured and straight-grained, making it favored for piano sounding boards and construction lumber. The cambium, boiled, dried or consumed raw, is a traditional survival food. Bright green new spring-growth at the branch tips are high in vitamin C and brewed as tea in many cultures. Spruce oil is known for relieving stress and lifting the emotions.

OLD-GROWTH FORESTS

Tall and majestic, old-growth forests are those that have reached a climax state in which a diversity of shade-tolerant species—typically spruce, subalpine fir and Douglas-fir in this area—have become dominant. Only 1% of America's original old-growth forests still exist, remaining as reservoirs of plant and animal biodiversity unique to their ecosystems and acting as natural laboratories for understanding ecological processes that take place in the absence of human disturbance. Distinguishing characteristics of old-growth forests are: • very old and/or large trees with bits of gray-green lichen, "usnea," often hanging from the branches • multi-aged stands • clearings where large trees have fallen • soft, uneven, often moss- and lichen-covered ground shaped by toppled and decayed trunks and other plant growth • better overall forest health, as multi-aged, multi-species stands are less vulnerable to disease and insect infestations.

Lodgepole Pine,
Rocky Mountain Lodgepole Pine

Pinus contorta var. *latifolia*

EDIBLE · MEDICINAL · WILDLIFE

Serotinous cones

Lifezone/ecosystem: Montane to subalpine. Large, even-aged stands usually occur from 8,200 to 9,300 ft. (2499–2835 m); random trees mixed with aspen, Douglas-fir, spruce and subalpine fir may occur from 7,000 to 9,800 ft. (2134–2987 m), or occasionally to timberline on south-facing slopes. **Female seed cone:** 1-2 in. (2.5-5 cm); cone scales bristle-tipped; winged seeds. **Male pollen cone:** In orange-red clusters. **Characteristics:** Common. Usually straight, slender, medium-sized tree, typically 70–80 ft. (21–24 m) in this area; free of branches on lower portion. May have thicker trunk with lower branches in open areas. Short-lived; 200-year-old trees rare, though some have been recorded up to 600 years. Sharp-pointed, 1–3 in. (2.5–7.5 cm), yellowish-green needles are in bundles (fascicles) of two.

Notice "bottlebrush" look of branch with needles and light-gray to blackish, scaly bark.

Cones of lodgepole pines come in two different types on the same tree. Serotinous cones have scales sealed tightly shut by resin, opening to release their seeds only when temperatures exceed 113 degrees F (45 degrees C), usually during a fire. This allows immediate seeding of a burned over area. Although common, many stands have less than 50% of this cone type. Non-serotinous cones open shortly after ripening in the fall. Cones do not start to appear until the trees are 5–10 years old, and the serotinous trait may not develop until 20–30 years of age. Spread by the wind, their winged seeds can travel 200 ft. (60 m) from the parent tree.

Like aspens, lodgepole pines are a pioneering species, adapted for growing in disturbed soil or after fire. Seedlings mature into exclusive stands of tall, slender, even-aged trees, which may give way to more shade-tolerant species. In some forests, without fire,

JOHN EMERICK

PONDEROSA PINE (*Pinus ponderosa*). Tall stately trees up to 130 ft. (40 m). Fairly common along the Roaring Fork River. Mature bark is cinnamon-colored to reddish-yellow with large, puzzle-like plates; needles are in clusters of 2 or 3, and are 5–10 in. (12.7–25.4 cm) long; cones are 3–6 in. (7.6–15 cm) long with most prickles curved out. Bark warmed by the sun has a wonderful vanilla fragrance.

Lodgepole cones are so tightly attached that old cones lining the branches are visible from a distance.

lodgepole stands become so dense that they are unusable to wildlife for 100–200 years until the trees reach the end of their natural lifespan.

Native Americans used the straight, slender poles of this species to support their lodges or teepees, thus the common name. The cambium was dried and powdered for food, sap was used to heal cuts and wounds and buds were chewed as a balm for sore throats. Lodgepoles are valuable to the timber industry, being used both for lumber and log homes. Wildlife benefits from considerable food and cover in mature, open lodgepole forests.

COLORADO PINYON PINE (*Pinus edulis*), 15-20 ft. (4.5-6 m). Occasionally found in oak-mountain shrubland. Needles in pairs. Drought-stressed trees suffer heavy mortality from pine engraver (or IPS) beetle.

DWARF MISTLETOE INTEGRAL TO FOREST ECOLOGY

Dwarf mistletoe (*Arceuthobium americanum*), a parasitic flowering plant, causes stunted growth and increased mortality in lodgepole pines. The plants produce slender, olive-green to yellow, leafless jointed shoots. Female plants produce the berry-like fruits. At maturity, the fruit's elastic outer case bursts under intense hydrostatic pressure, shooting single seeds into the air at up to 60 miles (100 km) per hour! Most seeds fall within 10–15 ft. (3–5 m) of the source tree, but can travel as far as 30 ft. (9 m). The sticky seeds cling to needles of other trees until rain moistens their viscous coating, allowing them to slide to the twig. There they establish root systems, but do not produce shoots for thirty-five years. Wildlife biologists are questioning the practice of clearing infested trees, as recent research shows that mistletoe brooms are an integral part of the forest, providing shelter and food for many wildlife species.

Subalpine Fir
Abies bifolia
EDIBLE · WILDLIFE

Life zone/ecosystem: Subalpine to tree-line. Spruce-fir. **Female seed cone:** 2¼–4 in. (6-10 cm); large-winged seeds. **Male seed cone:** Small clusters on underside of twig ends. **Characteristics:** Common. Steeple-shaped, 50–100 ft. (15–30 m). Life span 200–250 years (rarely 400); slow-growing. Soft, bluish-green needles, flat with small notch on rounded tip; grow from points surrounding the stem, but all curve upward. Deep purple cones stand erect on upper limbs; mature cone scales fall off; center spike remains. Pale gray bark with deep resin blisters; bark darker, scaly and fissured with age.

Steeple-shaped subalpine firs cluster among golden fall aspens (above), young bark with resin blisters (right)

Mature subalpine fir cone

Center core of cones remain upright on limbs after scales and seeds fall.

Subalpine fir's narrow spires stand out from the surrounding trees. In early fall, their upright cones spotted with resin sparkle in the sunlight. This is the smallest true fir, and one of the least fire-resistant western conifers due to its thin bark. A shade-tolerant climax species, it outnumbers Engelmann spruce in younger subalpine forests, but becomes dominated by spruce in older forests as fir seedlings grow more slowly, reaching only 4–5 ft. (1.2–1.5 m) in twenty to forty years. Cones appear the first spring only as microscopic primordia deep within vegetative buds near the tree's top, differentiating into seed-cone and pollen-cone buds in mid-summer. Not until late summer of the second year do cones reach maturity, dispersing their seeds from August to October. Only the candelabra-like spikes remain, perched erect on the branches. Pine squirrels cache large quantities of subalpine fir cones, while numerous small rodents and birds hunt for seeds on the ground. Blue grouse are partial to the succulent needles.

RED AND DYING SUBALPINE FIRS COMMON IN THE MOUNTAINS.
Together with the western balsam bark beetle (*Dryocoetes confuses*), the culprit is a fungus called "armillaria," a naturally occurring parasite that infects many tree species, but hits subalpine firs hardest in this area. Its fruiting bodies—"honey mushrooms"—are clustered at the base of infected trees, but armillaria lives mostly underground, sending out black shoestring-like filaments (mycelia) that invade tree roots to suck up water and nutrients. This eventually kills trees by interfering with their growth. On most conifers, infected portions of the lower stems are a bit enlarged and exude resin. Removing the bark reveals diagnostic white mycelial mats marked by irregular, fanlike striations. A giant patch of armillaria discovered in the Malheur National Forest of Eastern Oregon is believed to be one of the largest organisms ever found, covering 2,200 acres (890 ha) and extending about 3 ft. (9 m) below the surface. DNA testing shows that this enormous fungus originated from a single spore around 2,400 years ago.

BUDS SHAPE THE TREE.
Though subalpine fir is narrower and more spire-shaped than Engelmann spruce, both species are quite conical. A terminal bud dictates this type of growth from the top down. Auxins are plant growth regulators that flow rootward from the terminal buds, stimulating stems to lengthen while repressing the growth of lateral buds. The effect of auxins diminishes more or less uniformly with distance, so shoots at a given distance from the top tend to grow at the same rate each year, producing a conical tree. This shape enables trees to shed heavy snow the way A-frame chalet roofs do, a sensible adaptation in an environment where annual snowfall sometimes exceeds 25 ft. (7.7 m). These conical trees also keep the ground cool and shaded, which helps retain a deep snowpack and allows the much-needed moisture to be released slowly, recharging ground aquifers and feeding streams that flow to the Pacific Ocean from this side of the Continental Divide.

Flowering Plants

Without the gift of flowers and the infinite diversity of their fruits, man and bird, if they had continued to exist at all, would be today unrecognizable. The weight of a petal has changed the face of the world and made it ours.

—LOREN EISELEY

Flowering plants appeared during the Cretaceous Period, 145–65 million years ago. Their fragrance, color patterns, nectar, flower parts and form evolved to attract pollinators, which include insects, birds and mammals. This efficient strategy ensured that pollen would be carried from one flower to another to fertilize the ovary and produce seed-bearing fruit—thus confirming the next generation of plants. The beauty and food that humans derive from them are pleasurable by-products of this innovation.

BARBERRY FAMILY   *Berberidaceae*

Members of this family are generally shrubs, either deciduous or evergreen, with racemes of small yellow flowers bearing 6 sepals, 6 petals and 6 stamens. Use a hand lens to view their unique anthers, which open to release pollen by a pressure-controlled, flap-like valve, instead of splitting down the sides. Barberries grow primarily in northern temperate regions and in the mountains of South America. They have existed in Colorado since the Tertiary period, 30 million years ago.

A study of this family gives credence to the need to protect the full spectrum of plants on earth as a reservoir for potential use in human medicine. Berberine, a bitter yellow alkaloid contained in members of the barberry family, is a component in numerous effective herbal medicines.[7] Having strong anti-microbial properties, berberine is used in salves, teas and tinctures to treat liver and digestive disorders, infections and various parasites such as tapeworm and giardia. Two barberry genera, *Berberis* and *Mahonia*, are frequently used as ingredients in herbal medicines, while common barberry and the local Oregon grape share medicinal properties similar to goldenseal root, a popular but overharvested herbal remedy, and can provide useful alternatives to that increasingly scarce plant.

PROTECT NATIVE PLANTS

Unless there is better regulation of commercial wildcrafting, which supplies the herbal medicine industry, even wild populations of Oregon grape could suffer. It is very important to support those companies that sell only cultivated herbs. This will help protect the integrity of native plant populations.

Oregon Grape, Creeping Hollygrape
Mahonia repens

EDIBLE • MEDICINAL • WILDLIFE

Life zone/ecosystem: Montane. Oak-mountain shrubland, aspen and mixed conifer forests.
Flowering: May–June. **Fruit:** Berry.
Characteristics: Common. Low-growth shrub. Bright yellow fragrant flower clusters; holly-like leaves of 3–9 semi-evergreen leaflets. Leaves prickly; turn red in response to cold in fall and spring. Berries powdery navy-blue, tart.

Repens refers to the creeping habit of Oregon grape's rhizomes, while *Mahonia* refers to Bernard MacMahon, a pioneer horticulturist who wrote America's first garden encyclopedia in the early 1800's. Although Navajo tribes used woody parts of this plant to produce yellow dye for clothing and baskets, it is most noted for its medicinal uses in the treatment of liver and digestive orders. Scrape a stem or root of Oregon grape to reveal the inner bark containing bright yellow berberine (see family description, pg. 85). Though quite tart, the berries are edible. Black bears are fond of the berries, so take only a taste!

BELLFLOWER FAMILY   *Campanulaceae*

A family of forty genera and 700 species, bellflowers are found mainly in the northern temperate zone. Mostly herbaceous perennials, known for their ornamental uses, they are recognized by an inferior ovary, mostly united 5-lobed corollas and 3 branches on the style. Reproduction most often occurs by seed.

Anthers of most bellflowers produce pollen while still in the bud, before the stigma is ready to be fertilized—a special floral mechanism that minimizes self-pollination, thereby increasing genetic diversity in the population through cross-pollination. As soon as the flowers open, insects pick up pollen as they brush against pollen-laden anthers while probing for nectar. Upon leaving, they carry pollen away to mature flowers with receptive stigmas. Bellflower's stigma develops only after most of the pollen is gone. Look for newly opened buds with mounds of pollen already visible.

CREEPING BELLFLOWER (*Campanula rapunculoides*) is an ornamental plant with purple flowers that spreads rapidly by seeds and creeping rootstocks, thriving in sun or shade, and rapidly becoming a serious weed problem here as it has in Boulder, Colorado.

Mountain Harebell
Campanula rotundifolia
GARDEN · MEDICINAL

Life zone/ecosystem: Montane to alpine. Dry to moist soil in sunny meadows and rocky slopes. **Flowering:** July–September. **Fruit:** Nodding capsules. **Characteristics:** Common. Delicate, 4–20 in. (10–50 cm) tall—smaller in alpine areas. *Campanula* refers to bell-shaped blossoms (often several per stem); *rotundifolia* means round, referring to the basal leaves (actually more ovate than round); stem leaves alternate and linear. Obvious 3-lobed stigma indicates ovary's 3 seed-containing chambers. **Parry's harebell** (*C. parryi*), also common in mountain meadows, is more upright and open. **Alpine harebell** (*C. uniflora*), found in undisturbed alpine turf, is deeper blue with narrower petals. Both are usually single-flowered.

Above, Mountain harebell

Alpine harebell

These delicate bells dance to the slightest breeze on very slender stems, which are actually quite tough and fibrous. Mountain harebell grows all over the northern hemisphere. As the "bluebell-of-Scotland," it is celebrated in stories and songs in that country. The Haida people of Alaska knew harebells as "blue rain flowers" and children were warned that it would rain if they picked them. Early Navajos rubbed the dried and powdered plant on their bodies, believing it protected them from witches.[8] Mountain harebell, whose very appearance is a meditation on beauty and solitude, is long-blooming and does well in gardens. It provides food for deer, elk, pikas, bears and butterflies.

Parry's harebell

BIRCH FAMILY *Betulaceae*

Only three species of the birch family are found in the southern Rocky Mountain region—two birches and an alder—and all are shrubs or small trees growing among streamside willows. Their alternate leaves have conspicuous veins and their male and female flowers are in separate catkins on the same plant. Catkins of both alders and birches form within the bud of the previous season, opening in spring before the leaves unfold. Winged papery fruits contain a single-seeded nutlet and are dispersed far and wide by the wind.

In *Colorado Flora—Western Slope*, Dr. Weber notes "Birches in springtime yield a sweet sap that, while not collected for sugar-making, has been used to make vinegar." An infusion of birch bark was used by Blackfeet Indians to treat tuberculosis, while powdered birch bark was used by the Navajo people as a red dye and leaf tea from members of this family has been used to soothe minor skin irritations such as poison oak and insect bites.

Mountain Alder, Thinleaf Alder

Alnus incana var. *occidentalis*
[*A. incana* subsp. *tenuifolia*]
EDIBLE · MEDICINAL · WILDLIFE

Life zone/ecosystem: Montane to lower subalpine. Wet, well-drained soils, often rocky, along stream banks. **Flowering:** April–May. **Fruit:** Narrow-winged nutlets. **Characteristics:** Common. Multi-trunked shrub reaching 16 ft. (5 m). Mature female catkins resemble miniature pine cones; seeds are barely winged and solitary inside each "cone" scale. Slender, droopy male catkins appear on same plant as female catkins; pollen spread by wind. Wrinkled, wavy-edged leaves have double-toothed margins and appear dark green above and yellow-green on fuzzy undersides. Triangular pith, in contrast to round pith of river birch.

Alders are important to the ecology of river bank soils. Their roots contain bacteria that combine nitrogen with oxygen from the air, making it available in the soil for other plants. Decaying leaves also contribute nitrogen to the soil. Alders grow quickly, spreading by underground rhizomes, which may form almost impenetrable thickets along streams, providing habitat for wildlife. Marks on the smooth, gray bark are actually pores called lenticels, which allow oxygen to reach tissues underneath—an adaptation ensuring survival in wet, poorly aerated soils. Alders' flowering catkins are edible and high in protein, but not very tasty, so best eaten only in an emergency. People in Alaska have been known to brew a tea from the green female fruits to treat diarrhea and to make poultices of the astringent leaves for insect bites and stings. Deer and elk prefer the leaves and twigs of young plants, but will eat older ones during severe winters.

River Birch, Water Birch

Betula occidentalis [*B. fontinalis*]
EDIBLE · WILDLIFE

Life zone/ecosystem: Montane. Same riparian habitat as mountain alder, but more often at lower elevations. **Flowering:** April–May. **Fruit:** Broad-winged samara. **Characteristics:** Common. Multi-trunked shrub up to 16 ft. (5 m); in favorable sites, can occur as a small tree up to 33 ft. (10 m). Female catkins upright; males drooping and yellowish-brown. Round stem pith; bark shiny red-brown and smooth with pores resembling conspicuous white crosslines. Ovate or obovate leaves are not wrinkled and do not have the wavy edges specific to alders; may have similar double-toothed edges. Twigs sometimes scattered with resinous glands; tiny glandular dots on underside of leaves.

Springtime flocks of pine siskins can be heard chattering incessantly in river birches as they nibble away at the catkins. The catkins and tender young leaves of any species of birch can be mixed in salads along with milder greens. Sap from these shrubby trees is drinkable in springtime and the juice from the leaves can be used as a mouthwash.

Bog birch (*Betula glandulosa*), a small subalpine shrub of streambanks, willow carrs and beaver ponds. Has glossy green scalloped leaves, stems covered with resinous glands and catkins similar to river birch.

BORAGE FAMILY   *Boraginaceae*

This charming family of forget-me-nots and bluebells can be recognized by its unique flowers. Four distinct tiny nutlets at the base of the pistil, which contain the seeds when mature are easily seen with a magnifying hand lens. Members of the mint and verbena families share this feature, but only borage plants have radially symmetrical flowers, an inflorescence coiled in the bud (like those of the waterleaf family) and generally simple alternate leaves without stipules. Five stamens are attached to a 5-lobed corolla, which may be trumpet-shaped or bell-shaped. The mature nutlets are often considered a nuisance, as those of many species are adorned with bristles, allowing them to hitch a ride on shoe laces, socks and pets—an effective strategy for seed dispersal. Pikas and porcupines eagerly forage on these succulent plants.

One hundred genera and 2,000 species of borage are spread throughout temperate and subtropical regions, especially in the Mediterranean. Many of them have medicinal uses, and two common garden plants originally from Europe give the family much notoriety. Comfrey (*Symphytum officinale*) contains allantoin, believed to stimulate the growth of connective tissue, bone and cartilage and reportedly absorbed through the skin to help heal wounds. Common borage (*Borago officinalis*) is a garden herb used since the Middle Ages as a tea to increase perspiration during colds and flu. Gamma-linolenic acid (GLA) is derived from borage seeds and is apparently effective for Raynaud's disease when massaged into the fingers. Although both species contain small amounts of pyrrolizidine alkaloids (PAs), which are known liver carcinogens, there is supposedly little risk if using them externally.

Alpine Forget-Me-Not
Eritrichum nanum var. *elongatum*
[*E. aretioides*]
GARDEN

Life zone/ecosystem: High subalpine to alpine. Open rocky slopes. **Flowering:** June–July. Fruit: 4 nutlets. **Characteristics:** Common. Rarely reaches 3 in. (7 cm). Forms dense cushion. Sky-blue (rarely white) flowers diminutive, with leaves and stems covered in silvery hairs.

This woolly cushion plant hugs the ground, avoiding harsh winds and blowing snow where it grows in severe alpine environments. Spring buds can be almost purple with anthocyanins—red pigments that convert light energy into warmth for the plant. In early summer, brilliant blue flowers burst forth, embellished by golden crowns at the center and full of sweet fragrance. Pollinating bumblebees attracted by this flower's aromatic nectar look like giants in a Lilliputian flower meadow. Alpine forget-me-nots grow in mounds that contain flowers of two different sizes, an adaptation to decrease the chance of inbreeding. Larger flowers are male-dominant, with stamens poking out above the stigma, while smaller flowers are female-dominant, with larger stigmas. Plants are either one or the other, so pollinators are not likely to transfer pollen between flowers of the same plant.

Houndstongue
fruits

*Houndstongue, Beggar's Lice
Cynoglossum officinale

Life zone/ecosystem: Montane. Disturbed areas along trails, roadsides, in forest clearings. **Flowering:** May–July. **Fruit:** 4 prickly nutlets. **Characteristics:** Common. Weedy, Eurasian, branching biennial, 1–3 ft. (30 cm–1 m); appears as rosette of leaves first year. Small reddish-purple flowers on spreading stems at top of plant resemble forget-me-nots. Large and velvety alternate leaves have distinctive venation, decreasing in size up the stem; lower leaves stalked, upper ones almost clasping. Egg-shaped fruits like rough hound's tongue—covered in hooked bristles; cling tenaciously to fabric and fur.

Houndstongue's clusters of tiny flowers are so pretty, eager gardeners are occasionally duped into indulging what is in fact an aggressive weed. These plants should be removed as soon as possible if found, as they spread by seed and older roots are more difficult to remove. Houndstongue does have its uses. It is closely related to comfrey—one of the best-known medicinal herbs—and its leaves may be similarly used in salves and poultices to aid in the healing of burns, wounds or skin irritations. However, houndstongue also contains the same carcinogenic alkaloids, so internal use is not recommended.

Mountain Bluebells, Tall Chiming Bells
Mertensia ciliata
EDIBLE · GARDEN · WILDLIFE

Life zone/ecosystem: Montane to lower alpine. Wet meadows and shaded streamsides of aspen and spruce-fir. **Flowering:** June–early August. **Fruit:** 4 nutlets. **Characteristics:** Common. Grows 8–30 in. (20–80 cm) tall, with floral "bells" 0.4–0.7 in. (10–17 mm) long. Lance-shaped, bluish-green leaves with prominent veins are smooth and stalked with tapered bases. Lacks rough hairiness of other *Mertensia* species.

"Languid ladies," one of the other common names for this plant, seems appropriate for these dense stands of graceful nodding bells that impart an enchanting lushness to the landscape along streams. Delicate pink, pendent buds transform to beautiful sky blue as they blossom. Mountain bluebell leaves are somewhat succulent with an oyster-like flavor and may be eaten raw or sauteed as a vegetable. Be aware that chemical constituents they contain could be toxic in large quantities. Foraging hikers are not the only ones with their eye on this plant, as deer, elk, bear and pikas enjoy it, too!

Dwarf bluebell (*M. fusiformis*), common in mountain shrub habitat early in the spring, is less than 16 in. (40 cm) tall and has rough leaves with flattened hairs pointing away from the middle vein.

Stickseed
Hackelia floribunda

Life zone/ecosystem: Montane. Meadows and forest clearings.
Flowering: June–August. **Fruit:** 4 drooping nutlets with row of
2-barbed prickles around edge. **Characteristics:** Hairy, coarse,
weedy biennial (sometimes perennial), reaching to about 3 ft. (1
m). Attractive blue or whitish forget-me-not flowers with golden
centers. Alternate leaves lance-shaped (widest above the middle);
stalked on bottom of stem and stalkless near top of stem.

Although stickseed looks similar to several other
species in this family, its height and the pattern of
prickles on its fruits, or nutlets, are distinguishing
characteristics. Effectively barbed, the nutlets will
attach to any clothing, making the seed-distribution
method of this plant all too obvious. *Floribunda*
means "free-flowering"—a reference to the fact that
flowers and mature fruits can often be seen on the
same plant.

Wayside Gromwell, Lemonweed, Yellow Puccoon
Lithospermum ruderale
GARDEN · MEDICINAL

Life zone/ecosystem: Montane. Dry, open areas of
oak-mountain shrubland and sagebrush shrubland.
Flowering: May–July. **Fruit:** Shiny egg-shaped nutlets. **Characteristics:** Fairly common. Grows 8–24
in. (20–60 cm) in clumps of unbranched stems.
Inconspicuous pale-yellow to greenish-white flowers
tucked inside clusters of narrow, softly hairy, lance-
shaped leaves.

Lithospermum means "stone seed,"
referring to wayside gromwell's rock-hard
seeds. Shoshone tribes were known to take
gromwell root tea as a female contraceptive and recent studies on laboratory mice may have confirmed this use.[9] A European variety of the same
genus (*L. arvensis*) has been used as an oral contraceptive. Popular in
native wildflower gardens, gromwell can be grown in sunny areas with
moderately well-drained soil. It can propagated from cuttings, division or
by sowing seeds in early spring in a cold frame.

BUCKTHORN FAMILY *Rhamnaceae*

California lilacs (*Ceanothus* spp.) and common buckthorn (*Rhamnus cathartica*) are familiar horticultural shrubs in this family. Cascara sagrada (*R. pershiana*) is a well-known species used by herbalists as a laxative. Leaves with 3 prominent veins, and flowers with stamens opposite the petals, are two quite distinctive characteristics of the buckthorn family.

Snowbrush, Mountain Balm

Ceanothus velutinus

GARDEN • MEDICINAL • WILDLIFE

Life zone/ecosystem: Montane. Open hillsides, variable moisture. **Flowering:** Early July–August. **Fruit:** Glandular, sticky, with 3 distinct lobes bearing 3 hard nutlets; thread-like remains of styles protrude from tips. **Characteristics:** Fairly common. Spreading shrub, often growing in large masses. Alternate evergreen leaves, glossy dark green on top with somewhat sticky, resinous coating and 3 obvious veins. *Velutinus* refers to leaves' pale velvety undersides. Snowy clusters of tiny delicate, 5-petaled flowers adorn ends of branches.

Take a whiff of snowbrush's fragrant flowers before exploring the gland-tipped edges of its leaves with a hand lens. Native Americans and pioneers used the lacey flowers, which contain a natural soap called saponin, for washing. Red root is another common name for the plant, referring to its reddish-purple or brownish-red roots, which can be dried and brewed into a tea for tonsil inflammations, sore throats and enlarged lymph nodes. Deer like to bed down in snowbrush and eat the foliage and flowers year-round, whereas elk tend to browse this shrub during winter. A patient gardener can grow this beautiful shrub from seed.

BUCKWHEAT FAMILY *Polygonaceae*

Leaves of the buckwheat family are usually alternate and simple with smooth edges and the fruits are triangular nuts or winged seeds. Another identifying characteristic of the family is the papery, leaf-like appendage at the base of each leaf stem, which wraps around the stem node (except in the genus *Eriogonum*). About thirty genera exist worldwide, with around 750 species predominately found in the northern temperate regions. Rhubarb and buckwheat are both members of this family, with historical importance as food and medicine. Buckwheat grows luxuriantly and was one of the earliest grains to be cultivated as food. The red or pink stems of rhubarb, which are still found growing around old homesites in the valley, are delicious cooked as a sauce or filling for pies. The leaves contain very high concentrations of oxalic acid and are poisonous.

Alpine Bistort

Polygonum viviparum [*Bistorta vivipara*]
EDIBLE · WILDLIFE

Life zone/ecosystem: Subalpine to alpine. Moist meadows and along streambanks. **Flowering:** Late June–early August. **Fruit:** Bulblet. **Characteristics:** Common. Diminutive relative of American bistort, 4–9 in. (10–25 cm). Fluffy spike of tiny white to pale rose flowers atop simple stems; grows from woody root crown. Mostly narrow, oval leaf blades less than 6 in. (15 cm) on long petioles; upper leaves smaller; attached directly to stem.

Viviparum refers to the ability of this plant to "bear young" without producing seeds—in fact, alpine bistort has never been known to reproduce by seeds. Instead, a fascinating strategy to reproduce vegetatively circumvents the problems associated with setting seed quickly in a harsh alpine environment. Tiny claret-colored bulblets growing on flowering stalks detach and scatter liberally on the loose alpine soil, where they germinate easily. Sometimes a tiny green shoot will appear while the bulblet is still on the stem. Although smaller, rootstocks contain the same properties as American bistort and can be used interchangeably as food or medicine. The foliage is favored as forage by bighorn sheep and deer, while the starchy roots are sought by black bears and rodents.

Alpine Sorrel, Mountain Sorrel

Oxyria digyna
EDIBLE

Life zone/ecosystem: Alpine. Rocky crevices and talus slopes with moisture. **Flowering:** July–September. **Fruit:** Rust-colored to red, winged achene. **Characteristics:** Common herb 2–12 in. (5–30 cm). Somewhat succulent, round to kidney-shaped leaves on long stems originating from base. Minute green or reddish sepals are the "flowers"; inconspicuous without petals. Flattened, oval winged fruits, green or bright red, appearing mid to late summer.

The fleshy leaves of alpine sorrel are a great addition to any trail salad. They are tender and crisp, with a surprising, tart, lemony taste (due to the oxalic acid content) and are rich in vitamins A, C and E. Native Americans chopped them with watercress and other leaves, which they fermented like sauerkraut. Another option is to boil these "greens" for ten minutes or more.

American Bistort
Polygonum bistortoides [*Bistorta bistortoides*]
EDIBLE · GARDEN · MEDICINAL

Life zone/ecosystem: Subalpine to alpine. Moist meadows.
Characteristics: Common herb, 4–28 in. (10–70 cm). A compact cylindrical head appears as a single flower, which is actually a cluster of tiny 5-lobed "flowers" made up of white to pale rose-colored sepals (tepals) instead of petals. Leaves mostly basal, 4–10 in. (10–25 cm) long. Resembles diamond-leaf saxifrage, which is stouter, with 5-petaled flowers in a more spherical head.

Entire moist mountain meadows are often carpeted in American bistort, which appear as billowy cotton puffs bobbing in the breeze. Unlike alpine bistort, this species does not develop "bulblets," instead reproducing by seed. Green parts of both plants can be eaten raw or steamed. The seeds taste similar to the familiar buckwheat and can be used on breads in place of poppy seeds. *Bistortoides* refers to the contorted rootstock, composed of rosy flesh beneath a dark, scruffy outer layer. With its high tannin content, bistort root has been called

BEWARE! The starchy rhizomes are edible, but could be confused with poisonous death camas (*Zygadenus*).

"one of the strongest astringent medicines in the vegetable kingdom," and is used for all types of internal and external bleeding conditions as a tea, tincture, powder, poultice, injection or gargle. Bistort can also be propagated by dividing the rootstocks in spring or autumn and growing them in moist, rocky areas of your garden. Flowers and foliage are eaten by elk, deer and pikas, while bears favor the roots.

Polygonum translates as "many kneed," referring to the swollen nodes common to this family (except for the genus *Eriogonum*) and similar to those in the Pink family.

Sulfurflower, Wild Buckwheat
Eriogonum umbellatum
EDIBLE · GARDEN · MEDICINAL

Life zone/ecosystem: Montane to alpine. Sagebrush and oak-mountain shrubland, especially on Mancos Shale. **Flowering:** June–August. **Fruit:** 3-angled smooth achene. **Characteristics:** Common. Upright herb 4–12 in. (10–30 cm). Mat of leathery oval to spoon-shaped leaves, usually fuzzy beneath. Coppery-tinged buds appear prior to brilliant yellow flowers, tightly packed in shaggy globes on short stems originating from single point in umbrella-like cluster, with circle of leafy bracts beneath. Upright and leafless stems. Another species, **subalpine buckwheat** (*E. subalpinum*) grows in subalpine meadows; has tough, hardy leaves and off-white to rose-tinged flowers; sometimes considered a variety of sulfurflower, though they do not interbreed in Colorado.

Fossil records of this genus go back to the Eocene period, thirty-seven to fifty-eight million years ago. *Eriogonum* is the largest genus endemic to North America, with more than 300 species, fifty of them occurring in the Rocky Mountains. Wild buckwheat seeds are food for ants, rodents and birds, also found in the diets of the ancestral Puebloan peoples of Chaco Canyon and Mesa Verde. For the Navajo, the plant was known as "life medicine" and was eaten as an emetic to cleanse patients before ceremonies. It was also used for medicinal purposes, often during pregnancy, in many other Native American cultures.[10] With papery flowers that dry to a rich reddish-brown rather than withering, wild buckwheat provides a bright contrast to the dry areas it commonly inhabits, evoking memories of sunny summer days well into fall. It makes a great addition to any native plant garden.

*Yellow Dock, Curly Dock
Rumex crispus
DYE · EDIBLE · MEDICINAL · WILDLIFE

Life zone/ecosystem: Montane to subalpine. Moist disturbed areas. **Flowering:** Midsummer. **Fruit:** Achene surrounded by 3 heart-shaped wings. **Characteristics:** Common. Non-native, introduced from Europe. Hearty herb 1–5 ft. (30–150 cm). Wavy-edged, lance-shaped leaves. Although weedy, becomes attractive as branched spires of tiny green flowers ripen into winged seeds of copper, rust and red. Branched taproot, yellow-orange pith.

Rumex walmartsii should be the scientific name for this plant, because it is a veritable storehouse of wild food and medicine. People have eaten yellow dock for centuries—it has a higher nutritional value than spinach, being rich in vitamins C and A, calcium, iron and potassium. Yellow dock was used for food during the Great Depression. Its spring-green leaves are a tangy addition to casseroles, salads and soups. Just wash the leaves first to remove the naturally occurring chrysophanic acid, which can irritate the mouth. Most wilderness chefs recommend cooking the leaves in a small amount of water for ten minutes and seasoning like spinach to achieve an agreeable flavor. Dock seeds can be cleaned and eaten raw or toasted, ground as flour or cooked as cereals. Medicinal uses for yellow dock are recorded as far back as 500 BC. Modern herbalists suggest dock-root tea for cleansing the body of toxins (including lead, arsenic and other metals), resolving skin conditions and aiding digestion of fatty foods. A salve can be made from the roots to soothe skin irritations such as insect bites, or try treating irritated gums with powdered dock root. Dyes have been derived from

Dense-flowered dock (*Rumex densiflorus*) is a clump-forming native found in wet subalpine areas. Leaf margins are not wavy.

every part of the dock plant, yielding hues from rosy-beige to gold and gray-green. Rabbits are fond of the sour leaves, whereas birds draw energy from seeds still clinging to branches raised above the snowpack in winter.

BURREED FAMILY *Sparganiaceae*

S uch an unmistakable family needs little description. Burreed flowers are arranged in the shape of spheres, with female, seed-producing flowers growing on the lower parts of a zigzag stem and male, pollen-producing, flowers growing on the upper stem. Although normally inhabiting the muddy margins of ponds or lakes, with their "feet" in shallow water, burreeds will not produce flowers when growing in deep water. Their leaves may be linear, erect, immersed or floating, and the roots are creeping rhizomes.

Burreed, Emersed

Sparganium emersum (sometimes combined with narrow-leaved burreed, *S. angustifolium*)
RESTORATION • WETLAND

Life zone/ecosystem: Montane. Marshy meadows and ponds.
Flowering: July. Fruit: Bur-like. **Characteristics:** Fairly common. Floating aquatic (emergent). Foliage partially above water. Most leaves greater than 0.2 in. (5 mm) wide; somewhat spongy and triangular or 3-sided; not flat. Fruiting heads about 0.8 in. (2 cm) thick at maturity. Beaks on achenes greater than 0.08 in. (2 mm) long; need magnification.

With roots entwined in the smelly muck beneath the shallow water of a pond's edge, burreed casts an unusual reflection on the water's still surface. The thickened stem bases and rhizome tubers are edible in unpolluted waters. Muskrats find the whole plant tasty, while waterfowl and marsh birds readily consume the seeds.

BUTTERCUP FAMLY *Ranunculaceae*

Baneberry

Buttercups are abundant, with 1,800 species found primarily in the northern hemisphere. Flowers are either radially symmetrical or irregular. They have many stamens, many simple pistils with superior ovaries and 5 separate petals, not united at the base, which are often brightly-colored sepals instead of true petals. A typical flower will produce a cluster of follicles or achenes.

Leaves are usually alternate and compound. Clematis differs from the norm, having 4 "petals" and opposite leaves.

Although this family lacks a history of economic importance, countless members of the genus *Ranunculus*, the true buttercups, provide luxurious color in our gardens. Some common yellow buttercups may be confused with potentillas of the rose family. Buttercups, however, do not have 5 sepal-like bracts alternating with 5 larger sepals at the base of the flower as all rose family members do.

Though several botanists have separated the buttercups into three different groups, the botanical world has not yet reached a consensus on this subject. Here are brief descriptions of the basic traits of the other two proposed groups (or families) besides Ranunculaceae:

Hellebore group (Helleboraceae): Fruits of this group are follicles, which are dry fruits with single capsules that split open when mature, often containing many seeds (blue columbine fruits are examples of follicles). The flowers are often unusually beautiful, but many contain poisonous or irritating chemicals historically used as medicine or poison (e.g., aconite and belladonna). Delphinium, larkspur, monkshood, baneberry, columbine and marsh marigold are included in this group.

Meadowrue group (Thalictraceae): Members of this group are non-woody perennials with lacey leaves, no petals and no nectar. Local species have small, inconspicuous sepals and have male and female flowers located on separate plants. Fruits of this group are dry achenes, dry fruits that do not open and contain only one seed (ovule) inside of a single capsule (locule). Only one genus of this group, *Thalictrum*, occurs in this area.

Baneberry, Chinaberry, Doll's Eyes

Actaea rubra [*Actaea rubra* subsp. *arguta*]
POISONOUS

Life zone/ecosystem: Montane to lower subalpine. Aspen groves. **Flowering:** May–June.
Fruit: Berry. **Characteristics:** Common.
Erect herb up to 40 in. (1 m). Compound
leaves divided into 3 sections with sharp-
toothed, lance-shaped leaflets on long petioles.
Many tiny white flowers with 4–10 petals and
prominent stamens clustered atop the stem;
sepals fall off as flower opens. Poisonous shiny
red or white berries.

Baneberry's glossy red or white
berries appear lacquered, like bright
beads clustered on the stem. They're
alluring, but deadly. **Six of the fruits of the European
species have been known to kill a child; death would
come by cardiac arrest or respiratory paralysis.** Although
the roots and berries are poisonous, the toxic constituents

White-
berried
variation

have been used medicinally by Native
Americans and in very low dosages by modern trained professionals. On the other
hand, baneberry is a striking ornamental,
with the handsome berries usually remaining on the plant until the second frost.
Gather the seeds in late summer and sow
them in a moist, shady location. Viability is
limited, so sow them as soon as they are
mature.

> **BEWARE! Spring
> shoots resemble fern
> fiddleheads, and young
> plants are similar to
> sweet cicely, but do
> not have an anise
> smell when crushed.**

Blue Clematis,
Blue Virgin's Bower

Clematis occidentalis var. *grosseserrata*
[*Atragene occidentalis, Clematis columbiana*]
GARDEN · MEDICINAL

Life zone/ecosystem: Montane to lower subalpine.
Aspen, Douglas-fir, mixed-conifer forests and brushy
slopes. **Flowering:** May–June. **Fruit:** Achene with feathery style. **Characteristics:** Common. Woody vine up to
8 ft. (2.5 m) in length. Four lavender petal-like sepals surround numerous golden stamens
and styles. Compound leaves have 3 entire or toothed leaflets, sometimes deeply lobed.
Silvery seed clusters showy in late summer as styles transform into feathery plumes
attached to tiny seeds, which are easily dispersed by wind.

Sugarbowl, or **leatherflower** (*Clematis hirsutissima* [*Coriflora hirsutissima*]), is a local relative of blue clematis found in dry montane meadows of oak-mountain shrubland communities, with leather-like, urn-shaped flowers and finely dissected leaves cloaked in a silvery pubescence. Western white virgin's bower (*C. ligusticifolia*; not pictured), a cream-flowered relative, adorns fence posts, shrubs and trees along riparian corridors, irrigation ditches and roadsides at lower-elevations with fluffy white seed clusters in the fall.

Delicate as a butterfly's wings, drooping lavender flowers hang in the forest understory as this woody vine clambers over shrubs and small trees. *Clematis* comes from the Greek word *klema*, meaning "vine branch;" clematis leaf stalks are touch-sensitive, like tendrils, coiling around every object they encounter to secure the plant as it climbs. The entire genus contains chemicals known to cause severe skin irritation and possible internal bleeding if used in excess. These are reasons clematis is no longer used in mainstream medicine, though some herbalists still use it in tea for headaches. The fluffy seed heads might be used for building a fire. Native plant gardeners have discovered that clematis is easily grown from seeds gathered in the fall.

Blue Columbine
Aquilegia coerulea
EDIBLE • GARDEN

Life zone/ecosystem: Montane to alpine. Meadows, aspen groves, rocky slopes. **Flowering:** June–August. **Fruit:** Graceful furry pods (follicles). **Characteristics:** Common. 8–24 in. (20–60 cm). Flowers typically light blue to deep lavender-blue and white; possibly all blue or all white; funnel-shaped petals extend downward as slender spurs between sepals; bright yellow stamens clustered in center. Lacey, blue-green foliage often confused with meadowrue (*Thalictrum* spp.), which has smaller, more numerous scalloped leaflets and is usually prominent in understory vegetation of aspen groves.

Exotic and willowy, columbines are said to resemble doves dancing on the wind, and indeed *columbine* is derived from the Latin word for "dove-like." Blue columbine is Colorado's state flower and its graceful blossom is a fitting symbol and reminder of summer in the Rocky Mountains. *Aquilegia* is derived from the Latin for "water" and "to collect," referring to the slender nectar-laden spurs available only to long-tongued hummingbirds, butterflies and moths. Occasionally, tips of the funnel-shaped petals are nipped off by shorter-tongued nectar "thieves" such as bees, who use this devious method to reach the sweet prize. Botanists once thought this method did not lead to pollination because the bees bypassed the styles and stigmas. Recent studies indicate that flowers do get pollinated by these "robbers" when some pollen is gathered to feed the queen bee and is incidentally carried to the stigmas of other columbines.[11] Ripe seeds were once massaged into the scalp by Native Americans to discourage lice. They were also taken in wine to induce labor during childbirth. However, the seeds are no longer used as they are toxic in large amounts. Blue columbines are protected by law, though the flowers are edible and could be used in a survival situation.

A local favorite with stunning red and yellow flowers, **western red columbine** (A. elegantula) casts a crimson glow on moist shady hillsides of open montane and subalpine woods.

Fendler's Meadowrue
Thalictrum fendleri

Life zone/ecosystem: Montane to subalpine. Moist aspen, mixed aspen/conifer forests and moist open meadows. **Flowering:** May–July. **Fruit:** Dry 3-ribbed achene, somewhat flattened. **Characteristics:** Common. 1–3 ft. (30–90 cm). Loose branching clusters of inconspicuous flowers without petals; each plant either all-male or all-female flowers. Thin, greenish-blue leaves scalloped and much-divided; often confused with columbine, which have fewer divisions and larger leaflets. Similar species: **alpine meadowrue** (*T. alpinum*) and **few-flowered meadowrue** (*T. sparsiflorum*), distinguished by having perfect flowers (both male and female parts). While the former grows in alpine and subalpine peat bogs or wet tundra areas and has mostly basal, evergreen leaves, the latter may grow among Fendler's.

Loaded with pollen, the tassel-like male flowers shake in even the lightest breeze, assuring success by wind pollination.

Lacy and delicate, Fendler's meadowrue often dominates understory vegetation in the dappled sunshine of aspen groves. Fresh pendulous stamens of the male flowers are reminiscent of graceful golden tassels, while female flowers are star-shaped tufts of greenish pistils, maturing into ribbed fruits after pollination. A note from *Lone Pine Guide for the Rocky Mountains* says, ". . . meadowrue seeds and leaves keep their pleasant aroma when dried, and they were stored with clothing and other possessions as a perfume."

Female flowers are star-shaped tufts of greenish pistils.

Globeflower

Trollius albiflorus [*T. laxus* subsp. *albiflorus*]
POISONOUS

Life zone/ecosystem: Subalpine to alpine. Wet areas of forests and meadows.
Flowering: June–August.
Fruit: 10–20 beaked follicles (pods) with strong horizontal veins and tiny bumps, many seeds.
Characteristics: Common. 4–16 in. (10–40 cm) tall. Single cream-colored sepals (no petals) with bright yellow stamens atop multiple leafy stems. Leaves and stems hairless; leaves round in outline, divided into 5 deep lobes that are again deeply lobed. Mature pods have tiny bumps, prominent horizontal veins and many seeds.

Although our globeflower is really saucer- or cup-shaped, it's named after a European cousin that is globe-shaped (*Trollius* is derived from the German *troll*, meaning round). Typical of the buttercups, a golden starburst of stamens dominates the flower's center. However, unique to the globeflowers is an outer ring of stamens that is reduced to oblong, flattened segments that produce nectar instead of pollen.

Alpine anemone (*Anemone narcissiflora*) blooms later and has a bluish tinge on the underside of the white petals, hairy stems, 3-lobed leaves and a cluster of dry, non-hairy, single-seeded achenes instead of follicles. Compare with Marsh marigold.

Fruits of Alpine anemone

Graceful Buttercup

Ranunculus inamoenus
MEDICINAL

Life zone/ecosystem: Upper montane to subalpine. Moist meadows; pond edges. **Flowering:** June. **Fruit:** Pubescent achene. **Characteristics:** Fairly common. 6–8 in. (15–20 cm). Rounded basal leaves coarsely toothed; stem leaves deeply divided. A common alpine buttercup, snow buttercup (*R. adoneus*), has relatively larger, bright yellow, poppy-like flowers, brownish, hairy sepals; leaves divided deeply into narrow segments; blooms early near melting snowbanks.

Little buttercup (*R. uncinatus*), another local species, has leaves divided into three lobed segments and tiny yellow flowers.

Even though *inamoenus*, the species name, means "unattractive," this is a very pretty little spring-blooming buttercup, scattered throughout mountain meadows. Navajo tribes believed that drinking a tea made from the flowers protected them from dangerous animals while hunting. There are many other local buttercup species, very difficult to identify because they are distinguished by subtle details. Those who want to identify local buttercups to species should refer to Weber's *Colorado Flora—Western Slope*.

Water plantain buttercup (*R. alismifolius*) blooms in early spring.

Marsh Marigold, Elkslip

Caltha leptosepala [*Psychrophila leptosepala*]
EDIBLE • GARDEN • MEDICINAL • WILDLIFE

Life zone/ecosystem: Upper montane to alpine. Marshy meadows, streams. **Flowering:** June–August. **Fruit:** Follicle. **Characteristics:** Common. 1–8 in. (2.5–20 cm). Cup-shaped white flowers atop leafless stem; lustrous heart-shaped basal leaves very shallowly scalloped. Petals absent, 5–12 white sepals often streaked with lavender and green on the underside.

Marsh marigold's flowers—white and picture-perfect—are adorned with a spray of golden stamens. They form dense patches casting their bright reflections in pools and streams of marshy meadows near the base of melting snow banks amidst velvet-green moss and intense fuchsia clusters of Parry's primrose. Herbalists use a tea from the dried leaves, mixed with other herbs, as an expectorant for recovery from bronchial or sinus infections. Early Europeans, Native Americans and pioneers cooked marigold leaves as a potherb. The flower buds can be used in soups and side dishes, fermented for wine or pickled in boiling vinegar and used like capers. Alaska's Bristol Bay Eskimos even cook the spaghetti-like roots. Because of poisonous glycosides present in raw plants, all parts must be boiled or thoroughly dried before using. Elk are fond of this plant. The name marsh marigold dates back to the Middle Ages, when this genus was dedicated to the Virgin Mary and used in Church celebrations. The marigold of gardening fame is actually a member of the sunflower family.

Monkshood fruits

Monkshood, Wolfbane
Aconitum columbianum
GARDEN • MEDICINAL • POISONOUS

Life zone/ecosystem: Upper montane to subalpine. Along streams among willows, moist meadows. **Flowering:** June–August. **Fruit:** 3 follicles. **Characteristics:** Common. 2–6 ft. (0.5–2 m). Five elaborate, petal-like sepals conceal small petals; resembles hood of a purple monk's robe. Leaves resemble those of non-toxic wild geranium and very toxic delphinium; best to learn monkshood while in flower.

Found in moist mountain niches, monkshood often grows in clumps among twisted-stalk and mountain bluebells. A symbiotic relationship between monkshood and the queen and worker bumblebees helps prevent self-pollination. Flowers mature from the bottom up, with pollen-laden anthers appearing first and then fading as stigmas mature, so stigmas become receptive on the bottom flowers as anthers are ripening on the flowers above. Since bumblebees predictably visit lower flowers first, pollen is carried from one plant to the receptive stigma of the next.

Its association with the monastic life seems ironic, as the plants in this genus contain potent poisons, notably aconitine. In monkshood, the seeds and tuberous roots contain the highest degree of aconitine, which varies from species to species. Legend has it that monkshood sprang from the frothing saliva of Cerberus, the dog that guards the gates of Hades. It has been used for wolf and rat poison in Europe and in poison-tipped arrows to kill predators in China and India. Shakespeare's Romeo was referring to aconite when he wished for a "dram of poison." *Aconitum* is still used in traditional medicine in India, China and neighboring countries, where it is processed to reduce the toxicity. Some U.S. herbalists use monkshood in liniments for sciatic pain. Germany's *Commission E Monographs* recommend usage only in homeopathic doses due to the extreme toxicity. Monkshood can be propagated by root division or seeding and grows well in gardens.

Nelson's Larkspur, Spring Larkspur
Delphinium nuttallianum [*D. nelsonii*]
POISONOUS

Life zone/ecosystem: Montane and subalpine meadows. Oak-mountain shrubland, sagebrush shrubland. **Flower:** May–July. **Fruit:** Follicle. **Characteristics:** Common. Relatively small in stature, 4–16 in. (10–40 cm). Bright blue-purple, sometimes pink; bilateral flowers in elongated raceme of 3–10. Each flower has 5 showy sepals, possibly hairy and somewhat sticky; 2 unequal pairs of inconspicuous petals. One pair forms nectar-bearing structures; other is clawed, rounded and whitish marked by purple veins. Upper sepal forms prominent spur projecting backwards. Leaves mostly basal; palmate; divided into narrower segments than leaves of monkshood, subalpine delphinium and geranium.

Nelson's larkspur leaf

Nelson's larkspur is pollinated primarily by queen bees, solitary bees and hummingbirds. *Delphinium* comes from the Greek word for dolphin, possibly because the nectaries hidden inside the flower's spur resemble dolphins. "Larkspur" refers to the spur on a lark's foot, which the flower suggests. This larkspur was named for Aven Nelson (1859-1952), who founded the Rocky Mountain Herbarium at the University of Wyoming, where he taught botany for fifty years. Nelson's larkspur contains the same poisonous alkaloids as taller subalpine larkspur and can cause heavy losses of cattle on spring and early summer ranges; however, sheep do not seem bothered by it.

Subalpine Larkspur, Tall Delphinium

Delphinium barbeyi
GARDEN • POISONOUS

Life zone/ecosystem: Montane and subalpine. Wet areas of spruce-fir forests and moist meadows. **Flowering:** July–August. **Fruit:** Follicle. **Characteristics:** Fairly common. Robust, often over 5 ft. (1.5 m). Short dense racemes of deep purple flowers. Flowers resemble Nelson's larkspur, but spur's tip is bent. Broadly lobed, hairy leaves are short-stalked, mostly on the stem.

Clumps of 5–20 stems; grows in rich moist soil associated with other plants like false hellebore, mountain bluebells and cow parsnip. Upper stems and pedicels sticky due to spreading glandular, tawny hairs. Vaselike smooth seed pods have persistent tip (style), are slightly joined at the base and split open down the inside.

Delphinium contains poisonous alkaloids toxic to cattle if they consume more than three percent of their body weight, causing death by neuromuscular paralysis. Sheep do not seem affected unless they consume four to five times the amount toxic to cattle. "Green soap," still found in some pharmacies, is a concoction containing *Delphinium,* used as a shampoo to control lice on humans and animals. This has been the primary use of *Delphinium* since medieval days. Scientists believe that toxins such as those found in this genus evolved to protect plants from insects. The potency fades as the plant matures, probably because plant-eating insects have been deterred long enough for the seeds to ripen. Seeds of this plant are also toxic. Delphinium can be grown in the same manner as monkshood in gardens; however, children and adults should be made aware that they are very poisonous.

Seedhead

Pasqueflower, Wild Tulip

Anemone patens var. *multifida*
[*Pulsatilla patens* subsp. *hirsutissima*]
GARDEN • MEDICINAL

Life zone/ecosystem: Montane to subalpine.
Open forest, oak-mountain shrubland and sagebrush shrubland. **Flowering:** Early spring.
Fruit: Achene with feathery plume.
Characteristics: Common. Reaches 14 in. (35
cm). Delicate lavender, petal-like sepals surround
spray of golden stamens. Entire plant protected
by soft furry coat of silky hairs. Single flower of
5–7 sepals. Finely dissected basal leaves; whorl
of leaves cups the stem.

Pasqueflower blooms soon after the snow melts, its cheerful fuzzy flowers offering a hopeful sign of spring. The name
comes from the French word for Easter, when it often flowers.
Similar species of this genus have been used medicinally for
centuries, with the earliest records of use from China as an
antiseptic, diaphoretic and cure for eye ailments. Pasqueflower
was listed in the United States pharmacopoeia from 1882 to
1905 for similar uses. More recently, it has proven effective as
a sedative and restorative for the nervous system. In *Medicinal
Plants of the Mountain West*, Michael Moore recommends
pasqueflower for "distressful PMS and long, shaky periods
when it is hard to keep in touch with reality." However, inges-
tion of this herb is also known to reduce heart rate significantly. Pasqueflower can be started from seed and is a charming addition to native plant gardens.

Wind anemone
(*A. multifida* var. *multifida* [*A. multifida*
subsp. *globosa*])
Delicate rose-
colored tepals.
Fairly common in
montane and sub-
alpine dry meadows
and open forests.

EARS OF THE EARTH. Living so close to nature, early Native American tribes
had a genius for giving plants appropriate names. They called pasqueflowers "ears
of the earth," because these furry "ears" pushed up from the earth so soon after
snowmelt, to "listen for the faint rustle of summer."

CACTUS FAMILY   *Cactaceae*

Members of the cactus family are thick and succulent with clusters of
spines and brilliantly-colored flowers. Pricklypears are not endangered, but other members of this family are threatened because of their
popularity in home rock gardens. Some states, such as Arizona, have out-
lawed the collecting of wild cactus.

Potato Cactus
Opuntia fragilis
MEDICINAL

Life zone/ecosystem: Lower to mid-montane. Sagebrush and oak-mountain shrubland. **Flowering:** June–July. **Fruit:** Large, spiny and pulpy "berry." **Characteristics:** Fairly common. Spiny, small potato-shaped pads break off easily.

Pricklypear species interbreed, resulting in many different varieties. Potato cactus is easily recognized by the shape of the pads and the bright yellow of the flowers. Many other pricklypears, such as juniper

pricklypear, have the familiar wide, flat, "mouse-ear" pads. Fleshy parts of all *Opuntia* species are edible raw or cooked with special preparation. Big spines can be burned off, but tiny hair-like ones are hard to remove. A slit in the pad allows the outer skin to be pulled back, revealing a gel-like interior, similar to an aloe vera and with the same soothing quali-

Juniper pricklypear (*Opuntia polyacantha*), with mouse-ear pads, is found in similar habitat.

ties for bruised, burned or injured skin.

CATTAIL FAMILY *Typhaceae*

This is a small family of plants with a single genus, *Typha*, containing about fifteen species including reedmace, bulrush and cattails. Zealously hardy, they thrive in habitats of still or slow-moving fresh water of lakes, rivers, ponds and swamps all the way from the Arctic Circle to South America. They may dominate wetlands inundated with excess nitrogen found in runoff from agricultural fields or bluegrass lawns.

Female flower heads of the common local species are the familiar "cattail," recognized by anyone who has spent time in these habitats. This club-shaped terminal spike is green in early spring, later becoming a rich velvety brown as the flowers mature. Notice that the tops of the spikes look different, being composed of tiny male flowers that produce millions of pollen grains. These male flowers disintegrate soon after the pollen is dispersed on the wind, leaving behind a thin bare spike. Female flower ovaries mature into one-seeded achenes with tails covered in a tuft of hairs. This plume acts as a parachute, holding the fruit aloft as it is dispersed by the wind to land in an agreeable site for germination. These downy seeds have been used for everything from diapers to pillow stuffing. The strong, strap-like leaves of all species have been used throughout the world to weave baskets and water containers and to cane chairs.

Cattail
Typha latifolia
EDIBLE • WILDLIFE

Life zone/Habitat: Montane. Ponds. **Flowering:** May–July. **Fruit:** Achene. **Characteristics:** Common. 3–10 ft. (1–3 m). Coarse creeping rhizomes, cylindrical pithy stems. Long, bright green, flat leaves, usually greater than 0.4 in. (1 cm) wide. Parallel-veined leaves indicate close relationship with other monocots like grasses, rushes and sedges. Male (top) and female flower spikes (below) packed tightly together on the stem, differing from less common **narrow-leaf cattail** (*T. angustifolia*), which has at least a 2.5 in. (1 cm) separation between the two. Narrowleaf also has narrower leaves and early spring flowers with hairy bracts.

No wonder enthusiasts call cattails the "supermarket of the swamp." Classes on wild edibles have confirmed how tasty the young shoots are when sautéed and pollen from the male flower spikes can be mixed in equal parts with flour to create pancakes, muffins and biscuits. Connoisseurs of the wild say that boiling green female "cobs" makes a tasty substitute for corn. Be cautious if gathering young spring stem shoots, as they resemble shoots of toxic species in the orchid and lily families. Also avoid cattails growing in stagnant or polluted water. Historically, cattail roots were boiled and crushed to use as a poultice for burns and skin irritations, while Native Americans ate the astringent flower heads to relieve diarrhea. A cattail marsh is a whole ecosystem in itself. Muskrats and geese eat the rhizomes, and cattail stands provide nesting cover for birds such as red-winged blackbirds, ducks and rails.

DOGBANE FAMILY *Apocynaceae*

Of the approximately 200 genera and 2,000 species in the dogbane family, most are trees and shrubs, with only a few that are herbs. All have milky sap that can be toxic. Both the calyx and corolla of the flowers have 5 united lobes and the stamens are attached to the corolla tube, alternating with the petals. The leaves are without teeth or lobes and are opposite or whorled on the stem. Most gardeners are more familiar with tropical members of the dogbane family, such as oleanders and periwinkles. Indian hemp (*Apocynum cannabinum*), not the "hemp" related to marijuana, is a large, stout plant with greenish-white flowers and tough stem fibers historically used for ropemaking.

Spreading Dogbane
Apocynum androsaemifolium
MEDICINAL

Life zone/ecosystem: Montane to subalpine. Sunny, dry sites. **Flowering:** June–August. **Fruit:** Long pods with silky-haired seeds. **Characteristics:** Fairly common. 8–10 in. (20–50

cm). Erect, somewhat woody. Widespread, branching and droopy lance-shaped leaves appear very different from surrounding foliage. Pink, bell-shaped flowers grouped together on forked stems in open forked arrangement (cyme). **Indian hemp** (*A. cannabinum*), also found in the upper Roaring Fork Valley, has white flowers, erect or spreading leaves and opposite branching; found in more disturbed soil.

Dogbane's genus name means "noxious to dogs" in ancient Greek. The toxins contained in the milky sap actually deter browsing by most wildlife. The use of preparations of this plant as a diuretic and cardiac stimulant are confined to professionals, as misuse could be fatal. Recent laboratory studies indicate that dogbane may possess some anti-tumor properties.[12]

Dogbane fruits

DOGWOOD FAMILY *Cornaceae*

M any dogwoods are cultivated as ornamentals for their showy flowers, which are actually petal-like bracts surrounding clusters of tiny greenish flowers. A distinguishing characteristic of this family is the flower structure, which includes 4 to 5 sepals, petals and stamens, all of which are attached at the top of the ovary. The leaves are without lobes or teeth, and are attached on the stem in an alternate or opposite arrangement, while the flowers mature to produce a berry or stone fruit. Wood of this family is extremely hard and free of scratchy silica—so much so that jewelers reportedly used small splinters of it to clean out the pivot-holes in watches and opticians utilized it to remove dust from small deep-seated lenses.

Red-Osier Dogwood
Cornus stolonifera [*Swida sericea*]
GARDEN • MEDICINAL • WILDLIFE

Life zone/ecosystem: Montane to subalpine. Moist soil of streambanks, swamps and low meadows. **Flowering:** May–July. **Fruit:** Berry. **Characteristics:** Common. Spreading shrub to small tree, 10 ft. (3 m); bright red bark; flat-topped, creamy-white flower clusters. Opposite, broad, lance-shaped leaves with parallel veins converging toward the tip; veins exude latex substance.

Red-osier dogwood is a striking shrub no matter what time of year. Fall berry clusters are white and porcelain-like, creating an elegant display against the backdrop of colorful leaves. When the leaves drop off, only the blood-red stems remain, providing dramatic contrast with the white cloak of winter. This dogwood often grows in tangled thickets among other moisture-loving shrubs such as willow, alder and birch. These sheltered places provide valuable food, resting and nesting sites for wildlife. The berries, which resist rot due to their low sugar content, provide long-lasting food for winter. Deer, elk and mountain goats browse the twigs and foliage, while black bears, cottontail rabbits, snowshoe hares, racoons, squirrels and chipmunks eat the berries and foliage. Young stems and bark are consumed by deer mice, meadow voles and other small rodents. Numerous birds, such as flickers, woodpeckers, waxwings, vireos, thrushes, swallows, sapsuckers, grouse and band-tailed pigeons eat the berries. Though Northwest Indians ate the tart, bitter berries either fresh or dried, large quantities may be toxic. Apache, Cheyenne and other tribes dried the inner bark and leaves for use as a smoking mixture. Slim and flexible, the stems were also used for basket weaving and are still gathered today for this use.

EVENING-PRIMROSE FAMILY *Onagraceae*

Flowers of this fragrant family may be confused with those of the mustard family, whose flower parts also occur in fours—4 sepals, 4 petals and a 4-parted stigma. However, the ovaries of evening-primroses are inferior, while those of mustards are superior. Resplendent in their vivid pink and purple, ornamental fuchsias (native to the Andes) are related to local species. Although this family is not related to the true primroses of Europe, early botanists who named them were influenced by the similar sweet perfume characteristic of several species.

Evening-primrose oil is a source of gamma-linolenic acid, or GLA, which has been proven useful in the treatment of heart and vascular diseases, asthma, multiple sclerosis, arthritis, PMS, female hormone imbalances, dry skin and nervous disorders. Powdered seeds are also a source of tryptophan, used by naturopaths to treat Parkinson's disease. Yellow evening-primrose (*Oenothera biennis*), the source of this oil, is a common weed found growing along roadsides in North America.

Fireweed

Chamerion angustifolium
[*Epilobium angustifolium, Chamerion danielsii*]
EDIBLE • GARDEN • MEDICINAL • WILDLIFE

Life zone/ecosystem: Montane to subalpine. Moist and sunny disturbed areas along trails, ski runs, burned areas. **Flowering:** July–September **Fruit:** 4-celled capsule with 300–500 tiny plumed seeds. **Characteristics:** Common. Stately herb 3–9 ft. (1–2.7 m). Brilliant fuchsia flowers of 4 sepals and 4 petals arranged in a raceme; sparkling white styles taller than the 8 stamens. Alternate, willow-like leaves numerous along stem; prominent white mid-vein, side veins joining in loops on outer margins—useful in identification. A subalpine species of talus slopes and streamsides, **river beauty** (*C. latifolium* [*C. subdentatum*]) has less flowers, smooth styles (shorter than stamens), and grayish green leaves without veins.

Fireweed's fuchsia spires dominate the late summer landscape, often creating a colorful camaraderie with golden sunflowers also in bloom. Potandry—the phenomenon of flowering from the bottom up to prevent self-pollination—helps give fireweed flowers their characteristic appearance. As blooming proceeds, prominent white stigmas glitter in sunlight amidst already withered, pollen-bearing anthers. As final flowers fade and fruits mature, the leaves turn a burnished red and a transformation occurs. The former fuchsia spires become golden-brown sculptures of ram-like curls as the long capsules split and spill forth thousands of silky seeds, which often number up to 80,000 per plant! Fireweed flowers provide so much nectar that the Canadian and Russian honey industries are heavily reliant on this plant. Persistent underground rhizomes produce spectacular patches in the wild—a key factor in fireweed's critical role in stabilizing habitats disturbed by avalanches, road and trail building, fire or development.

Fireweed fruits split into graceful mahogany curls, spilling forth thousands of luxuriant silky seeds.

The spring shoots of fireweed can be enjoyed raw or cooked. High in vitamins C and A, they are still a popular food of indigenous Siberians. Modern herbalists treat systemic candida with fireweed leaf tea, which is also a gentle laxative. Native Americans rubbed the flowers into rawhide to increase water repellency and they ate the pith of summer stems. Elk, mule deer and bears favor fireweed as forage and the seeds provide sustenance for small mammals such as chipmunks and pikas.

Willowherb
Epilobium hornemannii

Life zone/ecosystem: Montane to subalpine. Wet soil of streams, springs and marshy areas. **Flowering:** Midsummer. **Fruit:** Capsule. **Characteristics:** Common. Slender herb 4–12 in. (10–30 cm). Ovaries mature to long capsules containing many tiny, tufted seeds; positioned beneath petals. Delicate pink flowers not easily spotted among tangled profusion of plants in wet areas.

Epilobium simply means "upon the pod," a reference to the flower's position atop the developing fruit. Willowherbs are so named because their long, tapering leaves with mostly smooth edges are reminiscent of willow leaves. As noted in Weber's *Colorado Flora*, recent genetic research has led botanists to reclassify willowherbs in a separate genus from fireweeds. This willowherb's foliage turns scarlet in autumn, as the seed pods ripen and split to reveal hundreds of cottony seeds. Its edible uses are similar to fireweed, and the fluffy fruits can be used as tinder.

Stemless Evening-Primrose

Oenothera caespitosa

EDIBLE · MEDICINAL

Life zone/ecosystem: Montane. Sunny, south-facing slopes. **Flowering:** May–August. **Fruit:** Woody capsules. **Characteristics:** Common. Low herb 6–8 in. (15–20 cm). Rosette of lance-shaped basal leaves, perhaps slightly toothed or lobed. Large, stemless white flowers turn pale pink upon withering. Thick woody roots. **Common evening-primrose** (*O. villosa*) is a tall, non-native yellow-flowered species up to 36 in. (91 cm); unlobed leaves; grows along roadsides.

This extravagant beauty graces dry hillsides and roadcuts where it flourishes in warm sunny soil, especially clay. As dusk deepens, the shimmering white flowers seem to glow from within. Having just opened, they will emit a delicate, sweet fragrance until noon of the next day, enticing mostly long-tongued moths to seek the sweet nectar. In the process, these moths and other night-flying insects are dusted with pollen, which they then deposit on the dramatic four-parted stigmas of the next stemless evening-primrose they visit. *Oenothera*'s thick roots can be cooked as an emergency food.

Long-tubed evening-primrose (*O. flava*) is a yellow-flowered native with narrow, irregularly pinnatifid (sometimes nearly entire) leaves. Look for it in moist meadows of oak-mountain shrubland and sagebrush.

FLAX FAMILY   *Linaceae*

Each delicate flower part appears in fives—5 roundish, wedge-shaped petals, 5 sepals that alternate with the petals, 5 styles and 5 stamens. Linen, the oldest textile known to man, is still in popular use today in the creation of very comfortable but easily wrinkled clothes. European common flax (*Linum usitatissimum*) has been the source of linen fibers for thousands of years, which are also used to fabricate nets and ropes. Seeds of the same plant are pressed to make linseed oil, used as a drying agent in paints and varnishes and in the manufacture of linoleum. Flax seeds are also pressed to obtain a nutritional oil, high in omega-6 and -3 fatty acids.

Wild Blue Flax

Linum lewisii [*Adenolinum lewisii*]
EDIBLE · GARDEN · MEDICINAL

Life zone/ecosystem: Montane to subalpine. Open meadows or hillsides. **Flowering:** May–August. **Fruit:** Round capsules. **Characteristics:** Common. Gray-green herb, 4–27 in. (10–70 cm). Alternate linear leaves line clusters of wiry, arching stems. Delicate, deep blue to whitish petals; drooping buds. Saucer-shaped flowers usually fade by midday, perhaps later on a cloudy day; new blooms daily.

Luminous ultramarine petals of wild blue flax lie sprinkled around each plant before the day is done. Because the flowers fade so quickly, the anthers ripen all at once, allowing the large golden pollen grains to be picked up by flies, butterflies and other pollinators. Wild blue flax is very drought-tolerant, grows well in clay soil and reseeds itself prolifically. Native Americans used the tough fibers in the stems for cordage. Although this is a desirable species for native plant gardens, seeds of this common native may be difficult to obtain commercially. Gardens and disturbed sites have in the past been seeded with a cultivar, "Appar" (*L. perenne* subsp. *perenne*). Research and monitoring are currently underway to ascertain if this plant spreads too easily, as some weed managers in Colorado maintain. These two species are difficult to tell apart without a technical plant key. Birds are known to eat the seeds of both.

FUMITORY FAMILY   *Fumariaceae*

Exotic flowers of pink bleeding hearts (*Dicentra spectabilis*), a member of this family native to Japan, add color and charm to shady areas of local gardens. Mysterious and peculiar, fumitory flowers have 2 tiny sepals beneath 4 petals, with the outer 2 petals flared at the top. One of these has a conical spur at the base. Smaller inner petals are joined over the stigmas, and the stamens are in 2 sets of 3. Sweet-scented fitweed (*Corydalis caseana*), with lush fern-like foliage and unique pink and white flowers, grows prolifically on moist soil around Crested Butte—but is rare in the Roaring Fork Valley. Both genera, *Corydalis* and *Dicentra,* are considered poisonous and are reportedly responsible for some livestock deaths. Some botanists include this family in the poppy (Papaveraceae) family.

Golden Smoke, Scrambled Eggs
Corydalis aurea

Life zone/ecosystem: Montane to subalpine. Sunny, south-facing slopes of oak-mountain shrubland. Often on disturbed soils, such as dirt mounds of pocket gophers and roadcuts; colonizes after fire. **Flowering:** May–August. **Fruit:** 2-valved capsule, resembles bean pod. **Characteristics:** Fairly common. Low-growing biennial 4–12 in. (10–30 cm). Reminiscent of scrambled eggs nestled amidst grayish-green parsley. Thinly succulent, finely dissected, fern-like foliage. Unusual yellow flowers, typical of this family, borne in short racemes. Curved, bean-like pods scatter among foliage as summer progresses.

Flowers of golden smoke are shaped so that insect pollinators automatically receive a dusting of pollen as they shove through the outer two petals to reach the nectar inside–a clever adaptation. *Corydalis* is Greek for "crested lark," referring to the flower's prominent spur. In *Medicinal Plants of the Rocky Mountain West,* Michael Moore says that a combination of golden smoke with a more specific herbal sedative like skullcap or valerian will treat nervousness, but is not safe alone or in large quantities. Foliage and seeds are eaten by songbirds, gamebirds and small mammals.

GENTIAN FAMILY　　　　*Gentianaceae*

Gentians' beauty has inspired people for millennia, eliciting poetry, art, folklore and exclamations of delight. They typically have opposite or whorled leaves without lobes or teeth on the edges and flowers with 4–5 united petals shaped like a bell or a slender tube spread flat at the top. Stamens are attached alternately with the corolla lobes and the ovaries are superior. Pollinating insects must crawl deep into these bell-shaped flowers to reach the nectaries lying at the bottom. Gentian species sometimes close during storms to protect their pollen, while some are so sensitive they close when touched. Gentians are native to mostly moist and cool habitats of higher elevations, with about seventy-five genera and 1,000 species around the globe.

Colorado species bloom in mid- to late-summer, in contrast to the spring- and early-summer-blooming species of Europe. Some of these gracious blooms will endure until killed by a hard frost or covered with early snows.

According to some legends in the Adriatic of southern Europe, it was Gentius, king of Illyria, who first discovered the medicinal values of gentian through his efforts to cure a fever taking over his army in the second-century BC. Gentian root has been used for centuries to prepare sweet bitters and tonics for treating digestive problems and malaria. Many people use Angostura bitters as an addition to cocktails, but may not realize that it is essentially a tincture of gentian roots from a related species, yellow gentian (*Gentiana lutea*). In *Natural Health, Natural Medicine*, Dr. Andrew Weil recommends a teaspoon of Angostura before or after meals in a little sparkling water, as a digestive remedy.

Green Gentian, Monument Plant

Frasera speciosa [*Swertia radiata*]

Life zone/ecosystem: Montane to subalpine. Openings in aspen or mixed-conifer forests to 10,000 ft. (3,048 m). **Flowering:** July–August. **Fruit:** Marginally flattened oblong capsules. **Characteristics:** Fairly common. 4–7 ft. (1.2–2.1 m). Monocarpic, living many years before flowering once and dying. Flowers have 4 pointed petals clustered in upper leaf axils among lance-shaped leaves in a whorl around the stout stem. Glabrous leaves progressively smaller upwards along stem.

The impressive flowers of these robust mountain giants deserve a closer look! Four greenish-white petals bear a sprinkling of purple spots, while elaborate nectar glands are covered by a pink-fringed flap. These ornate blossoms are embellished with a line of rigid glandular hairs down the center of the petal, giving the impression of contrivance by an ingenious sculptor. Only a rosette of green leaves, touched with a whisper of violet at the center, grow each season until the taproot has stored enough energy for reproduction to occur. Like the succulent agaves of desert environments, monument plants do not send up flowering stalks for twenty to eighty years.[13] Dried, golden-brown stalks of this plant often stand as sentinels along mountain trails for years after flowering.

Dried stalks of green gentian

KATHY DARROW

Rose Gentian, Northern Gentian
Gentianella amarella var. *acuta* [*G. acuta*]

Life zone/ecosystem: Montane to subalpine. Moist areas along streams. **Flowering:** July–September. **Fruit:** Capsule (spills seeds from tip). **Characteristics:** Fairly common. Small-flowered annual or biennial 2–16 in. (5–40 cm). Tubular flowers have 5 lavender petals, each bedecked with a feathery fringe at the base—possibly lacking in late bloomers. Calyx lobes united; lobes not visibly unequal. Leafy stem. **Dwarf gentian** (*G. heterosepala*), found in similar habitats, has unequal calyx lobes not fused at the base.

Although not as showy as other gentians, rose gentian's unusual fringed flower is quite charming. Take time to look for this delicate beauty along montane and subalpine moss-carpeted creeks, where they grow at lower elevations than most gentians.

Parry's Gentian, Bottle Gentian
Gentiana parryi [*Pneumonanthe parryi*]

Life zone/ecosystem: Upper montane to subalpine. Meadows and streambanks. **Flowering:** July–September. **Fruit:** Capsule. **Characteristics:** Common. 4–16 in. (10–40 cm). Flowers, usually in terminal clusters; deep to pale blue united petals. Each "pleat" ends in a single fine point, unlike **explorer's or bog gentian** (*G. calycosa*), a very similar species of other Rocky Mountain states, with pleats that end in 2 fine points.

Parry's gentian begins to bloom when most other plants are going to seed. Harbingers of fall, these flowers resemble graceful pleated goblets carved from lapis lazuli, pearl and peridot. Primarily visited by bees, these flowers represent a unique adaptation of flower to pollinator. The lower halves of each "goblet" are opalescent, welcoming insects attracted to light, inviting them to discover the nectaries at the base of the tumbler. Should a dark cloud shadow the ground or a storm threaten, this gentian slowly closes, perhaps to protect the fragile flower parts within or to hold the warmth.

Showy **arctic gentians** (*Gentiana algida*) appear in August and September, embellishing alpine turfs with papery, white to greenish blossoms, spotted inside and streaked outside with deep purple.

Rocky Mountain Fringed Gentian

Gentianopsis detonsa var. *elegans*

[*Gentianopsis thermalis, Gentiana thermalis*]

Life zone/ecosystem: Subalpine to alpine. Wet meadows.
Flowering: July–August. **Fruit:** 1-celled stalked capsule with persistent styles and stigmas. **Characteristics:** Common. Annual, 4–16
in. (10–40 cm). Several stems from a cluster of basal leaves, each
bearing 2–4 pairs of narrow lance-shaped leaves. Fringed petals
appear twisted together; four pointed calyx lobes with burgundy
central ridges hold each blossom. **Tufted gentian** (*G. holopetala*) of
the Sierra Nevada is considered a geographic variation; **eastern
fringed gentian** (*G. crinita*) is a different species.

Bounteous deep blue-violet blooms of fringed gentian inspired the poet William Cullen Bryant to
exclaim, "Blue, blue, as if that sky let fall a flower from
its cerulean wall." Fringed gentians were actually
chosen as the official flower of Yellowstone National Park because of
their abundance there in association with thermal basins—the origin of an
alternate species name, *thermalis*.

Star Gentian, Felwort

Swertia perennis

Life zone/ecosystem: Subalpine to alpine, most common in subalpine. Marshes and willow carrs. **Flowering:** July–September.
Fruit: 2-valved capsule with winged seeds. **Characteristics:**
Uncommon. Slender herb 4–20 in. (10–50 cm). Slate-blue to plum-
purple star-shaped flowers; prominent stamens alternate with the
petals. Lanceolate leaves taper to a slender stalk; are arranged opposite on stem.

Star gentian's dusky purple "stars" have two fringed
glands at the base of each petal, which appear to the
naked eye as miniscule marbles surrounding pillars that
are stamens slightly flared at the top. This species is
endemic to similar environments in western North
America, Europe and Asia. Steve Johnson, a member of
the Alaskan Flower Essence Project, believes that an
essential oil of star gentian "fosters cooperation
between the polarities that exist within the self to better focus one's energy towards goals of higher service; helps men reclaim their spiritual self-
image; supports men in serving the divine feminine; [and] helps bring
about a higher degree of balance and equanimity between men and
women as both are engaged in service to higher purpose." Seeds for this
unique native are available commercially and will germinate easily in wet
soil near ponds or along streams.

GERANIUM FAMILY *Geraniaceae*

W ild geraniums are difficult to identify when not in bloom, because their leaves are similar to those of toxic larkspur and monkshood (compare photos for each plant). Geraniums can be distinguished by two small leaf-like stipules attached where the leaf stalks join the stem and by their mostly basal or opposite leaves—whereas the others have alternate leaves on the stem. Dark pink veins on geranium petals serve as "nectar guides" (see box on the next page) and all geraniums have an interesting reproductive mechanism, which assures cross-fertilization and is also found in other flowering plants. Each anther matures and reproduces pollen before the stigma matures and becomes receptive to pollen for fertilization, ensuring that stigmas will receive pollen from another plant.

One common name for wild geraniums, "crane's bill," is derived from the fascinating fruit structure that develops as the ovaries ripen. Each of the five sections of the beak-like seed capsule contains a single seed and is attached by a single filament to the outer wall.

Cultivated geraniums, of the South African genus *Pelargonium,* domestic relatives of local wild species, are grown for cheery splashes of color worldwide. They also have aromatic uses. An oil distilled from rose geranium (*P. odorantissimum)* is said to soothe nervousness, uplift depression and alleviate skin irritations. By rubbing the somewhat similar leaves of wild geraniums between your fingers, you can detect a trace of the characteristic geranium scent. Geraniums contain high amounts of tannin in their roots, making them useful astringents in herbal medicine. Roots and leaves are brewed as tea to soothe insect bites and rashes, or as a mouthwash or gargle to treat sore throats and tonsillitis. Blackfoot tradition claims that powdered roots are a good herbal remedy to staunch bleeding of surface abrasions. Geranium foliage is not palatable, but does provide good forage for wildlife, particularly deer, elk and bear.

These drawings illustrate how fruits of native Geranium species change as they mature. Each seed capsule curls up along its section of style as the fruits dry and contract, creating the appearance of a carousel. During the process, the seeds are catapulted away from the parent plant.

Richardson's Geranium, White Geranium
Geranium richardsonii
GARDEN • MEDICINAL

Montane to subalpine. Moist meadows and aspen groves. Flowers June–August. Common. 8–32 in. (20–80 cm); 5–7 broadly lobed leaves arise mostly from the base, turning bright red as plants mature. Five white to pinkish petals; prominent red-purple veins; hairy on lower half. Magnification reveals ruby-tipped glandular hairs covering stems under flower cluster.

Sticky Geranium
Geranium viscossissimum
GARDEN • MEDICINAL

Autumn leaf of Richardson's geranium

Montane to subalpine. Tolerates moisture; prefers drier meadows near edges of aspen groves. Flowers June–August. Common. 1–3 ft. (30–90 cm). Stouter than Richardson's; thicker leaves. Sepals and pedicles usually covered with somewhat sticky, yellow-tipped glandular hairs. 5 deep-pink petals; hairy on lower quarter. Mature fruits longer than Richardson's. May hybridize with Richardson's where growing together.

*Crane's bill, Filaree
Erodium cicutarium

Montane. Common. Early spring weed. Up to 8 in. (20 cm). Small, non-native geranium of disturbed soil. 5 pink petals; 10 stamens, 5 without anthers. Fruit shaped like crane's bill; mature style hairy and twisted; straightens with moisture, drilling seed into ground. Pinnate leaves. Use hand lens for flower.

NEON SIGNS OF THE PLANT KINGDOM

Flowers possess unique visual cues which lead pollinators to the nectar source. Called "nectar guides," they represent a reciprocal relationship between flowers and insects. Both visible and invisible marks on the petals (such as stripes, rings or dots) appear to be there to direct a visiting insect toward the pollen or nectar once it has landed. Bees can detect ultraviolet light, which is not visible to humans without a special filter. It has been discovered that petals of many bee-pollinated flowers have stripes or spots that absorb or reflect ultraviolet light differentially. These patterns are visible to bees, which can detect ultraviolet light where invisible to the human eye. Examples of nectar guides visible to humans would be the reddish dots on monkey flowers and the dark pink stripes leading to the center of wild geraniums.

GOOSEBERRY OR CURRANT FAMILY

Grossulariaceae

Maple-like leaves of all sizes characterize this family, which is closely related to the Saxifrages. The gooseberry or currant family is represented in our area by a single genus, *Ribes*. Several species have parts covered in stalked hairs with tiny glands on the tip, inviting closer examination with a hand lens. These shrubs flower early in the spring, bearing petals that usually are much smaller than the sepals. When both are similar colors, it will appear that there are two layers of petals. Flower shapes—saucer, bell or tubular—help identify the species. Even after the flower's ovary has matured into a berry, flower parts persist at the tip providing clues to their former shape.

About 150 *Ribes* species inhabit the Northern hemisphere, also extending into the Andes mountains of South America. Several of them, such as red currant (*R. rubrum*) and golden currant (*R. aureum*), are widely cultivated in gardens. The raw berries of all currants and gooseberries are edible, although some are very tart or not palatable. The better ones have been used for jellies, jams and pies. Ute Indians mixed wild currants and gooseberries with fat, other berries and dried meat to make pemmican, creating the original "power bar!" Despite the temptation to eat them, berries are best left on the bush as they are a valuable source of energy for wildlife such as blue grouse, songbirds, black bears, small mammals and rodents. Elk and mule deer will forage on the leaves when other food is scarce.

Gooseberry or Currant Group

Ribes spp.

EDIBLE · WILDLIFE

Colorado Currant
Ribes coloradense [*R. laxiflorum*]

Upper montane to subalpine. Mixed conifer and aspen forests to 10,400 ft. (3,170 m). Flowers late June–July. Fairly common. Spineless sprawling shrub, usually less than 3 ft. (1 m). Reddish-brown flowers are saucer-shaped and arranged in a loose raceme emerging from previous year's growth. Ovaries, sepals and later the tasty dark purple or black berries are covered with stalked, gland-tipped hairs. Leaves have 5 fairly blunt lobes.

Mountain Gooseberry, White-stemmed Gooseberry
Ribes inerme

Montane to subalpine. Moist to wet meadows. Flowers May–early July. Common. Spiny, upright (sometimes sprawling) shrub to 4 ft. (1.2 m). Slender spines—1 to 3—at leaf nodes. Short reflexed sepals beneath greenish-white flowers in loose, droopy clusters of 1–4 flowers. Stamens protrude from short, tubular flower, longer than the style (with slightly hairy base). Very tart berry, smooth and dark red; matures August–September. Small roundish leaves with 3–5 lobes cut halfway to leaf's base. Leaves usually hairy in Colorado. Inerme means "unarmed," but there are thorns—nothing is set in stone with this shrub!

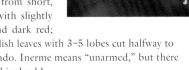

Red-fruited Gooseberry, Red Prickly Currant
Ribes montigenum

Upper montane to low alpine. Streams, wet forests, ravines. Flowers mid-June–July. Common. Spreading shrub grows to 28 in. (70 cm). Branches covered with stiff bristles, 1–9 small spines at leaf bases. Shallow, reddish-salmon, saucer-shaped flowers with glandular hairs, arranged in loose clusters of 4–12. Leaves glandular hairy with deep lobes and sharp-toothed margins. Red berries slightly ribbed and prickly with purple-stalked glands; greenish when young. Mature August to September.

Wax Currant, Squaw Currant
Ribes cereum

Montane to lower subalpine. Oak-mountain shrubland. Flowers May–mid-June. Common. Spineless shrub with stiff crooked branches, up to 5 ft. (1.5 m). Older bark gray to purplish. Long, tubular, pink—sometimes greenish-white with pink tinge—flowers with short non-glandular or glandular hairs, in tight pendant clusters of 1–6 at ends of stalks. Leaves broader than long with 3–5 shallow lobes, sometimes nearly heart-shaped, sparsely to densely covered with glandular hairs on both surfaces. Resinous secretions from glands on the leaves give them a waxy, shiny coating with age. Clear red to orange-red, bland berries are usually smooth-skinned (sometimes with stalked glandular hairs). Berries mature mid-July to August.

Wolf's Currant
Ribes wolfii

Upper montane to subalpine. Moist soil; aspen or mixed conifer-aspen forests. Flowers May–June. Common. Spineless, spreading shrub grows to 5 ft. (1.5 m). Older bark reddish to dark brown. Cup-shaped, creamy-white or yellowish-green flowers form long dense clusters on short leafy branches arising from year's new growth (not woody stems from previous years). Sepals showier than tiny petals. Large leaves; 3–5 nearly triangular lobes; smooth to sparsely hairy on both sides, especially on veins beneath. Dark purple, glandular berry.

GOOSEFOOT FAMILY *Chenopodiaceae*

Spinach, beets and Swiss chard are members of this family of 1,300 species that range from annual herbs to trees. Their inconspicuous greenish flowers lack petals, but some species make showy displays of their tiny, one-seeded fruits. Tiny granules—actually tiny hairs inside liquid-filled capsules—give the stems, flowers and leaf blades of some species a powdery or mealy look. "Chenopod" means goosefoot, and the wedge-shaped leaves of several chenopods do look somewhat like a goose's foot. Many of the wild species are edible and taste like spinach when cooked, though oxalic acid in the leaves can interfere with the body's absorption of calcium, so moderation is a good idea. Native Americans used the leaves of common lamb's quarters (*Chenopodium album*) to treat stomachaches and a cold tea made from the leaves to treat diarrhea. Quinoa (*C. quinoa*), another chenopod, is a nutritious grain considered a staple of people's diets in Peru, Ecuador and Bolivia. Saltbush (*Atriplex* spp.), a common evergreen shrub found in desert habitats on the Uncompahgre Plateau and in Rabbit Valley near Grand Junction (both in Colorado), provides valuable winter forage for wildlife and is an essential shrub for reclamation on oil shale and coal sites.

Netseed Lamb's Quarters, Goosefoot
Chenopodium berlandieri
EDIBLE · MEDICINAL

Life zone/ecosystem: Montane to subalpine. Disturbed sites. **Flowering:** May-August. **Fruit:** Pitted. **Characteristics:** Common. Up to 60 in. (150 cm). Tiny flowers grouped in an inflorescence of loose "spikes." Leaves succulent and thick-textured, irregularly toothed and lobed (at least lower ones), and densely mealy beneath. Identification requires hand lens to see distinctly pitted fruits.

Although the leaves of this species smell quite disagreeable when crushed, they still make a tasty pot of greens. Lamb's quarters are high in nutrition, reportedly containing higher amounts of vitamin A and C than most garden plants. Early settlers and Native Americans used the seed-containing fruits to make flour. They winnowed the dried plants twice, once to collect the fruits, and then again to separate out the seeds for grinding into flour. Because the flour was bitter, it was usually mixed with other types of flour before baking. Netseed lamb's quarters is more widespread in Colorado than the similar, non-native common lamb's quarters (*C. album*), which has smooth fruits.

GRASS-OF-PARNASSUS FAMILY *Parnassiaceae*

Although botanists once included grass-of-Parnassus as a subfamily of the saxifrages, new DNA sequencing indicates that the two groups have little in common. Obvious characteristics make these plants easy to recognize. The entire, smooth-edged leaves are all basal, except for a single leaf-like bract on the stem of some species. Peculiar sterile stamens with a fringe of glossy, golden, stalked glands alternate with the fertile stamens around a superior ovary.

Fringed Grass-of-Parnassus
Parnassia fimbriata

Life zone/ecosystem: Montane to alpine. Streamside, wetland areas of mixed-conifer, spruce-fir and tundra. **Flowering:** July–September. **Fruit:** Round capsule with angular seeds. **Characteristics:** Uncommon. Slender-stalked, 6–20 in. (15–50 cm). Glossy, heart-shaped to kidney-shaped leaves clustered at base, with another small clasping leaf at midstem. White to cream-colored flowers bear greenish or yellowish veins and fringes of "hair" near each petal's base. Five fan-shaped sterile stamens have crown-like projections tipped in golden glands, alternating with fertile, pollen-bearing anthers around the ovary. **Small-flowered grass-of-Parnassus** (*P. palustris* var. *montanensis* [includes *P. parviflora*]), found in subalpine wetlands, does not have fringed petals and the leaves are more egg-shaped to lance-shaped. **Kotzebue's grass-of-Parnassus** (*P. kotzebuei*), found on rocky ledges of the subalpine and alpine, has a leafless stem.

This elegant flower is truly a work of art. Grab a hand lens and look closely at its curious gland-tipped sterile stamens. Notice how the luminous striping on the petals converges to orient pollinating short-tongued flies to the location of the sweet nectar at the flower's center.

HEATH FAMILY   *Ericaceae*

ixie-like and evergreen, these perennials stimulate our imaginations
with their unusual flowers. Exquisite floral details appear delicately
carved in a waxy countenance of rose, white and green. All species have 8–10
stamens arranged in 2 whorls, opposite the petals and sepals respectively.
Ovaries are superior in local species, except for *Vaccinium* (inferior), and
mature into berries or else capsules that release many small seeds, easily dispersed by the wind. The leaves are simple, usually alternate and often leathery. Acid-rich, humus-laden soil created from generations of rotting conifer
needles and decaying logs provides the perfect environment for heaths to
thrive. Specific fungal mycorrhizae and other soil components are required
for these plants to germinate and survive—they do not transplant well to garden soil. Ericaceae includes Monotropaceae and Pyrolaceae, considered separate families by some botanists.

Well-known oil of wintergreen comes from the eastern wintergreen
species, (*Gaultheria procumbens*) and is used to relieve arthritic, rheumatic
and sciatic pain. The edible fruits of this family, such as blueberries, huckle-
berries and cranberries, are rich in flavonoid compounds known as antho-
cyanosides, which are potent antioxidants that help protect capillaries from
free-radical damage. Most members of this family contain ursolic acid and
the glycosides arbutin and ericolin, which are used interchangeably as ingredients in skin salves for irritations and shallow wounds and in teas for kidney problems. Native Americans often included cooked leaves in their diets,
though they are fairly tough and astringent. Because of this astringency,
they also used them as a treatment for mouth inflammations and sore
throats, hemorrhoids, insect bites and bleeding. Other heaths, such as azal-
eas and rhododendrons, are celebrated ornamentals. Step carefully as all
local species of this family are sensitive to trampling.

Bearberry, Kinnikinnik, Uva-ursi

Arctostaphylos uva-ursi

EDIBLE • MEDICINAL • WILDLIFE

Life zone/ecosystem: Montane to subalpine. Dry
rocky soil, spruce-fir and mixed conifer. **Flowering:**
May–June. **Fruit:** Berry. **Characteristics:** Fairly common. Low, mat-forming shrub up to 6 in. (15 cm). May
cover large areas; roots rigorously along spreading
stems. Pink petals are united, forming a bell shape,
resembling the chimney glass of a kerosene lamp; flow-
ers mature to bright red berries. Leathery spoon-shaped leaves with smooth
edges, often confused with **mountainlover** (*Paxistima myrsinites*), which has
teeth on the margins of lance-shaped leaves (see p. 217); both are evergreen.

The Latin, *uva-ursi*, literally means "bear grape," as the miniature, apple-like berries are favored by bears. Although mealy and bland, they are also important to non-hibernating wildlife such as songbirds, blue grouse and rodents as a source of nutrients that persists all winter. Deer and bighorn sheep eat the leaves and stems found beneath the snow. Native Americans smoked the bark together with red-osier dogwood and uncured wild tobacco in ceremony and for pleasure. Dr. Varro Tyler, dean of Purdue's school of natural products pharmacy, extols bearberry's use for urinary tract infections—the leaves contain hydroquinone, a powerful anti-microbial agent and require soaking in cold water for twelve to twenty-four hours to reduce the tannin content. Bearberry leaves are found in tea mixtures for bladder inflammations throughout Europe.

Bilberry, Whortleberry

Vaccinium myrtillus

EDIBLE • MEDICINAL • WILDLIFE

Life zone/ecosystem: Montane to subalpine. Spruce-fir. **Flowering:** June–July. **Fruit:** Berry. **Characteristics:** Common. Finely branched deciduous dwarf shrub 4–12 in. (10–20 cm). Thin, bright green leaves about 1 in. (2.5 cm) long. Greenish branches strongly angled, young twigs finely hairy. Flowers resembling delicate pink bells mature to tiny blue berries tucked beneath the leaves; miniature replicas of commercial blueberries. Two other species occur here: **Broom huckleberry** (*V. scoparium*) has red berries, leaves shorter at 0.5 in. (1 cm) long; branches more crowded; grows mostly in alpine areas. **Dwarf bilberry** (*V. cespitosum*) has blue berries; leaves widest above the middle; branches not as angled as other species.

Bilberry's thick foliage appears to hover above the ground, hiding the tiny sweet fruits dangling beneath. It is well adapted to cool, shady, acid soils, making it the primary ground cover in local spruce-fir forests. Birds, bears and small mammals feast on the berries, and mule deer and elk munch on the leaves and twigs, so don't be greedy. Different Native American tribes used fresh or dried berries for cooking. Daily supplements of bilberry and beta-carotene have been shown to improve night vision—a routine practice many pilots in World War II depended upon. As a tea, bilberry is mixed with other herbs to treat macular degeneration. Michael Moore, in *Medicinal Plants of the Pacific West*, reports that a tea of *Vaccinium myrtillus* leaves is

Dwarf bilberry—montane to alpine

effective in treating urinary-tract infections when the urine becomes too alkaline, and that a tea of the unripe berries can lower blood-sugar levels in certain types of diabetes.

One-sided Wintergreen

Orthilia secunda [*Pyrola secunda*]

GARDEN

Life zone/ecosystem: Montane to subalpine. Spruce-fir and Douglas-fir forests. **Flowering:** June–July. **Fruit:** Round capsule; withered style at tip. **Characteristics:** Fairly common. Evergreen, 2–8 in. (5–20 cm). Grows in patches, often in moist soil, at edges of cliffs or boulders. Flower stalks arch with weight of one-sided white to greenish flowers. Shiny round leaves with minutely scalloped edges, thinner than typical of this genus, alternating up lower half of stem.

One-sided wintergreen can be found in the northern regions of both the old and new worlds. *Ortho* is Greek for "straight" and refers to the long, straight style that protrudes from each dainty flower, while *secund* means one-sided. This species can be grown in rock gardens where it is cool and moist and the soil is rich in humus. Plants can be started by seed and then later divided as needed during the spring.

Pinedrops

Pterospora andromedea

PARASITIC

Life zone/ecosystem: Montane. Dry lodgepole pine/Douglas-fir forests. **Flowering:** Late June–August. **Fruit:** Spherical capsules. **Characteristics:** Uncommon. Parasitic plant, 1–3 ft. (30–90 cm). Lantern-shaped flowers dangle from pinkish, sticky, hairy stems that lack chlorophyll. Leaves reduced to small scales. Annual, though distinctive old stalks displaying pendulous brown fruits may persist several years; stems turn more reddish-brown with age.

Pinedrops are difficult to spot in the subdued light of the forest, but are very unusual and worth a careful search. Lacking chlorophyll, the green pigment necessary to make their own carbohydrates through photosynthesis, pinedrops attach parasitically to the roots of conifers and depend on their associated fungi to transform decayed plant material into usable nutrients. Often confused with parasitic orchids, such as spotted coralroot and striped coralroot, pinedrops have regular bell-shaped flowers instead of the irregularly shaped flowers characteristic of the orchid family.

Pink Pyrola, Bog Pyrola

Pyrola asarifolia var. *asarifolia*
[*P. rotundifolia* subsp. *asarifolia*]

Life zone/ecosystem: Subalpine. Mossy springs and creeks of spruce-fir, bogs. **Flowering:** June–August. **Fruit:** Many-seeded capsule. **Characteristics:** Fairly common. Evergreen 6–12 in. (15–30 cm). Extensive creeping rhizomes; creates colonies; occasionally inconspicuous amidst tall grasses. Slender raceme of pink, nodding, 5-petaled flowers spirals around leafless stem. Glossy green, spade-like basal leaves; heart-shaped bases and long stems.

Pink pyrola thrives in moist shady areas, producing pink flowers that seem to reflect the rose blush of an early morning sky. The petals are cupped at first, but spread wide as they mature. Curved green styles protrude from each blossom like a dangling elephant's trunk.

Pipsissewa, Prince's Pine

Chimaphila umbellata

EDIBLE · MEDICINAL

Life zone/ecosystem: Montane to subalpine. Spruce-fir. **Flowering:** June–August. **Fruit:** Capsule opens at tip. **Characteristics:** Uncommon. Semi-woody evergreen 4–12 in. (10–30 cm). Nodding, fragrant, rose-pink flowers in clusters of 3–8, each with a bright green fleshy ovary encircled by 10 burgundy stamens. 2–3 whorls of dark-green, toothed, leathery leaves.

CHARLES WEBBER, CALIFORNIA ACADEMY OF SCIENCES

As the nodding flowers fade, stems straighten and the fruits mature.

Pipsissewa, a treasure found in deeply shaded old-growth forests, is fast becoming overharvested by people exploiting it for food and medicine. Uses of this species have included the flavoring of root beer, candy and beer. Native Americans brewed a tonic high in vitamin C from the roots and leaves and used it to treat edema, kidney and bladder problems, coughs and fevers. The common name is thought to come from the Cree Indian word *pipsiskweu*, meaning "it breaks into small pieces," possibly referring to its use in remedies to break up kidney stones or gallstones. Found in nearly all northern regions, pipsissewa is indicative of a healthy forest and is considered a sign of healthy regeneration in moist conifer forests following fire or disturbance.

Wood Nymph, Single Delight
Moneses uniflora [*Pyrola uniflora*]
EDIBLE • MEDICINAL

Life zone/ecosystem: Subalpine. Spruce-fir, often near streams. **Flowering:** June–late July. **Fruit:** Capsule. **Characteristics:** Uncommon. Nodding single white flower atop a leafless stem 2–6 in. (5–15 cm). Nearly round basal leaves have tiny teeth above the middle.

Truly a delight, this charming wood nymph is a demure lady of shaded, mossy subalpine forests. Take a whiff of the alluring lily-of-the-valley fragrance. *Moneses*, the genus name, is appropriately derived from *mono* (single) and *hesis* (delight). Though the seeds are sometimes harvested, roasted and eaten, and medicinal uses abound, consider Janice Schofield's sentiment in *Discovering Wild Plants*—that wood nymphs are more valuable to humans as a "feast for the spirit."

HONEYSUCKLE FAMILY   *Caprifoliaceae*

Garden honeysuckle awakens childhood memories of carefree days wandering neighborhoods and woods near home. This family is best known for hardy ornamental shrubs such as honeysuckle (*Lonicera*), snowberry and coralberry (*Symphoricarpos*), elderberries (*Sambucus*) and viburnum (*Viburnum*). Obvious characteristics separate this family of mostly shrubs and vines from other similar plants. Honeysuckles' leaves are always opposite, usually lacking any small leaf-like appendages at the base of the leaf's stalk, though elderberry varies slightly by possessing stipules and pinnate leaves. Honeysuckles are most often confused with members of the madder/bedstraw family, which typically have stipules on the leaf stalks. The flowers have united petals and ovaries beneath the rest of the flower parts. A single style bears a cap-like or lobed stigma and they have 5 stamens, except for twinflower, which has only 4. Fruits of local species are berries, but again, not for twinflower (*Linnaea borealis*), which has a one-seeded capsule.

WARNING! Though some sources list snowberries as edible, they contain a toxic alkaloid, chelidonine, which can cause vomiting, diarrhea, sedation and depression.

Mountain Snowberry
Symphoricarpos rotundifolius (S. oreophilus)
GARDEN • POISONOUS • RESTORATION • WILDLIFE

Life zone/ecosystem: Montane. Moist to fairly dry soils of aspen groves, streamsides and oak-mountain shrubland. **Flowering:** May–July. **Fruit:** Berry-like drupe. **Characteristics:** Common. Deciduous shrub 2–4 ft. (0.6–1.2 m); fairly erect and dense; may have spreading or arching branches. Older bark shreds, looking slightly unkempt. Small gray-green leaves narrowly oval; not shiny. Though stiffly branched, leaves and pale-pink bell-shaped flowers are delicate in texture. White fruits contain 2 nutlets, each containing a single seed. Tip of berry often pink where flower withered.

Even on cool fall mornings after most other flowers have faded, snowberries coated with crystal dewdrops sparkle like jewels in the early light. Snowberry is one of the first shrubs to leaf out in spring, providing a good source of forage for elk and mule deer. Bears will seek out the bitter berries even when other food is available. Berries cling to the stem all winter, providing a valuable food source for grouse, pine grosbeaks, magpies and other overwintering birds. Navajo tribes used a tea of snowberry leaves for colds and sore throats and as a pre-ceremony emetic. Southern Paiutes smoked the leaves and also used the flexible stems to make the shade rim for baby cradleboards. Valuable in land restoration, snowberry persists once established and spreads vegetatively (stems touching the ground will take root). Plants are available commercially and can be propagated from stem cuttings or seed.

Red Elderberry
Sambucus racemosa var. *microbotrys*
[*S. microbotrys, S. racemosa*]
GARDEN • MEDICINAL • POISONOUS • WILDLIFE

Life zone/ecosystem: Montane to subalpine. Moist meadows, aspen forests. **Flowering:** May–July. **Fruit:** Berry. **Characteristics:** Common. Deciduous shrub 3–10 ft. (1–3 m). Pyramidal clusters of tiny white flowers; 5–7 pinnately divided, lance-shaped leaflets with slender tapering tips. Flowers and leaves have disagreeable odor. Small unpleasant-tasting, bright red berries of late summer and fall; seeds and raw berries are toxic.

Showing exuberant growth, red elderberry bushes evolve over the summer into graceful yet hardy shrubs. Elderberry is referred to as the "tree of music" because the pithy stems have traditionally been boiled and hollowed out to create flutes and whistles. "Sambuke," a similarly constructed Greek instrument, is the origin of the botanical name *Sambucus*.

WARNING! Cyanide poisoning can result from ingesting plant parts of red elderberry, causing vomiting and diarrhea. Although flowers and leaves have been used historically in medicine and cooked berries (with seeds removed) are still used in wine and jelly, toxicity can vary from plant to plant during various stages of growth. A person's age and health can also be a factor. Best to leave them for wildlife!

The showy blossoms have been famous from ancient to modern times, used in creams, lotions, steams and infusions to soften skin. Flower clusters have been battered and fried and recipes abound in folklore cookbooks. The stinky leaves have been used in dairies and by hikers to repel mosquitoes and flies. Chemical compounds in a black elderberry (*S. nigra*) are included in a patented Israeli drug (Sambucol) that has proven successful against flu viruses.[14] Berries are eaten by many birds, such as woodpeckers, warbling vireos and western tanagers, as well as rabbits, squirrels, foxes, mule deer and occasionally bears. In winter, porcupines and mice eat the buds and bark.

Twinberry, Bush Honeysuckle
Lonicera involucrata [*Distegia involucrata*]
WILDLIFE

Life zone/ecosystem: Montane to subalpine. Moist meadows and along streams. **Flowering:** May–July. **Fruit:** Berry. **Characteristics:** Common. Upright deciduous shrub to 6 ft. (2 m). Most easily recognized by paired yellow tubular flowers or paired blue-black berries surrounded by an involucre.

Involucrata means "with an involucre" and refers to the green bracts that surround the flowers. These bracts mature to a lustrous burgundy red and are covered with glandular-tipped hairs that sparkle in sunlight—a striking contrast to the glossy blue-black berries. Though not poisonous, these bitter berries are best left for the birds, bears and other mammals that seem to enjoy them.

Twinflower
Linnaea borealis
GARDEN

Life zone/ecosystem: Montane to subalpine. Moist to dry acid soils in spruce-fir forests. **Flowering:** June–September. **Fruit:** 1-seeded capsule. **Characteristics:** Evergreen shrub 4 in. (10 cm). Dwarf and creeping by nature, with stolons (slender horizontal stems) that root at the nodes; short erect stems that fork and bear paired, dainty pink bells. Small, opposite shiny dark green leaves are almost round; sometimes last for two years.

Twinflower's genus name, *Linnaea*, is in honor of Carolus Linnaeus of Sweden, the father of plant nomenclature, who claimed this was his favorite mountain plant. An abundance of seeds grow in each tiny capsule after the ovary is fertilized by pollen transferred from other twinflowers by native bees and syrphid wasps, although some plants do self-fertilize. Though usually found in shaded habitats, it tolerates a wide range of light intensity and may be found in full daylight in alpine meadows. Twinflower grows in rich soil full of humus, making it a charming groundcover for anyone lucky enough to have those conditions in their garden.

IRIS FAMILY $\qquad$ *Iridaceae*

Crocus, freesia, gladiolus and iris are familiar cultivated members of this family. Irises are widely appreciated for their exotic, sweet-scented flowers that have inferior ovaries. Irises can also be distinguished by their 3 stamens, compared with lilies' 6 stamens. Iris leaves are tough yet flexible and similar to those of the lily family, except they occur in two ranks at the plant's base in a flat plane forming a "fan." Underground storage organs are called corms, rhizomes, or bulbs and their fruits are capsules. Saffron, actually the 3 thread-like scarlet stigmas atop the style of one family member, *Crocus sativus*, is widely used as a dye and as a flavoring agent in cooking. *Iris versicolor* was the official medicinal species once included in the United States Pharmacopeia.

Wild Iris, Blue Flag

Iris missouriensis

MEDICINAL

Life zone/ecosystem: Montane. Wet meadows, streambanks and seeps. **Flowering:** Late May and June. **Fruit:** 3-parted capsules, many seeds. **Characteristics:** Fairly common. 8–10 in. (20–25 cm). Ornate flowers with 3 petal-like sepals curving downwards and 3 erect petals. Styles have evolved into 3 flattened petal-like structures, furnished with expanded showy "crests" curling over the surface of the stigma. Style branches curve outwards from the axis of the flower and form, with 3 of the floral segments, a shielding tunnel-like organ over each anther. Flowers sky-blue to lilac, with violet veins; patch of yellow in center. Narrow, sword-shaped leaves.

Iris was the goddess who relayed messages between heaven and earth for Zeus and Hera, using the pathway of a rainbow—Iris means "rainbow" in Greek. Elegant in stature, irises adorn marshy areas in early spring, followed by the growth of 3-parted cylindrical capsules which burst open when ripe to disperse abundant seeds. Bees attracted by the colorful yellow "signal patch" on the broadened sepal crawl along searching for nectar, where they inadvertently become dusted with pollen to fertilize the next flower visited. Wild iris was used as a digestive remedy by Native Americans and small doses of a tincture made from the less toxic dried rhizome are still used today. Sores from staph infections have been treated with a poultice of the boiled and mashed rhizomes and iris-arnica oils are used for bruises. The rhizomes contain an oleoresin (iridin) that can be extremely irritating to the liver and gastrointestinal tract, causing burning and diarrhea. Native Americans used the tough leaf fibers to make nets and other cordage.

LILY FAMILY *Liliaceae*

With close to 250 genera and 3,500 species, this is one of the largest plant families. Lilies have perfect symmetry, with flower parts alternating in 3's, and may have an inferior, superior or in-between ovary. Their sepals and petals are generally identical. These plants all have long, slender leaves with parallel veins; arise from bulbs, corms or thickened rootstalks; and bear fruit in the form of 3-celled capsules. Lilies, tulips and hyacinths are very popular as ornamentals, while onions, leeks, garlic and asparagus are found daily on the dinner table. Many of the plants considered lilies are now separated into other families by Dr. William Weber, author of *Colorado Flora—Western Slope*, whose research leads him to believe that their similarities are really only superficial (Alliaceae, Asparagaceae, Agavaceae, Convallariaceae, Calochortaceae, Melanthiaceae, Trilliaceae and Uvulariaceae). However, until further consensus is reached, species here are grouped in the traditional way.

Mountain Death Camas, Wand Lily
Zygadenus elegans [*Anticlea elegans*]
POISONOUS

Life zone/ecosystem: Montane to alpine. Moist meadows. **Flowering:** June–August. **Fruit:** 3-lobed capsule; 3 to many seeds. **Characteristics:** Common. 6–28 in. (15–70 cm). Greenish-white to white (sometimes pink) saucer-shaped flowers in loose, erect clusters (racemes). Each "petal" (actually a sepal) bears a green or yellow heart-shaped gland at the base; stamens not noticeably longer than "petals"; flower parts connected to sides of ovary instead of base. Leaves, growing from base, are long, flat and narrow with parallel veins. Bulbs somewhat round, coated with blackish scales. Seed capsules split along partitions that separate 3 sections of capsule, rather than down the back as in capsules of non-poisonous camas (genus *Quamasia*).

Zygadenus is derived from two Greek words, *zugon* (yoke) and *aden* (gland), which refer to the yoked glands at the base of the "petals." All North American species of this genus are poisonous to some degree, although mountain death camas appears to be comparatively less toxic to domestic grazing animals. Throughout history, bulbs of this genus have caused death to people mistaking them for bulbs of wild onion, camas or mariposa lily. Flowers of death camas have a strong, disagreeable odor and other plant parts smell nothing like onions. **A mixture of alkaloids concentrated in the bulb is responsible for the plant's deadly nature and can result in vomiting, lowered body temperature, breathing difficulty and sometimes death.** Its beauty is alluring, but do not be tempted by this toxic plant.

False Hellebore, Corn Lily
Veratrum californicum [*V. tenuipetalum*]
MEDICINAL • POISONOUS

Elk wallows are often found among patches of false hellebore.

Life zone/ecosystem: Montane to subalpine. Moist open meadows and along edges of aspen forests and streams. **Flowering:** June–August. **Fruit:** Capsules containing papery, winged seeds. **Characteristics:** Common. Tall and corn-like, 4–8 ft. (2–3 m). Large, robust leaves with pleated edges; distinct parallel veins. Showy flowering stalks at tops of leafy stems tower above non-flowering stalks. Greenish flowers lack petals; instead have 6 petal-like sepals, each with a V-shaped gland at the base. Lower flowers often male only; male and female flowers on separate plants.

Dr. David Inouye, of the Rocky Mountain Biological Laboratory in Gothic, Colorado, has made some fascinating discoveries regarding false hellebore. He found that rainfall and nutrient variability may be responsible for the spectacular flowering displays of false hellebore occuring only in certain years; besides reproducing by seed, the root system sends up shoots producing clonal patches possibly decades or even hundreds of years old that contain hundreds of genetically identical individuals; and that flies appear to be the dominant pollinators.

Dense stands of this lush, toxic lily lend a tropical air to the landscape. **All plant parts contain chemical components called alkaloids that depress heart function.** Native Americans and Europeans used it to poison arrows. The potency of these alkaloids is apparent in their severe effect on pregnant ewes: if false hellebore is consumed between the fourteenth and eighteenth days of pregnancy, deformed, one-eyed offspring are the result. These same alkaloids have been found useful in the treatment of lung cancer at the Sidney Kimmel Cancer Center at Johns Hopkins.[15] The root, which smells like rancid garlic, is also dried and powdered for use as an insecticide. Ironically, false hellebore was considered a love or passion talisman in North American folklore, possibly due to the voluptuous appearance of the flowers and leaves.

False Solomon's Seal, Solomonseal
Maianthemum racemosum var. *amplexicaule*
[*Smilacina racemosa*]
EDIBLE • MEDICINAL • WILDLIFE

Life zone/ecosystem: Montane to subalpine. Moist shaded woods and open meadows. **Flowering:** May–July. **Fruit:** Reddish (sometimes speckled) berries. **Characteristics:** Common. Robust herb 1–3 ft. (30–90 cm). Leafy, unbranched stem terminates in fluffy pyramid (panicle) of tiny creamy-white flowers. Broad alternate leaves lily-like with obvious parallel veins and wavy edges; bases partially embrace stem. Some leaves with short petioles. Grows from creeping rhizomes. Compare with star Solomonplume (p. 136).

False Solomon's seal stands out from the surrounding vegetation. Found in verdant patches interconnected by spreading rhizomes, the arching stems support smooth, bright-green leaves that appear almost succulent. Allantoin, mucilage and several saponins are the chemical constituents responsible for similar medicinal uses this plant's root and that of star Solomonplume. The roots are used in cough syrups that soothe sore throats and irritated respiratory tracts. A chewed piece of fresh root can achieve similar results. Native Americans used a poultice of the mashed fresh root to treat skin irritations such as bites, stings, burns and sunburn—the allantoin content supports healing, especially when mixed with curlycup gumweed. All parts of the plant are edible, however, the berries are rather bland and can cause diarrhea and the mature vegetation is fibrous and bitter. The young shoots closely resemble toxic species such as false hellebore. Birds, elk, bears and rodents are known to eat the foliage and berries, thus dispersing the seeds far and wide.

Glacier Lily, Avalanche Lily
Erythronium grandiflorum
EDIBLE • WILDLIFE

Life zone/ecosystem: Montane to alpine. Snowbank communities, aspen groves. **Flowering:** May–August. **Fruit:** 3-sided, club-shaped capsules. **Characteristics:** 12 in. (10–40 cm). Deep-seated bulb-like corms form large patches. Golden-yellow flowers hang beneath arching stems; 6 petal-like sepals (tepals) curl backward, revealing a pendent pistil and 6 yellow or red stamens. Two, somewhat lance-shaped, bright green leaves grow from base of plant.

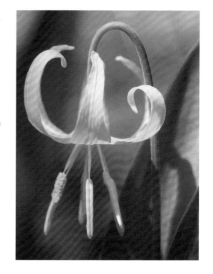

BARBARA MAGNUSON/LARRY KIMBALL

Walking a high mountain trail in search of this captivating beauty is a great way to spend a spring day. Sit quietly and you may be lucky enough to see a hummingbird hover to gather the plentiful nectar, getting dusted with pollen in the process. All parts of glacier lily were used by Native Americans. The corms are edible raw or cooked, as are the leaves and even the seed pods, which taste a bit like green beans. Only use this plant as an emergency food as eating too many corms causes vomiting and removing the corms destroys this lovely plant. Black bears and rodents dig and eat the corms and the seed pods are popular with elk, deer, bighorn sheep and mountain goats.

Alp Lily (*Lloydia serotina*) is another common lily found in alpine meadows.

Mariposa Lily, Sego Lily

Calochortus gunnisonii

EDIBLE · WILDLIFE

Life zone/ecosystem: Montane to subalpine. Meadows, aspen forests, oak-mountain shrubland. **Flowering:** May–June. **Fruit:** 3-sided capsule. **Characteristics:** 6–18 in. (15–45 cm). Bowl-shaped white or pale pink flowers have 3 petals, elaborately decorated with a broad purple band and golden, gland-tipped hairs above an elongated oblong gland at the base. Sepals are pale green and translucent. Leaves narrow and grass-like, making a "U" in cross section instead of the "V" characteristic of death camas. Plants dry up and disappear soon after flowering.

"Mariposa" is the Spanish word for butterfly. Indeed, the delicate cream-colored petals in contrast with lavender stamens and crescents of golden glandular hairs, create the illusion of a butterfly floating gracefully on the breeze. These "hairs" have glands that contain nectar and attract pollinators. *Calochortus* means "beautiful grass" in Greek, an allusion to the very slender stem and leaves. Many species of this genus have become rare or endangered because they were gathered for food by Native Americans and settlers. The bulbous roots are sweet and nutritious and were often dug and cooked like potatoes or ground as flour. Ute people taught Mormon pioneers how to eat the bulbs of *C. nuttallii*, a species of lower valleys, helping the settlers survive Utah's famine of 1848–49. Pocket gophers and other rodents also gather these bulbs and store them to eat during winter.

Star Solomonplume, Wild Lily-of-the-valley

Maianthemum stellatum
[*Smilacina stellata*]

EDIBLE · GARDEN · MEDICINAL · WILDLIFE

Life zone/ecosystem: Montane to subalpine. Moist woods, open meadows, even drier habitats of oak-mountain shrubland. **Flowering:** May–July. **Fruit:** Green with burgundy stripes first, ripening to purple brown. **Characteristics:** Common. 12–24 in. (30–60 cm); unbranched stem. Smaller and more delicate than false Solomon's seal; also narrower hairless leaves with straight edges, berries with stripes instead of speckles and open, few-flowered inflorescence (raceme).

Lovely patches of star Solomonplume in the sun-dappled shade of aspen groves seem so fresh and tidy, as if tended by some forest gnome. The dainty white flowers do indeed create an illusion of stars tossed at random across the patch. Wild lily-of-the-valley is another frequently used common name—European lily-of-the-valley, known from cultivated gardens, is a relative. See false Solomon's seal for uses.

Twisted-stalk

Streptopus amplexifolius [*S. fassettii*]

EDIBLE · GARDEN · WILDLIFE

Life zone/ecosystem: Montane to subalpine. Streamside in shaded forests. **Flowering:** May–August. **Fruit:** Oblong to oval red berry. **Characteristics:** Fairly common. Up to 4 ft. (1 m). Widely branched. Oval to lance-shaped alternate leaves, bright green above and soft gray green beneath; bases nearly surround stem. Bell-shaped, greenish-yellow flowers with curled petal-like sepals attached to stem by distinctly kinked or zigzag stalk; attached at base of leaves, not at stem tips. Jellybean-like, oblong berries are shades of gold when new, maturing to brilliant red-orange. Similar **bellwort** (*Disporum trachycarpum* [*Prosartes trachycarpa*]) has cream-colored flowers at tips of branches and red-orange velvety berries.

Above, Twisted stalk. Right, Bellwort.

Twisted-stalk's flowers hang from beneath the droopy leaves like Mandarin lanterns. Many Native American tribes thought this plant was poisonous, but in *Discovering Wild Plants*, Janice Schofield reports that many others, including the Bristol Bay Eskimos of Alaska, savor the delicious cucumber-like flavor of the spring shoots, both raw and cooked. Young shoots are often marked with pinkish tinges and purple spots similar to poison hemlock, but the growth form is different. Poisonous false hellebore inhabits similar sites, but is plump, pleated and more evenly green. Twisted-stalk's berries have a refreshing watermelon flavor, but can have a laxative effect. Taste, but leave the rest for the birds and mammals that depend on them for food.

Wild Onion, Tapertip Onion
Allium acuminatum
EDIBLE · WILDLIFE

Life zone/ecosystem: Montane. Oak-mountain and sagebrush shrublands. Dry open sites. **Flowering:** May–June. **Fruit:** 3-chambered capsule. **Characteristics:** Fairly common. 4–12 in. (10–30 cm). Erect, umbel-like flower head with 2 papery bracts at base; 7–25 reddish-purple sepals flaring to a slender sharp tip (or acuminate; thus species name). All basal, grass-like leaves; wither by flowering time. Egg-shaped bulb with fibrous outer layer.

Wild onion leaves and bulbs have a mild flavor and odor similar to cultivated onions. Both can be eaten raw or cooked, though they are sweeter when cooked. Native people historically steamed the bulbs in open pits. Wild onions are dug with relish by bears, pocket gophers and other wildlife.

MADDER FAMILY · *Rubiaceae*

Represented in Colorado by only one genus, *Galium*, the madder family is one of the largest flowering plant families in the world, with 6,500 species found mostly in the tropics and subtropics. Their leaves are simple, entire, opposite or whorled and have stipules. Flowers are radially symmetrical, 4-5 lobed with 4-5 stamens that alternate with the petals and have an inferior ovary. The inflorescence is usually a cyme. *Galium*, or the bedstraws, are unmistakable with their square stems and whorls of stalkless propeller-like leaves at each joint. Red madder is a rose-red pigment sometimes used by painters to enhance sunsets on canvas and is derived from the roots of plants in the genus *Rubia*. Northern Indians used stiff bedstraw (*Galium tinctorium*) to dye porcupine quills red for decorating clothing. Other members of this family give us gardenias, coffee, ipecac and the drug quinine.

137

Northern Bedstraw
Galium boreale
EDIBLE • MEDICINAL

Life zone/ecosystem: Montane to subalpine. Open, well-drained, often sunny meadows; aspen groves and oak-mountain shrublands. **Flowering:** June–August. **Fruit:** Pairs of short-haired nutlets. **Characteristics:** Common. Erect herb 8–32 in. (20–80 cm). Opposite, narrowly lanceolate leaves alternate with 2 leaf-like bracts (stipules) to appear as a whorl of 4. Stems square and basically hairless; sometimes rough on edges. Billowy mounds of tiny white flowers formed by forked clusters, with the terminal flower blooming first—an inflorescence called a cyme. Each flower has 4 petals and an inferior ovary. **Cleavers** (*Galium aparine*) is a delicate trailing annual with leaves and bracts appearing as whorl of 6-8. Curved, bristly stem hairs make foliage feel sticky and cling to other plants.

All *Galium* species are sweet both in taste and fragrance, and are used in herbal medicine interchangeably. Historically, people have found many practical and medicinal uses for this plant. "Bedstraw" refers to the use of a more fragrant species as mattress ticking by Europeans and pioneers. *Galium* species can be cooked as a vegetable, however the rough hairs of cleavers could be irritating raw. An acceptable caffeine-free coffee substitute is obtained by grinding roasted mature seeds of *Galium* fruits. Modern herbalists brew fresh plant teas of *Galium* as a tonic to drain swollen glands, as a diuretic and as a wash for skin irritations. There is evidence that cancerous tumors are healed by this herb.[16]

MALLOW or COTTON FAMILY   *Malvaceae*

This eclectic family includes showy hollyhocks—favorites in many local gardens—as well as hibiscus, cotton and okra. The remarkable flowers of the mallow family have a center column of fused filaments with yellow anthers that surround the pistil like a tube, resembling a child's newly-lit sparkler. Each flower has male and female parts, with 5 sepals and 5 petals that swirl together as the flower closes at night. Mallow fruits are capsules, berries, winged seeds or often have one-seeded segments arranged like tiny cheese wheels. The roots of all mallows contain water-soluble fibers called mucilage, which has been used for thousands of years to soothe sore throats, coughs and bronchial inflammations. Marshmallows were originally a confection made from the mucilaginous inner pulp of roots of the European marsh mallow (*Althaea officinalis*), and an abundance of mucilage gives cooked okra pods their characteristic slimy texture.

White Checkermallow

Sidalcea candida

GARDEN

Life zone/ecosystem: Montane to subalpine. Wet meadows, streambanks, and wetlands. **Flowering:** June–September. **Fruit:** Disc-like, resembling cheese wheel. **Characteristics:** Fairly common. 1.5–3 ft. (45–90 cm). White to cream-colored flowers resemble miniature hollyhocks, with spray of red stamens. Lower leaves nearly round with 5–7 lobes and coarse teeth; upper ones exotic-looking and deeply divided into 5–7 narrow lobes; upper surface not hairy. **Purple checkermallow** (*S. neomexicana*) has rose-purple flowers, hairy leaves and stems, lacks rhizomes, and also grows in montane and subalpine wet meadows.

Checkermallow is an indicator of wetland soils, through which it spreads easily by rhizomes. Seeds of this species are easily gathered and can be sown in wet areas. Variations of this handsome native plant are available from nurseries.

*Cheeseweed, Buttonweed

Malva neglecta

EDIBLE • MEDICINAL

Life zone/ecosystem: Montane. Disturbed areas, sunny south-facing slopes. **Flowering:** May–September. **Fruit:** Disc-like, resembling cheese wheel. **Characteristics:** Common, non-native and weedy. Sprawling winter biennial or perennial, up to 20 in. (51 cm). Miniature mallow blossoms resemble tiny white (or lavender) hibiscus with pink stripes; 5 lobed petals form cup-shaped flower. Crinkled leaves nearly round in outline with heart-shaped base and 5–7 shallow lobes. Plant is furry with a slippery, mucilaginous, okra-like quality when mashed.

Though often overlooked due to its weedy nature, cheeseweed is plentiful and quite useful. A tea made from any part of cheeseweed (chop and dry the whole plant for later use) yields a soothing treatment for sore throats, tonsillitis and respiratory and digestive ailments and a balm for skin irritations when applied externally. Fresh leaves can be mashed to create a poultice to reduce pain and inflammation from scrapes and bites. All parts of cheeseweed are edible. The tiny round "cheese-wheel" fruits make an amusing addition to salads. Allow space for these plants in your garden, so the fruits can be harvested all summer—the taste similar to a mild nutty cheese. Cheeseweed fruits can also be used as a substitute for thickening in soups and sauces.

Coppermallow, Scarlet Globemallow
Sphaeralcea coccinea
GARDEN • MEDICINAL

Life zone/ecosystem: Montane. Dry, south-facing slopes.
Flowering: May–August. **Fruit:** Disc-like, resembling cheese
wheel. **Characteristics:** Fairly common. Low-growing, may reach
20 in. (50 cm). Foliage covered with grayish velvety coating of star-
shaped hairs. Orange-red flowers with 5 petals. Leaves highly variable; usually deeply cut into 3–5 segments. Spreads by woody rhizomes, often creating wide patches. Entire plant secretes slimy,
mucilaginous substance.

Dried and powdered, this plant is a protective and
drawing poultice for skin irritations. A tea made from
any plant part serves the same medicinal purposes as
that of cheeseweed. Navajo tribes also used cop-
permallow powder to treat skin diseases, as a tonic to improve appetite
and as a ceremonial medicine. Navajo singers even used this mucilaginous
herb to strengthen their voices, while other Native Americans chewed the
leaves to apply as a healing salve for inflamed wounds and sores. Copper-
mallow is a colorful addition to dry, sunny areas of a native plant garden
and is easily propagated by seed.

Wild Hollyhock, Streambank Hollyhock
Iliamna rivularis
GARDEN • WILDLIFE

Life zone/ecosystem: Montane to subalpine.
Moist slopes and slopes, along streams.
Flowering: June–August. **Fruit:** Disc-like,
resembling cheese-wheel. **Characteristics:**
Uncommon. Shrubby herb, 3–6 ft. (1–2 m).
White to pink flowers in dense raceme; notched
petals not united; 5 sepals united at base; stamens in united column, 5 or more pistils, supe-
rior ovary. Star-shaped hairs (need magnification) cover most of plant. Alternate maple-like
leaves; 5–7 triangular-shaped toothed lobes; heart-shaped base.

Tall stalks of wild hollyhock flowers are a treat to discover on the
trail. Reproduction occurs only by the seeds, which have a very hard coat,
allowing them to remain viable in the soil for centuries. Patches of wild
hollyhock are often found growing in areas disturbed by wildfire, which
helps release the seeds for germination. Both elk and mule deer forage on
the whole plant.

MAPLE FAMILY

Aceraceae

M aples are the only locally occurring trees/shrubs that have opposite, lobed and usually simple leaves. Ovaries of maple flowers mature into dry, winged seeds joined in pairs called "keys." Many currants and gooseberries have maple-like leaves, but are easily distinguished from maples by their other characteristics. Only one species, Rocky Mountain maple, represents this family in the upper Roaring Fork Valley. Another, boxelder (*Acer negundo* or *Negundo aceroides*), is a familiar species at lower elevations.

Rocky Mountain Maple

Acer glabrum
GARDEN • WILDLIFE

Life zone/ecosystem: Montane to lower subalpine. Moist to wet sites along streambanks and mountain slopes. **Flowering:** May–July. **Fruit:** Winged. **Characteristics:** Common. Tree or multi-trunked shrub up to 33 ft. (10 m). Much variation in leaf form, stature and fruit shape has prompted some botanists to divide species into several varieties. May be tall and spindly or dense and bushy, depending on available sunlight. Male and female flowers appear in loose, fragrant clusters on separate plants in spring. Winged fruits, created by fusion of 2 samaras; each containing 1 seed. Opposite leaves are green above and shiny gray beneath, have 3–5 distinct lobes (occasionally 3 leaflets) and sharply-toothed irregular edges. Twigs opposite with thin, reddish-brown bark.

Rocky Mountain maple has been important to mountain wildlife and mountain people for thousands of years. Elk and mule deer browse on the twigs and leaves, especially during long, snowy winters, while seeds, buds and flowers provide food for many birds and small mammals. Blue grouse are partial to the buds, and squirrels and chipmunks will cache the seeds after removing the hulls and wings. Rocky Mountain maple provides excellent cover and bedding sites for elk, mule deer and black bear. It also supplies cover and nesting habitat for many small mammals and perching birds, including dusky flycatcher, MacGillivray's warbler, orange-crowned warbler and Lincoln's sparrow. This maple is sometimes planted to improve wildlife habitat and stabilize slopes and works well as low-maintenance landscaping. Navajo, Thompson and Okanagan-Colville

On a sunny day, use magnification to view mountain maple leaves where eriophyid mites have laid their eggs, creating patches of galls suggestive of tiny sparkling red rubies.

tribes used the flexible stems to create sweathouses, drying racks, snowshoe frames and spears. The fibrous inner bark was used to weave mats and rope.

MARE'S TAIL FAMILY   *Hippuridaceae*

O nly one genus and two species make up this family that occurs in most northern forested regions. It is characterized by heterophyllus leaves—meaning there may be two kinds of leaves on the same plant—occurring in whorls. Both of the species in this family have ground-level, underground horizontal and semi-horizontal stems that root in soft substrates. The aerial stems are erect or slightly curved and glabrous and without any petioles, or flowering stems. Inconspicuous flowers have one pistil and one stamen, but no petals and grow in the leaf axils. The calyx is reduced to an inconspicuous rim around an inferior ovary that produces a single seed.

Mare's Tail
Hippuris vulgaris
EDIBLE

Life zone/ecosystem: Montane to subalpine. Slow streams and ponds. **Flowering:** June-July **Fruit:** Nutlike. **Characteristics:** Grows from stout, spongy rhizomes, 4–20 in. (10–50 cm) above mud or water surface. Erect, sometimes curved, stems clothed in dense whorls of leaves. Emergent leaves stiff; submerged leaves limp. Inconspicuous tiny flowers without pedicels; have 1 large stamen and 1 slender style; occur in leaf axils.

This very strange plant appears, at first glance, to be some type of horsetail (see p. 74) and the genus name actually does mean "horsetail." However, mare's tail is a flowering aquatic plant that grows vigorously in very wet mud or quiet shallow water around the globe. The stiff upper leaves radiate to look like a small conifer, where the submerged leaves are flaccid. Although water quality is a concern, the whole plant can be cooked like spinach. Spreading by rhizomes, mare's tail will create a handsome "tiny forest of conifers" in garden ponds.

MILKWEED FAMILY   *Asclepiadaceae*

U nique and complex flowers, milkweeds deserve close attention with a hand lens. A milky sap is characteristic of this family whose members have flowers with 5 sepals, 5 united reflexed petals and 5 stamens united with 1 style to form a middle column. An example of the complexity in some species is the crown-like structure between the petals and stamens, composed of 5 inflated sacs or scoop-shaped hoods enclosing an arched appendage and 2 superior ovaries. Most of the world's nearly 2,000 species are tropical, and some of them, particularly those of the milkweed and butterfly-flower genera, are grown in North America as ornamentals. Silky hairs that billow from the mature seed pods were once used as low-quality down in the American South, and Navajo tribes used various species as ceremonial emetics and purgatives. Milkweeds are the most important plant to Monarch butterflies, as they give them lifelong protection from many predators. As a caterpillar they feed solely on the milky, acidic sap, incorporating it into their tissues, making them poisonous to some animals.

Showy Milkweed, Wax Flower

Asclepias speciosa
EDIBLE • MEDICINAL • GARDEN

Life zone/ecosystem: Montane. Gravelly roadsides, disturbed areas. **Flowering:** May–August. **Fruit:** Large velvety pod covered in small soft spines. **Characteristics:** Fairly common. Fragrant, stout herbaceous herb, 1–4 ft. (30–120 cm). Simple stems and opposite thick oblong leaves are covered in downy hairs, very prominent veins. Intricate pink flowers resemble pink globes. 5 petals and 5 sepals curve back toward the stem, adorned with 5 pink erect hoods in the center with incurved horns. Drooping pods, about 4 in. (10 cm) long, split along the side to reveal many silky-haired seeds. Milky sap.

Milkweed's complex flowers resemble wax sculptures, definitely deserving closer examination. With magnification, you can see "saddlebags" of pollinia (sticky pollen) connected by black thread-like structures protruding from vertical slits. These sticky "hooks" attach to the legs of visiting insects, which may lose a leg in the process or simply get trapped. In *Edible Native Plants of the Rocky Mountains*, Harrington refers to common milkweed as an edible species. Young spring shoots, flower buds, and even green fruits have been eaten when boiled in two to three changes of water to help remove bitterness and toxicity. Cheyenne and Lakota tribes peeled and cooked the flower buds and used the milky sap for chewing gum. Preparations of milkweed root have been used in expectorants, diuretics and poultices for swellings. Native Americans of Nevada used a tea steeped from milkweed seeds to draw out poison of rattlesnake bites. The silky fruit fibers were used to manufacture prehistoric cordage and cloth.

Mature fruit

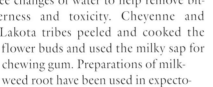

"Saddlebags" of pollina

WARNING! All milkweeds contain some toxicity, though showy milkweed is the least toxic, and can cause nausea and vomiting. Reactions vary with a person's health or age.

MINT FAMILY *Lamiaceae, Labiatae*

This family of fragrant and useful herbs holds a special place in human culture. Mint family herbs and shrubs are noted for their square stems, opposite leaves, usually fresh minty aroma and irregularly shaped flowers of 5 fused petals, 5 fused sepals and 2–4 stamens. The fruits mature from a superior ovary and have 4 nutlets. People sometimes confuse mints with borages, which have alternate leaves and regular flowers; snapdragons, which also have alternate leaves and fancy irregular flowers; or bedstraws, with their square stems.

Essential oils of relaxing lavender are found in powder, pillows and candles for aiding sleep and calming nerves. Chefs would suffer without sage, marjoram, basil, rosemary and thyme—all members of the mint family. Mints grow in most regions of the world, but are concentrated in the Mediterranean basin.

SELF-HEAL (*Prunella vulgaris*) is common in moist, shady montane forests and has been used in folk medicine for skin irritations. Leaves make a tasty tea to treat digestive problems.

*Dead-Nettle

Galeopsis bifida [*G. tetrahit*]
POISONOUS

Life zone/ecosystem: Montane. Shady or disturbed areas. **Flowering:** June–September. **Fruit:** 4 nutlets. **Characteristics:** Non-native, weedy annual. 4–20 in. (10–50 cm). White or pink flowers suffused with purple have 2 yellow spots; strongly 2-lipped; 3-lobed lower lip bears 2 tiny knobs at the base; 4 stamens. Few-flowered clusters in axils of upper leaves. Coarsely-toothed leaves broadly triangular with short stalks. Stems, corollas and calyx have bristles and long, straight, sometimes reflexed hairs. Erect plants; lack a strong odor.

Gale, part of the genus name, is Greek for weasel. People of ancient times imagined this flower to resemble the head of a weasel. According to a Russian scientist, V. L. Komarov, in *Flora of the USSR*, eating this plant can cause paralysis. Dead nettle "volunteers" in many local gardens.

American dragonhead
(*Dracocephalum parviflorum*) is a similar native species of moist or disturbed areas up to 10,000 ft. (3048 m).

Giant Hyssop, Nettleleaf Horsemint
Agastache urticifolia
EDIBLE • GARDEN • MEDICINAL • WILDLIFE

Life zone/ecosystem: Montane to subalpine. Moist meadows and hillsides, particularly in aspen zone. **Flowering:** May–August. **Fruit:** 4 nutlets. **Characteristics:** Common. Robust herb, 15–40 in. (40–100 cm). Dense thimble-shaped spikes of white to pink, 2-lipped trumpet-shaped flowers atop square-shaped stems; 2 obvious protruding pairs of stamens. Triangular leaves are nettle-like, hairless, with glands on lower surface; coarsely toothed edges. Branching woody root crowns and extensive fibrous roots. Occurs in scattered stands.

Although the leaves of other species in this genus have been used for flavoring and are steeped to make an anise-flavored tea, the fragrance of giant hyssop is musty and not particularly appealing. It can be used as an astringent, a diaphoretic and a somewhat sedative tea.[17] Giant hyssop is known as the most important western forage species in the mint family, for both wild and domestic animals. The leaves may resemble those of nettle, but the stinging hairs are missing. The seeds, which usually mature in August, are a favorite of small birds and were eaten by Native Americans both raw and cooked. The plant is easy to propagate by cuttings or root division.

Field Mint, Wild Mint
Mentha arvensis
EDIBLE • GARDEN • MEDICINAL

Life zone/ecosystem: Montane. Irrigation ditches, streambanks and meadows; wet or moist soil. **Flowering:** June–September. **Fruit:** 4 smooth nutlets. **Characteristics:** Fairly common. Strongly aromatic, 4–16 in. (10–40 cm). Pale pink to lavender flowers with 4 protruding stamens clustered where leaf meets stem. Stems square with opposite, finely toothed leaves, hairy veins beneath. Plant may be pubescent to almost smooth.

Field mint is often hidden among the lush vegetation in riparian areas, revealing itself only as the foliage is disturbed, releasing that heady scent—sweet, and just a bit softer than cultivated peppermint (*M. piperita*). This delicious mint has been treasured by cultures worldwide to flavor drinks, soups, vegetables and meat dishes. Cheyenne tribes loved the smell so much, they rubbed their bodies with the chewed leaves as perfume. Thanks to field mint's high content of menthol, the leaf tea is quite effective for settling upset stomach and digestive distress and the mashed leaves work well for soothing mosquito bites. Historically, the Kutenai people used it for treating rheumatism and arthritis and the Flathead people stuffed the leaves around aching teeth. Other tribes used mint tea for fevers, coughs and colds or sprinkled the powdered leaves on meat and berries to repel insects. Field mint is also a delightful plant for native plant gardens.

MORNING-GLORY FAMILY   *Convolvulaceae*

Funnel-shaped flowers and heart- or arrow-shaped leaves usually characterize this family of twining and climbing herbaceous or woody plants. The true sweet potato (*Ipomoea batatas*) is a highly valued family member. Although handsome cultivated morning glories (*Ipomoea purpurea*) create gorgeous cascades on garden fences, the local representative of this family is an unwanted visitor that wreaks havoc in native habitats.

*Field Bindweed

Convolvulus arvensis
NOXIOUS WEED

Life zone/ecosystem: Montane. Disturbed areas. **Flowering:** June–fall frost. **Fruit:** 4-seeded round capsule. **Characteristics:** Common. Aggressive non-native. Prostrate stems 1–3 ft. (30–90 cm) long, or more. Deep, creeping root systems create dense tangled mats. Alternate leaves somewhat arrowhead-shaped. Typical trumpet-shaped morning glory flowers, white to pinkish, with 2 tiny bracts growing about 1 in. below.

Introduced from Europe, field bindweed has become a great problem throughout Colorado and is one of the top ten on the state's Noxious Weed List. It adapts remarkably well to a variety of conditions and is found as high as 10,000 ft. (3048 m). Its long, deep taproots can store a two to three year food supply, making field bindweed very difficult to eradicate, and its seeds may remain viable in the soil for forty to fifty years. Rather than being lulled by its delicate beauty, take action as soon as you see this vine appear. At the present, herbicides appear to be the only effective means of control once a plant takes hold.

MUSTARD FAMILY   *Brassicaceae/Cruciferae*

From broccoli to horseradish, members of this spicy family are integrated into our daily lives as nutrition-packed foods and pungent condiments. About 3,200 species occur around the world, especially in the Mediterranean and southwestern and central Asia. Three major characteristics separate mustards from other plant families: 1) Flowers have 4 separate petals forming the shape of a crucifix (thus the alternate family name, Cruciferae); 2) 6 stamens, 2 shorter than the others; and 3) fruits with a translucent papery partition (replum) dividing the 2 halves of the capsule. Flowers of mustards may appear similar to species of the evening-primrose family, but the latter's ovaries are inferior while mustard's are superior.

Important foods from the mustard family include cauliflower, brussels sprouts, radishes, turnips, leafy greens, kohlrabi, rapeseed or canola oil, watercress and Chinese cabbage. Pungent culinary condiments are prepared as a paste or powder from ground seeds of white mustard (*Brassica hirta*) and black mustard (*B. nigra*). Seeds of all mustards can be dried or used fresh as a substitute for black pepper, stimulating the production of digestive juices in the stomach. They can also be mashed and made into a poultice for chest congestion; however, prolonged application to the skin can cause blisters. Many mustards—including sweet alyssum, wallflower, candytuft, rock cress and draba—have been beloved garden ornamentals for years.

Capsules are called a silique if at least three times as long as wide or a silicle if short, squatty and less than three times as long as they are wide.

Alpine Smelowskia
Smelowskia calycina
GARDEN

Life zone/ecosystem: Alpine. Rocky areas and tundra. **Flowering:** July-August. **Fruit:** Slender silique, pointed on both ends, sparsely hairy. **Characteristics:** Fairly common. Perennial, growing 6-12 in. (15-30 cm) tall. Spreading growth habit. Foliage covered in soft, sometimes branching hairs. Basal leaves pinnatifid to pinnately compound with 5-7 lobes, linear to narrowly egg-shaped, often attached at the narrow end. Stem leaves are reduced in size upward. Small, white flowers—often with pinkish veins—arranged in a raceme. Four pinkish to purplish sepals beneath petals that are 0.12-0.17 in. (3-4 mm) long. Pedicels covered with long, loose hairs.

This unmistakable alpine beauty is reminiscent of mountain candytuft, and is sometimes referred to as "fern-leaf wild candytuft." It also grows in Siberia, China and India, and was first named *Lepidium calcycinum* from

collections made in Siberia. Timotheus Smelowsky (1769–1815) was a botanist and Russian pharmacist from St. Petersberg. Found in similar habitats throughout the Rocky Mountains.

American Wintercress (*Barbarea orthoceras*) is one of many somewhat weedy native yellow mustards. Fairly easily identified by its alternate, fleshy leaves divided into numerous lobes or leaflets resembling a ladder that terminates in a larger, paddle-shaped lobe or leaflet. Leaf bases clasp reddish stems. Spicy leaves are edible in salads, and the dried seeds can be ground for a zesty seasoning.

Bittercress
Cardamine cordifolia
EDIBLE

Life zone/ecosystem: Montane to lower alpine. Streams and seeps, usually growing in water. **Flowering:** June–August. **Fruit:** Long, erect to ascending silique. **Characteristics:** Common. 4–32 in. (10–80 cm). Extensive system of runners. Vivid white clusters of cross-shaped flowers perched atop stems. Alternate, dark green, succulent leaves somewhat heart-shaped to triangular with wavy edges. Flat, slender seed pods, 0.75–1.5 in. (2–3.8 cm) long.

Bittercress's snowy-white flowers provide bright contrast to luxuriant masses of mountain bluebells (*Mertensia ciliata*) among which it often grows along high mountain streams—the color even richer when the plants are bespangled in morning dew. *Cordifolia* refers to the heart-shaped leaves. In *Wild about Wildflowers*, author Katherine Darrow suggests using bittercress leaves as a spicy addition to your trail sandwich, though they are a little bitter.

Mature plant with fruits

*Clasping Peppergrass
Lepidium perfoliatum
EDIBLE • MEDICINAL

Life zone/ecosystem: Montane. Sunny, south-facing slopes and roadsides. **Flowering:** May–July. **Fruit:** Round to oblong silicle. **Characteristics:** Common. Non-native weedy annual. Erect, up to 18 in. (45 cm). Margins of distinctive upper "leaves" completely surround reddish upper stem, which appears to pass through the leaf; lower leaves finely dissected. White to yellow flowers have slender pedicels (stems) and are clustered in racemes. Flowers ripen into typical round to oblong flattened capsules notched at tip; contain 2 reddish-brown, wing-margined seeds.

Clasping peppergrass's unusual upper "leaves" are actually modified petioles (leaf stems). The seeds, like those of many other mustard species, are said to relieve bronchial congestion if made into a paste-like poultice and sandwiched between layers of moistened flannel before being applied to the chest. The seeds can also be used like pepper. Other medicinal and edible uses are similar to those of shepherd's purse (see p. 152), with the younger leaves tasting less bitter.

Field pepperweed
(*Lepidium campestre*
[*Neolepia campestris*]),
a non-native weed.

*Common Watercress
Nasturtium officinale
[*Rorippa nasturtium-aquaticum*]
EDIBLE

Life zone/ecosystem: Montane. Water or mud of slow-moving ditches and creeks. **Flowering:** May–September. **Fruit:** Slender curved siliques. **Characteristics:** Common. Non-native aquatic. Stems up to 24 in. (60 cm) long. Stems floating or trailing, leafy and branched. Cross-shaped white flowers bloom in short racemes, mature to slender curved pods that point up. Leaves divided into 3–9 rounded (sometimes heart-shaped) leaflets with smooth, slightly wavy edges; terminal leaflet is largest.

Watercress stems often root at the nodes, creating bright green jumbled mats in shallow water. The peppery leaves are used fresh in salads, herb butters, sandwiches and marinades. **Beware of polluted water and mine tailings!**

*Dame's Rocket, Dame's Violet
Hesperis matronalis
NOXIOUS WEED

Life zone/ecosystem: Montane to lower subalpine. Riparian and wetlands, edges of trails and roadsides. **Flowering:** May–July. **Fruit:** Erect silique. **Characteristics:** Common. Aggressive non-native biennial or perennial weed, 1.5–4 ft. (45–120 cm). Racemes of large fuchsia flowers without bracts. Pair of glands at base of flower pedicle. Long slender silique somewhat constricts between seeds.

Dame's rocket was imported from Europe and has escaped cultivation to become an aggressive invader, threatening native wildflowers and wildlife habitats in the Roaring Fork Valley. Without the natural controls found in its native habitat, this beautiful plant has become a menace and its sale is now prohibited in Colorado both as nursery stock and as seed. Be sure to check wildflower seed mixes to make sure they don't contain dame's rocket and remove any plants from your garden. Try one of our native penstemons instead—such as Rocky Mountain penstemon (*Penstemon strictus*), which has similar colors and bloom times.

Drummond's Rock Cress
Arabis drummondii [*Boechera drummondii*]

Life zone/ecosystem: Montane to lower alpine. Dry rocky areas of oak/sagebrush, meadows, openings in aspen and spruce-fir forests. **Flowering:** May–July. **Fruit:** Flat, erect siliques. **Characteristics:** Common. Wiry, mostly smooth herb to 3 ft. (1 m). Few small flowers with 4 white to pinkish petals; alpine plants tend to have more purplish flowers. Leaves occur mostly at base and may be smooth or slightly hairy. Stem leaves have fanciful ear-shaped appendages (auricles) where attached to stem. Stiffly erect seed pods with stalks lying close to stem. Pods grow to 4 in. (10 cm), are flat and narrow with veined sides and have broadly winged seeds in 2 rows.

A springtime phenomenon occurs in Drummond's rock cress, an anomaly that has even confused professional botanists. A rust fungus, *Puccinia monoica*, infects the host plants and induces them to develop dense clusters of leaves at their stem tips that resemble flowers, the fungus even developing a fragrance. These pretty yellow "pseudoflowers" are actually rosettes of leaves covered in fungal spores, which are then spread to other flowers by pollinating insects fooled by the clever impersonation. Although other species of *Arabis* are found here, Drummond's is most common, and identification of others depends on technical characters such as amount of hairiness, length of basal leaves and position of the fruit at maturity (see Weber's *Colorado Flora—Western Slope*).

Pseudoflower

Mountain Tansymustard
Descurainia incana var. *incisa* [*D. incisa*]

Life zone/ecosystem: Montane. Open and disturbed areas. **Flowering:** May-August. **Fruit:** Linear glabrous siliques on slender spreading pedicels, acute to acuminate at both ends; remains of styles evident at tip; generally 1 row of seeds. **Characteristics:** Common. Native annual, sometimes branched above, 30 in. (20-5 cm). Tiny yellow to whitish flowers cross-shaped with 4 petals. The floral racemes elongate throughout season as fruits develop. Alternate leaves are pinnate and the pinnae are at least lobed; may be very deeply lobed; often less lobed on upper stem.

During the 1950's uranium boom, botanists recognized that species of *Descurainia* were indicators of uranium and vanadium, which they absorb by growing in soils rich in these minerals.

Western tansymustard (*D. pinnata*) has club-shaped siliques that are equal to or shorter than their stalks, and seeds usually in two rows.

Mountain Candytuft
Noccaea montana [*Thlaspi montanum*]
EDIBLE

Life zone/ecosystem: Montane to alpine. Oak-mountain shrubland, open aspen forests, meadows. **Flowering:** May–July. **Fruit:** Erect, heart-shaped silicle. **Characteristics:** Up to 10 in. (25 cm) Dense racemes of tiny white flowers with 4 spoon-shaped petals. Stem leaves alternate, smooth, heart-shaped and clasp stem. 4-pointed sepals green and white with purplish tinges.

Mountain candytuft is a common, hardy species adaptable to many habitats and one of our earliest spring-blooming plants. Its bright white flower tufts taste sweet like candy—just check for bugs first! Sample only a taste, leaving the rest to make seed for the next season.

*Pennycress, Fanweed
Thlaspi arvense

Life zone/ecosystem: Montane. Disturbed areas, roadsides. **Flowering:** May–August. **Fruit:** Roundish flat silicle. **Characteristics:** Common. Annual non-native, standing 6–18 in. (15–45 cm). Hairless plant similar to shepherd's purse (see p. 152), but with larger stem leaves; no basal leaves. Flowers white and arranged in raceme that elongates with age. Easily distinguished by broad, flat, penny-like fruits; papery and winged, tipped with heart-shaped notches. 2–8 seeds in each chamber of pod.

Pennycress is native to Europe and Asia and has become common throughout the West—to the distress of dairymen and cattlemen. The seeds contain a mustard oil called isothiocyanate that poisons cattle that are fed hay containing 25% or more of this plant. The rank smell you get from crushing pennycress is also responsible for causing dairy animals in some farm areas to produce a bitter-flavored milk.

Rollins' Twinpod, Double Bladderpod

Physaria rollinsii

Life zone/ecosystem: Montane to alpine. Dry, south-facing slopes and ridgelines of oak-mountain shrubland. **Flowering:** April–June. **Fruit:** Paired, inflated silicles with unequal sinuses; top sinus (indention) is deep; lower nearly nonexistent. Partition between two valves of silicle is a narrow upside-down egg-shape. **Characteristics:** Rare, endemic to Colorado. Floppy-stemmed herb 2–4 in. (5–10 cm). Bell-shaped, bright yellow flowers with 4 flaring petals resembling a cross, in tight showy racemes. Silvery foliage, covered in fine hairs, forms rosette at plant's base. Leaves somewhat linear to reverse lance-shaped (attached at the narrow end), less than 1.5 in. (4 cm) long; edges smooth to slightly toothed. Similar **pointtip twinpod** (*P. floribunda*) is common in local montane oak-mountain shrubland, but has divided basal leaves and a linear partition between the valves of the silicle.

Mature fruits

Spring arrives locally with a blast of color on slate-gray Mancos Shale transformed by scattered dollops of sunshine as the showy flowers of these two double bladderpods burst into bloom. Each golden flower matures into puffy twin pods before most flowers in the area have begun to emerge. The genus name comes from the Greek *physa*, meaning "bellows," referring to the swollen halves of the fruit. Rollins' twinpod is classified as "state imperiled" by the Colorado Natural Heritage Program. So far, populations of this species have only been located in six to twenty locations in this state. Given that status, Pitkin County Open Space is funding more research on populations here.

*Shepherd's Purse

Capsella bursa-pastoris

EDIBLE · GARDEN · MEDICINAL

Life zone/ecosystem: Montane. Disturbed areas, gardens, roadsides. **Flowering:** May–August. **Fruit:** Flattened, heart-shaped silicles. **Characteristics:** Non-native. Hearty annual weed, 6–16 in. (15–40 cm). Cross-shaped, inconspicuous white flowers appear to be in rounded clusters when young; transform to elongated racemes in fruit. Dominant leaves form rosette at base; lance-shaped and toothed or pinnately lobed, with largest lobe at tip; stem leaves alternate, clasping the stem; progressively smaller moving up the stem.

Shepherd's purse is named for its distinctive heart-shaped pods, which resemble the leather purses once carried by European shepherds. Harrington, in *Edible Native Plants of the Rocky Mountains*, extols its use as a cooked vegetable served with vinegar and salt, rating the taste better than spinach, without the bitterness often reported. These greens—high in vitamins A, C and K, along with calcium, potassium and sulfur—were introduced to the New World by the Pilgrims and cultivated by early settlers. The seeds can be dried and used as seasoning and have even been ground into a meal by Native Americans. Roots of shepherd's purse have been used as a substitute for ginger. Germany's *Commission E monographs* note the use of leaf tea as a treatment for symptoms of excessive menstruation. Packing the nostrils with mashed or powdered leaves can be a valuable trail remedy for high-elevation nosebleeds. The seeds are easy to gather and grow in your own garden.

Snowbed Draba
Draba crassifolia

Life zone/ecosystem: Subalpine to alpine. Rocky meadows and hillsides, open disturbed areas.
Flowering: June–August. **Fruit:** Glabrous silique.
Characteristics: Fairly common. Annual, biennial or short-lived perennial herb, 1–8 in. (2–20 cm). Slender forked stalks usually leafless; occasionally 1 leaf near base. Topped with tuft of tiny 4-petaled lemon-yellow flowers. Stems without hairs except at base. Basal leaves narrow, entire and ciliate; with few simple or forked hairs on upper surface.

Pixie-like snowbed draba is always a fun discovery along the trail and ideal for viewing under magnification. Look for simple or forked hairs on the leaves' upper surface—intricacies of nature not always visible to the naked eye. *Drabas* are common throughout the Rocky Mountains, with many similar species separated by only minor technical differences. See Weber's *Colorado Flora— Western Slope* or Beidleman and Willard's *Plants of Rocky Mountain National Park* for detailed descriptions.

Alpine tundra draba (*Draba streptobrachia*) is uncommon on rocky alpine areas.

Showy draba (*Draba spectabilis*), commonly found in moist meadows and forests of upper montane and subalpine; 4–16 in. (10–40 cm). Undersides of leaves are covered with sparse cruciform hairs of unequal arm lengths. Lanceolate basal leaves are stalked, while stem leaves are sessile and have small teeth directed outward. Hairless silique may be slightly twisted.

Thickleaf draba (*Draba crassa*) grows only on talus slopes and bouldery areas in the alpine. The lance-shaped leaves are thicker than most drabas.

NETTLE FAMILY   *Urticaceae*

The nettles make up a mid-sized family, with about forty-five genera and 1,000 species from mostly temperate and tropical regions, with only six of these genera native to the United States. Key nettle family characteristics include small green flowers with 4-lobed calyxes, no petals and 4–5 stamens opposite the calyx lobes. Flowers are unisexual, with a superior ovary on the female bloom. They occur in separate staminate or pistillate clusters where the leaves attach to the stem. Most species are herbs, semishrubs or rarely small trees, with fibrous stems, watery juice, and sometimes stinging hairs. Stinging nettle, perhaps the best-known member, may be painfully remembered by some, but has useful traits as well. Nettle stems contain small amounts of silky bast-fiber and were used for many years to make rope, cloth and paper. These fibers were actually considered preferable to cotton for making velvet and were thought to be more durable than linen. Ramie, or Chinese silkplant (*Boehmeria nivea*) from Southeast Asia, also in this family, produces a beautiful and strong fiber traditionally woven into fabric.

Stinging Nettle
Urtica gracilis
EDIBLE • MEDICINAL

Life zone/ecosystem: Montane to subalpine. Along trails, ditches, streams or disturbed areas in moist soil. **Flowering:** May–August. **Fruit:** Lens-shaped achenes. **Characteristics:** Common. Lanky native often reaching 5 ft. (150 cm). Flowers greenish and inconspicuous, either male or female in separate clusters on same plant or on separate plants, dangling between leaf and stem. Opposite leaves very coarsely toothed and lanceolate, with tapering tips on slender pedicels. Both stems and leaves armed with thousands of brittle, hollow, needle-like stinging hairs. Often forms clumps from spreading rhizomes.

If walking through an army of fire ants is unappealing, then learn to identify this plant! Needle-like hairs contain formic acid, the same stinging substance used to such painful effect by fire ants and bees. These hairs are very brittle and break off on contact, causing an immediate burning red rash with tiny blisters that may, depending on your sensitivity, last a few minutes or several days. Once identified, nettle can become a favorite edible. Sought after by backcountry connoisseurs, the tender young plants—often collected in avalanche paths just after the snow melts—are packed with protein, iron, potassium, calcium, manganese and vitamins A, C and D. Nettles are cooked like spinach, brewed as a pleasant-tasting tea, after straining, or made into beer and wine. What about that formic acid? It's neutralized by cooking or drying, although eating very large quantities can cause burning. Young plants are gathered before flowering, as the foliage becomes tough and develops small gritty crystals called cystoliths. Medicinally, clinical studies support nettle's effectiveness in treating prostate and urinary problems.[18] Nettle also contains boron, which may help in treating osteoarthritis and rheumatoid arthritis. Nitinaht Indians of Vancouver Island sometimes beat their arthritic joints with nettles to alleviate the pain.

OAK/BEECH FAMILY *Fagaceae*

V arious species of oak are dominant members in deciduous forests of the northern hemisphere, though their numbers have dwindled due to agricultural clearing, development and logging. Everyone loves an oak—many of us have played with acorns as children. The oak family yields some of the most valuable hardwood in the world. Oak has been used for everything from whisky barrels and furniture to sailing ships of old, while the Mediterranean cork oak (*Quercus suber*) is still cultivated for its useful

bark. And how many of us have sung "Chestnuts roasting on an open fire," or concocted stuffing, stews and desserts from the sweet chestnut (*Castanea sativa*), a family member of southern Europe? Locally, one of the first signs of autumn color is the rich red, orange and gold of scrub oak, painting wide swaths across the south-facing hillsides.

Scrub Oak, Gambel Oak
Quercus gambelii
EDIBLE • GARDEN • MEDICINAL • WILDLIFE

Life zone/ecosystem: Montane. Oak-mountain shrubland. **Flowering:** Early spring. **Fruit:** Acorn. **Characteristics:** Common. Multi-trunked shrub or small tree. Grows up to 25 ft. (7.5 m); averages less than 10 ft. (3 m) locally. Male catkins yellow-green, delicate, pendant, pollen-bearing. Female flowers, separate and inconspicuous, mature into acorns; woody basal "cup" on acorn develops from involucre of female flower. Lustrous green leaves have deep rounded lobes. Buds cluster at twig tips. Sometimes divided into different species based on leaf shape and hairiness.

Scrub oak spreads primarily by underground roots creating large thickets that are often impenetrable. Both foliage and stems provide crucial winter browse for mule deer and elk. Recent warming trends often cause leaves and flowers to emerge early, making them vulnerable to late spring frosts. This results in a lack of acorns in the fall when they are so important to black bears, which depend on them to put on enough fat for hibernation. When there is a lack of acorns, and berries for the same reason, there are going to be problems with bears in town, as they search for food they cannot find in the wild. Native Americans depended on acorns as a main source of nourishment, boiling them in several changes of water to remove some of the bitterness. Bark "tea," or water from boiling the nuts, has a high tannin content and is used as an astringent skin wash for skin irritations such as insect bites or stings and as a gargle for sore throats and gum problems. A powder from the dried inner bark is effective to stop bleeding.

OLEASTER FAMILY *Elaeagnaceae*

M ost shrubs and trees in the oleaster family have a unique satiny appearance, which comes from tiny scales on their stems, leaves and berries. These scales look like little umbrellas or shields under magnification. Called peltate trichomes, these structures prevent water loss in drier environments. Russian olive (*Elaeagnus angustifolia*), introduced from Europe, is a hardy, fast-growing tree that was often recommended for windrow and ornamental plantings at lower elevations in the Roaring Fork Valley. The yellow flowers emit a heavy, sweet fragrance that fills the air in springtime, then mature into berries that resemble tan olives by autumn. Although an appealing ornamental tree, Russian olive is now on the noxious weed list in Colorado, as it spreads aggressively and displaces native species, especially along river corridors.

Buffaloberry, Soapberry

Shepherdia canadensis

EDIBLE · WILDLIFE

Life zone/ecosystem: Montane to subalpine. Shaded, north- to northwest-facing rocky slopes in lodgepole pine, Douglas-fir and aspen forests. **Flowering:** Before leaves appear in spring. **Fruit:** Single-seeded berry. **Characteristics:** Native nitrogen-fixing, deciduous shrub up to 6.5 ft. (2 m). Male and female flowers are usually found on different shrubs; greenish with calyx of 4 fused sepals and no petals. Opposite, leathery leaves dark green above and lighter below, dotted with russet star-shaped scales. Egg-shaped berries yellowish-red to bright red when ripe. **Silver buffaloberry** (*S. argentea*), covered with silvery scales, grows up to 12 ft. (3.7 m); found along rivers up to 7,480 ft. (2280 m); silvered berries. Both are nitrogen-fixing shrubs.

Use magnification to see the interesting rust-colored scales covering this handsome shrub. Chinook tribes of the northwest call it "soopolallie" (soapberry)—chew on a berry and discover why. The initial sweetness rapidly gives way to an unpleasant soap-like bitterness, caused by an oily compound called saponin. Saponins could be toxic in large amounts, but are not readily digested by humans, passing through the body without harm. Despite the taste, Flathead tribes of Montana whipped the berries with water, sweetening them with other plants, to create a foamy dessert concoction like thick cream—said to taste like turpentine! There is a high percentage of carotenoids in buffaloberry, nearly 1% dry weight, providing wildlife with a good source of vitamin A. Snowshoe hares and mule deer will browse the foliage, while bears and blue grouse gorge on the berries in autumn.

ORCHID FAMILY   *Orchidaceae*

One of every seven flowering plant species on earth is an orchid, and the largest society in the United States devoted to a single plant family is the American Orchid Society, with 29,000 members. Elaborate flowers of usually 3 sepals and 3 petals distinguish this family. What appears to be the lower petal is really the upper, because of a 180 degree twist that occurs during development. This "lower" petal is referred to as the labellum, and may be contorted into many shapes and sizes, covered with bizarre combinations of plates, hairs, calluses or keels and have markedly distinct and vivid coloration patterns. Both style and stigma are united into a complex structure, the column, attached to the top of the ovary. Orchid fruits are capsules containing many minute seeds. Vanilla, a celebrated flavoring, comes from the dried seed pod of a vine-like tropical orchid, *Vanilla planifolia.*

Although second in size only to the sunflower family, the orchids, with some 20,000 species, exhibit less structural diversity in the flowers and leaves than many smaller families. What is remarkable about orchids is the tremendous variation in color and shape within the flower form, each an evolutionary strategy to lure pollinators. What tricksters! For example, the flower of one species actually mimics the appearance of the mate of the insect it wishes to attract as a pollinator. Insects and bats are attracted to the specific spot on the flower where the tiny pollinia or pollen packets can attach to their bodies. Pollinia may have waxy, horny or mealy surfaces, which attach to the pollinator's body by mechanisms such as quick-set glue on the pollinial stalk or an explosive apparatus that can project the pollinia up to 2 feet (60 cm) away. Orchids also require a symbiotic relationship with a specialized fungus in order for some of the thousands of miniscule seeds produced by a single plant to germinate. The fungus benefits by receiving moisture and nutrients as it is incorporated in root structures and other tissues as the plant develops.

While new orchid hybrids are entering cultivation at the rate of about 150 per month, many beautiful native species are in danger of extinction due to destruction of their natural habitats. Wild orchids are very specific to certain habitats, pollinators and soil conditions—making them especially vulnerable to disturbance. Not common in Colorado, they need our protection.

Calypso Orchid, Fairyslipper
Calypso bulbosa

Life zone/ecosystem: Montane to subalpine. Moist, slightly acidic to neutral soil, decaying needles or wood; filtered light of conifer forests; tolerates drier soils than other orchids. **Flowering:** May–early August. **Fruit:** 3-chambered capsule; 10,000-20,000 seeds. **Characteristics:** Uncommon. 8 in. (20 cm); arises from bulbous corm. Single pendant flower with inflated lower lip (labellum) resembles pointed slipper. Curvy, dark purple lines mark "slipper's" sole; tuft of golden hairs and maroon spots decorate its whitish top (apron). 2 petals and 3 sepals above labellum are rose-pink and lance-shaped. United style and stamen (column) is petal-like, overhanging opening of "slipper." Single stem has solitary oval leaf; withers after flowering; replaced in fall by another leaf, which survives under the snow until spring.

Only a bit of imagination is needed to envision a forest fairy slipping her foot gracefully into this dainty and elaborate orchid. Sweet scent and showy flowers, promising pollen and nectar within, are really deceptive advertising for unwary young bumblebees. While searching inside for nectar, sticky pollinia is glued to their backs from the upper petals, then carried off to the next orchid and deposited on its sticky stigma. Why do bees keep visiting these orchids when there is no nectar reward? Studies show that varied patterns of spots on each orchid's lip may make the bee believe it is visiting a different type of flower, one that possibly has nectar—so they continue to be fooled. In Homer's *Odyssey*, Calypso was the mysterious sea nymph who waylaid Odysseus during his journey home. Although common in some areas, this circumboreal orchid is in decline throughout North America, Europe and Asia. Picking or transplanting would destroy the root.

Green Bog Orchid
Platanthera huronensis
[*Habenaria, Limnorchis* or *Platanthera hyperborea*]

Life zone/ecosystem: Montane to subalpine. Moist to wet soil, especially streambanks. **Flowering:** June–early August. **Fruit:** Erect capsules. **Characteristics:** Common. Reaches about 1 ft. (30 cm). Leafy stems arrayed with dense spike-like racemes of tiny greenish-white flowers, each with small leafy bract at base; tubular nectar spur, almost equal in length to unlobed lip (labellum), projects behind flower. Pollinia remains visibly intact; carried off by insect pollinators.

Wet sites with patches of false hellebore are good places to search for these delicate, moisture-loving orchids. Tread carefully to protect the lush adjacent foliage that often hides them. In *Wild About Wildflowers*,

Katherine Darrow says the "sweet lusty fragrance" of bog orchids serves as an irresistible lure for pollinating bumblebees and moths. Three other, less common bog orchids, may be encountered in local montane and subalpine zones. Hard to tell apart, they may hybridize to produce offspring with a mix of characters.[19] The following detail may help:

Northern Green Bog Orchid
Platanthera aquilonis

Montane to subalpine. Uncommon. Lacks sweet fragrance of green bog orchid. Self-pollinating—the pollinia are not carried off intact, but visibly dribble their pollen onto their own flower's receptive stigma. Also greenish-white.

White Bog Orchid
Platanthera dilatata [*Limnorchis dilatata*]

Montane to subalpine. Fairly common. Pure white flowers, with spur only half as long as lip; more strongly inflated base than green bog orchid.

Short-Spurred Bog Orchid
Platanthera purpurascens
[*Habenaria saccata* or *Limnorchis stricta*]

Montane to subalpine. Uncommon. Contrasting, 2-toned greenish flowers with very short, bulbous spur only a third as long as lip.

White bog orchid

Striped Coralroot Orchid
Corallorhiza striata
MEDICINAL

Life zone/ecosystem: Montane to lower subalpine. Lodgepole, Douglas-fir or spruce-fir forests; fairly dry soil. **Flowering:** Late May–mid July. **Fruit:** Pendulous oblong, pointed capsule. **Characteristics:** Uncommon. Saprophytic herb 8–20 in. (20–50 cm). Translucent reddish-, yellowish- or purplish-brown stems bear tiny pink or yellowish flowers striped with purple to burgundy. Occasional albinos entirely yellow. Leaves reduced to sheathing scales. **Spotted coralroot orchid** (*C. maculata*) [see inset photo] has a whitish, pouty, 3-lobed lip bearing purplish spots.

True to their name, the tangled underground rhizomes of this orchid resemble a mass of coral. Like many orchids, this one is saprophytic, meaning it lacks chlorophyll and absorbs nutrients from rotting plant material through a symbiotic relationship with a fungus that is intricately entwined with the roots. A single anther bears four pollinia joined by an elastic thread with a sticky base that attaches easily to visiting pollinating insects. Their stems are very fragile, so step carefully when walking off the beaten path.

Western Rattlesnake Plantain
Goodyera oblongifolia
MEDICINAL

Life zone/ecosystem: Montane to subalpine. Dry to moist soil of lodge-pole, Douglas-fir and spruce-fir forests. **Flowering:** July–early September. **Fruit:** Erect capsules. **Characteristics:** Fairly common. Evergreen herb 4–16 in. (10–40 cm). Dark green leaves in basal rosette, each bearing obvi-ous white middle vein, sometimes with distinct white mottling. Tiny white flowers grow in loose spiral; flowers resemble miniature duck's head. Both flowers and rigidly erect stems covered in hairs tipped by miniscule glands. Short creeping rhizomes sprout, producing large colonies. **Dwarf rattlesnake plantain** (*G. repens*), rare in Colorado, is pos-sible up to 9,500 ft. (2896 m) in similar locations. Lacks prominent white leaf midvein; more bag-shaped floral lip.

Why such an intimidating name for this diminutive orchid? Early settlers believed the white-and-green mot-tled leaves resembled a rattlesnake's skin and could be used to treat snake bites. Although it is best to leave orchids undisturbed, these leaves have been brewed into a comforting tea for sore throats and coughs and applied to skin irritations. Pollination of western rattlesnake plantain has not been carefully studied, but dwarf rattlesnake plan-tain exhibits an interesting mechanism for thwarting self-pollination. In the beginning, the fragrant flower opens only wide enough to allow the long-tongue bee pollinators to reach the pollinia. Once the pollinia are removed, the flower opens further, allowing insects to reach the stigma that has now become receptive to pollinia from another flower.

PARSLEY or CARROT FAMILY *Apiaceae*

Can you imagine a world without carrots, parsley, parsnips, celery, cilantro, cumin, caraway, dill, fennel or anise? Our palates would indeed be impoverished. Correct species identification is critical, as this family includes some lethal plants that are often very similar to non-toxic ones (see poison hemlock and water hemlock). The Latin family name is sometimes referred to as Umbelliferae, so the plants are often called umbellifers or umbels, alluding to the shape of their inforescence. Local parsleys are perennial, often aromatic herbs with distinct attributes that set them apart from other families:

- umbrella-shaped flower clusters, called umbels, composed of tiny flowers with 5 petals and 5 alternating stamens.

- inferior ovary; calyx united with the ovary wall, generally so reduced it resembles tiny spikes on the ovary's apex.

- involucre circling the base of the umbels.

- mostly alternate leaves without stipules, frequently divided into many lacey leaflets- alternate leaf stalks may appear basal.

- leaf stalks with wide sheathing bases that surround the stem and stem piths that wither with age, resulting in hollow stem sections.

- fruits (called schizocarps) split into two, one-seeded nutlets when mature.

Botanists refer to parsleys as "promiscuous" because they are routinely pollinated by a wide range of insects—mostly flies, mosquitoes, gnats and some unspecialized bees, butterflies and moths. However, self-fertilization is the norm. Oddly, species of this complex family rarely hybridize.

About 3,000 species of parsleys (also called umbellifers, or umbels) are deeply entwined in our history, agriculture and medicine. Many members are used as treatments for gastrointestinal and cardiovascular ailments and as stimulants, sedatives, antispasmodics and more.

Alpine Parsley, Matted Spring Parsley
Cymopterus alpinus [*Oreoxis alpina*]

Life zone/ecosystem: Subalpine to alpine. Rocky areas of sub-alpine meadows and tundra turfs. **Flowering:** June–July. **Fruit:** 0.1–0.2 in. (3–6 mm) long, with corky-thickened wing-type ribs. **Characteristics:** Common. Nearly prostrate, mat-forming herb, 1–4 in. (2.5–10 cm). Minute yellow flowers crowded together into compact, flat-topped umbels, barely above finely dissected lacey leaves originating at base. Untoothed bracts below umbel are mostly united. **Baker's alpine parsley** (*C. bakeri*), a similar species, has purplish bracts below umbel that are toothed at the apex.

In *Land above the Trees,* Ann Zwinger and Dr. Beatrice Willard describe how the flat, umbrella-like heads of alpine parsley are fly favorites, and that each flower's two widespread stamens bend upward and inward with the insect's weight, powdering the underside of the fly with pollen. During warm summer days, an amazing number of flies busily patrol these alpine plants, giving them a polka-dotted appearance.

Fruit

Cow Parsnip

Heracleum spondylium var. *lanatum*
[*H. spondylium* subsp. *montanum*]

EDIBLE • MEDICINAL • WILDLIFE

Life zone/ecosystem: Montane to subalpine. Wet meadows and streamsides in aspen and spruce-fir forests. **Flowering:** May–August. **Fruit:** Papery ovals. **Characteristics:** Common. Robust herb reaching up to 6 ft. (2 m). Large compound umbels of tiny white flowers. Hollow, hairy stems and broad, hairy leaves divided into 3 coarsely toothed lobes. Fruits broader above the middle, marked with 4 dark stripes reaching halfway down, alternating with 3 delicate ribs; 2 one-seeded halves.

The broad, maple-like leaves and Herculean stature of this hearty plant add an almost tropical ambience to aspen forests and wet meadows. Late in the season, these giant umbels produce clusters of flat, tan seeds, used by herbalists as a tincture to settle gastrointestinal problems. A tea or tincture of dry or wilted roots is still used in poultices to stimulate nerve growth and to aid nerve function in cases of paralysis. Both chewed green seeds or tincture are considered good analgesics when applied to a sore tooth. Cow parsnip roots, peeled shoots and young leaves are edible when cooked and were eaten by Native Americans. Bears and elk find this plant a succulent source of nutrition; people of Kodiak, Alaska call it *pushki*, meaning a plant used by bears for early summer food and for play.

> **WARNING!**
>
> **Furanocoumarins are present in the sap and hairs of cow parsnip, causing skin irritation in some people, especially with sun exposure.**

Cowbane's pinnate leaves contrast with scalloped leaves of brook saxifrage.

Cowbane

Oxypolis fendleri

Lifezone/ecosystem: Montane to subalpine. Streamside in aspen and spruce-fir forests. **Flowering:** Late May–mid July. **Fruit:** Narrow oval with broad wings. **Characteristics:** Common. Slender, smooth herb, 20–40 in. (50–100 cm). Minute flowers of upright, bractless compound umbels, mostly white, sometimes tinged purple. Largest leaves once-pinnate (primarily at the base); stem leaves so reduced the single stem seems nearly naked.

These delicate plants can disappear, swallowed by lush surrounding foliage. They occasionally grow right in the water with mountain bluebells and bittercress. Cowbane resembles small and very fragile angelica.

Giant Angelica
Angelica ampla
EDIBLE MEDICINAL

Life zone/ecosystem: Montane to subalpine. Moist soil along streams, seeps, aspen forests and mixed-conifer forests. **Flowering:** July–August. **Fruit:** Flat and disc-like fruit, with narrow, winged ribs. **Characteristics:** Common. Towering herb, up to 6 ft. (2 m). Tiny white flowers form gumball-sized umbels, which together form an even larger globe with long pedicels all uniting at one point; inconspicuous bracts at base of umbels. Flowers fade to greenish-brown—in contrast to hollow, pink or purple with green or rhubarb-red stems. Large leaves divide twice into toothed leaflets, with veins reaching from main vein to tip of teeth. **Caution: don't confuse with water hemlock (see p. 167), whose veins terminate in angles between teeth on each leaf.** Another local, **pinnateleaf angelica** (*A. pinnata*) grows in moist montane zones, often along streams; smaller and more delicate, to 3 ft. (90 cm); white to pinkish petals; lacks bract under smallest umbel; pinnate leaves.

Please do not dig wild angelica roots for any purpose; cultivated roots are available commercially.

Regal and unmistakable, this giant parsley dominates many local streambanks. *Angelica* comes from the Latin for "angelic," referring to its long use as medicine and flavoring. Chinese angelica (*A. sinensis*), known as *dong quai,* has been venerated in Chinese medicine for regulating menstruation since before the time of Christ and angelica (*A. archangelica*) was used to treat bubonic plague during the Middle Ages. For centuries, seeds and roots of many angelica species have been boiled as decoctions, steeped for teas, soaked in alcohol for tinctures and ground into powder to treat minor respiratory ailments, menstrual cramps, nausea, heartburn and indigestion; recent research has revealed at least fourteen anti-arrhythmic compounds in angelica that may benefit the heart.[20] Even horses distressed by windy colic have been given ground angelica root. Cordials, such as Benedictine and Chartreuse, and gin owe their distinct flavor in part to angelica.

Gray angelica (*Angelica grayi*) grows in rocky subalpine and alpine areas. Much smaller than giant angelica, it has more noticeable bracts at the base of each umbel; petals purplish-brown or white.

Hemlock Parsley
Conioselinum scopulorum

Life zone/ecosystem: Montane to subalpine. Moist areas, aspen and spruce-fir forests. **Flowering:** July–early August. **Fruit:** Flattened oval. **Characteristics:** Uncommon. Unbranched, less than 3 ft. (1 m); 1–2 parsley-like stem leaves. Umbel of white flowers.

Common throughout the Rocky Mountain states, hemlock parsley is often hidden among sedges, rushes and grasses until it blooms. It is similar in appearance to osha, but is much smaller and less leafy, and its parsley-like leaves have a prominent middle vein on the ultimate leaf lobe. If in doubt, check the crown of the root, which lacks the unique "hairiness" of the osha plant.

Giant Lomatium, Fernleaf Biscuitroot
Lomatium dissectum
MEDICINAL

Please do not dig wild roots. Cultivated roots are available in health food stores.

Life zone/ecosystem: Montane. Oak-mountain shrubland, sagebrush; thrives in dry soil and clay. **Flowering:** May–June. **Fruit:** Oblong, flattened with stipes and narrow corky wings. **Characteristics:** Common. Stout, parsley-like herb, 12–36 in. (30–90 cm). Larger than other *Lomatiums*. Flowers usually yellow, sometimes purplish, in double umbel; flower stem usually taller than foliage. Stem hollow, purplish at base. Lacy leaves mostly basal and ternate, each leaflet divided again and lobed; ultimate leaf lobe has single midvein, compared to osha's pinnate veins. Plants wither once fruits mature.

Milfoil lomatium (*Lomatium grayi*) shares the same habitats as giant lomatium, but is shorter and has leaves very fine, thread-like divisions.

Giant lomatium is the earliest-blooming yellow parsley in this area. Native Americans had many uses for its pearly-gray, aromatic root, which exudes a milky sap in the spring. Eastern Shoshone tribes and northern Arapaho people of Wyoming's Wind River Reservation used a tea from boiled root to treat influenza and colds—they drank it, bathed with it and inhaled the steam. Herbalists today combine it with other herbs, such as grindelia, balsam root and echinacea, to treat viral respiratory infections, flu, pneumonia and tonsillitis. Lab tests have also shown preparations of the root to be effective against bacteria and fungi.

Mountain Parsley
Cymopterus lemmonii
[Pseudocymopterus montanus]
EDIBLE

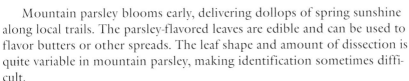

Life zone/ecosystem: Montane to lower alpine. Aspen and mixed-conifer forests, meadows, tundra turfs. **Flowering:** May–June. **Fruit:** Fruits have well-developed lateral wings. **Characteristics:** Common. 6–32 in. (15–80 cm). Tiny yellow flowers clustered in flat-topped umbel terminating the slender stem. Leaves deeply cut, parsley-like, growing from base of flower stem. Leaflets angled at both ends. Leaf-like bractlets usually protrude from secondary umbels.

Mountain parsley blooms early, delivering dollops of spring sunshine along local trails. The parsley-flavored leaves are edible and can be used to flavor butters or other spreads. The leaf shape and amount of dissection is quite variable in mountain parsley, making identification sometimes difficult.

Osha, Porter's Lovage, Bear Root
Ligusticum porteri
ENDANGERED · MEDICINAL ·WILDLIFE

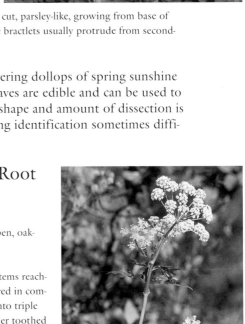

Life zone/ecosystem: Montane to subalpine. Aspen, oak-mountain shrubland, moist meadows. **Flowering:** June–August. **Fruit:** Double with ribbed wings. **Characteristics:** Common. Hardy, with hollow stems reaching 3 ft. (1 m) or more. Small white flowers clustered in compound umbels. Leaves large, parsley-like, divided into triple lobes, again dissected into smaller toothed or cleft segments. Leaves basal, with 1 or more well-developed stem leaves.

"Hairy," or fibrous, root crown ("hairs" being veins, or vascular strands, of previous years' leaves) and the root's unforgettable odor (like intensely spicy celery) are key identifying traits. Similar poisonous species, water hemlock and poison hemlock, lack these traits. **Fern-leaf lovage** (*L. tenuifolium* [*L. filicinium* var. *tenuifolium*]), is a similar native plant of moist subalpine areas; smaller in height, nearly all basal leaves, narrower leaf segments and only occasionally a reduced stem leaf.

Fern-leaf lovage

Osha means "bear" to some southwestern Navajo tribes, who have always revered the plant and believed it to be a gift of the great spirit bear. They have many medicinal uses for the root of osha, as fungicide, insecticide and as a remedy for headaches and

> No one has found a way to cultivate osha, and commercial exploitation is decimating wild populations, prompting United Plant Savers to place the species on its "At Risk" list.

indigestion. Modern herbalists consider the root an antiviral and antibacterial agent for upper respiratory infections and an expectorant and digestive stimulant. While working on his dissertation for Harvard, ethnobotanist Shawn Sigstedt gave osha root to bears at the Cheyenne Zoo in Colorado Springs. They chewed them up and smeared their bodies with the resulting mash, exactly as Navajo legends say the bears had taught humans to do and as brown and Kodiak bears are known to do. Researchers speculate that the fragrant coumarins in osha may repel insects for the bears.[21] Human cultures have often learned which plants to study for medicine by watching animals.[22]

*Poison Hemlock

Conium maculatum

POISONOUS

Life zone/ecosystem: Montane. Roadsides, ditches, disturbed areas. **Flowering:** Late May–July. **Fruit:** Round, flattened laterally. **Characteristics:** Common. Non-native. Tall, stout biennial up to 9 ft. (3 m). Coarse, hollow stems, freely branched and conspicuously covered with purple spots at all growth stages. Dark, shiny green leaves, finely dissected and fern-like. First-year growth a rosette; numerous umbrella-shaped clusters of tiny white flowers appear second season.

Imported from Europe, this is an extremely poisonous and aggressive plant that should be eliminated as soon as it is identified. Legend has it that rivals poisoned the philosopher Socrates with a brew from poison hemlock. All parts of the plant are deadly. **Be careful not to use the hollow stem as flutes or peashooters and take great care not to mistake these leaves for parsley or similar medicinal herbs.** Poison hemlock's tall, gangly shape, fern-like leaves, conspicuous purple spots and absence of the spicy celery odor help to distinguish it from friendlier parsleys.

Rocky Mountain Spring Parsley

Cymopterus planosus

GARDEN

Life zone/ecosystem: Montane. Sagebrush, oak-mountain shrubland. **Flowering:** May–June. **Fruit:** 2 halves with wings. **Characteristics:** Common. Ground-hugging herb. Umbels of tiny burgundy or yellow flowers. Bluish-green leaves spread out near or at ground level from long, slender, deeply buried pseudoscape. Similar species have more upright leaves and only a short pseudoscape not deeply buried.

Rich burgundy flowers and lacy bluish-green leaves distinguish this ubiquitous early-blooming parsley from others. The Ute people, who once hunted this valley during the summer season, still use the roots of a close relative, widewing spring parsley (*C. purpurascens*), as food at lower elevations. Spring parsley literally carpets sunny shale slopes in the montane zone. It could provide a good ground cover for local gardens plagued with shale soil. The seeds can be germinated, but not easily.

Water Hemlock

Cicuta maculata var. *angustifolia*

[*C. douglasii*]

POISONOUS

Life zone/ecosystem: Montane and subalpine. Standing water, wet soil of roadside ditches and slow-moving streams. **Flowering:** June–late July. **Fruit:** Flat, somewhat round with obvious ribs; side ribs largest; halves separate at maturity. **Characteristics:** Fairly common. Extremely poisonous, coarse herb 1.5–6 ft. (0.5–2 m). Hollow stems rise from a thickened, internally chambered base. Leaves similar to angelica's. Leaflets lance-shaped and sharply toothed, arranged opposite each other on midrib. Very important distinguishing characteristic: secondary veins appear to end in notches between the teeth on leaf margins. A small fork sometimes extends into tooth. Oily yellow sap has unpleasant odor.

Water hemlock retains the dubious honor of being the most poisonous plant in North America. A piece of its root the size of a marble can kill an adult in fifteen minutes, and children have been poisoned when attempting to use the hollow stems as peashooters. Needless to say, livestock, especially cattle and sheep, die each year by grazing on it. In *Edible and Medicinal Plants of the West*, Gregory L. Tilford recommends learning the following ditty: "Leaf vein to the tip, all is hip. Leaf vein to the cut, pain in the gut."

Western Sweetroot, Western Sweet Cicely
Osmorhiza occidentalis
EDIBLE • MEDICINAL

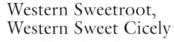

Mature fruits

Life zone/ecosystem: Montane to sub-alpine. Aspen forests, oak-mountain shrub-land. **Flowering:** June–late July. **Fruit:** Dark, narrow and smooth; few bristly hairs possible at base, no "tail." **Characteristics:** Common. Tall, leafy herb, 12–30 in. (30–75 cm). Leaves finely toothed and divided into several pairs of 3; arranged opposite each other along midrib. More simple leaves than most local parsleys. Inconspicuous pale yellow flowers grouped in loose umbels. Licorice smell distinguishes species from poisonous ones, such as water hemlock.

Both roots and leaves of sweetroot have a wonderful licorice fragrance and the young leaves are a true taste sensation. The leaves and fleshy green seeds can be dried and powdered to use as a flavoring in soups, teas, cookies, sauces, beer or wine. In *Medicinal Plants of the Pacific West*, Michael Moore recommends a tea of sarsaparilla, licorice and sweetroot for blood-sugar imbalances and as a laxative. Sweetroot also has anti-fungal properties and has been used as a douche and enema for fungal infections of the digestive tract and reproductive system.

Blunt-fruited sweet cicely (*Osmorhiza depauperata*) is similar to western sweetroot but is more fragile, has a milder licorice fragrance and has tiny sprays of white flowers that mature into club-shaped, bristly fruits with a definite narrow tail. Resembles a young, poisonous baneberry (see p. 99).

PEA FAMILY   *Fabaceae (Leguminosae)*

Distinct flowers, called "pea flowers" in this text, identify this family. Botanists describe pea flowers as being irregular, or bilaterally symmetrical, meaning that the opposite sides mirror each other. The broad upper petal is called the banner, the two lateral petals the wings and the two bottom petals joined and shaped like the prow of a ship are called the keel. The fruits are similar to garden pea pods.

This rather enormous family of some 13,000 species contains the legumes—vital food plants such as peas, beans, peanuts, lentils and soybeans—as well as species such as alfalfa and clover, which are grown as forage for domestic livestock. Many other species are cultivated as ornamentals, such as sweet peas (*Lathyrus odoratus*), treasured locally for their wonderful scent and intense colors. Exotic hardwoods and gum arabic are harvested from tropical tree species in this family, while astragalus and red clover have long been valued for their use in both Chinese and Western herbal medicine. Members of the pea family are often planted in revegetation projects for their nitrogen-fixing capabilities.

banner

wings

Pea flower   keel

NITROGEN FIXATION in plants is a phenomenon vital to the plant world. Special bacteria form a symbiotic relationship with some plants, invading the roots and multiplying within the cortex cells to form small nodules. The plant supplies nutrients and energy for the process, while the bacteria extracts nitrogen from the atmosphere to convert it into soil nitrates that are then available to these and other plants. As nitrogen is one of the three essential elements that plants need for growth, these plants are useful in agriculture, where species like alfalfa are rotated with other crops to replenish nitrogen in the soil.

*Alfalfa

Medicago sativa

EDIBLE · MEDICINAL · WILDLIFE

Life zone/ecosystem: Montane. Disturbed ground. **Flowering:** June–August. **Fruit:** Round spiral pod. **Characteristics:** Common. Non-native and persistent. Densely clumped, branched herb up to 40 in. (1 m). Appearance similar to a tall clover with 3-parted leaves, usually toothed on the apex portion. Flowers range from purple to white. Resembles yellow sweetclover until flowering.

Alfalfa, one of the oldest cultivated forage crops in the world, is thought to have originated in ancient Persia.[23] Livestock often thrives on dried alfalfa during winter or when grazing is unavailable, and it is added to oat and other types of hay to balance nutritional value. Alfalfa is known to have high nutritional value, containing fiber, protein, fats, minerals (calcium, phosphorus, iron), organic acids, vitamins K1 and C and various pigments including chlorophyll. However, some authorities feel that none of these are in high enough concentrations to be of great therapeutic value for humans. A tea is traditionally brewed from alfalfa leaves and flowers, mixed with lemon grass or mint for flavor, to treat ulcers, arthritis, colitis, anemia and liver damage. Some herbalists say that eating alfalfa improves digestion; however, research indicates that an amino acid, L-canavanine, in alfalfa seeds and sprouts may play a role in triggering lupus, or lupus-like syndromes, in sensitive people.[24]

Alpine Clover, Whiproot Clover
Trifolium dasyphyllum

Life zone/ecosystem: Subalpine to alpine. Spruce-fir; open rocky slopes and hillsides. **Flowering:** June–August. **Fruit:** Pod with 1–3 seeds. **Characteristics:** Common. Less than 4 in. (10 cm); tufted herb with tendency to form mats. Usually bicolored flower heads of 5–30 flowers; no circle of bracts at base. Banner pale, wings and keel pink- or purple-tipped. Leaves with 3 untoothed, lance-shaped leaflets that are less than 2 in. (5 cm) wide and somewhat hairy. Stems erect; no rooting at nodes.

Above, Alpine clover. Right, Dwarf clover.

Alpine clover is often confused with two other clovers growing in similar habitat. Dwarf, or deer, clover (*T. nanum*) has only 1–3 rather large flowers per cluster, is rose-colored and not hairy. It grows as a pioneer plant on alpine summits in Colorado, forming low, dense cushions. Parry's clover (*T. parryi*) prefers moist, sometimes gravelly, soil in the subalpine and alpine and has round, fragrant, pink to magenta flower heads on tall stalks. Parry's often grows where shallow snowbanks melt and recede, sometimes forming extensive colonies.

American Vetch
Vicia americana
WILDLIFE

Life zone/ecosystem: Montane. Aspen groves and meadows. **Flowering:** Late May–July. **Fruit:** Hairless flat pod. **Characteristics:** Common. Clambering vine, 2–4 ft. (60–120 cm) long. Reddish-purple pea flowers attach where leaf meets stem. Leaves usually divided into even number of opposite leaflets; leaf tip is curling tendril, sometimes forked. Ten stamens in 2 groups of 9 and 1; style, a slender stalk emerging from the ovary; circle of hairs around tip.

Delicate tendrils secure this common vetch to other plants, contributing to the tangle of vegetation in aspen groves and montane meadows. A choice forage for grazing livestock, these plants are fragile and can easily be decimated in a particular area. Although similar to peavines, species of the genus *Lathyrus*, they can be told apart with magnification. Pull down the keel of the flower to expose the style. In vetches, the bunch of hairs at the tip of the style resemble a shaving brush, while in peavines the hairs are attached along one side similar to a hairbrush.

Aspen Peavine
Lathyrus lanszwertii var. *leucanthus*
[*L. leucanthus*]
GARDEN • WILDLIFE

Life zone/ecosystem: Montane to subalpine. Oak-mountain shrubland, aspen forest, open hillsides of spruce-fir.
Flowering: May–July. **Fruit:** Hanging pod, widest at tip.
Characteristics: Common. Delicate trailing vine, 5–20 in. (12–50 cm) long. Large white, cream or white and pink, fragrant pea-like flowers. Pinnately compound leaves composed of 2–4 pairs of leaflets; curling tendril for climbing other plants at the end. May be confused with American vetch.

Clambering up and over shrubs and other vegetation in forests and along trails, aspen peavine is covered with voluptuous, fragrant flowers. It is a valuable forage plant for mule deer and elk. Local gardeners adorn their summer fences with a relative from Sicily, the delicately perfumed sweet pea (*L. odoratus*). These were often planted near outhouses, for obvious reasons. Peavines are easily distinguished from American vetch by the tip of the pistil, which has hairs along one side like a hairbrush. Vetch has hairs circling the tip like a shaving brush.

*Crownvetch
Coronilla varia
[*Securigera varia*]

Life zone/ecosystem: Montane. Disturbed soil. **Flowering:** June–September. **Fruit:** Erect linear pod with constrictions.
Characteristics: Non-native. Bushy herb with weak stems up to 4 ft. (120 cm). Variegated flower heads at ends of branches, rose-pink to white with keel tapering to narrow purple tip. Leaves pinnately compound with odd number of leaflets; no tendril.

Crownvetch is an introduced pasture plant from Europe and perhaps western Asia, which is planted for revegetation and in local gardens. It spreads quickly to form dense cover, escaping easily to invade land nearby.

Golden Banner, False Lupine
Thermopsis montana

Life zone/ecosystem: Montane. Open moist meadows, aspen groves. **Flowering:** June–August. **Fruit:** Slender erect pod, purple tinged, fuzzy. **Characteristics:** Robust and showy. 2–4 ft. (60–120 cm). Bright golden flowers resemble lupine. Leaf-like stipules where leaf stalk joins stem; lance-shaped leaflets attached at narrow end (oblanceolate); 3 leaflets per leaf. Exotic-looking seed pods.

Golden banner has a host of common names, including mountain goldenpea, buffalo bean and wild yellow pea, and is described by some botanists as a variety of the mega-species golden pea, *T. rhombifolia*. *Montana* is Latin meaning "of the mountains." Cheerful patches of golden banner are scattered across slopes of local ski areas.

Mountain Lupine
Lupinus argenteus

GARDEN

Life zone/ecosystem: Montane to subalpine. Moist to dry soil of aspen and mixed aspen/conifer forests and meadows. **Flowering:** Late May–August. **Fruit:** Hairy pod with 4–6 seeds. **Characteristics:** Common. Branched herb, 20–40 in. (50–100 cm). Leaves palmately compound (arranged like wheel spokes), with short, stiff hairs beneath. Leaf petioles close to same length. Main stems have short hairs flattened against the stem. Very pale to deep blue, pea-like flowers arranged in loose spike-like racemes.

What a visual feast! Luxuriant shades of blue inspire excited oohs and aahs as local lupine bursts into bloom in early summer. Petals of individual flowers flush to a deep fuchsia, as a signal to pollinating insects that the stigma has already been pollinated (see photo). *Lupinus* is a taxonomically complex genus, with much discrepancy among authorities concerning recognized subspecies, varieties and forms of mountain lupine. Although several other lupine species are present in this area, they are extremely variable and freely intergrade, making morphological characteristics used to separate them few and inconsistent. For now, just appreciate the beauty of these wildflowers, which may be grown fairly easily from seed gathered in the fall.

A burgundy blush on lupine's banner is notice to pollinating insects that they need not stop.

Colorado Loco, Lambert Locoweed
Oxytropis lambertii
POISONOUS

Life zone/ecosystem: Montane. Oak-mountain shrub-land, dry meadows and gravel slopes. **Flowering:** May–August. **Fruit:** Erect hairy pod. **Characteristics:** Fairly common. Up to 12 in. (30 cm). Silky-hairy tufted plant. Inch-long flowers, bright rose-purple or fuchsia, with sharply pointed keel; calyx not inflated. Each unbranched, leafless stem has 10–40 flowers; spike-like clusters actually racemes. Leaves pinnate, basal; tipped with leaflet, not tendril.

Colorado loco is just one of several locoweeds considered poisonous to livestock if large amounts are eaten over a period of time. However, the toxicity, which comes partly from selenium in the soil, does not seem to affect wildlife, and Navajo people made a tea from the plant to treat constipation. An individual crown may generate over a dozen stems, creating showy natural bouquets scattered across the landscape.

*Red Clover
Trifolium pratense
EDIBLE • MEDICINAL

Life zone/ecosystem: Montane to sub-alpine. Disturbed soil. **Flowering:** June–August. **Fruit:** Small pod with 1–2 seeds. **Characteristics:** Common. Non-native. Biennial or short-lived perennial herb at our elevations, 1–3 ft. (30–90 cm). Deep rose-pink pea flowers in large globe- or egg-shaped heads. Leaves, divided into 3 oval leaflets, usually marked with pale, jagged "V." Stems with soft hairs.

Red clover is grown as a legume pasture plant for livestock and poultry, and is often plowed under as "green manure" to improve the soil in cultivated fields. It was brought to America by British colonists. They had many uses for red clover, including as an alterative, antispasmodic, sedative and treatment for burns, rheumatism, ulcers and skin sores. Although its effectiveness is disputed in some cases, recent research does suggest it may have anti-cancer properties. Red clover contains an isoflavone called genistein, which is known to stop the formation of new blood vessels that feed tumors.[25] Isoflavones, having a weak estrogen-like activity, may reduce menopausal symptoms, as well.

*White Dutch Clover
Trifolium repens

Life zone/ecosystem: Montane. Disturbed ground. **Flowering:** May–September. **Fruit:** Pod. **Characteristics:** Fairly common. Non-native. Creeping herb, 1–3 ft. (30–90 cm). Tiny white or very pale pink pea flowers, clustered in round heads borne on leafless stalks. Compound leaves with 3 broad leaflets. **Alsike clover** (*T. hybridum*) is similar, but does not creep by rooting at the nodes and has darker pink flowers with tuft of hair at calyx lobe base.

Some people think of this species as the original Irish shamrock, whose three leaflets St. Patrick used to teach his followers about the Trinity. Leaves with four leaflets are not uncommon and have long been considered a symbol of luck. White Dutch clover is commonly included in grass seed mixes.

*Yellow Sweetclover
Melilotus officinalis
MEDICINAL · WILDLIFE

Life zone/ecosystem: Montane. Disturbed soil. **Flowering:** June–September. **Fruit:** Small 1- or 2-seeded pod. **Characteristics:** Common. Aggressive, non-native annual, winter annual or biennial herb, 2–6 ft. (0.6–2 m). Small yellow (or whitish) pea flowers. Leaves with 3 lobes like alfalfa, but leaflets more egg-shaped, and toothed halfway or more back from tip (alfalfa leaflets are toothed only near tip).

Like other legumes, yellow sweetclover helps increase available soil nitrogen, improves drainage, aerates the soil and increases water absorption in heavy clay soils. A native of the Mediterranean region, central Europe and Asia, it is quick to become established and grows rapidly, creating deep roots that are difficult to dig out. Because these characteristics are problematic in home landscapes and other sites, the popularity of including sweet-clover in grass/forb seed mixtures to help stabilize disturbed ground is changing. Sweetclover's use as a forage crop has also diminished due to its weedy nature; however, it is still favored by deer and elk and is used by birds for food and cover. Bees find it an excellent source of nectar for honey. Many cardiac patients rely on the drug Coumadin, which was discovered when farmers noticed their cattle were bleeding internally after consuming partially cured sweet-clover hay. It turns out that fungi were converting coumarins in the moist hay into dicoumarol—the powerful anticoagulant ingredient in the drug. Fresh dried bundles of sweetclover have a vanilla fragrance and were once hung in pioneers' homes to sweeten stale air.

PHLOX FAMILY
Polemoniaceae

Spring landscapes literally glow with showy displays of pink and lavender phlox (*Phlox* spp.). Species of this family first carpet shale slopes
among sagebrush and mountain shrubland communities in early spring,
soon followed by colorful scarlet gilia (*Ipomopsis aggregata*). Phlox family
flowers are mostly tubular and flare dramatically to 5 petals that are radially symmetrical or sometimes slightly bilaterally symmetrical. Each
flower has 5 united sepals, 5 stamens, a 3-lobed (may be 2-lobed) style and
a superior ovary. Phlox species are very popular with gardeners as a
ground-cover.

Narrowleaf Collomia
Collomia linearis

Life zone/ecosystem: Montane. Dry to moist
shaded sites of mountain-shrub and aspen forests.
Flowering: May–July. **Fruit:** 3-chambered capsule;
one seed per chamber. **Characteristics:** Common.
Leafy annual herb up to 12 in. (30 cm). Small
white, pink or purplish tubular flowers grow clustered in midst of leafy bracts at top of stem; stamens protrude unequally. Stems and narrow undi-
vided leaves usually covered with sparse gland-
tipped hairs.

Found throughout North America, this inconspicuous plant often
goes unseen. A close look reveals the dainty flowers clustered among leafy
bracts. *Collomia* is actually derived from the Greek *kolla*, or "glue," referring to the tiny seeds that become very mucilaginous when soaked in
water.

Showy Jacob's Ladder
Polemonium pulcherrimum
GARDEN • MEDICINAL

Life zone/ecosystem: Subalpine. Dry
spruce-fir forests. **Flowering:** June–August.
Fruit: Capsule. **Characteristics:** Fairly
common. Delicate herb reaching up to 10 in.
(25 cm). Blue-violet flowers have bright yellow throats surrounding 5 white stamens
and 3-parted stigma; furry, 5-pointed sepals.
Sprawling stems mostly at base, with pinnate
leaves. Leaflets and stems covered with tiny glands.

This plant's delicate violet to pale-blue flowers offer a colorful contrast to cinnamon-colored conifer needles carpeting subalpine forests. Its

ladder-like leaves are reminiscent of the ladder Jacob ascended to heaven in the book of Genesis. Crushing the thin glandular leaves releases a skunk-like smell, which becomes more intense on a rainy day. Gardeners say that Jacob's-ladder grows well if mature seed is sown in sandy, well-drained soil in the fall. European Jacob's ladder was grown in gardens for centuries as a medicinal. It was used for palpitations of the heart, anxiety and headaches. Thompson tribes of British Columbia prepared a head and hair wash from this herb.

Leafy Polemonium, Leafy Jacob's Ladder
Polemonium foliosissimum
GARDEN

Life zone/ecosystem: Montane to subalpine. Sagebrush shrubland, oak-mountain shrubland, open meadows of other plant communities. **Flowering:** June–July. **Fruit:** Capsule. **Characteristics:** Robust herb to 3 ft. (90 cm). Ladder-like leaves, gray-green and furry, predominately present along stem. Cup-shaped lavender flowers with yellow-orange stamens clustered at top of stem.

Leafy polemonium is an attractive, long-lived plant growing in clumps, popular in native wildflower gardens because it seldom becomes a nuisance by reseeding itself. Seeds can easily be gathered in late summer.

Multi-Flowered Phlox
Phlox multiflora
GARDEN • WILDLIFE

Life zone/ecosystem: Montane to alpine. Sagebrush shrubland and oak-mountain shrubland up to tundra. **Flowering:** Late May–June. **Fruit:** 1-seeded capsule. **Characteristics:** Common. Mat-forming herb up to 5 in. (13 cm). Sharp-pointed linear leaves are crowded along herbaceous branches emerging from woody prostrate stems. Each stem bears 1 flower, colored several shades of lavender to white. Plants often create mounds of blossoms, totally concealing foliage. Translucent membranes between calyx lobes (sepals) are flat.

In and among sagebrush, serviceberry and bitterbrush, showy mounds of multi-flowered phlox carpet otherwise drab shale slopes. The fragrant nectars of this species and of its cousin longleaf phlox (see photo) attract both butterflies and moths as pollinators. Deer sometimes eat phlox, though it has no nutritional value for humans. Phlox species are popular in gardens and are valuable for erosion control. Reproduction is usually by seed, but sprouting can occur from spreading rootstocks.

Longleaf phlox (*P. longifolia*), a less common species tucked among the shrubs and grasses, has more loose-growing, bright-pink flowers; translucent membranes between the calyx lobes appear folded.

Scarlet Gilia, Skyrocket

Ipomopsis aggregata

GARDEN · MEDICINAL · WILDLIFE

Life zone/ecosystem: Montane to subalpine. Sagebrush shrub-land, oak-mountain shrubland, dry meadows. **Flowering:** Late May–August. **Fruit:** Capsule. **Characteristics:** Common. Herbaceous monocarpic perennial, 6–21 in. (15–53 cm). Flowers, fruits and dies in 2–6 years. Trumpet-shaped, rich red to red-orange or pink flowers, often speckled on flower's face. Leaves grow in a basal rosette and along furry stem, are finely dissected and covered with miniscule silvery glands. Stems uncurl in spring from basal rosette, which persists through winter.

In late spring, from low valleys to timberline, dry meadows and sagebrush-dotted slopes appear to glow with the flickering flames of scarlet gilia's crimson-colored trumpets. Gilia's finely dissected leaves allow wind to pass through without uprooting the fragile plant, which smells slightly of skunk. Gilias

Leaf rosette

eaten by deer and elk will put up more flowering stalks, so grazing may actually stimulate the plants to produce more seed. Hummingbirds are frequent pollinators, hovering and lapping up nectar while getting dusted with showers of pollen. Navajo people prepared a tea of dried gilia leaves as a remedy for stomach problems, while both Navajos and Hopis swallowed a leaf extract to ensure good luck in hunting.[26] Sowing and lightly raking seeds of scarlet gilia into your native plant garden in the fall will produce a profusion of color in the second or third year.

Sky Pilot

Polemonium viscosum

Life zone/ecosystem: Alpine. Rocky soil. **Flowering:** June–August. **Fruit:** Capsule. **Characteristics:** Fairly common. Grows up to 7 in. (17 cm). Rich purple-blue (rarely white) funnel-shaped flowers with orange pollen-laden stamens clustered atop sticky, hairy stem. Ladder-like leaves spiral around stem.

Clumps of extraordinary purple-blue flowers, their stamens chock-full of brilliant orange pollen, brighten rocky areas in the alpine—especially where ground has been tilled by pocket gophers. Sky pilot's flowers are known for their pungent skunky odor, said to vary with altitude. Research has shown that the smell attracts bees, while detering nectar-robbing insects like ants. Orange pollen clings to the bees' legs as they fill up on nectar, then travels with them to cross-fertilize the next flower they visit—a useful exchange! The vivid contrast of petals and stamens also serves as a "nectar guide" for insect pollinators.

PINK FAMILY   *Caryophyllaceae*

Opposite leaves and swollen nodes are characteristics that make this family easy to recognize. Other family attributes include a branched or forked flowering stem in most genera and radially symmetrical bisexual flowers with a superior ovary. Flowers are composed of 5 (sometimes 4) separate or united sepals, usually 5 separate petals, 1–2 whorls of 5–10 stamens and 3–5 styles. The petals are often notched at the tip. The fruit is a dry capsule that releases the abundant seeds through valves at the top. Familiar flower-shop members of this family include carnations, sweet William and baby's-breath. Many hardy and attractive wildflowers and well-known garden plants are also pinks. Bouncingbet (*Saponaria officinalis*) is a fragrant, pink-flowered plant on the state noxious weed list that was innocently introduced for gardens.

Some botanists feel that the genera *Cerastium*, *Minuartia* and *Stellaria* are in a separate family—Chickweeds (Alsinaceae)—because their flowers have separate instead of united sepals and petals without the slender, narrowed base (claw) usually found in the pink family.

Alpine Sandwort
Minuartia obtusiloba
[*Lidia obtusiloba*, *Arenaria obtusiloba*]

Life zone/ecosystem: Alpine. Fellfields.
Flowering: July–early September. **Fruit:** Capsule.
Characteristics: Fairly common. Dense spreading plant up to 2 in. (5 cm). White flowers atop hidden wiry stems, appearing large in proportion to tiny moss-like leaves. Sepals and leaves blunt-tipped. Flowers have 10 stamens, 3 styles. Crowded stems have short, sticky hairs.

A diminutive treasure, alpine sandwort grows only in alpine sites consistently blown free of snow during the long winters. Roots develop wherever its branches touch the soil, creating a larger mat than the dense, tap-rooted cushion of the otherwise similar moss campion (see p. 180). Like moss campion, it is highly adapted to alpine environments, and helps stabilize the soil by collecting bits of blown soil and plant debris in its matrix. A phenomenon called floral sexual dimorphism is demonstrated in this charming sandwort. Notice how some plants have large flowers with showy anthers and undeveloped ovaries, while others bear smaller flowers with petals barely longer than the sepals, nonfunctional anthers and very developed ovaries. The former are more functionally male, the latter more female. Sexual dimorphism is thought to be a reproductive strategy to prevent self-fertilization and inbreeding in some plants.

Ballhead Sandwort, Desert Sandwort

Arenaria congesta [*Eremogone congesta*]

Life zone/ecosystem: Upper montane to sub-alpine. Rocky, dry soil in meadows and forest openings. **Flowering:** Late June–July. **Fruit:** Capsule. **Characteristics:** Common. 4–15 in. (15–40 cm). Sedge-like mat of sharp-pointed, grasslike leaves supports a slender-stemmed bouquet, arising from woody underground stems. Opposite leaves. 10 protruding stamens per flower give crowded (thus species name *congesta*) flower heads a ragged appearance. 5 separate sepals half the length of 5 white petals.

Pert and pixie-like, ballhead sandwort is tough and fairly flexible in its habitat preference, favoring sandy, rather dry soils that are often inhospitable to other species. Without flowers, when in bud or in fruit, it is often mistaken for a grass.

*Bladder Campion, Maiden's Tears

Silene vulgaris

Life zone/ecosystem: Montane. Disturbed areas. **Flowering:** July–September. **Fruit:** Round capsule with 6 teeth when open. **Characteristics:** Fairly common. Non-native weed, 24 in. (60 cm). Tap-rooted; stem base often woody. Stems usually branched, typically hairless and sometimes covered with waxy coating. Flowers solitary or on forked stems. Inflated, persistent calyx showing 20 veins, loosely enfolding ripe capsule. Large petals, usually whitish, deeply split into 2 lobes, with distinct claw- and crown-like scales. Opposite, egg-shaped or lance-shaped leaves generally have smooth edges and surfaces.

A handsome but invasive species introduced from England, bladder campion spreads easily by seeds or cut pieces of the root. This plant exhibits extreme variability in physical characteristics, resulting in conflicting descriptions by different authors. Slender and green when young, the calyx becomes inflated with age, displaying quite distinct burgundy (maybe purplish or greenish) veins. Flowers in this species may be perfect, bearing both anthers and pistils, or only the latter.

Drummond's Cockle

Silene drummondii
[*Gastrolychnis drummondii*,
Lychnis drummondii]

Life zone/ecosystem: Montane to alpine. Dry meadows.
Flowering: July–August. **Fruit:** Capsule. **Characteristics:**
Uncommon. Slender plant 8–20 in. (20–50 cm). Leaves
mostly basal, narrow-oblanceolate; stem glandular at least
on upper half. Calyx not inflated, marked by 10 burgundy
stripes. Pink or white petals only 0.25 in. (1–3 mm) long,
barely protruding from edge of calyx; 5 styles.

Meadows where this plant grows are
also home to wild strawberries, moonworts
and other rewarding discoveries. Bring along a
hand lens—and step carefully!

Long-stalked Starwort, Alpine Chickweed

Stellaria longipes

Life zone/ecosystem: Subalpine to alpine. Moist to dry
rocky meadows. **Characteristics:** Common. Low, fairly
compact plant less than 6 in. (15 cm). White flowers, generally only 1–2 per plant locally; 5 very deeply lobed petals,
appearing as 10. Smooth, green, keeled, linear lance-shaped
leaves; often waxy coating.

Fairly inconspicuous, delicate starworts are often
tangled with surrounding vegetation, their flowers
looking like tiny scattered stars. Long-stalked starwort
is very adaptable, making it a successful colonizer of different habitats.

Moss Campion

Silene acaulis
GARDEN

Life zone/ecosystem: Alpine. Fellfields.
Flowering: July–August. **Fruit:** Capsule.
Characteristics: Common. Dense, cushion-
forming herb, 1–3 in. (2.5–7.5 cm). Bright pink
flowers of 5 petals, 3 styles, 10 yellow stamens
and tough, tubular calyx. Short, sticky, densely
interwoven stems with tiny, narrow, sticky leaves.
Deep taproot.

These green, moss-like cushions, sprinkled with bright fuchsia stars, embellish cold, dry, wind-blasted alpine and arctic regions around the globe. Nestled flat to the ground, anchored by a deep taproot, moss campion has adapted to these harsh conditions. The dense cushion traps blowing bits of soil and plant debris over time, eventually providing an oasis for other species to sprout. After centuries or even millennia an alpine turf forms, which includes a diversity of plants. Two decades may pass before slow-growing moss campion flowers abundantly and single plants may grow to be 100–300 years old. As the flowers tend to cluster in the microclimate on the cushion's warmer south-side, hikers often refer to it as compass flower. Pollination is by specialized butterflies with mouth parts that coil into straw-like "tongues," able to siphon the slender tube's nectar. Sticky surfaces on the stems and leaves deter nectar-robbing ants and beetles, while a tough calyx thwarts short-tongued bumblebees. Moss campion is beautiful in rock gardens, but takes patience to grow.

Tuber Starwort, Sticky Chickweed

Pseudostellaria jamesiana

[*Arenaria jamesiana*, *Stellaria jamesiana*]

Life zone/ecosystem: Montane. Moist meadows, forest openings among aspen woodlands. **Flowering:** May–early July. **Fruit:** 3-valved capsule.
Characteristics: Common. Spindly herb, 6–8 in. (15–20 cm). Slender, erect stems are glandular-pubescent (at least above); often branch diffusely; upper 4-angled stem and 5-pointed sepals covered with tiny glandular-tipped hairs. Narrow, tapering, stalkless, lance-shaped leaves longer than 2 in. (5 cm). White flowers in terminal and axillary cymes (appear forked) bearing leafy bracts. Deeply lobed petals often twice as long as sepals; 10 stamens.

Common and quite a bit taller than other local chickweeds, this lanky starwort blooms early in moist aspen and oak-mountain forests. "Pseudo," or false, indicates that its physical similarity to another genus, *Stellaria*, is only superficial. Seeds are not produced from the showiest flowers, which have only anthers, but rather from the more inconspicuous fertile flowers pointing toward the ground. Valves of the seed capsule roll out at maturity, forming a flat shiny disk. *Jamesiana*, the species name, honors Edwin James (1797–1861), a surgeon-naturalist who explored the Rocky Mountains with the Long expedition in 1820.

*White Campion, White Cockle

Silene latifolia [*Melandrium dioicum*, *Lychnis alba*]

MEDICINAL

Life zone/ecosystem: Montane. Disturbed ground. **Flowering:** May–September. **Fruit:** Vase-shaped capsule with 10 teeth when opened. **Characteristics:** Common. Non-native. Winter or summer annual, biennial or short-lived perennial. Up to 4 ft. (1.2 m). Downy foliage. Male and female flowers on separate plants; showy, white, deeply notched petals. Inflated bladder-like calyx: cylindrical male calyx slender, burgundy-colored, with 10 lengthwise veins; spherical female calyx greenish, more inflated, with 20 lengthwise veins. Either yellow anthers or arching white styles of pistil are prominent. Lance-shaped to oval leaves taper to point; opposite at swollen nodes.

Introduced from Europe in the 1800's, probably in contaminated crop seeds, this beautiful "weedy" plant has fragrant flowers that open at night, releasing a sweet scent that attracts moths as pollinators. White campion is difficult to control because it produces so many seeds—each plant can produce fifty capsules, each containing approximately 500 seeds. It is also resistant to common herbicides and can spread from just a tiny piece of the root. Members of this genus were used in Elizabethan England to prepare a potion with sugar and wine to soothe the heart, while a worming medicine was made from the roots. Extracts from both roots and leaves are said to be extremely toxic to mosquito larvae.

PLANTAIN FAMILY   *Plantaginaceae*

Plantains appear in virtually every plant list around the globe. Despite the name, they are unrelated to tropical plantains, which are starchy relatives of the banana. Physical characteristics usually include:

- leafless stems and basal rosettes of simple, parallel-veined leaves not clearly separated into petiole and blade.
- small, papery flowers crowded into dense spikes or head-shaped clusters; flowers with 4 projecting stamens on wiry stalks.
- seeds that become mucilaginous when wet.

Psyllium—seeds from psyllium plantain (*Plantago afra*, native to Iran and India) or woolly plantain (*P. ovata*, native to northern Africa and western Asia)—is an ingredient in commercial laxative products. The seed coat contains a special mucilage that swells when soaked. This property enables psyllium to lubricate and absorb toxins in the digestive tract in the case of constipation or to absorb excess water in the case of diarrhea. Even animals are aware of plantains' curative powers. For example, Indian mongooses have been observed chewing plantain leaves to neutralize the venom of cobra bites.

*Common Plantain
Plantago major
EDIBLE · MEDICINAL

Life zone/ecosystem: Montane. Disturbed areas. **Flowering:** May–September. **Fruit:** Reticulated capsule. **Characteristics:** Common. Non-native. Weedy annual, biennial or perennial, to 16 in. (40 cm). Papery corolla lobes, densely packed in elongated spikes on leafless stems; 4 projecting stamens per flower. Alternate, broadly oval basal leaves; prominent veins, wavy margins. Reproduces by seed.

Thought to have originated in Europe, common plantain now grows almost everywhere. Although its pollen can irritate people with hay-fever, its long-standing value as an edible and medicinal more than makes up for that. Fresh plantain contains allantoin, a soothing substance that promotes healing of injured skin cells. A poultice of mashed leaves is considered effective for mild burns, bug bites, poison ivy, sunburn and stings. Herbalists have long recognized plantain's antibacterial nature, using it to treat sore throat, laryngitis, cough and bronchitis. The French soaked the mucilaginous seeds of some species in hot water to use for stiffening muslin, while Argentineans have used the same liquid for inflammatory eye problems. During the Middle Ages, the leaves were placed inside their boots to prevent blisters and hanging plantain in buildings was supposed to provide protection against evil.

English plantain *(P. lanceolata)* has darker, more grass-like leaves.

PRIMROSE FAMILY   *Primulaceae*

Showy primroses have been cultivated as colorful garden ornamentals since Elizabethan times. Cyclamen, a wild European species similar to North America's native shooting star, is a popular potted plant in this country. Our distinctive native representatives of this family are easily recognized by their united petals and stamens which are inserted opposite to each petal, rather than the more common alternate sequence. The family botanical name, Primulaceae, is based on the genus *Primula*, to which most of the popular garden varieties belong, and from which come many medicinal herbs in Europe.

Northern Rock Jasmine, Northern Fairy Candelabra
Androsace septentrionalis

Life zone/ecosystem: Montane to alpine. Sagebrush and oak-mountain shrublands; areas of pocket gopher disturbance; other gravelly, often disturbed soils. **Flowering:** May–August. **Fruit:** Capsules. **Characteristics:** Common. Miniature annual, 1–10 in. (2.5–25 cm); height varies with site conditions. Delicate, airy, umbrella-like clusters of tiny white flowers borne on slender stalks above rosette of glossy, dark-green leaves. Tiny, **alpine rock jasmine** (*A. chamaejasme*) also has a leafy, green rosette, but is perennial and has white flowers with yellow centers in dense cluster at top of stem; memorable, sweet fragrance. Common on local alpine tundra.

These sprays of tiny white, star-like flowers, with a fragrance like tropical jasmine, provide a facelift to dry ground in meadows and forest openings and are important early successional species common around pocket gopher mounds, ant hills and other disturbed soil sites. Rock jasmine is reminiscent of baby's-breath, found in flower arrangements. Imaginative minds can easily picture a fairy lighting her way with this delicate, branched "candelabra."

Parry's Primrose
Primula parryi

Life zone/ecosystem: Subalpine to alpine. Streambanks, moist meadows. **Flowering:** June–August. **Fruit:** Oval-shaped capsule. **Characteristics:** Fairly common. Up to 12 in. (30 cm). Sturdy leafless stems support umbel of 3–12 bright, magenta flowers splashed with sunny-yellow centers. Funnel-shaped flowers with 5 flaring, notched petals surrounded by cup-shaped calyx; 5 stamens opposite petal lobes; 1 pistil. Thick, smooth leaves with prominent mid-vein and toothed edges, grouped in basal rosette almost as tall as flowering stem.

Every hiker who loves the high country has vivid memories of these striking magenta flowers towering over the more ground-hugging alpine species. Since Parry's primrose thrives on moisture, the memory is usually associated with the sound of water tumbling and splashing through alpine meadows. Parry's primrose survives this exposed environment by inhabiting protected niches tucked amongst boulders and along streams. Although the flowers are sweet-smelling at first, they develop a skunky, disagreeable odor as they mature, probably an evolutionary strategy to attract insects. The bright-yellow centers alert the pollinators to the nectar source. This species was named after Charles Christopher Parry, a 19th-century plant collector who was named the "king of Colorado botany" by Joseph Hooker, director of England's Kew Gardens from 1865–1885.

WHAT'S THAT SOUND? Buzz pollination! About 8% of the world's some 250,000 species of plants have anthers that open by tiny pores at the top (poricidal anthers)—plants such as shooting stars, tomatoes and eggplants. Getting the pollen out requires a little extra effort, and is accomplished only by certain bees (not honeybees), which hold on to the usually downward-pointing flower and vibrate their thoracic muscles at about 300 cycles/second, producing the optimal vibration. These very high frequencies act like a tuning fork, producing sounds that are different than flying frequencies, causing the microscopic, smooth, dry pollen to explode in a cloud onto the female bee's belly. She uses her front legs to scrape the pollen into pockets on her hind legs, eventually delivering it back to the hive to be used as food. As she moves from flower to flower before heading home, pollination is accomplished.

Shooting Star
Dodecatheon pulchellum
WILDLIFE

BARBARA MAGNUSON/LARRY KIMBALL

Life zone/ecosystem: Subalpine. Streams and boggy areas in spruce-fir forests. **Flowering:** June–August. **Fruit:** Oval to cylindrical capsules, opening by pores on top. **Characteristics:** Fairly common. Distinctive herb, 4–16 in. (10–40 cm). Hot pink petals swept backward, revealing golden bases and beak-like projection of black stamens. Flowers in nodding cluster on slender, leafless stalk; fruits upright at maturity. Leathery basal rosettes of elliptical-shaped green leaves.

Discovering these floral shooting stars can bring as much delight as a sighting of their celestial namesakes. Here, lone plants may be scattered in subalpine meadows, whereas wet meadows elsewhere can be literally carpeted with shooting stars. The beak-like projection of black stamens around the stigma is an adaptation to buzz pollination. Pliny the Elder coined the genus name, believing the plant to be protected by twelve gods (*dodeka theoi*) of the Greek pantheon; *pulchellum* is derived from a word denoting "beautiful" or "handsome." Although shooting stars are not considered appealing forage, elk and deer will eat them when other nourishment is scarce.

PURSLANE FAMILY   *Portulacaceae*

Purslanes are herbs or shrubs whose succulent leaves contain large water-storage cells as well as betalains, which are red, nitrogen-containing pigments and lemon-tasting oxalic acid. Their roots are either sturdy taproots or fleshy roots. The "calyx" is actually a modified involucre of 2 bracts subtending the sepals that look like petals (tepals). Flowers in this family are usually radially symmetrical, with 2 of these bracts, 4–6 petal-like tepals and a superior ovary. Purslane fruits are capsules with a lid-like opening on top.

Native Americans, early settlers and other cultures throughout history have coveted the roots and leaves of this family for food and medicine. Two common species are still eaten today. Common purslane (*Portulaca oleracea*), a tenacious garden weed, is sometimes served in trendy restaurants as a tender, slightly peppery garnish, or included as a prized ingredient in traditional Turkish lamb and lentil stew. It is also known to be a good source of antioxidants and omega-3 fatty acids. Miners-lettuce (*Montia perfoliata* or *Claytonia perfoliata*), common in moist areas along the Pacific coast of North America, is a delicious addition to salads and sandwiches.

Lanceleaf Spring Beauty, Indian Potato
Claytonia lanceolata
EDIBLE • WILDLIFE

Life zone/ecosystem: Montane to subalpine. Moist ground in oak-mountain shrubland, aspen and spruce-fir forests. **Flowering:** May–June. **Fruit:** 3-chambered capsule; mature capsule forcibly expels shiny black seeds as margins roll inward. **Characteristics:** Common. Up to 6 in. (15 cm). 3–20 perky white flowers with distinctive pink or red veins, clustered atop stem above succulent pair of lanceolate leaves; basal leaves wither before plant flowers. Flower has 2 broad sepals, bright pink-tipped stamen attached to each of 5 petals and 3 stigmas. Corm walnut-sized or smaller; brown-skinned and white inside.

Soon after snowmelt, the drab spring landscape really comes to life when lanceleaf spring beauty's peppermint-striped flowers appear. Such dainty, cheerful plants should not be disturbed in a world where food is plentiful, although they can be eaten in an emergency. Locally, Native Ute people often camped in subalpine meadows to dig these shallow, pleasant-tasting corms, as did the Native Americans in other places—hence the alternative common name, Indian potato. Although usually eaten boiled or baked soon after harvesting, the corms were sometimes stored for a short time in holes lined with conifer needles and cottonwood bark, which prevented them from freezing and kept out rodents. Nowdays, the roots are dug by bears and rodents, while deer, elk and bighorn sheep browse the succulent foliage.

Big-rooted spring beauty (*Claytonia megarhiza*), a striking plant encountered in high alpine rockslides, has a basal rosette of large, spoon-shaped, succulent leaves, which collects and retains water in that dry, windy habitat.

Pygmy Bitterroot
Lewisia pygmaea [*Oreobroma pygmaea*]
EDIBLE · GARDEN

Life zone/ecosystem: Subalpine to alpine. Rocky to gravelly open areas, fellfields. **Flowering:** June–August. **Fruit:** Rounded capsule. **Characteristics:** Fairly common. Low-growing herb less than 2 in. (5 cm). Delicate, deep pink to white flowers nestle in basal rosette of fleshy linear leaves. 2 glandular-tipped sepals, 6–8 petals, 5–8 stamens, 3–5 stigmas. Minute pair of papery leaflets midway up stem.

This ground-hugging beauty can be found in cozy microclimates where rocks and soil are warmed by the sun, protecting it from freezing temperatures and harsh winds. In a survival situation, the roots of this species can be boiled or baked, but the skin must be removed or they are extremely bitter. The open, saucer-shaped flowers are especially accessible to insects; with the banquet of pollen particularly important to bees and bumblebees as food for young larvae. Pygmy bitterroot is favored for rock gardens because of its hardiness.

ROSE FAMILY   *Rosaceae*

Life would not be the same without the rose family, which includes many of our native plants and garden ornamentals. "Bon appetit" would not be as meaningful, either, without the luscious fruits of this family—apples, pears, plums, peaches, raspberries, strawberries and more. All northern temperate rose species have:
- radially symmetrical, perfect flowers with a conspicuous cup-like hypanthium, 10 to many stamens, 5 wavy-edged petals and 5 sepals.
- stipules, tiny leaflike bracts present at the leaf-stem attachment, which separate these plants from similar buttercups.
- no elaborate pollination mechanism, so the flowers depend on a generous production of pollen and easily accessible nectar to attract a large array of insects.
- potentially toxic, cyanide-producing compounds in the seeds, bark and leaves; berry pulp is safe; human digestive systems can break down plant cyanides into harmless compounds in very small amounts.

No blue or red roses are found in the wild because this family lacks the genes to produce those pigments. The range of color in cultivated roses is the result of genetic engineering, sometimes involving seven to nine species. Red roses, traditionally symbolic of love, became possible when a chance genetic mutation for the production of red pigment (pelargonidin) appeared in 1930 in some cultivated roses. This mutated gene began to be used to cultivate red roses. Local native species supply valuable food and habitat for wildlife and are excellent plants for wildlands restoration projects.

Alpine Avens
Geum rossii [*Acomastylis rossii*]

Life zone/ecosystem: Alpine. Tundra turfs.
Flowering: July–August. **Fruit:** Lance-shaped achene with hairs. **Characteristics:** Common. 2–8 in. (5–20 cm). Golden-yellow flowers with many stamens, similar to the genus *Potentilla* (see below); sepals sometimes red-tinged. Fern-like, pinnate leaves with uneven leaflets, cluster at base of rose-red stems. May be sparsley hairy beneath.

Lavish clumps of sunny yellow alpine avens are fly favorites, especially in the warmth of midday. Flies seem pervasive on many flowers in the alpine, but are especially attracted to flowers like avens, which are simple, open and somewhat flat, with easily accessible nectar and no fragrance. The pollen-laden stamens are numerous, so the insects cannot miss the dusting of pollen destined for the next flower. When the fern-like foliage of this dominant species turns copper and red in autumn, it creates vivid splashes of color across alpine tundra. Pikas can often be seen with their mouths full of avens leaves, busily scurrying to build their "haypiles" for winter.

Beauty Cinquefoil, Showy Cinquefoil
Potentilla gracilis var. *pulcherrima*
[*P. pulcherrima*]
MEDICINAL

Life zone/ecosystem: Montane to lower subalpine. Open areas of oak-mountain shrubland, aspen, spruce-fir. **Flowering:** June–August. **Fruit:** Small achenes, densely clustered.
Characteristics: Common. Showy herb, 1–2 ft. (30–60 cm). Open clusters of bright-yellow flowers, many stamens; orange spot at base of petal. Leaves mainly basal and palmately compound, with narrow leaflets atop long stalks; leaflets distinctly lighter colored and furry beneath. Lanky, larger **silvery cinquefoil** (*P. hippianna*) has lemon-yellow petals, silvery, pinnately compound leaves (usually 7 or more leaflets); found in sagebrush communities, sometimes large colonies; hybridizes with beauty cinquefoil.

The name *Potentilla* is derived from *potens*, Latin for "power," apparently referring to strong medicine created by many cultures from the roots, stems, leaves and flowers of this very astringent, tannin-rich genus. Cinquefoil tinctures and teas have historically been used to treat mouth inflammations, stomach ulcers, fevers and diarrhea. For generations, people in the Southwest have made a sun tea of the leaves to slosh over the backs of pack animals to prevent saddle sores. More recently, plant-savvy hikers put the leaves and flowers in their shoes to prevent blisters. In *Medicinal Plants of the Rocky Mountain West*, Michael Moore refers to this genus as "a botanist's nightmare of crossbreeding." To positively identify this or any other species of *Potentilla* often means making a difficult trek through a plant key. *Cinquefoil* is French for "5 leaves," which was characteristic of an old world plant. However, leaflets in local species may number from three to fifteen.

Alpine cinquefoil (*Potentilla subjuga*), common in the upper subalpine and alpine, has 3–5 leaflets toward the tip of each leaf with another 2–4 farther down the stalk.

Bitterbrush, Antelope Brush

Purshia tridentata

DYE • EDIBLE • MEDICINAL • WILDLIFE

Life zone/ecosystem: Montane. Oak-mountain shrubland, south-facing slopes. **Flowering:** Mid May–mid June. **Fruit:** Softly furry, spindle-shaped achenes. **Characteristics:** Common. Somewhat evergreen shrub, possibly reaching 12–15 feet (3.6–4.5 m), but usually averaging 3–4 feet (0.9–1.2 m). Fragrant, solitary yellow flowers with many stamens; cone-shaped calyx. Tiny dark green to gray-green leaves are wedge-shaped with 3 tiny lobes at tip (hence *tridentata*); densely furry beneath; alternate on stem. Short, spear-like branchlets gray to shreddy brown, possibly hairy when young (smoother with age); small, scaly buds. Drought-tolerant. Long-lived at 90–162 years.

Bitterbrush is most conspicuous in the spring when covered with hundreds of fragrant yellow flowers, whose abundant pollen was a vital source of nutrition for Native Americans. The extremely bitter, quinine-containing leaves provided medicine for the Hopis and Navajos, who chewed them to induce vomiting and steeped them as a tea to clean wounds and treat skin problems. The Utes made a potion from the inner bark for eyewash. Some tribes fashioned the stiff, straight limbs into arrow shafts, shredded the bark to create cradleboard padding or pillow stuffing, and boiled the twigs and leaves for a gold-colored dye. Most seedlings of bitterbrush sprout from the caches of small rodents and ants that gather the fat- and protein-rich seeds for consumption, leaving some uneaten. Bitterbrush shrubs can have nitrogen-fixing roots, a trait that is dependent on soil conditions such as salinity, moisture and available nitrogen (see p. 169). Though early-spring leaves are deciduous, leaves that emerge later in the summer remain all winter to provide important forage for elk and mule deer. Ranchers also consider bitterbrush an important browse for cattle.

Chokecherry, Puckerberry

Prunus virginiana var. *melanocarpa*

[*Padas virginiana* subsp. *melanocarpa*]

EDIBLE • GARDEN • MEDICINAL • WILDLIFE

Life zone/ecosystem: Montane. Dry to moist open sites of oak-mountain shrubland, aspen forest. **Flowering:** Late June–August. **Fruit:** Dark red to black cherry-like drupes, one pit; very sour. **Characteristics:** Common. Deciduous shrub to small tree up to 16 ft. (5 m). Fragrant, creamy-white flowers with tufts of golden stamens in dense droopy clusters (racemes). Leaves with finely serrated edges, waxy on top, grayish-green beneath; 2 tiny glands on petiole below leaf base.

Mature chokecherries

Just as showy displays of serviceberry are fading, chokecherry bursts into bloom with fluffy flower "caterpillars" speckled with golden "polka dots." Later, the flowers mature to clusters of black, sour berries that are edible and often used to make jelly. As with all rose species, the seeds contain toxic hydrocyanic acid and should not be eaten. Dried berries were a traditional addition to pemmican, a mixture of dried fruit, meat and fat that sustained different Native American tribes. Both settlers and native people concocted cough syrup from the berries and made preparations of the inner bark for sore throats, headaches and diarrhea. Chokecherries are very important to black bears, as they depend on them to put on extra winter fat. Birds and mammals relish the berries, and the twigs are a valuable browse for elk and deer in winter. This is one of the best shrubs for attracting birds to gardens and the burnished red, salmon and gold foliage embellish fall color displays. Fencing may be needed to keep elk and mule deer from eating them.

Greene Mountain Ash, Mountain Ash

Sorbus scopulina

EDIBLE • GARDEN • MEDICINAL

Life zone/ecosystem: Montane to subalpine. Moist, shaded hillsides and streambanks of aspen, mixed-conifer and spruce-fir forests. **Flowering:** June–July. **Fruit:** Berry-like pomes. **Characteristics:** Deciduous shrub or possibly small tree reaching up to 15 ft. (5 m). Fragrant white flat-topped flower clusters at end of branches, which mature into glossy, orange-red berries. Large leaves have 11–15 lance-shaped, pinnate leaflets with toothed edges. Young twigs have soft white hairs.

Frothy clouds of creamy white flowers followed by brilliant orange-red clusters of small apple-like berries characterize this beautiful native shrub. The inner bark of these plants was utilized by native cultures to treat various ailments such as colds, headaches, back pain and internal bleeding. Mountain ash berries are bitter but edible, cooked, dried or raw. They are considered one of the finest songbird foods, attracting evening and black-headed grosbeaks, cedar waxwings, robins, hermit and Swainson's thrushes and Steller's jays—remaining all winter for non-migratory birds. Black bears eat the leaves, twigs and berries, while mule deer and elk browse the stems. As nighttime lengthens during fall, the leaves stop producing chlorophyll, revealing the vivid red pigments that brighten our shaded hillsides. Mountain ash is a handsome addition to native gardens, though it may attract mule deer and elk.

Hawthorn, Red Haw

Crataegus erythropoda

MEDICINAL • WILDLIFE

Life zone/ecosystem: Montane. Streamside.
Flowering: Late May–June. **Fruit:** Haw; dark red berry-like pome containing 5 nutlets (seeds).
Characteristics: Fairly common. Tall shrub to small tree with thorns, 6–15 ft. (2–5 m). White flowers arranged in corymb. Numerous stamens with pink anthers, 5 petals and 5 styles. Leaves both lobed and toothed with appressed hairs on upper surfaces; mealy and lacking hairs beneath. Tips of leaf serrations blackish. Scattered hairs on petioles. Thorns average 1.5 in. (4 cm). **River hawthorn** (*C. douglasii* var. *rivularis*) and **willow hawthorn** (*C. saligna*—endemic to Colorado) are also found in this area. Leaves of river hawthorn toothed on edges, not distinctly lobed; berries, or haws, are dark red with age. Willow hawthorn not lobed; has 15–20 stamens (usually 10 on local species); blue-black berries.

Hawthorn has been used for centuries as a heart tonic. Modern research confirms that hawthorn leaves, flowers and berries contain compounds that gently strengthen heart muscles, improving blood circulation and reducing the need for oxygen. Varro Tyler, Ph.D., Dean and Professor Emeritus of Pharmacognosy (natural product pharmacy) at Purdue University, attributes these benefits to compounds in the plant, called oligomeric

Willow hawthorn

procyanidins (OPCs). Flavonoids, which dilate the smooth vessels of the coronary arteries, are also important. The German Commission E, a panel of experts that evaluates medicinal herbs for the government, approves hawthorn for various heart conditions as well. Thorns of hawthorn have been used by native peoples for piercing and hooking skins and other soft objects, while the strong, fine-grained wood has been crafted into tools and weapons. These thicket-forming shrubs provide good cover and secure nesting sites for small mammals and birds and the dried haws supply winter nourishment for mule deer, small mammals, blue grouse and various songbirds.

Large-leaved Avens
Geum macrophyllum
MEDICINAL

Life zone/ecosystem: Montane to subalpine. Moist meadows and streambanks in aspen and spruce-fir communities. **Flowering:** June–August. **Fruit:** Burr-like, hooked achenes. **Characteristics:** Common. Delicate hairy herb, up to 3 ft. (90 cm). Saucer-shaped yellow flowers, feathery styles, 5 petals, 5 recurved sepals in sparse, flat-topped clusters. Tiny stalked glands on bases of styles. Stalked basal leaves pinnately divided, the much larger terminal leaflet lobed but not divided into segments. Can be confused with herbaceous species of *Potentilla*.

Large-leaved avens is common in moist areas, often among horsetails. Each flower's style has an S-bend, or kink, near the tip that breaks off at maturity to create a persistent "hook" on the seed, helping it attach to passing animals—a handy dispersal mechanism. Avens have astringent properties and have been used in folk remedies for centuries.

Mountain Dryad
Dryas octopetala
GARDEN

Life zone/ecosystem: Alpine. Dry gravelly tundra, fellfields. **Flowering:** June–August. **Fruit:** Feathery-tipped achene. **Characteristics:** Common. Dwarf, prostrate evergreen shrub. Forms mats of trailing stems; roots freely with soil contact. Single creamy-white parabolic-shaped flower on leafless flower stalk; center spray of golden stamens. Leathery, wrinkled, dark-green leaves have scalloped, rolled edges.

A tough Lilliputian shrub, mountain dryad colonizes bare soil in local alpine areas, stabilizing, so other species can take hold. It also fills this important role at the edges of melting Alaskan glaciers, where it is abundant. Mountain dryad fixes nitrogen, which provides an ecological advantage in alpine soils where this element is limited. Hugging the ground close to sheltering and sun-warmed rocks, it survives severe temperatures and harsh winds. The evergreen leaves are ready to start photosynthesis immediately after snow melt as temperatures warm, signaling the onset of the short alpine growing season. Large, showy flowers seem to float above the mat of leathery green leaves, making mountain dryad a charming addition to sunny native rock gardens.

Mountain Mahogany, Alder-leaf Mahogany

Cercocarpus montanus

DYE • MEDICINAL • WILDLIFE

Feathery-tailed achenes

Emerging flower buds filled with red anthocyanin pigments for solar protection.

Life zone/ecosystem: Montane. Oak-mountain shrubland. **Flowering:** May–June. **Fruit:** Feathery-tailed achene. **Characteristics:** Common. Deciduous shrub grows up to 6.5 ft. (2 m). Inconspicuous greenish flowers with bell-shaped calyx and no petals. Leaves have large triangular teeth and wedge-shaped bases; green and sparsely silky above, pale and woolly beneath. Rigid gray to brownish branches marked with conspicuous ring-like leaf scars.

Mountain mahogany is most noticeable during autumn, when the shrub is covered with soft, wispy, spindle-shaped seeds. These form when the style of each flower matures into a long, feathery, somewhat curled tail attached to a furry achene. After dispersal, the plume-like tails twist in the wind, actually screwing the seed into the ground. Navajo people gathered the branches of this shrub to repel bugs under beds. They also used the twigs to brew a laxative, to make a reddish dye and to help women recover from childbirth. Mountain mahogany is typically associated with Gambel oak and serviceberry, becoming more prevalent locally on rocky soils along area ridge-lines. Although eaten year-round, this shrub is most important to mule deer and elk as a critical winter bowse species.

Pink Plumes, Prairie Smoke

Geum triflorum [*Erythrocoma triflora*]

GARDEN • MEDICINAL

Mature fruits

Life zone/ecosystem: Montane to subalpine. Dry, gravelly ground. **Flowering:** June–August. **Fruit:** Achene with long feathery tail from elongation of style. **Characteristics:** Common. Tufted herb up to 20 in. (50 cm). Spreads by rhizomes, forms clumps. Nodding, bell-shaped flowers with dusky-pink sepals and elongated bracts eclipse tiny off-white petals; reach skyward with maturity. Mostly fern-like basal leaves, stems covered with silky hairs; one pair of stem leaves.

Rosy-bronze plumed fruits develop after these enchanting flowers are pollinated, creating the illusion of smoke across the prairie. Winds easily disperse the fluffy fruits. The generic name is probably derived from the Greek *geno*, meaning "to yield an agreeable fragrance." Blackfoot tribes traditionally crushed the seed pods to rub on their bodies for fragrance and boiled the roots in water to treat sore eyes. The Thompson River Indians of British Columbia used pink plumes in sweat baths to relieve sore muscles, while other tribes and early European settlers used a decoction of the astringent roots for everything from sore nipples to horses' saddle sores—even as a beverage similar to weak sassafras tea. Pink plumes is host to a parasitic female moth (*Tetragma gei*) that possesses an elaborate telescoping abdomen, allowing her to deposit eggs in the deeply recessed ovaries of the flower. After hatching, the larvae feed on developing seeds. This is a great plant for local gardens, with seeds available commercially.

Red Raspberry
Rubus idaeus
EDIBLE • MEDICINAL • WILDLIFE

Life zone/ecosystem: Upper montane to subalpine. Rocky, disturbed soil, also streambanks in aspen and spruce-fir forests. **Flowering:** May–August. **Fruit:** Aggregate berry-like cluster of tiny, 1-seeded, fleshy drupes. **Characteristics:** Common. Prickly shrub 3–5 ft. (90–150 cm). Similar to garden varieties, but smaller. White, 5-petaled flowers in terminal or axillary clusters. Leaves compound; 3–5 sharp-toothed leaflets.

Raspberries are a culinary delight found throughout the world. Although delicious as trail nibbles, they are such a valuable food source for local wildlife that it is best to leave them on the bush. Centuries-old folklore attributes many medicinal uses to this astringent shrub. Women can drink a tea of the leaves and stems for morning sickness, menstrual cramps and labor pains. It also makes an effective mouthwash, gargle or treatment for diarrhea. There is some disagreement about whether raspberry-leaf tea really relaxes the uterus, though historical evidence indicates that it does help women prone to miscarriage carry babies to term.[27] Use only fresh or completely dried leaves, as mildly toxic substances develop during wilting. Keep in mind that dried herb potency decreases over time, so commercial sources of the herb need to be fresh in order to be effective.

Serviceberry, Saskatoon, Shadbush
Amelanchier alnifolia
EDIBLE • GARDEN • WILDLIFE

Life zone/ecosystem: Montane to lower subalpine. Aspen forests. Tolerant of variations in habitat: sun to moderate shade, infertile to nutrient-rich substrates and moist riparian areas to seasonally dry soils on mountain slopes. **Flowering:** Early spring. **Fruit:** Blue to blue-black pomes, resembling tiny apples. **Characteristics:** Common. Deciduous shrub 3–13 ft. (1–4 m). Terminal clusters of white flowers have 5 narrow petals, 12–20 stamens. Leaves narrowly oblong, the top half to two-thirds toothed; furry beneath when

young, becoming smooth with age (may remain furry along veins). Winter buds somewhat furry. **Utah serviceberry** (*A. utahensis*), found in oak mountain shrubland communities, has broadly oval leaves remaining furry beneath when mature.

A profusion of delicate white blossoms cloak serviceberry bushes in early spring, heralding a period of vigorous activity as all life welcomes the end of winter. Besides providing excellent cover for wildlife and nesting sites for birds, the berries are an important winter food source for birds such as robins and waxwings, which will winter here if enough berries are left dried on the bushes. Although chokecherries and acorns are the number one food choice of black bears, these berries are very important as they put on the fat they need for hibernation. Blue grouse will pluck the winter buds, hares eat the twigs and mice nibble on the bark. Native Americans combined dried ground meat with melted animal fat and dried berries to make pemmican, which lasted for months and sustained them on long journeys. They also crafted the hard, straight-grained wood into arrow shafts, spears and digging tools. Settlers traded the berries for needles, thread and other food items. Serviceberry reproduces mainly through suckering, but will also grow from seeds. This is a great shrub for native gardens.

Shrubby Cinquefoil
Potentilla fruticosa [*Pentaphylloides floribunda*, *Pentaphylloides fruticosa*]
MEDICINAL

Life zone/ecosystem: Montane to subalpine. Moist soils of aspen and spruce-fir communities. **Flowering:** July–August. **Fruit:** White hairy seed pods. **Characteristics:** Common. Hardy shrub, 6–60 in. (15–150 cm). Branches silky-textured when young, becoming shreddy, tough, twisted and brown with age. Small, compound leaves with 3–7 leaflets. Blazing yellow flowers have 5 broadly rounded petals nestled in silky cup of 5 sepals; about 30 stamens in center ring; tiny pistils, each a complete female reproductive structure, crowd the center.

Adaptable and showy, shrubby cinquefoil is easily grown in your native garden and can be obtained from nurseries in many colors. It grows commonly throughout the northern latitudes, preferring cool, moist but not wet environments, often between forest and wetland areas where the soil is slightly drier. Medicinal uses are similar to those of beauty cinquefoil (see p. 188).

Sibbaldia, Cloverleaf Rose
Sibbaldia procumbens
GARDEN

Life zone/ecosystem: Upper subalpine to alpine. Snowbank communities. **Flowering:** June–August. **Fruit:** Pear-shaped achene. **Characteristics:** Fairly common. Mat-forming herb, 1.5–3 in. (4–8 cm). Yellow flowers in flat-topped cluster (cyme) on leafless stems, spreading to erect; 5 petals, each about half the length of adjacent green calyx lobe and 5 stamens (unusual in rose family, where numerous stamens are the norm). Blue-green basal leaves covered with flat-lying wispy hairs, divided into 3 leaflets, each wedge-shaped at base; squared tips with 3–5 obvious teeth. Confused with wild strawberry or alpine clover.

Sibbaldia is distributed throughout the northern hemisphere, thriving in thick, organic soil layers fed by late snow melts. It is considered an indicator species for these areas. Scandinavians have long recognized that where sibbaldia grows, roads should not be built! This delicate, inconspicuous plant often goes unnoticed, but still can be an appealing plant for high-elevation rock gardens, appreciated when the leaves turn coppery-crimson in the fall. Seeds are available commercially.

Thimbleberry, Salmonberry
Rubus parviflorus [*Rubacer parviflorum*]
EDIBLE • GARDEN • MEDICINAL • WILDLIFE

Life zone/ecosystem: Montane to subalpine. Shady, moist to dry soil in aspen, mixed-conifer and spruce-fir forests. **Flowering:** Late May–July **Fruit:** A dome-shaped, loose aggregate cluster of 1-seeded red drupes, similar to raspberry; separate from the core when picked. **Characteristics:** Common. Robust, woody, deciduous plant, averaging 3 ft. (1 m). Large, maple-like leaves, usually soft-fuzzy on both sides. Stems with glandular hairs, lacking spines or prickles. Often forms thickets. Relatively large, white flowers that resemble wild roses; petals crinkled like tissue paper.

Although not as flavorful as raspberries, thimbleberries are very palatable—slightly sweet and a bit tart. Most Native Americans and early settlers ate the berries fresh, though some tribes prepared them in interesting ways, such as layering with roasted clams or pressing the berries into cakes that were sun-dried and stored. Creative uses for the large leaves have included lining cooking pits, making baskets, wrapping food for storage and natural toilet paper. Soap can be made from the boiled bark, and the young spring shoots can be peeled and cooked like asparagus. The medicinal uses of thimbleberry are similar to those of red raspberry. Birds and small mammals gorge on the fruits—watch for telltale red-stained droppings on rocks and limbs of trees and shrubs. Available commercially, thimbleberry adapts well to native plant gardens.

Wild Rose, Wood Rose

Rosa woodsii var. *ultramontana*
[*R. woodsii*]

EDIBLE • MEDICINAL • WILDLIFE

Life zone/ecosystem: Montane to sub-alpine. Aspen, mixed-conifer and spruce-fir forests. **Flowering:** June–August. **Fruit:** Red to orange-red hip; dried sepals and stamens remain with hip as a "tail." **Characteristics:** Common. Deciduous prickly shrub reaching 3–6 ft. (1–2 m). May form thickets from underground stems. Fragrant, saucer-shaped pink to rose flowers with ring of golden stamens and heart-shaped petals. Flowers more than 3 per branch. Prickles mostly with oval bases. Leaves alternate and pinnately compound with 5–7 oblong toothed leaflets and flat-winged stipules.

Misted with dew, wild roses are luminous in the clear light of early morning. Bumblebees are attracted to the open, saucer-shaped flowers and abundant stamens of wild rose, packing their leg pockets full of the nutritious pollen before returning to the hive. High in vitamins C and A, which increases after the first frost, the hips can be dried and powdered for soups, boiled for colorful jellies or eaten as survival food. Avoid eating the seeds, as the hairs can be irritating to the intestines. The Cheyenne people made a tea of this astringent shrub's leaves for treating diarrhea and stomach troubles, and boiled the buds, petals,

Fall frost turns leaves of wild roses remarkable shades of coppery red, gold and orange.

stems or root bark as a tea for eye problems, especially snow blindness. Rose buds and blossoms are traditional ingredients in moisturizing cosmetics and the moistened petals can be applied as a protective bandage over burns and minor wounds. Rose hips are a valuable source of energy and protein for squirrels, deer, coyotes and bears, and the persistent dry hips are important to birds and mammals during winter. Porcupines and beavers browse the leaves.

Wild Strawberry
Fragaria virginiana
EDIBLE • MEDICINAL • WILDLIFE

Life zone/ecosystem: Montane to subalpine. Dry soil in aspen, mixed-conifer and spruce-fir forests. **Flowering:** June–August. **Fruit:** Tiny replica of commercial strawberry, with seeds sunken in fruit surface. **Characteristics:** Common. Ground-hugging herb spread by stolons. Leaves in small basal clump, each with 3 thick, coarsely toothed leaflets; upper surface smooth, with blue-green cast; usually not hairy or prominently veined; terminal tooth of leaflet usually smaller than adjacent teeth. Flowers of 5 white petals, 20–25 gold stamens. Inflorescence usually shorter than leaves. **Woods strawberry** (*F. vesca*) prefers moister sites; has thinner, bright-green leaves grooved with veins and a silky-hairy surface; inflorescence at least as tall as leaves; terminal tooth of leaflet surpasses adjacent teeth; seeds on fruit surface.

Wild strawberry's soft red runners lace the landscape, producing new plants with small white flowers suggestive of wild roses. These strawberries, which ripen in cool temperatures at high elevation, are particularly sweet and flavorful, but be quick to taste them for they are soon discovered by a host of small mammals and birds who seek them out. The luscious, tiny "fruits" ripen only after the seeds are fully developed—a strategy that insures wildlife will disperse the seeds by consuming the fruit. Fruits typically result from the ripened ovary of a flower, but in this case the strawberry comes from the enlarged, fleshy mound, or receptacle, on which the single ovaries are attached. Each ovary develops into an achene that contains a single seed and is embedded in the strawberry's surface. Wild strawberry has many of the same uses as red raspberry. Strawberry-leaf tea, high in vitamins and minerals, is prescribed by herbalists to relieve diarrhea. Dried and powdered leaves were used by Native Americans to heal and prevent infection in the navel of a newborn baby or were mixed with deer fat to treat open wounds.

SANDALWOOD FAMILY *Santalaceae*

Sandalwood evokes the rich musky scent of incense and essential oil. Desire for these products was responsible for the near demise of the fragrant, wild sandalwood trees (*Santalum album*) of Australia and New Caledonia during the 18th and 19th centuries. Sandalwoods are grayish plants with greenish or pink "flowers," which are actually sepals (or tepals), as there are no true petals. Each stamen is aligned with a sepal and most ovaries are all or partly inferior. The leaves are simple and entire. Fruits maturing from the ovaries of this family are either a dry seed or a berry (drupe) with a stony seed. Sandalwoods may be herbs, shrubs or trees, but most are hemiparasites, meaning they have green leaves and make some food by photosynthesis, but require water and minerals from other plants.

Bastard Toadflax, Star Toadflax
Comandra umbellata
EDIBLE · MEDICINAL

Life zone/ecosystem: Montane. Dry soil of oak-mountain and sagebrush shrublands. **Flowering:** April–July. **Fruit:** Drupe. **Characteristics:** Fairly common. Hemiparasite. Up to 12 in. (30 cm). Stems branched and leafy. Flowers are white, pinkish or green-ish sepals; no petals; in dense clusters (cymes). Alternate, simple, pale-green to bluish-green leaves somewhat fleshy with pointed tips.

Although sandalwoods are abundant in the trop-ics, this is Colorado's only representative. *Comandra* comes from the Greek *kome* (hair) and *aner* (man), referring to hairs that are attached superficially to the base of each anther. Native Americans made a tea of the foliage to heal canker sores. The brown, slightly leathery, berry-like fruits are edible raw, though are reportedly better tasting when still a bit green. This species is not related to yellow toadflax of the snapdragon family.

SAXIFRAGE FAMILY *Saxifragaceae*

A family of small, fanciful flowers, saxifrages typically have 5 petals and 5 sepals combined with 5 or 10 stamens. Lobed or toothed, fleshy leaves are usually crowded at the base of the plant. The fruits—typi-cally oblong-shaped capsules with "horns" created by the mature pistils—are a good key to identification. Saxifrage means "rockbreaker," and was used for these plants because the belief was, as early as 1633, that medicine made from them could break up kidney stones. Besides being valued mem-bers of wild communities, this family boasts many horticultural varieties, such as *Astilbe*. The saxifrages formerly included several subfamilies that have recently been split off by botanists into separate families: the gooseberries, hydrangeas and grass-of-Parnassus.

Bog Saxifrage
Saxifraga oregana [*Micranthes oregana*]

Life zone/ecosystem: Subalpine to alpine. Moist meadows and streambanks. **Flowering:** June–August. **Fruit:** Reddish-purple, 2-horned capsule. **Characteristics:** Fairly common. Strong, erect herb averaging 12 in. (30 cm). Small, white to greenish-white flowers in branched clusters; pointed sepals are recurved by the time fruits mature. Stems usually short-hairy near base, becoming more glandular-hairy and sticky near the top; glands yellow, pink or purple. Somewhat succulent, spoon-shaped leaves longer than 2.4 in. (6 cm) with narrow to winged stalks; reddish, toothed margins.

Bog saxifrage is often confused with, and sometimes hybridizes with, snowball saxifrage (*Saxifraga rhomboidea* [*Micranthes rhomboidea*]). Both species seem to grow well in our subalpine and alpine life zones, often in similar habitats. Both have thick-skinned leaves containing interior cells filled with mucilaginous sap, which retain moisture—a distinct advantage in harsh alpine environments. However, snowball saxifrage does not have recurved sepals, is usually found in drier soil, has a more ball-like inflorescence and has shorter, diamond-shaped leaves (thus the species name, *rhomboidea*). Compare with American bistort.

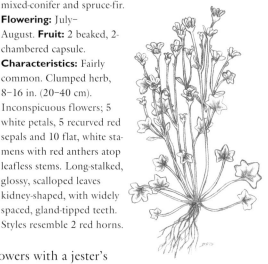

Snowball saxifrage

Brook Saxifrage
Saxifraga odontoloma
[*Micranthes odontoloma*]

Life zone/ecosystem: Upper montane to subalpine. Streambanks, wet meadows and seeps in aspen, mixed-conifer and spruce-fir.
Flowering: July–August. **Fruit:** 2 beaked, 2-chambered capsule.
Characteristics: Fairly common. Clumped herb, 8–16 in. (20–40 cm). Inconspicuous flowers; 5 white petals, 5 recurved red sepals and 10 flat, white stamens with red anthers atop leafless stems. Long-stalked, glossy, scalloped leaves kidney-shaped, with widely spaced, gland-tipped teeth. Styles resemble 2 red horns.

Delicate spires of tiny flowers with a jester's flair frolic above the scalloped leaves, often draped in mist from a cascading mountain stream. Lush brook saxifrage sometimes forms green, leafy mounds intertwined with the darker-green, more elongated foliage of bittercress, springing from old decaying logs and mossy soil midstream.

Weakstem saxifrage (*Saxifraga rivularis*) [*S. hyperborea subsp. debilis*] is a small, delicate plant of moist alpine ledges, slopes and rock crevices, no taller than 4 in. (10 cm); roundish leaves have 3–7 wide lobes. This pixie-like plant is easy to overlook.

Common Alumroot
Heuchera parvifolia
MEDICINAL

Life zone/ecosystem: Montane to alpine. Rocky slopes or outcrops. **Flowering:** May–August. **Fruit:** Multi-seeded capsule.
Characteristics: Uncommon. Averages 12 in. (30 cm). Tiny
white to greenish-white flowers, clustered atop leafless, erect
stems; styles and stamens shorter than petals. Long-stalked leaves
arise from base, mildly heart-shaped at base; roughly scalloped
margins. Large taproot; scaly brown surface.

Clumps of common alumroot display handsome, leathery leaves which are similar to those of
cultivated coral bells (*H. sanguinea*). The greens are edible, steamed or
boiled, but are quite sharp, sour and astringent due to the high tannin
content. Alum, a mouth-puckering additive used in pickling vegetables, is
probably the inspiration for this plant's common name. The Cherokee
drank a tea brewed from the plant roots for digestive complaints, hemorrhoids and diarrhea, and powdered the roots to treat ulcers and sores.
Herbalists today still use this powder as a styptic to stop minor bleeding.

**Flower of
common
mitrewort**

Side-Flowered Mitrewort
Mitella stauropetala var. *stenopetala*

Life zone/ecosystem: Upper montane to subalpine. Shady, moist places in spruce-fir stands.
Flowering: June–August. **Fruit:** Capsule.
Characteristics: Fairly common in suitable habitat.
Delicate herb, 4–16 in. (10–40 cm). White petals
divided into 3 linear segments about half their
length, resembling birds' feet; petals alternate with fused, petal-like sepals forming a shallow cup. Flowers dominate 1 side of unbranched, leafless
stem. Roundish, kidney-shaped,
long-stalked basal leaves, shallowly
lobed or toothed. Foliage usually mostly
hairy-glandular. Spreads by rhizomes.

Common mitrewort
(*M. pentandra*) has thread-
like greenish petals
resembling a tiny conifer's
skeleton, alternating with
5 triangular sepals.

With flowers like intricate
snowflakes, mitreworts are magical.
An excellent example of coevolution, side-
flowered mitrewort is the only host plant
for one of the oldest of all moth species, a
small Yucca moth, *Greya mitellae*. Feeding exclusively on the nectar of this slender plant, the female
moth also deposits her eggs in the stem, calyx or

201

flower-stalk tissue; during her nectar-seeking visits, she inadvertently pollinates flowers with her proboscis.[28] Like a miniscule bird's nest, mitrewort's fused sepals form a "splash cup" that holds the tiny seeds, which are dispersed by raindrops.

Fruit of common mitrewort

Spotted Saxifrage, Dotted Saxifrage

Saxifraga bronchialis
[*Ciliaria austromontana*]
GARDEN

Life zone/ecosystem: Montane to alpine. Cliffs, rocky places. **Flowering:** June–August. **Fruit:** Twin-beaked capsule. **Characteristics:** Fairly common. Evergreen, mat-forming herb, 2–6 in. (5–15 cm). White flowers with orange and dark red dots, suspended on reddish wiry stems above tiny rosettes of rigid, sharp-pointed leaves edged with bristly hairs.

Breaking through with delicate beauty, this moss-like mat cascades from rock crevices. Whether found perched precariously above a waterfall or hidden among rocky slopes, spotted saxifrage requires a closer look. The petals resemble china carefully painted with miniature violet-red and orange-yellow dots by a gifted hand. These colorful patterns act as nectar guides for pollinating insects. Easily started from seeds, spotted saxifrage is a charming rock garden plant.

Whiplash Saxifrage

Saxifraga flagellaris var. *crandallii*
[*Hirculus platysepalus*]

Life zone/ecosystem: Alpine. Moist, exposed and gravelly soil. **Flowering:** July–August. **Fruit:** Erect red capsules, 2-pronged top. **Characteristics:** Uncommon. Colonizing pygmy herb, 3–6 in. (4–15 cm). 1–3 flowers per stalk; 5 wedge-shaped, glistening-yellow petals per flower. Sepals and stems covered in gland-tipped hairs. Leaves rimmed with stiff gland-tipped hairs, mostly in basal rosette; stem leaves decrease in size moving up stem. Spreads by stolons (runners).

Like wild strawberry, whiplash saxifrage spreads vegetatively by stolons, elfin whips of red that conquer tiny obstacles in their path, colonizing even the tiniest pocket of bare soil near the mother plant. All foliage is cloaked with protective hairs, each tipped with a purplish-red gland, giving the leaves a jewel-like sparkle on sunny days. Once the tiny new rosettes have established firm roots, the "umbilical cord" disintegrates and they are on their own in the forbidding alpine climate.

Goldbloom saxifrage
(*S. chrysantha*), [*Hirculus serpyllifolius* subsp. *chrysanthus*] a yellow-flowered saxifrage of rocky tundra, has no stolons and is almost glabrous; leaf margins not ciliate.

SNAPDRAGON or FOXGLOVE FAMILY
Scrophulariaceae

Snapdragon's unique and colorful flowers are captivating and often, very unusual. The "scrophs" or "figworts"—as members of this family are often called—feature irregular flowers with united petals, 2 lobes up and 3 lobes down, and fruits that are many-seeded capsules. Their fascinating floral structures illustrate a number of specialized mechanisms for attracting pollinators, assuring pollination or encouraging cross-pollination:

- lower lips acting as landing pads for insects.
- various stripes, dots, colors or hairs acting as "nectar guides," leading pollinating insects from the outer lip to the nectar within.[29]
- infertile stamens covered in golden hairs (*Penstemon*).
- brightly colored bracts when actual flowers are inconspicuous (*Castilleja*).
- stigmas arranged so they touch the backs of visiting bees arriving with fresh pollen (*Linaria*).
- pollen that shakes easily onto a pollinator when it lands on the flower's lower lip (*Penstemon*).[30]

Many snapdragon flowers are so convoluted that "cheater" or "robber" insects bite right into the flowers to reach the nectar, completely bypassing the pollen. Many botanists, including Charles Darwin, have long believed these insects deplete the food available for actual pollinators and decrease the plant's reproductive success.[31] Although the issue is complex, Dr. David W. Inouye of the Rocky Mountain Biological Laboratory has shown that nectar robbers can have beneficial or neutral effects, sometimes acting as pollinators, too.[32]

In order to include the numerous species in this family, those of the larger genera, such as paintbrushes and penstemons, are listed here in the alternate format as groups and are alphabetical within the group.

Alpine Speedwell

Veronica wormskjoldii [*V. nutans*]

MEDICINAL

Life zone/ecosystem: Subalpine to alpine. Spruce-fir to tundra, streambanks and other moist to boggy soil. **Flowering:** July–August. **Fruit:** Glandular-hairy capsule. **Characteristics:** Unbranched herb, 4–16 in. (10–40 cm). Tiny, dark-blue flowers in compact terminal clusters above hairy-glandular foliage; 4 unequal petals, 2 stamens. Opposite, clasping leaves.

Legend has it that St. Veronica, offered Christ her handkerchief to wipe his brow on the road to Calvary. "Vera icon," meaning "true image," was the name the Church gave to this maiden because Christ's facial image was said to remain on the handkerchief. This genus was named in her honor as some species have markings that resemble a face. "Speedwell" alludes to the many medicinal uses credited to this plant, primarily for skin and respiratory problems.

American Speedwell, American Brooklime

Veronica americana

CEREMONIAL • EDIBLE • MEDICINAL

Life zone/ecosystem: Montane to subalpine. Wet soils, creeks and seeps. **Flowering:** May–August. **Fruit:** Smooth, flattened capsules. **Characteristics:** Fairly common. Trailing, multi-branched herb, 4–24 in. (10–60 cm). Pale violet, 4-petaled flowers with top lobe largest; 2 obvious, spreading stamens. Delicate curving flower stalks grow from opposite the leaf axils. Somewhat lance-shaped leaves are smooth, short-stalked and toothed.

When growing in clean water, this plant is a great emergency food. In parts of Europe and Japan, American speedwell is considered a delicacy in salads and served as a steamed green. It also makes a tea that is similar in taste to green tea. Being bitter, the herb may require a few changes of water during cooking. Historically, its main medicinal use was as an expectorant for respiratory problems. Navajo people used it as a ceremonial emetic, for purification purposes.

Blue-Eyed Mary, Blue Lips
Collinsia parviflora

Life zone/ecosystem: Montane. Aspen and mixed-conifer forest; tolerates moist or dry soil, shade or partial sun. **Flowering:** May–June. **Fruit:** Narrowly oval capsules. **Characteristics:** Fairly common. Delicate branched annual, usually less than 6 in. (15 cm). Blue flowers with white upper lobe; upper surface hump-backed; grow in leaf axils. Leaves narrowly lance-shaped; often strong purple to red tinge on stems and leaves.

Blue-eyed Mary's sky-blue flowers are bent at a slight angle to the stem as if listening to the latest gossip. Take a moment to lie on the ground and contemplate this intricate, tiny flower.

*Butter-and-Eggs, Yellow Toadflax
Linaria vulgaris

DYE • MEDICINAL • NOXIOUS WEED

Life zone/ecosystem: Montane. Aspen and mixed-conifer stands, disturbed soil of roadsides and trailsides, moist or dry. **Flowering:** June–September. **Fruit:** Round capsule. **Characteristics:** Common. Extremely aggressive non-native, 8–24 in. (20–60 cm). Clustered yellow flowers with orange lower lip resemble familiar garden snapdragons; fragrance bland to sweet. Alternate leaves narrow and pale green, pointed on both ends. Extensive underground root system of creeping rhizomes; also reproduces by seed.

Butter-and-eggs is a beautiful plant that has been revered for centuries in Europe for fabric dyes and medicinal uses. Some herbalists still recommend it for liver conditions. Although introduced into North America in the late 1600's as an ornamental and for folk medicine, local land managers now consider this species to be one of Colorado's worst threats to native plant diversity. Butterflies throng to butter-and-eggs to drink its sweet nectar, which is often visible in the tip of the spur when held up to the light.

KATHERINE DARROW

BARBARA MAGNUSON/LARRY KIMBALL

Goldtongue Owlclover

Orthocarpus luteus

DYE

Life zone/ecosystem: Montane to subalpine. Oak-mountain shrub-lands to spruce-fir, moist or dry soil. **Flowering:** July–August. **Fruit:** Capsule of many seeds. **Characteristics:** Uncommon. Skinny, unbranched annual, 4–12 in. (10–30 cm). Yellow tubular flowers with inflated lower lip, upper lip surrounding 4 stamens; flowers crowded near top of stem, interspersed with green to dark-reddish, leafy, 3–5-lobed bracts. Finely-haired foliage. Hemiparasite.

Owlclovers occur all over the West, with this species being the most common. Although goldtongue owlclover easily tolerates variable moisture and occurs where sparse plant life offers little competition, it also obtains some of its nutrition by slender taproots that attach and draw nutri-ents from other plants. Blackfoot tribes pressed its crushed leaves into feathers, skins and horsehair to dye them red.

James' Snowlover

Chionophila jamesii

GARDEN

Life zone/ecosystem: Alpine. Snowbank communi-ties, gravelly soil. **Flowering:** July–early August. **Fruit:** Capsule. **Characteristics:** Uncommon. Distinctive herb, 2–4 in. (5–10 cm). Greenish-white to soft cream-colored flowers, 1-sided on stem, flattened horizontal-ly—typical only of this genus. 5 stamens, one shorter and without anther. Leathery basal leaves suggestive of small rabbit ears; stem leaves more slender. Stem usual-ly minutely hairy. Found in similar locations, **Tweedy's snowlover** (*C. tweedyi*) is more delicate, with slender, flattened, pink to lavender flowers; also 1-sided on stem.

Each curiously flattened flower of this snowlover is suggestive of one of the long slender slippers worn by the gawky Ichabod Crane in "The Legend of Sleepy Hollow." Snowlover's leathery-leafed rosettes turn a warm salmon red in autumn, brightening the barren landscape. Found only in the Rocky Mountains, James' snowlover was first discovered on Pike's Peak in 1821 by Edwin James (see p. 181). *Chionophila* is Greek for "snow beloved." Adventurous gardeners may want to try planting snowlover, as seeds are now available through specialty catalogs.

Lance-leaf Figwort, Hare Figwort

Scrophularia lanceolata
MEDICINAL

Life zone/ecosystem: Montane. Ravines and trailside.
Flowering: June–July. **Fruit:** Round capsule. **Characteristics:**
Uncommon. Handsome but rangy herb, often taller than 3 ft. (1
m). Tiny greenish to reddish-brown, 2-lipped flowers, like miniature penstemons; upper 2 lobes fused and middle lobe of the
lower lip bent downward; of 5 stamens, 4 are functional and 1
reduced to a teensy scale attached to roof of upper lip. Triangular
leaves are coarsely toothed, opposite on short stalks that wrap
around square stem (like mints); cluster of small leaves may occur
where leaf stalk meets stem.

Wildflower enthusiasts often overlook this inconspicuous flower and the foliage is easily overshad-
owed by the lush undergrowth in aspen forests.
Figworts have a rich history of medicinal uses. A salve made from
lance-leaf figwort's foliage is believed to decrease premenstrual
breast pain and soothe hemorrhoids, vaginal irritations, cracked
skin and diaper rash.[33] Other figwort species have been used to
make mild anti-inflammatory salves and tinctures for low-grade
skin irritations, arthritis and swollen lymph nodes. Iroquois people drank an infusion of the roots to prevent colds and cramps after
childbirth and prepared a poultice from the plant for sunburn, sun-
stroke and burns.

Lousewort, Wood Betony Group

Pedicularis spp.

SUBSET OF SNAPDRAGON FAMILY   MEDICINAL • WILDLIFE

It was believed that animals grazing on marsh lousewort (*P. palustris*)
became infested with lice—hence the genus name *Pedicularis*, which translates as "little louse." Conversely, heads and wigs were once powdered with
Pedicularis to repel lice. Louseworts are often named after the animals their
peculiar petal arrangements mimic. These whimsical flowers
usually invite very specific mechanisms of pollination insects or sometimes hummingbirds.
Scientists classify most louseworts as hemiparasites (see p. 211), so they may be difficult, if not
impossible, to cultivate in your garden without
their needed host plants. Modern herbalists prescribe lousewort as a mild sedative and muscu-
loskeletal relaxant, especially for muscle strains
and twitches. The roots, tender spring foliage
and flowers can be used as survival food (raw or
cooked). The young flowers of several species are
consumed by wildlife.

USE CAUTION if using
louseworts for medicine or
food, for they can absorb
toxins from nearby plants.
For example, louseworts
growing with *Senecio* spp.
are known to contain their
toxic alkaloids.

Alpine Lousewort

Pedicularis sudtica subsp. *scopulorum*
[*P. scopulorum*]

Upper subalpine to alpine. Wet meadows in spruce-fir, moist alpine tundra. Flowers July–August. Uncommon. 4–8 in. (10–20 cm). Rose-colored flowers with hooded upper lip; lacks slender, upcurved beak of similar elephantella; crowded into short spikes, interspersed with cobwebby bracts (occasionally smoother). Typical Pedicularis fern-like leaves.

Bracted Lousewort

Pedicularis bracteosa

Subalpine to lower alpine. Moist, sometimes shady forest openings or meadows. Flowers June–August. Fairly common. 12–24 in. (30–60 cm). Stem smooth below flowers. Yellow, occasionally red-tinged flowers with hooded upper lip, style exposed; lacks upturned beak; packed in dense, often cobwebby spike among leafy bracts. Fern-like leaves mostly on stem, with individual toothed leaflets, unlike Parry's lousewort that has only comb-like lobes. Stems used in some Native American basket design.

Elephantella, Elephant-head

Pedicularis groenlandica

Montane to alpine. Boggy meadows, streambanks. Flowers June–August. Common. 6–24 in. (15–60 cm). Striking magenta "elephant heads" crowded in spike-like racemes; upper petal and curved beak resemble head and trunk, lower petals the ears and lower jaw. Fern-like leaves. Known hemiparasite of arrowleaf groundsel (Senecio triangularis), which indicates that leaves of this plant could also be toxic. Elk eat the flowers. Species name, groenlandica, means "of Greenland" where the plant supposedly originated. Ironically, elephantella is not found in Greenland.

Giant Lousewort

Pedicularis procera [*P. grayi*]

Montane. Aspen, mixed-conifer forest, moist soil. Flowers July–August. Common. Averages 3 ft. (1 m). Deer and elk nip off flower heads, leaving headless stems often mistaken for ferns. Red-streaked, somewhat dingy yellow or greenish to white, beakless flowers.

Parrot's Beak, Ram's horn, Curly Lousewort

Pedicularis race- mosa var. *alba*

Subalpine. Spruce-fir, dry soil. Flowers June–August. Common. 8–20 in. (20–50 cm). Lustrous, creamy-white flowers with curved, sickle-shaped beaks/horns. Coarsely toothed leaves tinged with red. Obvious clumps when blooming; hemiparasitic on firs and spruce.

Parry's Lousewort

Pedicularis parryi

Subalpine to alpine. Spruce-fir to tundra, dry/gravelly soil. Flowers July–September. Common. 4–16 in. (10–40 cm). White to yellowish (possibly pinkish) flowers; hooded upper petals resemble the profile of a Canada goose. Calyx lobes usually streaked with dark red. Leaves mostly basal and fern-like, with only narrow toothed lobes from winged central rib, not divided into leaflets; reddish stem with reduced leaves. Hemiparasitic on golden banner and chokecherry.

END OF LOUSEWORT GROUP

SNAPDRAGON FAMILY *continued*

Monkeyflower
Mimulus guttatus
EDIBLE • MEDICINAL • WILDLIFE

Life zone/ecosystem: Montane to alpine. Mucky areas, streams, seeps and springs. **Flowering:** June–August. **Fruit:** Oblong capsule. **Characteristics:** Common. Showy annual or perennial, averaging 8 in. (20 cm). Bright yellow tubular, 2-lipped flowers greater than 0.75 in. (1.9 cm) long; 2 upper and 3 lower lobes; lower, fuzzy throat with reddish-brown spots. Inflated calyx with pointed teeth. Square stems; opposite, somewhat oval leaves with coarsely toothed margins; no underground stems. **Subalpine monkeyflower** (*M. tilingii*), found in the same habitats and once considered the same species, is shorter, with larger flowers and sod-forming underground stems.

Along the trail, whimsical monkeyflower is nestled in a carpet of lush green moss, dripping with spray from the mountain stream. It has an ingenious pollination mechanism. Bumblebees land on the flower's protruding lower lip, crawl over the raised furry patch and follow the spotted "guide" to nectar within. Each 2-parted stigma closes when touched, trapping pollen deposited from the bumblebee's back. This prevents the flower from fertilizing itself as the insect backs out. If no pollen is captured, the stigma lobes reopen.[34] Native people of California and Arizona made monkeyflower a part of their daily lives as cooked greens, a source of salt, stomachache cure, crushed-leaf poultice for wounds and rope burn and a decoction in steam baths for sore backs. A Bach Flower Remedy of monkeyflower is sold for nervous conditions in pets. **Monkeyflower concentrates selenium from the soil, so Colorado may not be a safe place to eat this plant**; however, deer, elk, bighorn sheep, and even muskrats do eat it.

*Mullein
Verbascum thapsus
MEDICINAL • WILDLIFE

Life zone/ecosystem: Montane. Disturbed soil. **Flowering:** June–August. **Fruit:** Woolly capsules. **Characteristics:** Common. Non-native weed. Woolly biennial reaching 5 ft. (1.5 m). Torch-like clusters of yellow flowers with 5 open lobes. Woolly, rabbit-ear-like leaves in basal rosette first year, then also alternately clasping stem the second year.

Mullein is a familiar roadside weed introduced from Europe. Standing tall above the snow, its dried seed pods are a bountiful source of food for winter birds. Popular as a medicinal, mullein is used to treat asthma, hay fever, bronchitis and dry coughs. The leaves are, even now, smoked to relax the bronchial passages during the onset of infection, used as a base for smoking mixtures or powdered for use in wounds. **Mullein tea might irritate the throat if the hairs are not removed by straining, and the FDA warns that mullein should be used sparingly because it contains coumarin and rotenone.**

Paintbrush Group

Castilleja spp.

SUBSET OF SNAPDRAGON FAMILY

EDIBLE • MEDICINAL • WILDLIFE

Displaying all the shades of sunset, the flamboyant spires of paintbrush embellish our mountain meadows with a kaleidoscope of bright blooms. Flashy colorful bracts, or modified leaves, attract pollinators to the slender, lime-green flowers that remain tucked out of sight until maturity. Each flower is strongly 2-lipped, with the long upper lip enclosing 4 stamens. Although having little fragrance, they produce lots of sweet nectar—which was appreciated by Native Americans and settlers, who bit off the ends of individual flowers for the sweetness. Botanists theorize that paintbrushes and hummingbirds evolved together, as the birds are attracted by bright colors, have few taste buds and almost no sense of smell, but require copious amounts of nectar to support their active metabolism.

Although capable of making the majority of their food through photosynthesis, paintbrushes maintain hemiparasitic connections with lupine, sagebrush and members of the sunflower family—a trait that makes it possible for them to survive drought and extend their normal range. Various native tribes used paintbrush root decoctions as an emetic, contraceptive, cure for stomachaches and menstrual difficulties and for decreasing baby size for easier delivery. Paintbrush is a valuable source of food for deer, elk, small mammals and blue grouse.

HEMIPARASITES

Many plants—including paintbrush, elephantella, and toadflax—are hemiparasites, meaning they derive some of their nutrients, water and even chemical defenses from other plants by means of siphoning structures in their roots (haustoria). Unlike total parasites, hemiparasites have green leaves and can manufacture some or all of their own nourishment by photosynthesis, making it possible for them to live without their host plants.

Hemiparasites can also function as biochemical "bridges" between their host plants, which produce an array of defensive chemicals, and insect or mammal browsers that would not otherwise feed on that host plant to have access to those chemicals. For example, checkerspot butterflies lay their eggs only on specific plants, such as Indian paintbrush. Their main defense against bird predation comes from chemicals ingested as larvae while feeding on paintbrushes that have derived the protective chemicals from other plants, such as sagebrush. This biochemical bridge provides protection for many species against predators that would otherwise devour them.[35]

Paintbrush Group
Castilleja spp.

Narrowleaf Paintbrush
Castilleja linariifolia

Montane. Oak-mountain shrublands. Flowers July–August. Common. Usually branched, 18-36 in. (45–90 cm). Scarlet bracts often less conspicuous than the scarlet, finely-haired calyx and more deeply cut in front (below) than in back (above). Upper leaves divided into 3 very narrow lobes, lower leaves linear; all with 1 main vein; bracts usually deeply lobed.

Northern Paintbrush, Sulfur Paintbrush
Castilleja sulphurea

Montane to subalpine. Moist slopes and meadows in aspen, mixed-conifer and spruce-fir forest. Flowers June–August. Common. Usually more than 8 in. (20 cm). Occasionally branched. Pale-yellow spikes; lower lip of flower a green bump. Hybridizes with rosy paintbrush.

Rosy Paintbrush
Castilleja rhexifolia

Subalpine. Spruce-fir clearings and moist meadows. Flowers July–August. Common. Rosy-pink to magenta bracts covered with soft hairs, some shallowly lobed; leaves mostly without lobes. Such a beautiful contrast with the reds, blues, and yellows of midsummer subalpine meadows.

Fairly common hybrid between rosy paintbrush and northern paintbrush

Scarlet Paintbrush
Castilleja miniata

Montane to lower subalpine. Moist aspen and mixed-conifer forests. Flowers May-September. Common. 6-24 in. (15-60 cm). Some red/scarlet bracts with lobes more than half their length. Typically unbranched. Leaves may be lobed, but only very shallowly; noticeably wider than narrowleaf paintbrush.

Western Yellow Paintbrush
Castilleja occidentalis

Upper subalpine to alpine. Flowers July–August. Common. 2–8 in. (5–20 cm). Conspicuously fuzzy clumps of pale-yellow (may vary) spikes with reddish, unbranched stems. Western yellow paintbrush is a common ingredient in a pika's haypile (p. 385-386).

Penstemon Group
Penstemon spp.

SUBSET OF SNAPDRAGON FAMILY

GARDEN • WILDLIFE

Some of our most gorgeous local wildflowers are penstemons. Their tubular flowers trumpet showy displays in vivid jewel-tones of blue, purple, pink, magenta, red, white and yellow. Penstemons can thrive on roadsides and other inhospitable habitats—even in dense clay—flourishing with lots of sunshine and good drainage. With more than 250 species of perennial herbs and shrubs, this is the largest genus of flowering plants native to North America and one that is still actively evolving—closely related species in the same vicinity readily hybridize. An enormous number of species, subspecies and varieties makes exact identification often exasperating even for professional botanists.

All penstemons share similar traits. Each 2-lipped "trumpet" is formed from 5 fused petals flaring to 2 lobes above and 3 lobes below; 4 regular fertile stamens, 1 pair attached on the lower corolla wall and the other attached on either side of the ovary. Two anthers tip each stamen, splitting open at maturity in a multitude of ways, offering botanists technical charac-

Bumblebees in search of nectar and pollen often become immobile as temperatures drop at dusk and may still be headfirst in a flower at dawn.

213

ters for classifying diverse varieties. The staminode (sterile stamen) is attached on the upper wall, often wearing a bristly beard at the tip, generating another common name—beardtongue. Stigmas of penstemons do not bend to receive pollen from visiting pollinators until the flower is ready for fertilization, preventing self-fertilization. Pollinators include bees, wasps, butterflies, moths, flies and hummingbirds. The leaves are usually in opposite pairs and the ovary matures into a dry, 2-chambered capsule.

In *Northwest Penstemons,* Dr. Dee Strickler writes that the prefix *pen* means "almost," and combines with *stamen* to mean "almost a stamen," referring to the sterile 5th stamen that is characteristic of penstemons. This corresponds to the first description of the genus *Penstemon* by Mitchell in 1748 and contradicts a later belief that the derivation came from the Greek *pente* ("five").

Native Americans and pioneers prepared powders, poultices, ointments, suppositories and teas from penstemon for wounds, burns and coughs and also to treat sick or injured animals. Penstemons reproduce easily by seed when grown under conditions similar to their wild habitat.

Mat Penstemon
Penstemon caespitosus

Oak-mountain shrublands, thrives in clay on south-facing hillsides. Flowers in early spring. Common. Typically a low mat less than 6 in. (15 cm) high, but is variable; can be loosely erect.

Osterhout's Beardtongue
Penstemon ousterhoutii

Roadsides, oak-mountain shrublands, thrives in clay. Flowers in late spring. Common. Averages 16 in. (40 cm). Large lavender clumps brighten Brush Creek Road in late spring. Bearded, expanded staminode only barely protruding, or not at all; same holds true for active stamens. Anther sacs spread widely apart at maturity. Pale-green leaves broadly lance-shaped, clasp stem at narrower end; decrease in size upward. **Harrington's beardtongue** (*P. harringtonii*) is similar, except flowers are in looser spikes and 2 stamens clearly protrude past the petals. Harrington's beardtongue is considered vulnerable and threatened in Colorado.

Rocky Mountain Penstemon
Penstemon strictus

Oak-mountain shrublands. Flowers in midsummer. Common. Tall, straight herb up to 3 ft. (90 cm). Glowing lavender or blue-purple flowers; hairy anthers. Smooth, narrow stem leaves, lance-shaped basal leaves. Great for gardens; available commercially. Photo on right.

Subglaborous Penstemon, Smooth Penstemon
Penstemon subglaber

Oak-mountain shrublands. Flowers in early summer. Uncommon. Averages 15 in. (38 cm). Flowers deeper blue-purple than other local penstemons; arranged on 1 side of stem. Staminode with short golden hairs; anthers completely open at maturity, with short hairs. Calyx tips very thin and pointed; scattered glandular hairs. Narrow lanceolate leaves glabrous with wavy margins; upper leaves clasp stem; lower leaves petiolate.

Whipple's Penstemon, Purple Beardtongue
Penstemon whippleanus

Montane to alpine. Open areas and rocky slopes. Flowers in midsummer. Fairly common. Grows to 2 ft. (60 cm). Glandular-hairy flowers, deep red-purple to wine-burgundy (rarely white); bearded staminode. Glandular hairs make flowers really sparkle in sunlight.

ST. JOHN'S WORT FAMILY   *Hypericaceae [Clusiaceae]*

This family has received much recognition as an alternative to Prozac and other antidepressants. There are only three genera, with 356 species worldwide. Hypericaceae is sometimes considered a subfamily of the mangosteen family (Guttiferae). The yellow (sometimes pinkish) flowers typically have 5 petals with many stamens in tight clusters. The leaves are opposite, untoothed and dotted with glands.

Western St. John's Wort
Hypericum formosum

Life zone/ecosystem: Montane to subalpine. Wet meadows, stream-banks. **Flowering:** July–August. **Fruit:** Translucent capsules. **Characteristics:** Uncommon. Delicate herb, 8–12 in. (20–30 cm). Copious stamens extend beyond 5 soft cadmium-yellow petals; buds tinged rosy-red. Egg-shaped opposite leaves, 5 calyx lobes, 5 petals. Petals at least rimmed with glandular dots. Single stems usually branched near top; flowers terminating each stem. **Common St. John's wort** (*H. perforatum*) is an aggressive weed introduced from Europe. Flower has 70–100 stamens in 3–5 bundles. Lance-shaped leaves; slightly shrubby and multi-branched with profusion of flowers. Favors moist, disturbed soil.

St. John's wort has been a staple of folk medicine for at least 3,000 years, and has been used to treat "melancholia" since the Middle Ages. Medical studies have confirmed that St. John's wort is effective in treating mild to moderate depression and anxiety and may combat old-age dementias. Research is in progress regarding its general anti-viral properties and its efficacy against HIV.[36] In *Medicinal Plants of the Pacific West*, Michael Moore notes that fresh preparations of the herb are superior and that western St. John's wort has only half the potency of the common species. The oil is used topically for muscle and nerve pain (sciatica, back spasms), wounds, burns and hemorrhoids. Pregnant women or young children should avoid this herb, which was once used to induce abortions.

The flowers of St. John's wort bloom around St. John's Eve (June 24). People of some religious traditions believe that the red glandular spots on the petals represent the blood shed at the beheading of John the Baptist, while the translucent spots on the leaves represent his tears.

STAFFTREE FAMILY   *Celastraceae*

Members of this fairly large family of tropical to temperate shrubs, trees and vines display quite a bit of variation regarding stamen, fruit and seed characteristics. *Catha, Celastrus, Elaeodendron* and *Euonymus* are genera cultivated as ornamentals and *Maytenus* is a genus containing a toxic alkaloid that research indicates may be helpful in treating colon cancer.[37] Only one family member, mountainlover (*Paxistima myrsinites*), occurs in our area.

Mountainlover, Oregon Boxwood

Puxistima myrsinites

GARDEN · WILDLIFE

Life zone/ecosystem: Montane to subalpine. Tolerates dry to moist soil, sun or shade; needs cool sites. **Flowering:** May–July. **Fruit:** 1–2-seeded capsule. **Characteristics:** Common. Densely branched evergreen shrub, 8–24 in. (20–60 cm). Inconspicuous pink to reddish flowers of 4 petals alternating with yellow stamens, tucked in leaf axils. Opposite leaves are smooth and lanceolate with toothed edges above the middle. Compare with kinnikinnik, or bearberry, which has similar leaves with smooth edges.

Mountainlover is a fairly ubiquitous member of the understory vegetation in local montane and subalpine forests, but can also be found in forest openings and shrublands. Mountainlover provides valuable forage for mule deer and elk and is also browsed by bighorn sheep and grouse. The seeds are apparently spread only by gravity. Gardeners should try this handsome species in appropriate settings—the stems layer and root easily and root cuttings can be used to revegetate disturbed ground.

STONECROP FAMILY   *Crassulaceae*

Cascades of "hens-and-chicks" plants (*Sempervivum*), with their continuous rows of plump succulent leaves, tumble from the crevices of many a greenhouse. Members of the stonecrop family are usually succulent herbs and shrubs. Many of them, such as the omnipresent kalanchoes, are cultivated as houseplants. Their regularly symmetrical flowers are bisexual and typically have 4–5 petals and sepals, though sometimes 30 of each instead; 1–2 whorls of stamens, with the number of stamens in each whorl equaling the number of petals; and an ovary of 3 or more simple pistils. Each leaf readily starts a new plant. Stonecrops are found from tropical to arctic regions, usually in arid habitats. They photosynthesize in a modified way that enables their stomata to remain closed during the day—definitely an adaptation which reduces water loss in dry regions.

Young leaves and stems of the three local species are edible raw or cooked, especially before they flower and turn bitter. Succulent and containing vitamin A and C, young leaves of these plants can serve as a good emergency food and source of moisture. **Eating too much, especially mature leaves, can cause nausea.** Gardeners love the ease of growing cultivated *Sedum* varieties for their colorful flowers, unusual leaves and beautiful fall colors.

King's crown, Roseroot

Sedum integrifolium

[*Rhodiola integrifolia, S. rosea* var. *integrifolium*]

EDIBLE • MEDICINAL

Life zone/ecosystem: Upper subalpine to alpine. Moist rocky tundra, ridges or talus slopes, lake shores or streambanks. **Flowering:** July–August. **Fruit:** Erect capsules (follicles). **Characteristics:** Fairly common. Blue-green-tinged, succulent plant, 2–12 in. (5–30 cm). Flattened stems terminate in small, deep-red (rarely greenish-purple), 5-petaled flowers in flat to somewhat domed clusters. Flowers may be staminate or pistillate, or bisexual—all on same plant. Alternate, flat, fleshy, egg-shaped leaves; may have whitish coating; no grooves on upper surface. Scaly underground rhizomes.

King's crown is heady stuff—its fresh flowers glow like rubies and the smoky blue-green foliage turns an impressive salmon red in autumn. Many variations of king's crown exist, from the northern Yukon south to Colorado and California. Eskimos eat the foliage raw or fermented and make a beverage of the flowering tops.[38] Mucilaginous and mildly astringent, the plant also has medicinal uses. Eskimos chewed the roots, spitting out the juice when they had mouth sores and the Dena'ina Athabascans people of Alaska still use leaf teas and root decoctions for colds, sore throats and as a wash for sore eyes.[39] The roots have a scent similar to roses.

Queen's crown

Sedum rhodanthum [*Clementsia rhodantha*]

EDIBLE • MEDICINAL

Life zone/ecosystem: Upper subalpine and lower alpine. Moist rocky tundra, ridges or talus slopes, lake shores or stream banks. **Flowering:** June–August. **Fruit:** Capsule (follicle). **Characteristics:** Fairly common. Succulent herb, 4–14 in. (10–35 cm). Rose to whitish flowers attached where leaf meets flattened stem, creating an elongated cluster. Leaves alternate and grooved to the tip on upper surfaces. Foliage turns imposing orange-red in fall.

Succulent, rose-colored queen's crown often grows alongside king's crown, though usually at the lower end of the latter's range. Edible and medicinal uses are similar to those of yellow stonecrop.

Yellow Stonecrop
Sedum lanceolatum
[*Amerosedum lanceolatum*]
EDIBLE • GARDEN

Life zone/ecosystem: Montane to alpine. Rocky or gravelly soils of open areas. **Flowering:** June–August. **Fruit:** Capsule. **Characteristics:** Common. Succulent herb, 2–8 in. (5–20 cm). Sunny-yellow, star-like flowers sit atop thin leafy stems originating in densely clustered rosettes. Leaves are roundish with blunt tips, often reddish; may have a whitish coating.

Golden like sunshine, these bright stars are tucked in every nook and cranny of rocky ground at all elevations. Yellow stonecrop's reddish-bronze rosettes are attractive long after the flowers fade. Both foliage and flowers of this species are considered the best of the *Sedums* for survival food.

SUNFLOWER (or COMPOSITE) FAMILY
Asteraceae

Sunflower family members are called "composites," because they are composed of many tiny flowers (florets) crowded into a compact head (see Glossary, Fig. 4). When plucking one "petal" at a time to determine whether he/she loves you or not, each petal is actually an entire flower! An interesting evolutionary development, this compaction allows much-reduced flowers to become more visible to pollinating insects, primarily flies and beetles. When cutting a typical sunflower-style composite apart, there will be two different flower types. Tube-shaped disc florets in the center and ray (or strap) florets around the outside which simulate petals. Some composite flowers, such as dandelions, contain all ray florets, whereas others, like thistles, have all disc florets. Each floret is equipped with its own reproductive parts to produce a single seed, contained within a dry fruit called an achene or capsela, as in a snack package of sunflower seeds. A series of leafy bracts, called an involucre, at the base of each flower head assumes the role of a calyx. Attached to the base of each floret is usually a pappus, or modified calyx—a feature often used in technical keys to separate species. If present, the pappus may consist of soft hairs, stiff bristles, scales or a crown and may sometimes remain atop the ripe fruit. Composites are known for creative seed dispersal mechanisms, as illustrated by the parachute-like pappus of dandelion, or the velcro-like involucre of burdock. Such tactics help them thrive as colonizers of disturbed ground.

Extremely successful and pervasive, composites are the largest plant family in the world, with about 24,000 species. Huge variations within species, along with a preponderance of yellow flowers, have led those struggling with identification to call them semi-affectionately "DYC's" or "damned yellow composites." Fossil evidence suggests that composites originated only about 30 million years ago in South America. Since then, they have experienced an explosive radiation and diversification into most ecosystems, on every continent except Antarctica.

The composite family includes such economically important plants as lettuce, Jerusalem artichokes and sunflowers, medicinal plants such as echinacea and chamomile and ornamentals like chrysanthemum, zinnia, marigold and dahlia. A variety of insecticides and industrial chemicals are also produced from composites, including pyrethrum, derived from chrysanthemum and natural rubber, from the bark of the guayule plant.

Alpine Sunflower, Old-Man-of-the-Mountain

Tetraneuris grandiflora

[*Rydbergia* or *Hymenoxys grandiflora*]

Life zone/ecosystem: Alpine. Rocky, gravelly tundra. **Flowering:** July–August. **Fruit:** 5-sided achene. **Characteristics:** Fairly common. Woolly herb, 1–12 in. (2.5–30 cm). Large, bright-yellow flowers of both disc and ray florets. Leaves finely divided into very narrow lobes; leaves, stems and involucre all covered with woolly hairs.

Bouquets of these showy golden heads appear like giants in the Lilliputian alpine world. Poised upright in unison to face the rising sun, they are often referred to as "compass flower." Year after year, the woolly leaves of alpine sunflower sally forth to weather the elements, storing food and energy from the sun. Finally, after several years—how many is not yet known—they bloom, set seed and die. Every few years, a grand exhibition occurs when hundreds of alpine sunflowers bloom at the same time, creating drifts of gold across the tundra.

Arnica Group

Arnica spp.

SUBSET OF SUNFLOWER FAMILY

MEDICINAL • WILDLIFE

Arnicas cast a sunny spell wherever they are encountered. The local species have 2–4 pairs of opposite simple leaves. Hybridization makes this a somewhat confusing genus; however, they all have the typical sunflower appearance (except for Parry's arnica) and the distinct tiny petals of each disc floret have a ruffled appearance. Europeans and Native Americans have long appreciated the medicinal value of these herbs. More recently, research has revealed that they owe their anti-inflammatory, analgesic and somewhat antibiotic properties to chemicals called lactones. Salves, creams and tinctures of arnica (most commonly of *Arnica montana*) are used to treat bruises, sprains, muscle aches, acne, rheumatic pain, inflammation due to insect bites and swelling from fractures. Homeopathic uses are similar.

Daffodil Arnica, Clumped Arnica
Arnica latifolia

Subalpine. Spruce-fir. Moist soil, often disturbed or burned areas. Flowers July–August. Fairly common. Clump-forming herb, 3–24 in. (7–60 cm). Taller than heart-leafed arnica, with most stem leaves sessile, somewhat heart-shaped. Flower heads may nod. Involucre with only few, or no long hairs. Achenes usually smooth below, hairy or glandular-hairy elsewhere.

Subalpine Arnica
Arnica mollis

Subalpine. Spruce-fir. Flowers July–August. Fairly common. 3–24 in. (7–60 cm). Ray florets more blunt-tipped than in heart-leafed or daffodil arnicas. Pappus definitely brownish, not whitish, and somewhat feathery. Flower heads a bit orange-yellow, sometimes sticky. Achenes hairy or glandular all over, not smooth at base. Leaves somewhat lance-shaped, not mostly heart-shaped as in daffodil arnica.

Heartleaf Arnica
Arnica cordifolia

Montane to subalpine. Dry forests, especially spruce-fir. Flowers May–August. Common. 8–18 in. (20–45 cm). Sunny yellow flower heads on stem with one pair of sessile upper leaves, lower stem leaves petiolate; long-stalked basal leaves, heart-shaped and on separate short shoots. Involucre with long hairs near base. Stems and leaves covered with soft, sometimes glandular hairs. Hairs of white pappus have tiny barbs. Achene with short, stiff hairs. Able to produce seeds without fertilization; also spreads by underground rhizomes, producing colonies of offspring genetically identical to parents. Mule deer graze on this species.

Parry's Arnica, Rayless Arnica
Arnica parryi

Montane to subalpine. Open meadows, mostly in aspen, mixed-conifer and spruce-fir forests. Flowers July–August. Fairly common. 12–20 in. (30–50 cm). Flower head with disc florets only, often nodding when young. Flower stalks possibly very hairy and glandular just below flower head. Stem leaves opposite. Green involucral bracts glandular near tips. Compare with Bigelow groundsel, see p. 244.

Seed heads of Parry's arnica

END OF ARNICA GROUP   SUNFLOWER FAMILY *continued*

Arrowleaf Balsamroot
Balsamorhiza sagittata
EDIBLE • MEDICINAL • WILDLIFE

Life zone/ecosystem: Montane. Oak-mountain shrublands and sagebrush shrublands. **Flowering:** May–June. **Fruit:** 3- or 4-sided hairless achene. **Characteristics:** Common. Long-lived herb, 9–24 in. (20–60 cm). Bright yellow, sunflower-like heads on leafless stems; large, arrow-shaped basal leaves, silver-gray; dense covering of fine white hairs. Opposite stem leaves. No pappus.

Balsamroot creates a striking display of green and gold spring color just before mule's ears have reached their peak. Pre-emergent shoots, roots and seeds were eaten by various Native American tribes—the woody roots pit-cooked for twenty-four hours or more to produce a sweet, brownish treat. Peeled flower budstalks taste pleasantly nutty, raw or roasted, and the fruits can be roasted and powdered, hull and all. With chemical properties similar to echinacea, balsamroot is considered a mild stimulant to the immune system. A poultice or salve of dried and powdered leaves is effective in treating mild burns or chronic skin sores. Mule deer and bighorn sheep seem to prefer the flowering heads, but will also consume tender spring foliage.

Aspen Sunflower, Little Sunflower

Helianthella quinquenervis

Life zone/ecosystem: Mid-montane to lower subalpine. Aspen and spruce-fir. **Flowering:** July–August. **Fruit:** Flattened achene. **Characteristics:** Common. Nodding, rough-hairy herb, 2–4.5 ft. (60–140 cm). "Sunflowers" of light-yellow ray florets and darker-yellow to brownish-red disc florets, surrounded by leafy involucres of many overlapping bracts. Leaves tapered on each end, prominently 5-veined. Erect stems often in clumps. Pappus of short scales and 2 slender awns. **Common sunflower** (*Helianthus annuus*) a similar plant that grows along trails and roadsides, is a stout weedy plant with large leaves.

Ants gleaning nectar from involucre

At the Rocky Mountain Biological Lab in Gothic, Colorado, Dr. David Inouye has discovered that nectar secreted by special glands on the involucre of aspen sunflower is collected by ants, who in return protect the plant from herb-chewing insects and seed predators. He has proven that seed loss in plants not protected by these ant guards is at least 80% higher. An aspen sunflower plant lives about forty years.

Aster and Daisy Group   *Aster, Erigeron* and *Machaeranthera* spp.

SUBSET OF SUNFLOWER FAMILY   **GARDEN • WILDLIFE**

A dizzy profusion of lavender, pink and purple sunflower-like plants bloom throughout the summer and fall. The following photos and explanations of general characteristics and blooming times should help differentiate between the most common local species of this group, which are from three separate genera. Accurate identification depends on considering all of the characteristics together, as any one character may vary. Chipmunks, grouse, turkeys and birds eat the seeds and leaves, while rabbits and mule deer eat the leaves.

Asters (*Aster*)

- white, bluish, rose, violet or purple ray flowers.
- disc flowers possibly yellow to red or purple, sometimes whitish.
- stems more leafy than in *Erigeron* (next page).
- bloom late summer and fall.
- ray flowers fewer and broader; typically more flower heads per stem.
- involucre bracts (phyllaries) in 2 overlapping (imbricate) rows; leafier than *Erigeron*.
- pappus of white or tawny soft bristles.

Fleabanes and mountain daisies (*Erigeron*)
- white, pink or purple rays.
- disc flowers yellow or occasionally red.
- mostly perennial, bloom spring and early summer.
- narrow and more numerous ray flowers.
- 1–5 heads per flower stem.
- involucre bracts (phyllaries) in only 1–2 rows, narrow, often equal in height, rarely overlapping.
- pappus of fine hairs.

Tansy-asters (*Machaeranthera*)
- involucre bracts overlapping and curved outward.

Engelmann Aster

Aster engelmannii
[*Eucephalus engelmannii*]

Montane to subalpine. Spruce-fir and aspen forests. Flowers July–September. Common. Robustly elegant herb, up to 5 ft. (1.5 m). Sparse whitish to pinkish ray florets appear slightly awry, not orderly as in other asters. Involucre bracts papery and reddish. Obviously ribbed stems with many large, stalkless, lance-shaped leaves, not clasping stem.

Dwarf subalpine variety with brightly colored, showy flowerheads

Leafy Aster, Subalpine Aster

Aster foliaceus

Montane to subalpine. Flowers July–August. Common. Highly variable herb, 8–24 in. (20–60 cm). Open, forked flower clusters, fuchsia to lavender; many thinner ray flowers. Alternate leaves with usually smooth edges, stalked at the base (these may wither by flowering time), stalkless and somewhat clasping the stem higher up. Involucre bracts green and leafy, lower row typically wider and taller than inner bracts. Stems typically uniformly hairy beneath flower heads; sometimes hairs in lines down stem. Hairy achenes.

Pacific Aster, Long-leaved Aster
Aster ascendens
[*Virgulaster ascendens*]

Montane to subalpine. Pastures, along trails, and hillsides in disturbed soil. Common. 8–40 in. (20–100 cm). Spreads aggressively by underground rhizomes and by seed. Noticeably graduated involucral bracts, outer bracts shorter with cartilage-like edges and base. Long, narrow basal leaves, short thin stalks lay close to stem. Reddish stems wiry and rough with inconspicuous hairs.

Smooth Aster
Aster laevis var. *geyeri*

Montane. Open areas of aspen forests, dry or moist soil. Flowers July–September. Common. 12–40 in. (30–100 cm). Several upright stems from short rhizomes; many flower heads per stem. Involucral bracts graduated, with long, thin, somewhat sharply pointed green tips. Pappus often reddish. Foliage hairless, except for possible inconspicuous brief lines of fine hairs in the inflorescence; whitish waxy or powdery coating. Relatively stiff, alternate leaves, entire or toothed, can be egg- or lance-shaped; lower leaves stalked, often not persisting; upper leaves clasping stem. Achene usually hairless.

Smooth aster

Western Willow Aster, Skyblue Aster
Aster lanceolatus subsp. *hesperius* [*A. hesperius*]

Montane. Moist soil of stream banks, ditches and meadows. Flowers August–September. Common. Leafy herb, 20–60 in. (50–150 cm); creates patches from long rhizomes. Stems and branchlets have lines of hairs running from leaf bases downward; stalks never evenly pubescent below flower head. Involucre slightly overlapped, with inner bracts green-tipped and outer bracts completely green—not as leafy as in leafy aster (A. foliaceus); may have 1–2 leafy bracts below. Sometimes hybridizes with other species, making exact identification difficult.

Aspen Daisy, Showy Daisy

Erigeron speciosus
[*E. speciosus* var. *macranthus*]

Montane to subalpine forest openings and meadows. Common. 6–18 in. (15–45 cm). Showy clumps. Very numerous thin ray florets; many flower heads per stem; possibly some hairs and small glands beneath each head. Leaves lance-shaped, more or less triple-nerved, hairs only on edges; otherwise, smooth foliage. Stem leaves sessile, smaller than stalked leaves at or near base. Pointed involucre bracts finely glandular, narrow and equal in length.

Beautiful Daisy, Pink Erigeron

Erigeron elatior

Upper montane and subalpine. Flowers July–August. Common. Up to 24 in. (60 cm). Involucre graced with soft pink fur that sparkles with dew in early morning light. Abundant thin lavender to pink ray florets; sometimes whiter with maturity. Lance-shaped leaves are smooth without teeth; upper leaves clasp the stem. Only 1–3 flower heads per stem. Stems sticky-hairy toward top. Hairy achene.

Pinnateleaf Daisy

Erigeron pinnatisectus

Subalpine to alpine. Dry, rocky areas. Fairly common. Up to 5 in. (13 cm). Lavender ray florets. Only local daisy with deeply lobed, pinnately compound, hairy leaves. Hairy involucre bracts. Single conspicuous lavender flower head per stem. Involucre and stems glandular hairy. **Blackhead daisy** (*E. melanocephalus*), another small erigeron in meadows at similar elevations, has black to dark purplish, woolly hairs on the involucre; solitary flower heads with white ray florets; simple leaves.

Subalpine Daisy, Subalpine Fleabane
Erigeron peregrinus

Moist subalpine and alpine meadows. Fairly common. Distinctive tall herb, up to 20 in. (50 cm). Wider rose-purple ray florets than most daisies, resembling an aster. Involucre bracts covered in dark, red-tipped glandular hairs; bracts curved outward; contrasts with white to grayish, some glandular, hairs on stem beneath flower head. Leaves smooth, without hairs, mostly basal and stalked; stem leaves sessile, decreasing in size upward.

Whiplash Erigeron
Erigeron flagellaris

Montane to subalpine. Open sites, dry soils. Flowers May–August. Common. Slender biennial or short-lived perennial up to 16 in. (40 cm). Like a strawberry, produces sparingly-leafed stolons (runners) from plant's base that arc to root elsewhere. Small flowerheads; ray florets whitish on top, bluish beneath. Involucre bracts sticky, pointed and hairy. Stiff, straight hairs pressed close to stem, occasionally spreading near base.

Tansy Aster
Machaeranthera canescens

Montane to lower subalpine. Often in disturbed soil along trails and roads. Flowers July–October. Common. Biennial or short-lived perennial, 4–20 in. (10–50 cm). Dry soil. Involucre bracts well-overlapping, papery with short green curving tips. Bracts usually covered in fine, short hairs; sometimes also glandular; may be reddish. Flowers fuchsia-purple, bright gold centers. Branches terminate in several flower heads. Finely hairy foliage, often with stalked glands. Leaves with outward-spreading, spine-tipped teeth.

END OF ASTER/DAISY GROUP   SUNFLOWER FAMILY *continued*

PEGGY LYON

Broom Snakeweed
Gutierrezia sarothrae
MEDICINAL • WILDLIFE

Life zone/ecosystem: Montane. Oak-mountain shrublands.
Flowering: August–September. **Fruit:** Finely hairy achene.
Characteristics: Fairly common. Shrubby, broom-like bunches 4–28 in. (10–70 cm). Herb-like stems emerge from woody roots, crowns and bases. Tiny yellow flower heads with only 4–12 flowers of both ray and disc florets; both types fertile, producing seeds. Papery pappus. Heads in flat-topped, fine-textured sprays (cymes). Leaves slightly resinous, very narrow, almost threadlike, with prominent mid-rib and smooth edges. Thrives in dry, well-drained soil, but can grow in heavy clay.

A native plant that grows well on disturbed sites, this species is valuable for stabilizing soil and preventing erosion. High densities of broom snakeweed can occur in pastures because it is rarely grazed by livestock. Livestock will eat it only when nothing else is available, for it is toxic when consumed in large amounts. Mule deer, bighorn sheep and domestic goats are more resistant to the toxins. The seeds are a valuable source of food for small birds and mammals. Some Native American tribes made brooms from this brushy plant and found it useful for treating indigestion.

Rock Goldenrod (*Petradoria pumila*) is a similar species that grows in clumps (often forming large colonies) with numerous basal leaves, wider than those of snakeweed, and whorls of dead leaves from the previous year at the base. Florets have a hair-like pappus (capillary). Flowers mid-summer. Common on Mancos Shale.

*Chicory, Blue Sailors
Cichorium intybus
EDIBLE • NOXIOUS WEED

Life zone/ecosystem: Montane. Disturbed soil. **Flowering:** July–September. **Fruit:** Smooth achene. **Characteristics:** Fairly common. Non-native aggressive weed. May reach 6 ft. (2 m). Branched stems with milky juice. Flower heads blue or purple (rarely white); ray florets only. Leaves mainly basal, rough, dandelion-like. Deep taproot.

A native of the Mediterranean, chicory was brought to North America primarily as a source for salad greens and as a substitute for coffee. The roots are gathered before flowering to reduce bitterness, then dried and roasted. Chicory is closely related to cultivated endive. It is considered invasive in the West.

*Common Burdock
Arctium minus

EDIBLE · MEDICINAL · NOXIOUS WEED

Life zone/ecosystem: Montane. Disturbed sites. **Flowering:** July–September. **Fruit:** Spiny bur with curved prickles. **Characteristics:** Fairly common. Non-native aggressive weed. Coarse biennial often attaining a height of 2–6 ft. (50–200 cm). Purple or white disc florets occur in numerous heads, enclosed within involucre of many smooth or woolly bracts tipped with hooked spines. Forms only a rosette of leaves the first year. Very large leaves, dark green and smooth above, woolly-hairy beneath.

The story goes that Velcro was first conceived by an amateur Swiss mountaineer and naturalist, George de Mestral, when out on a walk with his dog through a field of similar "hitchhiking" burs. Introduced from Europe, burdock is considered a noxious weed, although it has many medicinal properties. A juice made from the foliage was used as a liver tonic and to treat cancer. The root oil may be massaged into the scalp for dandruff. Recent studies indicate that compounds in burdock juice exhibit test-tube activity against the HIV virus,[40] and that compounds in the fresh root possess bacteria- and fungus-fighting properties.[41] Young burdock leaves are also steamed and eaten as greens in Japan.

Coneflower (Colorado Rayless), Black Beauty
Rudbeckia occidentalis var. *montana*

MEDICINAL · WILDLIFE

Life zone/ecosystem: Montane to subalpine. Moist meadows in aspen and spruce-fir forests. **Flowering:** July–August. **Fruit:** Quadrangular achene. **Characteristics:** Common. 2–5 ft. (60–150 cm). Distinctive flower heads of purplish-black disc florets, maturing to cone shape 2 in. (4 cm) long; lacks ray florets. Large, grayish-green leaves, deeply lobed at least on lower half; somewhat heart-shaped at base; stalks wing-margined. Upper leaves stalkless.

Peculiar and distinctive, these cone-shaped flower heads contrast dramatically with other colors in the lush understory. A golden spiral of stamens encircles the blackish cone as the disc flowers bloom in an upward direction. The striking leaves stand apart from surrounding vegetation, providing a key to identification even before the flower heads form. Coneflower thrives in overgrazed areas.

Coneflower (Tall), Goldenglow

Rudbeckia laciniata var. *ampla* [*R. ampla*]

MEDICINAL • WILDLIFE

Life zone/ecosystem: Montane. Aspen and mixed-conifer forests, moist meadows, streambanks. **Flowering**: August–September. **Fruit**: Achene. **Characteristics**: Fairly common. Reaches 6 ft. (2 m). Large, cone-shaped flower heads with widely spaced, droopy yellow ray florets and greenish-brown disc florets. Involucre bracts in 2–3 series. Leaves have 3–7 large lobes, except near top of stem. Forms patches.

Along local mountain streams, patches of this striking tall herb do indeed seem to glow in the midst of surrounding foliage. Blooming disc florets create a golden swirl around the greener immature disc florets. Herbalists have been known to combine tall coneflower heads with goldenrod and giant hyssop flowers to treat burns. Songbirds and small mammals relish the seeds. A popular ornamental cultivar, called "Golden Glow," was developed from this species.

Curlycup Gumweed, Rosinweed

Grindelia squarrosa

DYE • MEDICINAL

Life zone/ecosystem: Montane. Disturbed soil. Oak-mountain shrublands. **Flowering:** July–September. **Fruit:** Achene with squared-off top. **Characteristics:** Common. Coarse, aromatic biennial to weak perennial, 1–3 ft. (30–90 cm). Underground rhizome system reaches depth of 6.5 ft. (2 m); drought-resistant. Yellow ray and disc florets. Involucre bracts covered in resinous glands; tips curled downward. Thick alternate leaves resinous, toothed, oblong with rounded tips. Pappus of 2–6 bristle-like scales. Multiple stems branch from single stem. Basal leaves wither by flowering.

A plant of dry, often disturbed sites, gumweed increases with grazing, because without competition from other plants, gumweed, which is not palatable to cattle, has the advantage. The Crow people and European settlers used preparations of the sticky flower heads for coughs, pneumonia, bronchitis and asthma and the Zuni pounded them as a poultice to relieve the itchiness of poison ivy.[42] Gumweed was officially listed in the *U.S. Pharmacopoeia* from 1882 to 1926, the *National Formulary* from 1926 to 1960, and is still listed in the German *Commission E Monographs* as a treatment for asthma and bronchial conditions. Herbalists in the United States also still prescribe this herb. A very odiferous infusion of gumweed yields greenish-gold to olive-green dyes.

Curlyhead Goldenweed, Western Goldenweed

Pyrrocoma crocea [*Haplopappus croceus*]

Life zone/ecosystem: Montane. Roadsides, meadows and aspen and mixed-conifer forests. **Flowering:** July–August. **Fruit:** Smooth achene with unequal bristles. **Characteristics:** Common. Hardy herb, 9–24 in. (25–60 cm). Golden-yellow flower heads; ray florets curl upward, disc florets secure the center. Tawny pappus. Bracts of involucre rounded, leafy and curled. Huge basal leaves smooth, inverted lance-shaped. Alternate stem leaves reduced in size upward, eventually clasping stem. Stem with woolly soft hairs (not matted) beneath flower head; rest of foliage smooth, mostly hairless. Thrives in clay soils. Compare with orange sneezeweed.

Large, cheerful clumps of curlyhead goldenweed appear elegantly sculpted, a midsummer reminder that art finds its inspiration in nature. *Pyrrocoma* comes from the Latin for "reddish hair" or "tawny mane," likely referring to the tawny pappus. *Crocea* is Greek for "saffron-yellow."

*Dandelion

Taraxacum officinale

EDIBLE · MEDICINAL · WILDLIFE

Life zone/ecosystem: Montane to alpine. Moist meadows and disturbed soil. **Flowering:** May–September. **Fruit:** Long-beaked achene. **Characteristics:** Common. Non-native. Herb with milky sap, 2–16 in. (5–40 cm). Sunny-yellow flowers consist of only ray florets. Basal leaves originate from the top of root crown, forming a rosette; jaggedly pinnate with lobes pointing downward; not prickly or hairy. No central stalk or branching of stems.

A sure sign of spring, huge patches of dandelions paint meadows throughout the mountains with gold. Imported from Europe and invasive in lawns, as well as some areas of the subalpine and alpine, dandelions have become common in most places, spreading by silky, parachute-equipped seeds that are easily carried on the wind. Dandelion root has long been touted as a cure for everything from high blood pressure to arthritis, but no well-documented studies have been done on its benefits. Dandelion is believed to increase bile flow, serving as a natural liver tonic to support liver function and purify the blood. Young dandelion greens have been cooked or eaten raw since ancient times, being rich in vitamins A, B-complex, C and E, as well as iron and trace minerals.[43] Green-tailed towhees, pine siskins and other birds love the seeds, while hares, rabbits and porcupines eat the foliage. Chipmunks, Wyoming ground squirrels and pocket gophers like the seeds and foliage.

Dusty Maiden, Douglas Chaenactis

Chaenactis douglasii

MEDICINAL

Life zone/ecosystem: Montane to subalpine. Dry, gravelly soil in oak-mountain shrublands. **Flowering:** May–September. **Fruit:** Hairy, club-shaped achene. **Characteristics:** Common. Leafy-stemmed biennial or short-lived perennial, 8–14 in. (20–36 cm). Long taproot. Rather gray-woolly, sometimes sticky-glandular, foliage; rosette of fern-like leaves withers as flower stems mature. White to cream, or pinkish, disc florets only; petals appear ruffled, stamens and pistils extend beyond flowers; outer disc flowers sometimes larger, almost mimicking ray flowers. **Alpine chaenactis** (*C. alpina*), a charming mound-forming species found in high scree fields, has leaves primarily in a basal rosette with similar thimble-like flower heads.

Often overlooked, this attractive grayish-green plant bears closer inspection. Its finely dissected leafy rosettes create the illusion of a dusty lace doily. Curled tips of the long, pink styles protrude from each disc floret. Its crushed leaves and other plant parts were used by some Native American tribes as a remedy for swellings and all types of skin problems, such as insect bites, acne and even snake bites. The Paiutes treated colds with *Chaenactis* tea.

Goldenrod Group   *Solidago* spp.

SUBSET OF SUNFLOWER FAMILY   DYE • GARDEN • MEDICINAL • WILDLIFE

Praise has been heaped on the curative powers of goldenrods since ancient times. The old English name, "woundwort," alludes to their use during the Crusades, when carried into battle to heal wounds. Their small flower heads with short ray florets make them easy to recognize. Both the ray and disc florets are yellow with a bristly pappus. Flower heads of some species grow predominantly on one side of the stems in the inflorescence. The leaves are relatively narrow and may have small teeth. Commission E, the panel of experts that advises the German government on herbal medicine, endorses drinking goldenrod tea for urinary-tract infections, kidney stones and bladder and yeast infections. A good herb for your first-aid kit or shaving kit, the powdered leaves help stop bleeding and the fresh leaves can be chewed for treating cuts and scrapes. Goldenrod is also used in dying, producing colors described as "screaming gold" and "bright green gold." Even though hay fever suffers will swear goldenrod is the culprit, it is usually some other plant that is responsible for their allergy—goldenrod tea is often prescribed to reduce allergy symptoms. Both songbirds and small mammals feed on goldenrod seeds and small mammals, rabbits, beaver and deer eat the foliage. Goldenrods make an attractive addition to any wildflower garden, attracting hummingbirds, bees, butterflies and wasps with their abundant nectar.

Mountain Goldenrod
Solidago multiradiata var. *scopulorum*

Subalpine to alpine. Rocky soil of open areas, ridges. Common. Clump-forming herb to 20 in. (50 cm); much smaller in alpine. Each flower head composed of 12–13 ray florets and many disc florets, arranged in extended panicle; resemble small bouquet. Leaves with smooth or toothed edges; basal leaves spoon-shaped, petioles edged with hairs (ciliate). **Dwarf goldenrod** (*S. simplex* var. *simplex*) is similar, but reaches only 10 in. (25 cm); flower heads have about 8 ray florets; petioles not ciliate. **Alpine goldenrod** (*S. simplex* var. *nana*) is small alpine race of dwarf goldenrod.

Parry's Goldenrod, Parry's Goldenweed
Solidago parryi [*Oreochrysum* or *Haplopappus parryi*]

Upper montane to subalpine. Open meadows of aspen, mixed-conifer and spruce-fir forests. Flowers July–August. Fairly common. 6–20 in. (15–50 cm); alpine version under 6 in. (15 cm). Flower heads larger than typical goldenrods, but small in comparison with rest of plant. Wide involucre bracts, greenish on tips. Leaves without teeth, relatively wide, lance-shaped; stems leafy, rough and purplish.

Slender Goldenrod
Solidago velutina [*S. sparsiflora*]

Lower montane. Oak-mountain shrublands. Flowers July–September. Common. 12–24 in. (30–60 cm) tall. Flower heads arranged on 1 side of stem. Foliage with short hairs. Leaves thin with 3 prominent veins; basal leaves wither by flowering time. Similar **Canada goldenrod** (*S. canadensis*) has tiny golden flower heads arranged on the top side of arched branches; grows up to 4 ft. (120 cm); forms clonal colonies. Stems somewhat hairy and uniformly leafy. Leaves large, lance-shaped,

2–4 in. (5–10 cm) long, with sharp-toothed edges; may be rough-hairy to almost smooth. **Giant goldenrod** (*S. gigantea* [*S. serotinoides*]), less common locally, is distinguished by smooth leaves and no hair on stem below inflorescence.

Goldenrod greens have been used in soups and quiches, seeds thicken stews and blossoms are added to pancakes.

END OF GOLDENROD GROUP   SUNFLOWER FAMILY *continued*

Hawkweed, Slender Hawkweed

Hieracium gracile

[*Chlorocrepis tristis* subsp. *gracilis*]

WILDLIFE

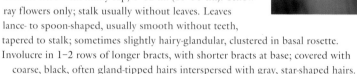

Life zone/ecosystem: Subalpine to alpine. Moist areas of spruce-fir forests. **Flowering:** June–July. **Fruit:** Cylindrical achene. **Characteristics:** Uncommon. Slender herb with milky sap, 4–12 in. (10–30 cm). Yellow ray flowers only; stalk usually without leaves. Leaves lance- to spoon-shaped, usually smooth without teeth, tapered to stalk; sometimes slightly hairy-glandular, clustered in basal rosette. Involucre in 1–2 rows of longer bracts, with shorter bracts at base; covered with coarse, black, often gland-tipped hairs interspersed with gray, star-shaped hairs. Pappus of tawny, hair-like bristles separates hawkweed from **hawksbeards** (*Crepis*), which have a white pappus.

The milky sap of this genus has been dried and used as chewing gum. The plants are eaten by rabbits, bighorn sheep, mule deer and elk. Blue grouse prefer the seeds.

Mule's Ears

Wyethia amplexicaulis

WILDLIFE

Life zone/ecosystem: Lower montane. Dry to moist soil of oak-mountain shrublands, sage-brush shrublands and aspen forests; thrives in dense clay soils. **Flowering:** June–July. **Fruit:** Flat achene. **Characteristics:** Common. Stocky, strongly aromatic herb up to 32 in. (80 cm). Bright-yellow, sunflower-like flower heads, usually several per plant. Pappus is a crown of tiny pointed scales at top of achene. Alternate leathery leaves resemble mule's ears. Plants grow in lush patches. Stout taproot. Compare to arrowleaf balsamroot.

When mule's ears bursts into bloom, brush strokes of spectacular yellow-gold brighten the landscape. Once mature, the hearty taproot, nearly 3 in. (7 cm) in diameter and up to 6 ft. (180 cm) deep in the earth, allows this plant to survive semi-drought conditions, which would discourage other species. Mule's ears has a clear advantage in range that has been overgrazed. For this same reason, biologists also consider this species ideal for erosion control and revegetation/restoration around old mine sites and other dry, disturbed sites. Extensive patches of mule's ears provide valuable cover for birds, particularly blue grouse and small mammals. Bear, elk and deer feed mainly on the young spring foliage, which turns tough and coarse in summer. The flower heads are popular with wildlife throughout the season.

Orange Agoseris
Burnt-orange False Dandelion
Agoseris aurantiaca

Life zone/ecosystem: Montane to alpine. Dry to moist meadows.
Flowering: June–August. **Fruit:** 10-ribbed or nerved achene, long beak;
attached to parachute of silky hairs (pappus). **Characteristics:** Fairly
common. Herb with milky sap, 4–24 in. (10–60 cm). Taproot. Solitary,
unmistakable orange heads of ray florets only, atop leafless stalks; cottony
hairs beneath flower heads; heads dry purplish. Leaves mostly long, narrow and basal, often
with randomly distributed teeth or small lobes. Involucre with erect, overlapping phyllaries.

Imaginative western Native Americans
used the solidified, somewhat rubbery sap
from the stem and leaves as chewing gum.
Agoseris is derived from Greek words
meaning "goat chicory." Yellow-flowered
members of the genus Agoseris are often
confused with non-native dandelions.
Dandelions have reflexed phyllaries.

Pale agoseris,
(*Agoseris glauca* var.
dasyphyllum) grows
from montane to
alpine; extremely
variable character-
istics in different
populations. Similar
to orange dande-
lion, but has yellow
flowers that dry
pinkish.

Orange Sneezeweed
Hymenoxys hoopesii [*Dugaldia hoopesii, Helenium hoopesii*]
MEDICINAL

Life zone/ecosystem: Montane to alpine. Moist meadows and
streambanks, aspen and mixed-conifer forests. **Flowering:**
July–August. **Fruit:** Tawny-hairy achene. **Characteristics:**
Common. Herb reaching 12–40 in. (30–100 cm). Orange-gold, sunflower-like heads with obviously droopy ray florets; several per stem.
Involucral bracts in 2 rows; stem furry just beneath. Thick, spatula-
shaped, parallel-veined, toothless leaves taper to stem. Smaller stem
leaves. Pappus of 5–10 papery bracts, visible atop mature fruit.
Differs from **mountain sneezeweed** (*Helenium autumnale* var. *montanum*), which has leaf bases that continue down the stem and no
fuzz beneath flower head.

Orange sneezeweed is a favorite for vivid color
among the lush aspen understory, giving the illusion of
large orange spiders. The plant is toxic to livestock,
especially sheep, causing what is called "spewing sickness." *Yerba del lobo* is a odd-smelling liniment made
from the foliage and flowers of sneezeweed. This preparation is weaker than arnica, but is used in a similar way to treat sore
joints, sprains, muscle bruises and arthritic joints. Arapaho tribes mixed
orange sneezeweed with other plants as an inhalant for headaches, and
chewed the fresh leaves for a "clearer voice and throat."[44]

235

*Oxeye Daisy
Chrysanthemum leucanthemum
NOXIOUS WEED

Life zone/ecosystem: Montane to subalpine. Disturbed soil, moist meadows of aspen, mixed-conifer and spruce-fir forest. **Flowering:** June–August. **Fruit:** 10-ribbed achene. **Characteristics:** Common. Non-native weed. Less than 3 ft. (1 m.). White ray flowers with center of yellow disc flowers. No pappus. Involucral bracts with thin dark band near edge. Leaves spoon-shaped with scalloped/lobed edges; stem leaves without stalk.

This beautiful but aggressive plant was introduced from Europe, where it had already become a plague on pastures and crop fields. Still included in so-called "regional wildflower mixes," oxeye daisy has escaped cultivation to invade and modify many natural communities in Colorado. It is extremely tenacious and difficult to eradicate—a single plant can produce as many as 26,000 seeds, or start a colony through its short spreading rootstocks. Be vigilant and keep these daisies from taking hold. At the very least, cut off flowering heads before they go to seed.

Pearly Everlasting, Strawflower
Anaphalis margaritacea
CEREMONIAL • MEDICINAL

Life zone/ecosystem: Montane to subalpine. Moist or dry, open rocky areas, sometimes disturbed or burned over. **Flowering:** July–September. **Fruit:** Rough achenes. **Characteristics:** Common. Clump-forming, rhizomatous herb, 10–24 in. (20–60 cm). Flower heads are straw-like, with only yellow disc florets and white involucral bracts; heads are luminous "pearls" even when dried. Unbranched, leafy, fuzzy stems with narrow green leaves sporting woolly undersides.

Known for its astringent, diaphoretic (sweat-inducing) and expectorant properties, this herb was used medicinally by several Native American tribes. Coastal Indians believed pearly everlasting was effective for tuberculosis and rheumatism. Mohawks prepared a tea from the flowers for asthma, and from the whole plant as a wash for external skin irritations and wounds. For the Cheyenne, it was used in ceremonial cleansing rituals, as a liniment rubbed onto arms and legs before battle and as a tobacco substitute. Although an unconventional practice, the Menomini tribe burned this herb with beaver gall bladders and blew the smoke into the noses of people who had passed out in order to revive them.[45] Pearly everlasting can spread aggressively along river corridors and in irrigated pastures.

*Perennial Sowthistle
Sonchus arvensis

Life zone/ecosystem: Montane. Disturbed soil.
Flowering: June–September. **Fruit:** Achene.
Characteristics: Common. Non-native weed.
Grows 1.5–4 ft. (45–120 cm). Erect, hollow stems
with bitter, milky juice. Flower heads with ray florets only; involucre and pedicel bristly with glandular sticky hairs. Alternate leaves are deeply-
toothed to nearly smooth, with prick-
ly edges and pointed lobes. Stem leaves clasp the stem and are smaller
than basal ones. Silky white pappus attached to end of oblong,
ribbed, wrinkled achene.

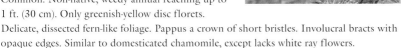

Perennial sowthistle spreads aggressively by horizontal, rhizome-like roots. Even though there may be up
to twenty flower heads per plant in one season, only a few
are blooming at a time. They open two to three hours
after sunrise and close around noon. Although responsible for reduced agricultural yields in some states, this
plant has a positive side. Rabbits, small mammals and
domestic animals feed on the foliage and flowers.
Because the milky latex is oil rich, sowthistle may have
potential value for use in oil production.

*Pineapple Weed
Matricaria matricarioides
[*M. discoidea* or *Lepidotheca suaveolens*]

MEDICINAL

Life zone/ecosystem: Montane. Sunny, disturbed
soils, trailside, roadside. **Flowering:** June–August.
Fruit: 2–4-nerved achene. **Characteristics:**
Common. Non-native, weedy annual reaching up to
1 ft. (30 cm). Only greenish-yellow disc florets.
Delicate, dissected fern-like foliage. Pappus a crown of short bristles. Involucral bracts with
opaque edges. Similar to domesticated chamomile, except lacks white ray flowers.

A sweet pineapple fragrance pervades the air when these plants are disturbed or crushed. Pineapple weed was strewn over floors during the
Middle Ages as an air freshener and stored in buckskin bags by Blackfoot
tribes for its fragrance. The dried flowers can be brewed as a mild
chamomile-like tea for calming nerves, inducing sleep (especially in children) and for soothing indigestion and relieving gas pain. Alaskan herbalists recommend the tea to relieve colds and rashes. **Anyone allergic to the
pollen of plants in the sunflower family could react to this tea. Do not
use plants from roads or trails that may have been sprayed for weeds.**

Rabbitbrush (Common), Golden Rabbitbrush
Ericameria nauseosus
[*Chrysothamnus nauseosus*]
DYE • MEDICINAL • REVEGETATION • WILDLIFE

Life zone/ecosystem: Montane. Oak-mountain shrublands. **Flowering:** August–September. **Fruit:** Plumed achene. **Characteristics:** Common. Aromatic, deciduous shrub up to 4 ft. (120 cm) locally. Erect branches give rounded appearance. Deep, often branching, taproot. Golden-yellow flower heads of 5 perfect disc florets; in large terminal clusters. Slender, white plumose pappus. Felt-like covering on stems and leaves. Many subspecies; some with smooth bracts under flower heads and more greenish leaves and stems; gray subspecies has more densely hairy bracts with gray to whitish leaves and stems. Compare with broom snakeweed on p. 228.

Sticky-flowered rabbitbrush, yellow rabbitbrush
(*Chrysothamnus viscidiflorus*). Leaves may be smooth or short-hairy, but are not woolly or silky. Easily identified by the greener, slightly twisted leaves.

As summer green fades from the landscape, rabbitbrush blooms in golden profusion on south-facing slopes, thriving in dense clay soils. Endemic from Canada to Mexico, it tolerates a wide range of environmental conditions. Germinating easily, it grows rapidly, making it beneficial for revegetation and erosion control. Rabbitbrush is used in the production of natural rubber, contains hydrocarbon resins that are potential insecticides and fungicides and is planted as an ornamental. Cheyenne people boiled the leaves and stems for soothing itchy skin, drank the same for smallpox and made a tea from rabbitbrush and sagebrush flowers to treat colds, coughs and tuberculosis. They also believed that burning rabbitbrush stems and leaves over box-elder coals would repel nightmares. Small mammals and nesting songbirds seek cover in rabbitbrush, while mule deer and elk forage on the leaves and flowers. A bright yellow dye is made from the flowers. **Livestock in California has been poisoned by common rabbitbrush. It would be unsafe to consume it in any form, as the level of toxicity for humans is unknown.**

Rosy Pussytoes
Antennaria rosea
GARDEN • MEDICINAL

Life zone/ecosystem: Montane to subalpine. Abundant in dry soil, most plant communities. **Flowering:** June–September. **Fruit:** Achene. **Characteristics:** Common. Mat-forming herb. Flower heads about 0.25 in. (4–6 mm.) wide, on slender stalks about 10 in. (25 cm). Heads composed of only disc florets, with pappus hairs predominant. Phyllaries of involucres white or pink. Tiny spatulate leaves gray-woolly both sides. **Alpine pussytoes** (*A. media*), common in the alpine zone, has dingy to blackish phyllaries.

Leafy rosettes of rosy pussytoes

The flower heads of pussytoes truly resemble a kitten's soft paws. Species in this genus easily hybridize, combining their characteristics, which frustrates even the most ardent botanist. Medicinally, pussytoes is considered a reliable remedy for liver inflammation and mild recurrence of former hepatitis symptoms. Some Native Americans chewed the tiny leaves as a cough remedy, also stripping and drying them for use in tobacco mixtures. Ground squirrels and chipmunks will eat the plant when nothing else is available. Pussytoes' dense, silvery mat of leaves makes it an ideal plant for native rock gardens—it is easily propagated in early spring or late fall by root divisions, seeds or cuttings.

Showy pussytoes
(*A. pulcherrima*). Fairly common in oak-mountain shrublands and sagebrush shrublands. Not mat-forming. Leaves have distinct parallel veins.

Sagebrush Group   *Artemisia* [*Oligosporus/Seriphidium*] spp.

SUBSET OF SUNFLOWER FAMILY   CEREMONIAL • GARDEN • MEDICINAL

Plants in this native group are also referred to as sageworts and wormwoods, distinguishing them from true sages of the mint family, which include culinary sage (genus *Salvia*). Crushed sagebrush leaves release a scent that conjures up the American West—there is an undeniable magic in their spicey smell. The genus was named after Artemis, the virgin Greek goddess of the hunt and the moon, whom the Romans called Diana.

Sagebrushes are usually aromatic shrubs or herbs that owe their pungent smell, medicinal uses and ceremonial importance to their high content of volatile oils. One of these oils, thujone, is the active ingredient in absinthe, the now-banned narcotic aperitif under whose influence it is now thought, Vincent van Gogh cut off his ear and mailed it to a lady friend. Absinthe is derived from wormwood (*A. absinthium*), found in the nearby Gunnison Basin. All species of wormwood were probably used for medicine by Native Americans at one time or another. Tribes such as the Lakota used an infusion of the roots of some species to treat constipation, complications in childbirth and urination problems.

Their roots form symbiotic relationships with mycorrhizal fungi in the soil, which are usually critical for their establishment and competitive success (see hemiparasites, p. 211). Sagebrush plant communities are very important ecosystems as cover and food for wildlife, and yet have become one of the most threatened by development in mountain areas.

Boreal Sagewort, Northern Sagewort

Artemisia campestris var. *purshii* [*Oligosporus groenlandicus, A. borealis*]

Boreal
Sagewort

Subalpine to alpine. Gravelly or sandy soils. Flowers July–September. Common. Fruit is a smooth achene. Red-stemmed herb, up to 16 in. (40 cm). Phyllaries without dark margins. Flowers small, reddish, in spike-like arrangement. Leaves basal and moderately hairy (sometimes smooth), divided in 2–3 slender segments. Foliage with minimum odor.

Mountain Sagebrush, Mountain Big Sage

Artemisia tridentata var. *vaseyana* [*Seriphidium vaseyanum*]

Montane. Oak-mountain shrubland. Adapted to cool, moist areas with late-melting winter snows and moderately deep, well-drained soils. Prefers full sun, but tolerates shade and higher levels of organic matter than other *A. tridentata* varieties. Flowers late July–September. Fruit is a fragile achene. Common. Evergreen, aromatic shrub up to 36 in. (1 m). Small, relatively few greenish-gray flower heads lack ray flo-rets; arranged in stalks of spikes or racemes, which appear equal in height from a distance, compared to the ragged appearance of other species. Persistent leaves widest at base of 3 rounded lobes, similar in size and shape. Plants single to 2-stemmed.

Rocky Mountain Sagewort, Dwarf Sagewort

Artemisia scopulorum

Subalpine to alpine. Open, rocky areas of tundra. Flowers. July–August. Fairly common. Fruit an achene. Silver-hairy herb, 2–12 in. (5–30 cm). Not mat-forming. Tall basal leaves divided once or twice (twice-pinnatifid) into narrow segments, few reduced stem leaves. Stems reddish. 5–25 flower heads, not nodding, each with 15–30 purplish-tinged disc florets. Phyllaries of involucre moderately covered in non-matted soft hairs. Receptacle densely covered with long white hairs. RockyMountain sage could be confused with other herbaceous sages, such as **fringed sage** (*A. frigida*). **Arctic sagewort** (*A. norvegica*) and **Michaux's sagewort** (*A. michauxiana*) are also similar, but their receptacles are not covered in hair. All the above have dark prominent margins on bracts of the involucre, except for Michaux, which may be slightly purplish. Michaux also has mostly stem leaves, the basal leaves being stunted. **Patterson's sagewort** (*A. pattersonii*) is similar, but has only 1–5 heads and the leaves are only once-pinnatifid. Pikas harvest all of these small sageworts for their "hay piles."

Michaux's sagewort

Fringed Sagewort
Artemisia frigida

Montane to subalpine. Oak-mountain shrublands, dry soils. Flowers July–September. Fruit a smooth achene. Common. Mat-forming, herbaceous stems from woody base, 4–16 in. (10–40 cm). Yellowish (some red-tinged) disc florets only, each with functional ovary, grouped into numerous silvery flower heads in slender clusters. Woolly-hairy cloak imparts silvery appearance to foliage. Receptacle with long hairs between florets. Both basal and flower-stalk leaves plentiful; divided into abundant tiny segments, conveying "fringed" appearance. *Frigida* means "of cold regions" in botanical Latin.

The most abundant species in the *Artemisia* genus, fringed sage is hardy and drought tolerant, due to a flexible root system that develops either as a taproot or as a fibrous system near the surface, depending on available moisture. Fringed sage tea was used by several Native American tribes to correct menstrual irregularity, and the Hopi used the leaves to flavor their corn. It is also an important winter forage for deer and elk.

Western Mugwort, White Sage
Artemisia ludoviciana

Montane to lower subalpine. Dry, open areas. Flowers June–September. Fruit is smooth, broadly cylindrical achene. Fairly common. Aromatic herb forming loose patches, 12–40 in. (30–100 cm). Disc florets only, attached to naked receptacles; densely woolly involucres; packed into numerous flower heads in slender branching clusters (panicles). Highly variable leaves (many subspecies), usually linear to lance-shaped with smooth, turned-under edges; may be toothed. Lower leaves usually deeply divided into narrow-lobed segments. Mostly white-woolly foliage; leaves may be darker green and less hairy on upper surface.

WHICH WHITE SAGE? Western mugwort was a ritual herb for many Native American tribes. Tying the stems together into a "smudge stick" to burn as incense was believed by the Cheyenne to drive away bad spirits and influences and even to improve respiratory problems. Others used the tea to cleanse the body during purification rites or washed with it after breaking sacred taboos. Cheyenne people also crushed dried leaves as snuff to treat sinus attacks, nosebleeds and headaches. Although this species is referred to as white sage, the plant preferred by many Native Americans is the true white sage (*Salvia apiana*) of the mint family. Deer, rabbits and small mammals will eat the whole plant, while songbirds love the seeds.

Wild Tarragon
Artemisia dracunculus
[*Oligosporus dracunculus* subsp. *glauca*]

Montane. Oak-mountain shrublands. Flowers July–September.
Fruit a shiny achene. Common. Tufted, herbaceous herb, 12–30 in.
(30–75 cm); near-woody rootstock. Light tarragon fragrance and
anise-like flavor. Disc florets only; inner florets with fertile stamens,
non-functional ovary; outer florets with fertile ovary, no stamens.
Young linear leaves finely hairy, maturing to almost hairless; greener than other local wormwoods; usually not lobed. Stems reddish;
numerous tiny flower heads tucked among leaves of upper stem.
Some Native American tribes burned the branches as a smudge to
drive away mosquitoes and other biting insects.

END OF SAGEBRUSH GROUP   SUNFLOWER FAMILY *continued*

*Salsify, Yellow Goatsbeard, Oyster Plant
Tragopogon pratensis

EDIBLE • MEDICINAL

Life zone/ecosystem: Montane. Semi-dry to moist meadows,
disturbed soil. **Flowering:** June–August. **Fruit:** Achene with
very minute spines. **Characteristics:** Common. Non-native.
Biennial, can be annual, herb with milky sap, 12–32 in. (30–80
cm). Slender, mostly 8 pointed phyllaries extend beyond
lemon-yellow ray florets, giving flower head a star-like appearance; no disc florets. Stalks not enlarged beneath flower heads.
Grass-like leaves taper from base, clasping hollow stem. Large,
dandelion-like seedheads with feathery pappus.

American colonists introduced salsify from
Europe, where certain species are still cultivated
as a parsnip-like food. Since then, winds have
blown their fluffy, parachute-like seeds far and
wide. Salsify is also called Jack-go-to-bed-at-noon because the flowers open
at dawn and often close around noon on a cloudy day. Another common
name, goatsbeard, describes the distinctive phyllaries, which droop after
fertilization and resemble a goat's beard. Although the roots are tough
and fibrous and the leaves bitter, salsify has an oyster-like flavor when
cooked, thus the name oyster plant. Changing the water several times
makes the greens more palatable. Both Native Americans and colonists
made a tea from simmered roots to relieve indigestion and liver problems.
They also chewed the dried sap for better digestion.

*Scentless Chamomile
Matricaria perforata [*M. inodora*]
NOXIOUS WEED

Life zone/ecosystem: Montane to subalpine. Disturbed soil. **Flowering:** July–October. **Fruit:** Ribbed achene. **Characteristics:** Common. Non-native weed. Annual, often reaching 2 ft. (60 cm). Showy, with 12 white ray florets surrounding center of yellow disc florets. Finely dissected and feathery alternate leaves only about 2 in. (5 cm) long; no odor. Stems branched near the top.

Scentless chamomile was introduced from Europe as an ornamental, but is an aggressive weed that should not be used in local gardens. This is not the same chamomile used for tea, and the leaves do not have the characteristic chamomile fragrance when crushed.

Senecio Group (Groundsels, Ragworts and Butterweeds)   *Senecio* and *Packera* [*Ligularia*] spp.
SUBSET OF SUNFLOWER FAMILY

Senecio comes from Latin *senes*, "old man." As the flower heads go to seed, they look conspicuously like small white- or gray-haired heads. *Senecio* is an immense genus worldwide with more than 1,000 species, and was long considered the single genus of this group. However, some botanists have proposed dividing it up into several genera based on morphological and genetic differences between species. As of this writing, botanists at the Rocky Mountain Herbarium agree that it should be two genera, *Senecio* and *Packera*, which is the system followed in this book.

Species of both genera are recognized by alternate leaves, yellow composite flowers and a single layer of greenish phyllaries surrounding the flower head like a picket fence, with a few smaller bracts often at the base. *Packera* has branched, fibrous roots instead of the unbranched ones of *Senecio*, is less than 20 in. (50 cm) tall, and rarely has the small, thick, hard teeth found on the margins of *Senecio* leaves. Hybridization often takes place when species within each genera occur together, blurring physical characters and making positive identification difficult.

Both *Senecio* and *Packera* contain pyrrolizidine alkaloids (PAs), which are liver toxins and potential carcinogens that can be fatal to humans and animals over time. Horses and cattle are most affected, sheep and goats less so. Coltsfoot and boneset are popular medicinal composites that contain PAs; fortunately, preparations from these herbs are believed safe for external use.[46] Oddly, two of our local species, arrowleaf groundsel (*Senecio triangularis*) and saw-toothed butterweed (*S. serra*), are not considered harmful to grazing livestock. There are some species of *Senecio* and *Packera* that are used for ornamental woods, aromatherapy and dyes.

243

Alpine Senecio, Holm's Senecio

Senecio amplectens var. *holmii* [*Ligularia amplectens*]

Alpine. Fairly common. Showy, 4–8 in. (10–20 cm). Resembles daffodil senecio, but smaller. Ray florets twice as long as phyllaries; heads nodding. Leaves mostly basal, oval to narrowly oval, widely toothed (dentate). Foliage without hair, not strongly succulent, may be reddish-tinged.

Arrowleaf Senecio, Triangularleaf Senecio

Senecio triangularis

Subalpine. Streams in spruce-fir forests. Prefers cooler and wetter areas. Common. Stout herb, 20–60 in. (20–150 cm). Similar to saw-toothed butterweed, but leaves are distinctly triangular.

Bell Senecio, Purple-Leaf Groundsel

Senecio soldanella [*Ligularia soldanella*]

Alpine. Rocky ridges, fellfields, scree slopes. Uncommon. Endemic to Colorado. Distinctive herb, less than 6 in. (15 cm). Comparatively large yellow flower heads, often slightly nodding. Ray florets short in proportion to center of disc florets. Rounded, purplish-green, fleshy leaves on short petioles are mostly basal. Seed available commercially—great for rock gardens.

PEGGY LYON

Bigelow's Groundsel, Rayless Senecio

Senecio bigelovii [*Ligularia bigelovii*]

Montane to subalpine. Meadows and open areas of aspen and spruce-fir forests. Fairly common. 12–40 in. (30–100 cm). Distinctive nodding flower heads, only disc florets; appear "in bud" when fully open. Fleshy, dark purplish-burgundy phyllaries. Alternate leaves. Crushed leaves have slight lemon fragrance.

Blacktip Senecio
Senecio atratus

Montane to subalpine. Spruce-fir forest. Plentiful on mountain road-sides and scree slopes. Common. Handsome herb, up to 3 ft. (1 m). Many flower heads of only 4–5 ray florets. Long, grayish-green leaves, widest near sharp tip; copiously hairy, at least when young; may or may not be toothed. Lower leaves taper to flat stalk. Involucre of 8 black-tipped phyllaries, plus outer layer of straw-colored bracts.

Cut-Leaved Groundsel, Western Golden Ragwort
Senecio eremophilus

Montane to subalpine. Disturbed areas of aspen and spruce-fir forest. Common. Tall, short-lived herb, 12–24 in. (30–60 cm). Yellow flower heads usually not less than 10 per stem. Phyllaries black-tipped. Distinct leaves, deeply and raggedly pinnate, each lobe with small teeth; spread equally along stem.

Daffodil Senecio
Senecio amplectens var. *amplectens* [*Ligularia amplectens*]

Subalpine. Endemic to Colorado. Spruce-fir forests. Meadows and openings in forest. Fairly common. 8–24 in. (20–60 cm). Meadows and openings in forest. Fairly common. Unique lemon-yellow, pointed ray florets; flower heads face out or nod downward; phyllaries dark-tipped. Lance-shaped leaves smooth, may be toothed or not. Stem leaves clasp stem.

Fremont's Groundsel, Dwarf Mountain Butterweed
Senecio fremontii

Upper subalpine to alpine. Talus slopes and other open rocky areas. Fairly common. Smooth-foliaged herb, 4–20 in. (10–50 cm). Stems branch freely from reclining bases, forming low mounds. Yellow flower heads, 1–3 per stem. Smallish fleshy leaves, somewhat oval and variously toothed.

Lambstongue Groundsel
Senecio integerrimus

Montane to subalpine. Oak-mountain shrublands and sagebrush shrublands to moist meadows. Fairly common. Variable stout herb, 12–28 in.
(30–70 cm). Foliage with patches of cottony hairs when young, possibly
becoming nearly smooth with age. Flower heads numerous, tightly
packed in inflorescence; small stalk of terminal flower head thickened
and shorter than others. Leaves mostly at base, somewhat egg-shaped
and smooth or irregularly toothed on edges, tapering to long stalks; size
inconsistent. Upper leaves small; attached directly to stem.

Lobeleaf Groundsel
Packera multilobata
[*Senecio multilobatus*]

Montane. Oak-mountain shrublands. Dry soils,
clay. Uncommon. 6–12 in. (15–30 cm). Flower heads yellow. Leaves
deeply and irregularly lobed, mostly basal, decreasing in size upward
on stem—may or may not be glabrous, but will not have cottony-tan-
gled hairs.

Cuttleaf Groundsel, Rocky Mountain Groundsel
Packera streptanthifolia
[*Senecio streptanthifolius*]

Montane to subalpine. Dry soils of oak-mountain
shrublands, aspen and mixed-conifer forest. Fairly common. 4–20 in. (10–50 cm). Smooth foliage, except for
cottony tufts in leaf axils and inflorescence when
young. Leathery leaves, basal leaves taper to long stalk,
narrowly oval to somewhat round blades with widely
toothed to a bit shallowly lobed edges. Stem leaves more sessile, narrower and raggedly
lobed. Extremely variable.

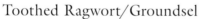

Toothed Ragwort/Groundsel
Senecio serra

Subalpine. Streams in aspen and spruce-fir forests.
Common. Mostly smooth herb, 24–48 in. (60–120
cm). Small flower heads crowded at top in somewhat
flat-topped inflorescence. Leaves thinly lance-shaped
and finely toothed on edges, mostly consistent in
size. Stems leafy. Overall look similar to arrowleaf
senecio, but a close look at leaves differentiates the
two. Both frequently occur in large stands.

Splitleaf Groundsel, Different Groundsel
Packera dimorphophylla var. *dimorphophylla*

Subalpine to alpine. Rocky slopes and tundra; occasionally in meadows or in talus. Likes drier soils; tolerates soils that are wet part of the year, and dry out later. Uncommon. Up to 8 in. (20 cm). Glabrous. Stems single or in several loose clusters. Ray florets yellow; 5–6 flower heads per stem. Tips of phyllaries sometimes burgundy. Lobed leaves clasp the stem; oval basal leaves narrow to a winged petiole. Easily confused with saffron groundsel (P. crocata), which has smaller flower heads and orange ray florets, is taller and likes wet soil. Both species have stem leaves that differ in shape from their basal leaves, but those of splitleaf groundsel tend to be more triangular in outline.

Thickbract Senecio, Mountain Meadow Groundsel
Senecio crassulus

Upper montane to subalpine. Open, dry to moist meadows of aspen, mixed-conifer and spruce-fir forests. Fairly common. 8–20 in. (20–50 cm). Only a few large, yellow-orange flower heads. Thickish green leaves with toothed margins, may be smoother), decrease in size upward, changing from longer winged stalks to sessile near top, nearly clasping stem; somewhat egg-shaped, attached at narrow end. Foliage smooth.

Wooton's Groundsel, Wooton's Ragwort
Senecio wootonii

Montane to subalpine. Dry soil in aspen, spruce-fir forests. Uncommon. 8–20 in. (20–50 cm). Foliage with pale, blue-green waxy coating (glaucous). Small yellow flower heads with few ray florets. Thickish leaves mostly basal, oblanceolate and tapering to narrow petiole; margins usually smooth, but may have tiny teeth.

END OF SENECIO GROUP

SUNFLOWER FAMILY *continued*

Showy Goldeneye

Heliomeris multiflora [*Viguiera multiflora*]

GARDEN

Life zone/ecosystem: Montane to subalpine. Aspen, oak-mountain shrublands, spruce-fir. **Flowering:** August–September. **Fruit:** Smooth, 4-angled achene. **Characteristics:** Common. Wiry-stemmed herb, 10–40 in. (25–100 cm). Branched stems short-hairy; leafy and erect. Flower heads small relative to other local yellow "sunflowers." Bristly lance-shaped leaves dark green, opposite, may be alternate toward top, usually without teeth; lower leaves on short stalks, upper leaves stalkless.

Showy goldeneye often produces a profusion of blooms in meadows and along trails and roadsides, adding a cheerful note to the late-summer landscape. Seed is available commercially, making this attractive plant very popular in native wildflower gardens.

*Tansy, Beggar's Buttons

Tanacetum vulgare

NOXIOUS WEED • POISONOUS

Life zone/ecosystem: Montane. Disturbed soil along roads and trails. **Flowering:** Late July–September. **Fruit:** Achene with short 5-toothed crown. **Characteristics:** Common. Non-native weed. Grows up to 4 ft. (1.2 m). Dark-green, alternate leaves are finely divided, appearing quite fern-like; rankly aromatic when crushed. Crowded, flat-topped clusters of golden disc florets resemble small buttons.

Originally introduced from Europe, tansy spreads quickly here, smothering native plant populations and taking over gardens. It is tenacious and should be eradicated or not allowed to set seed. Once the root system is established, digging it out is almost impossible. *Tanacetum* is derived from the Greek word *athanaton*, meaning immortal—possibly named for its use to embalm the dead until the American Revolution. During the Middle Ages tansy was hung in windows or strewn on floors as a flea and fly deterrent, its pungent odor filling the air when crushed. **Tansy contains volatile oils, principally thujone, making it potentially fatal in large doses.** In the old days, various preparations of this herb were used to expel roundworms and threadworms, as a poultice to relieve rheumatism and to cause abortion. Modern herbalists feel that tansy is dangerous and should not be taken internally.

*Tarweed, Mountain Tarweed

Madia glomerata

MEDICINAL

Life zone/ecosystem: Montane to subalpine. Disturbed soil. **Flowering**: July–August. **Fruit**: Achene enclosed within phyllary. **Characteristics:** Fairly common. Non-native weed. Resinous, tar-scented annual, 6–31 in. (14–70 cm). Glandular hairy foliage, yellow flower heads of few small ray florets, in small clusters; no pappus. Leaves opposite below, alternate above; without teeth.

Some moments one never forgets—such as the day you first discover tarweed and the disagreeable smell clings to your skin for the rest of the day! The Cheyenne were enamored with it—they inhaled the vapors to cure love sickness and carried the dried herb to attract women. It is now considered an undesirable and aggressive species that invades disturbed ground, often causing trouble for ranchers.

Tasselflower, Bricklebush

Brickellia grandiflora

MEDICINAL

Life zone/ecosystem: Montane to subalpine. Dry rocky areas, mostly of spruce-fir. **Flowering:** July–August. **Fruit:** 10-ribbed achene. **Characteristics:** Fairly common. Unusual herb with nodding heads, 12–40 in. (30–100 cm). Forms thick clumps; stems somewhat woody at base. Flower heads with disc flowers only; white to cream-colored or yellowish; fragrant. Triangular, slightly fuzzy leaves have toothed edges; alternate on stem. Pappus bristles whitish and minutely barbed.

A tea of tasselflower is known to regulate blood-sugar levels and may improve the functions of the digestive system and liver.[47] It is still used by some Mexicans, New Mexicans and Native Americans to treat type II diabetes.[48] Other common names of this plant include "prodigiosa" and "hamula."

Thistle Group

Cirsium and *Carduus* spp.

SUBSET OF SUNFLOWER FAMILY

EDIBLE • MEDICINAL • WILDLIFE

Many people think all thistles are weeds, yet native species fill important ecological niches. Their sweet nectar serves as essential food for butterflies and other insects, and most are edible or have medicinal uses. Members of the Cirsium genus have a feathery, plumose pappus, while that of Carduus is made up of simple hairs. At least fifteen thistle species are native to western Colorado, whereas only about five are "noxious weeds" introduced from Europe, mostly through contaminated hay and seed. Free from their natural biological enemies, these invaders adapt and spread rapidly in disturbed soil, crowding out native plants that wildlife depends upon for forage. Local governments are working to control Canada, plumeless and musk thistles, which are the worst offenders.

Most thistle roots can be eaten raw or cooked, the peeled stems can be roasted or boiled as greens and the leaves can be steeped as tea or eaten raw or cooked when young. Medicinally, boiled roots have been used for skin irritations and sores, while root tea is used for mouth sores.

Native thistles of the Rocky Mountains have not been adequately studied, so the following species designations are subject to interpretation.

Aspen Thistle, Osterhout's Thistle

Cirsium clavatum var. *osterhoutii*

Montane. Aspen, mixed-conifer forests and meadows. Flowers July–September. Common. Flower heads cream-colored. Leaves thin and flatter, less spiny than other thistles, with broad lobes and whitish mid-stripe; woolly on underside. Phyllaries have tan, straight spines; tips are not flanged, but phyllaries have purple centers and margins fringed with woolly hairs. Purple, hairy stems. This species has recently been described for the Flora of North America.

*Bull Thistle

Cirsium vulgare [*C. lanceolatum*]

Montane to lower subalpine. Flowers July–September. Uncommon. Non-native. Biennial, winter annual or annual. Flower heads are covered in tangled, long hairs; cobwebby. Leaves spiny and hairy on upper surface, cottony beneath; leaf bases decurrent, continuing winglike from node to node. Spiny leaf tips and bracts.

*Canada Thistle

Cirsium arvense
[*Dι ιuι uι vιιιsι*]

NOXIOUS WEED

Montane to subalpine. Flowers
June–October. Common. Non-
native. Flower heads pale lavender,
rarely whitish, but not pink or fuchsia as other weedy species. Plants
either male or female. Most abundant weed in Colorado. Spreads
aggressively by roots or seeds; even tiny root fragments start new plants. Systemic poisons
and biocontrol necessary. Vanilla fragrance attracts bees.

Eaton's Thistle

Cirsium eatonii [*C. tweedyi*]

Montane to lower alpine. Flowers: June–September. Common. Flowers
purple, rose-purple or whitish, heads in crowded terminal clusters.
Stems more slender upwards, leaves narrow and regularly pinnatifid,
very spiny. Spines not reflexed. Identification of varieties is difficult.

Elk Thistle, Colorado Thistle

Cirsium tioganum
var. *coloradense*
[*C. coloradense,*
C. scariosum]

Montane to subalpine. Meadows and streamsides in late summer. Common. White to reddish-purple flower heads in ground-hugging
rosette or at end of stem in dense cluster;

MIKE TYLER, JR.

additional flower heads possible in leaf axils. Phyllaries not reflexed, backs covered in
minute yellowish glands. Native Americans ate the roots after
baking them in a fire pit for a few hours. In 1870, Truman
Everts, a Yellowstone explorer with the Washburn Expedition,
became separated from his group for thirty-seven days. A
botanist had once told him that the root of elk thistle was safe
to eat, so he existed solely on the raw root and survived. Bears
love the low-growing version.

Mountain Thistle

Cirsium scopulorum [*C. hesperium*]

Upper subalpine to alpine. Rocky meadows and boulder fields.
Fairly common. Cobwebby flower heads look like frosty balls,
bringing to mind woolly sentinels guarding the tundra. Very
spiny. Large, yellowish or purplish flower heads, often nodding.
Leaves seem 3-dimensional.

REBECCA DAY-SKOWRON

*Musk Thistle
Carduus nutans
NOXIOUS WEED

Montane. Flowers late May to mid-July. Common. Non-native. Biennial, or rarely annual. Deeply lobed, spiny-margined, dark-green leaves; light-green midrib. Large, deep-rose flower heads that can reach 3 in. (8 cm) across; broad, rose-tinged, spine-tipped phyllaries.

Parry's Thistle
Cirsium parryi

Montane to lower subalpine. Moist meadows and streamsides. Flowers July to August. Fairly Common. Flowers greenish-yellow to yellow. Outer phyllaries with straight terminal spines and spiny margins. Involucre with long hairs, appearing cobwebby.

*Plumeless Thistle
Carduus acanthoides
NOXIOUS WEED

Montane. Flowers May–July. Common. Non-native. Winter annual or biennial. Grows 1–4 ft. (30–120 cm). Flower heads rose-purple to fuchsia. Stems very freely branching; covered with spiny wings extending to flower heads. Alternate stem leaves sessile, merging into stem. Young rosettes wavy-edged with yellow spines along margins.

END OF THISTLE GROUP

SUNFLOWER FAMILY *continued*

Western Hawksbeard, Largeflower Hawksbeard

Crepis occidentalis [*Psilochenia occidentalis*]

EDIBLE

Life zone/ecosystem: Montane. Oak-mountain and sagebrush shrublands. **Flowering:** May–July. **Fruit:** Achene with dense tuft of hairs about twice as long. **Characteristics:** Common. Milky-juiced herb averaging 12 in. (30 cm). Bright-yellow flower heads with 10–40 ray florets only (dandelion-like); 2–6 heads per stem branch; few to many branches. Leaves mostly at/near base of stem, up to 12 in. (30 cm) long, deeply lobed or toothed; several smaller stem leaves. Foliage usually grayish from short tangled hairs. Involucre thick and cylindrical with glandular hairs or bristles.

Distinctive leaves help identify the hawksbeards, which grow on drier, south-facing slopes in the Mancos Shale formation. Although there are no economic uses for western hawksbeard, Native American tribes did eat the leaves raw. **Tapertip hawksbeard** (*Crepis acuminata* [*Psilochenia*]), a taller species of similar habitats, has comparable leaves with long tapered tips, glabrous inner phyllaries, and only 5–10 ray florets per head. The Shoshoni people used this hawksbeard as a poultice of seeds or whole plant for sore breasts after childbirth, and powdered roots were sprinkled in inflamed eyes.[49]

Western Yarrow

Achillea millefolium var. *lanulosa* [*Achillea lanulosa*]

GARDEN · MEDICINAL · REVEGETATION · WILDLIFE

Life zone/ecosystem: Montane to alpine. Open meadows in all plant communities. **Flowering:** May–September. **Fruit:** Flattened achene. **Characteristics:** Common. 11–40 in. (30–100 cm). Whitish (rarely pinkish) flowers with pale-yellow centers, both ray and disc florets, tightly clustered together in flattened terminal clusters (corymbs). Blooms second year. Leaves dark green, soft, feathery, fern-like with pungent odor. **European yarrow** [*A. millefolium*], a native of Europe, has naturalized throughout North America. The two species are capable of interbreeding; difficult to differentiate. Medicinal uses similar.

Yarrow is an aromatic herb containing a complex mixture of over 120 chemical compounds that have made it popular as a medicine, fumigant and insecticide for millennia. *Achillea* is a historical reference to tales that the Greek hero Achilles healed the wounds of his soldiers with yarrow. During the Civil War, yarrow was known as "soldier's woundwort" for its curative properties, and is still mashed or chewed by hikers today and applied as a poultice to cuts and scrapes. References to yarrow are found in the *German Commission E Monographs*, the *U.S. Pharmacopoeia* from 1863 to 1882, the

1830 *Manual of Medical Botany of the U.S.* by Constantine Rafinesque, and the plant is still listed in the pharmacopoeias of Austria, Hungry, Poland and Switzerland. At least fifty-eight Native American tribes also used this herb. Yarrow has been used to treat menstrual cramps, colds, flu, fever, cuts and bruises, earaches, headaches, toothaches and sore eyes. It contains azulene, a blue volatile oil also found in German and Roman chamomile, that is likely responsible for the anti-inflammatory and anti-microbial properties. A "pioneer species," yarrow spreads easily from rhizome fragments and wind-dispersed seeds, readily colonizing disturbed soil and preventing erosion in revegetation projects. Bighorn sheep and deer eat yarrow leaves and flower heads. Cultivated varieties come in several colors and are popular in local gardens.

*Wild Lettuce, Prickly Lettuce

Lactuca serriola [*L. scariola*]

MEDICINAL

Life zone/ecosystem: Montane. Disturbed soil. **Flowering:** July–September. **Fruit:** Flattened achene; each side with 5–7 parallel ridges. **Characteristics:** Common. Non-native weed. Prickly biennial or winter annual with milky latex, 1–5 ft. (30–150 cm). Alternate, lobed leaves twist at base to lie in a vertical plane, clasping stem with 2 earlike lobes. Prickly spines on leaf edges and lower veins. Flower heads yellow ray florets only.

"Lettuce opium" is the title given to the milky latex extracted from this plant at flowering, which is said to look, smell and taste like the opium from poppies. It actually does contain minute amounts of morphine, but not enough to have much physiological effect on humans, according to Varro Tyler, author of *The Honest Herbal*. Nevertheless, the ancient Egyptians used the latex as a drug, believing it to have sedative properties, and Europeans made the dried latex into bitter, brownish cakes for the same reason. Lettuce opium has fallen in and out of favor over the centuries, becoming popular again for a brief time during the hippie years. Modern herbalists recommend a tea of the flowering stems as a weak sedative and cough suppressant for children and sensitive adults.

Woolly Golden Aster, Golden Aster

Heterotheca villosa

CEREMONIAL • GARDEN • MEDICINAL • WILDLIFE

Life zone/ecosystem: Montane to lower subalpine. Dry ground in aspen, spruce-fir forests. **Flowering:** July–September. **Fruit:** Flattened achene. **Characteristics:** Common. Furry, clumped herb up to 20 in. (50 cm). Golden ray and disc florets. Plant covered in silky hairs, often hiding small glands. Leaves lance-shaped, attached to leafy stem at narrow end; usually stalked at middle and lower part of stem. Double pappus, hair-like, with outer ring of short scales. Naked, pitted receptacles. Leaf form and size, amount of hair present, glands and attachment of flower heads all extremely variable; many varieties and species names, exact separations unclear.

Clumps of woolly golden aster appear lit from within on misty, cloudy days. Various uses were ascribed to this plant by Native Americans. The Hopi made a tea of leaves and flowers for chest pain. Navajo people made a ceremonial emetic and chant lotion, as well as leaf poultices for sore noses and ant bites and root poultices for toothaches. The Cheyenne used the plant as a sedative and as incense to rid homes of evil spirits. They also called this species "chickadee plant" because both chickadees and titmice relish the abundant seeds. Easily germinated, golden aster seeds are popular with native-plant gardeners.

VALERIAN FAMILY   *Valerianaceae*

Valerians of North America are plants with numerous small flowers in clusters, both basal and opposite leaves, roots with a strong scent and often fragrant flowers with tiny spurs, 5 united petals, 1–4 stamens and an inferior ovary. The sepals are barely noticeable. Though thirteen genera inhabit the planet, only three are native to North America. English valerian (*Valeriana officianalis*) is the official drug plant cultivated in Europe as medicine and is easy to grow if you are interested in valerian as medicine. Preparations of valerian are used as a sedative and carminative, and were also used as a condiment during the Middle Ages. Oils derived from the roots and rhizomes of valerians have been used in perfume.

Edible Valerian
Valeriana edulis
EDIBLE · MEDICINAL

Life zone/ecosystem: Montane to lower subalpine. Moist, sometimes rocky slopes and meadows of aspen, mixed-conifer and spruce-fir forest. **Flowering:** June–August. **Fruit:** Achene. **Characteristics:** Common. Up to 24 in. (60 cm). Inconspicuous white to yellowish flowers in open, branched arrangement (panicle). Somewhat fleshy leaves, lily-like, with side veins parallel to mid-vein; distinctive white line visible on leaf margin. Thick taproots, large and carrot-like, often branching.

Edible valerian is also referred to as tobacco root because of the odd taste of the roots when cooked. Their smell is reminiscent of dirty socks, somehow appealing to rats, so it was used as bait. Nevertheless, the roots are nutritious, and some Native Americans cooked them for many hours in a pit lined with hot stones and grass. Dried and powdered roots were used in breads and soups; however, the raw roots were considered poisonous. Medicinally, this herb is much milder than other valerians.

Western Valerian, Western Wild Heliotrope
Valeriana occidentalis

Life zone/ecosystem: Montane to subalpine. Moist, north-facing slopes, aspen and mixed-conifer forests. **Flowering:** Late May–July. **Fruit:** Ribbed achene. Calyx matures to parachute-like tuft of bristles on seed dispersed by wind. **Characteristics:** Common. 11–28 in. (30–70 cm). Tiny white flowers in round-topped clusters. Stalked basal leaves, spoon-shaped with smooth margins. Stem leaves opposite and stalkless with 3–9 lobes. Fibrous roots. **Subalpine valerian** (*Valeriana acutiloba* var. *acutiloba* [*V. capitata* subsp. *acutiloba*]) is more common in open, moist, rocky slopes near timberline into low tundra; the flowers are pinkish-white with one side distinctly more swollen; only 2–4 lobes on stem leaves; less than 18 in. (45 cm).

Some people actually find the earthy and pungent aroma of valerian root pleasing–it's definitely unforgettable! Prescribed since the 9th century by physicians, currently listed in the German *Commission E Monographs–Therapeutic Guide to Herbal Medicines* and still in use around the world, valerian can be trusted as a mild sedative to relieve nervous stress and sleeplessness. Although all have the same medicinal qualities, the different species vary in strength–western valerian is half the strength of English valerian and edible valerian is much milder still. No side effects or drug interactions are known; however, valerian is considered less effective for heavy people with high blood pressure. Tinctures seem the most reliable medicinal preparation. The dried herb will probably have no effect unless it has been dried and stored properly.

VERBENA or VERVAIN FAMILY   *Verbenaceae*

The verbenas comprise a family that includes cultivated ornamentals (*Verbena, Lantana*), teak wood (*Tectona*), flavorings and medicinal teas (*Aloysia, Verbena*). With their 4-angled stems, they can be confused with the mint family–but although sometimes aromatic, verbenas lack a minty fragrance. Verbena leaves are opposite or whorled and usually lobed or toothed. Flowers typically have 5 united sepals and 5 united petals and are sometimes 2-lipped, with 2 pairs of stamens. The ovary is superior with the pistil maturing into 2 or 4 nutlets, each with a single seed.

Prostrate Vervain
Verbena bracteata

Life zone/ecosystem: Montane. Roadsides, fields and other disturbed soil. **Flowering:** June–August. **Fruit:** Ridged, grayish-brown nutlet. **Characteristics:** Common, non-native. Prostrate annual or perennial, with spreading branches 6–18 in. (15–45 cm) long. Pinkish to pale blue-purple flowers arranged in dense spikes with leaf-like bracts extending past the flowers. Leaves typically 3-lobed and toothed; 4-angled stem. Reproduces by seed. Coarsely hairy.

Prostrate vervain is widespread throughout North America. A few patchy of this weedy plant occur locally in disturbed soil sites, but do not appear to be interfering with native vegetation.

VIOLET FAMILY   *Violaceae*

Violets are beloved by gardeners around the globe for their colorful and fragrant flowers, which resemble the faces of impish elves. About sixteen genera and 800 species of violet are mostly perennial herbs, but include some shrubs and a few annuals. The irregular flowers are bilaterally symmetrical and typically have 5 separated petals and 5 sepals. A large lower petal is sometimes bearded and may have a nectar-containing spur that extends backward. Those characteristic dark stripes on violet petals are there to guide pollinating insects to sweet nectar produced within, maneuvering them into a position that assures a dusting of pollen will be carried to the next flower. Violets possess quite a history, both in medicine and mythology. Pansies and Johnny-jump-ups are popular cultivated family members.

Violet Group   *Viola* spp.

EDIBLE • MEDICINAL • WILDLIFE

According to Greek mythology, when Zeus' lover Io was turned into a white heifer, Zeus commanded violets to grow wherever her tears fell, to console her and sweeten her diet. Violets still sweeten the diet of wildfood gourmets, who treasure the flowers and leaves as nutritious and colorful additions to salads, omelets and casseroles—but only in moderation as soaplike compounds in the leaves can upset the stomach. Violet wine was a popular brew in ancient Rome and violet-flower or leaf tea is still used as a beverage in England. Medicinally, violet leaves have been pre-pared in salves for skin irritations, poultices for bruises and teas and syrups for coughs, sore throats and constipation. The Greeks and Romans believed strongly in the medicinal value of violets. Hippocrates extolled the plant as a cure for headache, hangover and breathing problems. Violets also have a strong folklore tradition for treatment of cancer.

Canada Violet

Viola canadensis [V. scopulorum, V. rydbergii, V. rugulosa]

Montane. Aspen, mixed-conifer forest. Flowers May–July. Common. 4–16 in. (10–40 cm). White to pale-violet petals marked with delicate purple lines. Leaves broadly heart-shaped. A complex species not well understood.

Hooked Violet

Viola adunca

Montane to subalpine. Moist soil; aspen, mixed-conifer, spruce-fir forests. Flowers May–July. Common. 1.5–4 in. (4–10 cm). Violet petals marked by darker vio-let lines; white throat. 3 spreading lower petals and 2 backward-curving upper petals. Spur of lower petal obvious. Alternate leaves, egg-shaped with round-ed tips; heart-shaped base.

Lanceleaf Violet

Viola vallicola

Montane. Oak-mountain shrublands. Flowers May–June. Common. Up to 6 in. (15 cm). Cheery yellow petals with purplish-brown veins; 1 flower per stem. Leaves tapered, basal and somewhat lance-shaped, on long stalks. Grows in sun to partial shade.

Shelton Violet

Viola sheltonii [V. biternata]

Montane. Oak-mountain shrublands. Flowers May–June. Uncom-mon. Up to 6 in. (15 cm). More rare than lanceleaf violet, but also with yellow flowers and brown veins; leaves dissected into narrow segments.

WATERLEAF FAMILY *Hydrophyllaceae*

S ome of the most beautiful local wildflowers are waterleafs, easily recognized by their forked styles and their 5 stamens extending beyond the 5-petaled, saucer- or funnel-shaped flowers. Although the feature is not unique to this family, some waterleaf species collect rainwater and dew in the folds of their leaves, eventually channeling the moisture to their roots. Preliminary molecular analyses leads some botanists to believe this family is actually part of the borage family (Boraginaceae), because some species in each familiy share similar characteristics, such as immature seed placement on the walls of the ovary, coiled flower arrangements and bristly foliage.

Ball-head Waterleaf, Woolen Breeches

Hydrophyllum capitatum

EDIBLE

Life zone/ecosystem: Montane to subalpine. Moist, shaded soil of oak-mountain shrublands, aspen and mixed-conifer forests. **Flowering:** May–June. **Fruit:** Round capsule. **Characteristics:** Common. Dwarf herb, 2–8 in. (5–20 cm). Lavender (rarely white) flowers in tight round clusters; stamens exerted. Flower stalk shorter than leaf stalk. Leaves somewhat triangular-shaped overall; deeply lobed. Fleshy roots.

Clustered lavender spheres of waterleaf will often hide just out of sight beneath the leaves. A profusion of protruding stamens creates a fuzzy halo, probably leading to the plant's common name of woolen breeches. Although early American settlers cooked the tender young shoots and fleshy roots of this genus, these beautiful wildflowers should be disturbed only in a survival situation.

Fendler's waterleaf
(*Hydrophyllum fendleri*), a close relative of ball-head waterleaf, can be found locally in the subalpine. It grows up to 32 in. (80 cm), with the flower heads rising above the leaves, which are divided into 9–13 hairy, toothed segments.

259

Scorpionweed
Phacelia hastata

Life zone/ecosystem: Montane to alpine. Dry, open sites; trailside. **Flowering:** June–July. **Fruit:** Capsule. **Characteristics:** Common. Multi-stemmed herb, 8–20 in. (20–50 cm). White to dull-lavender flowers with 5 conspicuous brown stamens and a rough-hairy calyx; branched flowering spikes coiled like scorpion's tail. Both basal leaves and the alternate stem leaves are spoon-shaped and without teeth; may have small pair of lobes at base; grayish-green with dense, short hairs. Stems sometimes sprawling.

Plants of the *Phacelia* genus are cultivated in some countries for the mild white honey that bees produce from them. Science first received a description of this plant, although under a different name, from Nicolaus Joseph Baron von Jacquin (1727–1817), Professor of Botany and Director of the Botanic Garden in Vienna. Sometimes considered weedy, this native plant is actually important as an early successional species. An alpine variety is smaller and has more lavender-colored flowers.

Silky Phacelia, Purple Fringe
Phacelia sericea
GARDEN • WILDLIFE

Life zone/ecosystem: Subalpine to alpine. Gravelly open areas, disturbed soil. **Flowering:** June–August. **Fruit:** 2-chambered capsule. **Characteristics:** Fairly common. Aromatic, stout-stemmed herb, 4–12 in. (10–40 cm). Woody crown at base of stems. Violet to dark-purple flowers in dense, bottle-brush-like arrangements (actually, slightly coiled racemes). Obvious purple stamens with yellow anthers. Grayish-green leaves have deeply cut lobes covered in silky hairs; crowded at base of plant; also along stem. Taproot.

Silky phacelia's purple-flowered inflorescence sports a "fringe" of yellow-tipped purple stamens. Dr. Harry Warren, a pioneer in biogeochemistry, once discovered three gold-bearing areas in British Columbia by studying clues from the cyanide-bearing roots, which collect gold from the soil.[50] Elk, mule deer, mountain goats and black bear graze on silky phacelia. These striking plants are favored as a border in native gardens.

WILLOW FAMILY   *Salicaceae*

O nly three genera, but 300–500 species, make up this family of
shrubs and trees found primarily in cool, moist areas of the
northern hemisphere. Willows and cottonwoods like their feet wet,
thriving in the moist soil of streambanks, lake shores and in mountain meadows. Aspens prefer dry to moist, well-drained soils. All have
deciduous, simple, alternate leaves with stipules. Their tiny flowers
lack petals and are unisexual, meaning male and female flowers
appear in catkins on separate plants. The female flowers mature into
capsules filled with downy seeds, easily dispersed by wind. Members
of this family contain a variety of chemical compounds used medicinally in nearly every culture.

Narrowleaf Cottonwood

Populus angustifolia

GARDEN • WILDLIFE

Life zone/ecosystem: Montane. Riparian zones; grows
along streambanks and colonizes sandbars; needs wet soil,
full sun to germinate; either acid or alkaline soil. Up to
9,100 ft. (2774 m) in the Roaring Fork watershed.
Flowering: May. **Fruit:** Pointed capsule contains seeds,
each with tuft of fluffy, cottony hairs. **Characteristics:**
Common; exception is Brush Creek, where uncommon.
Deciduous tree up to 60 ft. (20 m). Trunk may exceed 30
in. (76 cm) in diameter. Bark yellowish-green to grayish-
brown; smooth on young trees, becoming furrowed into
broad, flat ridges with age. Buds can be somewhat sticky.
Male (staminant) and female (pistillate) flowers on separate
trees, both in pendent catkins. Alternate leaves simple,
lanceolate to ovate-lanceolate, rounded at base; hairless or
nearly so with glandular-toothed margins; dark green
above, slightly paler beneath. Petioles about ⅓ as long as
blade, flattened at base. Lives 100-200 years. **Balsam
poplar** (*P. balsamifera*), not native to this area, is found locally and
hybridizes with narrowleaf. Leaves much larger, ovate to ovate-
lanceolate, green above, paler beneath; buds very sticky-resinous.

Narrowleaf cottonwoods leaf out early along
streambanks, covering valley bottoms with clouds of soft lime
green, an eagerly awaited sign that spring has really arrived. These
important trees are found from southern Alberta to northern
Mexico. They are dominant in local montane riparian ecosystems
and are the most abundant wild cottonwood species in Colorado.
Riparian ecosystems occupy less than 3% of Colorado's total land
area, yet are home to approximately 40% of native plant species, as
well as 75% of the birds and 80% of the mammals that live in or

migrate through the state. Because wildlife depends on these areas for habitat, food, nesting sites, corridors for movement and cover from predators for all or part of the year, conservation of narrowleaf cottonwood and its streamside habitat is critical. Bald eagle, great-blue heron and sharp-shinned hawk nest in cottonwoods and beaver depend on them for food, lodge construction and dam building material. Twigs are browsed by mule deer, elk and rabbits, while buds and catkins are eaten by blue grouse.

Annual spring flooding is the controlling factor in the establishment of narrowleaf cottonwood communities. Peak river flows usually correspond with the flowering of cottonwoods, while the drop in river flow happens as clouds of the fluffy seeds are released, providing them with wet sand or newly deposited soil for germination. The seeds are only viable for two days, so timing is key. Already established trees reproduce primarily by suckering similar to aspens. This can be a great asset in streambank stabilization or erosion control in revegetation projects. It does present problems in home landscapes where the rapidly-growing roots invade gardens and penetrate pipes. A cottonwood can also be started from a root segment that already has lateral roots.

Some Native American people used the young cottonwood shoots to make baskets.

Quaking Aspen
Populus tremuloides
MEDICINAL • WILDLIFE
• RESTORATION

Life zone/ecosystem: Montane. Commonly grows up to 10,000 ft. (3048 m). **Flowering:** April–May. **Fruit:** Tiny capsules with cottony seeds. **Characteristics:** Common. Deciduous tree up to 90 ft. (27 m). Flowers in catkins appearing before leaves. Leaves roundish, or somewhat heart-shaped, with definite point. Leaf stalk flattened perpendicularly to blade, causing quaking, or fluttering, in slightest breeze. White to greenish bark mostly thin and smooth, but dark gray to black and roughly grooved at base of old trees. Buds without sticky resinous coating. Aspens often mistaken for birches, which are in a different family.

"Conifers have a majestic monotony, like someone who is always right. They are too timeless to mark the seasons. But aspen has eclat, a glorious brashness in defiance of the rules, the flapper who does the Charleston in the midst of the grand waltz. The landscape would be dull indeed without them."

—ANN ZWINGER, *Beyond the Aspen Grove*

Aspens have an intrinsic beauty, notably graceful and elegant, yet fragile—and are easily affected by wounds, disease, insects and fungus. To counter this vulnerability, aspens have developed a reproductive system called cloning, which allows them to recover from these events, even when besieged by such natural disturbances as fire or avalanche. Cloning occurs when a tree sends forth suckers, which grow rapidly, drawing needed nutrition and moisture from a network of established roots. Aspen forests are a mosaic of individual clones—forever dying and regenerating. While most aspens are short-lived at fifty to seventy years, an entire clone could be thousands of years old— some speculate even a million. Individual trees not

JUDY HILL

affected by disturbance or disease have been known to live 200 years. Aspen buds, inner bark and leaves were used medicinally by Native Americans and early settlers. Like willow, aspen contains salicin in the inner bark, which is an ingredient in aspirin. Cree tribes made a tea from the inner bark to treat rheumatism, liver and kidney conditions, diarrhea and coughs. A similar tonic, with the addition of tree fungus, eased earaches, and crushed leaves relieved the itch of insect stings. On the sun-facing side of trees, the photosynthetic bark makes its own protective powdery white coating, which was used by early people as a sunscreen. Current medicinal uses are similar to those described under willow. Today, aspens are mostly ground into pulp to be used in the manufacture of paper particle board. Historically, canoe paddles and tipi poles were made from the wood. See page 40 for more photos and a description of aspen forest ecology.

Aspens are critical to watershed health. They prevent erosion by controlling runoff, allowing water to filter down through the soil, cleaning it before it spills into our streams. In the arid West, aspen stands are second only to riparian zones in habitat importance for the essential role played in the lives of an estimated 500 species, from bears to fungi.

Willow Group

Salix spp.

SUBSET OF WILLOW FAMILY   **EDIBLE • MEDICINAL • REVEGETATION • WILDLIFE**

From the tall, bushy shrubs of lower elevations to the tiny, mat-forming plants of alpine heights, tenacious willows are perfectly attuned to their environments. Soft reds and tawny golds of bare winter branches provide welcome color against the snowy landscape and are the first to take on a fresh green blush in spring. As creeks and streams surge with snowmelt, female fruits burst open, filling the air with fluffy clouds of miniscule seeds, which have only a few days to germinate and survive. Willows grow rapidly, securing their "feet" into wet soil and forming sinuous thickets along mountain waterways. They spread aggressively by underground stolons and suckers, sprouting from even the smallest piece of stem, which makes them valuable for erosion control and stream-restoration projects.

Willow thickets fill with a riot of birdsong in spring and early summer, as yellow warblers, orange-crown warblers, song sparrows, and fox sparrows locate mates and establish nests. Elk and deer browse the spring twigs, while smaller mammals and birds nibble twigs and buds—the dense thickets providing important protection from predators. Beavers rely on willow when there are no aspens.

Willow was traditionally used as a pain reliever, and even now, herbalists still recommend willow bark for rheumatic and arthritic disorders, and the pain of non-acute inflammation. Although willow bark takes longer to be absorbed by the body than modern pain relievers, its effects are believed to last longer. For more information, refer to the books *Herbs of Choice, Beyond Cortisone* and *Medicinal Plants of the Mountain West.*

The inner bark of all willows has long been recognized as a food by native cultures and is considered safe to eat; however, not all species are palatable. According to the Alaska Cooperative Extension Service, the leaves contain seven to ten times more vitamin C than oranges.

Learning "which is which" among local willow species is definitely a challenge! In the descriptions that follow, willows are generally multi-stemmed shrubs unless noted. For an excellent technical willow key, visit the Colorado Native Plant Society's website.

FIRST AID FOR PAIN

The use of willow for pain relief goes back at least to ancient Sumeria, 6,000 years ago, but it wasn't until the 1820's that European chemists isolated willow's effective ingredient, salicin. Salicylic acid was first prepared from salicin in the laboratory in 1838 and soon became a panacea in Europe for pain. However, salicylic acid had a side effect—gastric discomfort. After much experimentation, Felix Hoffmann, a chemist for the German pharmaceutical company Bayer, produced a pure sample of a milder related compound, acetylsalicylic acid, which Bayer began distributing in 1897 under the name "aspirin."

Alpine Willow *Salix arctica*
var. *petraea*
[*S. petrophila*]

Alpine. 11,000–13,000 ft. (3353–3962 m). Dry or wet soil. Common. Creeping, prostrate shrub, less than 4 in. (10 cm). Catkins, 0.4–1.2 in. (10–30 mm) long, grow on side branches. Leaves usually hairy with pointed tips, without network of veins beneath. Thick twigs. Fruit is hairy capsule.

Bebb's Willow
Salix bebbiana

Montane, possibly lower subalpine. Wet areas, streambanks. Fairly common. Multi-stemmed to single-stemmed shrub to small tree, 3–13 ft. (1–4 m). Veins are sunken into the leaf surface and result in a textured appearance. Young twigs and more mature leaves are reddish with a soft fuzz, while older branches are frequently cracked, appearing white-streaked. Unique catkins with quite long stalks (stipes) for individual flowers, bristle out from the catkin. Bebb's willow has been used for making baseball bats and charcoal. Often called "diamond willow" because when the wood is carved, it results in diamond-shaped patterns. The sharp contrast between the reddish-brown heartwood and the white sapwood is responsible for these patterns.

Bebb's Willow

Booth's Willow
Salix boothii
[*S. pseudocordata*]

Montane to subalpine. 5,000–10,300 ft. (1524–3140 m). Springs and streambanks. Common. Broadly-rounded shrub, 3–13 ft. (1–4 m). Dubbed "Boring boothii" by willow whiz Gwen Kittel because its distinctive character-istic is that it has none. Catkins erect. Leaves somewhat lanceo-late, not glaucous; may be some-what hairy when young, smooth with maturity; mostly lack teeth on edges. Young twigs thinly hairy. Color of twigs varies.

Drummond's Willow, Silver Willow
Salix drummondiana

Montane to subalpine. Wet areas, ponds, streambanks (often steep) to 11,000 ft. (3353 m). Common. Grows 3–16 ft. (1–5 m). New and previous year's branches obviously glaucous. Leaves are dark green on surface, more than ½ in. (1.3 cm) wide, hairy and glaucous beneath.

Geyer's Willow
Salix geyeriana

Montane to subalpine. Streambanks (usually low gradient), wet areas, and ponds above 6,500 ft. (1981 m). Fairly common. Grows 3–16 ft. (1–5 m). New and previous year's twigs are strongly glaucous. Leaves pale yellowish-green to moderate green, less than ½ in. (1.3 cm) wide; glaucous and hairy beneath.

Mountain Willow
Salix monticola

Montane to alpine. 5,700–12,500 ft. (1727–3810 m). Streambanks and other wet places. Common. Grows 8–16 ft. (2.5–5 m). Difficult to distinguish from strapleaf willow, so compare all traits carefully, while looking at several leaves. Leaves yellow to yellowish-green, variably toothed to almost entire on edges, usually with rounded base; clearly broader in the middle. Twigs mostly yellow to yellowish-green, drying blackish.

Planeleaf Willow
Salix planifolia

Montane to subalpine. 8,000–13,000 ft. (2438–3962 m). Moist soil of valley bottoms, springs or seeps. Common. Subalpine shrubs only 16–40 in. (40–100 cm); montane shrubs may reach 16 ft. (5 m). Glossy, dark-green leaves, glaucous beneath, smooth to slightly hairy, margins rolled backward; edges seldom with teeth. Twigs shiny and colorful—bright red to dark red or purple to purple-black—and smooth to slightly hairy.

Sandbar Willow
Salix exigua

Montane. 5,600–9,200 ft. (1067–2804 m). Sandbars within streams, ditches and seeps. Common. Multi-stem thickets, up to 10 ft. (3 m), possibly taller. Only local willow with linear leaves, more than 6 times longer than wide. Leaf edges smooth to toothed with glandular tips. Leaf surfaces mostly smooth to silky hairy.

Scouler's Willow
Salix scouleriana

Montane to lower subalpine. Usually 8,000–10,000 ft. (2438–3048 m). Dry hill-sides in aspen and conifer forests, not in wet soil—only local willow growing away from water. Common. Sparsely branched shrub to 13 ft. (4 m). Spoon-shaped leaves are attached at narrower end; glaucous beneath. Crushed twigs usually have skunk-like odor.

Short-fruit Willow, Barren Willow
Salix brachycarpa

Montane to alpine. 7,500–12,000 ft. (2286–3658 m). Bogs, fens, sub-alpine willow thickets, talus slopes. Fairly common. Usually 16–40 in. (40–100 cm), but can grow twice as tall at lower elevations. Leaves appear grayish from the extremely hairy surface above and beneath; also glaucous on lower surface. Red-brown branches; new branches and capsules of catkins densely furry. Interbreeds with similar **gray willow** (*S. glauca*), whose leaves are more sparsely hairy. Mostly less than 3 ft. (1 m) and usually at or above timberline only.

Snow Willow
Salix reticulata [*S. nivalis*]

Alpine. 10,500–12,500 ft. (3200–3810 m). Common. Prostrate and creeping shrub, less than 16 in. (40 cm). Leaves are narrowly oval to egg-shaped with mostly rounded tips, glaucous and solidly net-veined beneath. Leaves often clustered at end of twig.

Strapleaf Willow
Salix eriocephala var. *ligulifolia*

Montane. 5,000–9,500 ft. (1524–2896 m). Streambanks and other wet places. Common. Leaves with fairly parallel sides (rather than being widest in the middle), are darker and more blue-green, more sharply pointed at tip, and usually more triangular and tapering at base than mountain willow. Both species may have some twigs that are reddish on one side, but observe dominant color of twigs overall. Younger twigs of strapleaf are more reddish to greenish.

Whiplash Willow
Salix lasiandra [*S. lucida, S. caudata*]

Montane to subalpine. 5,600–10,000 ft. (1250–3048 m). Wet areas and streambanks. Common. Tall shrubs or small trees, usually multi-stemmed, up to 20 ft. (6 m). Tips of lance-shaped leaves long and sharply pointed, appearing whip-like; edges have glandular-tipped teeth, upper surface shiny and smooth, lower surface either glaucous (var. lasiandra) or not (var. caudata). Can be confused with narrowleaf cottonwood.

Whiplash willow

Wolf Willow
Salix wolfii

Subalpine. To 11,000 ft. (3353 m). Wet soils of valley bottoms, seeps and springs. Fairly common. Low-stature shrub, less than 40 in. (1 m). Often forms large thickets. Olive-green leaves narrowly oval and sharp-tipped, uniformly hairy both sides; not glaucous beneath. Twigs yellow to orange when young, chestnut-brown when more mature; youngest may be slightly woolly, older are smooth and shiny.

NOXIOUS WEEDS—WHAT'S THE FUSS?

"Weeds" are often described as "plants out of place," having evolved in another part of the world, or as plants growing where they are not wanted. Non-native plants often become "noxious weeds," growing unchecked by natural enemies such as insects or diseases. These plants may spread aggressively, stealing precious moisture, nutrients and sunlight from surrounding plants and threatening biodiversity and ecosystem stability. Noxious weeds can also alter the structure of wildlife communities, which may not be able to adapt to rapid changes in habitat. Species that invade riparian or wetland areas rob waterfowl and mammals of their food sources, nesting areas and access to water, which is needed for protection from predators.

Many noxious species were brought to North America as ornamentals, later escaping to wreak havoc in native communities. Areas that once displayed a rich diversity of native plants are now dominated by such invasive species as Canada thistle, leafy spurge, yellow toadflax and oxeye daisy. Yellow star thistle, which has already devastated millions of acres in California, Oregon and Washington, has recently appeared in Colorado. The Colorado Noxious Weed Act of 1996 enables residents to play a bigger part in protecting natural resources and encourages taking responsibility for what grows on private land, including gardens. To learn more, contact Pitkin County Weed Control at 920-5214 or your Colorado State University Cooperative Extension Office (Garfield County Cooperative Extension, call 970-625-3969).

Adapted with permission from "Troublesome Weeds of the Rocky Mountain West," prepared by the Colorado Weed Management Association. Call 970-887-1228 or visit their website (http://www.cwma.org) for a complete list and photos of Colorado Noxious Weeds not included in this book.

Pitkin County Weed List (plants described in this field guide are marked with "•")

- Butter-and-eggs, Yellow toadflax (*Linaria vulgaris*)
- Canada thistle (*Cirsium arvense*)
- Common burdock (*Arctium minus*)
- Common tansy (*Tanacetum vulgare*)
- Dame's rocket (*Hesperis matronalis*)
  Dalmation toadflax (*Linaria genistifolia*)
  Diffuse knapweed (*Centaurea diffusa*)
- Field bindweed (*Convolvulvus arvensis*)
  Hoary cress (*Cardaria draba*)
- Houndstongue (*Cynoglossum officinale*)
  Leafy spurge (*Euphorbia esula*)

- Musk thistle (*Carduus nutans*)
- Oxeye daisy (*Chrysanthemum leucanthemum*)
- Plumeless thistle (*Carduus acanthoides*)
- Poison hemlock (*Conium maculatum*)
  Purple loosestrife (*Lythrum salicaria*)
  Russian knapweed (*Acroptilon repens*)
  Saltcedar, Tamarisk (*Tamarix parviflora*)
- Scentless chamomile (*Matricaria perforata*)
  Scotch thistle (*Onopordum acanthium*)
  Spotted knapweed (*Centaurea maculosa*)
- Yellow toadflax (*Linaria vulgaris*)

Hoary cress

Hoary cress is rapidly invading the upper Roaring Fork Valley. **Leafy spurge** is considered by some to be the most serious weed in Colorado. It is extremely difficult to control because of its extensive sprouting root system.

Leafy spurge

NOTE: Two species discussed in this guide are currently on the Colorado Noxious Weed List, but not yet on the Pitkin County list: Common St. John's wort (*Hypericum perforatum*) and chicory (*Cichorium intybus*).

GRASSES, SEDGES and RUSHES

These plants may all look like grasses, but they're not! Most of us usually overlook grasses (Poaceae), sedges (Cyperaceae) and rushes (Juncaceae), which, compared to showy wildflowers, trees and shrubs, seem mind-bogglingly similar in appearance and hard to identify. Despite appearances, these are also flowering plants, although the flowers are tiny and inconspicuous. These three families are often referred to as the "graminoids," meaning grass-like plants, the common traits among them being the radically smaller flowers and parallel-veined leaves. Use a hand lens to take a closer look at this fascinating hidden world. With a little attention to detail, it is easy to tell the differences between these three families—though without a good dose of perseverence, exact identification of the some 10,000 grass species, 4,000 sedge species and 400 rush species is best left to the professional botanists and extremely curious amateurs!

Grasses, sedges and rushes are of great ecological importance in controlling erosion, revegetating disturbed land and providing food and cover for wildlife. All are found growing in both dry and wet situations; however, grasses are more often found in all soil types, while, sedges and rushes are endemic to wetlands, where they provide shelter, food and breeding habitat for wildlife, as well as being an indicator of environmental health. The presence of a given species of wetland sedge, rush or grass reflects the soil and water chemistry, hydrology, history and other aspects of the site's ecology.

This book is not meant to be a technical guide for these groups, so what follows are brief descriptions of each family with a few photos of some common local species. The drawings are not from actual plants and are meant to loosely illustrate differences between the three groups whose technical details are extremely variable. For a more in-depth study, *How to Identify Grasses and Grasslike Plants* by H. D. Harrington is a good place to start. For simple identification keys, refer to *A Simplified Guide to Common Colorado Grasses* and *Illustrated Keys to the Grasses of Colorado*, both by Janet Wingate.

"Sedges have edges, rushes are round and grasses are hollow with nodes up and down," is an old botanical rhyme that may help you remember the main differences between them.

GRASS FAMILY

Poaceae

Cereal grains, including oats, rye, rice, wheat, corn and barley, come from this family, which forms the most important food group for humans and many other living things. Grasses have round stems that are typically hollow. The leaves are flat, with the lower section sheathing the stem, and the upper section, or blade, departing the stem from a swollen area called the node. The membranous or hairy appendage at this junction is called a ligule. The leaves are "two-ranked," which means two leaves grow opposite each other.

Fringed brome (*Bromus ciliatus*)

This trait is easily seen from above. The basic unit of a grass inflorescence is called a spikelet—a small cluster of one or more florets above 2 bracts (called glumes). Each floret is composed of a "bract-like" lemma and palea surrounding the flower parts. Each floret usually has 3 stamens and 2 stigmas. The spikelets are arranged in a 1- or 2-sided spike, raceme or panicle.

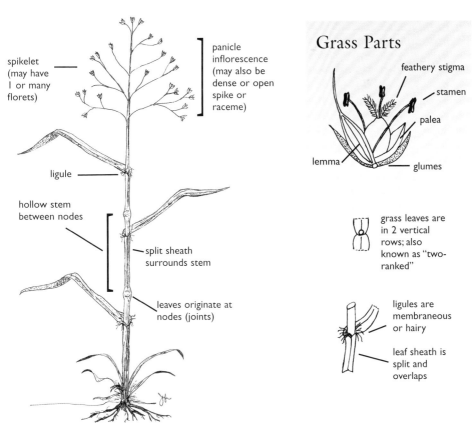

spikelet (may have 1 or many florets)

panicle inflorescence (may also be dense or open spike or raceme)

ligule

hollow stem between nodes

split sheath surrounds stem

leaves originate at nodes (joints)

Grass Parts

feathery stigma

stamen

palea

lemma

glumes

grass leaves are in 2 vertical rows; also known as "two-ranked"

ligules are membraneous or hairy

leaf sheath is split and overlaps

271

A Few Common Local Grasses

Blue wild rye
(*Elymus glaucus*)

Bottlebrush squirreltail
(*Elymus elymoides*)

Reed canarygrass
(*Phalaris arundinaceae*)
non-native

Indian rice grass
(*Oryzopsis hymenoides*
[*Achnatherum*])

Redtop
(*Agrostis gigantea*)
non-native

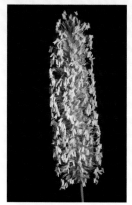

Timothy
(*Phleum pratense*)
non-native

Thurber's fescue (*Festuca thurberi*)

Shortawn foxtail (*Alopecurus aequalis*)

Thurber's fescue dominates many subalpine meadows.

Grasses, sedges and rushes are of great ecological importance for controlling erosion, revegetation of disturbed land and providing food and cover for wildlife.

SEDGE FAMILY

Cyperaceae

Water sedge (*Carex aquatilis*)

Sedge Parts

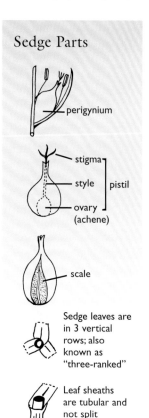

perigynium

stigma
style } pistil
ovary
(achene)

scale

Sedge leaves are in 3 vertical rows; also known as "three-ranked"

Leaf sheaths are tubular and not split

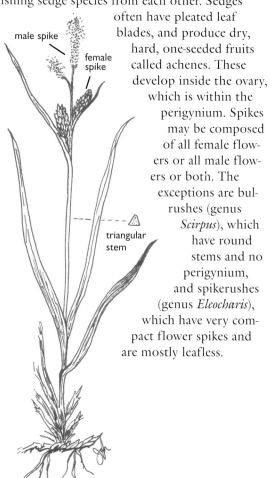

male spike

female spike

triangular stem

S edges usually have triangular, or 3-sided stems that are solid between the joints with leaves that are in 3 vertical rows (or 3-ranked). Look from above to see how the leaves are spaced about 120 degrees apart as they progress up the stem. Sedge flowers consist of a single dry scale with either stamens (male) or pistils (female), and are arranged in erect or drooping, green or brown flower spikes. Flowers typically lack sepals and petals, although these parts may be reduced to hairs or bristles. The pistil and single-chambered ovary are usually enclosed in a specialized sac-like bract called the perigynium, whose peculiarities of shape and surface texture provide the primary means of distinguishing sedge species from each other. Sedges often have pleated leaf blades, and produce dry, hard, one-seeded fruits called achenes. These develop inside the ovary, which is within the perigynium. Spikes may be composed of all female flowers or all male flowers or both. The exceptions are bulrushes (genus *Scirpus*), which have round stems and no perigynium, and spikerushes (genus *Eleocharis*), which have very compact flower spikes and are mostly leafless.

RUSH FAMILY

Juncaceae

I n general, rushes all have rounded stems with solid piths. Rush flowers are concentrated in terminal inflorescences, though some species may appear to have the flowers growing from the side of the stem—this upper "stem" is actually an involucral bract (see arctic rush below). The tiny flowers of rushes, unlike those of grasses, have distinct flower parts, which include 3 sepals and 3 petals (may look very similar), 2-6 stamens and a pistil with 3 slim styles. Rush fruits are 3-sectioned capsules containing many seeds.

Woodrush (*Luzula parviflora*)

Rush Parts

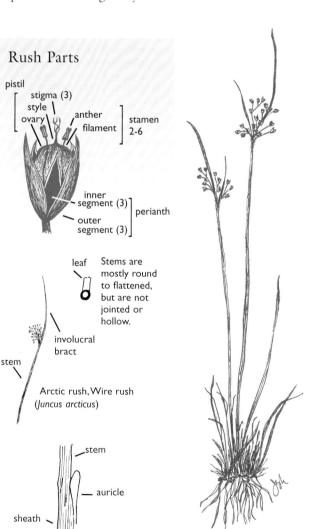

pistil
stigma (3)
style
ovary
anther
filament
stamen 2-6

inner segment (3)
outer segment (3)
perianth

leaf
Stems are mostly round to flattened, but are not jointed or hollow.

involucral bract

stem

Arctic rush, Wire rush (*Juncus arcticus*)

stem
auricle
sheath

Swordleaf rush (*Juncus ensifolius*)

BIRDS

Horned Owl
n Henry

Even the darkness moves with the passage of birds.
On soft spring midnights, the air is alive with the flight
notes of unseen warblers and vireos, thrushes and
orioles, sparrows and tanagers, filtering down through
the moonlight like the voices of stars.

—SCOTT WEIDENSAUL, *Living on the Wind:*
Across the Hemisphere with Migratory Birds

Imagine sitting by a mountain stream, mesmerized by an American dipper as it dives from its midstream perch into the frigid waters to retrieve a bill full of mayfly larvae. Suddenly a bald eagle swoops in to grasp an unwary trout and flies off, the trout now swimming on air as the eagle rises on powerful wings, its white head glistening in the early morning sun. Or perhaps, you discover a female robin patiently returning time after time with a bill full of mud, carefully placing it inside her nest of sticks and grass before she raises her wings and does a little belly dance to smooth the mud into the rounded inner surface.

What remarkable ability birds have to educate and inspire us about the interdependence of life. Their simple beauty, unique voices and diverse natural histories enrich our lives every day.

Learning to recognize bird songs takes birding to another level, enabling you to identify birds without direct sightings and also making it easier to associate them with their favored habitats. Each song is a distinctive feature of that species, and when combined with some species' non-vocal sounds, gives insight into their character and behavior. Spring, when the outdoors becomes alive with the sounds of males seeking to attract mates and define their territories, is the best time to develop an ear for bird songs. For practice throughout the year, there are instructional recordings available from bookstores, libraries, nature centers, and on the Internet. At first the numerous songs striking your ears will seem jumbled, but slowly, over time, they will become distinct and familiar, like the voices of old friends.

HOW TO USE THIS CHAPTER

All birds described in this chapter breed in our area unless otherwise indicated. The order in which families and species are listed is based on the one followed by *The Sibley Guide to Bird Life and Behavior* (2001 edition), by David Allen Sibley. Both the common and scientific names given are those designated as "official" by the American Ornithologists' Union (AOU). Although the "official" common name of a bird is traditionally capitalized, the lower case is utilized throughout this chapter to be consistent with the rest of this book.

Below each scientific name is a line indicating the species' seasonal status and abundance in this area, using the following terms:

RESIDENT, NON-MIGRATORY: Breeds and is a year-round resident in local ecosystems. Some species move to lower elevations during severe winter weather.

RESIDENT, MIGRATORY: Usually year-round residents, but part of population may migrate. There may be populations of these species that arrive from northern areas to winter here, supplementing local residents (e.g., bald eagle).

BREEDING, MIGRATORY: Nests in local ecosystems but migrates to warmer climates during winter. Some species occasionally remain for the winter.

MAY BREED: Unconfirmed in local ecosystems due to marginal habitat for that species' nesting and foraging needs.

ABUNDANT: Ubiquitous, very numerous and cannot be missed in appropriate habitat.

COMMON: Should be encountered frequently in appropriate habitat.

FAIRLY COMMON: Encountered fairly often, but not frequently, in appropriate habitat.

UNCOMMON: Present, but not always encountered, even in suitable habitat.

RARE: Not likely to occur.

Each species account begins with three sections:

- **Habitat/feeding** lists the local ecosystems and habitats favored by the species (including elevations where available), and describes its diet and feeding strategies.

- **Field ID traits** points out distinctive characteristics in the plumage, behavior, songs and calls that may be useful in identification. Songs are the most recognizable vocalizations, since birds sing to establish territories and secure a mate. Calls are short and quite variable, occuring throughout the year for different communication purposes. **Measurements refer to the average length of an adult male from the tip of the bill to the tip of the tail,** and are taken from National Geographic Society's *Field Guide to the Birds of North America.*

- **Breeding/nesting** describes courtship, nesting and certain associated behaviors as they occur in Colorado.

The final paragraph of each species description gives information on migration habits, recent research, conservation status and other noteworthy details. Each bird's conservation status was obtained from the *Colorado Breeding Bird Atlas,* Arvind Panjabi of the Rocky Mountain Bird Observatory, biologist Delia Malone, ecologist Jody Cardamone with the Aspen Center for Environmental Studies, or the Partners in Flight website.

BIRD VIEWING TIPS AND ETIQUETTE

- The best times to view birds are between sunrise and about 10 am, and late afternoon until dusk.
- Wear muted clothing and approach as quietly as possible.
- View from a distance through binoculars, spotting scopes or a telephoto lens so as not to disturb the birds.
- Make a quick mental note of the silhouette, and/or jot down characteristics such as bill shape, general size and color, wing-bars, eye-rings, and eyebrows to help in later identification.
- Being alert to behaviors and habitats of different species will help confirm the bird's identity.
- Steer clear of nests and nesting colonies, giving them plenty of room.
- If a bird shows any signs of distress—alarm-calling, tail-flicking, flying in short hops, scolding, dive-bombing, flushing from its nest, or trying to lead you away from the nest—you are too close!
- Do not try to "save" baby birds—Mom is usually somewhere nearby.

Conservation status is considered important in light of recent declines in some bird populations and changing attitudes toward conservation. During the early 1900's, birds were routinely shot for their meat or their brightly colored feathers. As populations began to crash in this country, Congress moved to protect most native birds through the Migratory Bird Act, signed by President Taft in 1913, which declared all migratory and insectivorous birds to be within the custody and protection of the Federal government. This act was eventually replaced by the Migratory Bird Treaty Act in 1918, signed by President Woodrow Wilson. Today, declines in migratory bird populations are more likely a symptom of a worldwide reduction in biodiversity caused by unprecedented damage to natural habitats. All migratory birds need safe places of refuge in order to feed and rest during their travels. The continued survival of billions of birds is dependent upon preservation of habitat. Help make the world bird friendly by learning which

Young robins

birds breed here, by understanding the issues that face them, and by becoming involved in local and international conservation efforts. It has been shown that protecting endangered species and their diminishing habitats ensures the survival of more common species (see References).

KEEPING YOUR CAT INDOORS IS NOT JUST FOR THE BIRDS!

There are an estimated 77 million pet cats in the United States and another 60–100 million stray and feral ones. Each year, they kill hundreds of millions of birds and an even greater number of small mammals.

True to their wild roots, domestic cats instinctively hunt and capture prey, even when well fed. Research shows that urges to hunt and eat are controlled by different parts of their brain.

While cats are natural-born hunters, birds and small mammals become unnatural victims. Wildlife in the Western Hemisphere did not evolve in the presence of such abundant small predators, so they never developed defenses against them. Even a "belled" cat can still kill wildlife, since cats learn to stalk without jingling the bell and in any case, wild animals don't necessarily associate the ringing of a bell with danger. Once caught by a cat, few birds survive even if they appear to have escaped. Infection from puncture wounds or the stress of capture usually results in death.

Keep cats indoors, especially in spring and early summer, when young birds are fledging. This will not only help preserve the birds, it will also greatly improve the cat's chances of survival. Coyotes, dogs, other cats, cars, diseases, parasites and a host of other hazards make the life of an outdoor cat dangerous and often short. There are statistics showing that the average life expectancy of an indoor cat is 17 years or more, compared with just 2–5 years for an outdoor cat.

Adapted with permission from a brochure by **CATS INDOORS!** The Campaign for Safer Birds & Cats. See also the American Bird Conservancy's website, http://www.abcbirds.org/.

HERON FAMILY *Ardeidae*

ROBIN HENRY

The largest heron, a great blue, stands 4 ft. (1 m) tall, but weighs only 5–8 lb. (2–4 kg).

Herons are large wading birds with long necks, long legs, spearlike bills, short tails and large, broad wings. In flight, their neck is held in a graceful "S" curve and the long legs extend behind. Great blue herons are the only local breeders. Bitterns and egrets are also included in this family. Though family members are primarily fish catchers, great blue herons are omnivorous carnivores, eating almost anything that fits in their gullets. Specialized feathers are used in a heron's preening. These feathers disintegrate into a powder that is rubbed into the body feathers to be combed out with the bird's flattened third toe. One hundred years ago, herons and egrets were hunted almost to extinction so their plumes could decorate ladies hats and soldiers helmets. The United States Audubon Society was formed in part to stop the slaughter, and federal laws were passed to protect these magnificent birds.

Great Blue Heron
Ardea herodias
BREEDING, MIGRATORY • COMMON

Habitat/feeding: Montane. Wetland/riparian areas in shallow water of ponds, streams, reservoirs and marshes. Diet is primarily fish, swallowed headfirst; also eat small mammals, nestlings and even human food scraps. **Field ID traits:** 46 in. (117 cm) tall; 6 ft. (2 m) wingspan. Sexes similar. Blue-gray body; two-toned upper wings visible in flight. Mostly white head in adult, black plume during breeding season; powerful, spearlike bill. Immature similar, except has black cap. Hoarse, trumpeting flight call, *fraaahnk* or *braak.* **Breeding/nesting:** Monogamous. Social colonies nest in tall trees usually close to water. Large platform nests of sticks lined with twigs and vegetation appear precariously perched in tree tops. Pair incubates 3-5 eggs up to 29 days; feed young mostly regurgitated aquatic species. Young remain in nest 2-3 months.

Poised motionless at water's edge awaiting an unwary fish, a great blue is the epitomy of grace and elegance.

Great blue herons return to the Roaring Fork Valley in early March and are nesting successfully in conifers above 8,000 ft. (2438 m). Their exquisite courtship ritual involves twig shakes, neck stretching and fluffing and short, straight-necked circle flights, as well as crest raising and bill clappering. A great blue's watchful golden eyes are monocular, meaning that each focuses independently. Since their eyes are placed close to the back of the head, slight movements provide 360 degree vision. They can refocus almost instantly in order to catch their dinner, their eyes acting as a telescope one moment and as a magnifier the next. Colonies are vulnerable to human disturbance, especially early in the season, and hawks and owls are among their few natural enemies. Being at the top of the food chain, great blues are excellent indicators of wetland health.

WATERFOWL FAMILY   *Anatidae*

Many members of this family enjoy riding the rapids as much as kayakers and rafters do. Local birders spend many enjoyable hours watching ducks bob through sections of rapids only to fly back to the top and do it over again! This colorful, varied family includes ducks, geese and swans. With webbed feet, oil glands at the base of the tail for waterproofing feathers, closely interlocking feathers which protect the soft insulating down beneath, and a subcutaneous layer of fat to seal in body heat, they are well adapted for a watery habitat.

Males of most North American duck species have brightly colored and distinctively patterned plumage, whereas females are usually drab, blending in with surrounding vegetation as they sit on the nest. Unlike other birds who need to continue flying, waterfowl molt all flight feathers at once, becoming flightless for several weeks. Realizing their vulnerability while flightless, they spend most of this time on the water, only

281

coming ashore to feed or rest. Open water is important to waterfowl, and local ponds—including those on the golf courses—provide good habitat if planted with appropriate wetland vegetation such as willows, sedges and rushes. Mallards are year-round residents, and green and blue winged teals, gadwalls, widgeons, and coots will nest in more secluded locations. A variety of species may be seen on local ponds in spring and fall. Only Canada geese are described here, as they are the most prominent waterfowl observed in our area.

ROBIN HENRY

Canada Goose
Branta canadensis
BREEDING, MIGRATORY • COMMON

Habitat/feeding: Montane. Wetland/riparian areas with ponds, streams and other open water; protected sites for nesting; prefers islands. Feeds on vegetation of lawns, golf courses and native plants; also corn, oats, other agricultural crops and aquatic plants. **Field ID traits:** 25–45 in. (64–114 cm). Sexes similar, male slightly larger. Exact characteristics vary geographically, but Canada geese generally have a taupe body, dark above, pale below; dark blue/black long neck, and head with bright white "chinstrap," dark bill; U-shaped white rump stripe visible in flight. **Breeding/nesting:** Lifetime mates; pair nests in feather-lined ground depression; goslings swim within 24 hours. Families remain together during migration and return to same nesting grounds each year; yearlings choose new areas, not mating or nesting for 3 years.

On brisk fall days when flocks of Canada geese fly overhead, their resonant honking inspires visions of freedom and wilderness grandeur. Although historically nesting and sometimes wintering in western Colorado's intermountain parks, they were extirpated with the arrival of Europeans. In 1953, the Colorado Division of Wildlife (CDOW) began a breeding and stocking program, with the geese reintroduced west of the Continental Divide in 1967 on the Colorado River about fifteen miles below Grand Junction. The program was so successful that Canada geese are now overpopulated and considered pests on golf courses, in parks, and anywhere else their numbers and resulting excrement have become a problem. Protected by the Migratory Bird Treaty Act of 1918, which gave the U.S. Fish & Wildlife Service the authority to set limits and regulations on hunting, Canada geese cannot be disturbed or killed without a federal permit. CDOW continues to research reasonable ways to handle the large population and associated complaints. Canada geese are now year-round residents in Colorado, only migrating to lower elevations for open water.

EAGLE, HAWK and HARRIER FAMILY

Accipitridae

Shakespeare once proclaimed, "One touch of nature makes the whole world kin." Who does not feel a sense of awe at the cry of a hawk filling the air, as it soars effortlessly overhead on buoyant thermals generated by the sun. Because they are predators, members of this family share similar specializations:

- exceptional vision for spotting prey from heights and for territorial defense.

- acute hearing, enabling them to find birds and small mammals that are vocalizing (alarm calling, etc.).

- long, sturdy digits armed with heavy, curved talons for catching, holding and killing their prey; and strong, hooked beaks to complete the kill and tear prey into small pieces.

- all raptors regurgitate pellets of undigested food.

Most accipitrids display some degree of reversed sexual dimorphism, meaning the female is larger than the male. This allows the mated pair to exploit a wider range of food sources, and provides the female with a greater body mass for producing large eggs and incubating them during cold weather. Many of the accipitrids routinely add fresh green leaves to their nest, which contain natural pesticides such as hydrocyanic acid. This may inhibit infestation by insect parasites. Most mate for life unless their mate dies—the exception being northern harriers and ospreys, which are sometimes polygamous. Most will defend a territory, the size determined by the abundance of prey. Their semi-precocial young hatch covered in down with their eyes open. After fledging, they depend on their parents for food until they aquire hunting skills, which typically takes a few months.

Migration in spring or fall is the best time to watch raptors as there are many different species in the air. Since they migrate during the day, they can be seen, unlike many birds that fly during the night. After flapping hard to reach the first thermal,

RAPTORS—BIRDS OF PREY

From the great eagle to the agile, pigeon-sized sharp-shinned hawk, raptors (Latin for "plunderer"), or birds of prey, are a diverse and striking group of birds. Most diurnal raptors—active during the day—are in the family Accipitridae, which includes kites, eagles, hawks, ospreys and harriers. This group also includes falcons of the family Falconidae and New World vultures of the family Carthartidae. Nocturnal raptors—active at night—are the owls, including family Tytonidae (barn owl) and family Strigidae (typical owls). Not all owls are solely nocturnal.

they may glide all day, soaring until darkness cloaks their path. Compare that to hummingbirds, which flap their wings seventy-five times per second during migratory flight!

Unfortunately, many birds of prey have become endangered or threatened due to poaching, pollution, hitting power lines and habitat destruction.

ACCIPITERS: BIRD HUNTING HAWKS

With long, rudder-like tails and shorter, rounded wings, accipiters—a subgrouping of the accipitrids that includes sharp-shinned and Cooper's hawks as well as northern goshawks—are well adapted for maneuvering rapidly through thick forest. These bird-hunting hawks prefer to sprint, and will abandon their prey if they fail to catch it within a short distance. They fly with a series of flaps interspersed with gliding, using thermals for lift and fanning their tails when soaring. Accipiters' eyes change color with age, from yellow in immature birds to orange and sometimes deep red in adults.

ROBIN HENRY

Sharp-shinned Hawk
Accipiter striatus
RESIDENT, MIGRATORY • FAIRLY COMMON

Habitat/feeding: Montane to subalpine. Dense foliage in coniferous, mixed and deciduous forests and woodlands up to the subalpine zone. In Colorado, small conifer stands within mature aspen forests appear to be important nesting habitat; also dense oak-mountain shrublands. Diet is 90% small birds, including yellow-rumped warblers, white-crowned sparrows and dark-eyed juncos; rarely takes amphibians, snakes and insects. **Field ID traits:** The smallest of accipiters, similar in size to a jay or pigeon; 10–14 in. (25–36 cm). The sexes have the greatest size difference of any North American bird. Compared to Cooper's hawk, tail is more squared-off at bottom; no distinct coloration difference in head and back; head and neck smaller in relation to size; more visible in flight. Tail may seem slightly notched when folded. Solid white undertail coverts. Adult slate-gray above, pale beneath, with obvious rust-colored barring. Flight consists of quick, deep strokes, with flapping motion at the "wrist." **Breeding/nesting:** Monogamous. Display flights above the forest, often near the nest; courting pair circles then lands in tree and calls; males sometimes fly high and dive steeply into the forest. Both sexes bring nest material, but female usually works alone on broad, flat platform well-hidden near conifer trunk, 20–60 ft. off the ground.

Very secretive behavior during breeding protects this small hawk from increased predation by Cooper's hawks, northern harriers and red-tailed hawks. During the fall, sharp-shinned hawks migrate singly or in small flocks to Central America and the Greater Antilles, often returning to their normal feisty behavior and harassing hawks larger than themselves. Sharp-shinned hawks are vulnerable to pesticide contamination as they eat primarily small birds, many of which feed on insects. This species saw a dramatic decline in the eastern United States during the early 1970's due to DDT-induced eggshell thinning. This is still a problem for birds wintering in Mexico and Central America, where the pesticide continues to be used. For this reason, the presence of sharp-shinned hawks is an indicator of ecosystem health. Additional problems they face include thinning of the dense forest habitats they require for nesting and suburban bird feeding stations, which are lethal for these small hawks—plate-glass doors and picture windows is the major cause of mortality.

> *. . . a small sharp-shinned hawk, not much bigger than a dove, coursed down the windward side of the ridge at treetop height. Its wings pulled back in a half-tuck, the hawk rode the updraft like a surfer riding a wave, scattering alarmed warblers in its wake like leaves in the slipstream of a car.*
>
> —SCOTT WEIDENSAUL,
> *Living on the Wind*

Cooper's Hawk
Accipiter cooperii
RESIDENT, MIGRATORY • FAIRLY COMMON

ROBIN HENRY

Habitat/feeding: Montane to lower subalpine. Mature deciduous forests, riparian woodlands and coniferous forests up to 10,000 ft. (3048 m); near openings or habitat edges. Compared to sharp-shinned, Cooper's less abundant in spruce-fir. Stealthy hunter; stalks prey by approaching perch to perch through dense cover, then pouncing with rapid, powerful flight; may fly low to surprise unwary prey. Both styles are effective for capturing small to medium-sized ground-feeding birds such as robins and jays, and small mammals such as rabbits, chipmunks, mice, squirrels and bats; some reptiles and amphibians. **Field ID traits:** 14–21 in. (36–51 cm). Reddish eye in adults. Similar to sharp-shinned hawk, except barred tail is longer and more rounded; head proportionally larger; coloration of adult's crown contrasts more sharply with back. Tends to be more solitary, not traveling in pairs or groups. Streaks on immature's whitish underparts disappear toward belly. Immatures of Cooper's and sharp-shinned are very brown. **Breeding/nesting:** Monogamous. In courtship flights, pairs fly slowly over territory with exaggerated wing beats, forming a deep arc. Males build nest, some with help from females, in conifer trees, 35–45 ft. from ground.

Because the Cooper's hawk preyed upon domesticated chickens, passenger pigeons, robins and flickers, also considered delicacies by early European colonists, there were many attempts to exterminate them. In the northeastern United States, their population declined precipitously in the 1940's due to the effects of DDT and other pesticides. Their numbers rebounded after DDT was banned; however, because DDT residues persist in the environment, and countries south of the United States still allow its use, these and other western raptors continue to be at risk.

SCOTT BUCKEL

Northern Goshawk
Accipiter gentilis
RESIDENT, MIGRATORY • UNCOMMON

Habitat/feeding: Montane to lower subalpine. Prefers mature coniferous, mixed and aspen forests up to 10,000 ft. (3048 m); occasionally somewhat open forests or along forest edges. Awaits prey on perches in mid-level forest canopy, attacking with a short burst of speed; also flies low, searching through forest. Aggressively pursues prey under shrubs or other cover on foot. Prey includes medium-sized birds and small mammals—especially grouse, crows, Steller's jays, robins, squirrels, rabbits and snowshoe hare. **Field ID traits:** 21–26 in. (53–66 cm). Largest of the accipiters, with proportionately longer tail and shorter wings. Adult's blackish crown and cheek separated by prominent white "eyebrow" that wraps to define the start of the blue-gray back. Tight, convoluted barring of whitish underparts appears gray at a distance; noticeable fluffy undertail coverts. Sexes similar, but female about ⅓ larger than male. Voice is a plaintive *ka ka ka* and a downward-inflected series of *kleet, kleet, kleet.* **Breeding/nesting:** Both sexes perform aerial displays, gliding and circling with white undertail coverts spread to the sides; may also perform a series of shallow dives and upward swoops. Pair mates about 10 times/day during nest building; builds bulky platform nest in major fork of tree (often aspen), 30–35 ft. off ground. Female fiercely protects nest, dive-bombing all intruders.

Northern goshawk populations may be threatened or endangered in the southern Rockies due to loss of the mature forest habitat they require. Unfortunately, these are the same types of forests desired by lumber companies. Goshawks need large, undisturbed territories for breeding and dispersing of young birds. They will not nest near a paved road, and often leave an area when human activity increases. Nest abandonment has been documented on National Forest lands in Colorado—caused by forest fragmentation. With populations declining, the northern goshawk is presently listed as a "sensitive species" by the U.S. Forest Service. In Colorado, they are more common on the western slope.

BUTEOS—BUZZARD HAWKS

Buteos (another subgroup of the Accipitridae) are also known as buzzard hawks. They have large, rounded wings and, compared to accipiters, relatively broad, short tails. They are frequently seen soaring in open places on thermals in search of food. When prey is spotted, they dive in for the kill. Buteos will also watch for prey from a high perch. Red-tailed hawks are the only members of this group which nest in this area.

Red-tailed Hawk

Buteo jamaicensis

RESIDENT, MIGRATORY • COMMON

Habitat/feeding: Montane to subalpine. Master of all open to semi-open habitats; not in densely forested areas. Mostly hunts from the air; will switch to perches in cold weather. Prey is primarily small to medium rodents, but may include small rabbits, birds and snakes. **Field ID traits:** 22 in. (56 cm). Females 25% larger than males. Cinnamon-red tail, very visible in flight, is not present in juveniles; occurs in second year after molt. Plumage highly variable with many coloration patterns, or morphs. Underside of adults usually has dark, mottled "belly band." Only hawk in North America with dark marks on underside of the patagium, located on wing between bird's body and wrist of wing. Dark morphs may make this trait difficult to see; also in juveniles.

Breeding/nesting: Monogamous. Courtship displays include talon drops, where male attempts to touch mate with his talons, circling together and preening each other. Pairs nest in aspens and spruce, on rocky cliffs and on top of utility poles.

RICHARD HOLMES

THE SHARPEST VISION

Raptors have the sharpest vision of any living organism. A hawks' eyes resolve 2–8 times more detail than those of a human. Hawks and eagles can magnify the image projected onto the central part of the retina by about 30%. This is possible because raptors have more pectin—a unique folded tissue that supplies nutrients and oxygen to the eye—and fewer blood vessels to scatter light entering the eye. Their vision is three-dimensional like ours; however, their eyes are extremely large relative to brain size and so require a bony internal support called the scleral ring.

A high-pitched descending cry—*kee-eeee-arrr*—is commonly heard in early spring as local air warms and thermals build, bringing the red-tailed hawk back from its wintering grounds at lower elevations. Often overhead, it searches for prey in mountain meadows. Snags provide perches with far-reaching views for this powerful raptor. They possess phenomenal eyesight, being able to recognize a deer mouse or vole from high overhead. Then, diving at speeds of 100 miles per hour (161 km per hour), they seize their prey with decisively sharp talons.

Red-tailed hawks are very versatile hunters, being able to sprint like accipiters and hover, kite and soar like buteos. As they are extremely territorial, they can sometimes be observed aggressively driving out intruders with quite an impressive aerial display. They normally mate for life, remaining in the same territory for years and are thriving in Colorado. Though they are usually migratory, individuals may remain year-round. Watch for their cinnamon red tail as they soar overhead.

THE EAGLE AND THE HAWK
A SONG BY JOHN DENVER

I am the eagle, I live in high country
In rocky cathedrals that reach to the sky
I am the hawk and there's blood on my
  feathers
But time is still turning they soon will be dry
And all those who see me and all who believe
  in me
Share in the freedom I feel when I fly
Come dance with the west wind and touch on
  the mountain tops
Sail o'er the canyons and up to the stars
And reach for the heavens and hope for the
  future
And all that we can be, not what we are.

CHARLES W. MELTON

Bald Eagle
Haliaeetus leucocephalus
WINTER, MIGRATORY • FAIRLY COMMON

Habitat/feeding: Montane. Mountain parks, lakeshores, rivers and streams in open areas. Dives for fish; also pursues waterfowl, rabbits and other small mammals. Will scavenge for fish, or steal them from ospreys. **Field ID traits:** 31–37 in. (79–94 cm). Sexes similar, but female slightly larger; adult wingspan typically 7 ft. (2 m). Adults have distinctive snowy-white heads and hooked, yellow bills, unique among birds. Larger heads and shorter tails than golden eagles. Immature bald eagles have mottled white visible on the underside of their wings during flight, whereas immature goldens have a more clearly defined white pattern. Not closely related to golden eagles, and not part of accipiters or buteos. **Breeding/nesting:** Long-term pair bonds (lifespan possibly 50 years). Breathtaking courtship displays include the pair locking talons and tumbling earthward, as well as impressive 360° aerial rolls. Choosing a secure fork high in a living tree, pairs build the largest nests of all avian species, composed of heavy sticks and twigs filled in with other foliage, and lined with their own feathers. Nests are often repaired and added to each year; some being used over 30 years, or until the tree dies and falls down.

Keeping our watersheds healthy encourages the recovery of this national symbol of wilderness and freedom. The toxic effects of chemicals like DDT, coupled with unregulated hunting, and campaigns to rid the West of predators, nearly drove this majestic bird to extinction. Thanks to the Endangered Species Act of 1973, the number of bald eagles in the United States has increased from 450 nesting pairs in the early 1960's to more than 4,000 today. Traditionally bald eagles went north to breed; however, there are now at least twenty-three nesting pairs living in Colorado year-round, and bald eagles have begun nesting locally. November is a time of excitement in the Roaring Fork Valley with the arrival of migratory eagles from northern states and Canada, who come to take advantage of relatively mild winters.

Bald eagles hold the record for the largest nest ever found. A nest in Florida was measured at 20 ft. (6.1 m) deep and 9 ft. (2.7 m) in diameter, and weighed greater than 2 tons (1814 kg).

Though bald eagles are no longer endangered, continued monitoring and protection of these predators at the top of the food chain is vital. They are valuable indicators of the health of our watersheds, their main prey being fish, which depend upon clean rivers and lakes to thrive. Preserving the large natural areas these birds of prey require for survival also provides an umbrella of protection for entire ecological communities. Listen for the slow, powerful wing beats as they cruise riparian habitats in search of food. Flying low along a stream, the feathers of its white head glistening in the sun, this splendid bird is an awesome sight to behold.

Golden Eagle
Aquila chrysaetos
BREEDING, MIGRATORY • FAIRLY COMMON

Habitat/feeding: Montane to alpine. Open spaces with varied topography up to 12,000 ft. (3658 m), on cliffs or in trees at edges of forests; avoids dense coniferous forests. Primary diet of rodents, hares, rabbits; lesser numbers of birds, reptiles and crickets. Carrion large part of winter diet. Consumes up to 12 ounces (340 grams) of food daily, year-round. May gorge and then fast, depending on food availability. Mostly crepuscular, but patrols for prey virtually all day when a hungry brood awaits. **Field ID traits:** 30–40 in. (76–102 cm). Magnificent bird, with wingspan up to 7 ft. (2 m). Rich dark-brown body with golden or coppery-colored feathers on back of head and upper neck; dark beak and eyes. Legs completely covered with feathers, and tail dimly banded with white in

ROBIN HENRY

adults. Sexes similar, female visibly larger than male. Closely related to buteos. **Breeding/nesting:** Evidently mate for life. Flight displays may involve courtship as well as territorial behavior, though the relationships are not clearly understood; nest may be 8–10 ft. (2.4–3 m) across and 3–4 ft. (1–1.2 m) deep. Female starts incubation after first egg, waiting sometimes 90–120 hours to lay the next, so young appear unevenly sized; Stronger siblings sometimes kill weaker. Parents may stockpile food near nest.

Only four large dark birds soar above us in this area—golden eagles, bald eagles, great blue herons and (more rarely) turkey vultures. The wing beats of goldens are slow and plodding, more shallow than those of bald eagles, and their heads are smaller. Goldens also hold their wings flat when soaring. Turkey vultures have featherless heads and legs, and a more discernible "V" shape to their wings during flight. A heron's long legs trail behind in flight.

Goldens' remarkable flight displays include joining with others to circle, dive, roll or fly in synchronized formations. They also perform "sky dances" composed of deeply undulating movements that increase with higher altitudes, possibly combined with rolls and dives and high-speed descents, as two birds lock talons and tumble downwards, wings folded, separating only seconds before hitting the ground to return to flight. Dive speeds often reach 150–200 mph! Golden eagles do not tolerate any sort of disturbance near their nests, and have been protected by law since 1962. There is evidence that increased recreational activities, such as rock climbing, can result in lowered rates of nesting success and increased nest abandonment for many birds of prey. Adult golden eagles are most susceptible to human related risks, which include shooting or poaching, being hit by cars while feeding on roadkill and electrocution by power lines.

FALCON and
CARACARA FAMILY
Falconidae

Falcons are distinguished from the other birds of prey by having narrow, pointed wings swept back with an angle at the elbow, a notched beak for crushing their prey's neck vertebrae, not building stick nests, and using their beaks to defend themselves. Falcons fly very fast, their physical size and shape allowing for incredible maneuvers and high-speed dives while hunting.

American Kestrel
Falco sparverius
BREEDING, MIGRATORY · COMMON

CHARLES W. MELTON

Habitat/feeding: Montane to lower subalpine. Exceptionally adaptable, found around open pastures, meadows and shrublands up to 10,000 ft. (3048 m). Favors riparian areas. Primary diet is insects, particularly grasshoppers; also hunts voles and other small mammals, small birds, snakes, lizards and some bats. Adept at hunting from perches, zeroing in on prey with rapid dives, hovering before plunging for the kill and pursuing on foot; also flushes prey to catch in midair. May rob swallow nests or rob other birds of prey in mid-flight. **Field ID traits:** 10.5 in. (27 cm). Handsome robin-sized raptor. Both sexes with cinnamon and slate-blue crown, 2 black vertical stripes on whitish face. Male has rich reddish-cinnamon back and tail, slate-blue wings and spotted breast; female has lighter cinnamon back with dark streaking, pale breast with vertical streaks. Most common vocalization is *killy, killy, killy*, when upset, during aggressive behavior or when unsuccessful at attempted kill. **Breeding/nesting:** Monogamous. Pairs nest in natural or manmade cavities, particularly old nests of flickers and other woodpeckers; may even force existing occupant to leave. Distinct division of labor, with male bringing food to female who spends most of her time in nest area and does most of the incubating.

American kestrels are the smallest falcons in North America, and their unique coloration and traits—hovering while searching for prey, bobbing their tails after landing on a perch—are unique among falcons. Both sexes perform interesting courtship displays. The male executes an impressive series of climbs and dives, uttering several *klee* notes at the peak. He also feeds the female, gliding toward her with fluttering wings and food in his mouth as she flies up and settles beside him. Then both flutter and bow to each other while she takes the food. The female typically invites copulation by bowing while holding her tail straight out or slightly up, and may "whine" during feeding or copulation.[2] Although kestrels are the most common falcon throughout North America (except in the very far north), and seem to have a healthy population in Colorado, they continue to be threatened by habitat loss, shooting, poisoning from pesticides and collisions with cars. A kestrel's richly-colored plumage makes them easy to spot from a distance.

OTHER RAPTORS POSSIBLE IN THE UPPER ROARING FORK VALLEY

Turkey vultures (*Cathartes aura*) may breed in the Roaring Fork Valley.

Female **northern harrier** (*Circus cyaneus*, formerly marsh hawk) is an excellent example of reversed sexual dimorphism in both size and plumage. The smaller male is strikingly different from the larger female; his pearly-gray back, black wingtips and mostly pearly-white belly offer a stark contrast to her brownish appearance. Harriers fly close to the ground with their wings held slightly above the horizontal; the prominent white rump is a good flight ID mark for both sexes. Although they may breed locally, they are rare due to a decrease in marshy meadows for nesting and foraging.

Immature **Swainson's hawk** (*Buteo swainsoni*). Swainson's are transient; seen mostly during migration.

Rough-legged hawk (*Buteo lagopus*) would be sighted in fall during migration and in winter.

CHARLES W. MELTON

Ospreys (*Pandion haliaetus*) nest at Ruedi Reservoir on the Frying Pan River, and are sometimes seen fishing at Hallam Lake and along the upper Roaring Fork River.

JACK BINCH

RICHARD W. HOLMES

Peregrine falcons (*Falco peregrinus*) may breed in the Brush Creek Valley and elsewhere in the upper Roaring Fork Valley.[3]

Prairie falcons (*Falco mexicanus*) are considered rare local breeders. They prefer remote sites in arid, open country on cliff faces up to 10,000 ft. (3048 m) in Colorado, but have even been known to nest above timberline.

293

GROUSE, TURKEY and ALLIES FAMILY
Phasianidae

⬦⬦⬦⬦⬦⬦⬦⬦⬦⬦⬦⬦⬦⬦⬦⬦⬦⬦⬦⬦⬦⬦⬦⬦⬦⬦⬦⬦⬦⬦

This large family, often referred to as upland game birds, includes sub-families for grouse (Tetraoninae), turkeys (Meleagridinae) and guineafowl (Numidinae). Species vary considerably in size, but share a similar chicken-like shape, and are all well adapted to life on the ground, where they feed on vegetation and insects. While foraging, they store food in a well-developed crop at the base of the neck, which is later emptied into the stomach for digestion during rest periods. A powerful gizzard grinds hard seeds and nuts. Quartz grit is purposefully consumed to help in the grinding. Most species have similar flight patterns, consisting of rapid bursts of flight interspersed with periods of glide.

RICHARD W. HOLMES

Blue Grouse
Dendragapus obscurus
RESIDENT, NON-MIGRATORY
• COMMON

Habitat/feeding: Montane to sub-alpine. Chooses both edges and interiors of oak-mountain shrublands, aspen, mixed-conifer and/or spruce-fir forests. Forages on the ground and gleans foliage. Diverse diet rich in bugs, plant matter and berries; includes aspen leaves, vetch, dandelions, clover, raspberries, elderberries, currants and strawberries. Winters almost exclusively in conifer forests, where its favorite food is Douglas-fir needles. **Field ID traits:** 20 in. (51 cm). Plump, chicken-like body, short, rounded wings and short, curved bill. Plumage is mottled grayish or gray-brown in both male and female. Dark tail is long, rounded or fan-shaped, with pale-gray bands. White flecks on flanks and under tail feathers. Feathers grow to base of middle toe. Adult male is more blue grey and larger than female, with eye-catching yellow-orange eye comb, and inflatable ruddy bare skin patch on the side of its neck; hidden, except during displays, by white feathers with dark gray to black tips. **Breeding/nesting:** Male mostly polygamous. Female cautiously builds simple nest scraped in the ground in thick vegetation under shrubs, at base of trees, under branches of fallen trees or next to rocks; well hidden from predators.

Blue grouse are the second-largest grouse species in Colorado. Males perform an entertaining array of courtship displays for potential mates and competing suitors, which include inflating the bare reddish skin on their necks, fanning their tails, hopping, strutting, hooting and fluttering their wings so loudly they can often be heard half a mile away. They make a deep drumming/booming sound when inflating the skin patch. In the summer, most grouse are found at higher elevations in forest with an understory of bilberry (*Vaccinium myrtillus*). Since these tame grouse spend most of their time on the ground, hikers are often startled by their quick, but short-lived bursts of flight. They tend to fly downslope, finding safety in trees. During winter, snowshoers and skiers are sometimes surprised by stumbling upon a grouse that has sought protection from the cold beneath the blanket of snow, causing it to explode into the air within a cloud of icy crystals.

White-tailed Ptarmigan
Lagopus leucurus
RESIDENT, NON-MIGRATORY • COMMON

Habitat/feeding: Alpine. Prefers moist areas such as edges of ponds, streams and marshy tundra. Males winter in krummholz areas or above, and females move down into the subalpine; both use willow thickets for protection. Willow tips and buds are the primary winter food, augmented by spruce and fir needles and some lichen. Summer diet is willow leaves and buds, bulblets of herbs, flowers and berries; scratches soil for lichen. Eats few insects, except while raising chicks that need the increased protein. Ingests grit to aid digestion. **Field ID traits:** 12.5 in. (32 cm). Sexes similar. Plump with short, rounded wings. White tail feathers not found in other ptarmigan species. Plumage changes with seasons: completely white in winter, except for black eyes and bill; summer plumage mottled dark-gray and brown, with white tail and outer wing feathers. Male has prominent crimson eye combs and white barring on breast. Female's eye combs are inconspicuous and pinkish, barring on breast is yellow. Feet and legs of both covered in stiff white feathers. Female makes soft low hoots, hen-like clucking; male courting call is scream-like. Droppings are skinny, 0.5 in. (1.3 cm) long, reddish-brown to chocolate-brown pellets.

Breeding/nesting: Monogamous. Breeds in early May in areas free of snow; pairs may rejoin in subsequent years using same breeding territory. Courting males strut, inflating eye combs. Pairs nest in natural ground depressions at the base of alpine bunch grasses or willows near water; base of talus slope near willows is ideal.

Summer plumage

RICHARD W. HOLMES

Winter plumage

CHARLES W. MELTON

Males aggressively defend territory, helping females conserve energy for foraging, nest-building and egg-laying. Move to summer habitat high above timberline, preferring rocky, moist meadows with abundant vegetation.

Fierce winter winds may howl, but hardy white-tailed ptarmigans continue to live only a few hundred vertical feet from their summer alpine habitat, finding warmth and protection from predators in snow burrows. These birds are equipped with their own "snowshoes"—their feet covered in stiff white feathers both above and below—allowing them to scurry quickly across the snow. Other species of ptarmigan inhabit the far north, but this is the only one found in the lower forty-eight states. Threats to ptarmigan populations are increasing. They include: construction of high-altitude reservoirs, ski-area development, snowmobiling, livestock grazing and road-building, all which cause disturbance to the willow thickets so important to the birds' survival. More recently, it has been discovered that cadmium, a heavy metal abundant in Colorado's ore belt, is taken up by willows where mine tailings are present. Eating these willows can cause irreversible kidney damage and bone weakening in ptarmigan when concentrations reach a certain level.[4]

COLIC CAECA? Ptarmigan and other birds that feed heavily on woody vegetation have dead-end pouches in their intestines called "colic caeca," which contain special bacteria that break down plant cellulose. This enables the birds to extract more nutrition out of their food. During the fall, a ptarmigan's digestive tract may increase in size by nearly half, shrinking again in spring when less woody, more easily digested food is available.

Two colorful males strut their stuff, one in full display.

RICHARD W. HOLMES

Wild Turkey, Merriam's Turkey
Meleagris gallopavo subsp. *merriami*
RESIDENT, NON-MIGRATORY • UNCOMMON

Habitat/feeding: Montane. Up to 8,000 ft. (2440 m). Open fields, woods and meadows adjacent to riparian zones where larger trees are available for roosting. Forages on the ground for seeds, sedges, fruits and bulbs; also consumes a variety of insects, such as grasshoppers and ground beetles; a few amphibians. **Field ID traits:** 37–46 in. (94–117 cm). Not quite as large as a domesticated turkey. Large body seems out of proportion with the thin neck and small head. Male more colorful, with bluish head, red wattle, long feather in center of breast (female also occasionally). Glossy feathers; tail feathers of western birds tipped in cream or white, as opposed to eastern birds with rufous tips. Female vocalization is a loud, abrupt *tuk*, and a slightly longer, whining *yike, yike*, repeated in a slow series.[5] Males make gobbling sound. **Breeding/nesting:** May wander in flocks of up to 60, except during breeding season when they break up into smaller all-male and all-female groups. Flocking discourages predators, which have a hard time sneaking up on a group of wary birds. During courtship, male spreads tail feathers and emits unmistakable gobbling. Does not establish territories. Nests are in well-hidden, shallow depressions on the ground, near edges of meadows or in open woods; female may lay eggs in another's nest.

Although native to Colorado, this subspecies of wild turkey has only recently appeared in the upper Roaring Fork Valley, after being nearly extinguished in the state in the early 1900's by unregulated market and subsistence hunting, disease and loss of habitat due to grazing. The Colorado Division of Wildlife started reintroducing turkeys to the state after 1930, eventually returning their populations to historical numbers. According to the *Colorado Breeding Atlas*, our "natives" may actually be feral descendents of domestic turkeys raised by pre-Columbian Native Americans. Turkeys definitely prefer life on the ground, though they can fly short distances to escape predators or roost in trees. This is the only native North American animal that has ever been domesticated; all others came from Europe. If it had been up to Benjamin Franklin, the wild turkey would have been our national emblem, instead of the bald eagle—only one Congressional vote made the difference!

PLOVER FAMILY
Charadriidae

Residents of coastal areas are familiar with these handsome shore birds that typically take several hurried steps across the ground, stop abruptly, then dash off again.

Killdeer
Charadrius vociferus
BREEDING, MIGRATORY • UNCOMMON

ROBIN HENRY

Habitat/feeding: Montane. Ground-dwelling bird of open pastures and fields (shorelines elsewhere); attracted to golf courses and airfields. Gathers on shores of ponds and streams late summer. Classified elsewhere as a shorebird. Probing bill perfect for finding grubs and worms just beneath ground's surface. Eats large variety of insects, many of them harmful to crops, humans and/or animals, such as mosquitoes and ticks. **Field ID traits:** 10.5 in. (27 cm). Robin-sized bird with long legs. Sexes similar; striking year-round plumage with 2 black bands across bright-white chest, dark band across forehead and behind red eye, white "eyebrow" band and brown cap. White face above bill, brown upper back and wings. Tail shorter than in plover relatives; held horizontal to body. Red-orange rump and white stripes on narrow, pointed wings visible during typical fast, straight flights. **Breeding/nesting:** Male courtship display includes rapid upward flight or ground display of crouching, leaning to one side, dropping the wings and fanning the tail to expose orange-red rump (may whirl around) while vocalizing a long trilled note. Nests in simple hollow scratched out by male with energetic backward kicks.

Killdeer are celebrated for their somewhat shrill, hysterical and repeated call, which sounds like *kill-deeah,* and for their strategy of feigning a hurt wing while uttering pitiful cries to draw predators away from the nest. Step carefully if this drama unfolds before you—a nest is nearby. A protective parent sensing danger will run with opened wings or fly directly toward a predator, even striking it. A killdeer's banded plumage is good camouflage for either rocky pastures or rocky shores. The female lays her eggs in a neat circle with the pointed ends toward the center. This works to camouflage the nest because the blunt ends have more splotches and blend better with the surroundings. Historically, killdeer were hunted for sport and food, but since 1913 have been protected under the Migratory Bird Treaty. Killdeer are vulnerable to storms that wash away nests, their nests or young being stepped on by domestic animals, recreational activities in their habitat, and predation by cats, dogs, foxes and hawks.

Often thought of as inhabiting only ocean coastlines, these small to mid-sized birds frequently breed on the edges of inland streams, ponds and wetlands. There they run along feeding on a diversity of insects, crustaceans and worms. Their nests are usually scratched hollows on the ground, barely lined if at all.

SANDPIPER FAMILY   *Scolopacidae*

Most of the forty-two sandpiper species in our western hemisphere migrate long distances, typically to wintering grounds in South America or islands of the South Pacific, and occupy a variety of ecological niches along the way. Places to feed and rest are critical for energy replenishment after migratory flights of thousands of miles. Unfortunately, much of the specialized habitats required by sandpipers are increasingly being lost to human wetland and shoreline development and recreation.

CHARLES W. MELTON

Spotted Sandpiper
Actitis macularia
BREEDING, MIGRATORY • COMMON

Habitat/feeding: Montane meadows to above timberline; streams, ponds and marshes with heavy adjacent cover. Prefers shallow streams with cobblestones and protective thickets of alders, willows and birches; reservoirs lack these features for nesting, but are used for foraging. Easily catches insects on the ground or in the air; catches small fish from shallows. **Field ID traits:** 7.5 in. (19 cm). Sexes similar. Female a bit larger, more spotted than male, and sporting definite breast spots of chocolate and obsidian with striking, barred back and wings during breeding season; spots disappear in winter. Short tail and short white wing-stripe. Call is a clear whistled *peet-weet*, accent on first note, and succession of *weet* notes during flight. **Breeding/nesting:** Female monogamous; occasionally polygamous. Sexual roles reversed with female more aggressive than male; holds territory and often performs elaborate courtship displays to male. Nests under bushes or ledges, hidden in grass or under steep banks; may nest in colonies.[6] Males do most incubating and care of young.

Noted for their interesting behavior and reversal of parental roles, spotted sandpipers vocalize while flying low over the water on stiffly downward-bent wings with shallow wingbeats. When walking, they hold their heads low and their bodies tilted forward, as they continually bob their tails up and down. You will find them scurrying up and down logs and over shoreline rocks, mostly alone or in small groups. Although normally seen scouring wet areas for food, sandpipers can be found perched in treetops or on utility wires. Their favorite roosting sites are old stumps, logs or rocks. The female has the shortest lifespan of any North American shorebird—3.7 years—which could be attributed to the very long migrations that some individuals make. Numbers of spotted sandpipers appear to be stable in Colorado, although they are declining in some parts of their range due to habitat loss.

Wilson's Snipe
Gallinago gallinago
(formerly Common Snipe)
BREEDING, MIGRATORY
• COMMON

CHARLES W. MELTON

Habitat/feeding: Montane to lower subalpine. Wet meadows and pastures, as well as moist areas near streams and ponds, up to 10,000 ft. (3048 m). Probes in wet mud; sensory pits at the tip of its soft, bendable bill detect larvae of crane flies, houseflies, mosquitoes, beetles and water bugs. Also feeds on dragonflies, damselflies, crickets, mayfly nymphs, earthworms, spiders, and seeds of sedges and grasses. Drinks lots of water and coughs up pellets of indigestible food. **Field ID traits:** 10.5 in. (27 cm). Handsome, stocky bird with uniquely striped head, rusty tail feathers and a long bill. Streaks and stripes of the plumage resemble vivid art deco paintings, while providing excellent camouflage. Eyes very laterally set, allowing maximum range of vision. **Breeding/nesting:** Both sexes perform aerial courtship displays. Female selects dry site, often on dry mounds of sedge or grass or floating islands, to scrape out shallow nest. Both mates perform distraction displays, appearing wounded and distressed, to draw predators and people away from the nest area.

The winnowing flight display of Wilson's snipes produces a weird, whirling-lasso sound—sometimes described as the "sighing of a wandering spirit."[7] As the snipe dives toward earth, the rushing air vibrates the stiffly spread outer tail feathers to make this eerie pulsating sound. These displays by both sexes include swooping and diving up to 360 ft. (120 m) in the air. Although the performances are mostly territorial in nature, they also occur during migration and on wintering grounds in more southern climes. Though Wilson's snipes were once hunted to excess, and are still fair game in some states (including Colorado), their numbers are on the increase again. Despite the loss of wetlands and other moist habitats nationwide, these birds have adapted well to irrigated farm and ranch land.

PIGEON and DOVE FAMILY   *Columbidae*

Although sizes are variable among species, ranging from very small doves to medium-sized pigeons, the overall shape of these birds is similar. Their bodies are fairly plump relative to short legs and small heads, and their short bills have a pliable base and hard tip with the nostrils covered by an enlarged fleshy area. The familiar pigeons of city parks are actually rock pigeons (*Columba livia*), introduced from Europe. The plumage of American species is predominantly earth-tone grays and browns, with some having colorful shimmering iridescence on the backs of their necks as well as some barring on wings and tails. Most species of this group are monogamous for at least a few years at a time. Passenger pigeons numbered from 3-5 billion when Europeans first discovered America, but became extinct in 1914 when the last known member of the species died in captivity. Traveling in flocks, they were easy prey for hunters, who held competitions that required killing a minimum of 30,000 birds.

FUN FACTS ABOUT PIGEONS AND DOVES

• Pigeons cool themselves off by blowing a "bubble" of inner-throat skin, which increases the bird's skin surface area, thereby decreasing body temperature.

• Both male and female pigeons and doves produce "pigeon's milk," a thick milky substance rich in protein and fat, from their crops, which they feed their nestlings during the first few weeks after hatching. The parents gradually add seeds and fruit, softened by the milk, until their young are ready for solids.[8]

• Pigeons and doves are the only birds in North America able to drink water without raising their heads to swallow.

Band-tailed Pigeon
Columba fasciata
BREEDING, MIGRATORY • FAIRLY COMMON

Habitat/feeding: Montane. Oak-mountain shrublands; also mixed-conifer and spruce-fir forests; 6,000 to 9,000 ft. (1830–2745 m). Favorite foods are acorns and pinyon nuts; also eats berries, insects and cultivated grains. Drinks large amounts of water—up to 15% of body weight daily. **Field ID traits:** 14.5 in. (37 cm). Sexes similar; female paler. Tail has both a dark band in mid-section and a wide pale-gray band at tip; more visible in flight. Body is purplish-gray on upper parts, darker slate-colored wings, remainder of body paler; iridescent greens and purples visible on neck and breast in bright sunlight. Vivid red eyes, yellow bill with dark tip, yellow legs and patch of greenish scalloped feathers on back of neck beneath thin white line. Vocalization is mellow, owl-like *who, whoo, hooo,* or 2-syllable *whoo uh.*
Breeding/nesting: Male feeds female during courtship as she beats her wings in a begging display similar to nestling eager to be fed. Nest is fragile platform on horizontal branch or forked tree branch; pairs return year after year to same area.

Our handsome wild pigeon is not as eager to associate with humans as its urban cousin is, although it is quite social when traveling in flocks outside of breeding season. Band-tailed pigeons often roost in treetops as they groom each other for ticks, fleas and lice. Strong birds, they have no problem flying through intense wind and rainstorms.[9] This species is on Partners in Flight's national "watch list," indicating a strong need for conservation throughout its range. Fortunately, because of the Migratory Bird Treaty Act and changes in hunting quotas, these birds are recovering from overhunting during the early 1900's. They often congregate at local bird-feeders, or can be seen foraging in the scrub oak during a good acorn year. **Mourning doves** (*Zenaida macroura*) are uncommon breeders in this area up to 9,000 ft. (2745 m). Gray-green with a pink cast, their tapered tail has white tips below a black band and the wings have black spots. Their soft, mournful hooting, *ooAAH-cooo-coo-coo,* may be heard at dawn and dusk.[10]

OWL FAMILY *Strigidae* and *Tytonidae*

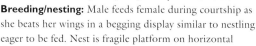
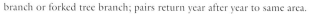

O wls are mostly nocturnal raptors, which have always intrigued humans with their ability to hunt under conditions where we are virtually helpless without technical aid. Avoiding competition with diurnal birds of prey, only a few owl species hunt at dawn and dusk, and even fewer hunt during the day. They further avoid competition by gulping prey whole, and then returning to protected areas to continue the digestive process. This involves compacting bones, fur and skeletal remains of prey into pellets that are regurgitated through the mouth, the bones wrapped inside the fur or feathers to prevent injury to the digestive tract. Piles of these pellets signify an owl's roost location. Owls are specialized for their unique lifestyle with:

- Extraordinary night vision—their large eyes extremely efficient at gathering light, with binocular vision similar to humans'; requires a bony sclerotic ring in the skull for support, limiting their range of movement. A flexible neck allows them to turn their head 180 degrees.
- A nocturnal owls' brain has more than 47,000 specialized hearing receptors (only about 11,000 in diurnal owls). This allows them to detect the slightest movement of prey in the dark, as well as high frequencies, such as a rodent's squeak, often beyond our hearing range.
- Relatively large wings and primary feathers, with a soft fringe at the leading edge, for efficient gliding and silent flight to surprise prey.
- Powerful grasping feet with stiletto-sharp talons.
- Plumage with a mixture of colors, bars and streaks for camouflage.
- Asymmetrical ears allow triangulation of sound, meaning it enters one ear before the other so that the owl can pinpoint the source.

Owls are ardent hunters helping to control rodent populations, yet they are needlessly harassed and killed by those not understanding their unique place in natural ecosystems. One study of 374 banded owls in the United States concluded that up to 86% may have been shot. Owls are usually resident birds, moving to other areas only occasionally to find more abundant food.

ROBIN HENRY

Great Horned Owl

Bubo virginianus
RESIDENT, NON-MIGRATORY
• FAIRLY COMMON

Habitat/feeding: Montane to subalpine. Highly adaptable to fields and forests, from riparian to dry hillsides; population decrease with elevation, so species is rare in subalpine forest and usually absent from the alpine. Prefers deciduous habitat, especially riparian, but will also breed in coniferous forests and wherever prey populations are high, including urban areas. Hunts in open terrain, making short flights from perches in trees or on man-made structures; dives with wings folded to snatch unwary prey. Nocturnal. **Field ID traits:** 22 in. (56 cm). Only large owl with feathered "ear" tufts, or "horns." Females 10–20% larger than males; juveniles resemble adults. Both sexes' vocalizations consist of 3–8 low, far-carrying hoots, with second and third hoots occurring more rapidly—*ho-hohoo-ho-ho*, or *who's-awake? me-too*—the female's being higher-pitched. Their low, mournful hoots vary individually and geographically in number, arrangement and accent. Capable of hair-raising shrieks. **Breeding/nesting:** Courting pairs bow to each other with wings spread; also rub and preen each other's bills. Pairs use old nests of other birds, particularly magpies, hawks, eagles or herons, or even old squirrel nests; may also nest in depressions of rocky ledges, caves, and infrequently on rocky ground or in hollow logs.

Great horned owls are one of America's most widely distributed owls, closely related to the Eurasian eagle owl; the two are thought to have originated from a single species and become separated only in recent times.[11] Great-horned owls use a wide variety of hunting techniques, and their range of local prey is diverse—they prefer hares or rabbits, but willingly take raccoons, porcupines, squirrels, skunks, muskrats, bats and many bird species (including other owls). Securing prey on foot is not a problem for these owls, who will even wade into ponds to grab frogs or fish. Their identifying "ear tufts" have nothing to do with hearing, but rather are used in visual communication. Individuals have lived thirty years in captivity, while those in the wild reach an average of thirteen years. One of the most interesting facts about these owls is that they have virtually no sense of smell, making them a skunk's primary predator—they are unaffected by skunk spray. Despite indiscriminate extermination by man, great horned owls have increased greatly due to their ability to adapt to urban areas.

Boreal Owl
Aegolius funereus
RESIDENT, NON-MIGRATORY • UNCOMMON

Habitat/feeding: Subalpine. Typically mature or old-growth spruce-fir and lodgepole forests above 9,000 ft. (2745 m). Needs open areas near streams or bogs, where prey population is higher. May move to lower elevation when food is scarce, sometimes as low as oak-mountain shrublands and pinyon-juniper. Diet is primarily red-backed voles, also other small rodents, birds and insects. Caches food, warming it later by sitting on top of it. Nocturnal. **Field ID traits:** 10 in. (25 cm). Sexes look alike, but female larger. Similar to northern saw-whet owl, but darker brown, lacking overall reddish-chestnut color. White facial disc with black border, white "eyebrows"; head spotted with white, larger spots scattered across back; bill a horn or yellowish color; feathered feet. Both sexes vocalize only during breeding—a quick sequence of hollow *hoot* notes, sounding snipe-like but more harmonic in quality. Male's song comes in two versions: a shorter, louder one (audible at least 1 mile away) used to lure female to territory, and a more prolonged (up to 3 minutes), softer one used to familiarize female with nest site.[12]

DAN AND CINDY HARTMAN

Its primary song (the staccato song) closely resembles the noisy winnowing of the common snipe. But whereas the snipe's winnowing emanates from an oatmeal box, the boreal owl delivers its song with the rich harmonics and pure musical tones of an orchestral hall.

—BILL LANE, *"Sirens in the Night,"* Birding Magazine

Flammulated owls (*Otis flammeolus*) also breed here, but are migratory and very secretive. They are only 6¾ in. (17 cm), a mottled gray or reddish-brown and have ear tufts and dark eyes. **Breeding/nesting:** Cavity nester, usually in used flicker or woodpecker holes; readily uses nest boxes in Colorado if in appropriate habitat.

Elusive boreal owls live in conifer forests around the globe, but since the male's flute-like staccato call is heard only during breeding season, this small nocturnal owl is quite difficult to locate—especially when its home territory is covered in deep snow and prone to avalanches. In efforts to encourage this species, nest boxes have been installed in Colorado's high country. Although the boreal owl is not under any particular protection program in Colorado, the U.S. Forest Service considers it a "sensitive species" that merits special management attention.

RICHARD W. HOLMES

Northern Saw-whet Owl
Aegolius acadicus
RESIDENT, NON-MIGRATORY • UNCOMMON

Habitat/feeding: Montane to lower subalpine. Diverse forest and woodland habitats with open understory and edge habitat; in Colorado, prefers mid-elevation habitats and bands of riparian forest in open shrubland; generally rare in dense spruce-fir forest. Hunts from low perches for small mammals and birds, particularly mice and voles. Nocturnal. **Field ID traits:** 8 in. (20 cm). Reddish-chestnut body with scattered white spots on upper parts; reddish streaking noticeably brighter on chest. Marks distinguishing it from boreal owl are its dark bill, darker facial disc and small white streaks (not spots) on crown. Amount of white on face is variable, but spreads from bill upward over eyes. Juvenile is tawny-rust colored below, lacking streaks. **Breeding/nesting:** Probably not monogamous, and probably rarely returns to same nesting area. Vocalizes only during breeding season; male's mating call is a monotonous whistled *hoop* that may last several hours. May present female with mouse after he attracts her to the nest. Nests almost exclusively in abandoned woodpecker (especially flicker) cavities.

Northern saw-whet owls have excellent hearing and very good night vision. If their relatively large heads look slightly off kilter, it's because their asymmetrical ears (an advantage in hunting) result in an asymmetrical skull. If threatened, a saw-whet will stretch out on a limb and bring a wing around the front of its body, transforming into a bump on the branch. The source of this owl's name comes from an alarm call it makes—*skiew*—which sounds somewhat like the whetting of a saw.

Forest management for snag retention and diverse stands of uneven-aged trees will help ensure the survival of Northern Saw-whet Owls and other members of the cavity-nesting guild.

—HUGH E. KINGERY,
Colorado Breeding Bird Atlas

Northern Pygmy-Owl
Glaucidium gnoma
RESIDENT, NON-MIGRATORY • UNCOMMON

TODD PATRICK

Habitat/feeding: Montane to lower subalpine. Aspen and riparian up to 10,000 ft. (3078 m). Hunts in daytime from tree perches; caches food for later consumption. Voles are the majority of diet; small birds a close second. Also dines on other small mammals, reptiles, insects and amphibians. Migrates to lower elevations in response to weather or food needs. Able to carry prey three times its own weight. **Field ID traits:** 6.75 in. (17 cm). Sexes similar. Large, rounded head, crown dotted with white; body chocolate, grayish or rusty brown above with white spots, white and boldly streaked beneath; long, dark tail with thin white bars; yellow eyes; pale bill. Black "eye spots" on back of head may deter predators; white throat visible if calling. Rapid wing beats, rounded wing tips. Vocalizations vary geographically; male call, primarily territorial, is sequence of repetitive whistled hoots; female vocalizes less frequently, call has cackling quality. If excited, emits high-pitched trill or rattle. **Breeding/nesting:** Solitary and unsocial most of the year, but pairs snuggle and feed each other during courtship. Nests in cavities; very dependent on abandoned woodpecker holes.

While sitting under an aspen tree, your reverie may be broken by feathers gently falling around your shoulders, and the sound of scolding songbirds. Looking up, don't be surprised to see this tiny owl calmly plucking feathers from a songbird—a common practice. Aggressive and quite ferocious for its size, this tiny diurnal predator plummets, piercing its prey's throat with a talon. When threatened, it flattens its feathers, narrows its eyes and faces the intruder. It attempts to drive off large predators by puffing its feathers and spreading its tail to look bigger. Large black "eye" spots on the back of the head, or nape, may help deter attackers from behind.

GOATSUCKER FAMILY   *Caprimulgidae*

Nighthawks and nightjars are jointly referred to as "goatsuckers"—a name that arose from a European belief that these weird, wide-mouthed birds stole into barns or pastures at night to suck milk from the teats of goats (Not true—they were after the insects hovering around the goats!).[13] These birds' camouflage coloring and dusk-to-dawn foraging habits make them difficult to observe. Goatsuckers are considered by many to be closely related to owls because of their coloration, curious vocalizations and nocturnal lifestyle; although not in the same order (or group) of birds, they are somewhat related biochemically. Most unusual are goatsuckers' similarities to bats—a good example of convergent evolution in very different animals. Both are night-flying vertebrates with erratic flight patterns, which consume the same prey in similar habitats although their methods of prey detection are different. They can also lower their body temperature and slow their metabolism to conserve energy, a common tactic when insects are scarce.

RICHARD W. HOLMES

Common Nighthawk
Chordeiles minor
BREEDING, MIGRATORY • UNCOMMON

Habitat/feeding: Montane to subalpine. Use open conifer forests, montane grasslands and oak-mountain shrublands. Gaping mouth adapted for catching insects in midair; hunt mostly dawn and dusk; also nocturnally or on cloudy days. Diet includes beetles, grasshoppers, flies and mosquitoes. Skims drinking water from lakes and streams while in flight. **Field ID traits:** 9.5 in. (24 cm). Sexes similar. Robin-sized bird, gray-brown mottled plumage; relatively large brown eyes. White patches on long, pointed, blackish wings, most visible in flight. Male has white bar on a slightly forked tail. Male's throat white, female's tan. Call is a nasal *peent*. Bouncing, erratic and darting flight.
Breeding/nesting: Male courtship display includes circling, hovering and soaring over nest site, usually at dusk, ending with a famously long dive and loud "boom." Although less intense, such flights may continue even into migration. Lays 2 eggs on open rocky ground, sometimes on gravel or tar roofs or burned-over areas from forest fires; uses no nesting material, but may scrape shallow depression in sand or gravel.

Although energetic in flight, birds of this rather curious species expend little energy in raising a family, choosing to lay their eggs on open, often barren ground. The mottled color of the eggs, plus leaves, pine needles and rocks, keep them well hidden. Nighthawks usually roost lengthwise on lofty limbs, their mottled gray and brown plumage providing intricate camouflage. The "booming" sound emitted at the bottom of the male courtship dive is created by air vibrating the primary wing feathers. The sound, which some have likened to a bull's snort, along with the species' erratic, bat-like flight, has earned it another common name, "bullbat." Nighthawk populations are declining, possibly because suburban development and grazing by livestock leave little safe open ground for nesting—the nest and eggs often get stepped on.

HUMMINGBIRD FAMILY *Trochilidae*

The smallest of all birds comprise one of the largest families in the western hemisphere. Calliope hummingbirds, the tiniest in North America, weigh in at only 0.1 oz (2.7 g), while the largest is the blue-throated hummingbird at 0.27 oz (7.6 g). Though tiny, these jeweled birds are well adapted for survival. Their normal heart rate is 250 beats/minute, and increases to a phenomenal 1,250 beats/minute while flying or foraging, allowing them to sustain their high levels of activity. On very cold nights, when conserving energy is especially important, hummingbirds do an amazing thing! They find protective cover and remain motionless with head tucked close to the body to preserve warmth as their metabolism drops into a temporary physiological state called torpor. Similar to hibernation, the heart rate drops to a mere fifty beats/minute, with little or no breathing for minutes at a time.

Hummingbirds' exquisite dances with flowers, acrobatic courtship displays and aggressive territorial behavior make for delightful entertainment. Irresistibly drawn to mostly red, orange or yellow tubular flowers, whose nectar only they and long-tongued moths are able to reach, they receive high-energy "rewards" in return for their pollination services. Hummers lap nectar, rather than sipping as through a straw, with the nectar moving up inconspicuous grooves in the tongue by capillary action. Evolutionary biologists believe the relationship between flowers and hummingbirds is a classic example of coevolution, where each party has adapted to the other, and both benefit. The hummingbird diet also includes some insects, taken from vegetation or caught while in flight.

HUMMINGBIRD FEEDER ETIQUETTE

Hummingbird feeders support unnaturally high populations of these birds, so it is important to learn feeder etiquette, and even better yet—plant a multitude of brightly colored tubular flowers in your gardens. To make your own nectar for feeders use one part white sugar and four parts boiling water. Red food coloring is not necessary, and may contain carcinogens! Mix well, allowing it to cool before filling feeders. Change every four days, or more often during warm weather, as sugar solutions will ferment if left too long and can sicken birds. Bring feeders in at night if bears discover the sweet food source. Bears may become a problem if they learn food is available around homes—often resulting in their death.

Male hummingbirds are extremely aggressive when defending their territories against other male hummers. They commonly use scolding vocalizations, increasing in pitch if ignored, while raising the brightly colored feather patches on their necks and heads, which catch the light, flashing iridescent colors as they engage in intense diving displays, occasionally knocking intruders to the ground.

These small birds are inordinately fond of bathing in mountain streams and using in-stream rocks as perches. Although nestlings may fall prey to snakes, squirrels, cats, ants, mice and jays, adult hummingbirds have few natural predators and may live as long as a decade.

LINDSEY KIRK

Broad-tailed hummingbird male lapping nectar from a Rocky Mountain penstemon.

Broad-tailed Hummingbird
Selasphorus platycercus
BREEDING, MIGRATORY
• COMMON

Habitat/feeding: Montane to subalpine, up to 10,300 ft. (3230 m). Aspen, spruce-fir, mixed aspen-conifer forests and riparian shrublands. Hover-feeds; catches insects in midair or gleans them from foliage; also eats spiders or prey trapped in their webs; feeds insects to young. **Field ID traits:** 4 in. (10 cm), 0.13 oz (3.6 g). Body is iridescent green above; male with fuchsia to red throat, whitish belly and green side patches; female with lightly mottled throat, dark peachy wash on flanks, rufous outer tail feathers. Male's narrowed wing-tip feathers produce persistent trill. Both sexes possess vocal repertory of chatters, chips and buzzes to signal locations, indicate mood and warn intruders. **Breeding/nesting:** Promiscuous males perform elaborate courtship flights above perching females. Sexes maintain separate territories, females carefully selecting those mostly in mountain valleys with protected nesting sites and plentiful food sources; males may range higher on the hillsides. Males offer no help to female in nesting/brooding process. Female feeds young by using her long bill to regurgitate food (mostly insects) directly into their throats.

Broad-tailed hummingbirds' cup-shaped nests are well-hidden treasures, often secreted away near streams beneath protective overhanging foliage. Intricately made, they are cemented together with pirated spider silk and disguised with lichens. Although many hummingbirds must perform special aerial displays to warn other hummers that they are trespassing, the male of this species has tapered outer primary feathers that cause an audible high-pitched vibration during his rapid flight—a strong non-vocal message announcing that he's around. Hovering broad-tailed males are able to beat their wings at fifty-two strokes per second, compared to twenty-seven strokes per second for chickadees. During the fall and winter, the little hummer that you have had so much fun watching is basking in the sun from central Mexico south.

Rufous hummingbirds (*Selasphorus rufus*) nest in the Pacific Northwest, arriving here around July 4th. They then hang out and guard individual feeders, creating splashy displays for the rest of the summer.

KINGFISHER FAMILY *Alcedinidae*

Both male and female have colorful waterproof plumage that is similar in appearance. In North America, they live mainly on fish, which they locate from a high perch, and capture by diving in headfirst with mouth open, bringing it to the surface while swimming with their wings. They are even known to dive underwater to escape predators. Kingfishers are loud, raucous birds, remaining fairly solitary except during mating season.

Belted Kingfisher

Ceryle alcyon
RESIDENT, NON-MIGRATORY
• COMMON

Habitat/feeding: Montane. Streams and ponds; mostly streams in Colorado; prefers clear, slow-moving water. Dives for small fish; diet also includes mice, butterflies, snakes, grasshoppers and berries. **Field ID traits:** 13 in. (33 cm). Chunky bird with short legs and stubby tail, proportionately large head with tufted crest, and long, spear-like bill. Body slate blue with white collar, blue cravat; female has bright rusty belly "belt." Juvenile's breast band more brownish. Call is a continuous series of loud clattering notes (resembles a wooden rattle); used during vigorous chases and attacks to defend territory. **Breeding/nesting:** Monogamous. Continuous mewing calls during courtship; female sits with beak up, fluttering wings and begging for food while male feeds her fish; also aerial displays. Pairs dig long horizontal burrows with their bills, 3–7 ft. (1–2 m), pushing dirt out with their feet, typically in banks of streams or ponds. Female lays eggs in round end of nesting chamber.

Found in riparian habitat throughout North America, belted kingfishers dive in the water to spear or capture fish with their dagger-like bills. Look for their unique profile as they perch over water, searching for prey, or hover twenty to thirty feet above just before a dive. They will often throw a fish into the air and swallow it headfirst—or, if necessary, hammer it into submission on a tree limb before devouring it. Kingfishers regurgitate pellets of indigestible prey parts, as birds of prey do, often leaving a pile of pellets beneath their favorite perches. Data from the Breeding Bird Survey shows an alarming 2% average yearly decline in belted kingfisher populations, possibly due to habitat degradation.

WOODPECKER FAMILY   *Picidae*

Woodpeckers make their *rat-tat-tat* sound on wood, or on some other surface, for three reasons: drumming, excavating and foraging. Drumming is a woodpecker's primary form of communication over long distances. It is used for territorial defense, social interaction and mate attraction. Both sexes drum, though males become specially active in the spring, loudly drumming on hollow trees to advertise a great nesting site to prospective mates. Drumming patterns are distinctive to each species, but are not a reliable identification aid. Most woodpeckers excavate cavity nests in standing dead or diseased trees. A pair will excavate a new nest cavity each season, and sometimes two—one for reproduction and one for fall nesting. Well-hidden cavity nests can be more easily defended against small predators like deer mice, and are less affected by weather. For further protection, woodpeckers have learned to excavate their nests near human habitation, where there are fewer snakes and other predators. Foraging includes probing for invertebrates in bark or wood crevices, in various fruits and food crops, as well as eating insects caught in sticky "wells" they previously drilled in tree trunks. Woodpeckers' foraging plays an important role in ecosystems, benefiting humans as well—a study in Mississippi found that northern flickers removed a large percentage of corn borer larvae from cornfields.

Woodpeckers' specialized adaptations include:

- a long, sticky tongue with a hard barbed tip for probing crevices in search of food.

- a skull with built-in shock-absorbing tissue between sutures.

- strong feet, usually with 2 toes forward and 2 back, for gripping tree bark.

- stiff central tail feathers for bracing against tree trunks when drilling or drumming.
- bristle-like feathers over the nostrils that act as a "dust guard" while drilling.
- exceptional hearing to listen for insect movements inside the wood.

Woodpeckers first appeared approximately 25 million years ago, and have evolved to become habitat specialists, rendering them very vulnerable to changes in their habitat due to development or logging. The current practice of selective logging of standing dead and diseased trees removes woodpecker's nesting and foraging trees. Fortunately, the forestry industry is beginning to recognize that standing dead trees, insects, disease and fire play an integral role in forest health.

Lewis's Woodpecker
Melanerpes lewis
RESIDENT, NON-MIGRATORY • UNCOMMON

Habitat/feeding: Mature montane and riparian forests; open canopy with brushy understory. Diet primarily of insects; also acorns, fruit and other nuts. Seldom excavates food from wood like other woodpeckers. **Field ID traits:** 10.75 in. (27 cm). Looks like a colorful crow, with ruby-red mask, dark head with neck wrapped in gray "scarf" extending onto the breast; belly with pinkish-red wash. Much quieter than other woodpeckers, with a crow-like flight of steady wing-beats rather than the typical undulating flight of woodpeckers. **Breeding/nesting:** Form permanent pair bond. During courtship, male utters quickly descending series of brief squeaks. Pairs build nest in decayed live tree, dead or burned tree, or in existing cavity (sometimes in old flicker hole). May return to same cavity year after year. Both sexes form brood patches.

The most specialized of North American woodpeckers, this species catches insects on the wing much like flycatchers, and gleans insects from tree bark like nuthatches or from vegetation as like wood-warblers do. It does not drill, having a weaker skull than other woodpeckers. Lewis's woodpeckers can even be seen soaring with swallows. Their low population density and patchy distribution make them especially susceptible to breeding habitat loss caused by development and logging. Fire suppression and salvage logging have cut down on their nesting and foraging opportunities in the burned areas they are attracted to, while human encroachment and degradation of riparian areas has led to the loss of cottonwood trees, which they also favor for nesting. In addition, their preference for agriculturally damaging insects such as ants, beetles and grasshoppers, and their penchant for choosing to live at lower elevations on ranches and farms, subjects them to the lethal effects of pesticides.

ROBIN HENRY

Red-naped Sapsucker

Sphyrapicus ruber (former subspecies of yellow-bellied sapsucker)

BREEDING, MIGRATORY • COMMON

Habitat/feeding: Montane to lower subalpine. Breeds almost exclusively in mature aspen stands containing trees infected with shelf or heartwood fungus, and feeds in associated willow and cottonwood habitats. Uses its tongue to lap up sap and insects mired in previously drilled "wells" in tree trunks; also eats inner bark of trees, and sometimes catches insects on the fly. **Field ID traits:** 8.5 in. (22 cm). Back (nape) of the black-and-white head always red in both sexes; red throat and neck of male extends to back tip of black "moustache," actually touching the white cheek and partially extending over the black breast patch; narrow white stripes down back broken by black bars; faint yellow wash on belly. **Breeding/nesting:** Excavates an 8 in. (20 cm) hole in about 6–10 days. Willingly shares nest tree with other species, such as mountain bluebirds, house wrens, tree and violet-green swallows, who often use abandoned woodpecker holes. Carries sap in bill to feed young.

To enter the magical world of the sapsuckers, spend some time quietly concealed near one of their sap-well trees and watch the show. These "wells," or holes, ooze sap, which is eaten by the sapsuckers along with the insects that are attracted to and then trapped by the stickiness. Typically drilled in aspens and willows, they are also visited by wood-warblers, hummingbirds, butterflies, moths and even chipmunks, squirrels and wasps—all share in the goodies provided by the woodpecker. An example of a "keystone species," sapsuckers provide essential and unique services within an ecosystem on which other resident species are dependent. This is a perfect example of the intricate web-like connections that develop in a healthy environment.

This female broad-tailed hummingbird is helping herself to sap and insects caught in one of the red-naped sapsucker "wells."

Williamson's Sapsucker
Sphyrapicus thyroideus
BREEDING, MIGRATORY • UNCOMMON

CHARLES W. MELTON

Habitat/feeding: Montane to lower subalpine. Prefers aspen forests, but also nests in spruce/fir, lodgepole and ponderosa; snags are critical. In aspen forests, avoids competition with red-naped sapsucker by choosing nesting sites closer to coniferous-dominated forest. Drills sap "wells," like other sapsuckers; occasionally catches insects in aerial pursuit. Sexes differ in feeding habits; female gleans for insects on tree trunks; male prefers limbs and the ground. **Field ID traits:** 9 in. (23 cm). Male and female so different in appearance ornithologists once thought them two separate species. Male has dark head with slender white stripes and red chin; solid black back, yellow belly, white rump, and noticeable white wing patches. Female has light-brown head with chocolate-brown and white barring on back, wings and sides; no red. **Breeding/nesting:** Males excavate nesting cavities. Young beg so boisterously unmated males are sometimes induced to feed them; the begging may also attract predators.

Sapsuckers' wintering grounds are primarily in Arizona and Mexico. Heavy logging in Mexico may be having detrimental effects on this species. With a seasonally specialized diet, this sapsucker feeds exclusively on conifer sap before nesting, switching primarily to ants, but also other insects after the young hatch.

Downy Woodpecker
Picoides pubescens
RESIDENT, NON-MIGRATORY • COMMON

RICHARD W. HOLMES

Habitat/feeding: Montane. Aspen forests, particularly with younger trees and low canopy. Forages for insects, including wood-boring beetles, carpenter ants, aphids, grasshoppers and spiders; also eats berries, mullein seeds and sap. Feeds at backyard stations on suet, corn bread, cracked walnuts, sunflower seeds and cracked corn. **Field ID traits:** 6.75 in. (17 cm). White back, bill about half length of head (compare with hairy woodpecker), white spots in wings, black markings on white outer tail feathers, red patch on back of head; lacking in female. According to the *Colorado Breeding Bird Atlas*, our subspecies has no or very few white spots on black wing coverts. Call is a quick, flat *peek*, much quieter than hairy woodpecker's call; also more piercing call like the "whinnying of a small horse." **Breeding/nesting:** Courtship in late winter; pairing bond is territorial-based and may last up to four years. Both sexes drum on trees, utility poles, etc., for territory establishment and courtship; maintain separate winter territories; intensely defend nests, sometimes becoming so disturbed they turn on each other. Female usually selects both her own and male's winter roosting cavity, either in live or dead trees or stumps.

Downy woodpeckers are the smallest of all North American wood-peckers, excavating a perfectly round nesting hole, exactly 1.26 in. (3.2 cm) in diameter. They winter at lower elevations, where they are known to "bathe" in snow. Separate feeding habitats reduce competition between the sexes for food during the winter—males feed in the tops of trees while females feed in the middle and lower parts. At other times of the year, the pair separates, feeding in different tree species and using different foraging techniques—males "peck" while females more often "probe."

RICHARD W. HOLMES

Hairy Woodpecker
Picoides villosus
RESIDENT, NON-MIGRATORY • COMMON

Habitat/feeding: Montane to lower sub-alpine. Our mountain subspecies breeds primarily in conifer forests; secondarily in aspen or riparian mixed woodlands, up to 10,200 ft. (3140 m). Prefers larvae of wood-boring beetles, spiders, ants, millipedes and beetles; will sometimes peel bark to find insects; occasionally eats nuts and berries. Similar to downy woodpecker regarding backyard feeding. **Field ID traits:** 9.25 in. (24 cm). Similar to downy woodpecker, but with larger, heavier bill about equal in length to head; white breast and back, black-and-white-striped head, black wings spotted with white, and clear white outer tail feathers. Back of male's head has red patch. Primary call a high-pitched *peek*; also produces a "rattling whinny," and a fast-paced *queek, queek, queek* during conflicts. **Breeding/nesting:** Mating begins in November or December, with female aggres-sively drumming up to 10 times per minute; male answers with only 4–5 drums per minute. Male usually locates nest site, and does most drilling of the 10–15 inch-deep cavity.

Hairy woodpeckers are one of the woodpeckers thought to find food by feeling the vibrations made by insects moving in or under the wood. They also may hear the insects eating wood.[14] This species appears to be more prevalent than the downy woodpecker in western Colorado, with population fluctuations tied to insect infestations and the availability of previously burned forests. In summer, families may wander to higher ele-vations after the young fledge, moving back to the lower elevations when winter comes.

American Three-toed Woodpecker

Picoides dorsalis [formerly *P. tridactylus*]

RESIDENT, NON-MIGRATORY • RARE

Habitat/feeding: Montane to subalpine. Primarily spruce-fir forest, but also aspen, lodgepole and ponderosa if wood-boring insects, such as spruce bark beetles, are plentiful in dead and dying trees; favors burned areas. Also eats spiders, inner bark and berries. Searches for insects by stripping bark off snags instead of drilling. **Field ID traits:** 8.75 in. (22 cm). Does not have inner rear toes. White back has irregular black-and-white barring down the sides. Yellow cap, lacking in female; both sexes have barred flanks. Fairly silent except for a few weak squeaks; call note is a soft *pik*. **Breeding/nesting:** Both sexes do lots of drumming and chasing each other during breeding.

CHARLES W. MELTON

The abundance of three-toed woodpeckers is tied to the availability of spruce bark beetles, which are plentiful in burned areas. As with some other woodpecker species, males lessen winter competition by foraging lower on trees than females. Three-toed woodpeckers are relatively inactive birds, frequently clinging to a tree trunk to rest for a while, and are fairly tolerant of human presence. Their drumming is also subtler than that of other species, echoing more softly through the forest.

> According to the *Colorado Breeding Bird Atlas*, 40% of Colorado birds depend on cavity nests, but only 8% of these birds are woodpeckers with the ability to drill holes. The other 32% are secondary cavity nesters—such as chickadees, swallows, house wrens and mountain bluebirds—which utilize the holes after woodpeckers are finished with them, usually in the second season.

Northern Flicker

Colaptes auratus

RESIDENT, NON-MIGRATORY • COMMON

Habitat/feeding: Montane to subalpine. Aspen, conifer and mixed aspen-conifer woodlands; riparian. Tolerates human-populated areas. Ants account for about 50% of its diet, making it more terrestrial than other woodpeckers; also hawks and gleans bark for insects; eats berries and nuts. **Field ID traits:** 12.5 in. (32 cm). Sexes similar. Two races, only the red-shafted version occurring in our area; sightings of yellow-shafted are unusual. Male has striking red moustache on gray face, cocoa-colored head; back and wings cocoa, barred horizontally with black; taupe breast and sides scattered with roundish spots; distinguishing black crescent on upper breast; white rump and salmon blush under wings obvious during deeply undulating flight. **Breeding/nesting:** Mates for life. Male's aggressive behavior toward other males during breeding and territorial disputes includes bill directing or bill poking (inclining head forward and sometimes pecking) and head bobbing or head swinging (side-to-side action of

CHARLES W. MELTON

head and body). Both sexes excavate nests; nest holes rather large and irregular compared to those of other species; after abandoned, cavities are popular with American kestrels and small owls.

Flickers' voices are distinctive, making them one of the easiest birds to identify by sound. The male flicker's powerful song reverberates through the forest for as much as fifteen seconds at a time, sounding like a low-pitched series of *kwik-wikwikwi*. Their distant contact call is a loud and high-pitched *keew*, while their call at close range is a softer *wik-a-wik-a-wik-a*. During mating, the female softly purrs and coos in the background. Flickers are declining, possibly due to competition with European starlings for nest sites and to the removal of dead and dying trees. This beautiful bird proves itself economically valuable by destroying insect pests such as European corn borers and aphids.

PASSERINES—SONGBIRDS, OR PERCHING BIRDS

The remainder of birds described in this chapter are in the Order Passeriformes, which means "sparrow-shaped," the largest order of birds in the world. Passerines are considered evolutionarily superior to other birds because of their complex vocal organs, adaptability and greater intelligence. They all have the same type of foot, which is well adapted for gripping a perch—with 4 toes, 3 facing forward and 1 backward—while their muscles and tendons function by tightening instantly if the bird starts to fall backwards off the perch (while sleeping). Songbirds have adapted to nearly every terrestrial environment and include about 5,100 species, as compared to only 3,500 species for all the other orders put together. Passerines are divided into two groups—subocines (1,100 species) and ocines (4,000 species). Suboscines, found chiefly in Central and South America (only the tyrant flycatchers of this group reach into North America), sing songs that are innate, or programmed from birth. Oscines, on the other hand, learn their songs. Not all passerines' "songs" are recognized as music by the human ear, but many birds in this order are known and loved for their melodic and heart-warming songs. Who has not been inspired by the trill of a red-wing blackbird or the rich warbling of a male robin at dusk.

TYRANT FLYCATCHER FAMILY *Tyrannidae*

Why *tyrant* flycatchers? These birds' aggressive behavior toward any perceived intruders to their territories is indeed tyrannical. They will mob both perched and flying hawks and crows, some going so far as to "ride" on the back of hawks, while insistently pecking at the back of their heads.

Visually identifying local flycatchers taxes even the most expert birder. Although some species in this family are quite colorful, the ones in this area are inconspicuous small birds with drab green to brown markings. The easiest way to distinguish them is by their short, simple songs. Unlike those of other North American songbirds, flycatchers' songs are thought to be completely innate, not learned, and do not vary geographically. Most flycatchers sing a special "twilight song" that differs from their daytime song, and is usually sung at dawn before the sun peeks over the horizon.[15] Learning the preferred habitat of different flycatchers can help with identification because they are habitat specific. Special foraging strategies provide behavioral clues in identifying flycatcher species as well.

Regardless of their preferred ecosystem, most flycatchers require open spaces—a natural forest clearing, a stretch of stream, or beneath a high canopy or above a low canopy—with snags on the edges to serve as perches from which to fly out and capture insects in midair, known as hawking. Most flycatchers will also hover over shrubs or grass to take insects.

A flycatcher's beak can reveal a lot about how it "makes its living." A broad, flattened bill, rictal bristles (specialized feathers) at the base of the bill, and small hooks at the bill's tip are common to most flycatchers, probably aiding them in the pursuit and retrieval of flying prey. Bill size varies depending on the prey. For instance, the willow flycatcher's small bill is perfectly suited to catching very small insects such as gnats and midges, while the olive-sided flycatcher's larger bill is better suited to accommodate bees, wasps and flying ants. Because their diet consists mostly of insects, flycatchers are forced to migrate to the warmer climates of Mexico and Central or South America in winter.

RICHARD W. HOLMES

Though not considered a resident, Say's phoebe (*Sayornis saya*) has been observed locally during breeding season on open south-facing slopes of Gambel oak. According to the *Colorado Breeding Bird Atlas*, Say's phoebe can be found in oak-mountain shrublands below 9,000 ft. (2745 m) and throughout mountain valleys up to 9,500 ft. (2896 m). Their memorable song is a mellow whistle, alternating *pidiweew pidireep, pidiweew pidireep*. The call is a soft, melancholy whistle *pdeeer* or *tueee*.

Olive-sided Flycatcher
Contopus cooperi
BREEDING, MIGRATORY • UNCOMMON

Habitat/feeding: Montane to subalpine. Aspen, mixed-conifer and spruce-fir forests from 7,000 to 11,000 ft. (2134–3353 m). Chooses natural edges with dead standing trees for foraging, especially along streams, rivers or lakes; prefers tops of tallest snags. Eats only flying insects such as bees, wasps, flying ants, flies, moths, grasshoppers and dragonflies; no spiders, caterpillars or other larvae. **Field ID traits:** 7.5 in. (19 cm). Olive-brown and larger than other local flycatchers; tail broad and short in proportion to body; notably notched. White feather tufts protruding from sides of rump not always visible; dark breast patches separated by slender creamy to yellowish strip. Most easily identified by distinctive, 3-syllable *quick-three-beers*; hurried birds may only vocalize the *three beers*. **Breeding/nesting:** Male chases female during courtship. Pairs usually nest fairly high in a conifer; female thought to select site and construct cup-shaped nest. Male energetically defends nesting territory from predators, including humans.

Olive-sided flycatchers complete the longest annual migration of any flycatcher breeding in North America, flying to winter habitats primarily in Panama's highlands and the Northern Andes, with the greatest abundance in the Andean portion of Colombia. Conservationists are concerned about this species, whose population has declined by 67% since 1966. Deforestation in its Andean wintering range combined with habitat loss in its North American breeding range could be the reasons. Species that produce only one brood per year, as olive-sided flycatchers do, are particularly susceptible to population declines.

Western Wood-Pewee
Contopus sordidulus
BREEDING, MIGRATORY • COMMON

Habitat/feeding: Montane to subalpine. Aspen, mixed-conifer and riparian woodlands, especially forest edges (rare in spruce-fir); up to 10,000 ft. (3048 m). Diet is mostly insects such as flies, wasps, bees and moths; some berries. **Field ID traits:** 6.25 in. (16 cm). Dusky gray-brown above, olive-gray on breast and sides. Lack of eye-ring and longer wings extending halfway down tail separates pewee from *Empidonax* flycatchers. Reedy dawn song, consists of 2 phrases—a hoarse *pheea* ending in a downward slur and a rising complex whistled syllable accented at the end.[16] Call is a descending, raspy *peeer*. **Breeding/nesting:** Female constructs cup-shaped nest, bound together with spider webs, on horizontal branch; nest reconstructed if destroyed; will reuse old nests from year to year, a trait uncommon in non-colonial perching birds.

JAMES R. GALLAGHER

CHARLES W. MELTON

The melancholy call of the western wood-pewee becomes very familiar to anyone frequenting local aspen forests. Unfortunately, significant population declines are occurring across the continent for this species. As with other flycatchers, this is probably due to a combination of factors including deforestation of its wintering grounds, fragmentation of its breeding grounds and its apparent sensitivity to disturbance.

Cordilleran Flycatcher
Empidonax occidentalis
BREEDING, MIGRATORY • COMMON

Habitat/feeding: Montane to subalpine. Adjacent to riparian in aspen or mixed-coniferous forests up to 10,000 ft. (3048 m). Diet of mostly moths, butterflies, small bees, wasps, caterpillars and occasionally spiders; some berries and seeds. Habit of foraging under 30 feet helps separate this species from similar Hammond's flycatchers (see description under dusky flycatcher on next page). **Field ID traits:** 5.5–6 in. (14–15 cm). Olive-green back, yellowish underparts (including throat) and 2 light wing-bars. Its bold, tear-shaped white eye-ring distinguishes it from other closely related flycatchers. Song is sequence of 3 continuously repeated high-pitched phrases, *te-see* (upward), *bi-da-dit* (rapid), *sit*. Call 2 two-pitched and diagnostic for this species—sounds like *bir-DEE*. **Breeding/nesting:** Female builds nest in a wide variety of locations, including cliff ledges, road cuts, tangled roots of upturned trees, under raised bark and in tree cavities; has a penchant for nesting on eaves, window ledges and porches of mountain cabins and other human structures; may build upon old remains from previous years.

RICHARD W. HOLMES

Cordilleran flycatchers begin to make the long trek to their winter habitat in Mexico during August. Due to their preference for forests in riparian habitat, populations are vulnerable to habitat loss from logging, livestock grazing and the development of recreational facilities with accompanying roads and trails.

Willow Flycatcher
Empidonax traillii
BREEDING, MIGRATORY • UNCOMMON

Habitat/feeding: Montane to subalpine, up to 10,000 ft. (3048 m). Thickets of deciduous trees and shrubs; favors extensive willow carrs, and willow and alder habitat along streams or around beaver ponds. Diet includes wasps, bees, winged ants, beetles, flies, caterpillars and moths; also some seeds and berries. **Field ID traits:** 5.75 in. (15 cm). Eye-ring faint, if present at all. Brownish to grayish-olive back, 2-toned bill with upper dark, lower light. Whitish throat, belly and undertail coverts; pale-olive breast, soft yellow wash on belly; 2 light-colored wing-bars; wings shorter and bill smaller than wood-pewee's. Most easily identified by its typical song of 2 syllables—*fitz-bew*, *fizz-bew*, or an alternate that's a rough, low *crrreeet*, rising sharply at the end. **Breeding/nesting:** Mostly monogamous. Both

JAMES W. GALLAGHER

male and female sing territorial song. Intruding males sometimes attacked by both mates; vigorous chases by pairs and trios during courtship. If perturbed, male flicks tail, raises crest, puffs breast, flicks wings and may fly at threat. Female selects site, accompanied by male, and builds a messy cup-shaped nest, with threads of grass often hanging from beneath.

Willow flycatchers' numbers are declining for several reasons. The most obvious are habitat degradation of their breeding grounds when willow and alder vegetation is removed for cattle grazing or developments, exposure to pesticides when ingested through insects and parasitism by brown-headed cowbirds, which frequent the same habitats. At lower elevations in Colorado, the invasive shrub tamarisk is replacing the native vegetation along streams and reservoirs, leading to a decline in nesting success for willow flycatchers. Tamarisks do not provide enough shade for successful nesting, and they concentrate salt in their leaves, which discourages the presence of insects the flycatcher depends upon for food. Willow flycatchers migrate to areas from southern Mexico to Panama and Costa Rica, where they prefer clearings and second-growth woodlands.

TODD PATRICK

Dusky Flycatcher
Empidonax oberholseri
BREEDING, MIGRATORY • COMMON

Habitat/feeding: Montane. Mid-elevations in mountains, especially in oak-mountain shrublands with scattered trees; also open conifer or aspen forests with deciduous shrub understory, and riparian woodlands. Diet consists of moths, bees, wasps, grasshoppers, damselflies and other insects. **Field ID traits:** 5.75 (14 cm). Obvious white eye-ring and whitish throat; pale-olive wash on upper breast. Lower bill mostly dark, yellowish to orangish near base. Larger body and paler beneath, with a longer tail, than **Hammond's flycatcher** (*E. hammondii*), a related species that is uncommon in this area. Song is composed of 3 distinct phrases: a clear *seput*, then a raspy *tesurrt* and finally a clear, high *chelup*. Call is a distinct *dew hic*, often repeated at regular intervals. **Breeding/nesting:** Female probably builds cup-shaped nest alone in crotch of small tree or shrub, up to 7 ft. (2.1 m) above ground. Male sings from perch to defend their territory, and may also resort to tail-pumping, bill-snapping and crest-raising.

The most common flycatcher in this area, this species winters as far south as southern Mexico. A big dilemma for bird watchers is that the dusky flycatcher is almost identical in appearance to Hammond's flycatcher. The two species are best separated in the field by habitat and behavior. Compared to the traits of dusky flycatchers listed above, Hammond's prefers a denser forest of mature conifers with little or no understory at higher elevations, up to 10,000 ft. (3048 m), and builds its nest on a horizontal branch up to 40 ft. (12.2 m) above ground. They are more inclined to include beetles in their diet and forage from 20–100 feet above the ground, or possibly right on the ground. Unlike dusky fly-catchers, they never include any clear high notes in their repertoire.

VIREO FAMILY *Vireonidae*

Vireos have a certain "gestalt" that is unmistakable. Members of this family have bodies like wood-warblers, but with thicker heads and legs, and more stout, handsome bills that are just a bit hooked at the tip, with two tiny notches on the upper bill near the tip. Although often confused with wood-warblers, the latter move more quickly and are less decisive in their movements. Vireos are divided into two somewhat different groups—one having spectacle-like eye-rings and wing-bars, and the other having eyestripes and no wing-bars.

Vireos exhibit a couple of interesting singing behaviors. They will use certain patterns of cadence and repetition of phrases, revealing their position relative to their nest, and also mimic songs of competing vireo species occurring within the same territories. It is speculated that these behaviors developed not only to deter males of the same species from entering the nesting area, but males of other vireo species as well.

Warbling Vireo

Vireo gilvus
BREEDING, MIGRATORY
• ABUNDANT

Habitat/feeding: Montane to subalpine. Aspen forests, willows and cottonwoods. Gleans insects such as caterpillars from foliage and bark; eats some berries. **Field ID traits:** 4.75 in. (12 cm). Sexes similar; slender, sparrow-sized. Olive-gray head, back, wings (no bars) and tail; whitish beneath, pale-yellow wash possible on belly or flanks; blue-gray legs and feet. White "eyebrow" and dark eye-line from back of eye; thick bill

CHARLES W. MELTON

has hooked upper mandible. Song a continuous sweet warble with husky quality—*viderveedeeviderveedeeviderVEET*. Calls have a rough nasal quality, sounding like a mewing *meeerish*. **Breeding/nesting:** Male sings and struts around female with wings and tail spread; female often quivers wings in response. Deep, cup nest built by both sexes; suspended between fork on horizontal branch of shrub or tree, a bit distant from trunk.

Warbling vireos seem to be everywhere in aspen forests, the males singing incessantly, their rising and falling phrases often ending abruptly on a high note. Constant singing from the nest by males can attract more parasitism by cowbirds; however, research indicates that benefits also result from this singing behavior. For example, vireos appear to use the song to maintain contact with each other and coordinate their movements on and off the nest.[17] Central and South America see an influx of this species during the winter migration. Although numbers appear to be increasing, long-term conservation of this species may depend on controlling the use of pesticides that bioconcentrate in the food chain.

CHARLES W. MELTON

Plumbeous Vireo

Vireo plumbeus

BREEDING, MIGRATORY • UNCOMMON

Habitat/feeding: Montane. Oak-mountain shrub lands and occasionally aspen and mixed-conifer forests; ponderosa and pinyon-juniper communities at lower elevations in the Roaring Fork Valley. May forage at different heights in the forest or select larger insects to reduce competition during rare overlaps with warbling vireo. Gleans insects from limbs and trunks, sometimes snatching insects from air; eats berries during fall/winter. **Field ID traits:** 5.5 in. (14 cm). Large, dark eyes contrast vividly with white "spectacles," bolder than those of other songbirds. Sexes similar. Slender bird with lead-colored plumage above, 2 white wing-bars, pale beneath; occasional pale yellow wash on flanks. Thick bill with hooked upper mandible. Song is high-pitched and slow—a purposeful *chu-weet, chu-wir, chu-weet.* **Breeding/nesting:** Hoping to entice the intended mate, plumbeous vireo male puffs out flanks, bobbing and bowing quite formally; sings as he follows female; she does bulk of work locating nest site. Nest a partially pendulous, open cup between branches of fork on horizontal limb; male may carry nest material; nest materials often trail from bottom of nest.

This species was once grouped with blue-headed vireos and Cassin's vireos as a single species, the solitary vireo. Plumbeous vireos have been in decline in Colorado since 1966, due to parasitism by brown-headed cowbirds and robbing of nests by magpies, jays, and other predators more tolerant of human disturbance. Identifying and protecting successful breeding populations is important to the conservation of this species. Hearing the plumbeous song, and spying those bright spectacles, are the best clues for a solid field identification.

MOLTING

Since feathers are lifeless material, like our fingernails, they cannot be changed or repaired without being replaced. That is why birds periodically molt, growing new feathers, which push the old ones out. Birds that wear their feathers out more quickly, due to long-distance migration or daily life in dense vegetation, may need to molt twice a year, whereas birds that put less wear and tear on their feathers molt only once a year or less.

Perching birds (see p. 316) lose only a few feathers at a time while molting, so as to maintain flight. Those that don't migrate to warmer climates molt into warmer winter plumage. Males of some species molt into their brighter-colored breeding plumage just prior to the mating season. Although molting usually takes five to twelve weeks in perching birds, with some raptors it may take two years or more. Ducks molt quickly, replacing their flight feathers in just two to four weeks. Being heavy and having difficulty flying with flight feathers missing, they go through the process quickly, while staying on or near water for safety from predators.

CROW, RAVEN, MAGPIE and JAY FAMILY
Corvidae

Members of this family—collectively known as corvids—are considered by ornithologists to be some of the world's most intelligent and curious birds. Their antics and entertaining social behavior have inspired and animated art, literature and mythology throughout world history. Corvids are found on every continent except Antarctica, and corvid fossils date back at least 25 million years. The largest songbirds on earth, they are relatively sedentary, migrating only short distances when food is scarce or during very cold winter weather.

Several characteristics are common to most species of this highly sociable family:

- both sexes are generally alike in appearance and share in nest-building and caring for their young.

- individuals tend to live in flocks outside of the breeding season.

- may nest in colonies, have group nests and/or breed cooperatively in extended families where "helpers" assist parents in feeding and caring for the young or defending territories.

- display many of the indicators used to define higher intelligence, including complex social structures; a proclivity for problem solving using available objects to make tools; the ability to play; an excellent memory, as demonstrated by their ability to cache food and retrieve it later; and often surprising communication and mimicry skills.

CHARLES W. MELTON

Gray Jay, Camp Robber, Canada Jay

Perisoreus canadensis

RESIDENT, NON-MIGRATORY • COMMON

Habitat/feeding: Montane to alpine. Spruce-fir and mixed-conifer forests, 8,500 ft. (2591 m) to timberline; may wander to lower elevations during fall or winter. Varied diet of insects, spiders, berries (especially mountain ash and bilberry), fungi, small rodents, birds' eggs and carrion. Caches food, which is often stolen by Steller's jays. **Field ID traits:** 11.5 in. (29 cm). Fluffy gray without crest. White to pearl-gray cheeks, forehead, throat and chest, with dark-gray partial cap on back of head leading into eye; sexes similar. Black bill, legs and feet. Song musical and muted, full of whistles and warbles.

Breeding/nesting: Pairs form long-term bonds, defending large permanent territory. Courtship feeding behavior begins early in breeding season; male presents female with solid or regurgitated food, which is thought to strengthen pair bonds, induce copulation and build nutritional reserves for egg-laying. Cup-shaped nest built in February or March; lined with thick insulation of feathers, lichen, down and animal fur.

They are the boldest of our birds, except the chickadee, and in cool impudence far surpass all others.
—*Birds Magazine,* April 1897

Gray jays, or "camp robbers" as they're commonly known, possess an uncanny ability to arrive the moment anyone pulls out a picnic in the vicinity of a spruce-fir forest. Confident and curious, they glide down fearlessly to steal bits of food with their feet—more often a trait of predatory birds. Instead of eating the morsel right away, they may create a sticky bolus by mixing it with saliva and hide it in a discreet location under bark or lichen for later retrieval. Considered clowns by most locals and visitors today, camp robbers were once despised by hunters and trappers, who lost bait and prey alike to these clever jays. Called *wiss ka tjon* by native peoples of Canada, they became known as "whiskey jacks" by lunching lumbermen who could not pronounce the indigenous name.

CHARLES W. MELTON

Western Scrub Jay

Aphelocoma californica

RESIDENT, NON-MIGRATORY
• COMMON

Habitat/feeding: Montane. Oak-mountain shrublands. Diet of acorns, fruits, berries and seeds most of the year; changes to insects, eggs and nestlings of other birds during the breeding season. The least dependent of corvids on food caches; carries only 1 seed at a time. **Field ID traits:** 11.5 in. (29 cm). Crestless jay, easily identified by remarkable blue coloration and obvious white "eyebrow;" sexes similar. Brown-gray patch on back, white throat streaked with gray, buffy underparts and long tail. Call is repeated *quick, quick, quick,* or a raspy *shreep* that may be in a short series. **Breeding/nesting:** Forms long-term pair bonds. Sets up year-round territories. A courting male will hop around the female with head erect and tail spread and dragging. Nest built by both sexes; well concealed, constructed 3–30 ft. (1–9 m) from the ground in tree or bush; compact and cup-shaped, made of twigs, moss and dry grasses; lined with hair and fine roots—no mud.

Usually considered a bit obstreperous, scrub jays become shy and reclusive during breeding season. They easily become accustomed to humans, and are quite common at bird feeders around houses within their habitat. Although they are not as dependent on food caches as much as some other members of this family, studies indicate that they have very precise memories, remembering what they hid and where and when they hid it. Being conciously aware of the passage of time is considered by some to be a more sophisticated form of memory.[18] Until the 1930's, many farmers held shoots to reduce jay numbers because of perceived damage to crops.

Clark's Nutcracker
Nucifraga columbiana
RESIDENT, NON-MIGRATORY • COMMON

Habitat/feeding: Montane to subalpine. Spruce-fir and mixed-conifer forests; also pinyon-juniper at lower elevations. Majority of diet is pine nuts, which it often collects at lower elevations and caches at higher elevations; also eats fruits, insects, small vertebrates, and other bird's eggs and nestlings. Gleans foliage for insects; also gleans them from ground and catches them in flight. Begins feeding on and caching coniferous seeds late summer and fall, relying on caches to survive winter. Feeds its young hulled and regurgitated pine nuts. **Field ID traits:** Bold, stocky gray bird, 12 in. (31 cm). Black bill, wings and inner tail feathers; white wing patches and outer tail feathers, especially visible in flight. Voice is nasal, raspy *kraaa* or *at-tat-tat-tat.* Often perches at very top of conifer trees. **Breeding/nesting:** Typically monogamous. Male follows female in long courtship flights; both build cup-shaped nest supported by platform of dry twigs and bark strips on horizontal limb in conifer, 8–45 ft. (2–14 m) above ground. Both sexes incubate, nestled within the deep cup, hesitant to leave, even if closely approached.

Clark's nutcrackers are capable of one of the most incredible mental feats known in the bird world. Each year a single nutcracker buries up to 33,000 food items in literally thousands of different sites on south-facing slopes, retrieving them months later with a fairly high degree of accuracy by making spatial references to surrounding objects such as boulders, trees or logs. Highly adapted for this behavior, this bird has a strong, sharp bill for opening cones and removing seeds, and a sublingual pouch that allows it to carry 90–150 pinyon nuts at once! Nutcrackers and pines are thought to have coevolved, with each influencing the other's evolution. Some pines depend on nutcrackers to distribute their large seeds at a distance from the parent tree, which nutcrackers inadvertently do when they cache seeds and occasionally fail to retrieve them. The impact of these birds on the landscape is immense.

LINDSAY KIRK

Black-billed Magpie

Pica hudsonia
[formerly *P. pica*]
RESIDENT,
NON-MIGRATORY
• ABUNDANT

Habitat/feeding:
Montane. Prefers open woodlands and thickets, and cottonwood bottom-land near streams. Unlikely to use conifers. Known as the most insectivorous North American corvid, 85% of its diet being insects; does consume carrion, invertebrates, small mammals and birds; also some fruit and seeds; common at bird-feeders. **Field ID traits:** 19 in. (48 cm). Striking black and white bird with quite long, greenly iridescent tail. White wing patches and white belly contrast vividly with black bill, head, back, rump, breast and tail underparts. Call is usually whining *mag* and a series of harsh *shek-shek-shek* notes; also combinations of variable sounds. **Breeding/nesting:** Forms long-term pair bond. Male struts and flashes its wings while chasing female during courtship. Once successful, builds an obvious, messy and bulky domed structure of heavy twigs enclosing a bowl of mud lined with finer stems, hair and rootlets; may take 40–50 days to construct; sometimes repaired and reused. Pairs mostly nest separately; occasionally found in loose colonies.

This unmistakable and gregarious panda-plumed bird attracts much attention from visitors to the valley. Campers napping outdoors may be awakened by curious chattering magpies. Unfortunately, shooting contests were held in an attempt to exterminate magpies through at least the 1930's, and thousands of these birds also died from poison bait originally intended for predators. Colorado populations have rebounded, but Christmas counts show a drop in their numbers again. Loss of riparian habitat may be responsible. Magpies roost in small flocks of eight to forty individuals when breeding season is over.

Common Raven
Corvus corax
RESIDENT, NON-MIGRATORY • COMMON

RICHARD W. HOLMES

Habitat/feeding: Montane to subalpine. Cliffs and rock outcroppings in aspen and aspen-mixed conifer, oak-mountain shrublands. Ravens are not picky about diet, eating mostly carrion, plus small rodents, insects, grain, and just about anything else they can find; will cache food temporarily. **Field ID traits:** 24 in. (61 cm). Black all over with shaggy throat; heavier bill, larger body and ganglier than crows. Tail slightly wedge-shaped. Soars frequently, rather than flapping, and has long wings that reach back toward tip of tail, unlike crows on both accounts. Vocalizations vary from strong and deep to higher and twanging. Makes drawn-out, hoarse *kraaah*, a lower-toned and hollow *brrronk*, and a deeper, more resonant *prruk*. **Breeding/nesting:** Monogamous. Courtship includes cooing and preening each other's feathers. Impressive aerial tumbling maneuvers from cliffs, similar to raptors', are presumably performed as play, or to strengthen bonds between mates. Both sexes build bulky stick nest, difficult to locate among cliffs; sometimes use trees or human structures; often return to same nest for years.

Many Native American legends involved ravens and crows. Pacific Northwest tribes called raven "the great trickster," and believed it to have created mankind, brought fire to deliver humans from darkness, created salmon for them to eat, and procured water for them during periods of drought. Like the crow, it was believed to be an intermediary between the spirit and material worlds. To honor the raven, tribes often carved its likeness on totem poles. Although some stories about corvids' intelligence may be slightly exaggerated, *The Sibley Guide to Bird Life and Behavior* describes how ravens have demonstrated true insight in solving problems, such as figuring out how to retrieve food dangling from a string on their first try.

American Crow
Corvus brachyrhynchos
RESIDENT, NON-MIGRATORY • COMMON

CHARLES MELTON

Habitat/feeding: Up to lower subalpine, about 10,000 ft. (3048 m). Aspens, conifers, montane riparian areas, urban and rural areas. Not present in upper Roaring Fork Valley until about ten years ago. Remarkably varied diet including insects, mollusks, carrion, frogs, mice, garbage, bird eggs, nestlings, seeds, fruit and nuts. Caches food for later consumption. Its primary predators are hawks and owls. **Field ID traits:** 17–21 in. (43–53 cm). Large perching bird. Black feathers, legs, feet and bill; plumage shimmers with iridescent purples in bright sunlight; sexes similar. Flies with steady, slow wing beats, rarely soars. Multiple calls communicate alarm, food availability, fighting behavior and summon to rally. Main vocalization raspy *carrr* or *caaw*. **Breeding/nesting:** Mates for life. In courtship, male performs acrobatic flights in pursuit of female; on ground or solid perch, male faces female, bowing while singing a short, rattling song with fluffed tail and spread wings.[19] Pairs prefer to nest high above ground in trees or on utility poles (thus, "crow's nest" of watercraft). Young return for up to four years as "helpers" with new broods. Prone to mobbing behavior, especially during nesting, congregating around predators to drive them away. Gather in huge flocks in late summer and fall to feed on insects in the alpine.

Crows figure in the spirit paths of many tribes, including the Paiute, Cheyenne, Arapahoe, Lakota, Navajo and Hopi. Believing crows to be messengers between this world and the spirit world, members of these tribes often wore ceremonial crow feathers, painted crows on garments, and carried crows in their dance circles. Called "black bandits" by farmers for their fondness of corn and young poultry, crows continue to prosper as one of North America's most plentiful birds, despite decades of intense efforts to eliminate them.[20] Crows did not appear in the upper Roaring Fork Valley until about ten years ago. Their numbers are increasing radically, causing problems with mobbing of raptors (especially red-tailed hawks), competition with native ravens and nesting songbirds as the crows eat their eggs and young. A "murder" is the poetic term for a flock of crows, possibly because they are scavengers and have historically been considered figures of ill omen in mystic and occult writings. Crows protect and defend one another, even showing affection and "grieving" when a group member is hurt or dies.[21] These resourceful birds also use tools to dig insects out of crannies and are observed using problem-solving tactics such as dropping mollusks or hard fruits on hard surfaces to break them open.[22]

CHARLES W. MELTON

Steller's Jay
Cyanocitta stelleri
RESIDENT, NON-MIGRATORY • COMMON

Habitat/feeding: Montane to subalpine, up to 11,000 ft. (3353 m). Spruce-fir and aspen forests; may extend range after breeding season into mixed-conifer woodlands, oak-mountain shrublands or developed areas. Nearly half of summer diet is insects, small vertebrates, bird eggs, nestlings and even small adult birds; seeds, fruits and berries make up the balance. Eats mostly cached seeds, nuts and other plant materials during winter; also steals from unwary picnickers. **Field ID traits:** 11.5 in. (29 cm). Striking sapphire with prominent black crest, forehead with white streaks and white brows; wings and tail with black bars.

Coloration and crest height varies geographically. Saucy *shack, shack, shack* often serves as alarm call for local birds and mammals. Adept at mimicry of other birds, particularly red-tailed hawks, but also of telephones and squeaky doors! **Breeding/nesting:** Monogamous;

changing mates only if the other permanently disappears. Male courtship display includes feeding female and hopping around her, changing direction in one hop. Very quiet and secretive while nesting, unless threatened. Bulky nest in crotch of tree or shrub up to 25 ft. (7.5 m) off ground.

A slightly raucous call is usually the first indication that a Steller's jay is present, but once it comes into view there is no mistaking this cobalt-blue bird with its distinctive crest and somewhat impudent manner. When threatened, a high crest signals attack, a low crest retreat. The only other crested jay in North America is the familiar blue jay, *Cyanocitta cristata*, which is only found east of the Rockies. Of interest is the Steller's characteristic way of climbing to the top of a tree, by hopping from branch to branch as if ascending a spiral staircase. Locals have observed flocks of over one hundred birds going to roost after feeding on acorns and berries in the scrub during fall and winter.

ANTING—THERAPEUTIC OR EUPHORIC!

More than 200 bird species, including many corvids, occasionally engage in a peculiar behavior called "anting"—literally wallowing in ants, or in bizarre counterparts such as beer, red wine (white won't do), onions, vinegar, mothballs and even hair tonic. After using its bill to spread these substances throughout its feathers, the anter typically appears mysteriously euphoric—or at least less concerned with its surroundings. Scientists speculate that formic acid sprayed by ants when attacked (and perhaps the same with the other concoctions) kills or repels parasites such as mites, relieves discomfort from new feather growth or possibly soothes irritated skin.[23]

LARK FAMILY   *Alaudidae*

Larks are smallish ground-dwelling birds of open spaces with subdued coloration in browns, blacks and white. The family includes two genera and two species, but the horned lark is the only species native to North America. There are twenty-six subspecies, or geographical variants of horned larks in the New World, extending from Mexico to the Arctic. The color of their plumage is typically keyed to the soil of their respective habitats. As an illustration, desert species have lighter backs, species from muddy areas have darker backs and species from places with red soil have reddish feathers on their backs. Larks share several traits, such as short legs and a rear claw that is quite long and straight—the "larkspur"—and a sturdy, pointed bill for eating small seeds and insects. The horned lark, our native species, is one of only four perching birds that nests above timberline.

Only five hardy birds are adapted to breed in this extreme alpine environment: American pipit, brown-capped rosy finch, horned lark, white-crowned sparrow and white-tailed ptarmigan.

CHARLES W. MELTON

Horned Lark
Eremophila alpestris
BREEDING, MIGRATORY • COMMON

Habitat/feeding: Alpine. Attracted to areas of open, bare ground for nesting, from short-grass prairies and agricultural fields to short-grass alpine tundra in this area. Forages for weed seeds and various insects in summer, including grasshoppers, caterpillars, ants and spiders. **Field ID traits:** 7.25 in. (18 cm). Taupe-colored bird with distinguishing coloration pattern on head; notice black forehead with feather tufts, or "horns," black moustache and black collar beneath pale throat. Females and juveniles similar to male, without black on crown. **Breeding/nesting:** Monogamous during breeding season. Elaborate courtship flight. Female builds shallow cup nest in hollow on ground, usually close to grass tufts in snow-free areas of alpine tundra; one side of nest may be rimmed with small pebbles or clods of dirt; incubates young alone; often nests in February and March, when freezing weather and spring snows lead to high mortality rates.

Larks are a common sight when visiting tundra areas—they run rather than hop, and will hunker down in depressions to avoid bad weather or predators. During courtship flights, the male climbs silently as much as eight hundred feet up into the sky, then circles while singing its high-pitched "tinkling" song—*pit-wit, wee-pit, pit-wee, wee-pit*—ending dramatically with a headlong dive to earth with wings tight to its side, when at the last second, it swoops sharply upwards before plunging back towards the ground. Anyone who has ridden in a stunt plane plummeting to earth would agree that the male of this species is one brave bird—tempting death to attract a mate! What female would not be impressed?

SWALLOW and MARTIN FAMILY *Hirundinidae*

S wallows congregate in open spaces around water, enchanting us with their aerial acrobatics as they swoop, arcing skyward in the search for insects. All swallows have certain physical adaptations, which are made for scooping insects out of the air. These include gaping, where the bird opens its mouth wide in flight; a broad flat bill; and well-developed wings and flight muscles. Swallows arrive early at their breeding grounds, which makes them vulnerable to cold snaps that deplete the insects they rely upon to survive. Much like hummingbirds, swallows can drop into a dormant state, called torpidity, during which their metabolism slows down to conserve energy. Frequently mistaken for dead, they will fly away completely unharmed upon being warmed up. Swallows are more fuel-efficient than most birds, with their aerodynamically-shaped bodies, swept-back narrow wings and short necks. Spending more time in the air than any other songbirds, they not only hunt insects and court during flight, but also drink water while skimming lightly over the surface of ponds.

Tree Swallow
Tachycineta bicolor
BREEDING, MIGRATORY • COMMON

RICHARD W. HOLMES

Habitat/feeding: Montane to subalpine. Prefers aspens and cottonwoods at edges of open areas near water, such as beaver ponds and streams; also open coniferous woodlands. Catches insects while in flight; also forages on berries in fall. **Field ID traits:** 5.75 in. (15 cm). Steely-blue to bluish-green irides-cent upper plumage, slightly greener after the breed-ing season; white underparts and cheeks do not extend above eyes (compare with violet-green swal-low). Streamlined appearance with long, svelte, slightly triangular wings; relatively short feet; slightly forked tail. **Breeding/nesting:** One brood/year (unless first fails). Female builds nest in cavity, with occasional help from male; lays only 1 egg/day within 2 hours of sunrise, not necessarily on consecutive days, until clutch of 4-6 eggs is complete. Incubation often postponed due to weather and food availabil-ity. Will take over bluebird nest boxes.

On cool, cloudy days, the warmer air above ponds is alive with these graceful birds. Tree swallows show a proclivity for feathering their nests, which researchers believe reduces parasite infestations. They also play a game with feathers, where one is dropped and then the bird who catches it is chased until the feather is dropped again. Although tree swallows are socially monogamous, females often engage in copulation with other males on the side. Research indicates that eggs are more likely to hatch in nests where the females have had multiple partners.

Violet-green Swallow
Tachycineta thalassina
BREEDING, MIGRATORY • COMMON

RICHARD W. HOLMES

Habitat/feeding: Montane to subalpine. Prefers edges of aspen-dominated forests, or open wooded areas, including cliffs and natural cavities near water; also open conifer forests. Catches flying insects such as bees, wasps, ants, flies and beetles. **Field ID traits:** 5.25 in. (13 cm). Male is vel-vety-green iridescent above, contrasting vividly with pearly-white underside; 2 white rump patches. Unlike tree swallow, white face reaches above eyes. Female more drab, bronze-green to purple above and grayish on forehead, side of head and upper breast; rump and tail dull green. **Breeding/nest-ing:** Female builds nest and incubates; male may contribute feathers. Both parents readily defend nest from same and other species. Nests primarily in natural cavities of cliffs and banks; also in abandoned tree cavities originally excavated by woodpeckers, particularly red-naped sapsuckers and downy woodpeckers. One brood/year. Female extremely loyal to breeding areas, returning year after year, often to same nesting site. Uses nest boxes, but may be evicted by fiercely competitive house wrens.

Bullets of iridescent green, these swallows reflect the sun as they dip and arc skyward, flashing bright-white rump patches. Although this species is a close relative of the tree swallow, not as much is known about its breeding biology and ecology. Violet-green swallows show a stronger inclination to nest in the crevices of cliffs than do other swallows, and they also use dead standing trees and live cavity-containing trees, which are not as prevalent due to logging. The females can be quite resourceful in finding alternative sites, such as openings in walls, ventilation systems or machinery.

Cliff Swallow

Petrochelidon pyrrhonota

BREEDING, MIGRATORY • COMMON

Habitat/feeding: Montane to alpine. Up to 12,000 ft. (3655 m). Cliffs and manmade structures with overhangs, including bridges, culverts and eaves of buildings. Needs open areas to forage, capturing insects in the air. Swarming insects carried upward on thermals provide good foraging. **Field ID traits:** 5.5 in. (14 cm). Striking plumage, white forehead diagnostic. More stocky and square-tailed than other swallows. Back is glossy, steely irides-cent blue, streaked lightly with white; buffy white beneath, rusty-colored rump, dark chestnut-red throat. **Breeding/nesting:** Courtship flights followed by ground copulation. Although socially monogamous, birds often copulate outside of pair bonds at mud-gathering sites. World's most colonial nesting swallow, colonies may number in the thousands; individuals tend to return to the same size colonies they were raised in. Usually return to same colony every year; may not reuse old nests. Females may lay eggs in adjacent nests or move eggs to other nests; nests lined with white feathers. Pair incubates and feeds young. Competes with house wren for nest sites.

A common sight in neighborhoods during the breeding season, cliff swallows relentlessly carry small daubs of mud to their chosen nest loca-tion on any structure with an overhang. The nest resembles an enclosed gourd-shaped structure with a spout-like entrance on the side. Populations of these handsome swallows are declining in many areas because their mud nests do not adhere well to painted buildings, and annoyed home-owners often remove the mud dwellings, considering them an eyesore. If they must be removed, it is important to wait until after breeding season to hose them down. Unlike many birds that winter in South America, these swallows fly around the Gulf of Mexico, effectively avoiding flight over long stretches of open water.

Barn Swallow
Hirundo rustica
BREEDING, MIGRATORY • COMMON

TODD W. PATRICK

Habitat/feeding: Montane to lower sub-alpine. Up to 10,000 ft. (3048 m). Open habitats near water with cliffs, caves, sheltered ledges along streams, or man-made structures close by. Primarily eats insects caught on the wing using a zigzag flight pattern; occasionally eats berries and seeds.
Field ID traits: 6.75 in. (17 cm). Sexes similar. Easily identified by deeply forked tail— even noticeable in juveniles. Rich chestnut-red throat separated from buffy underparts by blue-black "lapels." Glossy, iridescent steel-blue back, darker wings and iridescent blue-green tail. **Breeding/nesting:** More "romantic" in courtship than other swallows—male chases female in long swooping flights, later preening each other, interlocking bills or rubbing heads and necks together. Cup-shaped mud nest of about 1,000 mud pellets. Nests in small colonies.

There is speculation that the brightly colored plumage and long tail of a male barn swallow may have evolved through female preference, either as attractants or because they reflect the worthiness of the male. It appears to be true that males with larger tails survive longer and carry fewer parasites than their shorter-tailed counterparts. Barn swallow populations are currently increasing across the United States, as these birds seem to prosper around human development, choosing that over natural sites for nesting. They winter from Puerto Rico to the southern tip of South America.

CHICKADEE and TITMOUSE FAMILY
Paridae

Flitting from branch to branch, these bold little songbirds, referred to as parids by scientists, exhibit many signs of avian intelligence. They are also the epitome of animation and curiosity. On bright, cold winter mornings, their cheerful call notes bring life to mountain forests and local backyards. Chickadees and juniper (plain) titmice are both residents of the Roaring Fork Valley; however, only chickadees are common at the higher elevations covered by this book.

Chickadees bathe in water, snow and dew, and like many other species, sip drops from melting icicles to quench their thirst in winter when drinking water is scarce. Some of their major predators include sharp-shinned and Cooper's hawks, diurnal owls, raccoons and housecats. All parids share the following traits:

- males and females, whether immatures or adults, have similar plumage that does not change with molts.

- mate for life, nest in some sort of cavity in trees or nest boxes, and are very territorial (often mobbing intruders).

• have strong legs that support acrobatic feeding behavior as they glean insects and larvae from branch tips, and allow them to hold onto seeds while hammering them open with their bills.

• cache food for later consumption.

• flock with other non-migrating species during winter, often staying warm by huddling in groups inside cavity nests.

The chickadee is . . . the embodiment of cheerfulness . . . a symbol of faithfulness. It lives the year around in the same region. It never deceives its human friends, as so many birds do, by changing its coat and colors. In the summer, to be sure, it is not much seen...but with wintry blasts, time the others go south, the Chickadee begins to be noticed. Then there comes a time when it is almost the only thing to lend a touch of life and a note of gladness to a bleak outdoors.

—WILLIAM ATHENTON DUPUY, *Our Birds, Friend and Foe* (1925)

ROBIN HENRY

Black-capped Chickadee
Poecile atricapillus
RESIDENT, NON-MIGRATORY • COMMON

Habitat/feeding: Montane, up to 9,000 ft. (2745 m). Aspen and mixed-conifer forests; also riparian and oak-mountain shrublands. **Field ID traits:** 5.25 in. (13 cm). Black throat and crown with white cheeks, black bill, brown iris, bluish-gray legs and feet, greenish-gray back, dark-gray wings and tail. May hybridize with mountain chickadee. Song is 2 clear whistles, the first higher in pitch. Characteristic call is *chick-a-dee-dee.* **Breeding/nesting:** Courtship involves simple tactics where male chases female, then feeds her while she flutters like a nestling receiving food. Existing cavity nest is used; may excavate their nest further; tidily carry away wood chips, possibly to deter predators; both defend nest. Female covers eggs with nest fibers before she leaves to rest and feed.

Studies by Susan Smith, a leader in black-capped chickadee research, describe a social dynamic in chickadee winter flocks whereby male "floaters" move from one flock to another, waiting to take the place, and often the mate, of any high-ranking chickadee in the dominance hierachy if a vacancy occurs through predation or death.[24] This species is also known to flock by the thousands to faraway locations. Called "irruptions," these irregular migrations occur in reaction to food shortages. Research on the brain power of black-capped chickadees show that they may cache up to 100,000 food items each year, with the memory to retrieve them when needed. They will actually avoid locations where previously stored food was pilfered by rodents. Chickadees use memorized visuo-spatial cues, such as the arrangement of trees and other features, to find these food caches. It has been discovered that their brains show bursts of growth in the region associated with memory each fall, corresponding with the time when food storage behavior becomes critical.[25]

"CLEANING" UP THE FOREST OR ELIMINATING PRECIOUS NESTING SITES?

Logging of old-growth forests, or simply thinning old and rotten trees from any forest, has a profound impact on all cavity-nesting birds such as chickadees, woodpeckers, nuthatches, bluebirds, swallows and house wrens. The removal of trees with soft wood, which allows for easy excavating of cavity nests, compromises forest ecosystems and their associated food chains. More recently, the forestry practice of snag retention is one way to improve this situation.

Mountain Chickadee
Poecile gambeli
RESIDENT, NON-MIGRATORY · ABUNDANT

ROBIN HENRY

Habitat/feeding: Montane to subalpine. Up to 12,000 ft. (3600 m). Most abundant conifer specialist in Colorado after ruby-crowned kinglet; prefers spruce and subalpine fir to Douglas-fir and lodgepole pine; overlaps black-capped chickadee in aspen forest territory.[26] Diet of insects, larvae and insect eggs gleaned from tips of branches; also conifer seeds. **Field ID traits:** 5.25 in. (13 cm). Similar to black-capped chickadee, but has white "eyebrow" and slightly longer bill. Light-gray sides washed in peach in Rocky Mountain populations; gray under tail. May hybridize with black-capped chickadee. Song is 3–4 whistled syllables, *fee-bee-bee or fee-bee-bee-fee*; extra ascending syllable at end separates it from black-capped chickadee. Call is a husky *tsick-a-zhee-zhee*. **Breeding/nesting:** Only courtship display is sequence of high-pitched calls by both sexes. Uses natural cavities or abandoned cavities of other birds. When threatened, the female sits tight on the nest, hissing loudly while fluttering her wings.

Mountain chickadees do not exhibit excavating behavior, simply using an existing cavity instead. They have even been known to take up residence in old mammal burrows. When spruce and lodgepole cones open in September, mountain chickadees in the southern Rockies gather the seeds from dawn to dusk, storing as many as two or three energy-packed seeds per minute—wedging them in tight needle clusters or poking them into the ground. According to *The Sibley Guide to Bird Life and Behavior*, this species is undergoing a long-term decline in population numbers.

LONG-TAILED TIT (BUSHTIT) FAMILY
Aegithalidae

Although similar to chickadees and once included with parids, bushtits have been moved to the Old World family of long-tailed tits based on genetic and nest similarities. Their longer tails make it easy to tell them apart from chickadees and titmice. Bushtits are the only North American representative of this family, most of whose members are native to China and the Himalayas.

ROBIN HENRY

Bushtit
Psaltriparus minimus
RESIDENT, NON-MIGRATORY • UNCOMMON

Habitat/feeding: Montane. Usually below 8,000 ft. (2438 m) in the Roaring Fork Valley; oak-mountain shrublands and pinyon-juniper communities. Hops rapidly from branch to branch, gleaning aphids, beetles, wasps and caterpillars from foliage; also eats some fruit. **Field ID traits:** 4 in. (11 cm). Tiny gray bird, darker above than below, with long tail. Local subspecies has brown ear patch and gray cap. Juveniles and adult males have dark eyes, females have light eyes. No song, just squeaky high-pitched twittering—*tsit-tsit-tsit*, over and over again. **Breeding/nesting:** Monogamous 1 or more seasons. Courtship includes many trills, calls and posturing. Pair builds elaborate, hanging-gourd-shaped nest woven together with spider silk; decorated with lichens, flowers and feathers; takes 2–9 weeks to finish.

Bushtits maintain a multifaceted social system, both in and out of breeding season, with families forming sociable flocks that huddle together to generate warmth during cold weather and remain together in subsequent years. Chickadees, wrens and other species often join bushtit flocks, but may have trouble keeping up with their rapid foraging techniques. Flocks break up during the breeding season, though individual territory boundaries are not strictly enforced. Young or unpaired birds may help in building nests and raising the young of others. Some ornithologists speculate that females nesting communally and raising their young together are more successful.

NUTHATCH FAMILY *Sittidae*

Captivating small songbirds of the forest, nuthatches often forage in the same trees as chickadees, woodpeckers and creepers, but their different feeding techniques minimize competition. Nuthatches will climb up or down the trunk of a tree as they glean for insects in bark crevices. While foraging, they brace themselves against the trunk with the lower foot and grasp the bark with the other, unlike woodpeckers and creepers who use their tails to brace.

"Nuthatch" refers to their habit of wedging seeds or nuts into bark crevices before using their long bills to break or hatch them open. Insects, nuts and seeds are carefully cached in bark crevices during winter for later retrieval. Nuthatch migration patterns vary depending on food supplies. In years of good cone crops they will remain in their breeding territories, but may head south in search of food if cones are scarce. Those that stay as winter residents, will huddle in small groups for warmth during cold or stormy weather.[27] Conservationists report that forest fragmentation and logging practices that remove dead trees lead to declines in numbers of nuthatches.

ADAPTATIONS FOR LIFE ON TREE TRUNKS

- short stalky body.
- short sturdy legs with long toes and claws for gripping while climbing.
- strong, straight bill with upturned underside, for prying bark and seeds open.
- communal roosting for warmth in cold weather outside the breeding season.

Red-breasted Nuthatch
Sitta canadensis
RESIDENT, NON-MIGRATORY • COMMON

Habitat/feeding: Montane to subalpine. Mature spruce-fir forests, adjacent to or mixed with mature aspen stands up to timberline; prefers a supply of decaying trees for easier nest excavation. Found at higher elevation more often than white-breasted nuthatch. Probes bark for insects and spiders in summer; eats conifer seeds in winter; also hawks for insects. **Field ID traits:** 4.5 in. (11.4 cm). Black cap, with white "eyebrow" line above black eye line; blue-gray back; underparts washed rusty. Female and juveniles similar, but duller; female's head is blue-gray. Although uncommon, **Pygmy nuthatches** (*Sitta pygmaea*) occur in local conifer forests. Only 4.25 in. (10.8 cm) long; compared to red-breasted, pygmy's head looks larger in proportion to body, has plain gray back; lacks white eyebrow. **Breeding/nesting:** Interesting courtship behavior. Male turns away from female, sways side to side with back feathers fluffed and wings dropped while raising head and

ROBIN HENRY

tail; sometimes includes singing; also feeds female. Pair excavates nest cavities in soft or rotten aspen or conifer wood; may use abandoned woodpecker cavity in conifer.

Hikers are assured of this nuthatch's presence when they hear the rhythmic and nasal *hank-hank-hank*—sounding like a duck with a cold—or a toy trumpet-sounding *enk-enk-enk* reverberating through the forest. Red-breasted nuthatches are known for smearing sap around the entrance to their cavity nest, possibly to keep out invertebrates which can carry diseases. Areas of transition between conifer forests and aspen woodlands are often shared by this species and the white-breasted nuthatch.

CHARLES W. MELTON

White-breasted Nuthatch

Sitta carolinensis

RESIDENT, NON-MIGRATORY

• COMMON

Habitat/feeding: Montane to lower subalpine. Prefers lower-elevation conifers, using aspen woodlands and riparian areas as a second resource, up to 10,000 ft. (3048 m). Forages up, down and around trunks, probing for insects and insect larvae, including grasshoppers, moths, tent caterpillars, woodborers and aphids; eats mostly seeds in winter. **Field ID traits:** 5.75 in. (15 cm). Sexes similar. Clear white face and breast contrast vividly with black cap and nape; blue-gray above with fluctuating amounts of rusty wash beneath. Voice is rapid, low nasal whistled notes on one pitch—*whi-whi-whi-whi* or *yidi-yidi-yidi*. **Breeding/nesting:** Monogamous. Head feathers raised and tail fanned, male bows and struts while singing during courtship rituals; also feeds mate. Female builds nest in natural cavity or abandoned woodpecker hole; does not excavate her own cavity. Known to pluck hair from live squirrels to line nest.[28]

White-breasted nuthatches have an unusual habit of smearing crushed foul-smelling insects on the trunk around the outside of their nest cavity. This is a thought to be a vital survival technique, used to repel predators that might normally enter the nest uninvited. Normally year-round residents in this area, nuthatches roost singly, yet within calling distance of family members, when not breeding. During very cold periods they may roost communally for warmth.

CREEPER FAMILY　　　*Certhiidae*

S mall climbing birds, creepers have long, stiff tails with feathers pointed at the tips. Since they use their tails as a brace while searching
crevices for insects, they can only climb up trees. This distinguishes them
from nuthatches, who can climb in both directions. Leading quiet, inconspicuous lives, they sing only rarely, and their soft, high-pitched song is
difficult to hear when they do. Brown creepers are the only species found
in North America—the greatest variety being native to the Himalayas.

Brown Creeper
Certhia americana
RESIDENT, NON-MIGRATORY • UNCOMMON

ROBIN HENRY

Habitat/feeding: Montane to subalpine. Mature
spruce-fir or lodgepole forests; also aspens and mixed
conifers. Prefers shady, moist habitats, 9,000–11,500
ft. (2700–3500 m); lower outside of breeding season.
Diet of spiders, caterpillars, aphids and moths, including larvae. Unique adaptations include thinly pointed,
curved bill for extracting insects from bark crevices,
stiff tail for bracing and long toes with curved claws
for strong grip. **Field ID traits:** 5.25 in. (13 cm).
Sexes alike. Brown above, speckled with gray, buff and
black; obvious white "eyebrow"; white underparts;
rusty-colored rump. Song is high, thin *trees-trees-trees-
see-the-trees*—ending on a higher note. Call-note an
abbreviated soft *see*. **Breeding/nesting:**
Monogamous. Courtship displays include male chasing female in characteristic spirals around tree trunks,
courtship feeding, wing fluttering and display flights. Nest is crescent-shaped cup constructed beneath loose bark, typically not reused. Male brings food to female while incubating young. Fledglings roost in a circle, heads facing the center.

Cryptic coloration is the perfect camouflage for the brown creeper,
which neatly blends in with surrounding tree trunks, flattening itself and
remaining motionless if threatened. If not close enough to identify this
bird by the plumage, there is no mistaking its distinct climbing pattern—
flying to the base of a tree, it climbs in an upward spiral while probing for
insects, then flutters to the base of the next tree to repeat the process. By
foraging in dense stands of mature trees, brown creepers conserve energy
during the breeding season and stay in close proximity to nest sites.
Logging mature forests on which they depend has created a distinct conservation challenge for this species. Creepers will migrate to lower elevations during the colder winter months.

BROOD PATCHES

Bird feathers are such good insulation that when incubating, the bird must lose a few to ensure that enough heat from the body reaches the eggs. Typically, feathers on the belly are shed involuntarily near the end of the egg-laying period, and the skin becomes infused with extra blood vessels to bring more heat to the surface. Males can develop partial brood patches, though they rarely incubate as much as females. Geese and ducks pluck the feathers out, using them to soften the nest. An incubating bird will snuggle down over the eggs until contact is made with the brood patch—usually one large patch, but may be a series of smaller patches equaling the number of eggs laid. In species that hatch mobile young covered in down (precocial), the feathers may regrow soon after hatching. However, in those with young born naked or nearly so (altricial), the brood patches do not regrow feathers until just before the nestlings have fledged.

WREN FAMILY *Troglodytidae*

I f you have wrens nesting nearby, you undoubtedly are awakened by their energetic serenades, often way before sunrise. Probably the most vociferous of all songbirds, wrens sing so often throughout the day during breeding season, the song may become stuck in your brain! These lively little birds are insectivorous, gleaning their prey from every nook and cranny in rocks, plants and soil. Most wrens look similar, with relatively long tails (often cocked upward), slender curved bills for prying out insects and plumage that is darkish above and pale beneath with a combination of barring and/or spots. The sexes appear similar, and do not change color during molting.

CHARLES W. MELTON

House Wren
Troglodytes aedon
BREEDING, MIGRATORY • ABUNDANT

Habitat/feeding: Montane to subalpine. Favors wide variety of open habitats, usually with deciduous trees such as aspen and cottonwood, sometimes mixed with conifers; almost never present in treeless habitats such as tundra, fields or pastures. Forages in low, dense vegetation, gleaning insects and other invertebrates from foliage, twigs, branches, bark and soil; narrow heads and slender, pointed bills adapted for probing into deep crevices and crannies. May prey on eggs or young of other birds. **Field ID traits:** 4.75 in. (12 cm). Gray-brown above and pale beneath, with short rounded wings, and fairly long tail usually held upright; light eye-ring with faint "eyebrow" stripe, thin pointed bill. Wings, shoulders and tail faintly barred. **Breeding/nesting:** Male occasionally polygamous; arrives in territory first, cleaning out existing nests, possibly even those of other species; builds foundations for several nests from short, straight twigs. Female arrives and signals chosen mate by bringing material to finish only 1 nest; females may mate again later with male from another territory, leaving original mate to care for first brood.

House wrens are secretive yet saucy little birds, made quite conspicuous by their bubbly, enthusiastic song composed of a rich, descending warble of rattles and trills repeated many times. Some of the notes resemble chattering or scolding. When alarmed by a predator, the house wren will make short, buzz-like *zeeer–zeeer* calls. Song is their primary territorial defense strategy, however, males will also destroy the eggs of other birds nesting nearby. Competition for limited nest sites and food are probably the stimuli for this behavior. House wrens most often migrate at night, flying long distances to reach their wintering grounds in the southern United States and Mexico.

DIPPER FAMILY *Cinclidae*

Only four species of this extraordinary family exist worldwide—all found living along bodies of water. The most aquatic of all songbirds, dippers are particularly famous for their ability to walk underwater to secure prey.

American Dipper, Water Ouzel
Cinclus mexicanus
RESIDENT, NON-MIGRATORY
• FAIRLY COMMON

Habitat/feeding: Montane to subalpine. Mountain streams and ponds to timberline. Swims by paddling feet and flapping wings; walks underwater to forage for insect larvae, crustaceans, small fish and aquatic plants. **Field ID traits:** 7.5 in. (19 cm). Adult slate-colored, dark eye and bill, with short wings and short, upright tail. Juvenile whitish and mottled beneath, pale bill. **Breeding/nesting:** Usually monogamous, sometimes polygamous; 2 broods/year. Interesting courtship where male holds wings down and partly spread while stretching neck up, then struts around singing before female; sometimes performed together; concluded by touching breasts.[29] Mossy, dome-like nest built by pair on cliff face, under washed-out streamside roots or on mid-stream rock; especially moist places exposed to spray or under bridges. Semi-precocial young; can dive and swim underwater upon leaving nest.

Year-round residents, an American dipper can brighten a winter day with its wren-like musical chattering, vocalized at a frequency just enough

341

> *He [the American dipper] is the mountain stream's own darling, the hummingbird of blooming waters, loving rocky ripple-slopes and sheets of foam as a bee loves flowers, as a lark loves sunshine and meadows. Among all the mountain birds, none has cheered me so much in my lonely wanderings, none so unfailingly.*
>
> —JOHN MUIR,
> *The Mountains of California*
> (1894)

above that of rushing water to be heard. This fascinating bird will dive off a rock in midstream, swimming underwater to capture food in the frigid water of a rushing mountain stream. Most noticeable are the gymnastics they perform—an amusing up-and-down dipping—as they move along the stream. Why dippers dip has yet to be explained. It may be that this behavior, and the blinking of their white-feathered eyelids, are used for communicating with each other in a noisy world of rushing water. Another theory proposes that dipping deters predators by giving the dipper a physically fit appearance. Dippers are key indicators of stream quality because their favored meal of mayfly and caddisfly larvae are typically present only in clean, well-aerated water with a normal pH. These larvae won't survive in streams made acidic by past mining operations. Take time to observe these top-level specialists of mountain stream ecosystems and appreciate how they integrate a combination of physical adaptations allowing them to comfortably swim and forage underwater. These adaptations include:

• dense plumage for feeding underwater without excess heat loss.
• stout, strong bill for foraging between rocks.
• waterproof feathers.
• short wings for easier maneuvering; used like flippers.
• large strong clawed feet for walking in strong currents.
• nostril flaps to keep water out.
• elevated hemoglobin for more efficient oxygen consumption in water.
• vision that compensates for the refractive index of water.
• dark plumage for camouflage.

KINGLET FAMILY   *Regulidae*

Kinglets are miniature birds primarily inhabiting spruce-fir forests or other high-elevation coniferous forests around the globe—only hummingbirds are smaller. Kinglets dart around so quickly from branch to branch, they definitely challenge your binocular skills. Identification is easiest by learning the songs. Golden-crowned kinglets flit around in the tops of conifers, sounding much like musically inclined mosquitoes, while ruby-crowned kinglets belt out a cascading warble that is quite robust for such wee birds.

Golden-crowned Kinglet
Regulus satrapa
RESIDENT, NON-MIGRATORY • COMMON

RICHARD W. HOLMES

Habitat/feeding: Montane to subalpine. Open coniferous forests, especially old-growth spruce-fir stands to 11,600 ft. (3536 m). Diet of gnats, aphids, beetles, spiders and eggs of insects and spiders; some tree sap and fruit. Also hover at branch tips to obtain insects, or snatch them in midair. Forage for hibernating insects in winter. **Field ID traits:** 4 in. (10 cm). Bright crown patch—female's yellow, male's orange and edged in yellow. Boldly striped face; first white, then black stripe above eye; olive-gray above, pale gray beneath, darker wings and tail; wings have bold, dark wing-bar across the secondary flight feathers. High, thin call notes—a high ascending *tsee-tsee-tsee*, then dropping into a short chatter. **Breeding/nesting:** Though quite territorial, its non-aggressive solution to encounters is to raise its crown patch and sing (maybe a good lesson for us all). Female chooses nest site, building a petite, deep, spherical cup nest with a top entrance; hangs from a conifer branch; usually spruce. Deposits 2 layers of up to 11 tiny eggs, about 0.5 in. (13 mm) wide.

The golden-crowned kinglet is a vivacious social bird, constantly flitting from branch to branch with nervous flicks of its wings. Using its tiny, slender bill perfectly adapted for gleaning, and feet for clinging, this acrobatic master takes insects from twig tips, leaves or needles—often hanging upside down from the end of a branch. It is one of the smallest songbirds in North America, weighing in at less than a quarter ounce (7 g). Despite its size, a golden-crowned kinglet is undaunted by harsh winter temperatures, huddling all night with fellow kinglets and other winter residents such as chickadees and brown creepers. Golden-crowned kinglets remain in this area year-round, but those that summer farther north may migrate to warmer climes. Breeding Bird Survey (see p. 310) data suggests that the western United States is experiencing some decline in populations of this species, which, like its close cousin the ruby-crowned kinglet, is sensitive to the fragmentation of conifer forests.

Ruby-crowned Kinglet
Regulus calendula
BREEDING, MIGRATORY • ABUNDANT

Habitat/feeding: Montane to subalpine. Primarily coniferous forests or mixed aspens and conifers, at least to 11,000 ft. (3380 m). Unlike golden-crowned kinglet, uses open parts of forest more and rarely hangs upside down. Hovers, gleans and hawks insects from leaves and needles of trees; may feed from sap wells made by sapsuckers. **Field ID traits:** 4.25 in. (11 cm). Red crown patch of male visible only when excited, under threat or during rounds of full song; obvious broken white eye-ring. Olive-green upper parts, darker wings and tail; 2 bold white bars on wings; plumage shows yellowish wash, especially in fall. Dark legs with yellowish feet and a dark spot beneath lower wing-bar help distinguish this bird from similar Hutton's vireo on West Coast. Flicks wings continuously. **Breeding/nesting:** Male's brilliant red crown patch frequently raised during courtship displays while singing a wheezy subdued song. Inconspicuous

mossy, globular nest against trunk on horizontal branch; very tight entrance; deeper than wide.

Sounding like he has just conquered Everest, a male ruby-crowned kinglet's song is jubilant and oft repeated. It begins with 2–3 high clear notes, *tsee-tsee-tsee,* and 2–3 lower *churr* notes, before rolling into a musical cascade with a rhythm resembling *cheeseburger, cheese-burger, cheeseburger* or perhaps *look at me, look at me, look at me.* Females also sing, but it is a softer version of this song without the frolicsome ending. Like other forest species, logging and other disturbances that fragment woodland habitat put this bird at risk, also allowing access to predators and the parasitic cowbird. Ruby-crowned kinglets are not as hardy as golden-crowneds, migrating south in the fall.

OLD WORLD WARBLER and GNATCATCHER FAMILY *Sylviidae*

As its name suggests, this very large family of about 300 species is distributed mostly in the Old World. Its members are all small to medium-sized insectivorous songbirds, similar to wood-warblers and vireos but more delicate and active. North American species fall into two subfamilies; gnatcatchers and Old World warblers—the only local representative being the blue-gray gnatcatcher.

Blue-gray Gnatcatcher
Polioptila caerulea
BREEDING, MIGRATORY • UNCOMMON

Habitat/feeding: Montane. Typically breeds in drier, scrubby habitats of oak, sage and pinyon-juniper. Slender, pointed bill enables it to feed on a wide variety of small insects and spiders. Forages by hovering and gleaning on outer leaves and branches of deciduous trees; also on trunks and branches of conifers. **Field ID traits:** 4.5 in. (11 cm). Male blue-gray with distinctly dark-blue crown and well defined black forehead not visible outside of breeding season; pale gray beneath. Female pale gray with blue overtones. Long tail black above, trimmed in white outer tail feathers. Both sexes have bold white eye-rings and long narrow bill with prominent rictal bristles. Vocalization is a series of thin, wheezy notes—one local biologist affectionately calls them "little wheezers." **Breeding/nesting:** Monogamous. Male arrives first to establish territory; advertises for mate by singing. Once pair bond established, close contact maintained visually and vocally while foraging; male is primary defender of territory, but female chases intruding females. Small, compact cup nest camouflaged with lichens, built by pair in fork of small branches; anchored with spider webs or caterpillar silk.

This energetic little bird resembles a diminutive version of the northern mockingbird—some of its calls even mock other birds. Blue-gray gnatcatchers habitually flick and switch their tails back and forth, white outer tail feathers spread, possibly to flush insects out of hiding. Cowbirds frequently parasitize their nests, this being quite a surprise considering the size difference. Magpies, small mammals and scrub jays commonly rob nests, feeding on both the eggs and young of this species. Blue-gray gnatcatchers migrate to the southern United States and Central America for the winter. Researchers have found evidence that they are increasing and expanding their range further north.

THRUSH FAMILY *Turdidae*

Mostly small to medium-sized songbirds, thrushes have comparatively slender, blunted bills that are the perfect shape for dining on worms, insects and berries (but not for cracking seeds). Most species have prominently long wings and legs, feeding mostly on soft food, as they hop from place to place foraging on the ground or from low plants. The appearance of the sexes is usually dissimilar, with females being more muted.

Townsend's Solitaire
Myadestes townsendi
RESIDENT, NON-MIGRATORY • COMMON

Habitat/feeding: Montane to timberline and possibly above. Prefers coniferous forests; also nests in deciduous areas and along wooded streams. Frequent ground feeder, typically pouncing on terrestrial insects. During fall and winter, switches to diet of juniper, mountain ash, serviceberry and pine seeds; hovers to pluck berries from shrubs or hawks for insects. **Field ID traits:** 8.5 in. (22 cm). Sexes similar. Slender, long-tailed, misty-gray bird with peach to buffy wing-bars best observed in flight; white outer tail feathers; obvious white eye-ring. Song a melodious series of rising and falling fluty whistles; a rapid and prolonged sweet warble, similar but different in tonal quality and faster than black-headed grosbeak. Call a solitary clear, soft whistle—some say "piping note"—heard more often than song. **Breeding/nesting:** Exquisite flight songs during courtship. Socially monogamous; female will seek outside copulations; lays eggs in nests of other Townsend's solitaires. Physically struggles with any bird contesting territorial boundaries, chasing and displacing them from their perch by direct force. Female constructs shallow cup nest on ground among tree roots, on slopes or embankments, wherever an overhang offers protection and seclusion; nests also recorded below ground in abandoned mine shafts.[30]

345

Snow covers the landscape, yet the silvery song of this shy, ever-present solitaire floats from a juniper shrub—a reminder of glorious spring days filled with birdsong. The songs of male Townsend's solitaires vary from one individual to another and contain both innate and learned components. Although they sing throughout the year, there are peaks in spring and late fall, corresponding to the establishment of breeding and wintering territories. Townsend's solitaires serve an important ecological role in seed dispersal for the shrubs that support them during the winter. Solitaires are year-round residents in the Roaring Fork Valley, merely moving to a lower elevation in the colder months to feed on juniper berries. Elsewhere, however, they may migrate long distances to winter in the western United States and central Mexico—their destinations more associated with berry or fruit crops that persist all winter rather than any specific location.

A PIGMENT OF THE IMAGINATION?

Mountain bluebirds appear as blue as a brilliant summer sky, yet no blue pigment exists in their plumage. The intensely blue hue is created when light is refracted by the feathers' special inner structure—which disappears if the feather is crushed.

ROBIN HENRY

Mountain Bluebird
Sialia currucoides
BREEDING, MIGRATORY • COMMON

Habitat/feeding: Montane and subalpine. Undisturbed open country with scattered trees, open woodlands and forest edges adjacent to open space—especially aspen forests; also mountain meadows and grasslands found at the edges of ski runs or recently burned areas. Diet consists mostly of insects and other invertebrates, including beetles, ants, bees, wasps, caterpillars and grasshoppers. Hawks to catch insects, or hover feeds, dropping down on insects from above. **Field ID traits:** 7 in. (18 cm). Slim bird with long tail and wings. Male deep sky-blue above, soft blue from chin to belly, grayish-white from there to undertail coverts; black eyes, feet and bill. Female pale gray with blue wings, rump and tail; sometimes rufous wash on breast. Vocalization a series of clear, short, soft, burry warbles—*chur-chur-chur* or *jerrf-jerrf-jerrf*—murmured during flight. Calls are individual song syllables. **Western Bluebirds** (*Sialia mexicana*) are occasionally seen here during migration; have chestnut red on backs and breasts. **Breeding/nesting:** Mostly monogamous. Male guards mate during breeding season. Female selects site for loose cup nest in abandoned woodpecker hole, cliff crevice, hole in buildings or nest box. Male carries nest material, but never weaves it into nest.

Reflecting the brilliance of an azure summer sky, mountain bluebirds inspire the kind of wonder experienced seeing a rainbow emerge as storm clouds clear. The gorgeous males arrive early in the spring—making them vulnerable to late spring snows. Bluebirds compete with flickers, starlings, house wrens, house sparrows and tree swallows for cavity nest sites, though their populations are actually increasing, probably due to the national crusade to build more nest boxes. Putting up bluebird nest boxes can provide alternative nest sites when natural cavities are unavailable. Building instructions can be found on the Internet or at local nature centers. Mountain bluebirds are more migratory than other bluebird species, overwintering in the southern United States and Central Mexico.

Swainson's Thrush

Catharus ustulatus

BREEDING, MIGRATORY • UNCOMMON

CHARLES W. MELTON

Habitat/feeding: Montane. Streamside alder or willow thickets, especially with blue spruce, often in moist, steep ravines; also willow carrs, and aspen forests. Ground feeder, but also flycatches and hovers, or gleans insects and other invertebrates from foliage or branches; also eats wild berries. **Field ID traits:** 7 in. (18 cm). Rich brown-olive above, pale beneath, breast slightly buffy and spotted; buffy eye-ring, cheeks and breast. Flute-like song a rich ascending warble of varied whistles, often repeated; lacks long, lone introductory whistle of a hermit thrush, though may have one introductory note; sounds like *po rer reer reeer re-e-e-e-e*; tends to sing from damp, willow-lined stream bottoms. Common call a loud, sharp *whit*; flight call a single, clear note. **Breeding/ nesting:** Monogamous. Male courtship display includes wing flicking, crest raising and maintaining a sleek body while pointing bill upward.[31] Female builds bulky, cup-shaped nest in shrubs.

The song of Swainson's thrush is one of the most charming examples of a harmony in suspension which it is possible to find in all the realm of music. The bird deliberately chooses a series of even intervals and climbs up the scale with a thought entirely single to harmonious results.

—F. Schuyler Mathews,
Field Book of Wild Birds and Their Music (1904)

A Swainson's ethereal flute-like song, a rolling, ascending spiral of liquid whistles, echoes through the forest as solace for weary souls. These thrushes are long distance nocturnal migrants, wintering from central Mexico to northern Argentina and Paraguay. Numbers are declining, as they are particularly sensitive to habitat loss caused by logging, recreation and development in their summer range. Deforestation in the tropics, and the loss of fruit-rich "refueling sites" puts them at risk during migration and wintering. Moreover, like many other nocturnal migrants, they suffer increasing mortality rates from flying into unseen manmade obstacles such as tall buildings and TV towers.

O WONDERFUL! How liquid clear
The molten gold of that ethereal tone,
Floating and falling through the wood alone . . .
—HENRY VAN DYKE, *The Hermit Thrush* (1911)

Leaf litter is an important habitat component for hermit thrush foraging. In areas where litter has been removed, such as logged or developed areas (like campgrounds), hermit thrushes would likely be absent.

RICHARD W. HOLMES

Hermit Thrush
Catharus guttatus
BREEDING, MIGRATORY • UNCOMMON

Habitat/feeding: Montane to subalpine, 8000 ft. (2438 m) to timberline. Coniferous forest and mixed deciduous forests; likes forest edges and clearings or lakes surrounded by forest. Searches under fallen leaves, gleans foliage, or hovers for insects or fruit. Diet includes beetles, ants, spiders, earthworms, and small salamanders; also berries, especially in winter. **Field ID traits:** 6.75 in. (17 cm). Reddish tail, redder plumage overall and less pink legs key to distinguishing this species from Swainson's thrush. Olive-brown back, olive flanks, spotted buffy breast, distinct spectacle-like eye-ring. Flute-like song begins with long, clear introductory whistle (a "hermit" note), followed by two or three liquid twirling notes, fading at end; series of varied phrases. Interior west birds sound like *seeeeeee freediila fridla-fridla.* Call is a soft *chuck.*
Breeding/nesting: Monogamous. Arrives earlier, leaving later in fall than other thrushes. Displays include wing flicking and crest raising when being aggressive and tail raising and lowering when alarmed or landing on branch. Females east of the Rocky Mountains build cup-shaped nest 3–5 feet from the ground (0.9–1.52 m); western females nest 3–10 feet (0.9–3.0 m) feet above the ground in conifers, other trees or bushes.

Peace that only nature can instill follows the melodious flute-like song of the hermit thrush. Much research is being done to ensure that these birds will be around to delight future generations. Hermit thrushes depend primarily on unfragmented blocks of coniferous forests to breed: Project Tanager, a study by the Cornell Laboratory of Ornithology, found that hermit thrushes and western tanagers show a similar decline in attempted nesting when

When he sings there is no great need of a chorus; the forest has found a tongue . . .
—BRADFORD TORREY,
Footing it in Franconia (1901)

forest fragmentation increases.[32] A study in Colorado found that hermit thrushes declined by 14% in a selectively clear-cut forest while increasing by 12% in the unlogged control area. Hermit thrushes are big practitioners of "anting" (see p. 329), possibly to acquire the ants' defensive secretions for medicinal purposes or as a supplement to their own preen oil. Nocturnal migrants, they winter in the southern United States, Bahamas, Guatemala and El Salvador.

American Robin
Turdus migratorius
BREEDING, MIGRATORY · ABUNDANT

ROBIN HENRY

Habitat/feeding: Montane to subalpine. Alpine in late summer. Closed-canopy forests, open areas, woodland edges, riparian woodlands, gardens, parks and residential. Gleans a wide range of food items from ground, visually hunting for prey such as earthworms. **Field ID traits:** 10 in. (25 cm). Large, sturdy thrush with gray back and dark gray head, orange breast, white eye-ring, white under-tail coverts; limited white tail corners in western birds; female paler than male. Song several short warbled phrases, rising and falling in pitch—*cherlee-cherlup-cherlee-cherlup-cherlee*, a pause, then same series again. Sings from pre-dawn to mid-morning and again in late afternoon. Call is rapid *pit-tut-tut.* **Breeding/nesting:** Monogamous. Male arrives first to breeding territory, defending it by singing. Pair builds rather long, open-cup nest, cemented with mud, in virtually any structure with enough support, including trees (mid-canopy), shrubs, buildings; occasionally on the ground; sky-blue eggs. Parasitized by cowbirds; often recognize and destroy the cowbird eggs. See nest and young, p. 279.

Human alteration of the natural environment has given these generalists *par excellence* the advantage. Robins are one of the continent's most adaptable, and therefore most abundant, species. Their flexibility in foraging strategies, diet, breeding habitats and nest site preferences has allowed them to expand their breeding range onto the Great Plains and into drier areas of the West, thriving despite the conversion of natural ecosystems into farmland, orchards, irrigated pastures and tree-lined suburbs. This has not always been the case. Robin populations suffered when DDT was sprayed in the 1950's to kill beetles carrying Dutch elm disease, and it became concentrated in their food. Robins are diurnal, or daytime, migrants, wintering from southern Mexico to Guatemala.

European starlings (*Sturnus vulgaris*), not described in this guide, were introduced from Europe and compete with native local cavity nesters for nest sites.

BIRDS AND DDT

The insecticide DDT causes birds' eggshells to thin, with the result that incubating birds often crush their own eggs. DDT breaks down very slowly, accumulating and concentrating in organisms that ingest it as it moves through the food chain. Although it has been banned in the United States since 1972, it persists in the environment. Additionally, DDT is still widely used in tropical countries to control malaria-carrying mosquitoes, so birds that winter in the tropics are exposed to it there.

PIPIT and WAGTAIL FAMILY   *Motacillidae*

L ong legs and long tails that wag or bob are common traits of the small to medium-sized ground-dwelling birds in this family. Wagtails are mostly limited to northwestern Canada and isolated areas of Alaska, whereas pipits are common in the lower forty-eight states, preferring rocky alpine tundra or shortgrass prairie during breeding season. Wagtails also have comparatively bright-colored males, while pipits are cloaked in rather drab plumage and have shorter tails.

CHARLES W. MELTON

American Pipit

Anthus rubescens (former race of Water Pipit, *A. spinoletta*)

BREEDING, MIGRATORY • COMMON

Habitat/feeding: Alpine meadows. Ground foraging for insects and some seeds; may hawk for insects; searches shallow alpine puddles and ponds for mollusks and crustaceans. Adaptability to a wetter environments avoids competition with horned lark, also nesting in alpine meadows. **Field ID traits:** 6.5 in. (17 cm). Sexes similar. Sparrow-like bird distinguished by long, slender bill. Upper body grayish-brown, whitish to peachy-tan beneath; lightly to heavily streaked "necklace" across breast, extending onto flanks; wing feathers blackish with peachy-tan edges; dark eye, white outer tail feathers. "Eyebrow" matches paler body color. Flight call is familiar *pip-it, pip-it.* **Breeding/nesting:** Monogamous. Male performs courtship flights up to 200 ft. in air, floats down parachute-like, singing with tail held up and legs extended down.[33] Female builds small cup in shallow depression of alpine tundra, almost anywhere except talus and boulder fields, usually under overhanging rocks or vegetation; takes 4–5 days.

Always bobbing or wagging its tail, this behavior of the American pipit makes it easy to identify among alpine tundra birds. Mates will often form pair-bonds before arriving on the breeding grounds, which allows them enough time to raise their brood during the short alpine season. They sometimes move to lower elevations in severe weather. After breeding season, pipits wander, finding fields and beaches at lower elevations where they forage, forming into large flocks which migrate south to Guatemala and El Salvador.

ROBIN HENRY

CEDAR WAXWINGS (*Bombycilla cedrorum*), rich in their exotic attire, have traditionally bred below 7,000 ft. (2135 m) in the Roaring Fork Valley. They are now present in the upper valley year-round, being especially prominent when crabapples are ripe. As members of the waxwing family (Bombycillidae), they are closely related to thrushes, dippers and starlings.

WOOD-WARBLER FAMILY *Parulidae*

Migration is a remarkable phenomenon considering how small and delicate these birds are. Traveling from their winter habitat in the remote rainforests of southern Mexico and Central America to their summer breeding grounds in the Rocky Mountains is an amazing physical feat.[34] Many wood-warblers are appreciated for their dramatic and distinctive color patterns of chestnut, blue, yellow, black, gray, green and white. However, even the less colorful species gain attention with their songs, which range from sweet melodic warbles and musical trills to thin, high-pitched ringing or buzzy calls. Wood-warblers, forever active, with short, thin bills and short wings are highly adapted to a diet of insects. Many are important environmental indicator species, being habitat specific and sensitive to habitat degradation.[35] Their presence or absence indicates the environmental health of an ecosystem in the same way their cousin, the canary, once warned of bad air in coal mines. Several species—notably Wilson's, Virginia's and MacGillivray's wood-warblers—are declining in North America.

Orange-crowned Warbler
Vermivora celata
BREEDING, MIGRATORY · FAIRLY COMMON

CHARLES W. MELTON

Habitat/feeding: Montane to subalpine, up to 9,500 ft. (2900 m). Oak-mountain shrub, mixed-conifer forest and willow thickets. Insectivorous, gleans hanging dead leaves, and probes flower heads with sharply pointed bill; some berries in winter. Visits sapsucker wells (see red-naped sapsucker, p. 312), and hummingbird feeders in summer. **Field ID traits:** 5 in. (12.7 cm). Dull yellowish-olive, darker above;

Female and immature warblers look very similar during the fall and are difficult to differentiate.

orange crown patch very inconspicuous; split eye-ring and dark, thin eye-line; no notable wing markings or wing-bars; hazy streaks on sides of breast. Song a fast musical trill (too fast to count syllables); descends in pitch and weakens at the finish. Song possibly confused with Wilson's warbler, (less musical and slower), chipping sparrow (non-musical, constant pitch, too fast to count) or dark-eyed junco (slow musical trill of fewer than 20 syllables that can be counted). **Breeding/nesting:** Monogamous. Cup-shaped nest usually built on ground with rim flush to surface; occasionally up to 3 ft. (0.9 m) above ground, well concealed in vegetation. Little known about breeding biology.[36]

As if endowed with a magician's cloak, orange-crowned warblers seem to disappear at will, making them very difficult for a birder to locate unless familiar with their song. Nests of this species are so well concealed that ornithologists were once not sure if they even bred in Colorado. These wood-warblers nest a bit later than others and remain longer into the fall, eventually migrating to wintering grounds as far south as Guatemala.

P. DOTSON

Virginia's Warbler
Vermivora virginiae
BREEDING, MIGRATORY • UNCOMMON

Habitat/feeding: Montane. Mostly drier areas; dense undergrowth of oak-mountain shrublands, and along edges of brushy mountain streams; usually up to 7,000 ft. (2133 m); possibly higher in this area. Insectivorous. Primarily searches for insects through plant debris on ground; also hawks for insects and gleans foliage. **Field ID traits:** 4.75 in. (12 cm). Drab plumage overall; soft, darker-gray head and back; reddish crown patch usually imperceptible; distinct white eye-ring. Yellow wash on breast, rump and undertail coverts. Song a clear warble, usually a 2-parted phrase.[37] Call is a sharp *chink*. **Breeding/nesting:** Breeding biology not well understood. Female thought to build cup-shaped nest on ground in shallow hollows with rim even with surface; tucked under logs, rocky ledges, roots or edges of grassy mounds.

This well-camouflaged little wood-warbler darts swiftly among dense shrubs and undergrowth, often eluding even the most ardent and experienced birders. Its song is the most useful identification trait. The nest of the Virginia's warbler is extremely difficult to spot, impeding research on the breeding biology of this species. According to Breeding Bird Surveys (see p. 310), the number of Virginia's warblers is declining in Colorado. This may be due to parasitism by cowbirds as well as their adaptation to a narrow breeding range, which is easily affected by development.[38] As daylight hours decrease in the fall, they begin the long flight to central and southern Mexico.

Yellow Warbler
Dendroica petechia
BREEDING, MIGRATORY • COMMON

CHARLES W. MELTON

Habitat/feeding: Montane to lower sub-alpine. Riparian thickets and deciduous woodlands with dense understory. Eats insects, primarily by gleaning foliage and bark and by hawking; some berries. **Field ID traits:** 5 in. (13 cm). Flashy yellow beneath and green to yellow-green above; most significantly yellow bird in the United States (called canaries by some); male with red-brown streaks on breast; female without. Yellow wing-bars and yellow patches on inner tail feathers. Dark eye. Song a variable series of cheerful phrases, sounds something like *sweet sweet sweet, I'm so sweet*. Call note is a soft, clear *chip*. **Breeding/nesting:** Somewhat polygamous. Male chases female tenaciously 1–4 days. Female constructs orderly, streamlined cup nest of deer hair and plant materials in fork of shrub or tree 2–12 feet (0.6–4 m) and occasionally as high as 60 feet (18 m) up.

In his plumes dwells the gold of the sun, in his voice its brightness and good cheer. We have not to seek him in the depths of the forest, the haunt of nearly all his congeners, he comes to us and makes his home near ours.

—ARTHUR CLEVELAND BENT, quoting Dr. Chapman, *Life Histories of North American Birds*

Zipping from branch to branch with a brilliant yellow flash of tropical allure, yellow warblers are the most abundant wood-warblers in North America, and include many sub-species. Although not threatened or endangered at this time, yellow warblers' numbers are declining in some areas due to a loss of riparian thickets and parasitization by brown-headed cowbirds. To thwart cowbirds' cuckoo-like egg-laying strategy, female wood-warblers have evolved a counter-strategy where they build a new floor in the nest to cover the cowbird eggs before laying their own. They may have to do this as many as nine times. As winter approaches, yellow warblers head for warmer climates from Mexico to northern South America.

ARE WILD BIRDS HITTING YOUR WINDOWS?

Birds are fooled by reflections in the glass. When one crashes into your window, it may be attempting to chase that "other" bird from its territory, or may be fooled by reflections in the glass and/or houseplants hanging inside into believing the glass is an extension of the outdoors. These suggestions may help prevent injury to wild birds:

- **Close your curtains during times of the day when reflections are greatest.**
- **Don't place feeders close to windows, as alarmed birds may fly into the glass.**
- **Attach black silhouettes of hawks (available at nature centers) to your windows, or position statues of predator birds nearby.**
- **Attach strips of paper to windows to help birds see the glass.**

ROBIN HENRY

Yellow-rumped Warbler
Dendroica coronata
BREEDING, MIGRATORY • ABUNDANT

Habitat/feeding: Montane to subalpine. Mixed-conifer and spruce-fir forests up to 11,000 ft. (3353 m). Employs a greater number of foraging strategies than other wood-warblers. Main diet of insects—gleans from upper canopy of aspens or lower branches of conifers; searches bark like brown creeper; hawks from perch like flycatcher; hunts through leaf litter like towhee; swoops for over water like swallow; or forages on beaches like sandpipers.[39] Also eats juniper berries in winter. **Field ID traits:** 5.5 in. (14 cm). Comparatively large wood-warbler with sunny, yellow rump, throat and side patches. Tail long and somewhat flared, with significant white spots near tips of outer tail feathers. Dark breast, gray head and mostly black and gray body. Song a clearly whistled warble, usually in 2 parts; lowers slightly in pitch at the end.

Breeding/nesting: During courtship, male follows female making calls and fluttering while fluffing side feathers, raising wings and erecting its crest. Female constructs cup-shaped nest on horizontal branch of conifer, or in hollows of aspen; rarely behind dead bark. Practices unique trait of placing feathers at edge of inner lining to partially cover eggs.

JAMES R. GALLAGHER

BLACK-THROATED GRAY WARBLER (*Dendroica nigrescens*). Found mostly at lower elevations in the Roaring Fork Valley, but sometimes in higher oak and sagebrush shrublands if adjacent to mature pinyon-juniper habitat.

Yellow-rumped warblers are the most abundant bird of this group in Colorado. Relatively large and gregarious wood-warblers, they winter farther north than others—as far north as Seattle in the West. They are one of the first to arrive from wintering grounds and one of the last to leave, often not departing this area until late September or early October. In Colorado, parents of this species are known to practice "distraction" behavior, feigning injury to lure potential predators away from the nest. Yellow-rumped warblers come in two varieties, each so distinct that they were considered separate species until it was discovered that they freely interbreed where habitats overlap in the Canadian Rockies. The variety here, known as Audubon's warbler, occurs throughout much of the West. The other variety known as the myrtle warbler is found from Alaska to the eastern United States, though they are seen here occasionally.

MacGillivray's Warbler
Oporornis tolmiei
BREEDING, MIGRATORY · UNCOMMON

JAMES R. GALLAGHER

Habitat/feeding: Montane to subalpine to 11,000 ft. (3353 m). Dense, brushy undergrowth of oak-mountain shrublands or mixed-conifer forest near wet areas; also montane willow carrs; likes locations between steep slopes and wet areas. Eats insects exclusively, feeding on ground where protected by vegetation. **Field ID traits:** 4.75–5.5 in. (12–14 cm). Slate-gray head and olive body with pale yellow belly; female paler; black eye stripe separates obvious white eye crescents. Notes of distinctive song ascend for 4 notes, dropping for last 2; low-pitched, 2-parted; has a rolling quality, *tseetle tseetle tseetle tsur tsur tsur*. Hops rather than walks. **Breeding/nesting:** Pair constructs flimsy nests in dense shrubs near ground; also grassy clumps on ground.

Unless you are familiar with the song, spotting MacGillivray's among the dense vegetation it inhabits will be nearly impossible. Though each male sings a slightly different song, a sighting of this dapper bird will richly reward your efforts in learning to recognize its voice. These warblers winter in an area from west and central Mexico to Central America. The Breeding Bird Survey (p. 310) indicates a significant decline in MacGillivray's warbler populations in Colorado.

Wilson's Warbler
Wilsonia pusilla
BREEDING, MIGRATORY · COMMON

ROBIN HENRY

Habitat/feeding: Montane to alpine, up to 13,000 ft. (3962 m). Willow and alder thickets along streams and lakes, or in wet meadows; also spruce-fir and mixed-conifer forests where willows are present. Gleans foliage and hawks for insects; occasionally searches bark; eats some berries in winter. Some habitat overlap with yellow warbler, but generally breeds at higher elevations. **Field ID traits:** 4.75 in. (12 cm). Yellow beneath, olive above; tail comparatively long and olive, without spots or yellow patches; lacks wing-bars, streaks, tail patches or other markings. Male with distinctive black cap; mottled or absent in female. Song a chattery trill of 7 or so clear, staccato syllables along same pitch; sometimes drops at the end; similar to orange-crowned warbler's song, but much slower with individual syllables discernable. Known to raise and flip tail. **Breeding/nesting:** Mostly monogamous, male sometimes polygamous. Female crafts bulky, cup-shaped nest in tangled vegetation on or near the ground; includes inner-bark strips of willow and hair from deer or horses.

Wilson's warblers are unafraid and inquisitive. The dashing male has a sporty black cap, which easily identifies the breeding pair. Arriving on their breeding territories in late May, they are on the move again by mid-August to wintering grounds from the extreme southern U.S. to Panama. They often delight residents in this area when they pass through during migration, filling up on insects in the aspen trees. According to Partners in Flight, Wilson's warblers are experiencing significant declines in this region. They are sensitive to habitat degradation, losing high-elevation riparian ecosystems to development, cattle grazing, recreational use or decreasing water due to agricultural or municipal demands for the water.

TANAGER FAMILY *Thraupidae*

Tanagers are medium-sized songbirds with rather stout, pointed bills well adapted for eating larger insects and fruit. The males have striking plumage, in contrast to the rather drab females. Recent genetic studies indicate tanagers ought to be included in the Cardinalidae family.[40]

RICHARD W. HOLMES

Western Tanager
Piranga ludoviciana
BREEDING, MIGRATORY • COMMON

Habitat/feeding: Montane to subalpine. Mixed-conifer; especially common in Douglas-fir, much less so in lodge-pole pine; also oak-mountain shrublands and aspen forests. Prefers fairly dense areas broken by snags, natural openings, burns or clearcuts. Forages for insects in mid to upper canopy; primarily wasps, bees, beetles, moths and caterpillars; also hawks prey; eats berries and other fruit in late summer. **Field ID traits:** 7.25 in. (18 cm). In summer, male has red head and face, sunny-yellow body, black back, black wings with 2 white bars, and black tail. Female is dull greenish above and yellow beneath; both female and young have white wing-bars. In winter, both sexes molt to yellow-green plumage. Most easily detected by the dry, fast call note—*pit er ick*—vocalized by both sexes; song sounds like a hoarse robin, with similar up-and-down pattern. **Breeding/nesting:** Monogamous. Male sings loud and often during breeding season; very territorial. Breeding behavior not well documented, but male possibly carries food to female during courtship. Female builds shallow, compact saucer nest, placed carefully in the horizontal fork of tree, well away from trunk.

Western tanagers are so striking in their bright colors, they conjure up images of tropical havens—being the most exotic-looking birds in the Rocky Mountain region. Although fairly noisy and conspicuous as spring migrants, they are much quieter during the fall retreat to their wintering grounds in highland areas from central Mexico to Costa Rica. Although tanagers love birdbaths and are attracted to feeders stocked with fruit, feeders are not a good idea in this area because of the number of bears and raccoons. Populations of western tanagers appear to be stable in this state. Listen for the very distinctive call note to locate western tanagers in mixed-conifer forests and oak-mountain shrublands.

NEW WORLD SPARROW FAMILY *Emberizidae*

The Brits call these ground-dwelling songbirds buntings (reserving the name "sparrow" for members of a separate group, officially called the Old World sparrows), and authors occasionally call them finches (because this family was once lumped with the finch family). Generally, New World sparrows have rounded wings, conical bills built for cracking seeds, and come in unremarkable brown, tan and gray tones with various streaked patterns—the reason they are often just referred to as "LBJ's," or little brown jobs. Male and female sparrows are typically impossible to tell apart. Of course, there are always a few exceptions, such as the colorful towhees. Sparrow songs consist of whistles, trills and complex syllables and have a distinct "gestalt" that sets them apart from any others. Learning the songs, particular personalities and habitats of the species helps one look at each "LBJ" as something special.

Spotted Towhee

Pipilo maculatus

RESIDENT, NON-MIGRATORY • COMMON

ROBIN HENRY

Habitat/feeding: Montane. Oak-mountain shrublands, riparian thickets; prefers areas of dense thick undergrowth. Diet of snails, beetles, moths, millipedes, ants and many other insects; also seeds, berries and (in winter) acorns. Uses double-footed hopping motion, forward and backward, to uncover food on ground. Compare with similar black-headed grosbeak, which gleans insects from foliage. **Field ID traits:** 8.5 in. (22 cm). Robin-sized; referred to as "ground robin." Red eye. Male sports black hood and black-feathered back; white belly and flourish of deep rufous sides not extending above like black-headed grosbeak. Distinctive white spots across back and 2 white wing-bars; female similar, but duller overall with brownish back. Song typically depicted as *chick-chick trrrrrrrr* or *drink your teeeeeeee*.

Breeding/nesting: Monogamous. Female may sing in spring; finds site, builds nest and incubates young alone, protecting nest by feigning injury; will drop to ground in mouse-like scamper to run for cover. Scratches shallow depression in ground for cup-like nest, away from taller shrubs where male sings, possibly to avoid predators.

Shy and secretive, spotted towhees are difficult to locate except during times when the males are belting out their spring songs or when the young are fledging. Luckily, they eagerly respond to "pishing" (see p. 362). As they arrive, notice the flashy white corners showing on their long black tails, which are speculated to serve as an alert of impending danger to other towhees, or perhaps to fool predators into attacking the area behind the body rather than the vulnerable head area. You might know this bird by the name rufous-sided towhee, which is what it was called before being separated into two species in 1995—the spotted and eastern towhee—which differ somewhat in song and plumage; hybrids are found where their ranges overlap in the northern Great Plains. Spotted towhees may move short distances south or eastward if temperatures drop significantly.

RICHARD W. HOLMES

Green-tailed Towhee
Pipilo chlorurus
BREEDING, MIGRATORY • COMMON

Habitat/feeding: Montane to alpine. Oak-mountain and sagebrush shrublands; occasionally up to brushy alpine thickets. Prefers dry, open, shrubby areas; may occur in moist areas with gooseberry or currant bushes. Primarily feeds in leaf litter under shrubs, exposing seeds, fruits and insects by double-scratch movements with a quick jump forward, then backward; also gleans foliage of low shrubs for insects. **Field ID traits:** 7.25 in. (18 cm). Dapper gray bird with shimmering olive-green iridescence in wings and tail; rusty red crown and white throat. Relatively short wings and long tail. Vocalizations include a nasal, cat-like mewing call, a piping note and a song composed of several short, clear whistles, musical chips and burry notes.
Breeding/nesting: Monogamous. Fairly deep, thick-walled cup nest built under low shrub; may reuse for up to five years, with female adding more material. When incubating female is disturbed, will dart off in mouse-like fashion without raising wings.[41] Nest sometimes parasitized by brown-headed cowbirds.

Green-tailed towhees are fairly secretive except during the breeding season, when the males are heard singing their cheerful song atop low shrubs. According to researcher Hugh Kingery in 1998, 20% to 40% of the entire breeding population of this species lived in Colorado. Unfortunately, the preferred habitat of towhees is primarily south-facing mountain shrublands at middle elevations where a disproportionate amount of subdivision and road construction is occurring and mining and livestock grazing has occurred. The recent movement to preserve large areas of unaltered lands connected with wildlife migration corridors is vital to green-tailed towhees' survival. As fall approaches, these unique and colorful sparrows migrate south to central Mexico for the winter.

Brewer's Sparrow
Spizella breweri
BREEDING, MIGRATORY · UNCOMMON

Habitat/feeding: Montane. Sagebrush shrublands. Winter diet is mostly grass and other plant seeds; in spring and summer, eats more insects and spiders. Can survive up to 3 weeks on dry seeds without water.

Field ID traits: 5.5 in. (14 cm). Clear breast, delicately streaked crown, white eye-ring and dark-lined cheek patch. Longish tail is notched. Easiest ID is the amazing song—a very sustained series of long trills, which exhibit diversity in speed, pitch and quality.

Breeding/nesting: Believed monogamous. Nests late in season, producing only 1 brood/year; known to produce larger brood in wetter years. Cup-like nest is built in shrub or low tree. If danger is imminent, the female drops from her nest and runs away—instead of flying—to distract the predator.

JAMES R. GALLAGHER

The "King of Trills"—there is no mistaking this small bird's song. Brewer's sparrows arrive in Colorado in early spring and return to their wintering grounds in the southwestern states or Mexico by October. Because their preferred nesting sites are in areas of dense sagebrush cover, also very desirable in the mountain west for housing and livestock grazing, populations have suffered and are now on Audubon's National Watch List. They are unlikely to breed when this habitat is fragmented into areas smaller than 5 acres (2 ha). Partners in Flight recommends maintaining contiguous stands of at least 30 acres (12 ha) to assist in their recovery. **Sage sparrows** (*Amphispiza belli*), possible locally at lower elevations, are also on the National Watch List for the same reasons. They need extensive sagebrush habitat (320 acres or 130 ha). Sage sparrows are 6¼ in. (15.9 cm), are streaked with brown, have a pale gray head and white eyebrow, white mustache and a dark breast spot.

JAMES R. GALLAGHER

VESPER SPARROW (*Pooecetes gramineus*). Uncommon. Breed up to alpine elevations primarily in sagebrush shrublands, but also occur in other areas with scattered shrubs and a good cover of grasses. Notice rufous lesser coverts, pale center of ear coverts bordered by dark feathers and the cream-colored belly. Attracted to areas with trails, roads and cow paths, as it is fond of dust baths.

CHARLES W. MELTON

Chipping Sparrow
Spizella passerina
BREEDING, MIGRATORY • COMMON

Habitat/feeding: Montane to subalpine. Coniferous forest, oak-mountain shrublands; may occasionally breed in krummholz, bordering the alpine. Primarily a ground feeder; also gleans from foliage in low trees and shrubs, or hawks from perch; eats mostly insects, some spiders, also grass and other plant seeds. **Field ID traits:** 5.5 in. (14 cm). Sexes similar. Rusty-chestnut "beanie," white eyebrow, black eye-line, gray rump and ear patch, plus 2 white wing-bars. Song a long, rapid, mechanical trill of forty or so unmusical chips, too fast to count; similar to orange-crowned warbler's, but does not change pitch near the end. **Breeding/nesting:** Mostly monogamous; occasionally polygamous while mate is incubating. Female carries out nest-building and incubating activities; male sometimes feeds incubating female. Lines nest with horse, human or other animal hair. Parasitized by cowbirds.

The adult chipping sparrow is easily identified by its distinctive head pattern. Oddly, unlike males of most species these males are known to sing late into the evening and both sexes can survive on dry seeds for up to three weeks without water.[42] Chipping sparrows fly south to Mexico for the winter.

ROBIN HENRY

White-crowned Sparrow
Zonotrichia leucophrys
BREEDING, MIGRATORY • COMMON

Habitat/feeding: Mostly alpine. Riparian thickets, meadows, willow carrs and krummolz. Prefers shrubby understory. Primarily a ground feeder; usually scratches vigorously with both feet to find beetles, spiders, caterpillars and seeds of plants and grasses; also consumes fruiting bodies of mosses, willow catkins and blossoms. **Field ID traits:** 7 in. (18 cm). Black-and-white-striped crown, muted-gray face, neck and breast; white throat and belly; brownish back, rump, wings and tail; 2 white wing-bars. Song consists of 1 or more long whistles followed by 2 or more "twittery" trills. **Breeding/nesting:** Female chooses site, building cup-shaped nest usually on or near ground in dense woody vegetation; occasionally in small tree up to 35 ft. (10.7 m). Male and female socially monogamous; they defend territory and raise broods together, but genetic studies show that about a third of nestlings are fathered by other males. Female may challenge intruding females through behaviors that sometimes include singing.

Standing out from a crowd of similar sparrows, this species has a striking black and white crown that contrasts with the muted-gray and brown coloration of its body plumage. Males arrive first from the wintering grounds in Mexico, passing through local towns on their way to higher elevations. Unforgettable, their plaintive song often serves as a pleasant early-morning alarm clock. A multitude of regional dialects characterizes this species and has been intensely studied by ornithologists. The dialects are learned and enable a female to identify a male of the same subspecies and region for mating.

SAVANNAH SPARROW (*Passerculus sandwichensis*). Uncommon. Breeds up to 12,000 ft. (3658 m) in moist, dense vegetation of mountain meadows, pastures, willow carrs and marshes with emergent vegetation. Very secretive outside breeding season. If startled, may run like a mouse or jump and dive for cover. Look for yellowish lores, which is the area between the eyes and base of the bill, and crisp streaking on the breast.

CHARLES W. MELTON

Fox Sparrow

Passerella iliaca

BREEDING, MIGRATORY

• UNCOMMON

CHARLES W. MELTON

Habitat/feeding: Montane. Alder and willow thickets along mountain streams from 7,500 to 11,000 ft. (2285–3350 m). Noisily scratches for millipedes, spiders, insects and berries while well hidden in dense understory. **Field ID traits:** 7 in. (18 cm). One of the largest local sparrows. Stout bill. Slate-colored head and back, dull rufous tail and wings, whitish chin and throat; breast and flanks with a multitude of dark-brown triangular spots, melding into single center spot on breast. Compare with song sparrow (which has grayish eyebrow stripe), vesper sparrow (has white outer tail feathers, chestnut shoulder patches and white eye-ring) and Lincoln's sparrow (has a buffy breast with brown "necklace"). Clear, melodious, thrush-like song that first rises in pitch then falls to recognizable ending. **Breeding/nesting:** Both sexes sing; otherwise quite secretive. Female probably builds bulky, cup-shaped nest alone. Early-season nests tend to be slightly above ground, later ones on the ground—all well camouflaged. Female feigns injury to distract predators from young.

Fox sparrows are a variable species with as many as eighteen sub-species falling into three main groups, their differences often detectable only through DNA analysis. Fox sparrows winter in a wide belt stretching from the Pacific Northwest to lower elevations in the southwestern to the southeastern states and up to Newfoundland. Their preference for natural, undisturbed areas indicates the need to protect riparian areas from agriculture and livestock grazing.

ROBIN HENRY

Song Sparrow
Melospiza melodia
RESIDENT, NON-MIGRATORY • COMMON

Habitat/feeding: Montane, below 9,000 ft. (2743 m). Willow thickets, riparian woodlands of alder, cottonwood and willow; also emergent wetlands. Hops through ground debris for grass and other plant seeds or small berries, gleans foliage for insects; sometimes hawks from perch. **Field ID traits:** 6.25 in. (16 cm). Sturdy bill; upper bill is darker than the lower. Dark-brown head with white to gray median crown stripe and prominent gray eyebrow stripe; broad, wedge-shaped brown stripes on whitish throat. Heavy streaking on breast coalesces into conspicuous dark spot in center; long, rounded tail; pinkish legs and feet. Song begins with 3 clear notes, followed by 2–3 sets of trills (a few are buzzy). **Breeding/nesting:** Pairs may remain together several years. Energetic courting with male rapidly fluttering wings while chasing female; sometimes singing and flying among shrubs with neck outstretched, tail and head held high and wings aflutter. Female builds well-hidden cup-like nest in low, dense shrubs; may reuse for additional brood. Both tend young, readily carrying out displays to divert predators' attention. Males warble softly, fluff feathers and move one or both wings up and down when defending territory from a rival.

PISHING FOR WHAT?

Making sounds like *kksshh-kksshh,* **or** *psst-psst-psst* **to coax birds out of trees and bushy undergrowth for better identification is a field technique onomato-poetically called "pishing." This raspy sound arouses the curiosity of some birds, possibly because they think a predator is in the vicinity and other birds are giving an alarm call.**

Cheerfully heralding spring's return with their distinctive persistent song, these sparrows are common along the Roaring Fork River and its tributaries. Three clear beginning notes distinguish this bird's song from fox and Lincoln's sparrows, also found in riparian areas. During winter, song sparrows may move to lower elevations, staying for the most part within the United States. They are heavily parasitized by cowbirds; with eggs so similar, the cowbird's intrusion usually goes unnoticed by the host. Loss of wetland habitat, together with heavy grazing along stream corridors, has reduced song sparrow populations.

Lincoln's Sparrow
Melospiza lincolnii
BREEDING, MIGRATORY • COMMON

CHARLES W. MELTON

Habitat/feeding: Montane to subalpine. Boggy areas, willow-alder thickets and wet meadows from 9,000 to 11,000 ft. (2743–3353 m). Seeks cover in dense brush piles. Gleans insects and their larvae from ground, but also forages for insects from tips of shrubs and tree branches, and sometimes catches moths. **Field ID traits:** 5–6 in. (13–15 cm). Sexes similar. Like song sparrow, but more slight, with thinner dark whisker, thinner bill, and finer streaks on breast with obvious ochre "necklace" across upper breast. Ochre eye-rings and malar. Belly is white without streaks. Crown has central gray stripe with reddish-brown streak on each side, distinct wide gray eyebrow. Best ID trait is its sweet, wren-like song with a very recognizable ending—only learned by listening. **Breeding/nesting:** Relatively secretive bird, builds nest on ground in shallow depression concealed in moss, sedge or grass clumps, or occasionally low in shrub. Female runs rather than flies when predator threatens nest; also exhibits "broken-wing" display to distract predators.

The melodic bubbling song of the Lincoln's sparrow is unforgettable once recognized within the wet habitats this bird requires. Although normally secretive, these birds become curious in spring and early summer, and can be lured into the open by "pishing"—the sound birders make when hoping to attract a bird for identification purposes.

Dark-eyed Junco
Junco hyemalis
RESIDENT, NON-MIGRATORY • COMMON

CHARLES W. MELTON

Habitat/feeding: Montane to subalpine. Spruce-fir, lodgepole and ponderosa stands; also mixed aspen-conifer forests over 7,000 ft. (2134 m); prefers edges of wooded areas. Feeds on ground, scratching for grass and other plant seeds, green caterpillars and moths; also birdfeeder mixtures where available. Young are fed insects exclusively. **Field ID traits:** 6.25 in. (16 cm). Gray head barely contrasts with lighter gray chest and sides; rufous back, white belly and white outer tail feathers (a key characteristic when seen in flight). Song a musical trill with fewer than 20 syllables; slow enough that they can be counted; compare with chipping sparrow (song is too fast to count) and orange-crowned warbler (song is faster and changes pitch near the end). **Breeding/nesting:** Courtship displays include both sexes hopping with drooping wings, fanning tails to display white outer tail feathers; male sings softly from low perch in same posture. Cup-shaped nest built on or near ground, usually in protected depression surrounded by trees, shrubs, rocks or logs; sometimes in cavity along roads or streams. Both males and females furiously attack natural enemies such as chipmunks venturing too close to their nest.

This spunky little gray bird is one of Colorado's most common breeding species. The "gray-headed" form of this species is a resident of the Roaring Fork Valley, moving down in elevation when the weather turns cold. The "Oregon" form, with its sooty black head, is sometimes seen here during winter migration. Staying in constant communication, dark-eyed juncos' perky *dit* call is heard repeatedly. Juncos, as well as many other small sparrows, will land on the seed cluster of a grass stem and "ride" it to the ground in order to consume the seeds.

HOW SMART IS THAT?

Old World sparrows (family Passeridae) were once classified with weaver finches (family Ploceinae) and can be separated from New World sparrows by their stockier build and heavier bills. Their uncomplicated song has no special rhythm and really no beginning or ending—and is just repeated continuously all day long the year round. Locally, the only representative is the **COMMON HOUSE SPARROW** (*Passer domesticus*), which was introduced from Europe in the 1850's and is now considered the most widely distributed songbird on the planet. *The Sibley Guide to Bird Life and Behavior* notes its uncanny ability to learn to open automatic doors to grocery stores, cafes and other sources of food by hovering in front of the electric eye sensors!

RICHARD W. HOLMES

CARDINAL and ALLIES FAMILY *Cardinalidae*

Males of this family display some of the most colorful plumage in North America. Unusual in the bird world, females of several species—particularly the black-headed grosbeak—sing regularly, but at a lower volume than males. Cardinalidae is divided into three groups: cardinals, which have crests, stout bills and long tails; grosbeaks, which have no crests, stout bills and short tails; and buntings, which have small bills, short tails and no crests. This is an instance where common names can be confusing. While three of our local birds are called "grosbeaks," only the black-headed grosbeak is in this family. The others are classified as finches.

Black-headed Grosbeak
Pheucticus melanocephalus
BREEDING, MIGRATORY • COMMON

RICHARD W. HOLMES

Habitat/feeding: Montane. Diverse habitats primarily near riparian and wetland areas within oak-mountain shrublands, aspen forest, and even willow carrs; locally to just above 8,000 ft. (2440 m). Requires dense cover with varied plant heights and a low jay population.[43] Breeding diet comes mainly from gleaning beetles, scale insects, grasshoppers, bees, flies, spiders and wasps high in canopy; can crack conifer and other seeds with powerful bill; also likes fruits such as strawberries and elderberries. **Field ID traits:** 8.25 in. (21 cm). Thick bill has pale lower mandible and grayish upper. Burnt-orange male has a black head and black wings and a tail with white patches. Brownish female usually has tawny-buff to pale rust-colored breast, mostly lacking streaks, and striped head. Both sexes have lemon-yellow wing linings, visible during flight.
Breeding/nesting: Monogamous. Male courts by flying above female with tail spread, singing continuously. Male assists female building bulky, open, saucer- to cup-like nest 4–25 ft. (1–8 m) off ground; eggs sometimes visible; will rebuild nest after nest predation from Steller's jays and western scrub jays.

This bird's delightful trailside serenade is sweetly whistled, complex and variable. Songs of both the black-headed grosbeak and the western tanager have the robin's distinctive and melodic warbled syllables with an up-and-down cadence, but the grosbeak's is more mellow, fluent, varied and faster, while the tanager's sounds more raspy. The grosbeak also has a longer song. Its call notes are distinctive and helpful for field identification, sounding like *hic* or *pic*.[44] They winter in central Mexico, where they are known to gorge on toxic monarch butterflies, seeming immune to the poison's effects—even reducing their intake of the poison by disgarding the insects wings. Monarch caterpillars feed on a toxic milkweed, which helps them avoid most predators.

Lazuli Bunting
Passerina amoena
BREEDING, MIGRATORY • UNCOMMON

CHARLES W. MELTON

Habitat/feeding: Montane. Commonly said to occur from 5,500 to 7,000 ft. (1675–2135 m), but may breed up to 9,000 ft. (2743 m). Prefers oak-mountain shrubland thickets with adjacent riparian habitat. Forages for insects, seeds and some fruit; feeds on the ground and in aspen, cottonwoods, willows, chokecherries and serviceberries up to 65 ft. (20 m). Favors wild seeds, not inclined to visit feeders. **Field ID traits:** 5.5 in. (14 cm). Male has cerulean blue head, neck, throat and rump; toasty-cinnamon breast; dark wings with 2 white wing-bars with upper bar thicker. Female grayish-brown on top with greenish blue-gray rump, buffy wash on throat and breast fading to white on belly; 2 wing-bars. Stout, stubby bill. **Breeding/nesting:** Monogamous, except for about ⅓ of males who are polygamous. Crudely woven, open-cup nest, often lined with animal hair.

A sighting of this exquisitely beautiful bird is worth the search! Its song is lively and persistent, with several changes in pitch. It sounds like a wood-warbler, but the song is difficult to identify. Lazuli and indigo bunting males don't learn their songs as fledglings from their parents, instead copying older males from adjacent territories upon returning to the breeding grounds at one year of age. Lazuli buntings winter in southern California, Arizona and Baja California. Their populations appear fairly stable at the present time, although the species is adversely affected by the loss of thicket-type habitat and the accumulation of pesticides and herbicides in seeds.

BLACKBIRD, MEADOWLARK and ORIOLE FAMILY
Icteridae

Members of this family, collectively known as the icterids, have very strong, straight bills, though length and thickness may vary. They are divided into three main groups: the black and brown birds that include red-winged blackbirds, cowbirds and grackles; meadowlarks; and orioles. Unusual among songbirds, females of several species in this family also sing, although they may not sound exactly like the males. Most icterids do not migrate long distances, often remaining as year-round residents, at least at lower elevations. Members of this family have been able to take advantage of urbanization and human altered landscapes and their numbers are increasing in most cases.

ROBIN HENRY

Western meadowlark

Both **WESTERN MEADOWLARKS** (*Sturnella neglecta*) and **BULLOCK'S ORIOLES** (*Icterus bullockii*) probably breed in this area, but rarely. Meadowlarks need healthy open grassland habitat to breed, and are common at lower elevations in the Roaring Fork Valley. Colorful orange-and-black Bullock's orioles breed mostly in mature deciduous trees, preferring cottonwoods in riparian areas below 7,500 ft. (2285 m). They may occasionally be seen along the Roaring Fork River.

Brown-headed Cowbird

Molothrus ater

BREEDING, MIGRATORY • COMMON

RICHARD W. HOLMES

Habitat/feeding: Typically inhabits forest edges, and open areas with scattered trees. Habitat varies depending on particular "host." Uses robust conical bill to feed on insects, especially grasshoppers; also seeds such as dandelion and groundsel, and berries. **Field ID traits:** 7.5 in. (19 cm). Male has nut-brown head and black body; female grayish-brown above, lighter and slightly streaked beneath. Both have conical, sparrow-like bills. Distinctive vocalizations sound as if they are chuckling underwater—a bubbly *glug-glug-glee*. Call is a *chuck*; also emits clear high whistles in flight. **Breeding/nesting:** Courtship displays by male include: ruffling uppermost feathers, calling and bowing toward female while on ground; ruffling same feathers, bending head, singing and arching wings in flight; and pointing bill straight up, fluffing feathers on nape, breast and flanks while singing, then bowing while arching neck and spreading tail with wings raised—all on raised perch. Female lays eggs in nest of other species, leaving young to be raised by others.

Brown-head cowbirds are considered a parasitic species, because they depend upon another living organism to complete their life cycle. These females are adept at following birds of other species back to their nests, or "monitoring" their activities from high perches until discovering which birds are exhibiting nesting behavior, such as maneuvering through thick vegetation to find nest sites. Once the female cowbird has located a suitable nest, she lays her eggs in it, removing the "host's" eggs or even killing its nestlings if necessary. Cowbirds parasitize over 220 bird species in this way, and have been known to lay more than forty eggs per season. Their eggs hatch more quickly and the young are larger and grow faster than those of most hosts. These larger baby cowbirds dominate the feeding process, resulting in the death of the host's own young. Cowbirds once inhabited only the short-grass plains east of the Rockies and were called "buffalo birds" because they followed the buffalo herds eating insects disturbed by the pounding hooves. Humans have facilitated the spread of cowbirds by eradicating the buffalo herds and replacing native ecosystems with urban and agricultural landscapes. Cowbirds now hang out with their new "buffalo"—cattle—finding accessible food in farmer's fields and nearby urban areas.

Cowbirds are a major reason for the decline of some songbirds in the United States. Songbirds commonly victimized include Brewer's blackbirds, yellow warblers, song sparrows, chipping sparrows, American robins, and the tiny ruby-crowned kinglet.

ROBIN HENRY

Red-winged Blackbird
Agelaius phoeniceus
BREEDING, MIGRATORY • ABUNDANT

Habitat/feeding: Montane to lower subalpine. Prefers freshwater ponds and cattail marshes; may nest in other wet upland habitats. Feeds mostly on insects during the summer, switching to seeds and crop remnants in winter; commonly visits feeders. **Field ID traits:** 8.75 in. (22 cm). Glossy black male has wings with bright red shoulder patches trimmed in tawny gold. Chocolate-brown female has ruddy streaking above, dark eye stripes and bonnet; may have red blush on wing coverts or pink blush on chin and throat; breast and belly whitish with dark streaking. Bill, eyes and feet all black. Full adult plumage not attained until third year. Common call note is *chack*; alarm note is a whistle; melodic song sounds like *oak-a-leeeeee.* **Breeding/nesting:** Courting and territorial displays of male both involve spreading tail and wing feathers and raising the bright red epaulets, even in flight. Male defends territory and female the nest with equal ferocity, readily "escorting" your kayak or canoe through their territory. Strands of nest are woven around sections of existing vegetation, often cattails.

Brilliant scarlet epaulets on the male of this species offer a splash of daring color in the midst of midnight black plumage. Its thrilling musical trill of *oak-a-leeeeee* is a harbinger of spring wherever wet areas abound. This bird commands several superlatives: it is the most abundant North American bird, one of the most heavily researched and one of the most highly polygamous of bird species, and it congregates in some of the largest winter flocks—up to a million birds. Females choose males based on quality of their territory. Although the norm during breeding season is around two to six females per male, up to fifteen females have been found nesting in a single male's territory. Red-wings in this area migrate in winter only as far as the southern United States, where large flocks may sometimes damage crops. Even though these birds help control many harmful insects, people still attempt to exterminate them in some areas. Humans are partially responsible for increased number of blackbirds, because treated sewage and agricultural runoff promote the growth of rushes and cattails, which red-wings prefer.

Brewer's Blackbird

Euphagus cyanocephalus

BREEDING, MIGRATORY • UNCOMMON

CHARLES W. MELTON

Habitat/feeding: Montane to subalpine. Favors varied open areas such as pastures, mountain parks and urban areas near water as high as 10,000 ft. (3048 m). Primary diet of insects. Searches low vegetation, pecking, digging and probing in ground; will even wade into water up to its abdomen or hover over water to prey on aquatic insects; also consumes seeds and berries; typically forages in flocks. **Field ID traits:** 9 in. (23 cm). Male black except for neon-yellow eye; a shimmering iridescence on feathers in sunlight appears purple on head and neck, green on body and wings. Female dusky brown above and grayish below; brown eye. Walks while bobbing head forward in short, jerky movements. Vocalizations include a shrill, underwater-like shriek. **Breeding/nesting:** Forms monogamous pairs, but inclined to be polygamous; for breeding behavior, see below. Nests in colonies of 5–20 pairs at base of shrubs and clumped grasses, in small trees or up to 150 ft. (46 m) high in snags. Heavily parasitized by brown-headed cowbirds.

Brewer's blackbirds are content to nest in many different habitats, and are very flexible in their foraging behavior. As noted in the *Colorado Breeding Bird Atlas,* the male engages in complex behaviors—the male performing threat displays by pointing his bill straight up, flattening his feathers and pulling himself into an "iridescent column of arrogance," and courtship displays of "flirtatious feather-fluffing and tail-spreading," accompanied by vocalizations sounding like *squee* or *schlr-r-r-up.* Both sexes are intent on protecting their own—females the nest, males the territory—and will persistently mob hawks, owls and other large birds, as well as mammalian predators. Most Brewer's blackbirds migrate in flocks, mainly to Arizona and Mexico. Their populations, like those of other blackbirds, have increased as humans replace forests with agricultural land. Like red-winged blackbirds, they do cause damage to certain crops, so efforts to control them are carried out in some agricultural areas. Ironically, the majority of this species' diet consists of insects that are known to harm crops.

ROBIN HENRY

COMMON GRACKLE (*Quiscalus quiscula*). Uncommon. Occasionally breed in this area.

FINCH AND ALLIES FAMILY *Fringillidae*

Birds in this family vary in body and bill size, but have several features in common: sturdy conical bills, large jaw muscles, tough skulls, powerful gizzards, relatively short, forked tails and males more brightly colored than females. Many finches carry out complex courtship displays and sing wonderfully intricate melodies during breeding season.

A finch will wedge a seed in special grooves in the upper mandible of its bill before raising its lower jaw to crush it. The dexterous tongue then removes the husk, releasing the kernel to be swallowed. Nearly all North American finches—including goldfinches, grosbeaks, rosy-finches, pine siskins and crossbills—are assigned to the Carduelinae subfamily. Cardueline finches are renowned as nomads, following the yearly fluctuations in cone crops rather than regular migration patterns. The conservation of large expanses of forest with cone crops that produce in alternating years is essential for their survival. Finches often seek salt-impregnated soil, sand and gravel, a behavior observed on winter highways, which results in flocks being killed by vehicles.

ROBIN HENRY

Evening Grosbeak
Coccothraustes vesperitinus
RESIDENT, NON-MIGRATORY · UNCOMMON

Habitat/feeding: Montane. Coniferous and mixed-conifer forests, sometimes oak-mountain shrublands and aspen forests; prefer more open areas. Dine on spruce budworm and other insects, buds of conifers and deciduous trees, chokecherry seeds, dogwood berries and juniper berries; insects eaten only during breeding season. **Field ID traits:** 8 in. (20 cm). Striking bird with large pale-yellow to greenish beak, glossy cocoa-brown hood, golden-yellow body, black wings with white patches, black tail; forehead and eyebrow also golden yellow. Female subdued silver/gray/tan, but with enough of male's coloration pattern to be recognizable as same species. Large white wing patches visible during undulating flight. Song is infrequent short warble; call is loud *chirp*, *cleer*, or *cleer-ip*. **Breeding/nesting:** Female constructs well-hidden cup-shaped nest, far out on horizontal branch of conifer or deciduous tree such as aspen or willow; male may assist in gathering nest material. Research on nesting birds in Colorado found nests mostly placed on south and east sides of trees, undoubtedly to take advantage of sun's warmth.[45]

The handsome male evening grosbeak responds with elaborate court-ship displays after the female approaches him to be fed. In movements resembling an oriental dance, he puffs out his feathers, lowers his body to the ground and rapidly vibrates his spread wings, sometimes moving side to side, remaining silent. Then both male and female bow to each other.[46] Relatively quiet and secretive during breeding, they become more gregari-ous and quite unafraid of humans during winter. They do show aggres-sion when feeding stations become crowded, attacking and pushing other birds, creating quite a frenzy of noise and activity. The winter wanderings of evening grosbeak flocks are erratic and tied to food availability—a situa-tion becoming more complex with large numbers of available feeders. At the present time, the species is prospering and has expanded its territory.

> *... more than 150 grosbeaks at his feeders all winter ... stunning sight, a seething mass of cocoa and yellow, so raucous from inside the house you could hear the birds calling and screeching, like parrots. When a hawk cruised by, they would explode in every direction; the effect was vertiginous, like toppling into a field of sunflowers ...*
>
> —Scott Weidensaul, *Living on the Wind: Across the Hemisphere with Migratory Birds*

Pine Grosbeak
Pinicola enucleator
RESIDENT, NON-MIGRATORY · UNCOMMON

ROBIN HENRY

Habitat/feeding: Subalpine. Open spruce-fir forests, often with aspen patches. Dines primarily on spruce seeds; also buds of aspens, willows and cottonwoods, small flying insects, and mountain ash berries, snowberries and crabapples. **Field ID traits:** 9 in. (23 cm). Bill dark, heavy and conical, quite curved. Male head, back and underparts rosy-red to crimson; may be pink in fall. Female mostly gray with yellowish-brown head, nape and face. Both have black/gray wings with two dis-tinct white wing-bars and long, notched tail. Vocalizes both song and call during slightly undu-lating flight. Cornell researchers describe the song as varying "from a clear, loud carol full of trills to a soft, flowing warble." **Breeding/nesting:** Possibly monogamous. Male offers food to female as part of courtship and nesting; she leaves nest to receive food. Bulky, loose nest constructed in fork or on horizontal limb in dense foliage, within 25 ft. (7.6 m) of the ground.

"Talking aspens" along the trail during fall may turn out to be flocks of pine grosbeaks dining on aspen buds while chattering in their cheerful musical voices. These gentle birds will not flush easily, remaining hidden in the branches of spruce or fir as hikers approach. Subalpine specialists, pine grosbeaks are specially adapted to feeding and breeding in open spruce-fir forests mixed with aspen, and wintering there as well.

CHARLES W. MELTON

Brown-capped Rosy-Finch

Leucosticte australis

RESIDENT, NON-MIGRATORY

• UNCOMMON

Habitat/feeding: Alpine. Endemic to cliff areas of southern Rocky Mountains, mostly in Colorado. Favors remote spots during breeding season. Forages for insects and grass, sedge and other plant seeds around snowbanks and talus fields; often hover-feeds.[47] **Field ID traits:** 6.25 in. (16 cm). Male has black forehead; brown head, breast and back; pink belly, rump, undertail and wing feathers; female a pale mouse-gray overall and difficult to distinguish alone. Unafraid of humans, this species will continue feeding when skiers pass on-mountain winter feeders. **Breeding/nesting:** Monogamous during breeding season; male and female may arrive together on breeding grounds, not having much time to breed in short alpine season. Female defines territory, chooses nesting site and constructs grassy nest in rocky crevice; may reuse site each year. Very social species; even young flock together soon after fledging; adults return to flocking behavior once breeding season ends.

CHARLES W. MELTON

Gray-crowned rosy-finch (*Leucosticte tephrocotis*), above, and **black rosy-finch** (*L. atrata*), below. All three of these species will flock together in winter and are frequently seen at feeders on local ski areas. Once considered a single species, they regained individual species status in 1993 (American Ornithological Union).

CHARLES W. MELTON

While scrambling around in craggy alpine cliffs, this alpine virtuoso may be encountered. One of the few small perching birds that nest above timberline, and the only one choosing this rocky vertical habitat as its domain. Brown-capped rosy finch nests have been found as high as 14,200 ft. (4328 m). Descending to lower elevations during winter, but rarely below 7,000 ft. (2134 m), they are often seen in large flocks visiting on-mountain feeders at local ski areas. Males of this species outnumber females six to one, and those not lucky enough to be chosen for a mate spend the summer battling with other males. Rising temperatures in alpine areas due to global climate change are likely to have detrimental effects on this species, because it forages primarily on and around snowfields. Moreover, because its breeding areas are specific, it is vulnerable to human disturbances which include grazing, mining, recreation, road building and water storage projects.

Cassin's Finch
Carpodacus cassinii

RESIDENT, NON-MIGRATORY
• UNCOMMON

RICHARD W. HOLMES

Habitat/feeding: Montane to sub-alpine. Aspen and riparian woodlands to spruce-fir forests. Primarily forages on ground for seeds; supplements diet in spring with willow and aspen catkins, evergreen buds and insects; berries in fall. Common at feeders.
Location: Horse Ranch, Melton Ranch. **Field ID traits:** 6.25 in. (16 cm). Male has vivid crimson cap contrasting with brown nape; crimson wash on throat, breast and rump. Female strongly brown-streaked beneath, with marked face pattern. Both with clearly notched tail, heavily streaked undertail coverts. Bill longer and straighter than the similar **house finch** (*C. mexicanus*). **Breeding/nesting:** Monogamous. Cup nest usually built near end of large branch. Breeding locations vary according to food supply. Brown-headed cowbird host.

Cassin's finch is master of a very engaging and energetic courtship song. This fast warble is made up of short, complex syllables with sweet call notes at the end—or occasionally with phrases that mimic other local birds such as pine siskins, jays, western tanagers and flickers. The Cassin's two- or three-note flight call sounds like *soo-leep* or *cheedly-up*.

ROBIN HENRY

HOUSE FINCHES (*C. mexicanus*) are quite common in local urban areas. They are distinguished from Cassin's by a red (or possibly orange to yellow) "sweat-band," and red chin, upper throat and breast that fade into noticeably streaked sides. Their cheerful, warbling song usually ends with a distinct lower buzzy note.

RICHARD W. HOLMES

Red Crossbill

Loxia curvirostra

RESIDENT, NON-MIGRATORY

• UNCOMMON

Habitat/feeding: Subalpine. Spruce-fir, Douglas-fir and lodgepole pine forests. A crossed bill is an adaptation for opening conifer seeds; also eats insects, berries and buds of trees. **Field ID traits:** 6.25 in. (16 cm). Head and bill out of proportion to sparrow-sized body. Male various shades of red; may be yellow in first year; mostly brighter crown and rump. Female usually olive-green above and yellowish beneath. Male throat always red or yellow, female throat usually gray. Both with blackish-brown wings and tail; tail deeply notched. Call is sharp, repeated *kip*, usually during flight; other vocalizations sound like *chipa, chipa, chipa*, or *chee, chee, chee*. **Breeding/nesting:** Monogamous. Male puts on engaging courtship display, circling above female and serenading her. Breeds almost anytime, depending on food supply; may breed when less than 4 months old and still in juvenile plumage. Female builds shallow, saucer-like nest near end of horizontal branch in conifer. Raising of brood occurs even in cold weather; hatchlings can endure repeated cooling and even periods of torpor.

Capricious wanderers, red crossbills travel the continent year-round from Newfoundland to Alaska and south to Nicaragua in search of conifer seeds. With bills crossed like garden shears, these birds are specially adapted to pry apart the scales of conifer cones, which they hold with their feet while removing the precious seeds with their tongues. Their mandible tips slowly cross over within several weeks of fledging, and they become "left- or right-handed" in opening cones depending on which way the tips cross. Although known for chattering monotonously while foraging, red crossbills can move silently through the trees, using their bills and feet with parrot-like dexterity. At least nine separate geographic types occur in the United States, each with a distinct call, bill and body size—each adapted to feed on a specific conifer species, especially in spring and fall when feeding efficiency is critical. Individuals of the same dialect and conifer affinity tend to flock together, breeding only within that group. There are at least two of these types in our area, one found in lodgepole forests and one in spruce-fir forests. The survival of red crossbills depends on the preservation of large expanses of natural forest so that cone crops are consistent from year to year, guaranteed by variation in age and species of conifers.

Pine Siskin
Carduelis pinus
RESIDENT, NON-MIGRATORY · ABUNDANT

Habitat/feeding: Montane. Habitat generalist; nesting in lodgepole pine, spruce-fir, aspen, cottonwood and mixed-conifer forests; may nest in grassland or tundra. Forages in trees or on the ground for conifer, thistle and dandelion seed, and insects; drinks from sap wells drilled by sapsuckers. Common at feeders. **Field ID traits:** 5 in. (13 cm). Tolerates humans. Resembles a small, heavily streaked sparrow. Flashes of yellow on wings and tail during undulating flight. Chorus of long, buzzy *shreeee* notes while foraging in flocks. **Breeding/nesting:** Monogamous. Courtship begins as winter flocks dissolve; male circles over female with tail spread and wings flapping rapidly, singing continually; also feeds female. Female builds open saucer-type nest in thick foliage near ends of branches. May nest in loose colonies.

Flashy yellow on the outer primaries of the wing and on the base of the tail feathers easily distinguishes a pine siskin while in flight.

Pine siskins are very social year-round residents. They travel in small flocks during the breeding season, and much larger flocks during the winter, leapfrogging silently from treetop to treetop as they forage. Their buzzy chatter fills the air when they land, and again on departing. Like other finches, their breeding times are inconsistent and depend on food availability. Thus, late-summer breeding usually corresponds with periods when thistles, dandelions and related plants go to seed. According to the Cornell Ornithological Lab website, pine siskins are the most frequently seen member of irruptive winter finches—finches that breed in northern parts of North America, but sometimes make large winter invasions into central latitudes, probably when food is lacking in their typical winter range.

> *Those who contemplate the beauty of the earth find reserves of strength that will endure as long as life lasts.*
>
> —RACHEL CARSON

MAMMALS

*Our task is to widen our circle of compassion
to embrace all living beings and all of nature.*

—ALBERT EINSTEIN

Watching and learning about mammals adds to our enjoyment of the natural world. These vertebrate animals have hair and produce milk to nourish their young. Although sometimes elusive and hard to see, the search alone can lead to exciting adventures.

Begin by learning what time of day each species is active. Remember that most wildlife activity takes place at dawn and at dusk, so being outdoors at those times will improve your chances of an encounter.

Rather than actively pursuing wildlife, sit and observe from a hidden location or walk slowly and quietly using all of your senses. Binoculars can be a great tool, allowing a closer look without disturbing the wildlife.

While outdoors expanding your knowledge of animal habitats, behavior and tracks, there will be telltale smells, sounds, marks and movements that become a part of your mammal recognition vocabulary. Knowing that a badger or a bobcat lives in an area can be thrilling even if their wariness keeps them hidden from human eyes.

Had this guide been written a hundred years ago, it would have included descriptions of several majestic mammals that, sadly, have disappeared from our landscape:

- Gray wolves were hunted, poisoned and trapped to extinction in Colorado in the early 1900's. Several organizations in Colorado are undertaking extensive efforts to encourage gray wolf reintroduction into the southern Rockies. There have been sightings of wolves that are migrating into the state from Yellowstone National Park, where they were reintroduced from 1995 to 1996.

- Grizzlies were also killed off in our area during the early 20th century, the victims of hunting and loss of habitat caused by human settlement and livestock grazing.

- Wild bison historically roamed the upper Roaring Fork Valley. There are no longer any free-ranging herds in Colorado.

- Colorado is the southern limit of the wolverine's range in North America, and the Colorado Division of Wildlife's latest survey indicates there are probably no wolverines in the state.

- Canada lynx were trapped extensively for their pelts and became rare to extinct in Colorado. They are now being reintroduced in the southwest part of the state and will likely move back into this region as populations increase.

- River otters are currently considered endangered in Colorado. They were trapped for their pelts and suffered from poor water quality due to mining, agriculture and other pollution sources. From 1976 to 1991, otters were reintroduced into rivers throughout Colorado in their historic range. They have been seen on the Roaring Fork River above Glenwood Springs.

There are differing viewpoints on wildlife management, many of them quite controversial. By educating ourselves and making an effort to understand each other's needs—both human's and wildlife's—we can better share mutual habitat.

HOW TO USE THIS CHAPTER

This chapter groups local mammals by order and family, following the taxonomy or classification, presented in the Denver Museum of Natural History's *Mammals of Colorado*, by James P. Fitzgerald, Carron A. Meaney and David M. Armstrong. Both scientific and common names are listed.

General **abundance ratings** are listed beneath the scientific name. These may seem confusing with mammals that are common but rarely seen because they are secretive or nocturnal. For example, both marmots and bobcats are fairly common, but marmots are often seen sunning themselves along roads and trails, whereas bobcats are very elusive and actual sightings are infrequent. A mammal's abundance may also depend on the quality of habitat it experiences in a particular location. "Quality habitat" refers to habitat that is: appropriate for that species; undisturbed by humans; without an inappropriate abundance of predators; and not

WHAT HARM COULD A PEANUT DO?

Feeding wild animals is not a good idea. Salt-laden nuts, chips, pretzels and similar snack foods are poisonous to some animals' systems—and unhealthy for others whose normal diet consists of berries, plants or insects. Feeding wild animals can create a dependence on humans for food, decreasing their ability to forage successfully in the wild. Anyone attempting to feed animals by hand also runs the risk of being bitten and contracting diseases carried by that animal.

invaded by non-native plant or animal species. "Disturbed habitat" refers to habitat that has been altered in some way, by trails, roads or invasive non-native species. Some species may actually become more abundant in disturbed habitat because of increased food sources or accessibility.

Most species descriptions begin with a summary of four categories of the mammal's most important characteristics:

- **Habitat/feeding** has information on local habitat, diet and feeding strategies.

- **Field ID traits** covers the species' physical appearance and any behaviors that may be useful in identification.

- **Reproduction** details courtship, mating behavior and other related information.

- **Tracking notes** comments on tracks and signs to watch for.

A narrative paragraph follows, giving additional information on the natural history of the species, other distinctive behaviors and notes on its conservation status.

NOTE: When there are a number of similar species within a group, as with shrews, bats and rodents, the descriptions follow a shorter, alternate format without description headings or a narrative.

ANIMAL TRACKS are best found where the ground is soft, especially near water or along trails and jeep roads, where mud, sand or dust is present. The substrate can affect the apparent size of tracks. For example, melting snow can make tracks grow, while drying mud can make them shrink. A single track is rarely definitive, so look for additional tracks and other signs such as scat, scrapings and length of stride to help you determine the species. Many signs are territorial in nature, such as the large piles of brush a male mountain lion will scrape together and urinate on to mark his home range. Others may provide clues to an animal's behavior as it passed through an area, such as where a deer bedded down to rest. *Scats and Tracks of the Rocky Mountains*, by James C. Halfpenny, is a useful resource on mammal track patterns and sign.

MOLES, SHREWS and ALLIES
Order Insectivora

In general, insectivores have small brains, poor vision, unspecialized teeth, small ears, poorly developed eyes, high metabolisms and long, pointed snouts. Eating insects is not necessarily unique to this group, and its members do not necessarily eat only insects. They are the ancestral group from which all present-day placental (as opposed to marsupial) mammals evolved.

SHREW FAMILY
Soricidae

Shrews are tiny, ferocious insectivores that are active year-round, living their lives mostly unnoticed—far from the category of "watchable wildlife," though they are in many ways extremely interesting. The least studied of our native mammals, they travel on miniature trails beneath vegetation and snow, alternately foraging for food and resting to digest it, driven by their fierce metabolisms.

Some shrews have a secret weapon—poisonous saliva that partially paralyzes their prey so that it can be consumed or stored for later use. To make up for relatively poor vision, shrews use scent, whiskers for feeling and a high-pitched twittering as a form of echolocation. If food is scarce, they may enter a state of torpor, or temporary hibernation, lowering their metabolic rate by 50–80% for brief periods of time.

Although larger predators such as owls, kestrels, foxes, weasels and domestic cats hunt these tiny predators, two protective behaviors work in their favor. Glands in a shrew's skin emit a bad odor, turning this possible prey into a very foul-tasting tidbit that is often abandoned after the first bite.[1] Secondly, as they move about in the open, shrew mothers and their young sometimes form curious caravans, each clasping the tail of the one in front, which may deter predators by mimicking a snake.

These tiny brownish or grayish critters can be mistaken for mice, but a closer look reveals a long pointed snout and very tiny ears concealed within dense velvety fur. Shrews consume mostly eggs, pupae, larvae and adult insects, as well as some carrion, worms, snails, slugs, frogs and small fish. Local species do not exceed 7 in. (17.5 cm) in total length, or 1 oz. (30 g) in weight. Shrews are found almost everywhere except in the polar regions and are very important in the regulation of insect populations, especially snails and slugs. Larvae of insects that are active in winter are also consumed, helping to control insect infestations year-round.

THE FASTEST HEARTBEAT OF ANY ANIMAL

Studies have found that shrews maintain heart rates of up to 1,511 beats per minute—faster than any other mammal's. They will hunt and kill mice twice their size to fuel this energetically expensive lifestyle.

Masked Shrew

Sorex cinereus

COMMON

Montane to subalpine, up to 11,000 ft. (3350 m). Moist forests, particularly in willow thickets and moist meadows. Grayish to brownish above and slightly paler beneath—tail is noticeably bi-colored. Total length of 3–4 in. (82–105 mm). The most common shrew in appropriate habitat, and the most widely distributed shrew in North America.

Masked shrew. Although distinguishing between different species is difficult, this photo gives you an idea of a shrew's general appearance.

Pygmy Shrew

Sorex hoyi

UNCOMMON

Subalpine to alpine, mostly above 9,600 ft. (2900 m). Adapted to survive in a variety of habitats from spruce-fir and aspen forests to wet meadows. A very small shrew, with a total length of only 2.7–3.5 in. (70–90 mm). Dark brown above and paler beneath; bi-colored tail is relatively short. Our shortest mammal.

Montane Shrew

Sorex monticolus

COMMON • IN QUALITY HABITAT

Montane to subalpine, up to 11,500 ft. (3500 m). Prefers dense vegetative ground cover, logs or shrubs in forests and meadows that are neither particularly wet nor dry. Largest mountain shrew; total length 4-5 in. (90-125 mm). Tail is bi-colored, but not obvious; relatively long.

Dwarf Shrew

Sorex nanus

UNCOMMON

Montane to alpine. Variety of habitats above 5,600 ft. (1680 m). Total length is 3-4 in. (82-105 mm). Medium brown above, grayer beneath; indistinct bi-colored tail. The smallest mammal in Colorado (pygmy shrew has a shorter total length, including tail, but its body is larger).

Water Shrew

Sorex palustris

COMMON • IN QUALITY HABITAT

Montane to lower subalpine, up to 10,000 ft. (3048 m). Lives in riparian habitats near rivers, streams, ponds, lakes or marshes. Distinctly large at 5.5–7 in. (140–175 mm). Handsome charcoal-gray above, silvery beneath; obvious bi-colored tail. Toes and margins of large hind feet fringed with stiff hairs. Feeds primarily on aquatic insects and small fish. An adept swimmer, both in and under the water, often sighted by fishermen.

BATS
Order Chiroptera

Townsend's big-eared bat

These unique night-flying mammals evoke mixed emotions. Myths abound in the western world associating bats with evil spirits, whereas people of the Far East consider them symbols of good luck, fertility, happiness and long life.

The world's only true flying mammals, bats are thought to have evolved while dinosaurs still dominated the earth. Their reproductive biology is similar to that of humans and primates, with the females of most species having two teats and paired ovaries and usually giving birth to their young one at a time. Some bat species have the usual pattern of ovulation, mating, fertilization, implantation and then fetal development; while others have unique reproductive strategies in which fertilization, implantation or development are delayed to allow offspring to be born when there is an abundant insect supply, usually late spring or early summer.[2] Female bats give birth while hanging upside down, in some species grabbing the newborn with their tail and then swinging it into their embrace.

A bat's heart is capable of operating across an incredible range, from roughly ten beats per minute during hibernation to as much as 1,000 beats per minute in flight. They are renowned for their radar-like echolocation, which involves sending out ultrasonic calls and then navigating or locating prey with the returned echoes. In contrast, their social or communicative vocalizations are often audible to humans. They typically roost in human-made structures, caves or old mines, but can also be found in tree cavities, cliffs, crevices or under bark. Accessibility to water is key to the location chosen.

Bats are very intelligent creatures that pose little threat to humans, and are important not only to natural ecosystems but also to agriculture, science and commerce. A single little brown bat can catch up to 1,200 mosquito-sized insects in just one hour, and a colony of 150 big brown bats can eat enough cucumber beetles each summer to protect farmers from 33 million root worm larvae.[3] Some bats pollinate crops, while fruit-eating bats aid in the dispersal of seeds. In some countries, bat droppings called guano are commercially collected for use as fertilizer. Recently, bats have contributed to medical advances such as the development of navigational aids for blind people, artificial insemination and vaccines.[4]

Even so, humans kill millions of bats, often destroying entire cave ecosystems, mostly out of ignorance or fear. Threats to bat survival include cave explorers who disturb hibernating and maternity colonies, deliberate vandalism, loss of roosting and foraging habitat, and spraying of agricultural pesticides that contaminate the insects eaten by bats. More than 50% of bat species are endangered or threatened. Volunteers for the Colorado Division of Wildlife are doing an inventory of old mines to locate active bat populations. When discovered, they protect them from human intrusion by installing bat-friendly doors.

VESPERTILIONID FAMILY   *Vespertilionidae*

Bats in this area are all members of the Vespertilionidae, the largest family of bats, which are small to medium sized and have tails that are contained within the membrane between their legs. The best time to observe them is during the first four hours after sunset, when they fly overhead seeking their insect prey.

Numbers of bats in this area are often higher during fall and spring migration. Since a full key for bat identification is beyond the scope of this book, what follows are abbreviated descriptions of a few local bats.

Big Brown Bat
Eptesicus fuscus
COMMON

Montane to subalpine, up to 10,000 ft. (3050 m). Big brown bats are quite ubiquitous throughout the United States, including urban areas, often using attics of buildings, or cracks and crevices in rocky areas as roost sites. They forage for long distances from their day roost, leaving at dusk. Diet is primarily beetles. Reproduce by delayed fertilization.

MERLIN D. TUTTLE

Hoary Bat
Lasiurus cinereus
FAIRLY COMMON

Montane to lower subalpine. Occupies a variety of habitats up to 10,000 ft. (3048 m). White-tipped dorsal hairs give this largest of Colorado's vespertilionids a striking frosted, or hoary, appearance. Roosts in trees. Solitary bat, emerging well after dark. Reproduces by delayed implantation. Males usually stay in Colorado year-round, whereas females go further north to bear and rear pups.

Townsend's Big-eared Bat
Corynorhinus townsendii
UNCOMMON

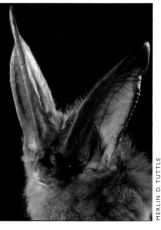

Montane forests, up to 9,500 ft. (2900 m). As its name suggests, this bat has extraordinarily large ears. Emerges well after dark and does not wander far in search of food. Females form nursery colonies to take advantage of the shared heat between individuals. Townsend's reproduces by delayed fertilization. Presence tied to available roosting sites in underground caves or mines.

Other local bats are: silver-haired bat (*Lasionycteris noctivagans*), long-legged myotis (*Myotis volans*), little brown bat (*Myotis lucifugus*) and long-eared myotis (*Myotis evotis*).

RABIES AND BATS

Contrary to popular belief, bats do not pose a significant rabies risk. Fewer than forty human deaths from bat-transmitted rabies have been documented in the United States in the past fifty years. Worldwide, deaths from bat-transmitted rabies are a small fraction of those from rabies transmitted by domestic dogs or cats.[5]

PIKAS, HARES and RABBITS
Order Lagomorpha

Lagomorphs are medium-sized vegetarians with lips that fold and meet behind their two upper, chisel-like incisors so that they can chew and gnaw without swallowing. As with rodents, their incisors grow continuously and are worn down at the leading edge. They have very short or rudimentary tails. Mammals in this order digest their food twice, in a practice sometimes compared to cow-like rumination. During early morning and again in the evening, they eliminate soft, sticky pellets, which they immediately reingest. This allows the absorbtion of nutrients missed the first time through. Later, they eliminate a dry, hard pellet that is left where it falls. Lagomorphs are preyed upon by a large variety of predators, making them an important member of many food chains.

PIKA FAMILY *Ochotonidae*

Pikas are small, short-eared mammals with tails so small they are usually not visible. This family has only one genus, with fourteen species worldwide, twelve in Eurasia and two in North America. Fossil remains indicate the pika family is about 15 million years old, and probably reached this continent by crossing the Bering Land Bridge during the last of the Pleistocene Ice Age, 23,000–16,500 years ago.

Pika, Coney, Rock Rabbit
Ochotona princeps
COMMON

Habitat/feeding: Subalpine to alpine. Talus slopes above 10,000 ft. (3048 m). Two distinct foraging strategies include grazing on grasses, as well as leaves and stems of herbaceous plants and shrubs, and "haying," which involves gathering and drying flowering plants, berries and conifer needles in "haypiles" for winter storage. Forages on some conifer needles and bark. Does not hibernate, burrowing under the snow for lichens and remaining meadow vegetation, while using haypiles as backup. Water mostly derived

Quite the ventriloquist, a pika's shrill *eeek* seems to reverberate from every direction as hikers approach.

from vegetation. **Field ID traits:** 8 in. (20 cm) total length. Guinea-pig sized, with small, rounded ears, which prevent heat loss. No visible tail. Most common vocalization a high-pitched *eeek*. Diurnal; most active morning and late afternoon/evening. Often confused with marmots (see p. 392). **Tracking notes:**

Furry soles provide better traction while scurrying across slippery rocks. Two types of scat are produced; spherical and dry; black and semi-liquid, which is reingested to recover remaining nutrients. **Reproduction:** Breeds April–June. Usually initiates 2 litters, produces only 1; average of 3 offspring. Very territorial; sexes maintain separate territories, often adjacent. Protects territory with vocalizations, scent markings on rocks (from glands in cheek/chin) and urine. Young are precocial; mature in 6 weeks.

Pika haypile

Mouthfuls of red elderberries and blue columbines seem no burden for this close relative of rabbits and hares, as it scampers among rocks and alpine meadows. With laser-like intent, pikas literally "make hay while the sun shines" during late summer and fall. After drying their "hay" in the sun to prevent rotting, pikas haul it into their dens and placed it in hard-to-reach crevices between rocks and boulders. They locate the haypiles near the center of their territory to become food for the long winter ahead. Haypiles of a single pika can cover up to 120 square yards (100 m²) and contain more than thirty different plant species. Researchers on Niwot Ridge in Colorado found that pikas included alpine avens in their piles to prevent rot. Though toxic when fresh, avens can be eaten when toxins degrade after drying. Pikas do avoid some plants early in the season, whose toxic nature could be a defense mechanism to deter cutting before seeds are set. Before haying begins, much of a pika's day is spent sitting motionless, perfectly camouflaged against the rocks, monitoring and protecting its territory.

PIKAS MAINTAIN THE BALANCE

A pika's constant grazing and "haying" activities help reduce interspecies competition, by preventing any one plant species from becoming dominant. This helps to maintain the diversity and abundance of plants in alpine meadows.

HARE and RABBIT FAMILY *Leporidae*

Relatively large and long-legged, hares live above ground and their young are born fully furred with eyes open. Rabbits are smaller, usually dig or use burrows for protection and their young are born furless, blind and vulnerable. Form often follows function in nature. Hares seek out sparsely-wooded habitat, where they can evade predators with speed and still find cover, whereas rabbits, with their shorter legs, rarely venture far from their burrows, and are found in thick vegetation where they can easily hide. All species in this group are listed as small game in Colorado.

Nuttall's Cottontail, Mountain Cottontail

Sylvilagus nuttallii

COMMON

TODD W. PATRICK

Habitat/feeding: Montane to timberline. Oak-mountain shrublands, forest edges. Avoids dense streamside vegetation and deep conifer forests. Less nocturnal than other rabbit species. Can be seen feeding early mornings and evenings if undisturbed. Diet of grasses and herbs in summer; twigs, young bark and buds in winter; also sagebrush, rabbitbrush and juniper berries. **Field ID traits:** Small rabbit, total length of 13–16 in. (34–42 cm). Short ears tipped in black; furry-white inside, grayish-brown in back. **Tracking notes:** Feet are fur covered. Tracks rarely show toe or pad marks. Usually hops with paired hind feet landing in front of offset front feet, most easily observed in snow. Scat is a small, dry flattened sphere. **Reproduction:** Mostly solitary. Does not form pair bonds. Nests are lined with soft grasses and fur plucked by the female from her own body; use burrows of other mammals instead of digging their own. Gestation 28–30 days, more than 4 young per litter, 4 litters per year. Young born March–July; atricial, weaned after 1 month.

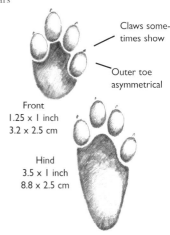

Claws sometimes show

Outer toe asymmetrical

Front
1.25 x 1 inch
3.2 x 2.5 cm

Hind
3.5 x 1 inch
8.8 x 2.5 cm

Dewdrops still glisten on surrounding vegetation as Nuttall's cottontail, the only rabbit in this area, nibbles warily on tender grasses and herbs, chewing in its side-to-side manner. At the sign of any threat, it dashes off to find cover or freezes briefly in a crouch, facing away from the danger. A prolific breeder, this local lagomorph feeds many of the resident carnivores, which include foxes, badgers, coyotes, great horned owls, hawks, eagles, weasels and bobcats. Average life expectancy is less than one year. Cottontails rest in shallow depressions, or "forms," among protective vegetation most of the day, where they nest.

HARRY WALKER

Snowshoe Hare
Lepus americanus
COMMON

Habitat/feeding: Upper montane to timberline. Prefers young coniferous forests, or old-growth conifer forests with openings. Especially abundant near willow thickets, which provide cover and forage. Diet of leaves, tender twigs and bark of shrubs and trees; also grasses and herbs; conifer needles and buds in winter. Mostly nocturnal and solitary, spends daytime resting in protected hollows among shrubs or conifers. **Field ID traits:** Total length of 13–21 in. (32–52 cm). Heavily furred, snowshoe-shaped hind feet. Turns totally white in winter except for black-tipped ears; often retains white stockings in summer.

White-tailed jackrabbit (*Lepus townsendii*) has white rump and tail, larger ears and still brownish above in winter; nearly extirpated from sagebrush and oak-mountain shrublands in upper Roaring Fork Valley, possibly due to loss of habitat.[6] **Tracking notes:** Typical hopping pattern, in which unmistakably large "snowshoe" rear feet land together in front of offset, smaller front feet; more easily observed in snow. Look for nipped branch tips, cut at a clean 45° angle, on both deciduous and conifer trees. **Reproduction:** Males feisty and aggressive during breeding season, though females most dominant in territorial disputes. Breeds mid-April to September; 2–3 litters averaging 3–4 precocial young. Dates and numbers fluctuate in relation to food availability.

Track is indistinctive because the foot is completely haired.

Hind feet are very wide to provide flotation on snow.

Front
1.75 x 1.5 inches
4.4 x 3.8 cm

Hind
4.5 x 3.75 to 4.5 inches
12.5 x 9.4 to 12.5 cm

Large, densely furred hind feet with toes that can spread wide provide this hare with excellent flotation over deep winter snow. The snowshoe hare's distinctive track pattern is a common sight from chair lifts during ski season. They are often overlapped by those of predators such as coyotes, foxes, bobcats, marten and weasels. Occasionally the hare's tracks disappear and those of the hunter continue, or the wings of an owl leave a clear impression in the snow, obliterating the tracks beneath. Both are sure signs of a successful hunt. In the Yukon, pine squirrels are known to prey on young snowshoe hares, although it is unknown whether they do this here.[7] Since snowshoe hare is a crucial food for Canada lynx, any lynx reintroduction effort will depend upon a healthy hare population.

RODENTS
Order Rodentia

Rodents, which first appeared about 65 million years ago, now occur in greater numbers, more diversity and wider distribution than any other mammalian family. They occupy almost every ecological niche in aquatic, subterranean, arboreal and terrestrial ecosystems. Though not often charismatic, these gnawing mammals play important roles in the web of life as both prey and predator. Rodent species run the gamut from herbivore to carnivore to insectivore, creating vital links in the flow of energy through ecosystems. Their sheer numbers and adaptability make them invaluable to the basic structure and function of ecosystems. More visible mammals such as bears, mountain lions, bobcats, foxes, coyotes and predatory birds would not exist without this food base of plant-eating rodents. With their burrowing and tunneling, rodents aerate the soil, recycle soil layers and improve water percolation; their feces fertilize the soil, and their foraging and storing plays a large role in the distribution of seeds and fungi spores.

North American rodents are threatened by extreme habitat loss from urbanization, grazing, fire suppression, logging, agricultural changes to habitat and other alterations. The Species Survival Commission of the IUCN—International Union for Conservation of Nature and Natural Resources—has developed a Status and Conservation Action Plan to assess the status of rodents worldwide and to establish conservation measures to save this important order of mammals.

SQUIRREL FAMILY   *Sciuridae*

Wherever raptors soar, you can rest assured that members of the squirrel family, which includes chipmunks, ground squirrels and marmots as well as the tree-dwellers, are somewhere below. Squirrels, like other rodents, play an important ecological role in supporting predators, and have adapted successfully to nearly every habitat available.

Tree squirrels, ground squirrels and flying squirrels have each found specific ecological niches. Tree squirrels have long bushy tails and occasional ear tufts; ground squirrels typically have strong front legs adapted for tunneling; and flying squirrels are equipped with a furry membrane between ankle and wrist that allows them to soar from tree to tree. While many other animals are elusive and/ or nocturnal, most members of this family are active during the day and are considered the most eminently watchable wildlife!

WHICH IS WHICH?

One of the easiest ways to tell chipmunks from golden-mantled ground squirrels is that chipmunks have stripes on their face, whereas ground squirrels do not.

ROBIN HENRY

Least Chipmunk
Tamias minimus
ABUNDANT IN DISTURBED HABITATS,
FAIRLY COMMON IN QUALITY HABITAT

Habitat/feeding: Montane to alpine. Found in more diverse array of habitats than other chipmunks in Colorado; more common in open areas or along edges. Excavates tunnel systems under rocks, logs, tree roots and shrubs. Eats fruits, berries, flowers, seeds, leaves and stems, plus insects and carrion, depending on availability. Dormant during winter, arousing occasionally to eat food cached in its den. **Field ID traits:** Colorado's smallest chipmunk, total length 7–8.5 in. (19–22 cm). Coloration variable, depending on location; usually has 5 dark stripes (center stripe reaches from head to tail) alternating with 4 whitish stripes across the back; 2 whitish facial stripes. Lateral stripes mostly darker than other Colorado chipmunks.
Reproduction: Gestation about 1 month; litter of 4–6 young.

Front
0.5 x 0.4 inches
1.3 x 1 cm

Hind
0.7 x 0.6 inches
1.8 x 1.5 cm

Heel not included in track measurement.

Least chipmunks are often confused with Uinta chipmunks (*Tamias umbrinus*). However, the less common Uintas are larger, with a total length of 8.5-9 in. (21-23 cm) and are not as brightly colored, with less distinct lateral stripes, grayish flanks and brownish fur on their back. Uintas are also found in montane to alpine areas, but tend to be more common in rocky areas such as talus slopes or forest-edge habitats, particularly lodgepole, up to 12,000 ft. (3660 m).

ROBIN HENRY

ROCK SQUIRRELS (*Spermophilus variegatus*)

Rock squirrels are found in the montane on rocky, south-facing slopes, bordering pinyon-juniper and oak-mountain shrubland communities. They are closely related to the ground squirrels on the following page and are relatively uncommon. Colorado's largest ground squirrel, measuring 17–21 in. (44–53 cm), they have a bushy tail that may mislead you. Rock squirrels look like tree squirrels, but spend most of their time on the ground. Their shoulders are obviously darker than the rump, and they have a white eye-ring.

Golden-Mantled Ground Squirrel
Spermophilus lateralis
COMMON

Habitat/feeding: Montane to alpine. Diverse habitats from open woodlands, riparian areas and oak-mountain shrublands to mountain meadows and forest edges. Diet mainly vegetation, seeds and fungi; also eats birds' eggs and young, insects and carrion. **Field ID Traits:** Gregarious and adaptable medium-sized ground squirrel, 9.5–12 in. (24–30 cm). Reddish-brown mantle cloaks head and shoulders. Two whitish stripes bordered by relatively wide black stripes reach from shoulders to back; white eye-ring. **Reproduction:** Nest in burrows. Usually breeds at 1 year of age. Gestation 28–30 days; litter of 2–8 young. Mostly solitary; sometimes congregates where fed by people. Typically lives 2–3 years.

ROBIN HENRY

These appealing ground squirrels are quite adaptable to the presence of humans. Local campers are very familiar with these friendly campground hosts! Western toads sometimes live in its burrows when the ground squirrel leaves.

1-2-1 toe spacing

1-3-1 toe spacing

Front
0.75 x 0.6 inches
1.3 x 1.5 cm

Hind
1 x 0.75 inches
2.5 x 1.9 cm

Wyoming Ground Squirrel
Spermophilus elegans
COMMON

Habitat/feeding: Montane to alpine. Grasslands, pastures, and disturbed areas of oak-mountain and sagebrush shrublands. Lives in large social groups in open grassy areas. Mounds of dirt mark the entrance to their extensive tunnels. Diet of herbs and grasses; also carrion. **Field ID traits:** Medium-sized with fairly long tail; total length 9.8–13 in. (25–34 cm). Brownish-drab to buffy-gray, lighter beneath. Visitors from prairie dog country may confuse this ground squirrel with **Gunnison's prairie dog** (*Cynomys gunnisoni*), which has a shorter tail and chunkier body. Though sometimes referred to as **Richardson's ground squirrel** (*Spermophilus richardsoni*), Wyoming is considered a separate species.[8] Reproduction: Male establishes and defends territory during breeding season; female may defend area around natal burrow. Gestation 22–23 days, litter averages 4–5 young.

CHARLES W. MELTON

Front
0.75 x 0.6 inches
1.9 x 1.5 cm

Hind
1 x 0.75 inches
2.5 x 1.9 cm

Heel not included in track measurement.

391

Wyoming ground squrrels have expanded in Colorado following human development and agriculture. Overgrazing by cattle may increase their habitat. Though considered pests due to the damage their burrows cause to landscaping and agricultural lands, their tunneling can be beneficial. Extensive tunnel systems channel precipitation deep into the water table, promoting deeper infiltration of soil moisture. Their digging also increases soil aeration and softens and loosens the soil. Known as "picket pins" for their upright alert-to-danger stance, they are quite entertaining to watch, constantly gathering food and interacting with each other. They retreat below ground to hibernate as early as mid-July, no later than mid-September, not returning sunnyside until March or April.

FROM GRASS TO COYOTE?

Wyoming ground squirrels are an essential part of the food chain in this area, providing food for many predators, from badgers to golden eagles. Some say that Wyoming ground squirrels are nature's way of turning grass into coyotes!

ROBIN HENRY

Yellow-Bellied Marmot, Whistle-Pig
Marmota flaviventris
COMMON

Habitat/feeding: Montane to alpine. Meadows with rocky outcrops up to 14,000 ft. (4267 m). Graze on a diversity of herbs, but prefer dandelions, chiming bells, cinquefoil, cow parsnip and brome (grass), forming obvious paths as they crawl on their bellies to gorge. Also eat flowers considered toxic, such as larkspur and lupine, apparently ignoring parts with higher amounts of toxins. Diurnal, most active mornings and evenings. **Field ID traits:** Housecat-sized; body length up to 24 in. (60 cm), tail length up to 10 in. (25 cm). Stout, thickly furred body; yellowish belly. Typically with white band across nose and buffy patches on side of neck. **Tracking notes:** Similar to beaver, but without webbing between toes. **Reproduction:** Male mates with a single female or entire harem. 1 litter, averaging 4 young, weaned by mid-July. Mostly social, living in somewhat stable colonies.

Front
2.2 x 1.8 inches
5.5 x 4.5 cm

Hind
2.8 x 2 inches
7 x 5 cm

Lounging in the sun atop large boulders along trails and roadways, these plump, furry mammals are a favorite with residents and visitors. Marmots that appear to be lounging are usually on the alert as sentinels to warn the colony of danger. Known for their sharp, loud, single-note whistle, marmots are affectionately called "whistle-pigs." Their high-pitched squeal is often confused with the pika's squeak; however, marmots are hibernating rodents with long tails and they inhabit a greater range in elevation. Possibly the epitome of the "couch potato," marmots spend 60% of their lives hibernating in their burrows. True hibernators, their winter sleep is so deep, construction workers have dug into their burrows without arousing them. Most marmots are quite social, living in colonies of a single male and several females with offspring. Social activities within the colony include playing, grooming, chasing and fighting.

Pine Squirrel, Chickaree, Spruce Squirrel
Tamiasciurus hudsonicus
COMMON

Habitat/feeding: Montane to subalpine. Conifer forests. Diet mostly of conifer seeds and mushrooms; also berries, buds and leaves. Active year-round; more in cooler times of day in summer, midday in winter. **Field ID traits:** Total length 12–14 in. (30–35 cm). Though called "red squirrel" elsewhere, the color in this area is only slightly reddish-brown in summer, and grayish in winter; bushy tail is sooty-gray to cinnamon (colors highly variable). Distinctive white eye ring. Small ear tufts.

Tracking notes: Slender toes of front foot arranged in 1-2-1 grouping; rear toes in 1-3-1 grouping. Fairly short claws. Track pattern shows rear feet land ahead of front feet. **Reproduction:** Nest of twigs, leaves and grasses nestled in conifer branches 10–66 ft. (3–20 m) above ground. Female able to mate 1 day only, mid-April to mid-June in Colorado; gestation 33–35 days. 1 litter/year, 2–5 young; leave nest after about 40 days, forage alone at about 1½ months.

CHARLES W. MELTON

Only tree squirrel in this area

Chattering and scolding, pine squirrels are the watchdogs of the forest, eagerly defending their territory against any perceived threat, which includes hikers. Many a camper has awakened to the continuous "plop, plop, plop" on their tent's roof, as one of these industrious rodents lops off still-green conifer cones to be buried for winter storage. A single squirrel may cut up to 16,000 cones per year, placing them in storage piles beneath the trees known as middens. As the squirrel shucks a cone from the branches above to eat the seeds, core and cone scales are discarded, adding to the midden below. Middens may become as large as 30 ft. (9 m) wide and 3 ft. (1 m) deep when used by successive generations of squirrels. The cool, damp conditions inside middens are ideal for keeping seeds fresh and preventing rot. Uneaten cones may eventually germinate,

Front
1 x 1 inch
2.5 x 2.5 cm

3 palm pads
2 heel pads

4 palm pads

Hind
0.9 x 1 inch
2.3 x 2.5 cm

Heel not included in measurement,

replacing the parent tree. Black bears sometimes invade these squirrel pantries in search of conifer seeds, and foresters often depend on them as a source of seed for reforestation. Pine squirrels are capable of burrowing beneath snow to reach buried cones, but rarely need to do so as heavy conifer boughs above these seed caches prevent deep snow accumulations. Pine squirrels are preyed upon by northern goshawk, great horned owl, red fox, lynx, weasel and marten. Healthy chickaree populations should encourage lynx recovery.

> *Though only a few inches long, so intense is his [the chickaree's] fiery vigor and restlessness, he stirs every grove with wild life, and makes himself more important than even the huge bears that shuffle through the tangled underbrush beneath him.*
>
> —JOHN MUIR, 1894

POCKET GOPHER FAMILY *Geomyidae*

Pocket gophers are the only true gophers, though the name is commonly given to a wide range of burrowing rodents. Powerful digging machines, these short-tailed creatures have strong front legs and sturdy claws. Unlike most other rodents, which have internal cheek pouches, their soil-carrying "pockets" are external, and come with fur linings to prevent soil from sticking to the inner surfaces. Pocket gophers are fairly isolated genetically, due to their sedentary habits and underground lifestyle. Populations only a few miles apart may have totally distinct gene pools.

PEGGY LYON

Northern pocket gopher eskers

Northern Pocket Gopher
Thomomys talpoides
COMMON

Habitat/feeding: Montane to alpine tundra. Roots, bulbs and tubers are winter diet. Spring and summer diet mostly leaves and stems of composites, legumes and other herbaceous plants; some grasses. Store cached food in side tunnels. **Field ID traits:** Rarely seen. Total length 6.5–8 in. (16.5–20 cm). Small and stocky, with small eyes and ears. Dark brown to nearly black in western Colorado. Yellowish-orange incisors are very visible because the lips close behind, allowing them to move rocks and soil with their teeth. **Tracking notes:** Evidence of their burrowing activity, called "eskers," is usually all that is seen of a pocket gopher. Signs of American badger or weasel, their main predators, may be found near areas of recent gopher activity. **Reproduction:** Tolerate other pocket gophers only during mating season. Little is known regarding reproduction. Only 4–7 young are born February–June each year; 2 litters possible.

Sinuous mounds of soil, called eskers, snake across the landscape wherever gophers tunneled during the winter, packing their trails beneath the snow with excavated soil. Tunnel excavation, as much as 16 in. (40 cm) below the surface, has a significant effect on the blending and vertical recycling of soil components. It also provides valuable aeration and allows water to penetrate into the soil. Where they occur in alpine habitats, pocket gophers are probably the most influential animal, because their constant nibbling of plants and tunneling prevents any one plant species from becoming dominant. These areas of intense gopher activity, called "gopher gardens," are the most diverse of alpine plant ecosystems (see p. 50).

DR. LLOYD GLENN INGLES

BEAVER FAMILY *Castoridae*

During the last Ice Age, nearly 2 million years ago, the beaver family consisted of gargantuan species, some as big as bears, weighing up to 700 lb. (320 kg). Today there are only two species, the American and European beavers, which continue to be some of the earth's largest rodents, weighing up to 100 lb. (45 kg).

Beavers are specially adapted for aquatic living, with their own "swim goggles" called nictating membranes, transparent inner eyelids that cover their eyes while underwater. They also have evolved valvular ears and nostrils to keep water out, dense waterproof fur, flipper-like webbed hind feet and baggy cheeks that suck in so that the lips close behind the incisors, allowing the beaver to carry and chew wood underwater.

AN INCREDIBLE ECOLOGICAL FEAT— COMEBACK FROM NEAR EXTINCTION

Before the arrival of Europeans there were at least 60 million beavers in North America. Colonists coveted their thick, silky, waterproof fur for coats and hats, even using the pelts as currency. By the early 1900's, trapping had reduced their numbers to about 100,000. Though managed as furbearers in Colorado, with thousands harvested annually, they have recovered in most places and are appreciated for the important role they play in water conservation and the maintenance of river ecosystems. In the Roaring Fork Valley, beavers are actively recolonizing former habitat. Up and down the Roaring Fork River and its tributaries, beavers are reengineering our riparian communities, which benefits many other species such as ducks, herons, voles and black bears.

CHARLES W. MELTON

American Beaver
Castor canadensis
COMMON

Habitat/feeding: Montane to alpine. Feeds mainly on bark, twigs, buds and leaves of aspens; also eats willows, cottonwoods and aquatic plants. Special microflora in the stomach digest woody material; also reingests its own feces to retrieve further nutrients. Crepuscular; sometimes diurnal. **Field ID traits:** One of the largest rodents in the world and the largest in North America, averaging 66 lb. (30 kg) and measuring 33–47 in. (84–120 cm) in total length. Flat, scaly, paddle-shaped tail unique in the animal kingdom. Small rounded ears, large orange-red front teeth, webbed hind feet. **Tracking notes:** Tracks of large, webbed, 5-toed hind feet frequently wiped out by dragging tail. Around ponds and along streams, watch for plunge holes emptying into underground canals and slippery ruts leading into the water, which allow a quick escape from predators. More obvious are their conical log and mud lodges surrounded by water contained behind skillfully engineered dams across creeks and streams. See p. 34. **Reproduction:** Monogamous. 1 litter per year. Breeds January–early March; young born about 110 days later; able to swim within a week and weaned by about 6 weeks. When the new litter is about to be born, even males and 1-year-old kits leave the lodge temporarily. Young leave the family at 2 years of age to find own territory, reducing competition for food resources. See lodge.

5th toe may not register

Front
3 x 2.75 inches
7.5 x 7.0 cm

Large broad nails; 2nd toe may not show.

Webbing

Hind
5 x 5.5 inches
12.5 x 13.8 cm

Beavers are very industrious in altering habitats to suit their own needs—only humans have a greater impact on the environment. Slow-moving on land, a beaver will not rest until it has dammed a stream, creating a pond for protection against predators and better access to food. Dug canals broaden its escape network and make ferrying of heavy logs easier. "Plunge holes" and tunnels under the banks provide further escape routes to the pond. An efficient chainsaw, the beaver braces its body with tail and hind legs to achieve a tripod effect, holds its head sideways and cuts at the top and bottom of a chip before tearing it out. A beaver's mud and log lodge can be partially on land or completely surrounded by water, with a hole for ventilation at the top. There is an underwater entrance opening onto a draining/feeding platform, which then leads to an upper level for sleeping. Willow, aspen and cottonwood sticks are gathered and stuck in the mud just outside the underwater entrance during late summer and fall. This is called a food whorl and serves as a "winter pantry." Occasionally, leftover willows take root and

A beaver can capably cut down a tree 4.7 in. (12 cm) in diameter in 3 minutes.

grow there. Ponds formed behind beaver dams slow spring runoff, reduce flooding, retain water for release during dry times of the year, and create improved habitat for other wildlife, all signs of a healthy watershed. Beavers may die from predation, disease, starvation or drowning, but man is responsible for most of their mortality, taking 5,000–10,000 annually in Colorado. They are killed for their fur or when considered pests in agricultural or residential areas. Otherwise, they can live up to twenty years.

INSTINCTIVE?
SUCH SUPERB ENGINEERING MAKES YOU WONDER

Fast-moving water does little to slow a beaver's fierce determination. A definite upstream bend is part of their design from the beginning, to counteract pressure from fast water, redirecting it to the more stable sides of the stream. Beavers laboriously maneuver stones and logs into position as a base for the dam, wider at the bottom where the water's force is greatest, then carefully wedge sticks under rocks and into mud with their free ends pointing downstream. Next, they weave a latticework of brush into the base, which catches debris and flotsam. They continue to weigh down the rapidly growing dam with logs and fresh mud.

RAT, MICE, VOLE and MUSKRAT FAMILY
Muridae

Members of the largest rodent family, consisting of 260 genera and at least 1,100 species, these small critters are usually the most abundant mammals in most ecosystems, having a large impact on energy flow. By consuming plants and then being consumed by larger predators such as foxes, mountain lions, hawks and owls, they in effect transfer energy from the sun up through the food chain. Only Antarctica and a few oceanic islands such as New Zealand and Iceland lack native species of this family. Mice, voles and muskrats in this area are active year-round. Mice and voles are busy tunneling beneath the protective snowpack in winter, while muskrats can be seen waddling along the frozen edges of creeks and streams during the day. Although they are not often seen and are difficult to differentiate without a detailed guide, short descriptions of members in this family are given in this section for readers interested in species found here.

Their very abundance, combined with their role as herbivores, converting plant energy to animal tissue, means that in the food web, they are like tiny Atlases holding up the world.

—MARY TAYLOR GRAY,
Gnawing Natives: Colorado's Mice & Rats

Rat, Mice, Vole and Muskrat Group

SHATTIL/ROZINSKI PHOTOGRAPHY

Deer Mouse
Peromyscus maniculatus
ABUNDANT IN DISTURBED HABITATS—
FAIRLY COMMON IN QUALITY HABITATS

Montane. Most common small mammal in North America, occupying all elevations and every native habitat except wetlands. Their generalist diet consists mostly of seeds, but also includes insects, fungi, carrion, bone, plants, even birds' young and eggs.[9] Total length 5–7 in. (14–18 cm). Relatively large eyes and ears, grayish-brown fur above, white feet and underparts, and a bi-colored tail shorter than the rest of their body. Tracks are tiny replicas of snowshoe hare tracks, most easily seen in snow; tail drag may be evident. Breeding begins when only 7–8 weeks old, with several litters of 2–8 young produced each year. Active year-round, they withstand cold weather by traveling in tunnels beneath insulating layers of snow, huddling together in nests for greater warmth, and sometimes entering a state of semi-hibernation that is called torpor. Deer mice are carriers of the airborne hanta virus, which can be fatal to humans.

Remnant pad

Front
0.3 x 0.3 inches
0.8 x 0.8 cm

Hind
0.4 x 0.3 inches
1 x 0.8 cm

Four toes on front;
Five toes on hind foot;
Typically shows tail drag.

> Deer mice are the quintessential disturbance species. Natural areas undergoing any type of disturbance, such as roads or trails, experience an increase in the deer mouse population.

CHRIS GRONDAHL

Bushy-tailed Woodrat
Neotoma cinerea
FAIRLY COMMON TO UNCOMMON IN QUALITY HABITAT

Montane to alpine. Forests to talus fields. Relatively large, 13–16.5 in. (34–42 cm), with a bushy tail; buff to gray fur with blackish wash; buffy sides and white hairs on chest and throat; tail dark gray and whitish beneath. Like other woodrats, this species builds a cup-shaped nest lined with thin plant fibers.

FENG SHUI EXPERTS THEY AREN'T. Bushy-tailed woodrats are the traditional high-mountain packrats. They hoard bottle caps, buttons, cans, plants, bones and scraps of material and metal, along with edibles such as leaves, conifer needles, berries and mushrooms, in their nest or midden. Some bushy-tailed woodrat nests are thousands of years old, enabling archeologists to document changes in climate and plant communities. Great climbers, these rodents prefer vertical crevices in cliff walls to horizontal habitats.

Meadow Vole
Microtus pennsylvanicus
COMMON

Montane to subalpine. Mostly associated with moist or wet meadows or bog habitats with a dense cover of grasses, herbs, sedges and rushes. Total length 6–7.5 in. (15.5–19 cm). Grayish brown on top, silvery gray beneath; bi-colored tail; dark, "beady" eyes. Good swimmer.

SHATTIL/ROZINSKI PHOTOGRAPHY

Meadow Vole (*Microtus pennsylvanicus*). Species of voles are difficult to distinguish from one another, but this photo shows how they differ from mice and shrews. It is also helpful to consider their size and habitat. Voles tend to have shorter tails than mice.

Front
0.3 x 0.3 inches
0.8 x 0.8 cm

Hind
0.4 x 0.3 inches
1 x 0.8 cm

Four toes on front;
Five toes on hind foot;
Seldom shows tail drag.

Heel not included in track measurement.

Southern Red-Backed Vole
Clethrionomys gapperi
COMMON IN QUALITY HABITAT

Montane to subalpine. Spruce-fir and lodgepole forests. Total length 5-6 in. (12.5–15 cm). A handsome vole with a reddish stripe down its grayish-brown back, contrasting with the buffy sides. Bi-colored tail. Red-backed voles typically select moist habitats, which may account for the reason that they consume more water than other small rodents. Burrows under rocks or logs; also tunnels beneath needle litter on forest floor. Sometimes lives in squirrel middens, a good source of seeds and fungi. Nests usually orange-sized, made from vegetation. Mostly nocturnal.

Heather Vole
Phenacomys intermedius
UNCOMMON

Montane to alpine. Not especially numerous, but adapts well to a number of different habitats, including aspen, spruce-fir and lodgepole forests, meadows and tundra. Total length 5–5.76 in. (12.5–15 cm). Fluffy fur, bi-colored tail is dark above and pale beneath with a sprinkling of white hairs. Stiff orange hairs in ears. Tail only a bit longer than hind foot. Often frequents areas with substantial ground cover of bilberry.

Long-tailed Vole
Microtus longicaudus
COMMON IN QUALITY HABITAT

Montane to alpine. Common in a wide variety of habitats in the mountains, usually near water. A small body compared to the long tail; total length 6.8–7.7 in. (17.4–19.6 cm). Reddish-brown to brownish gray with black-tipped hairs. Pale gray beneath.

Montane Vole
Microtus montanus
COMMON IN QUALITY HABITAT

Montane to alpine. Favors moist to wet habitats, where its well-developed run-ways used as foraging paths through vegetation can be seen. Total length 6-7 in. (15.5–18 cm). Grayish to grayish-brown with some yellow wash present; silvery gray beneath. Difficult to distin-guish from other voles.

Muskrat
Ondatra zibethicus
FAIRLY COMMON

Rudimentary 5th toe

Front
1.3 x 1.2 inches
3.3 x 3.0 cm

Long finger-like toes.

Hind
1.3 x 1.6 inches
3.3 x 4.1 cm

Riparian habitats in all ecosystems. Although often confused with beavers, muskrats are much smaller, at about 18–22 in. (45–56 cm) in total length. Their long, skinny tails are com-pressed from the sides, unlike the paddle-shaped tails of beavers, and they have webbed hind feet. However, like beavers, they are adapted to live a comfortable, semi-aquatic life. They typically inhabit bank burrows or small conical houses near the water's edge, composed of sedges, rushes and cattails. Muskrats maintain congenial relations with beavers, and sometimes even live in their lodges, thus not expending any energy themselves in construction of living quarters. Muskrats are sometimes controlled in waterfowl production areas, as they will eat all of the protective marshy vegetation. When vegetation is not available, they feed upon fish, crayfish, mollusks and carrion. Polygamous, or sometimes monogamous, they produce 2 litters per year of 4–8 young that are weaned by 4 weeks. Muskrats are North America's most valuable semi-aquatic furbearer. Active mostly dusk to dawn.

ROBIN HENRY

Muskrat

JUMPING MICE FAMILY *Family Zapodidae*

Jumping mice are naturally adapted for jumping movement with long hind feet and hind legs. They have been on the earth some 40 million years. Of eleven species, two are found in Colorado and only one in this valley. The other, Preble's meadow jumping mouse, is found on the Front Range, is listed as threatened, and protected under the Endangered Species Act. Lush, non-woody vegetation is their preferred habitat.

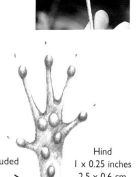

Western Jumping Mouse

Zapus princeps

COMMON IN QUALITY HABITAT

Habitat/feeding: Streamside communities up to 11,000 ft. (3353 m). Require high-energy diet of seeds, insects and spiders to gain enough weight to survive nearly 9 month hibernation. **Field ID traits:** Total length 8–10 in. (20–26 cm). Back is yellowish-gray with distinct blackish patch. **Reproduction:** Underground hibernating chambers lined with soft, dried plant matter; entrance may be plugged with soil. Only 1 litter of 3–8 young is born during summer.

Front
0.4 x 0.25 inches
1 x 0.6 cm

Long narrow hind feet.

Tail-drag is typical.

Heel not included in track measurement.

Hind
1 x 0.25 inches
2.5 x 0.6 cm

Western jumping mice live longer than any similar sized mammal. Some biologists believe that this species' long life span, which may exceed four years, is due to a low birth rate and deep hibernation, which removes these mice from the food chain and lowers their heart rate for an extended period of time. They are mostly nocturnal when not in hibernation.

NEW WORLD PORCUPINE FAMILY *Erethizontidae*

Porcupines evolved in South America during the Oligocene epoch (38–23 million years ago) but did not reach North America until the late Pliocene, 5–1.8 million years ago. They are best known for their sharp, penetrating barbed quills, which are actually modified guard hairs. Although there are five genera and twelve species in this family, this is the only porcupine north of the Mexican border.

TODD W. PATRICK

To me, [porcupines] are the Buddhas of the forest, quiet and looking down on you.

—MOLLY HALE, *University of Massachusetts researcher*

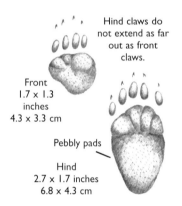

Hind claws do not extend as far out as front claws.

Front
1.7 x 1.3 inches
4.3 x 3.3 cm

Pebbly pads

Hind
2.7 x 1.7 inches
6.8 x 4.3 cm

Common Porcupine
Erethizon dorsatum
COMMON

Habitat/feeding: Montane to subalpine. Lodgepole pine, Douglas-fir and ponderosa pine forest; also oak-mountain shrubland. Summer diet of buds and leaves of trees, shrubs and ground vegetation; fall and winter diet of acorns and inner bark. Mostly nocturnal, but can be diurnal.
Field ID traits: Protective cloak of about 30,000 sharp, minutely barbed quills, yellowish with dark tips, up to 4 in. (10 cm) long. Weighs about 15 lb. (7 kg), possibly up to 40 lb. (18 kg). Lifespan in wild 5–7 years; up to 15 years in captivity. **Tracking notes:** Feet have a nobby surface for grip while climbing. Palm and heel pads seem to merge, leaving the impression of a single beaded-looking pad on soft surfaces. Rings of bark removed from trunks of trees are indicative of winter feeding and can kill the tree if bark is removed all the way around. **Reproduction:** Sexes remain apart except during mating season. Gestation about 210 days. Young born well-furred and soft-quilled; quills harden soon after birth. Young begin foraging with mother after 1–2 weeks; weaned in about 4 months.

Although plump and clumsy looking, a porcupine has feet endowed with bumpy, non-skid soles, a strong tail for bracing against tree trunks and long curved claws for gripping the bark. Slowly and deliberately they wind their way among the branches or perch precariously while dining. Apparently prone to falls that are sometimes fatal, biologists have found that porcupines' bones often bear evidence of many old breaks. Craving salt, they will lick and gnaw anything containing perspiration, including leather saddles and bridles left unprotected by backcountry horseback riders. Though their quills ward off most predators, coyotes, mountain lions, bears and bobcats can kill a porcupine by flipping it over and attacking the unprotected abdominal area.

THE BIG MYTH

The myth that porcupines throw their quills has been perpetuated for centuries. In fact, the loosely attached quills must come into contact with the object of attack. A porcupine achieves this by turning, raising the quills and whipping its hindquarters back and forth.[10]

CARNIVORES
Order Carnivora

C harismatic predators, carnivores are found at the top of the food chain. Conservationists are greatly concerned about protecting these apex species, as their survival is linked to complex interrelationships with all the other species, defining the ecological integrity of whole ecosystems. Unfortunately, a carnivore's requirement for large territories brings them into increased competition with humans for dwindling space and resources.

CANINE FAMILY—
DOGS, FOXES and ALLIES   *Canidae*

M embers of this family are often referred to as canids. They include coyotes, foxes and wolves, as well as domestic dogs. Most canids are adapted for living in very cold climates. Thick fur, walking repeatedly in the same trails in deep snow and a flexible diet allow them to conserve energy. Being long-legged and digitigrade, meaning they walk on their toes, gives them longer, faster strides so they are able to overtake prey more quickly. Adapted more for endurance than for speed over long distances, they can catch prey simply by tiring them out. Canids often hunt in packs, allowing them to bring down much larger prey than possible individually. Although sense of smell and hearing are acute, their eyesight is less well developed. They possess anal scent glands, which are important for identifying each other as well as scenting their urine for marking their territory. Sweat glands are present on the pads of their paws, which may help increase frictional contact with steep ground, and may serve as a type of scent communication with other canids.

Let's appreciate coyotes for the amazing beings they are. They offer valuable lessons in survival. Though coyotes try our patience, they're a model animal for learning about adaptability and success by nonhuman individuals striving to make it in a human-dominated world. Coyotes, like Proteus the Greek, who could change his form at will and avoid capture, are truly "protean predators." They're a success story, perhaps hapless victims of their own success. Coyotes: love them and leave them be.[11]

—MARC BEKOFF, Professor of Biology, University of Colorado

ROBIN HENRY

Coyote
Canis latrans
COMMON

Habitat/feeding: Montane to alpine. All habitats. An opportunist, exploiting whatever habitat and food sources available. Primary diet of small rodents, fruits, berries and carrion; especially juniper berries in winter. Thought to prey on young of elk and deer instead of healthy adults, but can kill an adult deer; also eats insects, including grasshoppers and beetles. Hunts mostly at dusk or dawn. **Field ID traits:**

Front
2.5 x 2.35 inches
6.3 x 5.8 cm

Hind
2.25 x 1.9 inches
5.7 x 4.8 cm

V-shaped
ridge on heel pads.

Adult male averages 30–50 lb. (13–23 kg) and has a total length of 3.5–4.5 ft. (1–1.5 m); larger than a red fox, but only about ⅓ the size of a wolf. Black-tipped tail. **Tracking notes:** Rear paws smaller than front ones. Prints are more oblong, less symmetrical and rounded than those of domestic dogs. Front and rear tracks often superimposed, looking as if left by a 2-legged animal. Scat is twisted and ropy-looking; hair from prey is often visible. **Reproduction:** Usually mates for life. Maintains den only during breeding season, February–March. May dig its own den, or give birth in abandoned dens of other animals, under large rocks or in caves. 4–7 pups born in April, nursed by alpha female. She is fed by regurgitation of food in small pieces by alpha male, and by remaining offspring from previous years; female offspring may even lactate and help nurse pups.[12]

Social structure based around this extended family unit, as they all care for pups together, teaching young to hunt at 8–9 weeks.

A haunting coyote chorus of yips, barks and howls echos across mountain valleys most nights. Music to the ears of many who live here or visit, it reminds us that we are still surrounded by wild country; that we are learning to coexist with wild predators.

Coyotes have been persecuted since the beginning of European settlement, blamed for the deaths of domestic livestock and pets. Despite aggressive efforts to eradicate them with poisons (which tend to accumulate and be dispersed throughout habitats when they are eaten by other wildlife), hunting from the ground and from airplanes, more coyotes roam the United States today than in the late 1800's. Biologists speculate that attempts by ranchers and wildlife agencies to reduce coyote populations may actually be having the opposite effect. Studies show that coyotes respond to persecution by having

A black-tipped tail, held down while running, distinguishes a coyote from the silver phase of the red fox with its white-tipped tail.

larger litters and reproducing at an earlier age. Extremely resilient and intelligent creatures, they learn from experience, training successive genera tions to avoid previous dangers. One of the most effective predators in North America, coyotes have colonized the entire United States, largely made possible by the elimination of their main competitors for prey—wolves and grizzlies.

Rather than look at coyotes as pests, it is important to consider the beneficial role they play in clearing carrion and controlling rodents. Where coyotes are present, domestic cats kill fewer birds, probably because the coyotes help control the number of cats.[13]

Gray wolves (*Canis lupus*), though not confirmed breeders in Colorado at the present, may move in or be reintroduced. They are up to three times heavier than a coyote and have several color variations.

Resourceful ranchers are finding some success protecting their herds using alternative means, such as guard dogs, corralling sheep and cattle during birth, cleaning up after ewes and cows and monitoring lambs and calves until they are older.[14] In some cases, deaths blamed on coyotes are natural deaths, with coyotes coming in to scavenge.

Cleaning up birdseed and dogfood and securing compost bins reduces the chances that coyotes will use our yards as hunting grounds and dine on our pets in the process. Coyotes rarely attack humans, posing less of a threat than domestic dogs.[15]

Coyotes are not adapted for deep snow, and will readily use trails packed for recreational use to access interior forest prey, such as squirrels and snowshoe hares. This can result in an unnatural competition between the intruders and forest interior predators, such as marten and lynx, who depend on these small mammals to survive. This type of stress from a predator that normally hunts in more open terrain could potentially lead to a decline of these interior species.

THE SLAUGHTER CONTINUES

The federal Wildlife Services (WS) program kills tens of thousands of coyotes each year (about 82,000 in 1999) because coyotes are blamed for livestock deaths.[16]

- Livestock protection programs cost U.S. taxpayers about $10–11 million annually, while 90% of WS money given to Colorado ($1.1 million) is spent on lethal control of native wildlife.

- 3.5 million coyotes have been killed in the U.S. in the past 50 years.

- Private hunters killed 26,000 coyotes during the 1999–2000 Colorado harvest season.

- Aerial gunning costs U.S. taxpayers from $180 to $800/animal. Sometimes, tens of thousands of dollars are spent to capture a single coyote, which might be responsible for a few hundred dollars worth of livestock damage.[17]

ROBIN HENRY

Red Fox

Vulpes vulpes

COMMON

Habitat/feeding: Montane to alpine. Open woodlands, meadows, forest edges, pastures; prefers areas near water. Hunts mostly small mammals (especially voles and deer mice), birds (especially ground nesters), reptiles and amphibians; also eats eggs, berries and nuts. Caches food under leaves, dirt or snow for later consumption. Acute hearing allows it to locate small mammals and insects underground. Active dusk to dawn when prey is active; more diurnal in winter. **Field ID traits:** Alert appearance with upright pointed ears, narrow nose. Total body length, including tail, 3–3.5 ft. (94–105 cm). Its tail, accounting for about 70% of length, is great protection from harsh weather when curled around body. Weighs 9–11 lb. (4–5 kg). Fur may be red, silver (blackish with silver tips on many hairs) or a cross between the two. Black or gray-black foxes have also been sighted. White-tipped tail. **Tracking notes:** Impressions of fur-covered paws often visible. Bar or line across heel pad is unique among canids. Hind tracks overlap front tracks when trotting. **Reproduction:** Mostly mates for life; male sometimes polygamous. Male competes for territory with other males with screaming threat duels, barking and scent-marking. Colorado foxes breed January–February and give birth in March or April; average litter size 4–5. Pups stay in den at least 1 month, fed milk only first 2 weeks, then given regurgitated food until ready to hunt at about 10 weeks. Non-breeding females may help raise young. Can excavate own den(s), but usually use old burrows of marmots or badgers, even cohabiting with original owners; may also use rock crevice. Den usually 20–25 ft. (6–7.6 m) long, though can be up to 60 ft. (18 m).

Front
2 x 1.8
inches
5 x 4.5 cm

Hind
1.9 x 1.7 inches
4.8 x 4.3 cm

V-shaped ridges on heel pads.

Often thought of as secretive, the red fox is one of the most visible wild residents, commonly seen absconding with balls on the golf courses. Long before modern biology proved otherwise, foxes were considered felines, because their pupils dilate elliptically like those of a cat, rather than circularly like a dog's. Foxes also crouch cat-like to stalk their prey. Gray foxes (*Urocyon cinereoargenteus*) even have semi-retractable nails and are able to climb trees.[18]

The white-tipped tail, held straight out when running, is key to identification.

The cleverness of a fox has been celebrated in literature and art for at least 2,500 years.[19] However, for all the respect we have accorded foxes, humans are still their fiercest predator, whether through hunting, or more recently, running them over. Red foxes are considered vermin in many parts of the world, and there are no particular conservation laws for their protection in the United States.

Both native and non-native red foxes occur in North America. Recent research suggests that the all-red fox is a non-native introduced from Europe, while the silver and cross-colored "phases" or races are the natives. This research indicates that native foxes are cold-adapted animals occurring in northern subalpine coniferous and montane habitats, whereas the non-natives, originally brought to the east and west coasts from Europe, are generalists found in a wider range of habitats, especially urban ones. Biologists believe that non-natives may displace native populations at higher elevations in the western United States. Despite apparent physical, coloration, behavioral and habitat differences between the two, they are currently considered the same species.[20]

BEAR FAMILY *Ursidae*

Bears are Colorado's biggest surviving carnivores, appearing relatively recently in the fossil record, about 29 million years ago during the Miocene Epoch. Most biologists recognize three genera and eight species in this family, with only one species remaining in Colorado. Grizzly bears, once common throughout Colorado, were eliminated as a result of conflicts with human settlement and livestock grazing. Adult male polar bears, weighing in around 1,430 lb. (650 kg), are the world's largest living land mammals. Bears have elongated, crushing pre-molar and molar teeth, suited for an omnivorous diet, non-retractile claws and heavy limbs. Bears walking is plantigrade, with the soles of their feet on the ground, moving more slowly than those mammals that move on their toes in a digitgrade fashion as coyotes do. Their slower mode of locomotion requires that they feed more on berries, roots, ants and carrion—food sources that do not run. Remember, however, they can run very fast for short distances.

Black Bear
Ursus americanus
FAIRLY COMMON

Habitat/feeding: Montane to alpine tundra. Most common in oak-mountain shrublands, aspen forests and lower subalpine, particularly where berries are abundant. Omnivorous, though primarily vegetarian, eating grasses, forbs, berries, fruits, acorns, insects and honey, including the bees and comb. Young deer and elk, small mammals and sometimes domestic animals make up about 10% of diet; carrion important when emerging from hibernation. Has color vision almost as sharp as humans, but depends more on keen sense of smell and hearing to find food and detect threats. Require 11–18 lb. (5–8 kg) of food/day. Active anytime; mostly

ROBIN HENRY

Front
4.5 x 4 inches
11.3 x 10 cm

Hind
7 x 3.5 inches
17.8 x 8.8 cm

diurnal. **Field ID traits:** Honey-colored, brown, blond or black in Colorado; elsewhere may be white (not albino), cream-colored or cinnamon.[22] Adult males average 300 lb. (135 kg), females 175 lb. (79 kg); average lengths are 4.5–6.5 ft. (1.4 – 1.95 m). Compared to grizzlies, black bears lack prominent shoulder hump, have shorter black claws sharply curved for climbing and longer ears in relation to head size. **Tracking notes:** Hind footprint resembles a human's; has wedge-shaped indentation lacking in grizzly; claws may or may not be visible. Watch for rotten logs and stumps ripped apart or large rocks overturned by bears searching for grubs, ants and other insects. Scat is quite large, averaging 7 x 1 in. (17.8 x 2.5 cm); usually full of grasses, plant leaves, partly digested berries, animal hair or seeds. **Reproduction:** Typically secretive and solitary, except during mating season or when female (sow) has cubs. Male (boar) breeds at 3 years, female typically at 5 years; mate in early summer; development of fertilized egg delayed until November; 2–3 cubs born from January to February during hibernation, usually every other year. Cubs weaned by September, often remaining with mother until next litter.[23] Female will not breed if food supply is insufficient or her body lacks the necessary fat.

> **Recreational berry picking by humans may compete with bears' pre-hibernation energy needs, especially in years when berries are sparse.[21]**

Bears are curious, shy, intelligent and have good memories. They can even learn to use "tools." Stories of their intelligence abound. A favorite one is told about a female bear that learned to use rocks to trigger traps. She would wait in a tree nearby while traps were being set, coming down later to trigger the traps and eat the bait![24] These human-like traits spawned early religions centered around bear worship. Evidence of ritual burials and reverence for bears is found in cultures throughout the world.

Black bears generally make their dens in rocky caverns or excavate their own holes up to 12 ft. (4 m) long under the dense protective cover of trees and shrubs, though they have been known to hibernate on top of the ground. Starting around late July, they must gain an average of 1.5 lb. (0.7 kg) per day to survive the long winter sleep. This period of gorging lasts as long as food is available. Denning may begin as early as the first week in October or as late as early December, with females usually hibernating a few weeks before males. Bears sleep for five to seven

months without eating, drinking, defecating or urinating. During this time, their heart rate drops from forty to fifty beats/minute to eight to ten beats/minute and oxygen intake is cut in half. Body temperature remains near normal, however, so they can rouse fairly quickly if disturbed. Bears have little appetite or thirst for two to three weeks after emerging from hibernation, coinciding with the scarcity of food in early spring.

There are an estimated 8,000–12,000 bears in Colorado. The number residing in the Roaring Fork Valley watershed is unknown, although they are common. Most bear deaths are caused by humans through hunting, illegal killing, habitat loss and fragmentation, and shooting of bears considered a threat to people or livestock. Black bears are listed as big game in Colorado, although current regulations prevent spring bear hunts when sows are with cubs, or the use of bait and dogs for hunting. Bears that are awakened by snowmobiles may not return to hibernation and often die. Natural enemies include mountain lions and male bears, who sometimes kill cubs. Protecting the biological integrity of large ecosystems with connecting corridors is important to the long-term survival of bears in North America.

TOWN OF SNOWMASS VILLAGE

BEAR TREES

Look for trees marked by the claws of bears, their teeth, or sometimes by body-scratching. An aspen's soft white bark often reveals these marks, whereas those on conifers are seldom seen (see "Aspen Forests" on p. 41). Black bears evolved in forested areas and will climb to avoid confrontation with non-climbing predators.[25] Climbing bears leave two different patterns, one when ascending and the other upon descent. Just as a telephone repairman "hunches" up a pole, a bear will kick its hind feet into the tree, leaving a neatly curved row of four to five punctures, using its front paws to pull itself up from the sides, which leaves diagonal slashes in the bark. Longer, parallel slashes show where the bear slid down. Bear marks are fairly wide because their claws are worn at the tips, in contrast with the narrow scratches left by the sharper retractable claws of mountain lions or bobcats. Bear expert Dr. Jim Halfpenny says bears climb for different reasons. Mothers send their cubs up trees for safety and may themselves climb to avoid contact with humans, dogs or larger bears. Bears also climb to eat spring aspen buds or rob a bird's nest of eggs.[26] As trees grow and bear "arborglyphs" age, they become blackened and distorted by scar tissue, appearing larger than when they were fresh. Fresh claw marks five inches across would indicate a fairly large bear.

FEEDING BEARS PUTS THEM AT RISK

Bears accustomed to human food often become "problem bears" and may return to the food source. In Pitkin County, bears get only one warning. If authorities are called to deal with a problem bear a second time, they will destroy it. Follow these tips to avoid tempting bears to their doom:

- Keep garbage in bear-proof containers and/or store inside at night—it's the law in Pitkin County.
- Put garbage out the morning of collection; bring container in before dark.
- Store barbecue grills inside at night or clean and bleach after use.
- Don't feed pets outside.
- Place bird feeders out of a bear's reach and/or take them down at night; clean up spilled seed.
- Leave meat or sweet food scraps out of your compost pile.
- If a bear is in your house, open the doors and stay clear of its escape route.
- Never intentionally feed bears—it's against the law!
- If camping, store food and toiletries in a locked car or hang them from a tree limb at least 10 ft. (3 m) above the ground and at least 4 ft. (1.2 m) away from the trunk. Keep tent and sleeping area free of cooking odors; clothes worn while cooking or eating should be stored with the food.

IF YOU ENCOUNTER A BEAR . . .

Bears rarely attack people unless threatened or provoked, but bears are individuals and may not respond predictably. The following tips generally apply if you meet a black bear:

- *Calmly* leave the area; talk aloud to make the bear aware of your presence.
- *Back away slowly.* Give the bear plenty of room to escape.
- If on a trail, step off the downhill side and leave slowly—don't run or make sudden movements likely to prompt the bear to give chase. Bears can run 35 mph—you cannot outrun them.
- *Speak softly.*
- If you see a mother bear or a cub, move away and be alert for other cubs.
- If a bear stands upright or moves closer, it may only be trying to detect smells in the air—this is not necessarily a sign of aggression. Once the bear figures out what you are, it may leave the area or it may try to intimidate you by charging to within a few feet before withdrawing.
- *Fight back if attacked.* Black bears have been driven away when people fought back with rocks, sticks, binoculars and even their bare hands.
- Pepper spray has been known to ward off an attacking bear.[27]

IN RECOGNITION OF THEIR INNOVATIVE BEAR MANAGEMENT, THE TOWN OF SNOWMASS VILLAGE WON AN AWARD FROM THE COLORADO WILDLIFE COMMISSION IN 2000, AND A CERTIFICATE OF APPRECIATION FROM THE COLORADO DIVISION OF WILDLIFE IN 2003, SERVING AS A MODEL FOR MANY OTHER COMMUNITIES.

RACCOON and RINGTAIL FAMILY *Procyonidae*

Long tails with rings of contrasting colors, pointed snouts and faces bearing distinctive markings are all traits of these medium-sized mammals. They first appeared in North America's fossil record some 18 million years ago during the Miocene Epoch. Procyonids, as members of this family are collectively known, walk flat-footed and have five toes and well-developed claws on each foot. This makes them capable climbers, enabling them to seek protection in trees or rock crevices. Though carnivores, they will eat vegetation. Ring-tail cats and red pandas are also considered members of this family.

Raccoon
Procyon lotor
COMMON

CHARLES W. MELTON

Habitat/feeding: Along streams and in neighborhoods throughout Colorado. Dens in hollow logs, rock crevices, brush piles, culverts, buildings and old burrows of other animals. Eats almost anything, including small mammals, frogs, snakes, bird eggs, berries, acorns, fruits, garbage and occasionally carrion. May cause a decrease in waterfowl populations by preying on eggs and young. Crepuscular and nocturnal, sometimes diurnal. **Field ID traits:** Total length 30–36 in. (75–90 cm). Masked face, very obvious rounded ears and bushy, black-ringed tail. Male slightly larger than female. **Tracking notes:** 5 slim toes, a bit bulbous at tips; front feet, especially, resemble slender human hands. Raccoon scat varies, but is typically a thick cord with blunt ends, 3 x 0.75 in. (7.5 x 1.9 cm). Scat may carry a parasite fatal to humans. **Reproduction:** Male polygamous. Capable of breeding December–June, mostly in February. Gestation about 65 days; young born April–May. Ears and eyes open in about 20 days, young leave den the eighth week; not weaned for 3 months. Young may stay with female until following spring. Most adults fairly solitary, hunt independently. Communal denning common in winter with females and offspring, possibly up to 23 in single den; rarely more than 1 adult male per group.

Front
2.5 x 2.5 inches
6.3 x 6.3 cm

Toes are bulbous.

Hind
4 x 2.3 inches
10 x 5.8 cm

Raccoons are highly adaptable and have actually thrived in the wake of human settlement. Benefiting from greater food sources and denning habitats, they have expanded in both numbers and range. Once confined to riparian corridors on the eastern plains in Colorado, they are now abundant everywhere, including the Roaring Fork Valley, first appearing in the late 1960's and early 1970's. They sleep for long periods during the winter, becoming active when temperatures rise above freezing. While appreciated for their appealing "masked" faces, dexterous front paws and playful natures, raccoons damage gardens, crops, trees and houses, and wreak havoc with trash bins in their search for food and den sites. They are very susceptible to canine distemper. A sick raccoon will appear lethargic, usually foam at the mouth, and typically have matted eyes. It should be reported and not handled. Raccoons swim and climb well, are fierce fighters when cornered, and can run at up to 15 mph. Their Latin species name, *lotor*, translates as "the washer"—appropriately enough, since they wash their food if near water. One local nimble-fingered raccoon opened the clamps on a camper's plastic food bin, removed a package of peanut butter cups and left only the wrappers by the stream.

WEASEL FAMILY   *Mustelidae*

Fearless and agile carnivores, weasels must consume up to a third of their body weight in meat daily. This explains their propensity for attacking prey up to four times their size and killing an excessive amount of prey when it is available, which they cache for later use.

The earliest weasels appeared about 35–40 million years ago. Members of the weasel family are now distributed on most continents, living in a wide range of semi-aquatic, terrestrial and arboreal habitats. They continue to be hunted for their soft, luxurious fur, an adaptation necessary for animals that remain active throughout cold winters.

Weasels are known for their anal scent glands, which they use for social communication and which skunks notoriously use for defense. Weasels make use of the reproductive strategy known as delayed implantation. The fertilized egg does not become implanted in the uterine wall and develop into an embryo until environmental conditions such as food availability and weather are right for the newborn to survive.

NEIGHBORHOODS BENEATH THE SNOW

Unpacked snow cover is important insulation for weasels and other small mammals that rest, live and/or hunt in this subnivean environment. Activities such as skiing, snowmobiling and snowshoeing pack the snow, destroying the space between the ground and the snowpack, where these animals live and move about during the winter. Extensive areas of packed snow can result in higher mortality rates for all small mammals active during winter.

American Marten, Pine Marten

Martes americana

FAIRLY COMMON

ROBIN HENRY

Habitat/feeding: Montane to subalpine. Mature spruce-fir or lodgepole forests needed for protected den sites. Prefers sites with varied understory and brushy open areas to enhance diversity of prey species. Occasionally inhabits montane forests or alpine talus slopes. Martens are generalists; diet of bird eggs and nestlings, fish, insects and young mammals in summer; berries, flower seeds and other fruits in fall; mice, voles (especially red-backed), snowshoe hares, pikas and squirrels in spring and winter. Travels well on ground or snow; climbs trees. Hunts rodents beneath the snow by following their routes along submerged branches and tree trunks; spaces that are also essential resting sites in cold weather. Active day or night, mostly dusk to dawn; rests in trees. Caches food. **Field ID traits:** Size of small housecat; male 20–40% larger than female. Slender body with short legs and long, slender, bushy tail. Fox-like face, obvious rounded ears. Glossy fur, reddish-tan to chocolate on body, dark on legs, cream to amber irregular neck or throat patch. Scent from glands less intense than that of other weasels. **Tracking notes:** Tracks similar to, but larger than, long-tailed weasel. Typical 1-3-1 grouping of 5 toes, chevron-like pad; semi-retractable claws. Easiest to track in winter when its gallop creates 2 x 2 paired tracks, with one foot registering slightly ahead of the other, and rear tracks falling almost directly on top of front ones, often ending at a tree that it has climbed. Burrows in snow sometimes evident. Scat is a long, narrow cord that tapers at each end and lays in twisted fashion.

Reproduction: Males promiscuous. Both sexes more aggressive during mating season; females may engage in vicious fighting with each other. Biologists recognize 2 types of dens: "maternity" dens for birthing and dens where the mother later lives with young. Dens located in tree cavities, hollow logs, rock crevices, burrows or under fallen trees. Female raises 1 litter of 1–5 young; eyes open in about 30 days; young leave den and become fairly active after about 6 weeks.

Front
2.1 x 2 inches
5.3 x 5 cm

Hind
2.3 x 2.1 inches
5.8 x 5.3 cm

Furry heel not included in track measurement.

Martens scamper along high conifer limbs with the agility of tightrope walkers, ever searching for the unwary pine squirrel. Although shy and seldom seen, they easily adapt to some human activity. Miners' tales from the late 1800's mention martens as excellent cabin mousers, and they may still take up residence in buildings. When mating or frightened, martens produce vocalizations ranging from "chuckles" to "screams." They also communicate through chemical signals released from anal, abdominal and paw glands, as well as through urine and feces placement. Martens are preyed upon by coyotes, red foxes, lynx, mountain lions, eagles, great-horned owls and by people, who have trapped them for their fur since aboriginal times. They are not protected under the Endangered Species Act, but are considered a sensitive species by the U. S. Forest Service, which means they can no longer be trapped in Colorado. Now, their main enemy is logging, which fragments old-growth habitat and clears brushy undergrowth, leaving them homeless. Current efforts to establish corridors between fragmented habitats is vital to their conservation.

ROBIN HENRY

Long-Tailed Weasel
Mustela frenata
COMMON

Habitat/feeding: Montane to alpine. Habitat type varies according to available prey; prefers brushy areas near water with large rodent populations. Eats mostly small rodents, pikas, birds, reptiles and some berries and vegetation. When hunting aboveground, wraps body around prey before delivering lethal bite to base of skull; belowground, bites prey in throat. Active year-round, day or night, especially at dawn and dusk. **Field ID traits:** Slender carnivore, much longer than wide. Male averages 12.5–18 in. (32–46 cm) total length, weighing about 5 oz.; typically 20% larger than female. White in winter, cinnamon-brown with yellowish to orange undersides in summer; black-tipped tail and eyes. **Tracking notes:** Small, furry paws and well-developed claws in asymmetrical pattern of 1-3-1. Track looks like a miniature dog's, possibly with only 4 toes evident; center pad is chevron-shaped, or an inverted "V." Common 2 x 2 track pattern, with one foot registering slightly ahead of the other, and rear tracks falling almost directly on top of front ones, indicative of typical "humping" (bounding) gait. Trails in snow very erratic and zigzagging; in deep snow, dogbone-shaped drag marks may be seen between tracks from food drag. **Reproduction:** Mating occurs July–August; implantation of embryo delayed until late winter. Gestation about 30 days; 4–9 young delivered April–May. Males and females establish separate territories and are mostly solitary except when breeding. Pairs remain together only a few weeks; females raise young alone. Young born blind; weaned at 6 weeks to learn hunting with female; disperse 1 week later.

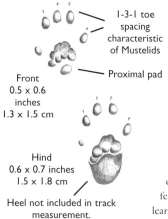

1-3-1 toe spacing characteristic of Mustelids

Proximal pad

Front
0.5 x 0.6 inches
1.3 x 1.5 cm

Hind
0.6 x 0.7 inches
1.5 x 1.8 cm

Heel not included in track measurement.

Inquisitive and fierce, these long, lean predators are perfectly shaped for diving beneath the snow, into holes or tight crevices. They can also climb and swim. If surprised during hunting, a long-tailed weasel may drop its prey and vanish, appearing again soon to retrieve its prize before diving back into hiding. During the ski season, weasels can be seen from the chairlift hunting in unpacked snow. Long-tailed weasels may den in the burrows of their victims or create their own under buildings, beneath rocks or fallen trees or inside rotten logs, lining it with grasses and their prey's fur. Their predators include coyotes, foxes, snakes, owls and trappers.

WHY CHANGE COLOR?

The change in a mammal's pelage, or coat, to winter white provides more than camouflage. White hair is filled with air instead of color pigment, greatly increasing its insulation value.

Short-tailed weasels (*Mustela erminea*), or **ermine**, are found mostly above 6,000 ft. (1830 m) and co-occur with long-tailed weasels. Both turn white in winter, but differ in size, ermines being only 7–9.5 in. (18–24 cm) in total length, and having a tail about a third as long as the body. They are a similar brown in summer, but have whitish undersides and are more nocturnal.

Mink
Mustela vison
UNCOMMON

Habitat/feeding: Montane to subalpine. Rarely strays far from riparian habitats along rivers, creeks, lakes, ponds and in marshes. Opportunistic predator, feeding on cottontails, muskrat, beaver kits, fish, small rodents, birds and frogs. Active year-round. Mostly nocturnal, but becomes more diurnal during winter. **Field ID traits:** Short legs on a long body, male averages 19–28 in. (49–72 cm) total length; tail a third to a half of total length. Male only about 10% longer than female, but often twice the weight. Beautiful, glossy chocolate-brown to blackish coat, occasionally with white spot under chin, chest or abdomen. Glands at the base of each hair produce oil to keep animal dry while swimming. Swims with head above water. **Tracking notes:** Five toes, 1-3-1 grouping; inside little toe may not show. Webbing between toes will show in tracks; heels usually do not. Pad shaped like a chevron. Scat slender and ropy; may smell fishy or contain fish bones. Narrow, muddy troughs in stream banks indicate where minks regularly slide down into water. Marks territory with very smelly discharge from the anal gland. Holes may be visible where the mink dives into the snow and comes up a small distance away. Moves with a bounding motion on land; pattern visible in snow. **Reproduction:** Polygamous. Builds den with numerous openings in hole or burrow along stream bank, typically under tree roots, or may use abandoned muskrat burrow or beaver lodge. Moves frequently. Breeds February–April; litters born late April–May. Early-breeding females often delay implantation of embryos until conditions are more

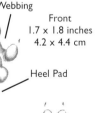

Webbing

Front
1.7 x 1.8 inches
4.2 x 4.4 cm

Heel Pad

Hind
1.8 x 1.9 inches
4.5 x 4.8 cm

415

favorable. Gestation 42–74 days; 1 litter of 1–8 altricial young; young stay with mother until dispersing in fall. See photo of mink young, p. 35.

A mink's glossy and luxuriant coat has led to a long history of being trapped for its fur. With most mink furs now grown on commercial farms, minks are slowly recovering in Colorado. There have been more sightings in the upper Roaring Fork Valley in the past couple years. Surprisingly, there have been no intensive studies of mink in the southern Rocky Mountains. They are vigorous hunters and avid swimmers, never straying far from water. Using air pockets to breathe, they even venture beneath the ice in winter to search for prey. Only during the coldest snowy days are minks inactive. Foxes, coyotes, Canada lynx, bobcats and raptors prey upon mink, but trappers are still a factor affecting their numbers. Protection of their habitat is critical. They cannot live in areas where cattle have eroded streambanks, and since they eat fish, are susceptible to waterborne environmental contaminants such as mercury and PCBs, which can cause reproductive problems. A healthy mink population is an indicator of a healthy stream ecosystem.

TODD W. PATRICK

Distinctive 'toed-in' with long claws.

Front
2.5 x 2 inches
6.3 x 5 cm

Hind
1.75 x 1.75 inches
4.5 x 4.5 cm

Heel not included in track measurement.

American Badger
Taxidea taxus
UNCOMMON

Habitat/feeding: Mostly oak-mountain shrublands in this area, but possibly in grasslands and open meadows of all life zones, even above timberline. Most numerous where its favorite prey, Wyoming ground squirrels and pocket gophers, are abundant; avoids dense forests. Also preys on rabbits, small rodents, marmots, ground-nesting birds and their eggs, reptiles and insects; sometimes carrion. Mostly nocturnal; occasionally hunts during the day. **Field ID traits:** Male 26–35 in. (66–90 cm); about 25% larger than female, but appearance is similar. Noticeably muscular, flattened profile; black face with white stripe on forehead, black patches (or "badges") on cheeks; thick hide. Muscular front legs and shoulders; front claws up to 2 in. (5 cm) long. Eyes have a special membrane that protects them from flying dirt. Waddling gait. **Tracking notes:** 5 toes, long claws visible, chevron-shaped pad, distinctly smaller rear foot. Scat similar to coyote, except smaller with blunt ends, 3 x 0.8 in. (7.5 x 2 cm); rarely seen because most often dropped inside burrow. **Reproduction:** Dens in burrows that may be 10 ft. (3 m) deep, contain 33 ft. (10 m) of tunnels and have special chambers for sleeping, defecation and maternity. Burrow openings elliptical, mimicking the badger's shape. Male and female maintain large, possibly overlapping territories, not aggressively defended; male's is larger. Sexes avoid contact except during mating. Breeds in late summer; embryo implantation delayed until about February; 1–4 young arrive early spring. Female raises young, which spend 6 weeks inside den and disperse by fall.

Badgers are ferocious if cornered and are highly adapted for digging. With amazing speed, they can utilize their powerful front legs and long curved claws for digging a protective burrow, obtaining their prey or excavating a home burrow. Few predators dare face these disagreeable, aggressive creatures; though coyotes, domestic dogs and golden eagles may kill juveniles. Although not true hibernators, badgers do enter a state of semi-dormancy during the winter, where their breathing and heart rate slows and body temperature drops. During this time, they remain in a single burrow for long periods, deviating from their typical pattern of moving from burrow to burrow about once a month. Humans are the biggest threat to their survival. Populations are dwindling in western states and Canada due to deliberate extermination as varmints because their holes can cripple livestock, accidental poisoning when they eat poisoned meat meant for other predators and loss of habitat. An interesting aside, badger hair once sold for eighty-five dollars a pound for use in expensive shaving brushes, which can still be found for sale today.[28]

> **Badgers have been observed hunting cooperatively with coyotes. The coyote guards a prairie dog's escape route while the badger digs. Then they share the meal.**

Striped Skunk
Mephitis mephitis
COMMON

CHARLES W. MELTON

Habitat/feeding: All habitats except alpine areas, including urban settings. Flexible diet: prefers beetles and their larvae, grasshoppers, crickets, earthworms and snails; also consumes ground-nesting birds and eggs, small mammals, carrion and some berries, fruit, grains and vegetables. Nocturnal. **Field ID traits:** Male larger than female, total length of 23–30 in. (58–77 cm). Familiar black-and-white body with bushy tail; single white stripe begins at nose and continues to nape of neck, splitting into 2 lateral stripes ending at the tail. **Tracking notes:** Half-dollar-sized prints; 5 toes, though inside little toe sometimes doesn't register; typical weasel 1-3-1 configuration with chevron-like pad. Both front and rear feet similar size; line across pad is distinctive. Rear track resembles small human footprint; wide claws on front foot distinguish this skunk from other skunk species.[29] **Reproduction:** Polygamous males may form harems for mating in February or March. Implantation of fertilized ovum often delayed in early breeders; births take place in May–early June. Can dig its own burrow, but usually borrows old ones belonging to marmots, foxes, coyotes or badgers. Lives aboveground most of year, resting in thick vegetation or under buildings; female rears litter of 5–8 young in underground den; may also have communal dens during cold winters; usually females with 1 male. Young's eyes open in about 3 weeks; are weaned at 8 weeks; on their

417

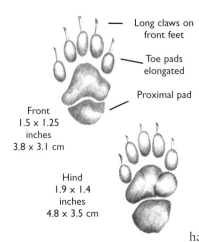

Long claws on front feet

Toe pads elongated

Proximal pad

Front
1.5 x 1.25 inches
3.8 x 3.1 cm

Hind
1.9 x 1.4 inches
4.8 x 3.5 cm

own after 2–4 months. They develop musk glands at birth; can spray soon after reaching 1 week of age.

Although everyone loves watching wildlife, no one wants to surprise a skunk. It can accurately eject a mist of nauseating, oily, yellowish musk from the anal glands up to 15 ft. (5 m). Mercaptans, the same sulfur-containing compounds used in natural gas for early detection of leaks, are responsible for the atrocious odor. Ironically, this musk, once descented, is used commercially in perfumes to enhance the clinging properties. The spray can burn badly and blind temporarily, though no lasting or serious harm results. Tomato juice has traditionally been used to rid pets of this intense odor, and carbolic soap and water are recommended for washing human skin. There are also commercial products on the market today. Male skunks may occasionally be active in winter; however, females and juveniles spend most of their time in a state of semi-dormancy, often in communal dens. This species is in no present danger of extinction, as most predators—except for owls, which have no sense of smell—leave them alone. Biologists examining the stomach contents of coyotes, foxes, bobcats and mountain lions, have occasionally found skunk remains, but it's likely that the skunks were already dead when consumed.

Skunks often contract rabies by feeding on carrion, and are now considered the chief carrier of rabies in the United States.

—NATIONAL WILDLIFE FEDERATION

CAT FAMILY

Felidae

Cats are the most specifically carnivorous members of the carnivore order. Formidable foes, they stalk, pounce and rapidly kill their prey. Although felids did not appear until the late Eocene, 56–38 million years ago, they are now found on almost every continent. The ultimate predator, they posses excellent night vision and keen hearing, sharp rear cutting teeth that close with a scissor-like action and jaws that open to almost ninety degrees.

Mountain Lion, Cougar, Puma

Puma concolor

FAIRLY COMMON

RICHARD W. HOLMES

Habitat/feeding: Montane to subalpine. Primarily oak-mountain shrublands and pinyon-juniper communities, wherever mule deer, the major component of its diet, are found. Also consumes a wide variety of small to medium-sized mammals (including some domestic pets) insects, fish, birds and berries; very rarely carrion. Adult lions will travel about 20 miles (32 km) a day in search of prey. Seldom needs to drink, obtaining most of its moisture from meat. Both nocturnal and crepuscular. **Field ID traits:** Male averages 145 lb. (66 kg), female 120 lb. (54 kg); both sexes average 5–9 ft. (1.5–2.75 m) total length. Slender, yet muscular body with short, thick fur is grayish-brown to cinnamon-tawny, pale beneath. Long, black-tipped tail, more than 50% of body length, is held low. Head appears small compared to body size. **Tracking notes:** Tracks larger and rounder than those of canines and the retractable claws leave no marks. Central pad has 2 lobes at the front and 3 at the back. "Scrapes," which are piles of dirt, leaves and other debris that may also include urine and scat, are territory markers. Mountain lions also pile dirt and debris over remains of a kill they plan to return for later. **Reproduction:** Male polygamous, breeding throughout the year with females of overlapping home ranges; usually in winter or early spring. Female usually only mates with 1 male; gestation about 92 days; litter of 2–4 black-spotted kittens born with eyes closed; open after about 10 days; weaned in 2 months, remain with female 12–22 months; spots disappear in about a year. Litters mostly 1.5–2 years apart. Availability of den sites critical to female's range size. Chooses cave, overhang or hollow under deadfall for den; no special birthing den.

Two lobes on front of planar pad

Front
3.5 × 3.6 inches
8.8 × 9.0 cm

Hind
3.25 × 3 inches
8.2 × 7.5 cm

Shy and secretive, mountain lions are solitary animals that require large expanses of wild terrain, with a single male maintaining a home range of 46–320 square miles (120–830 square km), and a female 15–270 square miles (40–700 square km). They don't even associate with other lions, except during breeding season. Females with cubs will not tolerate adult males, as they often kill the cubs. This intolerance of each other

We feel that the increase in attacks upon humans [by mountain lions] is part of the problem with the rampant development now taking place. . . . Most of these [attacks and conflicts] are warning flags reminding us of the real problems, which are habitat loss and degradation and fragmentation... The real threat to the future of mountain lions isn't hunting, it's the tremendous land conversion that's taking place all over the West.

—STEVEN TORRES,
*cougar biologist with the California
Department of Fish and Game*

maintains the spacing of their ranges.

Mountain lions are relatively quiet, emitting only soft whistle-type mews, purring, or meowing-like calls. Louder growls and cries are heard only when they are mating or fighting. Lions rely on stealth when hunting, as their lungs are too small to sustain an extended chase. They stalk and ambush their quarry, leaping on its back and using their powerful jaws and forepaws to crush the vertebrae at the base of the skull. Though not normally aggressive toward humans, increasing development and recreation pressure on their natural habitats have led to more close encounters—a few of them fatal. Of the humans killed by mountain lions in the United States, two were in Colorado during the 1990's.

As with other large predators, habitat fragmentation and degradation are the most serious threats to mountain lion survival. Roads block the dispersal of sub-adults, necessary for maintaining genetic diversity, which encourages inbreeding. Roads also enable greater access by poachers and hunters. Mountain lion populations now fill the predatory role once occupied by wolves and grizzlies, which is important to a healthy ecosystem. Though 1,500–3,000 mountain lions live in Colorado, most of us will never get a glimpse of anything but their tracks. Just knowing that these magnificent cats still survive is enough to inspire hope that we will find ways to coexist with them.

LEARNING TO COEXIST WITH MOUNTAIN LIONS

PRECAUTIONARY BEHAVIOR IN MOUNTAIN LION COUNTRY

- Make sure young children are supervised; running and squealing on the trail could trigger an attack. Keep pets on a leash when outdoors.
- At night, keep pets indoors or in a kennel with a secure top, and keep domestic livestock in an enclosed space.
- Prune heavy shrubbery away from the house; close off open spaces below porches or decks, because lions might hide or den in these areas.
- Don't hike, jog or mountain bike alone.
- Leave the area immediately if you find an animal carcass partially buried beneath sticks, leaves or dirt.

IF YOU MEET A MOUNTAIN LION

- Never approach the cat or attempt to pick up kittens if found alone—females ferociously defend their young.
- Avoid placing yourself downhill of the lion—the animal will be more tempted to pounce.
- Speak loudly and firmly, making yourself look as large as possible by holding your hands above your head or opening your jacket. Do not crouch or bend.
- Make eye contact—failure to do so will be viewed as a sign of submission or weakness.
- If attacked, fight back with sticks, rocks, camera or whatever you can find— people have defended themselves with nothing more than a ballpoint pen! Lions will hunker down and swing their tails back and forth if considering an attack.
- Never turn and run, as this may trigger the lion's predatory chase response.[30]

Bobcat
Lynx rufus [Felis rufus]
COMMON

SCOTT BUCKEL

Habitat/feeding: Montane to lower sub-alpine. Easily adapts to various Colorado habitats. Prefers pinyon-juniper, but also frequents aspen, mixed-conifer and open spruce-fir forests in summer; mostly avoids wetlands. Preys mainly on rodents, snowshoe hares and cottontails; also eats chipmunks, mice, Wyoming ground squirrels, porcupines, amphibians and some small domestic animals. Vegetation probably consumed as purgative, not a food source. Both nocturnal and crepuscular, resting during the day in dense forest with light understory; may occasionally hunt during the day. **Field ID traits:** Male averages 28–40 in. (70–100 cm) long, including tail; 35 lb. (16 kg); 30% larger than female. Twice the size of a housecat, with long legs and bobbed tail. Streaked, spotted fur is grayish-tan in winter when the facial "ruff" is most noticeable; more reddish in summer. Young spotted mountain lions could be confused with bobcats, but their tails are much longer (see following page for comparison with lynx). **Tracking notes:** Bigger print than domestic cat's, smaller than mountain lion's or lynx's. Toes point in different direction than heel pad. Retractable claws leave no impression. **Reproduction:** Polygamous. Social only during mating. May breed anytime, but usually February–March; litter of 2–3 kittens arriving in April–May; young remain with mother until the next spring. Eyes open in about 10 days, eventually turning from blue to golden yellow. Dens in cave, rock overhang, crevice between large rocks or even under dense shrubs.

Front track round with one toe leading.

Claws usually retracted, not showing in tracks.

Leading edge of pads have two lobes.

Front
2 x 2.1 inches
5 x 5.3 cm

Hind
2.1 x 1.9 inches
5.3 x 4.8 cm

DALE FRANZ

Canada Lynx (*Lynx canadensis*) is being reintroduced to Colorado. Notice the huge paws for rapid travel over deep snow of subalpine areas in pursuit of their favorite prey—snowshoe hare. The end of their short tail is completely black.

A true phantom of the landscape, this elusive cat is rarely seen even though it is fairly common. A male bobcat's home range may slightly overlap that of the female, though he will not tolerate sharing except to allow adolescents to pass through. This social separation seems to be an evolutionary survival strategy, resulting in less competition for food, less energy lost in fighting and probably less disease.

421

Bobcat mothers typically teach their kittens to hunt and kill during their second spring. First they bring them dead prey to practice on and later deliver small live prey. Hissing, growling and spitting behavior is learned at the same time. Adult bobcats will slink along, belly nearly on the ground, rapidly ambushing their prey, often from above. They swiftly sever the spinal cord with a bite to the neck, or puncture the jugular vein of larger prey. Sitting for hours along a game trail waiting for their next meal to appear is no problem—extremely keen vision gives bobcats the advantage in dim light. If the cat does not land its quarry fairly quickly, it will probably give up the chase and start over. Although coyotes and mountain lions pursue bobcats, their populations are usually decimated by legal trapping and poaching.

Compared to **CANADA LYNX** (*Lynx canadensis*), a bobcat has smaller feet, shorter, darker ear tufts, a longer tail with more black markings, more reddish fur in most areas and a more aggressive nature. Grayish fur of the southern Rockies subspecies can cause confusion with a grayish lynx. Both have a black-tipped tail, but the bobcat's is black only on the top half.

EVEN-TOED HOOFED UNGULATES
Order Artiodactyla

These hoofed animals are called ungulates because they walk on their ungules, or "nails," which are the hooves. They are the most successful group of large herbivores, built to cover long distances quickly in order to take advantage of diverse plant resources. All the wild ungulates in our area are members of the Artiodactyla order, which includes cattle, sheep, goats, pigs, camels, llamas, giraffes, antelope, gazelles and hippopotamuses. They range in size from the lesser Malay mouse deer at barely 5 lb. (2.5 kg), to the hippopotamus at up to 10,000 lb. (4500 kg).

Members of this diverse group are ruminants, which means they have complex stomachs with three or four chambers, permitting them to swallow large quantities of food in a short time, digesting it later while resting under protective cover. These aid digestion by providing bacteria to break down woody plant material and supplying moisture to form a cud—a bolus of food that returns to the mouth for more chewing. When food finally arrives in the "true" stomach, digestive juices break it down further. Proliferation of noxious weeds competes with native vegetation, reducing the quality and quantity of summer forage for ungulates. This can limit the accumulation of body fat needed for winter survival. Ungulates play a vital role in many ecosystems, and where domesticated are the backbone of agricultural economies around the world. Human cultures have relied on them for food, hides, fiber and sport for thousands of years.

DEER FAMILY

Cervidae

Members of this family, known as cervids, include deer, moose, caribou and elk. Many of these slender-legged species have antlers, ranging from short spikes to complex branched structures, which are covered with living "velvet" that later dies and is rubbed off on vegetation. In most species only the male grows antlers, which are used during breeding season for defending territory.

Most cervids live in herds as this affords better protection from predators and are polygamous, with males generally larger than females. Scent glands on the face, feet and legs are used for intraspecies communication.

American Elk, Wapiti

Cervus elaphus

COMMON

RICHARD W. HOLMES

Habitat/feeding: Migratory. Females prefer aspen woodlands for abundant forage and better cover during spring calving; in summer/fall, elk migrate to subalpine and alpine meadows; in late fall/winter, they move down to oak-mountain shrublands and south-facing slopes at lower elevations. Graze on grasses and forbs from late spring through fall; also browse on shrubs, conifers, aspen bark and twigs winter into early spring (see photo under "Aspen Forests," p. 41); have been known to prey on bird young and eggs.[31] **Field ID traits:** Second-largest member of deer family in Colorado (after moose). Mature bull about 700 lb. (320 kg), cow about 500 lb. (230 kg); bull 4–5 ft. (1.2–1.5 m) tall at the shoulders. Shaggy, khaki-colored winter coat contrasts with dark-brown legs; winter coat is shed in spring, fur becoming sleek and deep cinnamon-brown. Both sexes have buff-colored rump patch ringed in dark brown and a narrow tail without black tip; male has especially dark head and neck.

Tracking notes: Tracks larger and more rounded than mule deer's. Besides feeding marks, long scars on trees result from elk rubbing the velvety skin from their antlers, late August–September. Dried blood and bark compounds responsible for brown color of antlers. Winter scat is elongated or bell-shaped pellets, often with tiny points; summer scat is clumps of softer pellets, resembling small cow patties. "Wallows" are shallow depressions dug with hoofs and antlers, where male elk rub their scent glands and urinate, then wallow to cover their bodies with the odiferous mud. Some speculate that older bulls assert their dominance over younger bulls in this way; smells may also help induce estrus in females. Daily bedding grounds can be located by the peculiar musky odor and trampled vegetation. **Reproduction:** Males begin whistle-like bugling just prior to the fall rutting (mating) season, apparently to challenge other males and attract females. Most aggressive bulls collect harems of 5–15 females,

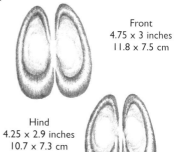

Front
4.75 × 3 inches
11.8 × 7.5 cm

Hind
4.25 × 2.9 inches
10.7 × 7.3 cm

CHARLES W. MELTON

Cow elk and calf

protecting them from unattached males with mild to dramatic antler-sparring; higher male mortality rate often attributed to energy expended during rutting season. Breeding mostly mid-September to mid-October; females deliver single calf (occasional twins) around first week of June. Cow elk have attacked humans perceived as a threat to their calves. Males tend to congregate in separate groups except during breeding season; older females typically lead herds during migration or to new feeding areas.

When European colonists arrived, elk were the most widely distributed member of the deer family on the North American continent.[32] Although elk were not as prized as the American bison, Native Americans valued them for their meat, skin, bones and teeth. They used the thick neck hides as shields against enemy arrows, the oversized canine teeth as ornamental jewelry and the bones as needles and awls.[33] Colorado has an estimated 300,000 elk—more than any other state—but this was not always the case. During the late 1800's, uncontrolled market hunting to feed miners and Colorado's booming population severely depleted the herds. The decline was reversed by a statewide ban on hunting from 1903–1929 and the reintroduction of a few hundred elk shipped down from Yellowstone by train.

A bull elk's dominant feature is the dramatic antlers, which are made of bone and weigh up to thirty pounds. Only single points, or "spikes," grow the first year. Although the number of points increases with age, there is not necessarily a direct correlation. Antlers are shed by late winter, with next year's growth beginning within two weeks. Antlers are rarely found because small mammals, particularly rodents, gnaw on the mineral-rich bone, recycling it back into the ecosystem.

Wapiti is Shawnee for "white," referring to the white rump. Early settlers mistakenly called this animal an "elk," as that is what Europeans call their moose, which is closely related to the American moose. The European red deer is a variant of our wapiti species.

Elk deaths in Colorado are primarily due to human hunting and predation on young calves by mountain lions, black bears and packs of coyotes. Some die from starvation during the winter. Most elk bagged by hunters are five years old or less, though elk can live to be twenty years old. About 40,000–50,000 elk are killed by hunters each year in Colorado—more than in any other state.

GIVE 'EM A BREAK

Most everyone living in or visiting this part of the southern Rockies stops to watch elk or deer in the wild. The future of this opportunity depends on conserving the health and numbers of these animals. Snowmass Village is in the historic migration corridor for the Burnt Mountain elk herd. As a result, both its Town Council and residents have undertaken extensive efforts to incorporate standards in the Land Use Code that foster the survival of the herd. Since loss and fragmentation of their habitat due to development pressures disrupts breeding grounds and migration routes, please consider the following:

- Observe trail closures in elk migration corridors and calving areas. These limit disturbance to the herds as they migrate to subalpine and alpine areas from their wintering grounds on lower, south-facing slopes, and ensure the survival of newborn calves in the spring.
- Help keep winter range undeveloped and available for winter survival. South-facing slopes are most critical, as they remain free of deep snow in the harshest of winters.
- Make sure that fences between winter and summer ranges are designed so young calves and fawns can pass through without getting tangled or trapped.

Important dates: spring migration, April 15–May 31; fall migration, October 15–November 30; calving season, May 15–June 30.

Mule Deer

Odocoileus hemionus

COMMON

CHARLES W. MELTON

Habitat/feeding: All Colorado ecosystems. Summer ranges are a mixture of aspen woodlands and forest edges from the montane to the alpine. Diet depends on availability of browse species; favors serviceberry, mountain mahogany, chokecherry, bitterbrush, grasses and forbs; also eats sagebrush in winter. Crepuscular and nocturnal—may feed more during the day in winter. **Field ID traits:** Males average 154 lb. (70 kg), but can reach 440 lb. (200 kg); larger than females. Shoulder height is about 39 in. (1 m). Gray in winter, cinnamon in summer; darkish forehead, white throat and rump patch, black-tipped tail. Conspicuously large ears. Male has antlers, divided once and then again. When alarmed, uses a stiff-legged bounding gait—as if on pogo sticks—called "pronking" or "stotting," with tail held down. **Tracking notes:** Hooves are 2 crescent-shaped halves, creating a heart shape, with the point showing the direction of travel. Hooves have 2 appendages called dewclaws just above the hoof, which may register with track. **Reproduction:** Male pursues single receptive female, protecting her aggressively until breeding in November–December. Approaches rivals with stiff-legged gait as glands on legs give off an odor; may thrash shrubs or trees or make bluffing charges, but antler-locking battles are rare.[34] Male sheds antlers during early winter. Female undergoes repeated

Front
3.25 x 2.6 inches
8.2 x 6.5 cm

Hind
3.1 x 2.5 inches
7.8 x 6.3 cm

RICHARD W. HOLMES

Doe and fawn

estrus cycles, each lasting only a few hours. Doe bears 1 fawn, though older doe may bear twins, after gestation that averages 203 days; fawns begin foraging in a few weeks; weaned in fall. Doe remains solitary while fawning; later forms small group with other females and their young. Adult males congregate in small groups outside of mating season.

Meriwether Lewis first spotted mule deer along the Missouri River in 1804, naming them for their conspicuous mule-like ears. Mule deer are more abundant in Colorado than in most other states, even though populations declined for a time from the 1950's through the mid-1970's due to a combination of overhunting, shrinking habitat and conversion of shrub habitat to pasture. Predators include mountain lions, golden eagles, bobcats, coyotes, black bears and domestic dogs—fawns are especially vulnerable. In the Roaring Fork Valley, competition pressure from increasing elk populations is definitely a threat. Warmer winters and an intensive management plan by the Colorado Division of Wildlife have helped reverse the downward population trend.[35] More recently, chronic wasting disease, discovered in Fort Collins in 1967 and endemic to northeastern Colorado, is a growing concern for native deer herds. Local mule deer migrate seasonally, summering at higher elevations, then moving lower for the winter, especially to south-facing slopes where snow cover is scarce. Herd migratory movements depend on weather and snow depths, snowfall greater than 14 in. (36 cm) being the catalyst for the late fall migration to wintering grounds.

ELK VS. DEER

Mule deer numbers are down in Colorado, but elk numbers are up. Why? Habitat generalists, elk are more flexible, adapting better to development pressure. Habitat specialists, mule deer return year after year to particular breeding grounds, so are not as flexible if these areas disappear. Deer are not as large as elk, so are more affected by loss of nutritious forage because of a smaller rumen. They also have trouble digging through deep snow to find food and are easier prey for predators. Being more solitary, deer are vulnerable, not having the safety in numbers that living in a herd affords elk.

BOVID FAMILY *Bovidae*

B ovids are a diverse family of browsing or grazing ungulates that range from slender and graceful species like gazelles to heavy, massive cattle. Their characteristics include permanent, unbranched horns with a bony core and keratin sheath—in most cases on females as well as males—and four-chambered, ruminant stomachs. Evolutionarily speaking, bovids' hooves have evolved from the third and fourth digits, with the second and fifth digits absent or present only as highly reduced hooves or dewclaws. Humans have hunted bovids for meat and hides since prehistoric times, while cattle, sheep and goats were domesticated early in man's history and are still major sources of milk, meat and fiber.

Mountain Goat

Oreamnos americanus

FAIRLY COMMON

ROBIN HENRY

Habitat/feeding: Alpine. Steep talus slopes combined with grassy alpine meadows; cliffs. Diet variable depending on season; grazes on grasses and forbs; browses on shrubs, conifers and lichens. Active dawn to mid-morning, then late afternoon to evening. **Field ID traits:** Male (billy) weighs 100–300 lb. (46–135 kg) and is 3–3.5 ft. (1–1.1 m) at the shoulder; female (nanny) approximately 15% lighter and smaller. Blocky build with straight sides, short legs and powerful shoulders adapted for maneuvering and climbing in steep rocky terrain; outer coat of long, hollow (insulating) guard hairs and thick, fluffy wool undercoat. Both sexes have thin, slightly curved, black conical horns; females are not as curved or tapered. **Tracking notes:** Squarish track due to somewhat splayed hooves—they are divided into 2 movable halves, making them slightly more agile on steep, rough terrain; tracks differ from similar species by having point of hoof centered in each half. Tracks show the convex, pliable pads— versus concave in other ungulates—that extend slightly beyond hard outer rim of hoof, providing extra grip in precipitous terrain. Dewclaws present but not visible in track. **Reproduction:** Polygamous. Billies mostly solitary or in small groups until rutting season, November–December; rarely fight, but do paw shallow depressions, use threat postures possibly involving horns, and become more aggressive toward other males. Occasional fights can inflict serious injury. Billies wipe heads against ewes to "mark" them with scent glands found near base of horns. Nannies usually have 1 kid (occasionally 2) in late May or early June, every other year. Very precocial; kids able to follow mother and eat vegetation within 1 week; weaned in late August–early September.

Front
3 x 1.9 inches
7.5 x 4.8 cm

Hind
2.6 x 1.5 inches
6.5 x 3.8 cm

Mountain goats are not true goats, but are closely related to the chamois of the Alps and the African antelope.

They look like cloud tatters snagged by the sharp summits. Mountain goats drift across the highest, most remote places in Colorado. Their world is made up of dizzying heights, cold wind, blue sky, white snow, and gray rock. They live out their lives, for the most part, beyond the reach of human eyes, just one step below the sky.

—Jeff Rennicke,
Colorado Wildlife

Called "white buffalo" by Northwest Indians, this shaggy creature is legendary for its climbing prowess. Descending below tree-line only in the very worst weather, mountain goats are supremely adapted to their unforgiving environment. Mountain goats were in fact introduced to Colorado from Montana in the 1940's to increase the number of available game animals. The first transplant occurred in 1948 when four adult females, two adult males and three kids were released at the southern end of the Collegiate Range.[36] Since then, mountain goats have expanded their range throughout the Colorado high country, being declared a resident species by the Colorado Division of Wildlife in 1993. Although exact numbers are not known, populations are thought to be increasing, with some biologists concerned that goats are competing for habitat and food with native species, particularly bighorn sheep. Life in the cliffs precludes most problems with predators; however, eagles, bobcats, mountain lions, coyotes and bears will occasionally prey on young or weak individuals. Most deaths are accidental, caused by falls in steep, icy terrain or by avalanches—whole herds have been found at the base of avalanche chutes during the spring thaw. As mountain goats are considered a big game species in Colorado, hunting is allowed, with about one hundred animals taken each year.

ROBIN HENRY

Bighorn Sheep, Mountain Sheep
Ovis canadensis
FAIRLY COMMON

Habitat/feeding: Typically in steep terrain of higher mountains; some bighorns have become habituated to humans and highways (e.g., on I-70 near Georgetown, Colorado). Prefer open meadows of grasses and low shrubs for safety from predators. Diet primarily grasses, sedges and some forbs; browse on alpine willows and other shrubs in winter. Seasonally, migrate only short distances, seek windblown, south or southwest-facing slopes during winter. **Field ID traits:** Male (ram) weighs 150–250 lb. (68–114 kg), female (ewe) 120–200 lb. (54–90 kg); male about 3 ft. (1 m) at the shoulder, female a bit less. Ram has massive spiraling horns, ewe only slightly curved spikes; neither are shed. Coat brownish to grayish taupe, depending on the season; pale beneath. Buff-colored muzzle and rump. Lifespan of 20 years possible; typically 10–12. **Tracking notes:** Hooves leave almost rectangular prints, with points on each half toward the inside, as opposed to tips at center on mountain goats. Front hooves slightly larger than hind. Tracks less heart-shaped than those of deer, with straighter sides and less pointed tips. **Reproduction:** Promiscuous. Males engage in spectacular displays during rutting season (November–

December) to exert dominance over other males and to control ewes. Usually only one ewe of herd in estrus at a time, pursued by several dominant males. Ewe moves to traditional lambing grounds for about a week during May or June to deliver single lamb. Young forage on their own within a few weeks; weaned in 5–6 months. Herd separates in spring and summer into small groups of bachelor rams older than 3–4 years and larger groups of younger rams, ewes and lambs.

Front
3.5 x 2.5 inches
8.8 x 6.3 cm

Hind
3 x 2 inches
7.5 x 5 cm

Symbol of remote mountain wilderness, and Colorado's state mammal, a bighorn's silhouette with its massive curled horns is most impressive. Males engage in spectacular displays during the rutting season, which occurs from November through December. Two males begin the display by interacting with subtle aggressiveness, touching and pushing each other before walking away as if nothing had happened. Abruptly, one of them wheels first, and then both rear up on their hind legs and plunge toward each other, at speeds up to 40 mph (64 kph), ramming their horns together with tremendous "whacks" that can be heard over long distances. Their skulls are double-layered and reinforced with a bone matrix to help absorb the intense shock.

Regardless of such power, they are not immune to predators such as mountain lions, coyotes, bobcats and golden eagles, but lambs are most often the targets. When not grazing, bighorns retreat to inaccessible cliffs for resting. Soft, concave hooves with hard outer rims allow them to move gracefully and securely on perilous, rocky terrain, and camouflaged coloration makes them difficult to spot.

Colorado bighorn sheep populations were severely depleted by early settlers and market hunters, resulting in a ban on hunting from 1887 to 1953. Although some herds are still in decline, many herds have been reestablished in their native habitats through intensive management efforts, with Colorado now home to the largest population of bighorn sheep in North America.

BIGHORNS: NOT OUT OF THE WOODS YET

While bighorn sheep have staged an impressive comeback in Colorado over the past half-century, they still face several threats related to human activities. Parasites, perhaps spread by domestic sheep, can eventually lead to pneumonia in populations where immune systems are suppressed. Year-round mountain recreational use is disturbing bighorns, which in some places are so harassed they are hiding in the woods they once avoided. Even mild alarm, caused by the approach of a backpacker, cross-country skier or ice climber, increases a bighorn's energy expenditure and stresses its immune system for seventy-two hours.[37] Trophy hunting of mature rams is believed to have an unhealthy effect on the gene pool and on learned behavior. People can help ensure the survival of these magnificent animals by viewing them from a distance.

APPENDIX

END NOTES

(Complete citations for some of these references are found on pages 445–447.)

Geology

1 Photos taken by Garrett E. Zabel. Flight time for aerial photo courtesy of Greg Rippy, Glenwood Springs, Colorado, fall 2001.
2 Hoy, R.G. and Ridgeway, K.D., 2002, "Syndepositional thrust-related deformation and sedimentation in an Ancestral Rocky Mountains basin, Central Colorado trough, Colorado." *Geological Society of America Bulletin*, v. 114, p. 804–828.

Ecology

1 Shinneman, Doug, Roz McClellan, and Rocky Smith, *The State of the Southern Rockies Ecoregion* (P. O. Box 1182, Nederland, CO 80466: Southern Rockies Ecosystem Project, 2000) 1-3.
2 Carsey, K., G. Kittel, K. Decker, D.J. Cooper, and D. Culver. *Field Guide to the Riparian and Wetland Plant Associations of Colorado* (Ft. Collins, CO: Colorado Natural Heritage Program, 2003).
3 Cooper, David J., *A Handbook of Wetland Plants of the Rocky Mountain Region*. EPA Region VIII. (contact Dr. Gene Reetz at Reetz.Gene@epamail.epa.gov). Reprinted by Federal Highways Administration, 1996.
4 *A Classification of Riparian Wetland Plant Associations of Colorado* (Ft. Collins, CO: Colorado Natural Heritage Program, 1999). See website http://www.cnhp.colostate.edu/reports.html. Accessed March 2004.
See also Fitzgerald, James P., Carron A. Meaney, and David M. Armstrong, *Mammals of Colorado* (Denver Museum of Natural History, 1994).
5 Partners in Flight website, http://www.partnersinflight.org, Click on PIF Maps, then Physiographic Area Plans, Region 62: Southern Rocky Mountains. Accessed January 2003.
6 FEIS website, Fire Effects Information System, http://www.fs.fed.us/database/feis/, search Latin name of plant Accessed March 2004.
7 Johnson, Douglas W. 1999. Biogeography of Quaking Aspen (San Francisco State University Department of Geography website) http://bss.sfsu.edu/geog/bholzman/courses/fall99projects/aspen.htm. Accessed September 2004.
8 Jeffrey B. Mitton and Michael C. Grant. 1996. Genetic variation and the natural history of quaking aspen. *Bioscience*, 46(1):25-31. University of Colorado at Boulder.
See also Gymnosperm Database, edited by Christopher J. Earle, 2001, http://www.conifers.org/. Accessed October 2004.
9 Armstrong, W.P. 2001. Wayne's Word Online: 9 January 2002. http://waynesword.palomar.edu/wayne.htm). Accessed February 2002.
10 Partners in Flight website, http://www.partnersinflight.org, Click on PIF Maps, then Physiographic Area Plans, Region 62: Southern Rocky Mountains, 2003. Accessed January 2003.

Plants

1 Jamieson, Michael (of the Missoulian). 2002. Mysterious Moonwort: The search continues in Glacier Park for an elusive and rare plant, despite the death of the man who found it (Davenport, IA: Editorial Matters, Lee Enterprises). http://editorialmatters.lee.net/articles/2002/11/03/stories/top_stories/anews095.txt. Accessed September 2004.
2 Schofield, Janice, *Discovering Wild Plants* (Seattle, WA: Alaska Northwest Books, 1989) 113-114. See also Caldwell ME, Brewer, MR. Possible hazards of eating braken fern (letter). *N England J of Medicine* 1980; 303:164.
3 Pryer, Kathleen M. et al. February 1, 2001. Horsetails and ferns are a monophyletic group and the closest living relatives to seed plants, *Nature* 409:618-622.
4 Kershaw, MacKinnon and Pojar, *Plants of the Rocky Mountains* (Edmonton, Alberta, Canada: Lone Pine Publishing, 1998) 47.
5 Weber, Dr. William, *Colorado Flora—Western Slope* (Boulder, CO: University Press of Colorado, 2001) 30.
See also: One bristlecone pine in California's White Mountains has been dated at more than 4,780

years old—see Rocky Mountain Tree-ring Research, Inc. website, http://www.rmtrr.org/oldlist.htm. Accessed September 2004.

6   Personal communication with Dr. Ronald Hartman, curator of the Rocky Mountain Herbarium, University of Wyoming, Laramie, WY, November 2002.

7   Ausubel, Kenny. 2000. Tempest in a Tonic Bottle: A Bunch of Weeds? *HerbalGram* 49: 37. See American Botanical Council website, http://www.herbalgram.org/. Accessed January 2003.

8   Kershaw, MacKinnon, Pojar, *Plants of the Rocky Mountains*, 185.

9   Brinker, Francis, N.D. 1990. Inhibition of Endocrine Function by Botanical Agents. *Journal of Naturopathic Medicine*, Vol. 1, No. 1. http://www.healthy.net/Library/Journals/naturopathic/vol1no1/endo.htm. Accessed January 2003.
     See also Kershaw, MacKinnon and Pojar, *Plants of the Rocky Mountains*, 205.

10 Dunmire, William W. and Gail D. Tierney, *Wild Plants and Native Peoples of the Four Corners* (Santa Fe, NM: Museum of New Mexico Press, 1997) 203-204.

11 Maloof, J. E., and D. W. Inouye. 2000. Are nectar robbers cheaters or mutualists? *Ecology* 81(10):2651-2661.

12 Tilford, Gregory L., *Edible and Medicinal Plants of the West* (Missoula, MT: Mountain Press Publishing Company, 1997) 206.

13 Personal notes from field class with Dr. David Inouye, Rocky Mountain Biological Lab, Gothic, CO (July 2002).

14 Duke, *The Green Pharmacy*, 136.

15 Ettinger, David S., research summary, Sidney Kimmel Comprehensive Cancer Center at Johns Hopkins, Baltimore, MD (September 22, 2004). See website http://www.hopkinsmedicine.org/, then type *Veratrum* in the search engine. Accessed October 2004.

16 Schofield, *Discovering Wild Plants*, 134.

17 Moore, Michael, *Medicinal Plants of the Pacific West* (Santa Fe, NM: Red Crane Books, 1993) 290.

18 Tyler, Varro E., *Herbs of Choice* (Binghamton, NY: Pharmaceuticals Products Press, an imprint of The Haworth Press, Inc., 1994) 84.

19 Sheviak, Charles J. 1999. The Identities of Plantanthera hyperborea and P. huronensis, with Description of a New Species from North America, Lindleyana 14(4):193-203.

20 Duke, *The Green Pharmacy*, 118, 239, and 246.

21 Andrews, Rebecca. March 16, 1992. Western Science Learns From Native Culture, The Scientist, 6 (6).

22 Mahale Mountains National Park, Tanzania, Africa. Medicinal Plant Use by Chimpanzee in the Wild. See website: http://jinrui.zool.kyoto-u.ac.jp/ChimpHome/mahaleE.html, or type the National Park name in a search engine. Accessed October 2004.

23 Moore, Michael. *Medicinal Plants of the Mountain West* (Santa Fe, NM: Museum of New Mexico Press, 1979) 20.
     See also: Tieraona Low Dog, M.D., A.H.G, *Gifts of the Earth—The Healing Way of Herbal Medicine* (No location available, may be out of print: Herbal Press, 1991) 201.

24 Bengtsson AA, Rylander L, Hagmar L, Nived O, Sturfelt G. 2002. Risk factors for developing systemic lupus erythematosus: a case-control study in southern Sweden. *Rheumatology* (Oxford) 41(5):563-71.
     See also: Alcocer-Varela J, Iglesias A, Llorente L, et al. Effects of L-canavanine on T cells may explain the induction of systemic lupus erythematosus by alfalfa. *Arthritis Rheum* 1985;28(1):52-57.
     See also: Natural Standard Patient Monograph, *Herbal Plant Therapies: Alfalfa: Medicago sativa* (Houston, TX: The University of Texas MD Anderson Cancer Center, Complementary/Integrative Medicine Review of Therapies, 2004). See website, http://www.mdanderson.org/.
     See also: Duke, *The Green Pharmacy*, 324.

25 Ausubel, Kenny, Tempest in a Tonic Bottle, 37.
     See also Duke, *The Green Pharmacy*, 399. See note #7.

26 Dunmire, William W. and Tierney, Gail D., *Wild Plants and Native Peoples of the Four Corners* (Santa Fe, NM: Museum of New Mexico Press, 1997) 247.

27 Duke, *The Green Pharmacy*, 167, 331, and 361.

28 Olle Pellmyr, Tree of Life Web Project: *The Yucca Moth Family*, Department of Biological Sciences (University of Idaho, P.O. Box 443051, Moscow, ID 83844-3051, 1996). See website: http://tolweb.org/tree/eukaryotes/animals/arthropoda/hexapoda/lepidoptera/neolepidoptera/prodoxidae/prodoxidae.html. Accessed October 2004.

29 Attenborough, David, *The Private Life of Plants* (Princeton, NJ: Princeton University Press, 1995) 103.

30 Heywood, V. H., *Flowering Plants of the World* (Oxford, England: Oxford University Press, 1993) 243-245.

31 Buchman, Stephen L., and Gary Paul Nabhan, *The Forgotten Pollinators* (Washington, D.C.: Island Press, 1996) 57-58.

32 Maloof, Joan E., and David W. Inouye. 2000. Are Nectar Robbers Cheaters or Mutualists? *Ecology*, 81(10):2651-2661.

33 Holmes, Peter, *The Energetics of Western Herbs* (Boulder, CO: Snow Lotus Press, 2nd edition, 1994) 654-656.

34 Martin, Noland H. 2004. Flower size preferences of the honeybee (*Apis mellifera*) foraging on *Mimulus guttatus* (Scrophulariaceae). *Evolutionary Ecology Research* 6:777-782.
     See also Robertson, Alastair W. Robertson, Claire Mountjoy, Brian E. Faulkner, Matthew V. Roberts, and Mark R. Macnair. 1999. Bumble Bee Selection of Mimulus Guttatus Flowers: The Effects of Pollen Quality and Reward Depletion. *Ecology*, 80: 2594-2606.

35 Mitton, Jeff (professor of biology at University of Colorado, mitton@colorado.edu), Stealing food and defenses (Boulder, CO: Daily Camera, April 14, 2002). Accessed January 2003.

36 Barnes J, LA Anderson, and JD Phillipson. 2001. St. John's Wort (*Hypericum perfoliatum*): A review of its chemistry, pharmocology and clinical properties, Centre for Pharmagognosy and Phytotherapy, School of Pharmacy, University of London, *J Pharm Pharmacology* 53(5):583-600. See website: http://www.biopsychiatry.com/stjohnrev.htm. Accessed January 2003.

37 L. Watson and M. J. Dallwitz (1992 onwards). The Families of Flowering Plants: Descriptions, Illustrations, Identification, and Information Retrieval. Version: 14th December 2000. See website: http://biodiversity.uno.edu/delta/. Search for title above. Accessed January 2003

38 Anderson, J. P. 1939. Plants Used by the Eskimo of the Northern Bering Sea and Arctic Regions of Alaska, *American Journal of Botany* 26:714-716 (715).
     See also: Ager, Thomas A. and Lynn Price Ager. 1980. Ethnobotany of The Eskimos of Nelson Island, Alaska, *Arctic Anthropology* 27:26-48 (36).

39 Scofield, *Discovering Wild Plants*, 227-229.
     See also: Ager, Thomas A. and Lynn Price Ager. 1980. Ethnobotany of The Eskimos of Nelson Island, Alaska, *Arctic Anthropology* 27:26-48 (36).

40 Duke, *The Green Pharmacy*, 154, 269 and 366.

41 Tyler, *The Honest Herbal* (New York: Pharmaceutical Products Press, an imprint of Haworth Press, Inc., third edition, 1993) 63-64.

42 Kindscher, Kelly, *Medicinal Wild Plants of the Prairie* (Lawrence, KS: University Press of Kansas, 1992) 119-121.

43 Duke, *The Green Pharmacy*, 39.

44 Kindscher, *Medicinal Wild Plants of the Prairie*, 177.

45 Willard, Terry Ph.D., *Edible and Medicinal Plants of the Rocky Mountains and Neighboring Territories* (Calgary, AB, Canada: Wild Rose College of Natural Healing, 1992) 199-200.

46 Dharmananda, Subhuti, Ph.D. (director), Safety Issues

Affecting Herbs: Pyrrolizidine Alkaloids, article online. (Portland, Oregon: Institute for Traditional Medicine, November 2001). See website: http://www.itmonline.org/arts/pas.htm. Accessed January 2003.

47 Miller, Francis, Cuauhtemoc Rios, Forrest Ross, *Brickella grandiflora*, Medicinal Plants of the Southwest website, New Mexico State University, 2002. See website: http://medplant.nmsu.edu/brickellia.htm. Accessed September 2004.

48 Moore, *Medicinal Plants of the Pacific West*, 293.

49 Moerman, Dan, University of Michigan-Dearborn, Native American Ethnobotany Database. See website: http://www.umd.umich.edu/cgi-bin/herb/, type Latin name of plant in search engine of website. Accessed September 2004.

50 Harry Verney Warren, Pioneer of Geochemistry, a commemoration of his life. Researched *Phacelia sericea*. Earth Sciences Department, University of Waterloo, Ontario, Canada. See website or type name in search engine: http://www.sci.uwaterloo.ca/earth/waton/s003.html. Accessed September 2004.

See also: Ager, Thomas A. and Lynn Price Ager. 1980. Ethnobotany of The Eskimos of Nelson Island, Alaska, *Arctic Anthropology* 27:26-48 (36).

Birds

1 Personal communication with Arvind Panjabi, Rocky Mountain Bird Observatory, Brighton, CO, 2004. See website http://www.rmbo.org.

2 Snake River Birds of Prey, Raptor Information. See BLM website: http://www.birdsofprey.blm.gov/. Accessed March 2004.

3 Personal communication with Jonathan Lowsky, Pitkin County Wildlife Biologist, Aspen, CO; who observed these birds in courtship flights, in the upper Roaring Fork Valley, during 2001.

4 Milius, S. 2000. Metal in Diet Harms Colorado Birds. *Science News* 158 (6):90.

5 Sibley, David Allen, *The Sibley Guide to Birds* (New York: Alfred A. Knopf, National Audubon Society, 2000) 149.

6 Swarth, C., B170, *Spotted Sandpiper*, California Wildlife Habitat Relationships System. California Department of Fish and Game, California Interagency Wildlife Task Group, http://www.dfg.ca.gov/whdab/html/B170.html. Accessed January 2004.

7 Bent, Arthur Cleveland. 1927. *Smithsonian Institution United States National Museum Bulletin* 142 (Part 1):81-98. United States Government Printing Office. See online book, *Life Histories of Familiar North American Birds*, http://birdsbybent.netfirms.com/ch61-70/snipe.html. Accessed March 2004.

8 Gingras, Pierre, *The Secret Lives of Birds* (Buffalo, NY:

Firefly Books, 1997).

See also: Skutch, A., *Life of the Pigeon*. (Cornell University Press, Cornell, New York, 1991).

9 Hammon, J. 2001. Columba fasciata" (On-line), Animal Diversity Web. See website: http://animaldiversity.ummz.umich.edu/site/accounts/information/Columba_fasciata.html. Accessed October 03, 2004.

10 Sibley, *Sibley Guide to Birds*, 255.

11 Burton, John A. editor, *Owls of the World* (E.P. Dutton, New York, 1973) 78.

12 Lane, W.H., All About Boreal Owls. See article online at website, http://www.mindspring.com/~owlman/index.htm. Accessed March 2004.

13 Line, Les, Goatsuckers get some respect. *National Wildlife Federation Newsletter*, August/September 1998.

14 McQueen, Larry, Hairy Woodpecker. Online article at Cornell Ornithology Lab website, www.birds.cornell.edu/. Accessed March 2004.

15 Saunders, Aretas A., *The Lives of Wild Birds* (Garden City, New York: Doubleday and Company, 1954) 157.

16 Jim Travis, board member and editor of the New Mexico Bird Atlas project. References in text refer to notes taken in a Bird Song Workshop given by Jim Travis in 2000 at Aspen Center for Environmental Studies, Aspen, Colorado.

17 Howes-Jones, Daryl. 1985. Relationship among song activity, context, and social behavior in the warbling vireo. Wilson Bulletin 97:4-22.

18 Phillips, Helen, Space-time for bird brains. *Nature* (magazine): Science Update, (September 24, 1998). See website: http://www.nature.com/news/bysubject/celland molecularbiology/980921.html. Accessed January 2004.

19 Erlich, Paul R., Dopkin, David S., and Wheye, Darryl. *The Birder's Handbook* (New York: Simon & Schuster, Fireside, 1988) 416.

20 McGowan, Kevin J., Reproductive and Social Behavior of two Crow Species in New York—Ecology and Systematics, Cornell University, 12 December 1997, Termination report for US Department of Agriculture, http://birds.cornell.edu/crows/hatchrep.html. Accessed March 2004.

21 Elston, Catherine Feher, *Ravensong—A Natural and Fabulous History of Ravens and Crows* (Flagstaff, AZ: Northland Publishing 1991).

22 Lipton, James, *An Exaltation of Larks* (New York: Penquin Books, 1993).

23 Kilham, Laurence, *The American Crow and the Common Raven* (College Station, TX: Texas A & M Press, 1989).

24 Line, Les, Total Recall, *National Wildlife Newsletter*, February/March, 1998. See website: http://www.nwf.org/nationalwildlife/1998/recall.html. Accessed October, 2004.

25 Sherry, D. 1996. Behavioural and neural bases of orientation in food-storing birds. *J. of Experimental Biology* 199:165-172.

See also: Model Systems in Neuroethology, Food Caching

Two local red fox kits

in the Black-capped Chickadee, 1996. http://soma.npa
uiuc.edu/courses/physl490b/models/bird_caching/
bird_caching.html.

26 Kingery, Hugh E., *Colorado Breeding Bird Atlas* (Denver,
CO: Colorado Bird Atlas Partnership and Colorado
Division of Wildlife, 1998) 350.

27 Coverstone, Nancy. Cooperation is Survival in Nature.
University of Maine Extension Educator, Wild About
Nature online, October 2000, University of Maine
Cooperative Extension. See website: www.umext.maine
.edu/WildaboutNature/1000.htm. Accessed October 2004.

28 Bent, A.C., Life histories of North American nuthatches,
wrens, thrashers, and their allies. Washington, DC: United
States National Museum Bulletin 195, 1948).

29 Erhlich, Dopkin, and Wheye, *The Birder's Handbook*, 482.

30 Andrews, R., and R. Righter, *Colorado Birds* (Denver, CO:
Denver Museum of Natural History, 1992).

31 Ehrlich, Dopkin, Wheye, *The Birder's Handbook*, 458.

32 Hames, S. 1999. Early Looks at Thrush Relationships.
Birdscope, 13 (3):11-13. Cornell Laboratory of Ornithology,
Ithaca, New York. See website: www.birds.cornell.edu.
Accessed January 2003.

33 American Pipit online article. See Stanford alumni website,
http://www.stanfordalumni.org/birdsite/text/species/
American_Pipit.html. Accessed January 2004.
Also try http://www.stanfordalumni.org/ and type
American pipit in the search engine.

34 Weidensaul, Scott, *Living on the Wind–Across the Hemisphere
with Migratory Birds* (New York: North Point Press, 1999)
introduction.

35 Simons, Theodore. 1999. *The Role of Indicator Species:
Neotropical Migratory Songbirds.* See website: http://
www.srs.fs.fed.us/pubs/rpc/1999-03/rpc_99mar_36.pdf.
Accessed January 2004.

36 Ehrlich, Dopkin, Wheye, *The Birder's Handbook*, 504.

37 Notes from Jim Travis, board member and editor of the
New Mexico Bird Atlas project. References in text refer to
notes taken in a Bird Song Workshop given by Jim Travis
in 1999 at Aspen Center for Environmental Studies,
Aspen, CO.

38 Partners in Flight, Conservation Plans, Physiographic
Region 62: Southern Rocky Mountains, Mountain
Shrublands: Virginia's Warbler. See website: http://
www.rmbo.org/pif/bcp/phy62/mt-shrub/viwa.htm.
Accessed January 2004.

39 McQueen, Larry, Yellow-rumped Warbler. Online article at
Cornell Ornithology Lab website, www.birds.cornell.edu/.
Accessed March 2004.
See also: Blom, Eirik, Species Profile: Yellow-rumped
Warbler, *Bird Watcher's Digest*, M/J (1997): 32.

40 Sibley, *Sibley Guide to Bird Life and Behavior*, 512.

41 Erlich, Dobkin, and Wheye, *The Birder's Handbook* (Simon
& Schuster, Fireside, 1998), 564.

42 Ibid., 586.

43 Lynes, Michael, California Partners in Flight Riparian Bird
Conservation Plan for the Black-headed Grosbeak,
February 1, 1998, Point Reyes Bird Observatory, 4990
Shoreline Hwy, Stinson Beach, CA 94970. See website:
http://www.prbo.org/calpif/htmldocs/species/riparian/
black_headed_grosbeak_acct.htm. Accessed September
2004.

44 Notes from Jim Travis, board member and editor of the
New Mexico Bird Atlas project. References in text refer to
notes taken in a Bird Song Workshop given by Jim Travis
in 1999 at Aspen Center for Environmental Studies.

45 Blom, Eirik, Evening Grosbeaks, *Bird Watcher's Digest*, J/F
(1997):28.

46 Speirs, Doris Huestis. 1968. Evening Grosbeaks,
*Smithsonian Institution United States National Museum
Bulletin* 237 (Part 1):206-237. United States Government
Printing Office. See online book, *Life Histories of Familiar*

North American Birds, http://home.bluemarble.net/
~pqn/ch41-50/grosbeak.html. Accessed September 2004.

47 Brown-capped Rosy Finch (040415), Biota Information
System of New Mexico (Bison), New Mexico Game & Fish
website, http://fwie.fw.vt.edu/states/nmex_main/
species/040415.htm, version January 2004. Accessed
October 2004. Author unknown.

Mammals

1 Gray, Mary Taylor, Shrews. See Denver, CO: Colorado
Division of Wildlife website: http://www.wildlife.state
.co.us/education/mammalsguide/shrews.asp, Accessed
April 2004.

2 Lollar, Amanda, and Barbara Schmidt French. *Caring for
Pregnant and Lactating Females, from Captive Care and
Medical Reference for the Rehabilitation of Insectivorous Bats.*
(Mineral Wells, TX: Bat Conservation International, 1998).
See website: www.batcon.org. Accessed October 2004.

3 Whitaker, J. 1995. Food of the Big Brown Bat, Eptesicus-
Fuscus, From Maternity Colonies in Indiana and Illinois.
American Midland Naturalist 134 (2): 346-360.

4 Barnes, Thomas G., Bats-Information for Kentucky
Homeowners. (Lexington, KY: University of Kentucky,
Department of Foresty, no date available). See website:
www.biology.eku.edu/bats/Kybatinfo.html. Accessed
October 2004. Or, use search engine and enter: bats, med-
ical advances.

5 Internet article, Answers to Questions about Bats, Rabies,
and Other Health Issues (Mineral Wells, TX: Bat
Conservation International, 2003). See website: http://
www.batcon.org. Accessed August 2004.

6 Personal communication with Jonathan Lowsky, Pitkin
County Wildlife Biologist, September, 2004, regarding the
near extirpation of the white-tailed jackrabbit in the upper
Roaring Fork Valley, possibly due to loss of habitat, human
development and increased number of coyotes due to previous extirpation of wolves.

7 O'Donoghue, Mark. 1994. Early Survival of Juvenile
Snowshoe Hares, *Ecology* 75(6): 1582-1592.

8 Gibson, L. J. 1984. Chromosomal Changes in Mammalian
Speciation-A Literature Review. *Origins* 11(2):67-89.
See also: Nadler, C. F., R. S. Hoffmann and K. R. Greer.
1971. Chromosomal divergence during evolution of
ground squirrel populations (Rodentia: *Spermophilus*).
Systematic Zoology 20:298-305.
See also: Jonathan Lowsky, Pitkin County Biologist, Aspen
Times Letter to the Editor, June 18, 2001.

9 Boyd, David, Herbivores' Busted Preying on Bird Nests
(Casper, WY: *Casper Star Tribune*, August 20, 1998).
Available through archive department.

10 Wolkomir, Richard and Joyce, Prying Into the Life of a
Prickly Beast, *National Wildlife*, December/January 1994.

11 Marc Bekoff, Professor of Biology, University of Colorado-
Boulder, Tireless Tricksters, protean predators, coyotes
adapt to wasteful human extermination ploys (Boulder,
Colorado: The Daily Camera, November 18, 2001).

12 Wilkinson, Todd, *Track of the Coyote* (Charlottesville, VA:
NorthWord Press, Inc., 1995) 122.

13 Crooks, K.R. and M.E. Soule. 1999. Mesopredator release
and avifaunal extinctions in a fragmented system. *Nature*
400:563-566.

14 Ibid.

15 Rezendez, Paul, *Tracking and the Art of Seeing* (Richmond
Hill, Ontario, Canada: Firefly Books, 2nd edition 1999)
194.

16 Marc Bekoff, Professor of Biology, University of Colorado-
Boulder, Tireless Tricksters, protean predators, coyotes
adapt to wasteful human extermination ploys (Boulder,
Colorado: The Daily Camera, November 18, 2001). See

website: http://www.wolfpark.org/ICRC/
article_bekoff.html. Accessed September 2004.

17 Ibid.

18 Rezendes, Tracking and the Art of Seeing, 176.

19 Wassink, Jan L., *Mammals of the Central Rockies* (Missoula, MT: Mountain Press, 1993) 56.

20 Kamler, Jan F., and Warren B. Ballard. 2002. A review of native and nonnative red foxes in North America. *Wildlife Society Bulletin* 30:370-379.

21 Joslin, G., and H. Youmans, coordinators. 1999. Effects of Recreation on Rocky Mountain Wildlife: A review for Montana, 7.18, 307. Committee on effects of recreation on Rocky Mountain wildlife. Order from: Montana Chapter of the Wildlife Society, 2763 Grizzly Gulch, Helena, MT 59601.

22 Vince Schute Wildlife Sanctuary, American Bear Association online article, A Closer Look at the Black Bear's Fur. See website, http://www.americanbear.org/FUR.htm. Accessed October 2004.

23 Halfpenny, Jim, Ph.D., Tracking the Great Bear: Breaking the Rules, *Bears and Other Top Predators*, Vol. 2 (1):11-12. See website: http://www.bearmagsales.com or call (206) 938-4969, Seattle, WA.

24 Young, Mary Taylor, Bears, *Colorado's Wildlife Company* newsletter. Write or call Colorado Division of Wildlife, Public Information, 6060 Broadway, Denver, CO 80216.

25 Smith, Dave, Hey, You're Crowding Me! *Bears and Other Top Predators*, Vol. 2 (1):16. See website: http://www

.tracknature.com. Accessed April 2004.

26 Halfpenny, Jim, Ph.D., Bear Art, *Bears and Other Top Predators*, Vol. 1 (1):11-13. See website: http://www.bearmagsales.com or call (206) 938-4969, Seattle, WA. Accessed October 2004.

27 Living with Wildlife—In Bear Country. Colorado Division of Wildlife brochure, Denver, CO, 303-297-1192.

28 Cahalane, V.H., *Mammals of North America* (The Macmillan Company, New York, 1961) 226.

29 Halfpenny, Jim, *Scats and Tracks of the Rocky Mountains* (Helena, MT: Falcon Press, 1998) 36.

30 Living with Wildlife in Mountain Lion Country. Colorado Division of Wildlife, Denver, CO, 303-297-1192.

31 Boyd, David, Herbivores' Busted Preying on Bird Nests (Casper, WY: *Casper Star Tribune*, August 20, 1998). Available through archive department.

32 Living with Elk. Colorado Division of Wildlife brochure, Denver, CO, 303-297-1192.

33 Rennicke, Jeff, *Colorado Wildlife* (Helena, MT: Falcon Press Publishing, 1990) 79.

34 Rennicke, *Colorado Wildlife*, 54.

35 Personal communication with Snowmass Village biologist, Larry Green.

36 Rutherford, W.H., 1972. *Status of Mountain Goats in Colorado*, Department of Natural Resources, 4. See website: http://www.dnr.state.co.us/.

37 Bama, Lynne, Bringing back the bighorn, *High Country News*, Vol. 29, No. 2, February 3, 1997.

GLOSSARY

The following drawings and definitions relate to terms as they are used in this book.

Achene. Hard, dry indehiscent fruit with a single seed (ovule); attaches to the ovary wall at a single point. Figure 10.

Acuminate. Leaf or fruit, for example, that tapers to a sharp point with concave sides along the tip.

Alkaloid. Organic, nitrogenous molecule found in plants (e.g. pyrrolizidine alkaloids of the borage family) and animals (e.g., shellfish) that has a pharmacological effect on humans and animals. Many are poisonous (e.g., alkaloids in poison hemlock). They are also used in traditional and/or herbal medicine (e.g., morphine, opium, caffeine and the berberine in Oregon grape, or Mahonia).

Allantoin. Protein with hormonal-like qualities, known to result in cell proliferation. Plants containing allantoin are used for healing wounds and skin irritations (e.g. false Solomon's seal).

Alterative. Tonic that affects the liver, helping the body eliminate waste products.

Alternate leaves. Leaves spaced at uneven intervals on the stem of a plant. Figure 5.

Alternation of generations. Ferns, pg. 71.

Altricial. State of development at birth; animals or birds born with eyes shut, without fur or feathers, needing parental care to survive. These young spend little energy on staying warm and no energy at all on foraging (e.g., rabbits are altricial, hares are precocial).

Andromonoecious. Having flowers with only stamens (staminate) and flowers with both male and female parts (perfect) on the same plant.

Annual. Plant that germinates, flowers, fruits and dies within twelve-month period.

Anther. Pollen-bearing sac or sacs of a plant's stamen. Figure 1.

Anthocyanins. Blue, purple or red water soluble pigments responsible for the red tinge in early spring plants; convert light energy into warmth for the plant.

Antimicrobial. Capable of destroying or inhibiting growth of disease-causing microorganisms.

Antirheumatic. A plant with the reputation of alleviating or preventing rheumatism.

Antispasmodic. Helps control involuntary muscle contractions, such as coughing.

Apex. The tip; that point that is most removed from the point of attachment.

Apomixis. Production of seeds without fertilization.

Appressed. Lying close and flat against, as a bud against a twig.

Auricles. Ear-shaped appendages, as at the base of some leaves.

Auricular. Having auricles.

Awl-like. Very pointed, shaped like a narrow triangle; short, sharp and stiff (e.g., leaves of young junipers).

Basal. Occurring at the base of a plant stem (e.g., leaves of many plants in heath family). Figure 5.

Bastfiber. Strong wood fiber obtained mostly from the phloem, or food-conducting tissue, of plants.

Berry. A fleshy fruit that develops from the ovary. The seeds are surrounded by pulp inside of a thin skin. Figure 10.

Biennial. Plant that flowers during second year of its life cycle, with only a set of leaves during the first year. A biennial that blooms again in the third or fourth year is called a "short-lived perennial."

Bilaterally symmetrical. When one half of a plant is the mirror image of the other (e.g., Calypso orchid). Figure 2.

Bioconcentrate. Referring to the accumulation of chemicals in animals or humans through the food chain; when a contaminated plant or animal is eaten by another, passing the chemicals to the next individual.

Bisexual. Plant with both stamens and pistils on same plant. Also called "perfect."

Bog. Type of wetland with acidic soil, characterized by spongy ground of decomposing vegetation that has less drainage than a swamp; moisture sometimes solely from rainwater; often dominated by peat, or sphagnum, moss.

Bolus. In this book, a mixture of food and saliva from a special enlarged gland in birds; often tucked into discreet location for later retrieval. In general, is a small, rounded mass of food made ready by the tongue and jaw movement for swallowing.

Boreal. Pertaining to northern regions, including a wide band of coniferous forests reaching from New England to Alaska.

Bract. Small leaf-like appendage at the base of a flower or inflorescence. One of the main structures coming off a conifer cone's axis.

Brood. Collective young of a bird.

Brood patch. Bare area on the abdomen of a bird where feathers are plucked or dropped so that warm skin is adjacent to eggs for incubation.

Browse. Typically refers to an animal feeding on woody plants.

Bulb. Spherical underground bud with thick, fleshy scales (e.g., onions).

Cache. A store of food concealed in a hiding place for later retrieval. Also used to mean the act of making a cache (e.g., Clark's nutcracker is famous for doing this).

Calyx. Collective term for all the sepals of a flower. Figure 1.

Cambium. Inner bark of woody plants.

Carnivore. Any species that feeds on flesh of other species.

Carpel. Simple pistil formed from a modified leaf (e.g., pea pod), or one member of a compound pistil formed from a modified leaf; where seeds are attached.

Carpophore. Slender extension of the receptacle forming a central axis between carpels (e.g., fruits in parsley family, such as mature fruit of western sweetroot).

Carr. Shrubland community composed of species such as willow, alder and birch growing in wet soil.

Catkins. Type of inflorescence without petals in the willow or birch family, composed of either male or female flowers; also called an "ament."

Cere. Raised, fleshy part at the base a bird's bill (e.g., a raptor's bill).

Chrysophanic acid. Bitter yellow substance found in roots of yellow dock and rhubarb. A glycoside used in herbal medicine for skin irritations.

Ciliate. Having a fringe of hairs on the margin (e.g., edge of a leaf).

Circumboreal. Surrounding the Northern Hemisphere in forested regions, appearing in both the Old and New Worlds.

Circumpolar. Distributed around the world.

Clasping. When the base of a leaf wholly or partly surrounds a stem. Figure 6.

Climax species. Species in equilibrium with the surrounding ecosystem—not likely to change without disturbance such as insect infestation, fire or avalanche. For example, Engelmann spruce is a climax species in the subalpine zone. When an avalanche opens a path through dense forest, aspen or lodgepole pine trees (successional species) will colonize the disturbed area, taking advantage of the sunlight. However, these trees are eventually replaced by spruce, a more shade-loving species that will remain until the next disturbance.

Coevolution. When two species change together throughout time, the change in one necessitating a change in the other; a change that makes that species increase or maintain its fitness (e.g., hummingbirds and red flowers with long tubes that fit their long bill are said to have co-evolved.)

Figure 1 · PARTS OF A GENERALIZED FLOWER

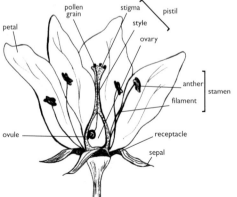

Figure 2 · FLOWER SYMMETRY

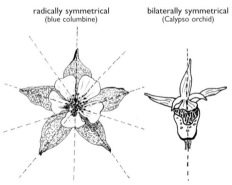

Column. Structure resulting from the union of filaments (e.g., mallow family), or filaments and the style (e.g., orchid family).

Compound leaf. Leaf separated into two or more leaflets. Figure 8.

Contraindicated. Word used to indicate a substance that should not be used under certain circumstances.

Convergent evolution. Where two unrelated structures evolved in unrelated species to perform the same function (e.g., wings in birds and bats).

Cordate. Heart-shaped, referring to the outline or base of a leaf. Figure 7.

Corm. Solid, short, vertical underground stem with thin, papery leaves (e.g., iris family).

Corolla. Collective name for the petals of a flower. Figure 1.

Corona. Structures appearing crown- or petal-like; attached to the inside of the corolla, as in milkweeds.

Corymb. A flat-topped or convex, open flower cluster, the outer flowers opening first. Figure 3.

Coverts. Small contoured feathers that cover the base of a bird's flight feathers. Figure 11.

Crepuscular. More active at dawn or dusk.

Cruciform. Shaped like a cross.

Cyme. Inflorescence, usually with opposite branching; terminal bud blooms first, preventing any further elongation. Branching can be alternate or opposite. Note: A cyme with alternate branching resembles a corymb, but the fruits of a cyme mature first in the center, not on the outside branches as in a corymb. Figure 3.

Decurrent. Describes the base of a leaf that extends down the stem below where it is attached (e.g. leaves of some thistles), or hairs that extend in a line down the stem from base of leaf (e.g. some asters). Figure 6.

Delayed development. When mating is immediately followed by fertilization and implantation, but fetal development is delayed until spring. Some development may occur earlier in some species, but slowly.

Delayed fertilization. After mating in the fall, the male's sperm is stored in the female's uterus until spring, when ovulation, fertilization, and then embryonic development take place.

Delayed implantation. A suvival mechanism of mammals that allows young to be born early enough in the spring to be old enough and strong enough to survive the following winter. To achieve this, mating occurs in the fall and is followed by fertilization of the egg, but there is only minimal development of the embryo, and then a period of relative dormancy. This young embryo is not implanted in the uterus until females emerge from hibernation in the spring; further development then takes place. Mating in the spring would not allow enough time for many species, as males often do not recommence sperm production for many weeks following hibernation.

Diaphoretic. Induces perspiration.

Dioecious. Imperfect flowers; stamens and pistils are on different plants of the same species.

Disc floret. Small flowers of the sunflower family that make up the center of a typical sunflower. Figure 4.

Diurnal. Active chiefly in the daytime.

Drupe. Fleshy fruit with a single, stony seed; as in a cherry. Figure 10.

Emergent. Coming from, but standing out of, the water.

Endemic. Confined to a particular geographic area.

Entire. Smooth on the edges, without serrations.

Eskers. Long, ropy dirt "snakes" made by pocket gophers during winter while digging and shoving dirt into tunnels in the snow; lay exposed on the ground as snow melts.

Evergreen. Fallen needles are constantly being replaced by new ones, ensuring evergreen foliage.

Extirpated. Eliminated or exterminated.

Fascicle. Small bundle, such as clusters of pine needles joined at the base.

Fellfield. Rocky alpine areas blown free of snow most of the winter.

Figure 3 · FLOWER ARRANGEMENTS—THE INFLORESCENCE

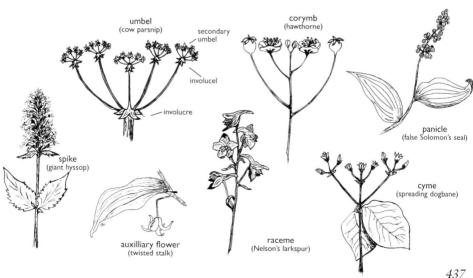

umbel
(cow parsnip)

secondary umbel

involucel

involucre

corymb
(hawthorne)

panicle
(false Solomon's seal)

spike
(giant hyssop)

auxilliary flower
(twisted stalk)

raceme
(Nelson's larkspur)

cyme
(spreading dogbane)

Fen. Wetlands that form peat; receiving their nutrients from sources other than precipitation, often from groundwater; may be alkaline or acidic, though less acidic and with a higher nutrient level than a bog—thus a greater diversity of plants. Important to watersheds for water quality, flood control and as a unique community; often subalpine.

Filament. Slender stalk supporting an anther. Figure 1.

Flavonoids. Antioxidants that protect living cells against free-radical damage.

Floret. Small flower, typically used in referring to sunflowers, sedges and grasses. Figure 4.

Follicle. Dry fruit composed of a single carpel, opening at maturity along a single side (e.g., milkweed, columbine, delphinium). Figure 10.

Food chain. Refers to the way living things get their food. Some animals eat plants (herbivore), and some animals eat animals (carnivore). Each link in this chain is food for the next. A large mass of living things at the base of the food chain (vegetation) is necessary to support a few at the top (animals).

Fruit. Structure that ripens from an ovary, including any other parts connected to it; contains the seed or seeds. Figure 10.

Furanocoumarins. Toxic chemical compounds found primarily in the parsley family (locally), which often cause skin irritations in humans. Ultra-violet radiation sometimes enhances their negative effect.

Gametophyte. The self-sustaining, individual plant that develops from a spore in the sexual phase of the alternation of generations—two completely different phases that occur in the life cycle of some plants (See ferns and horsetails, pg. 71). The heart-shaped gametophyte of ferns is only a few mm in diameter and lays flat on the ground; rarely seen.

Gametophytes produce the sperm and egg that meet in fertilization to form the fertilized egg that develops into the non-sexual phase, or sporophyte (e.g., visible fern). Sporophytes produce spores that will again grow into the gametophyte. Gametophytes are usually the inconspicuous part of a vascular plant's life cycle. See prothallus.

Glabrous. Smooth and hairless.

Glaucous. Covered with a whitish or bluish coating (e.g., Drummond's willow).

Glycoside. Group of plant compounds that often have medicinal properties; yield different sugars when broken down.

Grazing. Feeding on growing grass or herbs.

Gynodioecy. When species have pistillate flowers and flowers with both pistils and stamens (perfect); flowers on separate plants.

Habitat specific. Usually found living in a particular habitat, not flexible to variable conditions.

Half-inferior ovary. An ovary that neither appears superior or inferior because the hypanthium of the flower is fused to the lower half of the ovary, making it look like the flower parts are arising from the middle of the ovary (e.g., rose family). Figure 9.

Hand lens. Magnifying lens available from nature centers.

Haustoria. Specialized root-like organ that connect roots of a parasitic or hemiparasitic plant to its host plant, allowing transfer of water and minerals.

Hawk. Method of feeding. Refers to a bird that darts from the ends of branches to capture insects in flight - soaring and striking like a hawk.

Figure 4 · Parts of a Typical Sunflower *(continued next page)*

Flowers in this family are composed of many individual flowers, called either ray or disc florets.

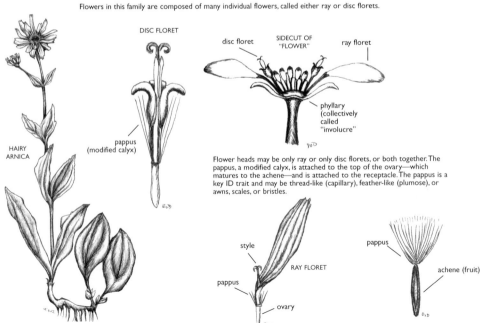

DISC FLORET

disc floret

SIDECUT OF "FLOWER"

ray floret

phyllary (collectively called "involucre"

HAIRY ARNICA

pappus (modified calyx)

Flower heads may be only ray or only disc florets, or both together. The pappus, a modified calyx, is attached to the top of the ovary—which matures to the achene—and is attached to the receptacle. The pappus is a key ID trait and may be thread-like (capillary), feather-like (plumose), or awns, scales, or bristles.

style

RAY FLORET

pappus

pappus

achene (fruit)

ovary

Hemiparasites. Plants with outer roots that produce haustoria, or structures that penetrate the roots of other plants to absorb some of their nutrients, water, and even chemical defenses (typically alkaloids)

Herbivores. Animals that eat only plants.

Hexaploid. When each cell has six full sets of chromosomes.

Home range. Area an individual covers in its daily round of activities.

Host plants. Individual, plant or animal, that provides another individual with food/and or abode.

Hypanthium. Cup formed by the fused bases of a flower's stamens, petals, and sepals; typical of the rose family.

Hyphae. Thread-like structures forming the mycelium of a fungus.

Indehiscent. Remaining closed at maturity (e.g., fruit or anther, which does not open along definite pores or lines).

Indicator species. Species representative of a particular environment (e.g., warbling vireos are indicator species for aspen forests).

Inferior ovary. Whether a flower's ovary is superior or inferior depends on placement. An inferior ovary is beneath the attachment of stamens, petals and sepals (e.g., parsley and evening-primrose families). Figure 9.

Inflorescence. Arrangement of the flowers on a plant. Figure 3.

Insectivore. Animal that eats only insects.

Invertebrate. Animals without backbones, such as insects, spiders and snails.

Involucel. Secondary involucre, when there are secondary umbels within a larger umbel (e.g., parsley family). Figure 3.

Involucre. Whorl of bracts (phyllaries) at the base of a flower or flower cluster (e.g., parsley and sunflower families). Figure 4.

Irregular flowers. Bilaterally symmetrical, all sides of the flower are not the same (e.g., monkeyflower).

Irrupt. An often unpredictable, large and sudden movement of birds into an area where they are normally uncommon (also called an invasion).

Keystone species. Species that provide essential and unique services within an ecosystem (e.g., red-naped sapsucker); without them, other resident species might disappear.

Krummholz. Stunted tree zone that is the transition from the subalpine zone to the alpine zone; comes from the German word for "crooked wood."

Labellum. Outstanding lip-like petal of an orchid.

Life zone. Area with boundaries determined by the extent of particular plant communities and their associated ecosystems.

Locule. Hollow space or chamber inside an ovary where seeds form, or inside an anther where pollen forms; typically referred to as a cell.

Mandible. Either the upper or lower segment of the bill of a bird. Figure 11.

Mantle. Feathers grouped in the center of a bird's back. Figure 11.

Marsh. Wetland ecosystem characterized by poorly drained mineral soil and dominated by grasses.

Marsupial. Order of mammals characterized by premature birth, with the young continuing development while attached to nipples within a pouch on the mother's belly.

Mericarp. One of two halves of a fruit in the parsley family.

Midden. Mound of cones and cone scales at the base of conifers. These result from generations of squirrels removing the scales from cones to get to the seeds, while sitting on branches in the conifer above the midden. Middens include whole cones stored for future use.

Mobbing. Behavior that occurs when birds are aggressive toward or actually attack a perceived enemy, often a predator (e.g., crows attacking a hawk, chickadees scolding an owl, blackbirds chasing a crow). May occur to warn others of the predator's presence, distract the predator from nest or young, or drive the predator from the area.

Figure 4 · Parts of a Typical Sunflower (*continued*)

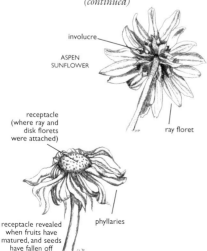

involucre

ASPEN SUNFLOWER

receptacle (where ray and disk florets were attached)

ray floret

receptacle revealed when fruits have matured, and seeds have fallen off

phyllaries

Figure 5 · Leaf Arrangements

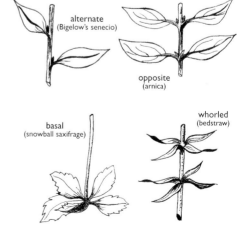

alternate (Bigelow's senecio)

opposite (arnica)

basal (snowball saxifrage)

whorled (bedstraw)

Molt. Periodical shedding and replacement of a bird's worn feathers.

Monocarpic. Plants that may live many years before blooming only once and then dying.

Mordant. Chemical that helps a colorant bind to a fabric for which it otherwise has no affinity.

Mucilage. Gelatinous substance of many plants used in herbal medicine, containing proteins and polysaccharides (e.g., mallow family; okra also has the same type of mucilage).

Muslin. Any of several plain-weave cotton fabrics, the sturdier variety used for sheets; originally fabricated in Mosul, a city in Iraq.

Mutualism. An interaction between species that benefits both participants; one individual provides another with food or abode in exchange for a beneficial service.

Mycelium. A complex network of threadlike tubular filaments (hyphae) that function in nutrient absorption and transfer for fungi. The non-reproductive part of the body of a fungus.

Mycorrhizae. Hyphae of certain fungi (mycorrhizal fungi), which are symbiotic with the plant roots on which they are found. May be used to refer to the symbiotic combination of the hyphae and the plant roots to provide benefit to the associated plant.

Nape. Feathers at the back of a bird's neck.

Native. A plant species "that occurs naturally in a region, state, ecosystem or habitat without direct or indirect human actions" (Federal Native Plant Conservation Committee, 1994).

Neotropical migrant. Bird species that nest and reproduce in the United States and Canada during spring and summer and then migrate to Mexico, Central and South America and the Caribbean during the non-breeding season.

Niche. The role/place a particular organism occupies in the community of organisms in its habitat.

Nitrogen-fixation. When special bacteria nodules form a symbiotic relationship with some plants, attaching themselves to their roots and extracting nitrogen from the atmosphere to convert it into soil nitrates that are then available to other plants.

Nocturnal. More active at night.

Node. That part of the stem where leaves or branches originate.

Non-native. A species that has immigrated from another region, usually within the past 250 years. The words "alien" and "exotic" are synonyms.

Non-serotinous. Lodgepole pine cones that are not tightly bound together by resin; open at maturity to disperse seeds. See serotinous.

Nut. Fruit similar to an achene, since it is a one-seeded fruit with a leathery or stony covering (e.g. acorn of oak family, or nutlet of the borage family). Figure 10.

Oblanceolate. Inverse of lanceolate, where the leaf attaches to the stem at the narrower end. Figure 7.

Omnivore. An animal that eats both plants and meat.

Opposite leaves. Two leaves that originate across from each other at the same node on the stem. Figure 5.

Ovary. Expanded base of the pistil, which holds the growing seeds, and eventually produces the fruit. Figure 1.

Ovule. Structure in the ovary that becomes the seed after fertilization.

Oxalic acid. Organic compound in the family of carboxylic acids, which gives many plants a tart taste; toxic in large amounts, but safe when used moderately.

Pair-bonds. Bond formed between two birds for the purpose of mating, which usually lasts as long as they feed and care for their young. The character and duration varies greatly. Although the extremes are wide-ranging, with some birds

Figure 6 · LEAF MARGINS AND ATTACHMENTS

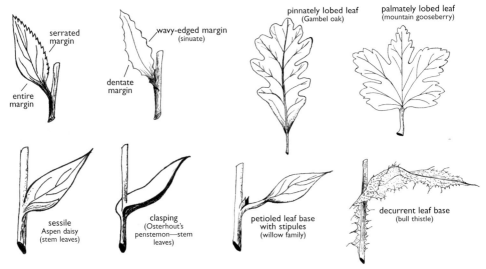

serrated margin

entire margin

wavy-edged margin (sinuate)

dentate margin

pinnately lobed leaf (Gambel oak)

palmately lobed leaf (mountain gooseberry)

sessile
Aspen daisy
(stem leaves)

clasping
(Osterhout's penstemon—stem leaves)

petioled leaf base with stipules
(willow family)

decurrent leaf base (bull thistle)

separating soon after mating and others remaining together throughout the year, most pairs separate sometime after the breeding season and spend migration and winter apart, even if they do pair again with the same individual the next breeding season.

Panicle. A cluster of associated spikes, racemes or corymbs. Often applied to any complex cluster. Figure 3.

Parthenogenesis. Reproduction by development of an unfertilized gamete; occurs especially among lower plants.

Patagium. Area on wing between bird's body and wrist of wing. Figure 11.

Pectin. Peculiar structure in the eye of all birds, fishes and reptiles; a fan shaped tissue attached to the retina; extends into the central part of the eye. Full of blood vessels, it may supply oxygen to the retina.

Pedicel. Stalk of a single flower in an inflorescence.

Peduncle. Stalk of a single flower or of an inflorescence.

Pelage. Furry, hairy or woolly coat of a mammal; important to insulation, protection or coloration.

Pemmican. Mixture of dried fruits, meats, and fats that sustained Native American tribes.

Perennial. Plant that lives for more than a few years. May or may not die back each year to a storage organ, such as a taproot, bulb or corm.

Perfect flowers. Flowers having both male and female parts.

Perfoliate. When a leaf surrounds a stem so that the stem appears to go through the leaf.

Perianth. Both the petals and sepals together, especially when they look similar.

Periderm. Outer layer of bark.

Perigynium. Scale-like bract that encloses the ovary in sedges.

Petal. Whorl of flower parts inside or above the calyx; collectively called the corolla.

Petiole. Leaf stalk.

Pharmacopoeia. An official compilation of medicinal substances and/or articles with descriptions, tests and formulas for preparing them, recognized by a particular authority. A country often issues a pharmacopoeia that is the legal standard for that nation.

Phyllary. One of the bracts of an involucre in the sunflower family. Figure 4.

Phenolic glycoside. Organic compounds that include the plant salicylates (e.g., willow family).

Pinnate. A compound leaf blade with rows of leaflets on opposite sides of the main axis. If twice-pinnate, it means the leaflets themselves are branched. Figure 8.

Pinnatifid. Leaf with lobes that reach halfway to the midrib, called pinnately-cleft.

Pinnule. Last division of a leaf that is more than twice pinnately compound.

Pistil. Female reproductive organ. Collective term for the stigma, style and ovary. Figure 1.

Pistillate. Having one or more pistils but lacking stamens.

Pith. Soft inner tissue of some stems and roots.

Placental. Mammal that grows within the uterus of the mother, supplied with blood vessels by the placenta.

Pollinium. Clump of waxy, coherent pollen grains (e.g., Milkweeds and Orchids). Plural is pollinia.

Polyandry. Breeding relationship where a female is mated to more than one male during a season.

Polygamy. Mating system whereby one sex attempts to form pair bonds with several members of the opposite sex. Polyandry and polygyny are both types of this system.

Polygyny. Breeding relationship where a male is mated to more than one female during a season.

Pome. Fleshy fruit that does not open at maturity; derived from a compound inferior ovary; like an apple. Figure 10.

Potash. Mined salt containing potassium in water-soluble form; used primarily in agriculture for fertilizer.

Figure 7 · LEAF SHAPES

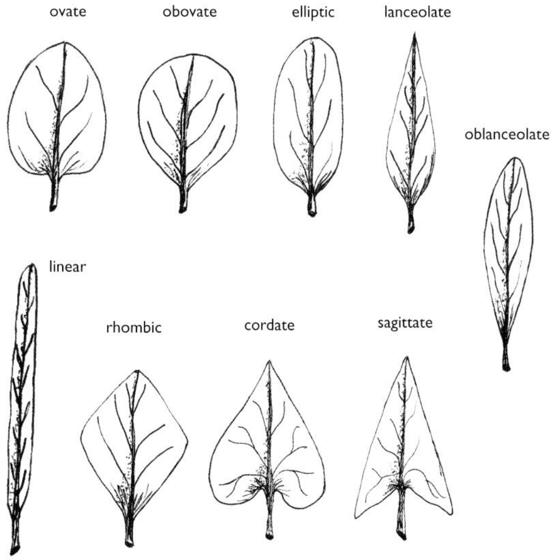

ovate obovate elliptic lanceolate

oblanceolate

linear

rhombic cordate sagittate

Figure 8 · COMPOUND LEAVES

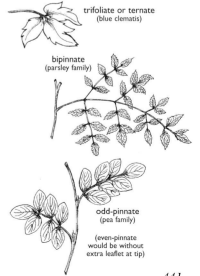

trifoliate or ternate
(blue clematis)

bipinnate
(parsley family)

odd-pinnate
(pea family)

(even-pinnate
would be without
extra leaflet at tip)

Figure 9 · OVARY PLACEMENT

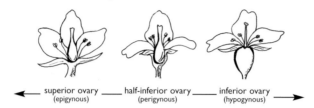

superior ovary ——— half-inferior ovary ——— inferior ovary
(epigynous)   (perigynous)   (hypogynous)

Poults. Young turkey, chicken, etc.

Precocial. Birds or animals born with fur or feathers and with their eyes open; leaving parents soon after birth to search for food on their own.

Primordia. Organ or part in its most rudimentary stage of development.

Proboscis. Biological term that applies to the long feeding structure, or tongue, of an individual (such as butterflies or moths).

Promiscuous. Indescriminate regarding sexual partners.

Protandry. When the anthers of a plant release their pollen before the stigma is receptive.

Prothallus. Small, typically flat, growth that germinates from a spore; the gametophyte generation in the alternation of generations (e.g., ferns and horsetails).

Pseudoscape. When all leaves are not really basal as in a true scape, even though they appear to all originate at the base of the plant; a 'fake' scape.

Pubescence. Soft, short hairs covering plant parts.

Raceme. Unbranched inflorescence with flowers that have pedicels; blooms from the bottom up. Figure 3.

Radially symmetrical. Parts radiate from a central point, like spokes of a wheel. (e.g., blue columbine) Figure 2.

Ramet. Individual member of a clone. For example, every individual stem of an aspen clone is a ramet.

Ray floret. Strap-shaped flower (floret) in a sunflower, resembling the petal of typical flowers. Figure 4.

Receptacle. Enlarged top of the stem; supports the flower parts. Figure 4.

Recurved. Curves backward (e.g., involucre of the curlycup gumweed).

Reflexed. Bent downward or backward.

Rhizomes. Horizontal underground stem.

Rictal bristles. Hair-like, modified contour feathers that extends from the corners of a bird's mouth, each controlled by its own muscle. Figure 11.

Riparian. Habitats occupying moist soil along creeks, streams, lakes and ponds.

Ruminant. Animal with multiple stomachs able to chew food again that has already been swallowed (called "chewing the cud"); able to digest cellulose.

Sagittate. Shaped like an arrowhead, with the basal lobes of the leaf pointing downward. Figure 7.

Salicylates. Plants produce chemical constituents called salicylates, which help protect them from soil bacteria. Salicylates are one of the active ingredients in aspirin responsible for reducing inflammation (e.g., Willow family).

Sallying. Flying out from a branch to catch insects "on the wing."

Samara. A hard, non-opening fruit with one seed (basically an achene), which has wings. (e.g., maple family fruits are two joined samaras that break apart after they are dispersed by the wind). Figure 10.

Figure 10 · FRUITS

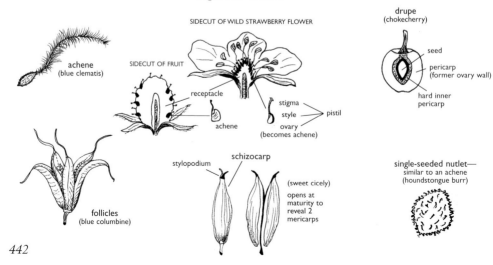

achene
(blue clematis)

SIDECUT OF FRUIT

SIDECUT OF WILD STRAWBERRY FLOWER

receptacle

achene

stigma
style   } pistil
ovary
(becomes achene)

drupe
(chokecherry)

seed

pericarp
(former ovary wall)

hard inner
pericarp

follicles
(blue columbine)

stylopodium

schizocarp

(sweet cicely)

opens at
maturity to
reveal 2
mericarps

single-seeded nutlet—
similar to an achene
(houndstongue burr)

Saponin glucosides. Also called saponins. Chemicals that form soapy emulsions when the plant is crushed in water. Plants containing these soapy emulsions began to be used at least 2,000 years ago to clean wool before weaving it into cloth. Also used as a purgative by herbalists.

Saprophyte. Plant lacking chlorophyll; living on dead or organic materials.

Scape. Leafless stalk of a single flower or of the entire inflorescence, typically arising from a basal rosette of leaves.

Schizocarp. Dry fruit that does not open at maturity, but splits into separate one-seeded segments; like the two segments of a mature fruit of the parsley family. Figure 10.

Scree. Often given as a synonym of talus, but usually considered rock rubble smaller than talus.

Semi-precocial. Young of a bird born with open eyes, down feathers, and the ability to leave the nest; continue to be cared for in the nest by the parents until nearly the size of adults.

Sepal. A single "leaf" of the calyx. Figure 1.

Serotinous. Late in opening, flowering or leafing; cones that remain closed on the tree with seed dissemination delayed or occuring gradually (e.g., lodgepole pine).

Sessile. Immediately adjacent to the stem; referring to leaves without a stalk, or petiole.

Sexual dimorphism. Having the male and female flowers on the same plant.

Silique. Fruit of a plant in the mustard family.

Skirting. Vegetative reproduction of conifers, where limbs touch the soil and take root.

Socially monogamous. When a male and female cooperate to hatch, and sometimes raise a brood when they may not both be the genetic parents. Scientists are finding that copulations outside the breeding pair are common for both male and female birds.

Sorus. Plural sori. Cluster of spore-bearing sacs (sporangia) on a fern leaf.

Spike. Unbranched, elongated inflorescence when the flowers are attached directly to the stem (or almost), without a pedicel. Figure 3.

Sporangium. Spore-bearing sac. Plural, sporangia.

Sporophyte. Spore-producing generation of a plant's reproductive cycle. This is the plant you see in vascular plants (as well as the typical, more visible fern and horsetail). See gametophyte.

Spur. Hollow, saclike appendage of a petal or sepal (e.g., columbine).

Stamen. Male reproductive organs, which provide the pollen to fertilize the pistil, or female organ. Collective term for the anther and filament. Figure 1.

Staminate. Having only male flowers; thus only stamens.

Staminode. Stamen that is modified and does not produce pollen (e.g., penstemon).

Stigma. Upper part of a flower's pistil; receives the pollen, and aids in its germination. Figure 1.

Stigmatic. Having the traits of a stigma.

Stipules. Leaf-like appendages located at the base of the petiole in some leaves.

Stolon. Long horizontal stem that creeps along the ground to root at the tip or a node to produce a new plant; identical genetically to the 'mother' plant.

Stomate. Pore in plant tissue that allows the exchange of gases. Plural, stomata.

Subnivean. Environment beneath the snow; often warmer than the outside air.

Successional species. Species that often take over after some type of disturbance (e.g., avalanche or fire), but eventually give way to other species. See climax species.

Figure 10 · FRUITS *(continued)*

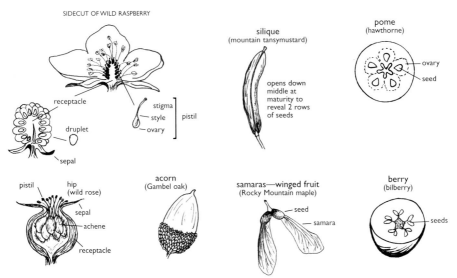

SIDECUT OF WILD RASPBERRY

receptacle
stigma
style
ovary
pistil
druplet
sepal

silique
(mountain tansymustard)

opens down middle at maturity to reveal 2 rows of seeds

pome
(hawthorne)

ovary
seed

pistil
hip
(wild rose)
sepal
achene
receptacle

acorn
(Gambel oak)

samaras—winged fruit
(Rocky Mountain maple)

seed
samara

berry
(bilberry)

seeds

Supercilium. "Eyebrow" of a bird. Figure 11.

Superior ovary. Ovary placed above where petals, stamens and sepals are attached (e.g. mustard and mint families). Figure 9.

Symbiosis. Relationship between two species where at least one side benefits.

Talus. Large areas of angular, broken rock at the base of a slope or cliff. See scree.

Tepal. Sepal that appears petal-like; there are no actual petals on a plant with tepals.

Terminate. At the tip.

Territory. Portion of a home range defended against members of the same species.

Tetraploid. With four complete sets of chromosomes in each cell.

Torpor. State of semi-hibernation or dormancy; allows organisms to save energy. Not as great a reduction in metabolic activity as hibernation; organisms awakened more easily.

Umbellifer. Plant with an inflorescence composed of umbels (e.g., parsley family).

Umbel. Inflorescence with all of the pedicels arising from a single point, as in an umbrella. Figure 3.

Understory. Vegetation under the canopy of trees.

Unisexual. Having either male (stamens) or female (pistil) flower parts, but not both.

Watershed. Land area that drains into a stream; may include surface or subsurface runoff. A large watershed (e.g., Roaring Fork River) may have several smaller watersheds that supply it (e.g., Brush Creek).

Whorled. Leaf arrangement where three or more leaves arise from a single node on the stem (e.g., northern bedstraw). Figure 5.

Willow carr. Willow thicket in a wetland.

Winter annual. Plant whose seed germinates in late summer or early fall, then completes the flowering cycle in spring or summer of the next season before dying.

Figure 11 · PARTS OF A GENERALIZED SONG BIRD

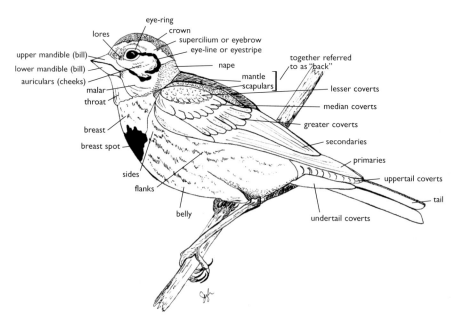

REFERENCES

Trails

Molvar, Erik, *Hiking: Colorado's Maroon Bells-Snowmass Wilderness* (Guilford, CT: Falcon Publishing, 2001)

Ohlrich, Warren, *Aspen and Central Colorado, Trails–A Hiking Guide* (Aspen, CO: Who Press, 1993).

Ecology

Benedict, A.D., *A Sierra Club Naturalists Guide: The Southern Rockies* (San Francisco, CA: Sierra Club Books, 1991).

Benyus, Janine M., *Biomimicry-Innovation Inspired by Nature* (New York: Perennial, an imprint of HarperCollins Publishers, Inc., 2002).

Cronin, John, and Robert F. Kennedy, Jr., *The Riverkeepers* (New York: Simon & Schuster, 1997).

Geology

Bryant, B. Geologic map of the Highland Peak quadrangle, Pitkin County, Colorado, U.S. Geological Survey Geologic Quadrangle Map GQ-932, 1972.

Bryant, B., and Freeman, V.L. 1977. "Geologic summary of the Aspen area, southern Rocky Mountains, Colorado." Rocky Mountain Association of Geologists, 820 16th Street, Suite 505, Denver, Colorado 80202. Phone (303) 573-8621.

Colorado Geological Survey, *Messages in Stone: Colorado's Colorful Geology* (Denver, CO: Colorado Geological Survey, 2003).

Dawson, L. W. *Colorado Backcountry Skiing*, Vol. 1. (Colorado Springs, CO: Blue Clover Press, 2001).

Laing, D. and Lampiris, N., *Aspen High Country: The Geology* (Aspen, CO: Thunder River Press, 1980).

U.S. Forest Service. Forest Visitors Map, White River National Forest, Colorado, 1979.

U.S. Geological Survey. Highland Peak quadrangle, 7.5 minute series, topographic. Pitkin County, Colorado, Map no. 39106-B8-TF-024, 1987.

Plants

Attenborough, David, *The Private Life of Plants* (Princeton, NJ: Princeton University Press, 1995).

Attenborough, David, *Life on Earth* (Boston, MA: Little, Brown and Company, 1979).

Barth, Friedrich G., *Insects and Flowers–The Biology of a Partnership* (Princeton, NJ: Princeton University Press, 1991).

Bliss, Anne, *North American Dye Plants* (Loveland, CO: Interweave Press, 1993).

Beidleman, Linda H., Richard G. Beidleman, and Beatrice E. Willard, *Plants of Rocky Mountain National Park* (Helena, MT: Falcon Publishing, 2000).

Blumenthal, Mark, *The Complete German Commission E Monographs* (Boulder, CO: American Botanical Council, 1998).

Brown, Tom, Jr., *Tom Brown's Guide to Wild Edible and Medicinal Plants* (New York: Berkley Books, 1985).

Buchman, Stephen L., and Gary Paul Nabhan, *The Forgotten Pollinators* (Washington, D.C.: Island Press, 1996).

Darrow, Katherine, *Wild About Wildflowers* (Crested Butte, CO: Heel and Toe Publishers, 1998).

Dowden, Anne Ophelia, *From Flower to Fruit* (New York: Ticknor & Fields Books, 1994).

Dowden, Anne Ophelia, *Poisons in Our Path, Plants that Harm and Heal* (New York: Harper Collins Publishers, 1994).

Duke, James A., Ph.D., *The Green Pharmacy* (Memmaus, PA: Rodale Press, 1997).

Dunmire, William W. and Tierney, Gail D., *Wild Plants and Native Peoples of the Four Corners* (Santa Fe, NM: Museum of New Mexico Press, 1997.

Elpel, Thomas J., *Botany in a Day* (Silver Star, MT: Hops Press, 2000).

Emerick, John C., *Rocky Mountain National Park–Natural History Handbook* (Niwot, CO: Roberts Rinehard Publishers, 1995).

Gellhorn, Joyce, *Song of the Alpine* (Boulder, CO: Johnson Books, 2002)

Harrington, H.D., *Edible Native Plants of the Rocky Mountains* (Albuerqueque, NM: University of New Mexico Press, 1997).

Heywood, V. H., *Flowering Plants of the World* (New York: Oxford University Press, 1993).

Holmes, Peter, *The Energetics of Western Herbs* (Boulder, CO: Snow Lotus Press, 2nd edition, 1994).

Kershaw, Linda, *Edible & Medicinal Plants of the Rockies* (Edmonton, AB, Canada: Lone Pine Publishing, 2000).

Kershaw, Linda, Andy MacKinnon and Jim Pojar, *Plants of the Rocky Mountains* (Edmonton, AB, Canada: Lone Pine Publishing, 1998).

Kindscher, Kelly, *Medicinal Wild Plants of the Prairie* (Laurence, KS: University Press of Kansas, 1992).

Komarek, Susan, *Flora of the San Juans* (Durango, CO: Kivaki Press, 1994).

Meeuse, Bastiaan and Morris, Sean, *The Sex Life of Flowers* (London: Oxford Scientific Films Ltd., 1984).

Moore, Martha, *Beyond Cortisone: Herbal Alternatives for Inflammation* (Lincolnwood, IL: Keats Publishing, 1999).

Moore, Michael. *Medicinal Plants of the Pacific West* (Santa Fe, NM: Red Crane Books, 1993).

Moore, Michael. *Medicinal Plants of the Mountain West* (Santa Fe, NM: Museum of New Mexico Press, 1979).

Nelson, Ruth Ashton, *Rocky Mountain Plants* (Niwot, CO: Roberts Rinehard Publishers, 1992, fourth edition, revised by Roger L. Williams).

Schofield, Janice, *Discovering Wild Plants* (Seattle, WA: Alaska Northwest Books, 1989).

REFERENCES

Schultes, Richard Evans, *Ethnobotany-Evolution of a Discipline* (Portland, OR: Dioscorides Press, 1995).

Seebeck, Cattail Bob, *Best-Tasting Wild Plants of Colorado and the Rockies* (Englewood, CO: Westcliffe Publishers, 1998).

Stark, Raymond, *Guide to Indian Herbs* (Surrey, B.C. Canada: Hancock House, 1984).

Stuckey, Maggie and Palmer, George, *Western Trees* (Helena, MT: Falcon Publishing, 1998).

Tilford, Gregory L., *Edible and Medicinal Plants of the West* (Billings, MT: Mountain Press Publishing Company, 1997).

Tyler, Varro E., *Herbs of Choice* (New York: Pharmaceuticals Products Press, an imprint of Haworth Press, Inc., 1994).

Tyler, Varro E., PhD, *The Honest Herbal* (New York: Pharmaceuticals Products Press, an imprint of Haworth Press, Inc., 3rd edition, 1993).

U. S. Department of Agriculture, *Common Weeds of the United States* (New York: Dover Publications, 1971).

U. S. Department of Agriculture, *Range Plant Handbook* (New York: Dover Publications, Inc., 1988).

Waldbauer, Gilbert, *Insects Through the Seasons* (Cambridge, MA: Harvard University Press, 1996).

Weber, William A., and Ronald C. Wittmann, *Colorado Flora-Western Slope* (Boulder, CO: University Press of Colorado, 2001).

Western Society of Weed Science, *Weeds of the West*, (Laramie, WY: University of Wyoming, 2001).

Willard, Terry Ph.D. *Edible and Medicinal Plants of the Rocky Mountains and Neighboring Territories* (Calgary, AB, Canada: Wild Rose College of Natural Healing, 1992).

Zomlefer, Wendy B., *Guide to Flowering Plant Families* (Chapel Hill, NC: The University of North Carolina Press, 1994).

Zwinger, Ann H., and Beatrice E. Willard, *Land Above the Trees* (New York: Harper and Row, 1972).

Birds

Bent, Arthur Cleveland. *Life Histories of North American Woodpeckers* (Bloomington and Indianapolis, Indiana: Indiana University Press, 1992).

Burton, John A., editor, *Owls of the World* (, New York: E.P. Dutton, 1973).

Erlich, Paul R., David S. Dopkin, and Darryl Wheye. *The Birder's Handbook* (New York: Simon & Schuster, 1988).

Harrison, Hal H., *Western Bird's Nests*, (Boston, MA: Houghton Mifflin Co., 1979).

Kingery, Hugh E., *Colorado Breeding Bird Atlas* (Denver, CO: Colorado Bird Atlas Partnership and Colorado Division of Wildlife, 1998).

Lanner, Ronald M., *Made for Each Other* (New York: Oxford University Press, 1996).

Short, L.L. *Woodpeckers of the World* (Greenville, DE: Delaware Museum of Natural History, Monograph Series No. 4., 1982).

Sibley, David Allen, *The Sibley Guide to Birds* (New York: Alfred A. Knopf, 2000). National Audubon Society.

Sibley, David Allen, *The Sibley Guide to Bird Life & Behavior* (New York: Alfred A. Knopf, 2001). National Audubon Society.

Weidensaul, Scott, *Living on the Wind—Across the Hemisphere with Migratory Birds* (New York: North Point Press, 1999).

Mammals

Armstrong, David M., *Rocky Mountain Mammals* (Boulder, CO: Colorado Associated University Press, 1987).

Cahalane, V.H. *Mammals of North America* (New York, NY: The Macmillan Company, 1961).

Fitzgerald, James P., Carron A. Meaney, and David M. Armstrong, *Mammals of Colorado* (Denver, CO: Denver Museum of Natural History, 1994)

Halfpenny, Jim, *Scats and Tracks of the Rocky Mountains* (Guilford, CT: Falcon Press, 1998).

Jones, Stephen R., Cushman, Ruth Carol. *Colorado Nature Almanac* (Boulder, CO: Pruett Publishing Company, 1998).

Joslin, G., and H. Youmans, coordinators. 1999. Effects of Recreation on Rocky Mountain Wildlife: A review for Montana. Committee on effects of recreation on Rocky Mountain wildlife. Order from: Montana Chapter of the Wildlife Society, 2763 Grizzly Gulch, Helena, MT 59601.

MacDonald, Dr. David, *The Encyclopedia of Mammals* (New York: Facts on File, Inc., 1995).

Rennicke, Jeff, *Colorado Wildlife* (Helena, MT: Falcon Press Publishing, 1990).

Rezendez, Paul. *Tracking and the Art of Seeing*, (Westport, CT: Firefly Books, 2nd edition, 1999).

US Forest Service, The Scientific Basis for Conserving Forest Carnivores, American Marten, Fisher, Lynx, and Wolverine, in the Western United States, general technical report RM-254. Contact USDA, NRCS, Suite 300, Bldg. A, 2150 Centre Ave., Fort Collins, Colorado 80526.

Wassink, Jan L., *Mammals of the Central Rockies* (Missoula, MT: Mountain Press, 1993).

Wilkinson, Todd, *Track of the Coyote* (Minocqua, WI: NorthWord Press, Inc., 1995).

Conservation and Research Organizations

American Bear Association
P. O. Box 77
Orr, MN 55771
http://www.americanbear.org/main.htm

Aspen Center for Environmental Studies
P. O. Box 5776
Aspen, CO 81611
970-925-5756
http://www.aspennature.org

Audubon Society
700 Broadway
New York, NY 10003
212-979-3000
http://www.audubon.org/

Bat Conservation International
P.O. Box 162603
Austin, TX 78716
Phone: 512-327-9721
http://www.batcon.org

Colorado Division of Wildlife
6060 Broadway
Denver, CO 80216
303-291-7227
http://www.wildlife.state.co.us/

Colorado Native Plant Society
P. O. Box 200
Ft. Collins, CO 80522
http://www.conps.org

Colorado Natural Heritage Program
Colorado State University
8002 Campus Delivery
Fort Collins, CO 80523-8002
970-491-1309
http://www.cnhp.colostate.edu/

Conservation International
1919 M Street, NW Suite 600
Washington, DC 20036
Telephone: (202) 912-1000
toll-free (within the US) 1(800) 406-2306
http://www.conservation.org/xp/CIWEB/home

Cornell Lab of Ornithology
159 Sapsucker Woods Rd.
Ithaca, NY 14850
1-800-843-BIRD (8473)
http://birds.cornell.edu/

Ethologists for the Ethical Treatment of Animals
Citizens for Responsible Animal Behavior Studies
(EETA/CRABS)
Jane Goodall and Marc Bekoff
http://www.ethologicalethics.org

Natural Resources Defense Council (NRDC)
40 West 20th Street
New York, NY 10011
212-727-2700
http://www.nrdc.org/

Roaring Fork Conservancy
P. O. Box 3349
Basalt, CO 81621
970-927-1290
http://www.roaringfork.org

Rocky Mountain Bird Observatory
14500 Lark Bunting Lane
Brighton, CO 80603
303-659-4348
http://www.rmbo.org/homenon.html

Southern Rockies Ecosystem Project (SREP)
1536 Wynkoop St., Suite 309
Denver, CO 80202
970-946-9653
http://www.restoretherockies.org/

The Nature Conservancy
4245 N. Fairfax Dr., Ste. 100
Arlington, VA 22203
http://nature.org/

The Wilderness Society
1615 M St. NW
Washington, DC 20036
800-843-9453
http://www.wilderness.org/

Wilderness Workshop
P. O. Box 9025
Aspen, CO 81612
http://www.wildernessworkshop.org

Other Selected Websites

Audubon, Protecting Our Natural Heritage,
http://www.audubon.org/campaign/invasives/index.shtm.

Centers for Disease Control. Hanta virus in deer mice,
http://www.cdc.gov/ncidod/diseases/hanta/hps/.

City of Boulder Open Space and Mountain Parks,
http://www.ci.boulder.co.us/openspace/index.htm.

Colorado University, Research and Collections, http://
cumuseum.colorado.edu/Research/.

Native American Ethnobotany Database, Dan Moerman.
University of Michigan-Dearborn, http://www.personal
.umd.umich.edu/~dmoerman/.

NatureServe, A Network Connecting Science with
Conservation, http://www.natureserve.org/.

Partner's In Flight,
http://www.rmbo.org/pif/bcp/overview/overview.htm.

Rocky Mountain Herbarium, University of Wyoming,
http://www.rmh.uwyo.edu/.

Southwest Colorado Wildflowers, Ferns & Trees,
www.swcoloradowildflowers.com.

The Wildlands Project, http://www.wildlands
projectrevealed.org/.

United Plant Savers, http://www.plantsavers.org/.

USDA Forest Service, Fire Effects Information Service
(FEIS), http://www.fs.fed.us/database/feis/.

GEORGE P. HUGGINS

INDEX

A

Abies
  bifolia, 83–84
  lasiocarpa, 83–84
Accipiter
  cooperii, 285–286
  gentilis, 286
  striatus, 284–285
accipiters, 284
Accipitridae (EAGLE, HAWK and HARRIER FAMILY), **283–290**
Aceraceae (MAPLE FAMILY), **141**
Acer glabrum, 141
Achillea
  lanulosa, 253–254
  millefolium, 253
  millefolium var. *lanulosa*, 253–254
Achnatherum hymenoides, 272
Acomastylis rossii, 188
Aconitum columbianum, 104
Actaea
  rubra, 99
  rubra subsp. *arguta*, 99
Actitis macularia, 298–299
ADDER'S TONGUE FAMILY (Ophioglossaceae), **72**
Adenolinum lewisii, 113
Aegithalidae (LONG-TAILED TIT (BUSHTIT) FAMILY), **336**
Aegolius
  acadicus, 304–305
  funereus, 303–304
Agastache urticifolia, 145
Agelaius phoeniceus, 368
agoseris
  orange, 235
  pale, 235
Agoseris
  aurantiaca, 235
  glauca var. *dasyphyllum*, 235
Agrostis gigantea, 272
Alaudidae (LARK FAMILY), **329–330**
Alcedinidae (KINGFISHER FAMILY), **309–310**
alder
  mountain, 88
  thinleaf, 88
alfalfa, **169**
Allium acuminatum, 137
Alnus
  incana subsp. *tenuifolia*, 88
  incana var. *occidentalis*, 88
Alopecurus aequalis, 272
alpine zone, 31, 46–50
alumroot, common, 201
Amelanchier
  alnifolia, 194–195
  utahensis, 195
Amerosedum lanceolatum, 219
Anaerobic Nightmare Trail, 15–16
Anaphalis margaritacea, 236
Anatidae (WATERFOWL FAMILY), **281–282**
Anderson, Hildur Hoagland, 4, 7
Androsace
  chamaejasme, 184
  septentrionalis, 184
anemone

alpine, 102
wind, 106
Anemone
  multifida subsp. *globosa*, 106
  multifida var. *multifida*, 106
  narcissiflora, 102
  patens var. *multifida*, 106
angelica
  giant, 163
  gray, 163
  pinnateleaf, 163
Angelica
  ampla, 163
  grayi, 163
  pinnata, 163
animals, feeding/tracks, 378, 379
Antennaria
  media, 238
  microphylla, 238–239
  pulcherrima, 239
  rosea, 238–239
Anthus
  rubescens, 350–351
  spinoletta, 350
Anticlea elegans, 132–133
anting, 329
Aphelocoma californica, 324–325
Apiaceae (PARSLEY or CARROT FAMILY), **160–168**
Apocynaceae (DOGBANE FAMILY), **108–109**
Apocynum
  androsaemifolium, 108–109
  cannabinum, 108, 109
Aquila chrysaetos, 289–290
Aquilegia
  coerulea, 100–101
  elegantula, 101
Arabis drummondii, 150
Arceuthobium americanum. See dwarf mistletoe
Arctium minus, 229, 269
Arctostaphylos uva-ursi, 124–125
Ardea herodias, 281
Ardeidae (HERON FAMILY), **280–281**
Arenaria
  congesta, 179
  jamesiana, 181
  obtusiloba, 178–179
Armillaria, 84
Armstrong, David M., 378
arnica group (*Arnica* spp.), **220–222**
  clumped, 221
  daffodil, 221
  heartleaf, 221
  Parry's, 222
  rayless, 222
  subalpine, 221
Arnica spp. (Arnica group), **220–222**
  cordifolia, 221
  latifolia, 221
  mollis, 221
  montana, 221
  parryi, 222
Artemisia spp. (Sagebrush group), **239–242**
  borealis, 240
  campestris var. *purshii*, 240
  dracunculus, 242
  frigida, 240, 241

Maroon Bells, Pitkin County, Colorado

*One touch of nature makes
the whole world kin.*

—WILLIAM SHAKESPEARE

About the Author

Janis Lindsey Huggins' passion for plants and the natural world has been a driving force in her life as long as she can remember. She moved to the Aspen/Snowmass area in 1970, and has spent more than 30 years exploring the upper Roaring Fork Valley, studying the plants, wildlife and ecosystems. For her, this connection means feeling exhilarated about life and inspires her to share this enthusiasm with others. For many years here she has guided naturalist tours, worked as a freelance botanist in survey fieldwork, taught others in sports such as alpine skiing, cross-country skiing and windsurfing. She also worked

with her family's commercial real estate development company for five years during this eclectic work history. Janis received a B.S. in Natural Sciences with an emphasis in Botany from the University Without Walls at Loretto Heights College (Denver) in 1981, where she was chosen "student of the year" for work on a Crystal River Valley field guide. Because she has a love of travel, her education was accomplished through study at several universities—the University of Denver, the University of California at Santa Barbara, and the Biological Station at Flathead Lake in Montana. Janis also holds a degree in Clinical Herbal Therapy from the Artemis Institute of Natural Therapies in Boulder. She hopes that readers of this field guide will be inspired to look at the landscape "through new eyes," to cherish the fascinating species with which we share our surroundings, and to seek new ways to secure the future of those species as they are a part of the matrix that enriches life. ■

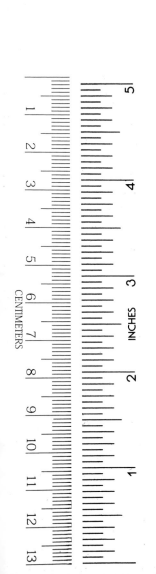